The Letters of
Virginia Woolf

Volume III: 1923-1928

The Letters of Virginia Woolf

Volume III: 1923-1928

Edited by Nigel Nicolson
and Joanne Trautmann

A Harvest/HBJ Book
Harcourt Brace Jovanovich
New York and London

Originally published in England as *A Change of Perspective*

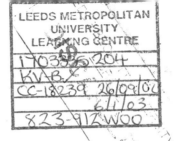
Editorial Note and Introduction copyright ©-1977 by Nigel Nicolson

Letters copyright © 1977 by Quentin Bell and Angelica Garnett

Printed in the United States of America

Library of Congress Cataloging in Publication Data
Woolf, Virginia Stephen, 1882–1941.
The Letters of Virginia Woolf.

(A Harvest/HBJ book)
Vol. 1 first published under title: The flight of the mind.
Vol. 2 first published under title: The question of things happening.
Vol. 3 first published under title: A change of perspective.
Includes bibliographical references and indexes.
CONTENTS: v. 1. 1888–1912 (Virginia Stephen).—v. 2. 1912–1922.—v. 3. 1923–1928.—
1. Woolf, Virginia Stephen, 1882–1941—Correspondence.
2. Authors, English—20th century—Correspondence.
PR6045.072Z525   1977   823'.9'12 [B]   76-40422
ISBN 0-15-650883-4

First Harvest/HBJ edition 1980
A B C D E F G H I J

"To write a novel in the heart of London is next to an impossibility. I feel as if I were nailing a flag to the top of a mast in a raging gale. What is so perplexing is the change of perspective. . . ."

Virginia Woolf to Vita Sackville-West
2 *March* 1926

Contents

Illustrations

Between *pages 328 and 329*

2a and 7a were loaned by Professor and Mrs Quentin Bell,
3b by Milo Keynes and George Rylands and 6a by Barbara
Bagenal. The remainder are the copyright of the Editor.

Editorial Note

THERE were only four people, all women, with whom Virginia Woolf corresponded at great length. Her sister Vanessa Bell, to whom she wrote throughout her life; Violet Dickinson, whom she knew best during the period covered by the first of these volumes; Vita Sackville-West, who became her most intimate friend between 1925 and 1929; and Ethel Smyth. whom she did not meet until 1930.

Today the original letters to all four of them are carefully preserved in a single place, the Berg Collection of the New York Public Library, together with very many of their replies. Outside New York, the main collection of Woolf letters, both from and to her, is in the library of Sussex University. The Editors wish to thank the curators of these two great collections, Dr Lola S. Szladits of the Berg, and Peter Lewis and A. N. Peasgood of Sussex, for their courtesy and help. Together the two libraries contain about two-thirds of Virginia Woolf's surviving letters. The remainder have been loaned to us for copying, or sent in the form of xeroxes, by a large number of individuals and public or semi-public institutions. Their names are given at the foot of each letter in this printed edition, and this information is also a method of expressing our thanks.

The copyright in all the letters written by Virginia Woolf belongs to her nephew and niece, Quentin Bell and Angelica Garnett, at whose invitation we have undertaken this edition.

In the Editorial Notes attached to Volumes I and II we have explained our methods of transcription and annotation, and only a few points need be added here.

As we approach nearer our own times, the risk of libelling or deeply offending some living person becomes greater. A few of Virginia Woolf's surviving friends have told us that they do not mind the publication of her remarks about them, knowing that occasional maliciousness was a recognised Bloomsbury habit of which they were all both victims and perpetrators, and that a sneer would often be expunged by an affectionate salute a few letters later. In other cases, when we felt that it would be too cruel to publish an item of gossip about a person still alive today, we have deleted the words or lines, always making it clear when we have done so and to what extent.

Virginia Woolf's closest friends like Roger Fry, Lytton Strachey, T. S. Eliot, E. M. Forster, Duncan Grant and Desmond MacCarthy are too well known to require separate identification in footnotes, and the reader's knowledge of such people has been assumed. In the case of people more obscure, an identification is given when they are first mentioned, and the reader who uses this book as a quarry is advised to consult the index for names unfamiliar to him.

In the 1920s Virginia Woolf began to use a portable typewriter more frequently for her letters. In spite of much practice (for she typed out her own manuscripts too), she never became expert, and we have corrected obvious errors, unless she draws specific attention to them. She occasionally illustrated her letters to Vita Sackville-West by a fanciful signature. One example has been reproduced (Letter 1862), but in other such cases the signature has been printed normally, with the indication 'squiggly design' alongside it.

About thirty short notes and postcards have been omitted from this volume because they were nothing more than arrangements for social meetings, many of which are mentioned again in another context.

Our work has once again been greatly eased by the help of other people. Foremost among them are Quentin and Olivier Bell. They have read this volume in typescript, and again in proof, and by correcting errors and supplying additional information, they have enhanced the usefulness of the book immensely. Olivier Bell is simultaneously editing Virginia Woolf's *Diaries* (the originals are also in the Berg Collection, New York), and we have been able to examine it ahead of publication, in order to avoid any inconsistencies between the dating and annotation of the two sets of documents. However, we have quoted nothing from the *Diaries* which has not already been published in Leonard Woolf's abbreviated edition, *A Writer's Diary* (1953), or quoted by Quentin Bell in his biography.

Another close collaborator has been George A. Spater. Formerly a leading business executive in the United States, he now lives near Rodmell and devotes part of his retirement to the study of Leonard Woolf's papers in Sussex University. He has let us draw on his profound knowledge of Leonard's career and the publications of the Hogarth Press, and we acknowledge his generosity with much gratitude.

Juliet Nicolson has spent many hours in libraries searching for, and with few exceptions finding, clues to the identification of the most obscure people, publications and events mentioned in the Letters.

Three books in particular have answered many of our questions: *A Bibliography of Virginia Woolf* (revised edition, 1967, now in course of further revision), by B. J. Kirkpatrick, who has also given us much of her time personally; *A Checklist of the Hogarth Press*, by J. Howard Woolmer, 1976; and *Virginia Woolf: The Critical Heritage*, edited by Robin Majumdar and Allen McLaurin, 1975.

For allowing Dr Joanne Trautmann to spend part of her academic year working on this volume, we are grateful to the Department of Humanities and its Chairman E. A. Vastyan, the Pennsylvania State University College of Medicine, Hershey, Pennsylvania. We also acknowledge with thanks the grant of travel funds to Dr Trautmann by the Institute for the Arts and Humanistic Studies, Pennsylvania State University, directed by Professor Stanley Weintraub.

Mrs Norah Smallwood of the Hogarth Press has again been the most understanding of publishers, and T. & A. Constable the most painstaking of printers.

The following have willingly responded to our requests for information: Charles Anson; Mark Arnold-Forster; Lady Ashton (Madge Garland); Barbara Bagenal; Enid Bagnold; Dr Wendy Baron; Kildare Bourke-Borrowes; Gerald Brenan; Lady David Cecil; Angus Davidson; Mrs T. S. Eliot; Angelica Garnett; David Garnett; Katherine Hill; Richard Kirby; James Lees-Milne; Paul Levy; the staff of the London Library; Raymond Mortimer; The National Book League; Benedict Nicolson; George Rylands; Daphne Sanger; Anne Scott-James; Desmond Shaw-Taylor; Richard Shone; Dame Janet Vaughan; Ursula Vaughan Williams; and Julian Vinogradoff.

The typing of the letters has been shared between Valerie Henderson, Gretchen Hess Gage and June Watson in the United States; and Pamela Kilbane and Jane Carr in England. Their accuracy and expertise in deciphering Virginia Woolf's often difficult handwriting has been invaluable to us. In preparing the book for press we owed much to the secretarial help of Jane Carr and Lyn Dunbar.

NIGEL NICOLSON
JOANNE TRAUTMANN

Introduction

WITH the third volume of Virginia Woolf's letters we step into the middle of her life. All her friends were assembled (or almost all), her literary career and the Hogarth Press well launched, and she had developed a method of living and a style of writing which she had little desire to change. In 1923 she was 41. She had published three novels, several short-stories and much literary criticism. She was not yet famous. But during the six years covered by this volume, when she wrote *Mrs Dalloway*, *The Common Reader*, *To the Lighthouse* and *Orlando*, and gave as two lectures *A Room of One's Own*, her name became one to drop. She wanted fame, enjoyed within limits the social notoriety it imposed on her, and was encouraged by the acclaim of the people whose opinions mattered most to her. Long before one book was finished, she was conceiving the next. "Why does one write these books after all?" she asked herself in a letter to Edward Sackville West (No. 1906). "The drudgery, the misery, the grind, are forgotten every time; and one launches another, and it seems sheer joy and buoyancy."

Her delight in writing, and the pain of it, her artistic loneliness, are seldom reflected in her letters. What was intended to be most public must be composed in greatest privacy, like the conception and carrying of a child. Just as Charlotte Brontë could manufacture out of her simple life innumerable letters which never mention her novels and poetry, and even Byron could record for his friends every mood and emotion when he was in Italy, without saying one word about *Manfred* and *Childe Harold*, so Virginia Woolf kept silent about what meant most to her. "I'm terrifically egotistic about my writing", she told Jacques Raverat when he asked her about it (1496), "think practically of nothing else, and so, partly from conceit, partly shyness, sensitiveness, what you choose, never mention it." When she went for walks on the Sussex Downs or through the streets of London, she was 'thinking, thinking, thinking about literature', but on returning home she wrote letters about other things, unpremeditated, uninhibited, unrehearsed. She set down from moment to moment whatever came into her head, provided that it was not too solemn. Her melancholy and worries were siphoned off into her diary. Her letters, she told Gerald Brenan, were 'a tossing of omelettes'. They mopped up chance impressions, aerated her lightly ironic style. Her phrases were always newly minted; she never felt comfort or self-satisfaction in a cliché, and it soon ceases to be a surprise to be surprised by her. "I can only write letters if I dont read them", she said. "Once think and I destroy" (1416). Her letters were expendable, ideas caught on the wing, intended to give pleasure, to provoke a reply, to start or resume an argument. She spun them off the top of her mind.

Yet she could say, "I *hate* and *detest* writing letters" (1913). How could she, when she wrote so many? Only if she wrote from duty does her manner appear forced, her pen pushed. The general flow of her correspondence is easy, a flight from twig to twig. She slides, oscillates, meanders, becomes exhilarated, gets bored, as in conversation. She can break off the discussion of something which deeply interests her, with the excuse of no space or no time; but she can write to her sister Vanessa a long and brilliant description of her mother-in-law's tedious chatter (1919), having just been exhausted by it. The telephone made little difference: she continued to write just as many letters after it became available to her, even when she was ill. She took to typing; disliked it, felt herself to be pecking at the machine, it at her, and the great majority of these letters were written in her own hand. A friend's long absence (Raverat's in France, Vita Sackville-West's in Persia, Brenan's in Spain) made her all the more eager to write, and write more personally, partly out of kindness to an exile and to sustain a friendship, but mainly because absence deepened the affections, and dammed the news. To Raverat, if to nobody else, she expressed a certain unease about the 'unreality' of her letters. They become "inevitably jocular. I suppose joviality is a convenient mask; and then, being a writer, masks irk me; I want, in my old age, to have done with all superfluities" (1501). But she didn't. Although her letters became a distraction more than a relaxation, an interruption to her central purpose, the wonder of her correspondence is that it never drooped, in quantity or vitality, as long as she lived.

These years, 1923 to 1928, were happy and successful for the Woolfs. Everything, in the end, turned out right. Virginia experienced a few mental stabs, enough to remind her of the threat, but though often ill, she was never mad. It was on her insistence, against Leonard's misgivings, that they moved in 1924 from Richmond back to Bloomsbury, so that he could live nearer his work, she nearer the friends whose parties might exhaust her but without whom she felt deprived. The Hogarth Press gained much in reputation, though little in profit. Leonard became Literary Editor of the *Nation and Athenaeum*. Virginia would soon be able to afford to write only what she wanted to write. They bought a car; added to the comforts of Monk's House; travelled, to Spain, to Italy, several times to France. By this time their life had settled to an annual rhythm—two summer months and frequent weekends at Rodmell, the others in London—and often they contrived a longer break, in Cornwall or abroad. Virginia much enjoyed these expeditions. More than once she and Leonard were tempted by a milder climate, a more colourful scene, to throw up their London life for at least half the year, as Vanessa did, but the Press, Leonard's political and journalistic work, and Virginia's pining for the society she loved, always reclaimed them.

She seldom resented the demands made on her time by the Hogarth Press. Except at moments of greatest pressure before a publishing season, she was not expected to do much more than advise on manuscripts or commission jackets, and in the memory of the young men who rapidly succeeded each other as 'managers' under Leonard, she sat for most of the morning over a gas fire, writing on her knee, emerging to pack a parcel, interview a bookseller, set or distribute a tray of type, more because the occupation took her mind off her work or allowed it to simmer than because her help was needed. She could work in discomfort; in fact, she told Vita, preferred it. The clanking of the heavy printing-press next door, the constant intrusion of people to fetch a book (her 'studio' at Tavistock Square was also the stock-room), did not disturb her. Her equanimity had a stabilising influence on the Press. She was seldom irritable, always clear in her literary judgements, and she spread around her the confidence she felt in Leonard. She may have questioned, but never challenged, his decision to continue the Press in spite of its low return on time and nervous energy, and when he proposed to add to it a bookshop, she agreed with acclamation.

Leonard does not figure largely in this volume. When one reads the corresponding pages of his autobiography, it becomes clear that for much of the day he and Virginia were inhabiting different worlds. She scarcely mentions his political work, but supported it, vaguely, and was roused to excitement only by the General Strike, when, under his influence and without much thought, she took the strikers' side. Only twice in these pages does she mention the massive book he was writing, *After the Deluge*. The rarity of her letters to him, since they were seldom apart, and her reluctance to discuss him or his work with other people, may create a false impression of their relationship. He was essential to her. She loved him deeply. They shared much—literature, friends, houses, travel, music, garden, car, dogs—and their marriage was woven into a strong fabric by these common interests. It comes as a sudden revelation, but it should not be, to read the chain of letters which she wrote to him in September 1928, when she was in France with Vita, and to discover not only how greatly she missed him, but how private, how soppy even, their relationship had become. 'Dadyka' he now was; 'dusky, darky marmot', 'mongoose'; and she puts in a claim 'for an hour of antelope kissing' the moment she gets back. That Leonard, apparently so austere a man ('solitary and grim' were Vita's words, but mistaken) should have been her accomplice in such animal-baby talk, and that Virginia, never a sentimentalist, could have lowered her guard to this extent, can have been known to nobody else.

Not even to Vanessa. How, in spite of Vita, she takes hold of this volume! Friends come and fade, but Vanessa is rocklike in Virginia's life. Teasable, yes—why, she could not be expected to know that the Sierra Nevada are mountains in Spain, what *viz* means, who wrote *Antony and Cleopatra*—but she is right in everything she does and thinks, makes no attempt to conciliate, has 'a marmoreal chastity', 'purrs with happiness' at her children, her painting. She enjoys parties, gossip, charades, picnics; she can design a book-jacket, a fire-place, a chair-cover, a dress; is unjealous, manages her life with magnificent abandon, and creates around her, whether at Charleston or at Cassis, 'an atmosphere of ragamuffin delight'. Virginia never lost her amazement at Vanessa's certainty of touch. She almost ceased to envy her her children, because they had become so much part of her own life, but wondered at Vanessa's apparently effortless success in bringing them up, demanding to know from her whether she, Virginia, could have done the same. Vanessa thought not. When Virginia wrote about her painting, she did so diffidently, distrusting her own judgement; but when Vanessa wrote to Virginia about her books, also protesting a lack of comprehension, Virginia found her comments more rewarding than the most sophisticated criticism, because she was so honest and unhysterical. She was never quite convinced that Vanessa returned her love with equal strength. If she did, how could she spend months in France away from her? "My love for you remains hot and strong: yours for me thin and weak" (1703). Of course this wasn't true, and Virginia knew it. But she recognised that Vanessa had somehow achieved an independence, a style of living, an astonishing reservoir of sympathy and common-sense, which she could never quite manage herself. She was "a bowl of golden water which brims but never overflows" (1743). She was beyond challenge.

Nothing of the same sort emerges from Virginia's letters to any other person. She could be fiercely critical of people, and did not mind being thought formidable in their company. Old friends were dropped quite gently, or less gently ridiculed, like Ka Arnold-Forster, Violet Dickinson, Saxon Sydney-Turner, because she had outgrown them. Others were permanencies, but few immune: Roger Fry ('the only civilized man I have ever met'); Morgan Forster (who alone 'lays hold of the thing I have done' in literature); Lytton Strachey, who had drifted slightly apart from her but to whom she could suddenly write a letter of intense affection; the MacCarthys, Desmond and Molly, solid friends but vaguely disappointing; T. S. Eliot, firmly established in her life, though he drove her to distraction by his inability to make up his mind. Clive Bell amused her; she liked him most when he was with her: he had a style, a gift for sharing enjoyment. Ottoline Morrell was always vulnerable to a biting simile; so was her husband Philip, whose sudden declaration of love for Virginia she found gratifying but pathetic. Middleton Murry, with 'his rolling oleaginous eyes', alone came near to being an enemy. And then there was the group of society women who lionized her—Sibyl Colefax, Lady Cunard, the Bibescos, Dorothy Wellesley. They represented to her a world which she half, but only half, despised.

She was ambivalent. In writing to or about the same person she could veer from genuine affection to a kind of contempt, according to mood, as if she was not quite certain of her own values. She could present a sympathetic portrait of Mrs Dalloway, when she had grown to despair of Mrs Dalloway's original, Kitty Maxse. When she came to write of her own much loved mother as Mrs Ramsay in *To the Lighthouse*, she describes her as a woman more touching than admirable. Perhaps she began to wonder whether her high intellectual standards might not be denying her a great deal of pleasure, and giving others too much pain. "Why do I pity and deride the human race", she wrote (1622), "when its lot is profoundly peaceful and happy?" Even about Sibyl Colefax, the epitome of the type which in theory she most disliked, she can find good to say, mixed with the bad: "Every value is different. . . . Yet I respect, even admire. . . . She skated over everything, evaded, palliated, compromised; yet is fundamentally kind and good" (1687). But such self-questioning was rare. She tended to fasten on the weakest side of a person, unless they were unhappy, or ill, or abroad, and then she saw the best in them, and they in her. She confessed to Rebecca West that she found it difficult to appreciate contemporary writers. Her attitude to them often verges on the arrogant, not out of jealousy (she lost that with the death of Katherine Mansfield in 1923), but from her conviction that while she tried so hard to create something new, they tried so little. She made new friends warily: George Rylands, Raymond Mortimer, Rose Macaulay, Hugh Walpole, Edward Sackville West. But she could find little to admire in the young, particularly young men, particularly if they came from Oxford. She thought them insipid, weakened by mutual admiration. Young women, like Janet Vaughan, Frances Marshall, Carrington and Rebecca West, had more spunk, more pride, were less anxious to please.

One of them was Vita Sackville-West. She is central to this volume. She grows through it like a plant. Virginia's first letter is written to her: so is the last. Beginning as 'Dear Mrs Nicolson', she ends as 'Darling honey'. How can one explain this remarkable metamorphosis? It was the deepest relationship which Virginia ever had outside her family. In her girlhood there had been Violet Dickinson; in her thirties, Katherine Mansfield; in her fifties there was to be Ethel Smyth. But none of them aroused in Virginia the emotions for which Vita, half-inadvertently, was responsible. Their friendship began slowly, leaving time and space for retreat if either of them came to regret it; and it ended slowly, without recrimination, indifference or damage. Both benefited greatly from it. Virginia was moved more than she cared to admit, even to her diary; while to Vita it was the most important event in her life except her marriage, giving her warm companionship, literary stimulus, and, as she once expressed it to her husband Harold Nicolson, 'a treasure and a privilege'.

It was a friendship which might have disintegrated before it became an intimacy. There was much in Vita—Vanessa felt this—that was alien to Bloomsbury. She was interesting because Virginia adored her, because she had broken with the philistine tradition of her family, and had been daring to the point of recklessness in her private life. But she was not clever in the way of Virginia's other friends; she found it difficult to inflate conversational balloons. Bloomsbury alarmed her (she called it 'Gloomsbury'), and on certain subjects which they thought important, she was downright ignorant, about modern painting, for example, and the history of ideas. Early in their acquaintance Virginia asked her, unkindly: "Ever heard of Moore?" "George Moore, the novelist?" "My dear Vita, we start at different ends" (1440). So they did. That their friendship survived this sort of thing was due, in the first place, to mutual admiration. Vita's for Virginia was explicit: Virginia's for Vita more guarded. Vita was dazed by the brilliance of Virginia's talk and books, flattered that such a woman should choose her—why her?—as a person she wanted to meet again. She could easily be repulsed, and when she failed to steer Virginia into a world smarter and more organised than she wanted, they did not meet again for nine months, and then it was on Virginia's initiative. For she too found something irresistible in Vita. She could do things which Virginia could not do,

> being so much in full sail on the high tides, where I am coasting down backwaters; her capacity I mean to take the floor in any company, to represent her country, to visit Chatsworth, to control silver, servants, chow dogs; her motherhood . . . her being in short (what I have never been) a real woman. (*Quoted from Virginia's diary by Quentin Bell, Vol. II, p. 118.*)

But there was much more to it than that. Vita was very beautiful. Her beauty was dark and lustrous, ripe as a fig; tall and graceful, the two elements in her nature, feminine and masculine, combined into an appearance which was both ravishing and strong. There was shyness, but no awkwardness, in her. She moved with confidence. Virginia often returned to her image of Vita in a fishmonger's, ordering this, countermanding that, imperious yet with a natural courtesy, a veritable Sackville, a daughter of Knole.

Nor could Virginia suppress a certain admiration for Vita's writing. "A pen of brass", as she once described it to Jacques Raverat, should not be allowed to stand as her verdict. She discovered in Vita's books a darting imagination, a gift for imagery, which she did not recognise in her conversation. Her 'rich dusky attic of a mind' continually surprised her. Virginia wrote with immense care, constant alteration. Vita produced her books at speed, and this Virginia somehow envied, wondering whether Vita might not be right to assume that the first thought to be put down on paper is probably the best. Her story *Seducers in Ecuador*, which the Hogarth Press published in 1924, was written in the Dolomites each night of a walking-tour, when she was tired, but it was so well-turned, so audacious in Virginia's own manner, that she wondered once again whether she might not have underestimated her friend. So with Vita's two Persian books, and *The Land*, and *Aphra Behn*, such different shapes formed out of so great a variety of material. Virginia had her reservations ('a central transparency lacking', 'something that does not vibrate'), but there was no doubt that Vita was a writer. They had a craft in common, and could discuss it, endlessly, on terms which Virginia did not find too unequal to be fun.

Books, glamour, heritage, adventurousness, admiration for Virginia—this was quite a lot to find in one person. But the reason why they formed so close an attachment was that Virginia needed someone like Vita in her life. "If one could be friendly with women", she wrote in her diary on 1 November 1924, before Vita had swum deep into her life, "what a pleasure—the relationship so secret and private compared with relations with men." Had she become, perhaps, too isolated and cynical? In Vita she found exactly the remedy she was seeking. She was 'cool, fruitful and delicious', comfortable to be with, a butt for teasing and flattery, yet sometimes 'standoffish', which added the stimulus of challenge. She 'glowed': but she could also be 'virginal, savage, patrician', and 'fitful, sudden, remote'. Virginia had begun her game of 'making Vita up', attributing to her at different times every quality except that of genius, sometimes to her credit, more often with simulated reproach, until she flung them all together in *Orlando* to produce a man-woman who strode masterfully through life but remained vulnerable and aloof. Each of them saw in the other this pathetic quality. They protected each other. "She has a sweet and childlike nature", Vita wrote to Harold, "from which her intellect is completely separate. But of course nobody would believe this except Leonard and Vanessa." Virginia's letters, particularly when Vita was in Persia, are implicit appeals not to abandon her; and Vita by her replies gave her what she needed, the reassurance of unalterable love. In return she never demanded too much from Virginia, knowing that she could be shattered by an emotional storm, and fearing to touch in her a spring which could precipitate madness. It was Vita who kept their relationship under control, not Virginia.

They loved each other. Set down those words and they provoke questions which their discreet letters do not answer directly. But the facts are clear from other sources, Vita's diary (not Virginia's), and her confessional letters to Harold. They slept together perhaps a dozen times, in Vita's house and later in Virginia's, while their husbands were away. It happened first at Long Barn, on 18 December 1925. Recollecting the scene three years later, Virginia wrote to Vita: "The night you were snared, that winter, at Long Barn, you slipped out Lord Steyne's paper knife, and I had then to make the terms plain: with this knife you will gash our hearts I said" (1976). There was no gash, either then, nor at any later time. Vita was entranced: Virginia was curiously unalarmed. When Vita once threatened to leave a Hampshire house-party at midnight, drive to Rodmell, accost Virginia by throwing gravel at her window, and drive back in the dawn, Virginia sent a telegram: 'Come then' (1774). She found it flattering to be thought, at 45, desirable by so glamorous a woman, ten years her junior. She felt neither shock nor self-reproach, never feared that Leonard would think her treacherous, for he knew, as Harold knew, that there was no threat to either marriage.

For Virginia the affair was a strange and pleasurable experience, but unintoxicating, terminable. Only for a short period was it central to her life. This was also true of Vita. In her last novel *No Signposts in the Sea* (1961) she quoted the lines,

> *Love one another, but make not a bond of love.*
> *Fill each other's cup but drink not from one cup.*
> *Let there be spaces in your togetherness.*

This was her lifelong philosophy of love and marriage, and it suited Virginia too. Both were too independent, both had too much else to occupy them, to leave room for a monopolising passion. Their affair lasted, intermittently, for about three years. When they travelled to France together in the autumn of 1928, they slept in separate rooms. Vita sensed that the time had come to end it. She had other friends—Mary Campbell, Dorothy Wellesley, Margaret Voigt, Hilda Matheson—and Virginia surrendered Vita to them, not without some jealousy, particularly of Campbell. Against their hotter, thinner love, she employed her art to reassert her claim on a different Vita. She wrote *Orlando*. It was her most elaborate love-letter, rendering Vita androgynous and immortal: it transformed her story into a myth, gave her back to Knole. Without shame on either side, she identified Vita as her model by the dedication and the photographs. *Orlando* defused their affair, and they remained friends till Virginia died. Perhaps it was the only occasion in her middle life when Virginia was physically aroused, and then but slightly. The precipice which she had feared turned out to be nothing but a step, and she did not even stumble.

NIGEL NICOLSON
Sissinghurst Castle, Kent

The Letters of
Virginia Woolf

Volume III: 1923-1928

Letters 1341-1373 (January–March 1923)

Virginia and Leonard Woolf were living at Hogarth House, Richmond, and went for occasional weekends and longer holidays to Monk's House, near Lewes. They ran the Hogarth Press from the Richmond house, and it was there that Virginia set up the type for T. S. Eliot's The Waste Land *with her own hands. In two other ways she was deeply involved at this time with Eliot's career. First, she was still helping to organise the fund which would make it possible for him to leave his job at Lloyds Bank and concentrate on literature. Secondly, she tried to obtain for him the post of Literary Editor of the* Nation *and* Athenaeum, *now under Maynard Keynes's control, and when her efforts failed, largely owing to Eliot's indecision, the post was unexpectedly offered to Leonard, who accepted it on 23 March. Virginia was bed-ridden for part of January with influenza, and her depression was deepened by the death of Katherine Mansfield on 9 January. Having published* Jacob's Room, *her first experimental novel, in October 1922, she was making slow progress with* Mrs Dalloway, *and collaborated with Koteliansky on translations from Tolstoy. Her friendship with Vita Sackville-West, whom she had first met in December 1922, developed through the exchange of books and occasional visits, but after March they did not meet again till 1924.*

1341: To V. Sackville-West   *Hogarth House, Paradise Road, Richmond, Surrey*

3rd Jan. [1923]

Dear Mrs Nicolson,

I should never have dared to dun you if I had known the magnificence of the book.[1] Really, I am ashamed, and would like to say that copies of all my books are at your service if you raise a finger—but they look stout and sloppy and shabby. There is nothing I enjoy more than family histories, so I am falling upon Knole the first moment I get.

I am shameless enough to hope that the poems[2] won't go to the wrong address. I was prepared to sniff at Eddie's Georgians,[3] and so I did; but not at yours.

I wonder if you would come and dine with us? Say Monday 8th, 7.45.

1. *Knole and The Sackvilles*, by Vita Sackville-West, which she had published in 1922.
2. Vita's *Orchard and Vineyard* (1921).
3. The fifth and last volume of *Georgian Poetry* (1922), an annual anthology of contemporary verse edited by Edward Marsh.

We don't dine so much as picnic, as the press has got into the larder and into the dining room, and we never dress.

I would look up a train, and give you directions if you can come, as I hope.

Yours very sincerely
Virginia Woolf

Berg

1342: To Molly MacCarthy

Monks [error for *Hogarth*] *House, Richmond*

Jan 3rd [1923]

Dearest Molly,

It was indeed a surprise, a pleasure, and a consolation for all the troubles of life to find your letter waiting here. We are just back from eating our turkey at Rodmell, and it's quite true what you say—the thighs are gigantic —and then there are pockets of flesh under the armpits. We arrived on top of Mr and Mrs Lucas,[1] of Kings, who had come from Blackheath to see us—a tribute which I can't imagine paying to anyone at Blackheath—but that's my damned unsocial nature. I was wanting to ask Michael, Desmond and Rachel[2] here, and then we plunged into the very hell of domestic catastrophe: both servants in bed simultaneously with the German measles, and all the chars of Richmond fleeing from the plague and leaving us to empty the slops. We are still infectious, and I find that only the faithful, like Molly and Roger [Fry], will remain faithful to friendship and run the risk. Tomorrow, however, I dine with Clive [Bell] to meet Goldie.[3] You were going to say something witty and spiteful about Goldie—then you crossed yourself and refrained. But couldn't you uncross yourself?

Did you write the article on Mrs Inchbald in the Statesman?[4]

Well, we went to tea in Rodmell Rectory and discussed fox-trotting and canker. I read 20 dozen books, but have forgotten them all—except by Gwendolen Cecil[5] who has the style not merely of a man, but of a guardsman. I mean virility fairly sticks to the particles. When do you come back?—and

1. F. L. Lucas, the critic and poet, a Fellow of King's College, Cambridge, and his wife Topsy.
2. Desmond MacCarthy was literary editor of the *New Statesman* 1920-27. Michael was Desmond's and Molly's elder son, and Rachel their only daughter.
3. Goldsworthy Lowes Dickinson, the historian and philosopher, and a fellow of King's College, Cambridge.
4. Elizabeth Inchbald (1753-1821), the novelist, dramatist and actress, best known for her novel *A Simple Story*, 1791.
5. The *Life* of Lord Salisbury by his daughter, Lady Gwendolen Cecil.

is it to the ghost of old Miss Clough, or to your native Chelsea?[1] This lovely blue sheet will hold no more—so good bye.   V.W.

Mrs Michael MacCarthy

1343: To Hope Mirrlees   *Hogarth House, Paradise Road, Richmond, Surrey*

[6 January 1923]

My dear Hope,

I ought to have thanked you ages ago for your letter, which gave me the greatest pleasure. I went away, and meant to write, and found I had left your letter and address here.

I think you are too generous, but I am very pleased to find that your generosity had to overcome the boredom of the first chapters.[2] I wish we could talk the matter over, instead of writing. I don't feel satisfied that I have brought it off. Writing without the old bannisters, one makes jumps and jerks that are not necessary; but I go on saying that next time I shall achieve it. I suppose one is always buoyed up in this way. Anyhow, I find your praise a great comfort. Sometimes I can't help feeling that its too much in the air, and that though I can see something ahead, I must leave it to other people to carry out what I see.

Are you writing your book again?[3] I very much want to read it.

I grow more and more dissatisfied with my contemporaries. None of them seems able to carry the thing through—for the most part because they will not or cannot write I think. But this won't apply to you.

I have chosen the worst hour possible for answering you, and, so I see, convey nothing—nothing. We are half dressed for a fancy dress ball:[4] a cold night; and we have to travel to London. But I have left you too long unanswered and so, without saying any of the things I meant to say, shall send you this.

Shall you be in Paris in March—the end?—or the beginning of April?

We have a plan for going to Spain via the [Jacques and Gwen] Raverats

1. The MacCarthys had lived in Wellington Square, Chelsea, until 1922, and then, for the sake of economy, took lodgings with a Miss Anthea Clough, the owner of a gloomy house in Ladbroke Grove, W.8, before moving to Wiltshire.
2. Of *Jacob's Room*, Virginia's third novel, which had been published by the Hogarth Press on 27 October 1922.
3. Probably her novel *The Counterplot* (1924). Hope Mirrlees was living in Paris with her friend Jane Harrison, the classical scholar. The Hogarth Press had published Mirrlees' *Paris: A Poem* in 1920.
4. A Twelfth Night party, given by Maynard Keynes at 46 Gordon Square, Bloomsbury, where Duncan Grant had a room.

3

at Vence, and might spend a night, in our speechless British way, in Paris, and see you.

Don't forget your play for the Hogarth Press.[1] We are taking on a manager,[2] and hope to become more and more professional.

Do write sometime.

"Oh but I *can't* write letters—shouldn't dream of it". Those were your very words to me in the Charing X Road!

Yours ever,
Virginia Woolf

Mrs T. S. Eliot

1344: To V. Sackville-West *Hogarth House, Paradise Road, Richmond, Surrey*

Sunday [7 January 1923]

Dear Mrs Nicolson,

It is extraordinarily good of you to send me Hassan,[3] and I am ashamed that you should take this trouble, owing to my laziness, for I have meant to get it for ever so long.

I shall start reading it and testing my theories of modern poetry directly I am in a fit state, but having sat up till three this morning watching other people dance, I am sunk in the depths of stupidity.

I hope you'll come and look at my great aunt's photographs[4] of Tennyson and other people some time. My sister has many of them at her house.

Yours very sincerely
Virginia Woolf

Berg

1345: To V. Sackville-West *Hogarth House, Paradise Road, Richmond, Surrey*

[10 January 1923]

Dear Mrs Nicolson,

Yes, do come tomorrow, Thursday—it will really suit us better than Monday, if you don't mind finding us alone, and our maids out.

1. The Press never published a play by Mirrlees.
2. Marjorie Thomson (who was living with C. E. M. Joad, the philosopher, and used his surname before she married him) joined the Hogarth Press on 29 January, overlapping Ralph Partridge, who left the Press in March.
3. The play by James Elroy Flecker, published posthumously in 1922.
4. Julia Cameron (1815-79), the photographer, was an aunt of Virginia's mother.

Will you catch the 7.10 at Sloane Square, which comes straight to Richmond. I will meet you and show you the way, which though short, is difficult to explain.

If I dont hear, I shall expect you then.

Yours sincerely
Virginia Woolf

Berg

1346: To Dorothy Brett   *Hogarth House, Paradise Road,*
                                 Richmond, Surrey

Friday [12 January 1923]

My dear Brett,

Yes, I quite agree that a meeting should be made. What about next Wednesday, 4.30? I think that seems my only day, so please manage it.

I wanted to write to you about Katherine, but all I could say seemed futile; but that does not mean that my feeling is. I am glad to find how many of her letters I have, so don't let us become strangers, and believe how I have thought of your sorrow.[1]

Ever yours
V.W.

University of Cincinnati

1347: To Violet Dickinson   *Hogarth [House, Richmond]*

Postcard
Wednesday [17 January 1923]

I'm in bed with the flue, so can't come, alas, on Friday, but hope to one day next week, if that suits you.

VW.

Berg

1348: To Molly MacCarthy   *Hogarth House, Paradise Road,*
                                   Richmond, Surrey

Friday [19 January 1923]

Dearest Molly,

I was just taking up my pen when struck down by the usual old temperature, which sinks my head fathoms deep in the mud. Ought one not to

1. Katherine Mansfield died in France of a pulmonary haemorrhage on 9 January 1923. In August 1922 she and her husband, Middleton Murry, had stayed for six weeks in the Hampstead flat of Dorothy Brett, the painter, who was one of her intimate friends.

5

find one's father's eyes when one sinks fathoms deep [*The Tempest*, I, ii]? But no such luck.

This is, primarily, in answer to your letter to the Hog. Press. Of course we will bully the old wretch.[1] Perpetual letters? Telegrams? Telephone? What do you advise? He must be coerced. I hate to think that all his words vanish into the cesspool (a horrid figure of speech—but then, I sometimes think we ladies, of the old guard, you and I, that is, the solitary survivors, ought to invigorate our language a little)—I've been talking to the younger generation all the afternoon. They are like crude hard green apples: no halo, mildew or blight. Seduced at 15, life has no holes and corners for them. I admire, but deplore. Such an old maid, they make me feel. "And how do you manage not- not - not - to have children?" I ask. "Oh, we read Mary Stopes of course."[2] Figure to yourself my dear Molly—before taking their virginity, the young men of our time produce marked copies of Stopes! Astonishing! Think of Aunt Gussie![3]

This is all incoherent drivvle: but then I'm above normal. You want news of that old bubble, now flown over St Paul's and far away, Nessa's party. Well, we were all awfully nice: I kept thinking of Shakespeare. We were so mellowly and good fellowly: not any intensity or bitterness, but all serene and melodious. Miss [Ethel] Sands; [Walter] Sickert; Roger [Fry]; then dancing, acting; it's a great thing to have done with copulation and to be merely a bag of pot pourri. Do you recognise any of your friends in that? Bunny Garnett went away and had a son the very next morning.[4] Everyone was so clever too. They sang. Marjorie Strachey acted, and her obscenity was really sublime. I want very much to come down. I figure us two, old friends, ladies, straying hand in hand down the glades of Savernake[5]—talking. Harry Norton[6] was at the party: very very old, no teeth: no flesh, no lusts. I felt that he was nothing but a pouch, a sort of puff ball, gone dry—but so amiable it made one weep. How is Mona Wilson?[7] Please write to me, a

1. Desmond MacCarthy. Virginia never managed to persuade him to write a book for the Hogarth Press.

2. Dr Marie Stopes, author of *Married Love* and *Wise Parenthood*, both published in 1918. The latter dealt with methods of contraception and was a huge popular success.

3. Mrs Douglas (Augusta) Freshfield, a sister of Sir Richmond Ritchie, who married Anne Thackeray. She was related by marriage to the Stephens, and was Molly MacCarthy's aunt.

4. David Garnett had married Rachel Marshall in 1921. Their son was christened Richard Duncan.

5. The MacCarthys lived at Oare, Wiltshire, near the Savernake Forest.

6. H. T. J. Norton, the Cambridge mathematician. In January 1923 he was only 36.

7. The writer, who also lived at Oare in Wiltshire, with G. M. Young, the historian.

diary letter: beginning "I was woken by a sunbeam at 8 a.m." going on through every detail until the schoolmaster calls in the evening.

But I must stop.

Ever Yr.
V.W.

Mrs Michael MacCarthy

1349: To Richard Aldington
Hogarth House, Paradise Road,
Richmond, Surrey

Typewritten
21st Jan. 1923

Dear Mr Aldington,

Mr Eliot has been here, and discussed the question of the fund[1] as I think he had already done with you. He asked me various questions which I could not answer and said I would ask you.

—whether it is our intention to give him an annual sum or to make him presents, like this £50, from time to time?

is the collection still going on in England?

how much he could count upon annually from our fund, if it is to be given annually?

I take it for granted that he told you, as he told us in confidence, of his decision to leave the Bank if he could get any reasonable means of living. Therefore of course the answers to these questions are very important to him. Probably it would be simpler if you wrote direct to Mr Eliot—I expect there are other things he wants to know, but I was not well and we could not go into it very thoroughly.

Then, I saw Mr Norton, the other Member of our Committee, who feels very strongly that we ought now to amalgamate with Mr Pound's committee and asked me to suggest this to you and Lady Ottoline.

If you think it would make matters any easier to talk instead of writing, please suggest any time, either to come here or to meet me in London.

Yours sincerely,
Virginia Woolf

Texas

1. In the summer of 1922 Virginia collaborated with Lady Ottoline Morrell, Richard Aldington, and H. T. J. Norton to collect a sum of money which would enable T. S. Eliot to leave his job at Lloyd's Bank and concentrate upon his writing. They issued an appeal, but by December 1922 had raised only £77 in cash, of which they gave Eliot £50. Ezra Pound was simultaneously attempting to raise money for Eliot on the Continent.

7

Hogarth House, Paradise Road,
Richmond, Surrey

[21? January 1923]

Dearest Ottoline,

I am ashamed not to have written before—I've been waiting for Tom to come to a decision—and saw him at last yesterday.

He wants to put the money in the Bank, invest it, and keep it, with his £400 from the dial,[1] to use when he leaves the Bank, which (but this is confidential) he feels now he must do before long. He was extremely grateful, full of hesitating and scruples of course.

I saw Harry [Norton] too. He feels strongly that we ought to amalgamate with the French Committee, and urges us to write to Ezra Pound and get him to take over our fund.

What do you think?

We should very much like to come to Garsington.[2] At this moment I'm in bed again with the usual influenza, and rather fear the dr may insist upon some more drastic measures [removal of her tonsils]—so that I can't make definite plans. But I look forward to coming; and so does L.

We are turned off the Nation, I suppose, with Massingham—This, too, is doubtful.[3]

I wish I'd kept up with Katherine [Mansfield], as you did—I found it too difficult. But I keep thinking of her now.

Ever your

VW.

Texas

1351: To Violet Dickinson   *Hogarth House, Paradise Road,*
Richmond, Surrey

[23? January 1923]

My Violet,

You are the most faithful of subscribers. Many thanks for your cheque. Next week we start an all-time Manager [Marjorie Joad], and we become more and more full of works to print. I wish we had something of yours.

1. In 1922 Eliot's *The Waste Land* won the $2000 prize from *The Dial*, where the poem was first published.
2. The Morrells' country house near Oxford.
3. Maynard Keynes had just became a major shareholder and Chairman of the Board of the *Nation*, which had been edited, since its foundation in 1907, by H. W. Massingham. Leonard had been a regular contributor to the journal, but Keynes now intended to change the editorial policy and staff, and Leonard was threatened with the loss of an important part of his income.

Yes, it is very tragic about Katherine [Mansfield]—She wanted to live so much. They thought she was getting better, and had talked of living in England again next summer. One can't help feeling rather a brute to go on living.

Shall I come to tea someday?—if you don't insist upon white gloves, which I can no longer scrape together. The Press is in the dining room, in the larder, and soon will be in bed with us.

Jacob [*Jacob's Room*] has gone into his second edition, and is going to be translated into French. (This is dreadful boasting). Leonard never wanted to get in—only to annoy Herbert Fisher; and we were both thankful when the results came out.[1]

I go on having a mild temp. They vaccinated a guinea pig with my spittle. It died, but no one knows what of—anyhow not tuberculosis which one idiot of a doctor discovered.

How are you? and your dog?

I like Mrs Nicolson: no nonsense about her.

Yr VW.

Berg

1352: TO RICHARD ALDINGTON

Hogarth House, Paradise Road,
Richmond, Surrey

Typewritten
26th Jan. 1923

Dear Mr Aldington,

Many thanks for your letter. I have sent the pass book to the Bank and have asked them to return it to me when made up.

I shall be seeing Mr Norton shortly and will tell him what you say about Mr Pound.

Am I right in thinking that Mr Eliot would object to my mentioning the possibility that he will leave the Bank? I find that when I ask people to subscribe, many of them object that he is staying in the Bank and drawing what many of them consider a good income. They would be much more ready to give, I think, if they knew that he would leave. I would tell them, of course, in confidence.

---

1. Leonard Woolf had stood for Parliament in the General Election of November 1922, as Labour candidate for the Combined English Universities. He came fourth in the poll out of six candidates, and one of the two sitting Members re-elected was Virginia's cousin H. A. L. Fisher, who stood as a National Liberal.

I do not know Mr Schiff[1] at all. Mrs Hutchinson[2] does I think and I will ask her to ask him to circularise. Also I will press this on Mr Norton. I will do my best, but find people full of objections.

Yours sincerely
Virginia Woolf

Texas

1353: TO CLIVE BELL   *Hogarth House, Paradise Road, Richmond, Surrey*

[February 1923?]

Dearest Clive,

I have to see my sister on Thursday, and should come round too late for a prolonged and animated conversation: so why shouldn't you come here on Friday or Saturday: or why shouldn't I come to tea with you on Tuesday?

Please settle one or t'other.

I can't face your blasted telephone, which kicks in my ear like an infuriated mule.

Yours
V.W.

Quentin Bell

1354: TO CLIVE BELL   *Hogarth House, Paradise Road, Richmond, Surrey*

[early February 1923]

Dearest Clive,

Yes, please, come to tea on Tuesday.

Streams, not of tears, but of disgusting rheum descend from either eye, and may, I feel, gush from the drums of my ears. I am in bed again, and my cold is a match for any in Bloomsbury. That's my first boast. Second, of course I've read the Cahier Rouge: but am slightly bemused—I've read Adolphe: Cahier Rouge: (forgive my crapulous repetition, and its not crapulous I mean either, but some word signifying the numb spasm which vibrates in a head with a cold): but what then is the Journal Intime? My memory is of a young man travelling in England—a diary? Please bring any I haven't read, but which?[3]

1. Sydney Schiff, the novelist and translator of Proust's last volume, who wrote under the name Stephen Hudson.
2. Mary Hutchinson was the wife of St John Hutchinson the barrister, and an intimate friend of Clive Bell.
3. These were all books by Benjamin Constant, the French politician and writer (1767-1830). The records of his travels through England in 1787 were contained in *Le Cahier Rouge*, published posthumously in 1907.

Boast three Scott Moncreiff pesters for a few words—any words from *you*, Mrs Woolf—it don't matter if you haven't read—invent.[1] But, unlike someone [Clive] I could not, unfortunately, touch with a short stick, I refuse. But do you realise who your colleagues are?

Boast four I've forgotten. Remind me when you come,—I'd like to remember it.

Who is Simpson?[2] What is she?

That Clive, my dear, adores him [*sic*]?

As for Tom [Eliot], we had a sitting: costive, agonised, but we were too ill to penetrate. What was said was confidential. And have you read the Criterion?[3] Mary writes a charming grumble on that head this morning.

Yes, I've fallen in love with [Marjorie] Joad, and given her my fountain pen to mend.

What else?

Tea Tuesday.

V.W.

Quentin Bell

1355: To MAYNARD KEYNES   *Hogarth House, Paradise Road, Richmond*

Typewritten
12th Feb. 1922 [*error for* 1923]

Dear Maynard,

May I lay the following facts about Eliot before you? of course in the strictest confidence.

He has now decided to give up the Bank. It is obvious that it is impossible to collect enough money to provide him with anything like a sufficient income. He is anxious therefore to get some permanent job which would bring him in £3 or £400 a year. If possible he would like work in some way connected with literature. Is there any chance that the Nation could give him employment as literary editor, or in any capacity which would bring him in an assured income? I suggested the very vague possibility of such work, and he said it was of all others what he should prefer.

If this is out of the question could you give us any advice or suggestions?

1. C. K. Scott Moncrieff was translating the second volume (1924) of Proust's *A la recherche du temps perdu*.
2. F. A. Simpson, a Fellow of Trinity College, Cambridge, had been attacked in the *TLS* for his book *Louis Napoleon and the Recovery of France*, 1923. Clive Bell had defended it.
3. The literary journal which Lady Rothermere and Cobden Sanderson founded in 1922 and of which T. S. Eliot was the first editor.

He has a degree at Harvard, where he studied philosophy; then went to Paris and Oxford but left without taking a degree. He would prefer not to teach, but would do secretarial or librarian's work. He is clearly getting into a bad state of health, and the efforts of the Eliot fund are so slow that it is useless to wait, on the chance that that will eventually support him. At present, the fund would pay him £300 a year, perhaps, for three years or so. If he could rely on a small certain income from regular work he would risk giving up the Bank. If it were not for his wifes constant illness he would have left the Bank before now.

His address is,

9 Clarence Gate Gardens, N.W.1.

I told him I was writing to you.

If there is anything you would like to ask me, I am on the telephone, or would come up.

Please excuse this pestering on my part, which is to relieve my own conscience, for I feel we have made a muddle and ought to try and do something sensible if possible.

Yours Ever
Virginia Woolf

[in Virginia's handwriting:]
He is, of course, extremely anxious that none of this should be talked about.

Marshall Library, Cambridge

1356: To Ethel Sands   *Hogarth House, Paradise Road, Richmond, Surrey*

Monday [12 February 1923]

Dear Ethel,

Fate seems determined against us. I'm having pneumonia germs injected into me to stop a mild sort of influenza which I go on having, and the doctor insists upon doing this on Thursday which means I shall be shivering and shaking on Friday night and intolerable as a companion. Then Tom Eliot says he can't possibly come, and really he is so worried that he's not much good either.

So I feel it would be useless to ask you to come all this way, and can only hope we haven't upset any of your plans.

Please forgive me, and promise to come another time instead.

Yours very sincerely,
Virginia Woolf

I hope to come on Wednesday.

Wendy Baron

1357: To Lady Ottoline Morrell

Hogarth House, Richmond

[mid-February 1923]

Dearest Ottoline,

This is merely to say that we look forward very much indeed to seeing you and Philip, on Sunday, 18th, about 6; and hope you will stay and dine—and excuse our having no dining room. It will be great fun, and let us postpone till then the eternal Eliot discussion—except could you send or bring some forms. I am making a last attempt before subsiding in despair

We should like ever so much to come to Garsington—May we leave it vague? We are completely unsettled in our plans by this Nation business, and may go abroad almost at once, or not, as things turn out. Their plans change from day to day, and ours with them.

Ever your
VW.

Texas

1358: To Vanessa Bell   [*Hogarth House, Richmond*]

[18 February 1923]

I forgot to say that Tom is fearfully anxious that no one should know of this scheme,[1] as it might damage him at the Bank if it got known—so please don't mention at all except to Duncan

Also he wished me to convey his extreme gratitude to you, which he could hardly express.

Philip [Morrell] posts this.

Berg

1359: To Ethel Sands   *Hogarth House, Paradise Road,*
                                    Richmond, Surrey

[21? February 1923]

My dear Ethel,

I find that Mr Eliot can't come on Saturday, but would like very much to meet you on Tuesday, 27th. Would that suit you? I hope so. I will send full directions if you will come. It is really as easy as can be even by train.

1. To obtain for T. S. Eliot the literary editorship of the *Nation*.

Did you say I might come and meet Leo Myers[1] one day. If Wednesday, I could come, with pleasure.

Yours very sincerely,

Virginia Woolf

I rather hope that there is a chance of some project for Tom Eliot; otherwise I must try to inveigle Mr Myers—his state is so depressing.

Wendy Baron

1360: To Lytton Strachey   *Hogarth House, Paradise Road, Richmond, Surrey*

Feb. 23rd 1923

Private and Confidential

I have to approach you on a delicate matter—to wit, poor Tom [Eliot]. The state of affairs is this; Maynard is trying to get him appointed literary editor of the Nation. He has to meet with great opposition from his fellow directors, who have none of them ever heard of him. His hands would be immensely strengthened, he says, if he could say that Tom is well thought of by writers of the highest importance, like Mr Lytton Strachey; and that in the event of Tom becoming Editor, Mr Lytton S. would contribute. As you are aware, the Eliot fund business has proved a fiasco; and this certainly seems to be the only possible solution of the problem. In fact, the poor man is becoming (in his highly American way, which is tedious and longwinded to a degree) desperate.[2] I think he will be forced to leave the Bank anyhow.

So if you could write me a line giving some sort of promise that you would write, or at least would be more inclined to write for him than another, we should all be very grateful. Only could I have it without delay, as Maynard is polishing off the whole affair in a series of distracted interviews early next week? Perhaps indeed it would be better if you wrote straight to Maynard at Kings.[3]

Please forgive me; still, this is cheaper than contributing the £100 which is your due; your conscience will be placated; and English literature, which we both have so much at heart, resents intensely, so I hear through Mr

1. Leo Hamilton Myers, the novelist and author of *The Orissers* (1923).
2. Virginia wrote in her Diary (19 February 1923) that she "could wish that poor dear Tom had more spunk in him, less need to let drop by drop of his agonised perplexities fall ever so finely through pure cambric". In March Eliot refused the offer of the literary editorship, mainly because the *Nation* could not guarantee more than six months employment.
3. In November 1919 Maynard Keynes was appointed Second Bursar at King's College, Cambridge, of which he had been a Fellow since 1909.

14

Gosse,[1] your prolonged indifference to her charms. What way of escape remains?

Yr
V.W.

It is said that Maynard is going to pay his contributors highly.

Berg

1361: To Lady Ottoline Morrell

Hogarth House, Paradise Road,
Richmond, Surrey

[23? February 1923]

Dearest Ottoline,

We were greatly disappointed not to see you,—perhaps you'll be up again?

At present our plan is to go to Spain about the 15th, which would I'm afraid make it difficult to manage a week end on the 10th—But with the Nation perpetually changing its plans, we really dont know from week to week. I think if you would let us come later it would be much pleasanter. We are rather distracted at the moment. We shall have to find some other job,—not journalism I hope.

Anyhow, we count on coming in May It was a great pleasure seeing Philip [Morrell].

By the way, Mrs Nicolson (Sackville-West)[2] wished to meet you; and was then disappointed.

Yours Ever
Virginia Woolf

I am talking to Quentin at the moment, so forgive this scrawl.

Texas

1362: To Maynard Keynes   Hogarth House, Paradise Road,
Richmond

Typewritten
24th Feb. [1923]

Dear Maynard,

I obeyed your instructions and did not reveal Miss Royde Smith[3] or any

1. Edmund Gosse, the critic.
2. Vita dined at Hogarth House on 22 February.
3. Naomi Royde Smith (d. 1964), the novelist, had been literary editor of the *Westminster Gazette*, 1912-22, and was a candidate for the literary editorship of the *Nation*.

other confidence to Eliot. He was a good deal concerned to think that he had not put before you the following point which had only struck him later: The Bank requires him to give three months notice. As his work is so specialised, he would not like to press them (unless absolutely forced) to relax this in his favour (as I gather they generally do.) Also he feels that he would do better work if he had a holiday first. Thus it seems certain that he would not be able to start in April, and he thought that you ought to know this before making any offer. He had tried to write to you, but being consumed with gratitude and diffidence had failed, and so asked me.

I think you'll find, if the arrangement can be worked, that Eliot has great influence with the younger writers, and would give the literary side of the Nation much more character than any of the ordinary literary hacks. Anyhow, it is a great relief to me that you have offered him something,—and something much better than he could expect—and I add my gratitude to his.

Yours ever
Virginia Woolf

[*in Virginia's handwriting:*]
I wrote to Lytton giving him an outline of the circumstances; and asked him to write to you.

No answer is required.

Marshall Library, Cambridge

1363: TO RICHARD ALDINGTON

Hogarth House, Paradise Road,
Richmond, Surrey

25th Feb [1923]

Dear Mr Aldington,

I am sorry I have not answered your letter before. I wrote to Mr Schiff myself, and enclose his reply (which I do not want returned.)

After talking to Mr Eliot I feel more and more that we should aim at finding some congenial post for him, so that he could leave the Bank without waiting until we collect sufficient for him to do so safely. I think our position with would-be subscribers is much stronger if we can say that he means to give up the Bank anyhow. They object (so I have found in two cases at least) to his staying on, with an income which they merely supplement.

But I will send out more forms, and hear from Mr Norton that he is making an effort at Cambridge.

Yours sincerely,
Virginia Woolf

Texas

1364: To Lady Ottoline Morrell

Hogarth House, Richmond

Feb. 28th [1923]

Dearest Ottoline,

I saw Tom yesterday and he was very anxious that I should write to you and ask you not to take any further steps about getting subscriptions to the Fund. He says that he can't take any more money so long as he is in the Bank, and I dont think there is any prospect of his being able to leave it for some time.

He feels very strongly (as you can imagine) about this, so will you tell your friend that the fund is now closed.

I'll tell Mr Aldington when he comes back.

Ever Yr
VW.

Texas

1365: To Dorothy Brett

*Hogarth House, Paradise Road,
Richmond, Surrey*

March 2nd [1923]

My dear Brett,

No you didn't tire me in the least—of course not. It was selfish of me, I felt, to make you talk about Katherine. I have wanted to so much since she died. But it must be very difficult for you. I've been looking in my diary and see that I must have written to her sometime in March 1921. From what you say, perhaps she never did get my letter. It makes me sorrier than ever that I did not simply persist—and yet I like to think that she had not, as I thought, taken some dislike to me, or got tired of hearing from me. I had been meeting [John Middleton] Murry, who was just going to join her, and he said she was lonely, and asked me to write. So I wrote at once, a very long letter, saying that she need only send one line, and I would go on regularly writing.[1] It hurt me that she never answered, and then, as I was telling you, those gossips assured me that this was her game, and so on, and so on; until though I wanted to write, I felt that I no longer knew where we stood together; and so waited to see her—as I thought I certainly should.

I have been typing out her letters this morning,[2] and it is terrible to me

1. Only two of Virginia's letters to Katherine Mansfield are known to survive, of which one is number 1156 in Vol. II of this edition.
2. She sent the typescripts to Katherine's widower, John Middleton Murry, who published twelve of them in his 2-volume edition of the Mansfield letters (1927-8). See letter 1387.

to think that I sacrificed anything to this odious gossip. She gave me something no one else can. But here I am being selfish again. No one of my friends knew her, except you; and that is why I cant help going on to you.

Whenever you like, please come again, or I'll come up to you.

Remember the photograph, some day.

Ever yours
V.W.

University of Cincinnati

1366: To Dorothy Brett   *Hogarth House, Paradise Road,*
Richmond, Surrey

[5? March 1923]

My dear Brett,

It was very good of you to write to me. I'm sure what you say is really true [about Katherine Mansfield]; but then you never wasted your chances as I did mine. Still, I'm sure, as I say: we always did get straight the very moment we met. Of course, don't dream of sending me a photograph if they are scarce—I have one I took somewhere, in Sussex, but can't find it. I'm afraid someone's coming on Saturday: and so don't think it's worth your while to come all the way—unless you're near, which I don't suppose is likely. But come another day if not that.

This ink is Waterman's fountain pen ink. Cheap, violet, indelible. (Which sounds as if I were paid to write their advertisements.)

But I didn't think you looked well: so why make yourself out a stolid carcase? Nonsense. I'm being driven by Kot^{sky} to translate Russian,[1] and have no time to write.

Ever yr
V.W.

University of Cincinnati

1367: To V. Sackville-West   *Hogarth House, Paradise Road,*
Richmond, Surrey

Tuesday [6 March 1923]

Dear Mrs Nicolson,

Do you think that you and your husband would dine with us, at my sister's house, 46 Gordon Sqre, on Thursday, 15th at 7.45?[2]

1. Virginia was correcting S. S. Koteliansky's translation of *Tolstoi's Love Letters*, and *Talks with Tolstoi* by A. B. Goldenveizer, both of which were published by The Hogarth Press in 1923.
2. At the dinner, besides Virginia and Leonard and the Nicolsons, were Duncan Grant, Clive Bell and Lytton Strachey.

She would have the [Cameron] photographs, and would very much like to see you.

There would be no party, and please dont dress—

Yours very sincerely
Virginia Woolf

Berg

1368: To S. S. Koteliansky   [*Hogarth House, Richmond*]

Postcard
[9 March 1923]

I'm greatly interested in the Tolstoi[1]—almost the best we've done, I think: and hope to finish it this week.

It's being typewritten; and I'll let you know when I have it back, and either come to your fire, or ask you to mine. Then I'll see whether an article could be made—but Squire[2] is certainly full for April, and, I expect, May.

V.W.

British Library

1369: To Vanessa Bell   Hogarth [*House, Richmond*]

Monday [12? March 1923]

I'm sorry I couldn't write yesterday.

The facts about the paper seem to be as follows:

one ream of paper costs 8/- From this you could make 1000 covers of the size of the stencils you have.

Or for 5/- you could get 500 covers of that size.

We want 300 covers for Read (of the size I gave you)

500 covers for Eliot (size not yet settled). We would commission you to do us 300 for Read; 500 for Eliot, at one penny each cover. (Eliot would be smaller than Read).[3]

We have chosen a cheap paper, and I'm not sure that it will be suitable.

1. *Love Letters*. See p. 18, note 1.
2. J. C. Squire was the founder and editor of the *London Mercury*. He did not publish Virginia's and Koteliansky's article.
3. She is referring to the forthcoming publication by the Hogarth Press of T. S. Eliot's *The Waste Land* (September) and Herbert Read's poems, *Mutations of the Phoenix* (May). Vanessa did not in fact do 'designs' for the first editions of these two books, which were bound in marbled paper boards with pasted-on labels, but she may have supervised the marbling.

I could bring you up samples to look at; but the difference in price is not very great. We should have to order through the Press in order to get wholesale prices.

I dont know whether you'll think this worth your while.

I should like to come and put the colours on under your direction, as I said.

What did you think of the marbling colours?

Would the firm of Grant and Bell give me an estimate for making a design for a simple wall paper to be stencilled?—something I could carry out myself.

VW.

Berg

1370: TO MAYNARD KEYNES   *Hogarth House, Richmond*

Typewritten
March 13th 1923

Dear Maynard,

Once more I come to bother you, for the last time, I hope, and very unwillingly.

Eliot rang me up last night, (apparently on the verge of collapse, but that is neither here nor there) and explained the present, and very satisfactory, state of affairs. But there still remains the one great obstacle which makes us hesitate to advise him to accept—the question of guarantee. If the paper [*Nation*] were to fail or you were to dismiss him within the year he would have had no experience to qualify him for another post as journalist, and would have lost his other work. Bruce Richmond [Editor, *TLS*], whom he consulted, assures me that all journalists would think his an exceptional case, as he is coming straight from the Bank, and has no experience to depend upon in case of disaster. On the Times each man on the staff has now a contract for five years. Do you think it would be impossible to assure him a guarantee for the first two years at any rate? and after that he could be treated in common with the others?

Some security would I think make all the difference to him and his work; and if he had that one could have no possible doubt in urging him to accept.

I know what difficulties you have already overcome, and wouldn't press you further unless I felt this rather vital.

Yours Ever
Virginia Woolf

[*in Virginia's handwriting:*]
I am writing without consulting Eliot.

Marshall Library, Cambridge

20

1371: To Lady Ottoline Morrell

Hogarth House, Paradise Road,
Richmond, Surrey

Saturday [17 March 1923]

My dear Ottoline,

I was in company with a young man yesterday called Sebastian Sprot[1] who said that his great wish was to meet you. He is a friend of Lyttons, a psychologist, and apparently (this was our second meeting) agreeable and intelligent. So, as you guess, I said I would risk annoying you by repeating this, in the hope that perhaps you might ask him to Garsington one day and so gratify his ambition.

His address is Clare College, Cambridge. I really think he is very nice, and very young.

But of course don't take any notice if it is inconvenient—and no answer is needed.

Ever Yours
Virginia Woolf

Texas

1372: To Maynard Keynes   *Hogarth [House, Richmond]*

Friday [23 March 1923]

Dear Maynard

I'm very sorry not to see you today, but I have the typhoid [inoculation] germs strongly.

In justice to Eliot, I think that there were difficulties which made it very hard for him to decide, and he could not give his real reasons for delay. Nevertheless, I can't help feeling he was not the right person for the job, so on the whole I'm relieved.[2]

It was very good of you to take so much trouble.

Ever yours
V.W.

Marshall Library, Cambridge

1. W. J. H. Sprott was then an undergraduate at Cambridge and a friend of Maynard Keynes, with whom he had travelled to Algeria in 1921, and of Lytton Strachey, whom he often visited at Tidmarsh. He had been to Venice with Lytton in the summer of 1922. In 1926 he went to Nottingham University as Lecturer in Psychology.
2. When T. S. Eliot turned down the job, Leonard was offered the literary editorship of the *Nation* on this very day, and he accepted it.

Hogarth House, Paradise Road,
Richmond, Surrey

[26 March 1923]

My dear Brett,

I haven't tried to see you, as the chaos of affairs has been too great and I've had to spend a good deal of time with injections and mild temperatures. We are off to Spain tomorrow till May 1st.

This is merely to say I hope to see you, and think of you in the fragmentary but sincere way one does of people one wants to—oh but this sentence will never come right. I'm packing. You will see what I meant to put. How are you?

Let us meet with time to talk when I get back.

Ever yours,
V.W.

University of Cincinnati

Letters 1374-1382 (April 1923)

On 27 March Virginia and Leonard went abroad for the first time since their honeymoon in 1912. They travelled by train through France and Spain, to Madrid and then Granada, where they spent a few days with Charles Temple and his wife, and continued by bus and mule to the remote cottage in the Sierra Nevada belonging to Gerald Brenan. Brenan, a wartime friend of Ralph Partridge, who introduced him to Bloomsbury, had chosen to live in this isolated place for the sake of economy and to study English and French literature. Partridge, with Lytton Strachey and Carrington, had visited him there in 1920. The Woolfs' visit was a great success. "Virginia seemed", wrote Brenan in South from Granada *(1957), "though quiet, as excited as a schoolgirl on holiday". They spent ten days with him, and then went home, Virginia remaining in Paris three days longer than Leonard, who returned to London to take up his new duties as Literary Editor of the* Nation and Athenaeum.

1374: TO JACQUES RAVERAT   *Hotel Ingles, Madrid*

Good Friday [30 March 1923]

My dear Jacques,[1]

    Domestic uncertainties have prevented me from writing to you—that is to say, the Nation, the newspaper for which Leonard wrote, has been bought by Maynard Keynes, and Leonard first lost his job, which ruined us, and has now been made literary editor, which is almost as bad. It means that we must be back punctually on April 27th, and thus shan't get to Vence. This is a great disappointment; but next year? It will have to be arranged somehow. Will Gwen be over again? Don't let her choose August if she is. Meanwhile, I hope you will occasionally send a letter. Only friendship dictates this. Never was there such a pen, and as for Hotels, the spirits of the damned inhabit them. It is a superb country all the same, as we came through yesterday. Still, I was impressed by the South of France—not by the midlands. I felt a kind of levity and frivolity and congeniality upon me with the first sight of Dieppe. How much more enjoyable in some queer way France is than England! But how does one learn the language? I must and will. I want to know how the French think. After the English, they seem so natural, so much akin to all one likes.

1. Jacques Raverat, the French painter, had married Virginia's friend Gwen Darwin in 1911. He had been educated in England, but they lived at Vence, near Nice.

23

Here we have been following the Crucifixion and the Last Supper through the streets, and again I felt entirely sympathetic, which one couldn't imagine doing in Piccadilly say, or the Earls Court Road—where you and Gwen once lived, if I remember, before you made your grand attack upon Bloomsbury and left us. Is this right? You see I am still reconstructing your past, from fragments, mostly false, I daresay. You were a man of convictions, in which you were confirmed by marrying a Darwin, of all races the most monolithic. I was in Cambridge last month, and there started up, in the Shoves'[1] drawing room, a military man, of upright bearing and manly spirit, whom I thought to be a friend of Gerald's youth, quite out of place in literary society—but it was Mr Cornford!![2] Good Heavens! Last time he was wearing a French peasant's blouse and a red tie. There is a great deal of mystic religion about. I wish one had the cruelty of youth. I've been asked to advise a woman [Brett] as to the souls of the dead—can they come back? As I'm never quite sure which is which—spirit, matter, truth, falsehood and so on—I can't speak out as roundly as a Darwin should. Or is Gwen not an agnostic?

Are you painting? Will they be shown in London? Are they good? And in what direction are you tending? I wanted to buy a seascape by Matisse the other day, but the price was tremendous.

But this is trivial gossip, and we must go out and dine. I find you easy to write to, however—which I mean as a very great compliment. (You remember how vain I always was).

Now we go on for 10 days to the Englishman's castle near Granada, and then home to Maynard, to politics, to printing, to whatever life may be said to be. I've no room to go into the matter further, alas.

Love to Gwen.

Yrs ever,
V.W.

Sussex

1375: To V. SACKVILLE-WEST   *Hotel Ingles, Madrid*

Good Friday [30 March 1923]

Dear Mrs Nicolson,

(But I wish you could be induced to call me Virginia). I got your letter

1. Gerald Shove, the Cambridge economist, married in 1915 Fredegond Maitland, the daughter of Virginia's cousin Florence Fisher, who married F. W. Maitland, the biographer of Leslie Stephen. Fredegond was received into the Catholic Church in 1927.
2. Francis Cornford had been a Fellow of Trinity College, Cambridge, since 1899, and was appointed Lecturer in Classics in 1904. He married the poet Frances Darwin, Gwen Raverat's cousin.

as we left Richmond. I am much flattered that the P.E.N. should ask me to become a member.[1]

I would do so with pleasure, except that I don't know what being a member means. Does it commit one to make speeches, or to come regularly, or to read papers or what? Living so far out, dinners are apt to be difficult, and I cant speak. But we shall be back the first week in May, and if you would then enlighten me I would at once let you know. It was very good of you to propose me, and I shouldn't be cautious at all if I didn't remember some reason that made it seem, when I was asked once before, difficult to manage.

We have been tramping round Madrid after the figure of Christ in a purple dressing gown, The Last Supper, The Crucifixion and so on, and are half dazed with noise, but it is all very exciting,—the country as we came through Spain yesterday was incredibly beautiful. Tomorrow we are off to Granada.

Yours very sincerely
Virginia Woolf

Berg

1376: To Vanessa Bell *Carmen de los Fosos, Generalife, Granada, Spain*

1st April [1923]

Dearest,

We arrived here last night, and are staying with the Temples;[2] she being a Miss McLeod, lord of the Scottish Isles, who says she once met you. Anyhow they're very anxious that you and Roger [Fry] should come here, which I said I would pass on to you at once, and hereby do. It's an awful long journey—and we still have 2 days on mules and in diligences before we reach Gerald's [Brenan] house, up in the Sierra Nevada—mountains, I may tell you, always with snow on them. Nevertheless I am determined never to live long in England again. The rapture of getting into warmth and colour and good sense and general congeniality of temper is so great. I was overcome by the beauty of Dieppe—don't you think we might share a Chateau, so large that we never met? Not to run up against suburbs and old respectable creatures at every step is such a joy. I shall learn French at once.

1. Vita was a member of the Committee of P.E.N., the international authors' society, and had proposed Virginia for membership. She described the scene in her letter to Virginia of 26 March: "There was a little shout of excitement from the Committee about you, and Galsworthy (so to speak) got up and made a curtsy." Virginia had received a previous invitation from P.E.N. in the autumn of 1921, and had refused it.
2. Charles Lindsay Temple, formerly Governor of Northern Nigeria. His wife was Olive, daughter of Sir Reginald Macleod, 27th Chief and Baron of Dunvegan, Skye. He was 52; she was 37.

We had no adventures to speak of. Travelling is very easy. I managed to avoid the Aldous Huxleys who crossed with us. I can't think it right to look precisely like an illustration to Vogue; and I daresay they thought the same t'other way round about us. Spain is quite different from France, but I leave all that for you. There was a great religious festival at Madrid, and stuffed images of great beauty (emotional, not aesthetic) were parading; and Christ was showered under with confetti. Why not bring the children up Roman Catholics? I think it induces to warmth of heart. Gerald is staying here, and we have been walking in wind and rain through the Generalife gardens, which I visited in 1904 with Adrian. Much has happened since. The Temples are an elderly couple, he racked with malaria, always wrapped in a great coat, and was at Cambridge and knew the Ll. Davies', and used to be taken to Roger's studio in Battersea. He jumped at the mention of him. He said he understood he had become very advanced; but himself stuck to Corot. She is a Scottish gentlewoman, clean, discreet, shabby, with blue eyes like poor Marny's [Margaret Vaughan], but is a woman of character, since her betrothed died exploring Lake Chad, when she was a girl in the Isle of Skye, and was buried (naturally enough) on the spot without a tomb. She at once went to Edinburgh, bought a marble slab, had it engraved, and started for Lake Chad, against the wishes of all her family; deposited it on the very spot and married the governor. Mrs [Margot] Asquith is coming on Tuesday, but we shall be gone.

Leonard and Gerald are at a bull-fight. I am afraid I am not going to be offered any tea. It is a wonderful modern house, with electric saucepans in every room. Mr Temple is an engineer. I regret to say that I had difficulty with the W.C. this morning. Remember, if you come, to screw the handle round and round—otherwise nothing happens.

I ought to be writing an article for the Nation;[1] but the worst of travelling for writers is that it freezes all their functions. To write to a dolphin is all very well—perhaps though Leonard's terms are rejected.[2] I hope not. I think it might be great fun. Does it strike you that we are all now elderly?—elderly, accomplished, successful, looked up to? It doesn't reach to Granada however. Murry wrote me a wormish letter, by the way, about the differences between us, and our memories and so on. I tried to imitate you, and replied that our differences are too great to admit of any further communication; so that we had better rely on the past. Poor Tom [Eliot] said he was only capable of creeping into the country. His problem still remains[3]—

1. Virginia's article *To Spain* was published in the *Nation and Athenaeum* on 5 May 1923, the first issue after its reorganisation under Keynes.
2. His terms were: first, that he would attend the office only part-time; second, that the literary side of the journal would be autonomous, subject to Keynes's ultimate decision. These conditions were accepted.
3. Mrs Eliot's mental illness had worsened, and Eliot's future was still undecided.

God knows what we can do about it. Please, however, be as discreet as marble. Mary, I gather, is the [person] they most dread[1]—she wrote me a most affectionate letter about looking at the cliffs of Dover and thinking of her, which is more than I get out of some people I could touch with a short stick.

Did you think Rodmell very inferior to Charleston?[2] I suppose so: but then what a pleasure that was! How the Wolves can live here: how stuffy; how ridiculous their decorations are etc etc. That was what Dolphin said to Duncan when they settled in at night.

Yr
B.

The Posts are apparently most prolonged here, so it would be best to write to me at Hotel de Londres, Paris, to say if you're coming and when. L. has to be back on 27th; we shall get there 25th; and I shall stay on 5 or 6 days. Mrs Temple is of course a cousin of the Vaughans.[3]

Berg

1377: To David Garnett   *Carmen de los Fosos, Generalife,*
                                        Granada, Spain
April 2nd [1923]

Dear Bunny
    I enclose a letter from the headmaster's wife of Rugby. (She was Symondse's daughter)[4]
    I have just written your biography, shortly, but amiably. At the same time, it is very difficult to write to Rugby when one is at Granada. I have told her that if she will buy a book, you will tie the parcel with your own hands.
    She is an incredible figure from the Victorian past.
    We go to Brenan's tomorrow.

Yr
Virginia Woolf

Berg

1. Mary Hutchinson was an intimate friend of T. S. Eliot at this period.
2. During Virginia's absence abroad, Vanessa and Duncan Grant stayed with her children at Monk's House.
3. Through Sir Vere Isham Bt., who married Millicent Vaughan, Virginia's cousin.
4. Madge Vaughan, who had written to Virginia praising David Garnett's novel *Lady into Fox* and asking for information about the author. She was the daughter of John Addington Symonds, and her husband was William Wyamar Vaughan, who had previously been Headmaster of Wellington College.

Murcia, Spain
April 15th 1923

Dear Madam,
I have just had forwarded to me your letter saying that I have been elected a member of the P.E.N. Club.

As I have been travelling, I did not know that Mrs Nicolson had proposed me, and so could not let her know in time that, much though I should like to be a member, circumstances at present make it impossible.

I regret very much that you should have had the trouble of writing to me, and hope that you will be so good as to express my thanks and regrets to The Committee.

Yours faithfully
Virginia Woolf

Texas

Murcia, Spain
April 15th 1923

Dear Mrs Nicolson
The secretary of the P.E.N. club has written to me to say that I have been elected a member. Very regretfully I have had to decline—since I see from the club papers that it is wholly a dining club, and my experience is that I can't, living at Richmond, belong to dining clubs. I've tried two dining clubs, with complete disaster. But I'm very sorry, as I should like to know the members, and see you also.

But this last I hope can be managed in other ways.

I'm sitting in a Café with a band, ten million Spaniards playing dominoes, and old men trying to sell lottery tickets, so forgive this scrawl. We've had a splendid time up in the Sierra Nevada, staying with a mad Englishman [Brenan], who does nothing but read French and eat grapes.

There never was such a lovely country.

Yours very sincerely
Virginia Woolf

Berg

Murcia [Spain]
16th April 1923

My dear Roger,
This is an invitation from Brenan—he is very anxious that you should come and stay with him at Yegen—also from the Temples, who want you to

stay with them at Granada. Brenan says you are the greatest living critic—But besides that his house is comfortable, and the country strange and amazing, and I kept wondering where you would pitch your camp stool and what you would say. But I shan't commit myself to descriptions.

It has been the greatest success so far. I am amazed that we should live in England and order dinner every morning and edit the Nation and catch trains when we might roll in bliss every moment of the day and sit and drink coffee on a balcony overlooking lemon trees and orange trees with mountains behind and every sort of colour and shade perpetually changing which I do now: then a delicious lunch off rice and bacon and olive oil and onions and figs and sugar mixed, then off to a place where cypresses and palm trees grow together.

How is your show doing?[1] I'm very anxious for news, but never see papers, and can't get any more letters. I've been reading the life of Cézanne (and Rimbaud and lots of the French whom Gerald has, being disgusted with my own language and in love with theirs). So if you never sell a picture till you're 70 you will only be like Cézanne—but I hope you are selling.

I'm afraid I shall exactly miss you in Paris. We get to Hotel de Londres on the 22nd, and I shall stay on alone till 28th, but Nessa seemed to think you and she would be certainly later. What a bore! I look forward to Paris with the excitement of a girl of 16, and intend to talk French like a native by the light of nature. I know the words, but can never think how to make them into sentences.

Gerald is very nice; we discuss literature 12 hours every day; unfortunately your praises are sung too often for my taste, but he has an enthusiasm for your criticism—which reminds me I hope you're getting on with your lectures. And remember the Nation.

Ever yours
V.W.

Temple (Charles) ex-governor of Nigeria, said he used to visit your studio with the [Llewelyn] Davies'—rather a nice man, slightly cranky, always dressed in 2 overcoats; also admiring, but out of date.

Sussex

1381: To Molly MacCarthy   *Hotel de France, Montauban*

22nd April 1923

Dearest Molly,
    I snatch this moment while Leonard is in the W.C., to wish you good morning. I wish you were here. We are travelling home after staying with

1. Roger Fry's one-man show at the Independent Gallery.

Brenan on the top of the Sierra Nevada. But how dull travellers' stories are! I omit all about the adventures with the mule, the vulture, and the wolf. Your imagination can play freely upon them. This is an old French town. One lives very cheap. I should rather like to transfer life here. I don't want to come back to meat meals, servants, and telephones. But my French is insufficient to carry on human communication, so one dries up in the founts of one's being and must return.

How are you? When shall I see you? Two days before we left it was sprung on us that Leonard was to be lit. editor of the Nation. (I continue, if I can, in the train). Should this take place, which is not quite certain, he wishes to get hold of your memoirs.[1] Would you consent? Very slight alterations would be needed; and how delightful to humanise the Nation, which is dry and bald as bone, with the Cornish[2] family and its eccentricities!

You must consider this and let me know.

We are now about to enter Paris, in the dark.

There I shall stay a few days and meet Jane Harrison and Hope Mirrlees . . . [*six words omitted*], while Leonard returns.

But the train is crowded with these exquisite French ladies—all un-reproachable, elegant and composed, while I feel like a farmyard boy who has lately rolled in the gorse bush.

Ever yrs
V.W.

Mrs Michael MacCarthy

1382: To Leonard Woolf   *Hotel de Londres* [*Paris*]

Tuesday [25 April 1923]

Dearest Mong[oose],

Here I am already in bed at 10.30, and I shall be asleep within the half hour. I've had quite a successful though a lonely day. I wrote—found nothing to do to my Nation article, so began Gissing;[3] lunched at a new place; good; 3 courses; bought china and went to the Louvre; took bus to Notre Dame; was there pursued by the Headmaster of Eton and wife and family whom I knew,[4] and had to escape; had tea; again pursued—hid

1. Her memoirs were serialised in the *Nation* later this year, and published in book form as *A Nineteenth-Century Childhood* in 1924.
2. Molly MacCarthy was the daughter of Francis Warre-Cornish, vice-Provost of Eton College.
3. Review of *George Gissing: An Impression*, by May Yates (*New Statesman*, 30 June 1923).
4. Cyril Alington, Head Master of Eton, 1917-1933. His wife was Hester Lyttelton, whom Virginia had known in her youth through Violet Dickinson.

behind a pillar; bought more china; again pursued, hid behind a pot; so home by bus; rung up by Hope [Mirrlees], who wants to treat me to ices at Rumpelmayers tomorrow, and asks me to dine on Thursday; says I shall easily get tickets for the Misanthrope. Now I've dined at our usual place— omelette, ham and pots, and spinach; suisse, coffee and cream, then choco- late, very good, at the orchestra café, but the music was such that even I could dream no dreams, so came away, got straight into bed, and finished reading my Gissing book; which brings me to the present moment. You, I suppose, have arrived, and are surrounded by innumerable letters. I'll now put out the light and fall fast asleep—it being 25 to 11. Goodnight, sweetest tiny mouse.

Wednesday

Here I am on Wednesday morning, having had a very good night, no aspirin—slept till 7.45.

I have written at Gissing, and now I am going to dress and go about my business. It is fine, almost hot. I must go first and get money changed: then to the [Galeries] Lafayette, and then home to meet Hope and have tea. I'm already rather lonely, and home sick. No letter from Nessa, so I shall come certainly on Friday. So far I've found my way without difficulty. Just before I came to the Boul. St Germain a drunk taxi driver drove straight onto the pavement into a tree and knocked five people down and bent the tree right over. But I was too late to see it.

I long to hear from you. It was bitterly cold here yesterday; how is your cold? and I wonder how Margery [Joad] has done, and what news there is,— if I've many letters—but it's no use asking questions.

I must now get ready; and kiss my Mong a thousand times.

I am honestly being very good, shall go to bed again tonight and read till 10.30, then sleep: and of course the way to make me want Mong is to be away from him: It is all rather pointless and secondrate away from him.

                                                                        MANDRILL

Sussex

31

Letters 1383–1414 (May–July 1923)

The Woolfs returned from their Spanish holiday to intensive work. Leonard was editing the literary columns of the Nation, *running the Hogarth Press, acting as Secretary to two Labour Party Committees, and writing, when he had time, his major work* After the Deluge. *Virginia helped Mrs Joad with the Press every afternoon, reading manuscripts, setting type, packing parcels, and contributed regular reviews to the* Nation. *But her most important activity was the writing of the two books which she had started in 1922. The* Common Reader *required much new study for the articles which were not reprints.* Mrs Dalloway (*then named* The Hours) *had hung fire for several months, but after a visit to Ottoline Morrell at Garsington in early June, she returned to it energetically, foreseeing 'the devil of a struggle' with it.*

1383: TO VANESSA BELL   [*Hogarth House, Richmond*]
Saturday [28 April 1923]

Dearest,

I got your letter in Paris just as I was starting back. Oddly enough, the first person I ran into at Victoria was Duncan, who was dining somewhere, and already an hour late, so I hadn't much talk. Please stay on at Rodmell as long as you or the children want. We certainly shant be able to come down yet—the Nation keeps us in a rush at present; and all its politics.

I hope I shall see you next week. I didn't write, as I thought you were touring in the north of France. I had a very amusing time in Paris, and saw a good deal of Hope [Mirrlees] and Jane [Harrison] and met various oddities —among them a humpback painter Maria Blanchard,[1] who said that Vanessa Bell was one of the few women to take art seriously. She didn't know I was your sister—She is humped in front, not behind, Spanish, almost unintelligible. There were also some friends of Clive's friends—and a lot of chatter, which I will tell you about but haven't time now.

We are in a frightful turmoil with our books coming out, and now Maynard wants a special literary supt. in a hurry. Wont you write something? or Duncan? I saw the Poussins at the Louvre—the only pictures I liked: also the Alingtons, who aren't pictures: she was Hester Lyttelton. They chased me about; till I went into a china shop and hid behind po's. No good.

1. The Spanish painter (1881-1932). She met Roger Fry in 1916, and exhibited with the London Group in 1923.

Hester bobbed up as usual, grown fat and blowsy with ankles like the thick end of asparagus. I'm sorry you don't like Rodmell nearly as much as Charleston, but it aint my fault.[1] I don't think the children could spoil anything, as there's nothing to spoil.

Yr devoted and loving faithful furry dear

B.

Mary wrote me a letter of affection so of course I answered.[2] I always do. Try. We're dining with Maynard on Tuesday. What about Lydia? I hope to God Maynard has been restrained—a fatal, and irreparable mistake.[3]

Berg

1384: To Clive Bell

Hogarth House, Paradise Road, Richmond, Surrey

[May? 1923]

Dearest Clive,

Your paramour rashly whetted my curiosity to see your pamphlet.[4] May I read it? May the Press consider it for publication? If so, may I have it instantly? Anyhow, I want to read it; but it would be even more to my taste to read it as Woolf & Co with a view to our future glory.

Please excuse the scrawl.

V.W.

Quentin Bell

1385: To Vanessa Bell

Hogarth House, Paradise Road, Richmond, Surrey

Typewritten
[early May 1923]

Dearest Dolph,

Here is a cheque for £36. 7. 8. £33. 6. 8. is Wallers money.[5] £1. 1. is

1. In fact, Vanessa had written to Virginia: "It has been the greatest blessing having it for the children who are very happy there and I hope not too destructive" (25 April 1923, *Berg*).
2. Vanessa had complained that Virginia had written to Mary Hutchinson and not to her.
3. Maynard Keynes had fallen in love with Lydia Lopokova in the summer of 1922, and married her in August 1925.
4. *On British Freedom* was published in the summer of 1923 by Chatto and Windus.
5. When his wife, Virginia's half-sister Stella Duckworth, died in 1897, John Waller Hills made over her marriage settlement from the Duckworths to the Stephen children until he remarried in 1931.

Hogarth Press payment for your drawing. The remaining two pounds I should be very grateful if you would lay out for me on a cotton dress, of the greatest charm, not too bright or startling, but cool, exquisite, as long in the leg as possible; and to be sent here as soon as so you can. The rest of the money I should like to buy china with. I want six soup plates; six sweet plates. I leave the choice entirely to you. Of course, plates are always useful, if any money is over.

Don't bother. If you cant get the dress, would you let me know, as I must get one. Let me know if these items come to more than £2.

Did you read your praises in the New Statesman?[1] best woman painter living, wonderful, lovely and so on. I like you to be praised, chiefly because it seems to prove that I must be a good writer. Oh dear, why does Lydia always come in—and why must she beg me to believe that she thinks seriously every day of her life, as she says? when her brain is a cage of canaries?

The china shop is on the left just before you get to Notre Dame. Please write; take care of yourself; etc etc. Kiss Duncan whom I adore more and more. Do you like him better than I do? I dont believe—but hush.

Your affectionate sister,
Virginia Woolf

A copy of the wood cut was sent as requested to Mr Furst.[2]

Berg

1386: To Janet Case   *Hogarth House, Paradise Road,*
                                      Richmond, Surrey
Friday [4 May 1923]

My dear Janet,

We came back from Spain last week, and I found your letter. Two days before we started Leonard was offered the Literary Editorship of the Nation: with the result that we find ourselves bombarded with proofs, reviewers, books and turmoil of all kinds, as nothing is ready, no one is experienced, and the old Nation has left a litter of odds and ends behind it.

---

1. On 5 May John Alton, writing about the London Group, had said of Vanessa: "There is always a beautiful character pervading all the work of this the best of our women painters."
2. Herbert Furst, the art critic and editor of the *Woodcut*, an annual publication. In 1924 he included one of Vanessa's illustrations for *Kew Gardens*.

But this sounds all very trivial compared with your forest trees.[1] I'm not sure that it isn't, and don't at all want to see Leonard engulfed in wretched little chatter about new novels. But he is a masterly man: in two days he does what a thoroughly good editor spreads over a week.

I have just seen Harry Davies' death in the paper.[2] Poor Margaret! How one tragedy follows another! How are you? and Emphie? and the china, and the house? I've been freshening up my furniture, and tea cups—in vain imitation of you. Why, with a passion for nice tea cups, am I destined to drink forever out of chipped earthenware? But I have no time to go into this profoundly interesting question, as I must read Miss Dorothy Richardson,[3] having been bribed by very large sums of money to do what of all things I have come to detest—write reviews for the Nation. All I say is commonplace: reading the books is sheer agony: it is warm and seductive; apples are out, and bees are busy, but in order to make large sums of money here I must sit at my books. As a matter of fact, she interests me rather.

So goodbye,—the blessed germs have started again, after leaving me for 4 weeks—I suppose I must have more pneumonia injected, but feel too well to bother. Excuse the handwriting.

Ever yrs
V.W.

Sussex

1387: To John Middleton Murry

Hogarth House, Paradise Road,
Richmond, Surrey

May 11th [1923]

My dear Murry

This is just to say that I am back here again, if you have done with Katherine's [Mansfield] letters, and would like to send them back. Brett said that you would let me have a photograph of her one of these days. It would be very good of you, and I should prize it very much. The one I had, a snapshot I took at Asheham, is lost, much to my sorrow.

Yours ever
Virginia Woolf

Berg

1. Janet Case, who had been Virginia's tutor in Greek, lived in the New Forest with her sister Emphie.
2. Harry Llewelyn Davies, who died on 1 May at the age of 57, was Margaret's brother. He had been a businessman. Another of Margaret's brothers, Theodore, and her nephew Michael, had both been drowned.
3. The English novelist, whose 'stream of consciousness' method had some resemblance to Virginia's own. Virginia's review of her *Revolving Lights*, appeared in the *Nation and Athenaeum* of 19 May 1923.

1388: To Gerald Brenan   *Hogarth House, Paradise Road,*
                                          Richmond, Surrey
Sunday, it may be 12th [13th] of May [1923]

My dear Gerald,

If I don't seize this moment, inauspicious as it is, I shan't write. Every cranny of my day is filled with the most degrading occupations. I think of you as a Saint on a hill top—someone who has withdrawn, and looks down upon us, not condescendingly but with pity. Indeed, all my memories of you are of an extraordinary pleasantness. What do the old ladies at Granada say about you? So sweet a nature, such tact, combined, my dear, with all an Englishman's dignity, and never in the way, and so considerate, with charming manners too. I can well believe that he will write something very very wonderful one of these days. With all these sentiments I entirely agree.

Please let me know exactly what your allowance comes to.[1] Is it enough for travel? Shall you alter your way of life? Here we are with our noses to the grindstone. The grindstone is made of innumerable books which have to be transubstantiated into precisely the right number of articles, containing the right sentiments, views and facts, in the right number of words at the right moment. This not once, but weekly, every week, every month, every year— till all our precious time is over, and life, which surely has other uses, has poured in cataracts of printers ink, down the main gutter to the Thames. Perhaps the horror will mitigate. I have had only 4 days writing at my novel[2] since I got back. Tomorrow, I say to myself, I shall plunge into the thick of it. But how does one make people talk about everything in the whole of life, so that one's hair stands on end, in a drawing room? How can one weight and sharpen dialogue till each sentence tears its way like a harpoon and grapples with the shingles at the bottom of the reader's soul? Did we discuss dialogue at Yegen? I lose myself in metaphors when I begin to write, being dissipated, interrupted,—here is Leonard with the title page of the Feather Bed, a poem in the manner of Browning by Robert Graves. We are printing all day long, Mrs Joad and I, while Leonard goes to his office. No news, except a postcard from Palermo from Carrington.[3] I am sending Valéry's poem which I got for you in Paris. The Nation with a poor article by Lytton and a poor article by me.[4] This is to fulfil my promise—not to make you think well of me as a writer. Then, I shall send the Proust book, which one day I should like back again.

1. Gerald Brenan was receiving £50 a year from his great aunt Addie, Baroness von Roeder, and a further allowance from his father.
2. *Mrs Dalloway* (see introductory note to this section).
3. Dora Carrington, with Lytton Strachey and Ralph Partridge, was on her way back through Sicily from visiting North Africa.
4. Lytton's article was *Sarah Bernhardt*, and Virginia's, *To Spain*.

Did I not say this was an inauspicious moment? The church bells are ringing, through a watery evening atmosphere: I sit by a solid coal fire, and hear vaguely the motor buses accumulating power to return to London stuffed with wet clerks and girls in bright woollen dresses. To your eye, these girls might have something attractive. I wonder whether your manly passions are a help to your writing? I wonder what your father and mother do and say? I shall recoup myself for the extreme coldness, colourlessness, and insipidity of the external world by going to the Italian marionettes[1] tomorrow: by having Tom Eliot to dinner; by dining at the Cock with some brave sprit like—can't think of anyone at the moment: and with luck, some small adventure will turn up. This I say to lure you here. Beevor Bevan[2] makes his appearance in about 2 weeks time. Let me have your Aunt's address and a copy shall go to her.

Your
Virginia Woolf

George Lazarus

1389: TO THOMAS HARDY   *Hogarth House, Paradise Road,*

Richmond, Surrey

17th May 1923

Dear Mr Hardy,

I was once so bold as to write and thank you for your poem upon my father, Leslie Stephen.[3] I have always treasured your reply.

My husband, Leonard Woolf, has just been made Literary Editor of the *Nation and Athenaeum*, and I am writing to say how proud it would make us if you would send us anything of yours for the paper. It would be impertinent for us to try to tell you how great an honour we should think it. There is, of course, no other writer who could give the paper the distinction that you could give it.[4]

Please excuse me if I bother you in making this request. I cannot help thanking you once more for the profound and increasing pleasure which your writings give me.

Yours sincerely,
Virginia Woolf

Trustees of the Hardy Memorial Collection,
Dorset County Museum, Dorchester

1. The Marionette Players of Teatro dei Piccoli, who were performing Charles Perrault's *Puss in Boots*.
2. A satirical article by Gerald Brenan which Leonard had accepted for the *Nation*.
3. Letter 719 (17 January 1915).
4. Hardy contributed nothing to the *Nation* until his poem, *Coming Up Oxford Street—Evening* (13 June 1925).

1390: To Roger Fry   *Hogarth [House, Richmond]*

Saturday 18th May [1923]

My dear Roger,

I had just come in thinking of you, from the local Heal show,[1] and meaning to write to you, when I found your letter.[2] It was a great pleasure. I'm very pleased that you liked the article [*To Spain*]. I had been feeling that it wasn't quite suitable for a first number. Journalism is altogether such a beastly business, but your praise has set me up. One of the things I wanted to tell you was how our apprentice [Marjorie Joad] broke out the other day about your show [Independent Gallery]—how she admired your works, in particular a portrait of Mme M[uter]: and a picture of a vineyard, and wanted to go again; then found that the show was over—So I said that I'd ask you if she might go up to Dalmeny [Avenue, N.7] one day and see some more. I always like it when the young volunteer praises—so don't be scornful of her ignorance. She was genuinely enthusiastic anyhow.

I try to pity you; indeed, I am much concerned about the damnable intestines;[3] only conceive England at this moment—leaden grey at half past five, so cold one wraps in wool to cross the hall, fires blazing, tents at the dog show blown over, the first class of Pekinese irretrievably mingled with the second to the despair of a thousand hearts: and to cap it all, Murry abroad again—I should say in Fleet Street again—blowing the enclosed nonsense through a megaphone.[4] That bloodless flea to talk about life! that shifty ruffian who can't keep his hands out of other people's pockets to prate of honesty! But there is a charm in complete rottenness. Leonard met him in the street, and Murry at once lied so splendidly about his duty to Massingham, and "sticking to the old Nation" (he offered to edit the new) that Leonard couldn't help loving him.

What gossip is there? That strange figure Eliot dined here last night. I feel that he has taken the veil, or whatever monks do. He is quite calm again. Mrs Eliot has almost died at times in the past month. Tom, though infinitely considerate, is also perfectly detached. His cell, is I'm sure, a very lofty one, but a little chilly. We have the oddest conversations: I can't help loosing some figure of speech, which Tom pounces upon and utterly destroys. Never mind: I loose another. So we go on. But at my time of life, I begin to resent inhibitions to intercourse; and these poor damned Americans so

1. The Spring Show of the London Group, at which Roger Fry was exhibiting.
2. Letter 532 in *Letters of Roger Fry*, ed. Denys Sutton (1972).
3. "I am marooned in Nancy, tied by my intestines which have rebelled again" (RF to VW, 13 May 1923).
4. In 1923 John Middleton Murry issued a prospectus for the *Adelphi*, the journal which he founded and edited until 1930. In 1919-21 he edited the *Athenaeum* until it merged with the *Nation*, edited by H. W. Massingham.

respect them. But I can't really hit it off with Lady [Sibyl] Colefax. Can you advise me how to acquire the social manner—neither cold nor hot? When I go to these tea parties, they all seem like people enchanted, and chained to a particular patch of the carpet, which they can't cross for fear of death—But you know it all of old. What irritates me is to see—anybody, Mrs W. K. Clifford[1] it may be—possessed of a sense which I have not. And I believe—but here you mightn't agree—that it is one essential for a writer. I think Proust had it.

We've been on the edge of violent rows—journalism again. Poor old Desmond[2] thinks that his writers will desert him for higher pay on the Nation. Then of course Bob[3] who is at large—with Donald Tovey swollen to the size of the Prince Consort in Hyde Park—makes it all infinitely worse by turning up at impossible hours, foaming at the mouth, apparently charged to the lips with diplomatic secrets, which set us all by the ears, and are entirely of his own concoction. Really, he is going quite mad! "I think, Morgan [Forster], you ought to go round and see Goldie [Dickinson]. I *think* Goldie has taken offence—well I may be wrong." By this time of course, Morgan is flying across Cambridge to see Goldie, whom he finds . . . [*five words omitted*] entirely oblivious of all earthly matters. This is not strictly accurate; but substantially so. In spite of Bob's enormous assiduity, the row with Desmond is now over. But I assure you, the atmosphere is full of coal dust.

Importunate old gentlemen who have been struck daily by ideas on leaving their baths, which they have copied out in the most beautiful, and at the same time illegible, handwriting, dump these manuscripts at the office, and say, what is no doubt true, that they can keep it up for years, once a week, if the Nation will pay £3. 3. a column. And there are governesses, and poetesses, and miserable hacks of all kinds who keep on calling—So do for God's sake, write us something that we can print.

Two nights ago I went to the Opera with Saxon [Sydney-Turner]; both in attenuated evening dress, for he takes stalls. There was Sir Claude Phillips,[4] Mrs Norman Grosvenor; Mrs Strep; and so on and so on. We had a divine Bach, Phoebus and Pan; towards the end of which, with the lights

1. Lucy Clifford, the novelist and playwright, whose husband had been a friend of Leslie Stephen.
2. Desmond MacCarthy had been literary editor of the *New Statesman* since 1920.
3. R.C. Trevelyan, the poet, essayist, and classical scholar. He was attempting to mediate between the *Nation* and the *New Statesman*. His friend Donald Tovey had been Reid Professor of Music at Edinburgh University since 1914 and Trevelyan had written the libretti for several of his operas.
4. The art critic, and Keeper of the Wallace Collection, 1897-1911. In 1923 he was 77, and died in the next year. Caroline Grosvenor was a novelist and painter who founded The Colonial Intelligence League for Educated Women.

still low, that old goat Sir Claude, only kept by the tightness of his white waistcoat from gushing entrails all over the carpet, took it into his head to leave. The whole audience saw him move down the gangway. Suddenly he disappeared. There was a sound of coal sacks, bounding and rebounding. Then dead silence. He had fallen down a complete flight of stairs; but is *not* hurt.

This is my only news of the great world. So cherish it tenderly. Brenan is engaged to be married: I'm afraid to a pretty American girl, who will bore him:[1] Lytton has come back: I'm going to tea with her Ladyship [Ottoline Morrell] on Tuesday: Garsington looms ahead; and as I began by saying, the Richmond dog show ended in irretrievable confusion, owing to the violence of the gale, which is now dissipating itself in the steady rain.

So my dear Roger, don't go palming yourself off on me as a broken down failure, because such shifts are utterly unworthy: and I now can't, for very shame, tell you how much I liked—but I know I liked all the wrong things, the colour, the charm, the sentiment, the literary power—your little landscapes at Heals. I think you've probably broken through into another partition of your art, in which there may be properties of an entirely different kind—we shall see.

But Lord! lord! what a chatterbox I am!

Yours Ever
V.W.

Sussex

1391: To Lady Ottoline Morrell

Hogarth House, Paradise Road,
Richmond, Surrey

21 May [1923]

Dearest Ottoline,

You asked us to come to Garsington one weekend early in June—but which, I cannot remember. Might it be one in the middle, or towards the end? Leonard wants very much to come, and his work at the Nation has so muddled his work at the Press that he can't take a weekend off just yet. We rushed off to Spain chaotically, and I can't find any letter from you about it. But do let us come some time. What has been happening to you? Shall you be in London? The depression of Bank holiday is too great to allow me to write a letter.

Ever your
Virginia

Texas

1. Brenan had flirted with an American girl in Granada who repulsed his advances. He protested that there was never any question of marriage between them. See *Carrington*, ed. David Garnett (1970), pp. 245-7.

1392: To MOLLY MACCARTHY   *Hogarth House, Paradise Road,*
                                                Richmond, Surrey
Whit Monday [21 May 1923]

Dearest Molly,

I'm afraid we can't come next week end, as we've arranged to go to
Monks—if we go away at all, but what with the Nation and with the
Hogarth Press we are at the moment in a state of uncertainty. Might we
come later? I should be completely happy in your house.

The question of your Memoirs[1] must be decided. Leonard says if you
let him have it, he would cut it up, and make himself responsible for every-
bodies feelings.

A little comb and brush is all thats needed. You know how Clive conceals
his bald patch? Well, that's how to treat your memoirs. I'm glad Squire is
going to print your story,[2] though Squire seems to me the common horse-
pond. Forgive this abrupt and what they call—I shan't remember my own
name next—style. When you leave out everything that makes sense, they
say you write *elliptically.*

We've just been to see the Polo at Hurlingham, and my wits are gone.
How I wish I were the Duke of Peneranda and could play polo! And what
d'you think they're like to talk to?—the D. of Peneranda, the Marquis of
Cholmondeley? Imagine their conversation.

                                                                    Yr V.W.

Mrs Michael MacCarthy

1393: To DORA CARRINGTON   *Hogarth House, Paradise Road,*
                                                Richmond, Surrey
Tuesday [22 May 1923]

Dearest Carrington,

Do come, any day you like, if you will let me know first. I'm generally
alone, as this d—d Nation keeps Leonard up in London. We go to Rodmell
for the week end.—but come back on Monday.

I want to see you—I don't want to write letters. Gerald tells Leonard
that he has just got engaged to an American girl at Granada.[3] Have you
heard? Perhaps its a joke.

1. See p. 30, note 1.
2. *Humanity Martin, M.P. for Galway* was published in the *London Mercury* of
   January 1924. It was not a short story, but an article about Richard Martin
   (1754-1834), a founder of the RSPCA.
3. See p. 40, note 1.

I can't think why home comings are so upheaving, generally for the worst.[1] But I'm through mine, and we are now in the usual press chaos.

Love to Ralph and the Serpent [Lytton]

Your V.W.

The ribbon[2] is entirely to my taste—moreover just like you.

Robert H. Taylor

1394: To Lady Ottoline Morrell

Hogarth House, Paradise Road,
Richmond, Surrey

[23? May 1923]

Dearest Ottoline,

We will stop the printing and come on the 2nd (Saturday week) if you do not mind Leonard going back on Sunday night, as he is afraid he must. I should like to meet Puffin Asquith[3]—

Yours in great haste, but looking forward to seeing you.

V.W.

Leonard says that if you feel his going will disturb the party, please say so. Otherwise he hopes you will let him come even for the short time.

Texas

1395: To Vanessa Bell

Hogarth House, Paradise Road,
Richmond, Surrey

24th May [1923]

Dearest,

I have several times written to you in spirit, but interruptions always occur. Really, you only want to know about your family.[4] Quentin[5] came down 2 weeks ago, in a snowstorm; very flourishing—indeed I've never seen such superb children as you breed: we walked, and Karin[6] and Ann came

1. Carrington had just returned from her Mediterranean journey, and had written to Virginia that she felt depressed on returning to Tidmarsh.
2. Which Carrington had bought for Virginia in Rome.
3. Antony Asquith, son of the former Prime Minister, and later the distinguished film director. He was then 20, and at Balliol College, Oxford.
4. Vanessa was in Spain with Duncan Grant and Roger Fry.
5. Quentin Bell was then aged 12. His sister Angelica was 4.
6. Karin Stephen, and her husband Adrian (Virginia's brother), both qualified as psychoanalysts in 1925. Ann was their daughter, aged 7.

to tea, and then Quentin, still remaining very polite, but slightly bored, superintended Ann's games. He told me that Angelica treats the Stephens as if they were dirt beneath her feet—so does he rather. I tried to get him for Whitsuntide, but he had gone yatchting [*sic*] with the Stephens. We go to Rodmell this weekend, (and I suppose its no good trying to take him?) and to Garsington next, so I've not much chance of seeing him. I wish I could. I make him discuss the Bells. 'Of course Aunt Dorothy's[1] the best of them, but shes very nuggety'—'What d'you mean by nuggety—?" "Oh she's one of those people you can't depend upon. Sometimes she's very un-pleasant . . . But theyre all very dull. In fact we would rather stay in London than go to Seend." [2] Karin gave me an alarming account of Adrian's spiritual state. Apparently he has been broken down by the psycho-analysis (mentally) and has now to be put together. In 3 months he may be entirely different, the dr. says; resolute, vivacious, pugnacious, amorous, and manly. I gather that his tragedy—as the dr calls it—is all our doing. He was suppressed as a child. As for Karin, her emotions are being humanised.

Carrington and [Ralph] Partridge turned up yesterday. They are all just back, rather discontented, I thought, and Lytton was being given his Benson medal by some society,[3] and then they all retire to the [Tidmarsh] Mill; and breed chickens. The pink dress, I should have said, arrived last week, just as I thought it lost. It is lovely, and exquisite, and I depend upon it to impress the youth of Oxford—Puffin Asquith that is to say. But at Ottolines. She is frantic, sends express letters, confutes my lies (we tried to put her off) by returning my own promise to go, which was made in March. But I can't have given you enough money. We must settle. By the way, its a *strict rule* that you bring me no present from Spain.

Life is rather dull at the moment. We have to spend most of our time printing; and the Nation is rather burdensome. Morgan [Forster] takes up the line that Maynard has no particular end in view; and being an ascetic (he was much pleased by your compliments though) won't be tempted to write by money. Unfortunately, talking to Lydia [Lopokova], I called Maynard 'your husband' I see this is not the thing to do. Poor little parrokeet—there she sits at the window in a pink kimono awaiting him, I suppose. "Maynār liked your article so much Leonār. What a good paper it is! Noā noā, I cant come out to tea. I am awaiting someone!" I suppose she has to read the Nation now. What tragedies these parrokeets go through!—not however your couple [Clive Bell and Mary Hutchinson]. Clive's just written me a prodigious letter all about his compliments, and his parties, and his ladies,

---

1. Clive's younger sister.
2. The village in Wiltshire where Clive Bell's parents had a house.
3. The Royal Society of Literature. The medal (endowed by A. C. Benson) was awarded to Lytton for his achievement as biographer and critic.

and gentlemen, and Derain,[1] young Oxford men who admire Mrs Woolf so much—for, of course, I am sprinkled with compliments too, and I suppose its all part of the game, but at our time of life it seems a little noisy and splashy don't you think. (vain as I am). By the way, here's a compliment for you: only that I went to Heals [London Group Exhibition] and thought your big picture [Charleston interior] very lovely; especially from the end of the room. But its like putting a necklace of daisies round the neck of an elephant, praising you. Brenan is engaged to an American girl: Ld. Carnarvon has left George's sons £25,000 each.[2] No more news.

Love to Duncan, and Roger.

B.

Berg

1396: To Lady Ottoline Morrell

[Hogarth House, Richmond]

Thursday [31 May 1923?]

Dearest Ottoline,

I'm afraid I can't come on Friday, but I'm much looking forward to Saturday. I shall arrive at Wheatley at 6.44, and find my way up—I remember what to do.

It will be a great pleasure—but there is no time to go into that properly now. Leonard says he is writing to say how sorry he is not to come—his sub-editor[3] is away, and he has all the work to do. She has no teeth, but she is very useful.

Your aff^{ec}
V.W.

Texas

1. André Derain (1880-1954), the French painter, whom Clive was meeting in Paris.
2. George Duckworth, Virginia's half-brother, had married the sister of the 5th Earl of Carnarvon in 1904. They had three sons, Henry, Auberon, and Anthony, who in May 1923 were aged respectively 17, 16, and 9. Their uncle died on 5 April.
3. Miss Crosse. See *Downhill all the Way*, pp. 92-3. It is possible that this letter was written on Thursday 19 June 1919, when Virginia was also about to visit Garsington. In that case, the sub editor would be Miss Matthaei, Leonard's assistant on the *International Review*.

1397: To T. S. Eliot   *Hogarth House, Paradise Road,*
                                          Richmond, Surrey

[4 June 1923]

My dear Tom,
    I enclose the two stories I told you about.¹ Mrs Dalloway doesn't seem
to me to be complete as she is—but judge for yourself.
    Last night, dining in high society [at Garsington], I sat next a young
Lord at Oxford² who said that Mr Eliot was his favorite poet, and the
favorite of all his friends. Why didn't he republish his poems? Had he
written prose? etc etc. Mr Eliot's poems, he said, amused him more than
anybodies, though he found them very difficult. He takes in the Criterion,
and is the descendant of Lord Dorset who knew Shakespeare and so on and
so on.
    Forgive this scrawl. I'm rushing to catch post.

                                               Ever yours
                                               V.W.

Houghton Library, Harvard University

1398: To Lady Ottoline Morrell
                                          Hogarth House, Paradise Road,
                                          Richmond, Surrey

7th June [1923]

Dearest Ottoline,
    This is a very belated letter, but I have been lunching with Lady Colefax,
which makes it hard to collect one's wits for a day or two.
    And really it is impossible to convey any sense of the weekend at
Garsington—it still overwhelms me, and I can't conceive what genius is
yours to manage as you do to make us all so happy and pleased with ourselves. I think of the thirty seven young men, and you waving your wand
among them. Lady Colefax, was very humble about not being asked, and
had of course heard all about it—heaven knows how.
    Leonard says that he enjoyed himself thoroughly—a very great compli-
ment from him: but I shan't pay you any compliments, as they are, I expect,

----

1. One of the two stories was *Mrs Dalloway in Bond Street*. The other is unidentified. Neither was published in the *Criterion*.
2. This was Virginia's first meeting with Edward Sackville West, the writer and
   music critic. He was Vita's first cousin, and was then aged 21, an undergraduate
   at Christ Church, Oxford.

rather too common when the post comes in: My post contains one letter
from Mary Sheepshanks,[1] who wants to see me!
Yours Ever
V.W.

Texas

1399: To Molly MacCarthy   *Hogarth House, Richmond,*
                              Surrey
[7? June 1923]

Dearest Molly,
    This is no answer, only a plea that you shall write again, and also I must
despatch some matters of business. May we come in July? May we meet
somewhere in the [Savernake] forest and spend Saturday night and go home
on Sunday?
    Still to business.
    First, where is your article for the Nation? Second, I've just had a
brilliant and fruitful idea. You must write a book about your mother—
letters, anecdotes, memories of Tennyson and Watts, photographs, descriptions—not a respectable life, but merely a general collection. I've read
Benson in the Mercury;[2] and find him repulsive. Even so, I can imagine what
a book might be made. We would bring it out with exquisite illustrations.
Please do consider this seriously and let me know. I go on repeating "I was
born in wedlock. I'm on dry land" and find the greatest comfort. The book
should be begun *at once* and should be ready to print next spring. I missed
Desmond, at Ly Colefax's, and want to press him on with his articles.
    Let's write again. It is a great joy to see your hand.
Ever
V.W.

Mrs Michael MacCarthy

1400: To Lady Ottoline Morrell
                              Hogarth House, Paradise Road,
                              Richmond, Surrey
June 19th [1923]

Dearest Ottoline,
    I have extracted this from Leo Myers.[3] It is a great effort, and leaves one
humiliated. Would you give the form to Philip [Morrell], as I think he keeps
them.

1. Daughter of the Bishop of Norwich and effective Principal, 1899-1913, of
   Morley College in South London, where Virginia had taught 1905-7.
2. In the June issue of the *London Mercury*, A. C. Benson had written a lengthy
   and sentimental obituary of Blanche Warre-Cornish, Molly's mother.
3. A contribution to the Eliot Fund.

46

Thank you very much for the photograph which seems to me highly flattering (not of Goldie, I agree) If there are any of me that would bear enlarging and reproducing I wish you would send me copies—*I insist upon paying for them*. I've said I'll send one to America to go in advertisements [for *Jacob's Room*], and yours come out so much better than the professionals.

I'm so sorry you're in bed again. The prescription is I am sure rest; and that is replied to by 37 undergraduates and Mrs Lindsay[1] coming in for a moment! Ever yours

V.W.

I open this to say that I've just seen [Hubert] Henderson, the editor of the Nation, who says that Murry never offered to edit the Literary side, only to write. It was from Maynard I got that impression. I think I maligned him therefore to that extent.[2]

Texas

1401: TO RICHARD ALDINGTON
Hogarth House, Paradise Road, Richmond, Surrey

Typewritten
21st June [1923]

Dear Mr Aldington,
I enclose an order for a subscription of Ten pounds from Mr L. H. Myers, as I'm not sure what the procedure is. Lady Ottoline tells me she has sent you the other part of the form.
I hope the [Eliot] fund has made some advance lately.
Yours sincerely,
Virginia Woolf

Texas

1402: TO SYDNEY WATERLOW
Hogarth House, Paradise Road, Richmond, Surrey

Friday [22 June 1923]

Dear Sydney,
I want to clear up one point which got wrong in talking to you the other day. I said, I think, that [Middleton] Murry had written offering to be

1. Norah Lindsay, the celebrated gardener, who lived near Garsington at Sutton Courtenay.
2. See p. 38.

literary editor until one was appointed. I hear from Hubert Henderson that he never saw such a letter, and thinks that there cannot have been one. This merely corrects my inaccuracy, and does not alter what Leonard said—that is, that Maynard said that Murry, apart from offering to write (in truth he did), had previously made a vague offer of help during the difficult time of taking over at the beginning.

No answer is needed.

Yours
Virginia Woolf

John Waterlow

1403: TO RICHARD ALDINGTON

Hogarth House, Paradise Road,
Richmond, Surrey

June 24th [1923]

Dear Mr Aldington,

This is only a line to say how pleased I am that you should like my book [*Jacob's Room*].

I am always surprised when people like what I write, and therefore must thank you for saying so.

I saw Tom the other day. I don't see what we can do now, yet I feel that money is more wanted than ever. Perhaps it would be a good thing to offer another lump sum to tide over this latest illness [of Mrs Eliot]?

But don't bother to answer. I will try to find out when I see him next how things are.

Yours sincerely,
Virginia Woolf

Texas

1404: TO KATHERINE ARNOLD-FORSTER

Hogarth House, Paradise Road,
Richmond, Surrey

Sunday June 24th [1923]

Dearest Ka,

I was very glad to get your letter, but I have absolutely no wish to answer it. There was a day when I liked writing letters—it has gone. Unfortunately the passion for getting them remains.

We shall be here till August: that is the first question answered. So come and see us, and dont retire to the usual surgeon's home.[1]

"I think the Adelphi[2] is rather good" K.A.F.

"I think the Adelphi is mildly bad" V.W.

"but then I'm always carried away by any vague declaration about life" K.A.F.

"But this is only a declaration that Murry wishes he were alive, but is dead" V.W.

"And your literary editor—does he like the job?"

Parts. Very busy; amused; annoyed; but we get some fun out of it. We are embroiled with some, endeared to others; but I'll tell you the story by word of mouth.

"No, I dont think I really liked In the Orchard."[3] K.A.F.

That's the best news I've heard for many a day. It would take too long to explain why, however.

Pots of cream are always acceptable. I don't like symbolical granite, if thats what you offer me.[4]

There! Every question answered, more or less.

It has turned very hot, and I am feeling very stupid. Barbara[5] has the scarlet fever in hospital; and I have to write and *amuse* her. What does one say?

Will never turned up, so far as I know. Yes, I wish he would write about the Ruhr, but thats in Hubert's [Henderson] department.[6] What I long for is a literal account of something like a badger. Now turn your paw to that, facts not fiction.

Leonard's love to you both; and he much wants the garden article.

Ever yr
V.W.

What did Will think of Duncan's pictures?

So now you must write again and answer my questions.

Mark Arnold-Forster

1. When in London, Ka usually stayed with her brother-in-law, Harold Wilson, the senior surgeon at St Bartholomew's Hospital.
2. The new journal edited by John Middleton Murry.
3. A story by Virginia which Eliot had published in the *Criterion* in April 1923.
4. In her letter of 17 June (*Sussex*), Ka had written, "I would send you some cream and a morsel of granite", from Zennor, Cornwall, where she lived.
5. Barbara Bagenal. See next letter.
6. Leonard had asked Will Arnold-Forster to write him an article on gardening, and he had replied that he would prefer to write on the Ruhr.

1405: To Barbara Bagenal   *Hogarth House, Paradise Road,*
                             Richmond, Surrey
24th June 1923

My dear Barbara,

I should have written to you before, but I have had so many disasters lately from writing letters,[1] that nothing short of death or bankruptcy will in future draw one from me. I hope scarlet fever isn't about as bad as going bankrupt. I have often thought of you in your hospital, as I take my way about the streets in comparative freedom. Yet I would have changed places with you last Sunday fortnight, when Ottoline completely drew the veils of illusion from me, and left me on Monday morning to face a world from which all heart, charity, kindness and worth had vanished. How she does this, in 10 minutes, between 12 and 1, in the best spare bedroom, with the scent of dried rose leaves about, and a little powder falling on the floor, Heaven knows. Perhaps after 37 undergraduates, mostly the sons of Marquises, one's physical life is reduced, and one receives impressions merely from her drawl and crawl and smell which might be harmless in the stir of normal sunlight. Only is the sunlight ever normal at Garsington? No, I think even the sky is done up in pale yellow silk, and certainly the cabbages are scented. But this is all great rubbish. We've had a desperate afternoon printing, and I'm more in need of the love of my friends than you are. All the 14pt quads have been dissed into the 12 pt boxes! Proof taking has been made impossible; and Eliots poem [*The Waste Land*] delayed a whole week. I'm sure you'll see that this is much more worth crying over than the pox and fever and the measles all in one. Do you have horrid old gamps who come and cheer you up? by which I mean tell you stories about their past grandeur, and how they have come down in the world or they wouldn't be nursing the likes of you—by which they mean that you haven't got silk chemises. I could write you a whole page of their talk, but refrain.

Here is a quotation from a letter I've just had from Roger, in Salamanca. "I was really rather surprised to see Saxon Turner approach the table at Segovia where I was seated with one Trend, a Cambridge musician; he approached the table in perfect style with just a little guttural noise, a sort of burble which expressed everything the moment demanded and sat down and we went about very happily for some days. He became quite talkative. And really what a nice creature he is."[2] So our poor Saxon is moving among the

---

1. See Letter 1416.
2. These lines are part of Letter 535 in *Letters of Roger Fry*, ed. Denys Sutton (1972). Saxon Sydney-Turner had proposed to Barbara Hiles, as she then was, in 1918, but she had refused him to marry Nicholas Bagenal. At that time she was an assistant at the Hogarth Press.

living. He disappeared in such gloom, owing to your loss,[1] that I've since thought of him as a kind of sea gull wailing forlornly round the coast on windy nights. You won't be lacking though in letters from him. And they will tell you every detail. London is spasmodically gay, that is to say I dine out in humble places and went to the opera one night, and one night to the Italian puppets, and one night to see Nessa, and another to dine with Maynard, and Leonard is frightfully busy. We meet on the stairs oftener than anywhere, and I'm not sure that the glories of the Nation are quite worth so much energy.

Mrs Joad is doing very well—much better, to be honest, than dear Ralph, but then she is a daily worker, enthusiastic, sanguine, and much impressed by small mercies. If only she didn't scent herself, rather cheaply, I should have nothing to say against her. She is a character so entirely unlike my own that I can't help gaping in astonishment, as we sit at lunch. Fancy playing tennis in Battersea Park! Fancy having a mother who lives at Harpenden! Fancy eating up all the fat, because it's good manners! Carrington insisted upon meeting her—I don't think they received good impressions of each other. How is that couple doing at Tidmarsh? I hear that Ralph [Partridge] is to become a bookbinder: also that he is to write articles, say on the hibernation of toads, on the maternal instinct of weasels, for which he is to be paid £50 guineas an article, if Lytton will co-operate. Of course Lytton won't, and so we shall soon read "Saturday, with the Buff Orpingtons" by Lytton Strachey: or "Hints on Wireworm," by the same author. Oh how glad I am I'm not married to Ralph (he's in love with Mrs [Bonamy] Dobrée!).

Duncan was very severely treated by Simon Bussy in the Nation.[2] Nevertheless he has sold almost every picture, I hear: and they say this will revive poor Roger's miseries about his own failure; but Roger, of course, is far the nicest human being of any of us, and will as usual be incomparably more generous than one could suspect Christ to be, should Christ return, and take to painting in the style of Cézanne at the age of 56. Clive, who has nothing Christlike about him, has had to give up eating tea, because, when Lady Lewis gave a party the other night and Rosenthal[3] played Chopin, a waistcoat button burst and flew across the room with such impetuosity that the slow movement was entirely spoilt. The humiliation, which would have killed you or me—the room was crowded with the élite of London—only brushed him slightly—he won't eat bread and butter any more: but his

1. Barbara had planned to go to Spain with Saxon, but was prevented by her illness.
2. On 9 June Bussy had written of Duncan that he had "a manner of using paint which makes the canvas look more like stuff that has been dipped in a dye than like a painted picture".
3. Moriz Rosenthal, who was born in Austria in 1862 and was Court Pianist to the Emperor of Austria and Queen of Roumania.

spirits are superb, and he says that life grows steadily more and more enchanting, the fatter one gets. Mr Bernard Shaw almost agreed to review his book[1] for the Nation; and said so on a postcard, but Clive is very touchy about postcards from Bernard Shaw, and has never forgiven Carrington,[2] nor ever will. Lydia has got a new bed: Very tactlessly I asked her if it was a double one. No it isn't yet, she said; I saw that one must not make jokes about beds . . . [*Thirteen words omitted*]. Her respectability is something your gamps would revere. But I find that talk about the Ballet has its limitations. Not indeed that she dances anymore: unfortunately she sometimes writes.

I hope you realise that though I am chattering like a pink and yellow cockatoo (do you remember Mrs Brereton's[3] poem, Pink and yellow, pink and yellow?) I'm a chastened raven underneath: I mean I am very much concerned at your miseries, which besides being in themselves odious, show a mean malignity on the part of Providence which makes me, for one, a Christian and a believer. If there were not a God, of course you would have gone to Spain with Saxon: as it is, there you are in bed at Maidstone. Our only alleviation of HIS afflictions is to send you our latest, Talks with Tolstoi—a very amazing book, even when it has passed through the [hospital] furnace, which I suppose it must do, before reaching you.

Leonard is still trying to take proofs in the basement. I have cheered myself up by writing to you, so please don't say that I've plunged you into despair, as another invalid [Vivien Eliot] did the other day, when I cheered myself up by writing to her.

Please get well, and come and see me. Barbara Chickybidiensis[4] is one of those singular blooms which one never sees elsewhere, a rare and remarkable specimen. I wish I could write an article for Outdoor Life about you, and get £50. £25 should then be yours.

Love to Nick.

Let me know how you are.

Yr V.W.

Sussex

1406: To Margaret Llewelyn Davies

Hogarth House, Paradise Road,
Richmond, Surrey

[27 June 1923]

Dearest Margaret,

Leonard says he is writing to you—but wont have time for a day or two, so I will send a page meanwhile—

1. *On British Freedom* (1923).
2. See Volume II of these *Letters*, pp. 507-8.
3. The governess to the Bell children at Charleston in 1917.
4. See Letter 1287, Volume II of this edition.

In the first place, can you help me to a speaker for the Guild[1] on Tuesday 2nd [3rd] July? I make no apologies for bothering you. It is all your fault. Never should I have undertaken this appalling business if it hadn't been for you—I want a speech on the Strike.[2] We have had nothing but brilliancy and charm the last 3 months—Morgan Forster on India, Bob Trevelyan on China, Mary Sheepshanks on Peru: now we must attend to the horrid facts. Heavens! Its next week! Don't forget.

This being off my mind, what else is there to say? The truth is, we meet so seldom its no use writing letters. For example, where am I to begin about the Nation? We've been so bullied, so lectured, so encouraged and so worried by all our friends that I'm inclined to nail my flag to the mast and go down with the ship. Really, I don't think it matters a straw what paper one writes for, if one speaks one's mind. That Leonard could spend his time better, is another question. We must wait, anyhow till the end of the year. But Massingham and his supporters and his principles leave me cold. There he is writing for the New Statesman[3]—

The Webbs [Sidney and Beatrice] are active. We badly want some Davies to balance them. Printing is ferocious. Mrs Joad very willing, but makes awful howlers of course. Ralph is becoming a bookbinder. Two books are sold out this week; and it becomes more and more difficult to manage in one house. Writing and people are also lively.

Perhaps we shall soon see you, which will be better than letter writing. As I grow old I hate the writing of letters more and more, and like getting them better and better.

Last year I saw Harry [Margaret's brother] for the first and only time in a theatre, and felt as I do for all your family affection and respect. I am sorry—but that you knew without my saying it.

Leonard sends his love

Ever yr
V.W.

Sussex

1. For several years Virginia had acted as speakers' secretary for the Richmond Branch of the Women's Co-operative Guild, an association for working women, of which Margaret had been Secretary.
2. It was a period of great social unrest. There had been strikes among miners and the farm labourers in March and April of this year, and fear of a general strike.
3. H. W. Massingham joined the Labour Party in November 1923 and transferred his *Wayfarer's Diary* from the *Nation* to the *New Statesman* when he was replaced by Hubert Henderson as editor of the *Nation*.

1407: To Margaret Llewelyn Davies

Hogarth House, Paradise Road,
Richmond, Surrey

Thursday [28 June 1923]

Dearest Margaret,

It was very good of you to wire, and made me feel very guilty for having bothered you, and in such a disagreeable way. I had had six dreary letters, on Press business and so on, to write, and so, as one always does on those occasions, inflicted another on you. Please forgive me, and let me indulge my own desire to write to you again, since I'm always wanting to write to you, and checking myself.

I rang up Miss Enfield.[1] She thinks she can supply a speaker, but Leonard has now offered his services, so I begged her not to bother. I stupidly mistook the week—hence this hurry.

I ought to explain about the Guild here—I only get a speaker once a month; they have their own speakers, either one of themselves, or someone they get themselves, every week. I've not been on the Committee for 4 years, so I can't resign from it, but I have twice offered to resign my task of getting a monthly speaker, but they voted that they wanted me to go on. They said they liked a change of subjects, and that is why we have travels, as well as education etc. But I shall again suggest giving it up in October, as I dont feel specially fitted, and also the difficulty of keeping up the supply is great.

This is a mere explanation, and I wont launch out upon Hardy and life in general as I should like.

I dont think Frank Rutter[2] has much reputation—nor, in my circles, has *William* Nicholson: I don't know anything about Ben.[3] David Garnett wrote a book called Lady into Fox which had a great success. He kept Bees at Charleston, Vanessa's house. Leo Myers is the son of the man who saw ghosts.[4] But I must stop.

Ever yr
V.W.

Sussex

---

1. Possibly Mrs Hood, from Enfield in Middlesex, a former president of the Women's Co-operative Guild.
2. The art critic of the *Sunday Times*.
3. William and Ben Nicholson, father and son, the painters.
4. F. H. W. Myers (1843-1901), a founder of the Society of Psychical Research.

1408: To DAVID GARNETT   *Hogarth House, Paradise Road,*
                                Richmond, Surrey
[Summer 1923]

Dear Bunny,
    At last, at last, the Hawthornden has chosen the right book.[1] A thousand
congratulations, and please spend the £100 in writing another.
    Dont bother to answer.

                                        Yours ever
                                        Virginia Woolf
Berg

1409: To W. J. H. SPROTT   *Hogarth House, Paradise Road,*
                                  Richmond
[early July 1923]

Dear Sebastian
    (I hope you don't mind, and will call me Virginia)
    We shall like very much to see you on Tuesday, 10th., and it is quite
easy to give you a bed.
    Dinner is 7.30; but come earlier if you like. I shall be in.

                                        Yours Ever
                                        Virginia Woolf
King's

1410: To BARBARA BAGENAL   *Hogarth House, Paradise Road,*
                                  Richmond, Surrey
Sunday, July 8th [1923]

My dear Barbara,
    I hope this sun is not adding to your torments. But now they will soon
be over; and your sympathies enlarged, which is very nice for your friends,
so as Nessa would say it's an ill wind that spills the milk. Perhaps you didn't
know how fond she is of proverbs; but not being of a literary turn, she often
tacks one on to another—not that it matters much. If I were you I should
write to Ka Arnold Forster, Eagles Nest, Tregerthen, Zennor, St Ives,
Cornwall for lodgings. She found us some very good ones with a Miss
Hosken (I think) at Zennor:[2] but Ka would know. I would have a mild attack
of the fever in order to go to Cornwall for 2 weeks. One cant ever go away
with out some such reason. I assure you the Press is worse than 6 children at
breast simultaneously. Consider the Sow. She shows no embarrassment. But

1. The Hawthornden Prize, for young writers, was awarded in 1923 to David
   Garnett's *Lady into Fox*.
2. Where Virginia and Leonard had stayed in 1921.

Leonard and I live apart—he in the basement, I in the printing room. We meet only at meals, often so cross that we can't speak, and generally dirty. His triumphs always coincide with my disasters. When one's up, the other's down. Then you and the sow say that maternity is worse!

I have just finished setting up the whole of Mr Eliots poem [*The Waste Land*] with my own hands: You see how my hand trembles. Don't blame your eyes. It is my writing. Roger is back, but has not swum into my life yet: though swimming scarcely expresses his descent—its more like having an aeroplane on the roof. Pamela[1] has started both to have a baby and to make coloured papers. She intends to sell the coloured papers to the Press, and so support the Baby. If the Baby dies, it will be all our fault. Diamond, as the husband is called, can't even cut his initials on a pane of glass. Roger says he's completely idle—but that may mean only that he stays in bed till 8.30. Roger, Nessa says, likes to begin sightseeing at dawn, and used to pinch poor Duncan awake every morning at 4. The consequence was that Duncan often fell asleep standing, like a horse, before the pictures in the Prado. This made Roger angrier still. But Saxon suited him exactly.

I went to Tristan the other night; but the love making bored me. When I was your age I thought it the most beautiful thing in the world—or was it only in deference to Saxon? I told many lies in Covent Garden Opera house. My youth was largely spent there. And we used to write the names of operas in books. But I must not write the whole history of my life. I must fish Leonard out of the basement—Think what happened this afternoon! A mouse fell into the servants W.C. Lottie[2] came rushing to Leonard. What was to be done? Like a man of action, without saying a word, he pulled the plug. Had it been a rat, the consequences might have been fatal. The drains wd. have been stopped, I say: Leonard says not. He says—but it is too disgusting. You can imagine what Leonard said, as we were having tea.

Let me know how you are, and forgive this dreadful scribble. Love to Nick.

Yr
V.W.

Berg

1411: TO VIOLET DICKINSON   *Hogarth House, Paradise Road,*
                             Richmond, Surrey
[July 1923]

My Violet,
A thousand thanks for your cheque—I'm afraid the Hogarth Press has been raining its fruit on you rather too frequently lately—but take heart—

1. Pamela Diamand, Roger Fry's daughter.
2. Lottie Hope had been Virginia and Leonard's parlourmaid since 1916.

there's only one more to come this summer—Mr Eliot [*The Waste Land*]. Then we disappear to Sussex, which will be a treat after reviews and books— not but what the Nation is amusing so far.

How are you—and dogs and cats and plants and widows and great ladies, and all the rest of your marvellous caravan.

Ask me to tea in October. Dont forget—And I will bring you your pot of jam.

Leonard's love.

Yr
Sp[arroy]:

Berg

1412: To V. Sackville-West   *Hogarth House, Paradise Road,*
                              Richmond, Surrey

[end of July 1923]

Dear Vita,

We had been hoping we might see you, but every week end, save one, has been sacrificed to the Hogarth Press, which grows daily and hourly more exacting.

Next week we go down to Rodmell. If you should be anywhere near, do come and see us.

I so much enjoy your reviews.[1]

Yours very sincerely
Virginia Woolf

Berg

1413: To Clive Bell   [*Hogarth House, Richmond*]

Postcard
[29 July 1923]

Your wishes about Poll [Mary Hutchinson] shall be attended to. Have you got my copy of a book of Conrads—Notes on Life and letters?[2] I lent it to Nessa, who denies possession: if you find it, and would either leave it out on Monday or bring it to Charleston, eternal gratitude etc etc.

Quentin Bell

1. In 1923 Vita started reviewing regularly for the *Nation & Athenaeum*.
2. For an article on Conrad in the *Nation* (1 September 1923).

57

July 30th 1923

My dear Jacques,

I only got your letter two hours ago, on my English breakfast tray, with its bacon and egg: and I will answer at once. No, no, no. Nothing you said offended me: all delighted me; and I should have written ages ago if I had not always said "I'll write Jacques a nice long letter"—and so waited for the proper moment, and wrote meanwhile myriads of dreary drudgery. I find I never write to people I like. Jacques and Gwen require a good state of mind: whereas,—now you shall fill in the names of our old friends who can be put off with miserable relics.

We are all packed to go to Sussex tomorrow. This conveys nothing to you who have never seen the Hogarth Press. We travel with a selection of our books packed in hampers. Add to this a dog and a tortoise, bought for 2/- yesterday in the High Street. My husband presides with considerable mastery—poor devil, I make him pay for his unfortunate mistake in being born a Jew by discharging the whole business of life. This induces in me a sense of the transitoriness of existence, and the unreality of matter, which is highly congenial and comfortable. Now what do *you* think real? Gwen used to have views about that. Gwen was a highly dogmatic woman. Her breed is, alas, quite extinct. I assure you I can knock over the freeest thinker and boldest liver with the brush of a feather—nincompoop though I am, as far as logic goes.

This brings me, rather helter skelter, (but forgive thimble headedness in your old friend)—to the question of the religious revival: which concerns you both a good deal more nearly than you suspect. On my way back from Spain I stayed a week in Paris and there met Hope Mirrlees and Jane Harrison. This gallant old lady, very white, hoary, and sublime in a lace mantilla, took my fancy greatly; partly for her superb high thinking agnostic ways, partly for her appearance. "Alas," she said, "you and your sister and perhaps Lytton Strachey are the only ones of the younger generation I can respect. You alone carry on the traditions of our day." This referred to the miserable defection of Fredegond [Shove] (mass; confession; absolution, and the rest of it.) "There are thousands of Darwins" I said, to cheer her up. "Thousands of Darwins!" she shrieked, clasping her mittened hands, and raising her eyes to Heaven. "The Darwins are the blackest traitors of them all! With that name!" she cried, "that inheritance! That magnificent record in the past!" "Surely", I cried, "our Gwen is secure?" "Our Gwen," she replied, "goes to Church, (if not mass, still Church) every Sunday of her life. Her marriage, of course, may have weakened her brain. Jacques is, unfortunately, French. A wave of Catholicism has invaded the young Frenchmen. Their children are baptised; their —" Here I stopped her. "Good God", I said, "I will never speak to them again! Whats more, I've just written a flippant, frivolous, atheistic letter to that very household, which will arrive precisely as the Host is elevated; they'll spit me from their lips, spurn me from their hearts—and, in short, religion has accomplished one more of her miracles, and destroyed a friendship which I'm sure began in our mother's wombs!" All this eloquence left me dejected as a shovelful of cinders. Next week arrived your letter, which was the greatest relief in the world. Gwen is a militant atheist: the world renews itself: there is solid ground beneath my feet. I at once sent word to dear old Jane, who replied, a little inconsistently, "Thank God".

But speaking seriously, (and I need not say that the hand of art has slightly embellished the preceding) this religious revival is a glum business. Poor Middleton Murry has had a conversion, which has had an odious Bantam—the Adelphi—which I wish you'd take in and comment upon monthly. I'm too much prejudiced to be fair to him. As literature, it seems to me worthless—(only strong words are out of place): it seems to me mediocre then. The spirit that inspires it, with its unction and hyprocrisy, and God is love, which still leaves room for flea bites, pin pricks, and advertising astuteness, would enrage, were it not that there's something so mild and wobbly about that too that I can't waste good wrath. Most of my friends find it deplorable. Ka, the usual exception, rather likes it. But the story of the Murrys, is long and elaborate, and I'm getting so harassed by household affairs that perhaps I'd better stop.

Leonard: Here's a man from the typewriter shop. Shall we be rash and buy a new one?

Cook: I think I'd better make the pie tomorrow. Monday meat is never trustworthy.

Virginia: I shall have to take my pink dress, if we're going to stay with Maynard.

Leonard: Well you can't take your pink dress, because the luggage has gone.

Virginia: Gone? Good God! Gone?

Leonard: I told you twenty times it was going at eleven.

etc. etc. etc.

I knew both the Murrys. Please read Katherine's works, and tell me your opinion. My theory is that while she possessed the most amazing *senses* of her generation so that she could actually reproduce this room for instance, with its fly, clock, dog, tortoise if need be, to the life, she was as weak as water, as insipid, and a great deal more commonplace, when she had to use her mind. That is, she can't put thoughts, or feelings, or subtleties of any kind into her characters, without at once becoming, where she's serious, hard, and where she's sympathetic, sentimental. Her first story which we printed, Prelude [1918], was pure observation and therefore exquisite. I could not read her latest.[1] But prejudice may be at work here too. As for the Sitwells, though I

1. *The Canary*, published in the *Nation*, April 1923.

paid 3/6 to hear Edith vociferate her poems accompanied by a small and nimble orchestra, through a megaphone, I understood so little that I could not judge.[1] I know Osbert slightly. They take themselves very seriously. They descend from George the IVth. They look like Regency bucks. They have a mother who was in prison. They probably need careful reading, which I have never given them, and thus incline to think them vigorous, but unimportant, acrobats. Literature is in a queer way, however: as I shall explain next letter. By the way, do send me your version of Mrs Litchfield's remarks on my article.[2] Gerald Brenan's aunt [Baroness von Roeder] sent him the same unfortunate work, picked out with red lines in ink. She was outraged. (She is 85). She said it was done for notoriety and was only printed because "Mrs Woolf has the dibbs, and would cut Mr Woolf short if he didn't". But Mrs L., being Gwens Aunt, is much too refined to say that.

What a letter! What a letter! It is like the interminable monologue of an old village woman standing at her door. Each time you say good day and try to move off, she bethinks her of something fresh and it all begins again. And my hand shakes, so I cant write legibly. I have a queer illness, which consists of a permanent slight fever, which the Dr. diagnosed consumption, but have almost cured now by injecting pneumonia germs in multitudes. This must be my excuse for febrile verbosity. Please write to Monks House, Rodmell, Lewes.

Ever Yrs.
V.W.

Sussex

1. This performance was given at the Aeolian Hall on 12 June 1923.
2. The article was *To Spain*, published in the *Nation*. Mrs Litchfield was Gwen Raverat's aunt, Henrietta Darwin, who married R. B. Litchfield.

Letters 1415-1434 (August–December 1923)

The Woolfs spent August and September at Monk's House, where Virginia was able to work alternately on her two books The Common Reader *and* Mrs Dalloway, *without telling her friends, either in her letters or when they visited her, how great an effort of composition both entailed. To relieve the tension, she contrived two breaks. She drafted a comic play,* Freshwater, *about Mrs Cameron and her circle, of which another version was acted by her friends and family many years later. And in early September the Woolfs joined Maynard Keynes in a large seaside house which he had rented in Dorset. Lydia Lopokova, Keynes's future wife, was there; and so were two young men who soon became closely linked to Bloomsbury, George Rylands and Raymond Mortimer. Back at Richmond, Virginia urged on Leonard the need to leave Hogarth House for central London. The strain on Leonard of almost daily travel to and from the suburb, and the sense of social deprivation which Virginia experienced there, eventually persuaded him, and in the late autumn Virginia was house-hunting.*

1415: TO PERNEL STRACHEY
          Monks House, Rodmell,
          Lewes [Sussex]

3rd Aug. [1923]

Dear Pernel,

This is the voice of your old, alas forgotten friend, Virginia—
Will you come here on Sept. 15th, for the week end?

It strikes me that you will then be back from France, where you're going I hear, and not yet inducted into your lofty seat.[1]

Of course, I have myriads of things to say to you, but your silence, which has now lasted 10 years, 56 days and twenty minutes, rather appals me. Everything I can think of appears trivial against that mighty and impressive wall. Only a tragic death can possibly break it down, or a divorce, or some catastrophe—none of which has happened. I saw Jane [Harrison] and Hope [Mirrlees] in London—thats true; and we talked about death in the boudoir of Lady Arthur Russell's[2] old house till a University woman, M.D. B.A.

1. Pernel Strachey was Lytton's elder sister. In 1923 she became Principal of Newnham College, Cambridge, the 'lofty seat' which she held until 1941.
2. Whom Virginia described as "a rude tyrannical old woman with a blood-stained complexion and manners of a turkey cock" (*Moments of Being*, edited by Jeanne Schulkind, 1976, p. 149). Her house was 2 Audley Square, which became the University Women's Club in 1921.

D.Sc., I should think, blushed, flushed and faded. Anyhow we got rid of her. Hope's novel[1] will soon be out, I suppose.

Since I last saw you, we have climbed onto our very low throne (compared with yours, that is to say). You don't know what I'm talking about? Only the Nation. This means that we wallow around among books and proofs,* like porpoises not so much reading or writing but dipping and snorting and some say losing a good deal of our character for distinction and high mindedness. This naturally brings me to the Adelphi—Murry's organ—which is full of both and morality too. Come, and let us discuss all these matters in my garden house, which (as I must have told you) overlooks first the flats and then the downs. Do you like descriptions of nature? I have really forgotten what you like; but not in the least how you put me in mind of one of those elegant fawn coloured creatures, who, at the slightest sound, gently tap the ferns with their front feet and gaze ahead of them with large, apprehensive, yet slightly sardonic eyes—Then, somehow, we must get in the pearl buttons and the dusty ears.

I'm waiting for the good woman to bring dinner, so excuse this drivel and dribble—I've been trying to read Tennyson, by Harold Nicolson.[2] I threw it onto the floor in disgust. To purify myself I said I will at once write a letter to Pernel. She won't answer, I said. But then thats why I write, I said. For these mysterious figures who never quite come out of the wood, and carry on such intrigues in the gloom are always the pursued and desired. That, I said, I shall never be myself. For I always say too much—I always rush out and jump in. Its dreadful that one can't sometimes be Pernel; and not always Virginia. This train of thought is becoming a little depressing—but its due to Harold Nicolson. Of course, he's due to Lytton; and Lytton is more or less due to you. What these skilful imitators dont realise is that it is absolutely essential, if you are going to[3]

I have just had dinner—ham and eggs and an odious pudding called Canary with a mop of bright red jam on its head,—so I can't think what I was going to say. Its a sprawling floundering book; then suddenly the poor wretch remembers Lytton and tries to cut a caper. But I am engulphed in the works of Conrad, who is a much better writer than all of us put together, don't you agree? Will you sacrifice your brother if I sacrifice myself, Clive Bell, Morgan Forster, Tom Eliot, and anyone else I can think of? Why is there much more difference between 1st rate and 2nd rate than between 3rd

* But how wallow, yet on a throne?

1. *The Counterplot* (1924).
2. *Tennyson: Aspects of His Life, Character, and Poetry*, published on 15 March 1923.
3. The sentence breaks off here, uncompleted.

rate and 2nd rate, or any other rate? As I say, I could go on writing for hours, but must alas, respect your privacy.

Ever yr
V.W.

One word on a post card about the 15th.

Strachey Trust

1416: To Pernel Strachey

Monk's House, Rodmell
[Sussex]

August 10th [1923]

My dear Pernel,

Any words of flattery are, as you know, precious above pearls to me, but still I cannot believe that you would really like me to yield to my impulse which is to write to you *daily* a letter as long as the Times. "Oh another! Oh defend me! Oh take it away! Take it away! Take it away!" (The last words are uttered with increasing quickness, culminate in a shriek, and have issue in vomiting, convulsions, and death). So I spare you, for the sake of Newnham. Moreover, I'm breaking myself of the habit of profuse and indiscriminate letter writing. I can only write, letters that is, if I don't read them: once think and I destroy. Several sent off lately on this system (the unthinking one) have had semi-fatal results: poor Mrs Eliot had a relapse; Margaret Davies wired at once; someone else has cooled and hardened; others have fired and irrupted. Letter writing as a game is not safe. And serious letters cease to be possible when 40 has struck, and life is more like trampling at random through a jungle than treading gingerly through tiny thorns and intense thickets, as it was when we were young, and met, I think, in the Quaker's[1] drawing room. Poor old lady! There she sat in grey alpaca, with her geraniums and cyclamen about her, talking and talking. What was it all about, I wonder?

But I must not begin to reminisce, or I shall have Leonard coming to tell me dinner is getting cold—eggs and ham and junket tonight.

Will you then write and propose a suitable day—not necessarily a week end, if they are occupied. The 7th Sept. wont do; nor yet the 1st; but choose any other and then let me see. I own I am a little vague, having thrown invitations into the air, and they fall to earth, anywhere, as the poet said of an arrow—but what poet?[2] How I long to discuss the matter, or indeed any

1. Caroline Emelia Stephen, Virginia's aunt, who lived at Cambridge and died in 1909.
2.   "I shot an arrow into the air,
              It fell to earth I knew not where."
              Longfellow, *The Arrow and the Song*

63

matter, with you. The 2nd rate question is most enthralling: leads to heat, coldness, fits, too. But I am giving you a violent view of this place, which is everything rural and clerical that a place can be. Has not Leonard just played tennis with the Vicar's daughter, and are we not roused from our junket by a voice in the road "Are you believers in the Lord?" Twelve young men then stand in a circle and sing Washed in the Blood of the Lamb.

But enough—anon, anon—what does anon mean? But a pox on these questions.

Yrs V.W.

Strachey Trust

1417: To Gerald Brenan *Monks House, Rodmell, Lewes [Sussex]*

10th Aug. 1923

My dear Gerald,

It pleases me to think that no apologies are needed—if I don't write, then I don't write; if I do, I do. The same applies to Don Geraldo [Brenan]. But like a donkey I left your letter in London, and can only remember two remarks out of the many I meant to attend to upon an auspicious occasion. First I must clear my character—was I not the only sceptic when your engagement was announced?[1] It's a joke, I said—a mild, Buffon[2] joke. Then I yielded on hearing (which was a mistake) how you had written seriously to the Partridges [Ralph and Carrington]. Never mind. Only don't use this particular stone in building your temple to the honour of women. The other matter is also, I see, remembered from vanity—your aunt's strictures [on *To Spain*]. A week later another friend [Raverat] wrote that his Aunt had sent him out the same article, marked with the same abuse, in the same red ink. So clearly I am poison to Aunts. Tell yours, though, that she is out in her reasoning. Its Mr Woolf who forces Mrs Woolf to write. The Americans now offer her £25 for a short article. Naturally Mr Woolf keeps her at it. Your Aunt will see the sense of this. Whats more, her opinion of me will rise so high that I expect to be asked to dinner. But the truth is that being offered £25 I now cannot write a line (this is true of me, physically speaking this moment—pen, ink, paper, all are bad: and I am sitting hunched in a chair with the board which is used for rolling flour upon my knee.)

1. To the American girl (see p. 40, note 1). Carrington, who was in love with Brenan, had written him a letter of sad congratulation. On 1 June Brenan wrote to Virginia: "I hear you've been putting romantic notions about me into Carrington's head. . . . Wherever can you have got all that from, unless (as I suspect) you were being a trifle malicious" (*Sussex*).
2. On 4 August Brenan had published an article in the *Nation* under the pseudonym 'B. Buffon'. It was a parody of natural history writing.

64

Buffon's remarks came out last Saturday. Have they sent you a copy?—or has your Aunt supplied you? I like Buffon. He amuses me, and I envy him his natural running style. But I am afraid of expressing these opinions, since my jocose remarks upon your character seemed to you so beside the mark.[1] Remember, I was writing in the person of a poor old woman, to whom you had been kind: her view was made rosy on purpose. As a fact, my own view, not of you in particular, but of humanity in general, falls and falls. Some base perfidy set me off, and now I can see little good in the race, and would like to convey this in writing. I should like to make odious, mean, lying characters. I should like to make the world so detestable that it seems better to desert it. But, I expect, to do this needs more power than I have at command. What started this misanthropy I cannot now remember—unless it were a visit to Garsington coupled with my view of journalists—their malice, cringing, and emptiness. I have many stories to tell you, but then, (this is my weakness) tolerance keeps breaking in, and I excuse the creatures instead of blighting them.

I have seen Saxon: I have seen the Partridges: I have seen Lytton: and Eliot. Undoubtedly Carrington is happier, even with Ralph entirely on her hands. I thought him a little surly, but I daresay in self-defence—I mean he did not wish us to think he regretted us[2]—nor does he, I daresay. They lead a rural life; many ducks and kittens in and out of the rooms; Lytton visiting the Duke of Marlborough at weekends, and coming back to the Tidmarsh atmosphere and telling his stories—infinitely affable and at ease reminding me of some dragon-fly, which visits dahlias, limes, holly-hock and then poises, quite unconcerned, in the lid of a broken tea-pot. Carrington and Ralph are the broken pot, in this fantasy—you can imagine how brown and robust they look. They're off to France now, and then, so it's said, Ralph bends his enormous fists to binding books.

We came down here last week, and here we remain till October, a very happy life, on the whole, though I become rather restless with my desire to write, my desire to read, my desire to talk, and to be alone, and to explore Sussex and find a perfect house, and arrive at some conception of the meaning of all things. Why nature dangles this ancient carrot before me, I do not know. Every book is to me a glass through which I may possibly behold—I don't know what; and so with people; and so with my solitary walks on the downs, when suddenly I find I am breaking through myriads of white convolvulus, twined about the grass, and then I think there are more flowers here than in Spain. . . . I will write to Gerald when I get home.

Eliot will come and stay with us. At first I shall find him very pompous and American. Later, rather young and simple. I will send you The Waste Land when it is out—in a week or two. All marked styles are to be avoided,

1. See Letter 1388.
2. Leaving the Hogarth Press.

I think, because they limit one. He begins to repeat himself. He creaks: he angles, (if there is such a verb from angular) but I insist, against his many detractors that these are only the impediments of a very good brain. You have heard, I suppose, of Murry's religious revival.[1] I am tired of him and his works. Again, I wish I could end, as usual, by excusing. Not that I excuse a word of his writing; but the creature himself is a paltry weakling, and I know if I met him I should at once succumb to his feebleness. Shall you change your way of life now you are a man of property? As for your writing: it is now clear that Ralph's press is given up[2] (so I imagine). Therefore, can't you deal with us? I am also to say from Leonard (who is playing tennis with the Rector's daughter while I sit at home with my bitch, Grishka, who is on heat, and all the dogs of the village throw their noses up and whine and snuff and come prowling about the house after dark till it seems like a rustic and impoverished version of Helen of Troy). I am to say that he wishes you to send him any sketch you do.

Well, I am running out of sense. Tonight I shall read the plays of Marlowe; tomorrow I shall walk across the meadows to Lewes and buy a chicken. Does this sketch in great blobs produce any likeness of a character? or what do you get out of these careless, random diluted letters? I can no longer write careful letters. Moreover I am too sleepy with the heat (it is as hot to-day as it was in Alicante) to visualise you, your room, Maria [servant at Yegen], the brassero, the mountains, the little begging children, the pigeons, the mules, the figure of Don Giraldo, in corduroys, with a knotted tie, sitting by a plate of grapes, from which he picks a handful now and then, while he reads—Then he jumps up. Then he goes to the other room. Then he writes. Then he tears up. Then he runs out up the mountain alone making phrases? stories? deciding profound matters of art? or scarcely thinking at all?—God knows. I do not pretend to know much about that young man, whom, at this moment—the church has just struck 6—I see with extreme plainness. Yes, but what is he thinking? How does it feel to be inside him? I am tormented by my own ignorance of his mind. And there is something absurd, and perhaps even insincere, in keeping up this semblance of communication in purple lines upon great white sheets.

I have been reading Tchekov this afternoon,[3] and feeling good Lord why does he mention *this?* There is a perpetual unexpectedness in his mind, which is, I rather think the interest of him. Perhaps all the Russians have it. It is only in France and England that events seem threaded like beads on a

1. The mystical element in his writing intensified after Katherine Mansfield's death.
2. Before leaving the Hogarth Press, Ralph Partridge planned to start the Tidmarsh Press, but the project never matured.
3. For her essay, *The Russian Point of View*, in *The Common Reader*.

string—for which reason our best stories are so dull. How dull Mérimée is!
—Try Carmen—said to be a masterpiece.[1] Please write.

V.W.

George Lazarus

1418: To Vanessa Bell   *Monk's [Rodmell,*
                                          Sussex]
Friday [17 August 1923]

Dearest,

What an awful bore—we've got Molly Hamilton[2] here for the week end,
and as she has to go on Sunday night, I don't suppose we can bring her over,
or come ourselves, much though we should like to. If we did come, we'd
come for tea, and bring our food—but I dont think its likely. A very small
[birthday] present will come for Quentin. If he doesn't like it, I want it for
myself.

Wont you and Duncan come over?—any day except Wednesday, or
Tuesday. I want to read you my play,[3] as soon as possible, as, if it is to be
finished, I'd better do it here.

Also, would my nephews come over for lunch and spend the afternoon
in water hunting? We are invaded by the dullest of dull people in Shoals—
Nick [Bagenal] among them,—I can't think why. So a little human society
would be acceptable. But how is it that M. H. [Mary Hutchinson] is only
spending one night? A triumph for Dolphin's [Vanessa] implacable character,
as usual. But discretion forbids me to say more.

I do think its time Roger [Fry] ceased to be in love with you, and to
resent my presence. After all I'm your only surviving sister, and knew you
long before he did.

Oh my sister in law [Flora] and Mr [George] Sturgeon are now arriving!
Nelly and Lottie[4] are back, frenzied (but secretly delighted) at the dirt of the
house. Thanks to you, the mattresses are now absolutely perfect, like the
best Heal.

I don't offer you and Duncan beds, as they would be repudiated. But
beds there are.

Let me know about the children, if I dont see you? Are you shopping in
Lewes on Tuesday?

V.W.

Berg

1. *A Story of Spanish Gipsy life* (1847) by Prosper Mérimée, and the basis of
   Bizet's opera.
2. Mary Agnes Hamilton, the novelist and biographer, and later Labour M.P.
3. *Freshwater*, a comedy about Mrs Cameron, Tennyson, etc., which Virginia
   had conceived in January 1919 and written in the summer of 1923.
4. Nelly Boxall and Lottie Hope had been respectively cook and parlourmaid to
   the Woolfs since 1916.

1419: To Margaret Llewelyn Davies

Monks House, Rodmell
[Sussex]

Aug. 17th [1923]

Dearest Margaret,

I can't tell you how deeply I share your passion for old letters; the ones you sent kept me full of them for a whole day.[1] Of course, Mr Croom Robertson played a great part in our childhood—as a name—for we never saw him: I can remember his death; and how much I was impressed by the feeling that he was somebody extremely great and venerable. But I could go on for pages—I do wish you would collect your brothers and mothers letters—anyhow to let me read them. It seems such a waste to destroy what has—as it certainly does have—this extraordinary power of bringing back a whole group—a whole attitude—more, I mean, than mere facts. I found some from Arthur [Margaret's brother] to my mother.

I am sitting in our garden room, trying to keep up an intelligent conversation with Molly Hamilton—do you know her?—Bradsfords sub-editor—so pardon faults of spelling and taste. However, I can't help wishing you were here; yes—why don't you come? and let us discuss everything in the whole world, the past and the future.

The whole world does nothing but shower manuscripts upon us. A lady from the North arrived in a motor laden with stories of passion. She was stone deaf, middle class,—with a kind of sultry character; a husband with yellow moustaches and a dog.

But I am getting into difficulties with my guest.

Please send me any memories of the past—not that I expect you want to do anything but bask.

Leonard's love.

Ever yr
V.W.

Sussex

1420: To Roger Fry

Monks House, Rodmell
[Sussex]

Friday [24 August 1923]

My dear Roger,

I think your little book[2] is a perfect triumph. I don't deny that in parts the writing might be tightened with advantage, but as a whole it seems to me

1. The letters were written by Margaret's uncle-in-law George Croom Robertson (1842-92), Professor of Philosophy at University College, London, founder-editor of *Mind*, and a great friend of Leslie Stephen.

2. *A Sampler of Castile*, published by the Hogarth Press in November 1923.

68

an amazing production, so subtle, so suggestive, so full of life, and sweeping together every kind of thing in such a way that it is perfectly easy to follow— I couldn't stop reading it. There's nothing quite like it that I know, and perhaps you've done nothing that so makes me stand in amazement at the sweep and range of your astonishing mind. I know you'll suspect me of flattery—but this is quite true—ask Clive if it isn't.

I think you would be very ill advised to leave out anything. The whole is so penetrated with interest of one kind or another that to break would merely be to mutilate. I have marked a very few slips which I have written on a sheet enclosed.

Indeed, I do think the Press is extremely lucky to get this book. You must go on and do more. I want to see you write about literature. I think you have found a genuine and most successful way of giving shape to all sorts of things which normally run off in talk or thinking to oneself. And its odd and surprising to me how completely you have evolved your own language.

Ever yr V.W.

I've just, once again, found Crown in shield's card.[1] I see he asks for the lectures you are doing for the Press. Am I to make any reply?

Sussex

1421: To Clive Bell   *Monks House, Rodmell*
                                              [*Sussex*]
Sept. 11th [1923]

Dearest Clive,
    You have given me one hour and a half of pure delight—reckoning that it takes half an hour to read your essay[2] and I have just read it for the 3rd time—so in spite of resolving never to write another letter, I must now write and thank you. It is far and away the best (don't think I merely mean the most complimentary) criticism I have ever read of my own works, and happens to come at an extremely convenient moment to light up the particular maze I am in. I think I could beat up an argument on the question of 'feeling' which is observed and feeling which is shared—But to do that you must come over, or invite me to walk across the downs. However, I'm really warmed to the cockles of my heart that you should have so much good to say—for when I thought of you wading through those interminable and

1. Frank Crowninshield (1872-1947), American editor of *Vanity Fair*, 1914-35.
2. Clive Bell's essay, *Virginia Woolf*, was not published until December 1924, when it appeared in the *Dial*. It is reprinted in *Virginia Woolf: the Critical Heritage*, ed. Robin Majumdar and Allen McLaurin (1975), pp. 138-47.

faded works I thought one withered laurel was all you could probably pick for my gray hairs—a laurel the size of a leaf of mint. As it is, I begin to write in the morning with a glance in your direction for comfort. But I can't be 'beautiful'—the beautiful daughter etc. . That I have struck out: I will try to find a better quotation tomorrow, and send back (unless you and your paramour who wrote me a charming note on a tender theme this morning) will be coming this way. You'll be amused to hear that when the discussion got upon the Nation at Studland,[1] I vociferated that Clive Bell was the best journalist, possibly critic, of the day; and got the table to agree. But this gives you no sort of pleasure.

We had rather a strenuous time, all sorts of walks and talks; loves and qualities were debated while we raced over Dorsetshire, grilled, baked, moralised among ruins, and saw the very spot [Lulworth Cove] where in 1910 Rupert lay in bed because of Noel [Olivier]. The poet Rylands was there.

I see this ought to be re-written; 10 years ago it would have been. But not now.

Moreover, I shall never explain to you, in words, exactly how, and for what reason, not all of them purely literary or even wholly vain, I like you to like what your affectionate sister in law writes; but perhaps as I approach a subject upon which you say I have *no* knowledge, I had better be silent.[2] Ha! ha!

V.W.

Quentin Bell

1422: To LADY OTTOLINE MORRELL   *Monks House, Rodmell,*
                                       Lewes [*Sussex*]
Typewritten
Monday [24 September 1923]

Dearest Ottoline,
    The typewriter, as you know, is always a sign of the Eliot Fund. I cannot approach it by any other means.
    I have heard from [Richard] Aldington who wishes to know whether we think it would be a good thing to declare that the fund is now closed. I have

1. Leonard and Virginia were at Studland, Dorset, from 7 to 10 September. Their companions were Maynard Keynes, Lydia Lopokova, Raymond Mortimer, and George ("Dadie") Rylands. The idea of Rylands joining the Hogarth Press was first mooted on this occasion.
2. In his essay on Virginia, Clive had written that she could observe lovers dispassionately: "Assuredly, she feels the romance of the situation, but she does not share the romantic feelings of the actors."

said that I do. Do you? Then, what is to happen next? I propose to ask Tom whether he would like the money handed over now. Aldington says we must communicate with [Ezra] Pound. He has quarrelled with Pound and wants you or me to write. I will do this, if you like—unless you know him, and could make him say what money he has got, and what their plans are.* I have never seen him; and only hate his works.

How are you? what are you doing? and thinking, and have you seen anyone exciting? Instinct tells me that Mr Sprott[1] was not a success—partly because of his name. But he is Lytton's Sebastian—not mine. I only handed on his request. I hope you'll like the poet Rylands who said he hoped to be received about now. He is Lyttons Dady—but a very nice young man I thought. What an interesting letter I could write if it weren't for this appalling machine! Not only does it misspell; it talks nonsense.

We go back to Richmond next Saturday.

Ever yours
V.W.

[*in Virginia's handwriting:*]
* Aldington says, we ought to "obtain from Pound an account of their results and intentions" address: 70 bis Rue Notre Dame des Champs, Paris.

Texas

1423: To George Rylands   *Hogarth House, Paradise Road,*
                                  Richmond
Sept 30th [1923]

Dear Dadie,

Yes, we are hoping you will come on Saturday, Oct 6th. Is there anybody (within reason) you want to meet? My address is a lie; we are still for 2 hours more, at Rodmell, on the hottest day of the year.

I don't agree with you about Tom Eliot, and I'm sure I'm right; but this we will argue. I see Desmond has returned to his vomit this week, without bringing up anything that convinces me about Ruskin.[2]

Leonard is quite ready to buy you a press at any moment.

Bring, I need not say, no clothes, except perhaps the cornflour suit.

Yours
Virginia Woolf

George Rylands

1. See Letter 1371.
2. Desmond's article was a review of A. C. Benson's *Selections from Ruskin* (*New Statesman*, 29 September 1923).

71

1424: To LYTTON STRACHEY   *Hogarth* [*House, Richmond*]
Postcard
Thursday [4 October 1923]

I should be very grateful for a line to say whether you advise me to buy the new Congreve.[1]

Does it give more (of importance) than the usual editions: or prove that they are bowdlerized? It is a serious matter to part with £3/3 but I would, in a good cause.

Yr.
V.W.

Frances Hooper

1425: To VANESSA BELL   [*Hogarth House, Richmond*]
Saturday [6 October? 1923]

Dearest

Here is a copy for you [of *Freshwater*]—perhaps you and Duncan could use the same one?—Could we arrange something with the Stephens on Tuesday night? Leonard is dining with Maynard,—I could either dine with you or with them; and read it to Adrian—Perhaps you'd be bored, so I'd better go to them.

Ring me up and say which. I'm writing to Desmond to suggest his coming here, and Lydia has her copy, so the thing is now on foot. I can get other copies typed.

Yr B.

Berg

1426: To DESMOND MACCARTHY
                              Hogarth House, Paradise Road,
                              Richmond
Sunday [7 October? 1923]

My dear Desmond,

Nessa says that you may consent to stage-manage a skit upon our great aunts, which we want to act for Christmas. If this is true, either I could send you a copy of the MS or perhaps we could contrive a meeting in order to discuss it? There are six parts: Lydia, Adrian, Nessa, are already cast. The rest await your decision.

I gather that Hawk[2] is hovering over a farmyard.

1. *The Complete Works of William Congreve*, in 4 volumes, edited by M. Summers for the Nonesuch Press.
2. "Affable Hawk" was Desmond MacCarthy's pen-name in the *New Statesman*.

I can't write a letter, though there are millions of things I want to say. So let me know if anything can be arranged. The idea is to have masses of Cameron photographs, shawls, cameos, peg-top trousers, laurel trees, laureates and all the rest.

By the way, tell Molly [MacCarthy] I won't appear in the same number of the Nation with her again. Her praises never cease ringing in the oddest quarters—Leonard's mother, Rylands' mother, elderly ladies of discretion, burst out in enthusiasm, and say M.M.'s memoirs are by far the best thing yet appeared in the Nation: and the young men too, seem enthusiastic—but all this is not balm and lavender to me.

Are you ever jealous? Of course, it's only skin deep with me, but I do cry out as the pin goes in—Molly's praise, that's to say. How I enjoy the description of the Grand Livre, and Mrs Cornish's sarcasm about the parrot![1] Of course, truth beats fiction hollow. One pinch of it scatters cartloads of the most carefully made up romance.

But this is developing into an essay, and may lead much further than I intend.

Logan [Pearsall Smith] was here yesterday, gone a little grey about the gills; Roger is hovering over us; Clive is in Paris; and the [Charles] Sangers are as usual.

So write and say what is to happen.

Your affte
Virginia

Mrs Michael MacCarthy

1427: To David Garnett   *Hogarth House, Richmond*

[9 October 1923]

Dear Bunny,
        Lytton advises me that the Congreve is more for people of wealth than for hungry students like myself, (which of course is a nasty one for the Nonesuchers) so, with a thousand thanks for your offer, I won't spend my £3/3 on that, but lay it out, I swear, upon other books.[2] There are any number I want; so I'll look in soon, and see.

1. Molly MacCarthy's memoirs appeared at intervals in the *Nation* from 1 September 1923 to 31 May 1924. In the 3 November instalment, she described her father's account book (known as 'Le Grand Livre'), his tyrannical attempts to economise, and her mother's retaliation against his parrot.
2. David Garnett, together with Francis Birrell, ran a bookshop which was patronised by all Bloomsbury.

Come and dine soon again. I want to hear about your book;[1] not merely to talk about mine.

Ever Yr
Virginia Woolf

Berg

1428: To Molly MacCarthy [*Hogarth House, Paradise Road, Richmond*]

Wednesday [10 October 1923?]

Dearest Molly,

I ran out and got you this tiny inadequate token this afternoon. It has "L'Amour nous unit" written upon it—that is exactly what I feel. Please forgive me for being so inconsiderate and vain. I don't mean it. At heart I am your most constant and affectionate

Virginia

who loves you in spite of all her imperfections.[2]

Sussex

1429: To Richard Aldington

Hogarth House, Paradise Road,
Richmond S.W.

Typewritten
12th Oct. 1923

Dear Mr Aldington,

I'm afraid I must have explained myself badly. Last year about this time I gave Mr Eliot fifty pounds, having got, as I thought, both your consent and Lady Ottolines. He told me then that he was putting the money in the bank, to keep as long as he could untouched. I'm afraid, from something he said, indirectly, that his wifes illness made it necessary for him to spend it.

The pass-book I sent you has just been made up to date. I saw there is sixty pounds to our credit (more or less) and what I want to decide with you is whether I am to give Mr Eliot a cheque for this amount now, or tell him how the fund stands, and ask him to decide what he wishes done.

Also, could you let me know how much will be paid us yearly so I may explain this too to him. It is a matter of some importance to him, I am sure,

1. *A Man in the Zoo* (1924).
2. The date of this letter is very doubtful. Virginia's gesture of contrition may have resulted from her semi-jocular expression of jealousy of Molly's memoirs in the letter to Desmond of 7 October (?).

to know what he can count on. I agree with you that so long as we are receiving subscriptions—that is for the next three or four years—we may as well keep the fund open. We shall have to sign cheques and so on, and keeping the Fund open means no extra trouble for anyone, so far as I can see.

I didn't mean that Mr Eliot was giving up journalism for good; only that he hopes to do none for three or four months and write poetry meanwhile.

We are very glad to hear that you liked the article on your book [*Exiles and Other Poems*], and hope it will lead you to do more.

Yours sincerely,
Virginia Woolf

Texas

1430: TO VANESSA BELL   *Hogarth House* [*Richmond*]

[mid-October? 1923]

Dearest,

On thinking over the play, I rather doubt its worth going on with.[1] It seemed to me, when I read it last night, that its so much of a burlesque, and really rather too thin and flat to be worth getting people together at infinite trouble to act. I could write something much better, if I gave up a little more time to it: and I foresee that the whole affair will be much more of an undertaking than I thought. I dont think this is vanity on my part: more common sense. So I shant take any further steps till I hear from you. I am willing to abide by any decision that you, Duncan, and Adrian, come to together. But I think it ought to be considered carefully before we start.

My own feeling is, as I say, that its not enough of a play to be worth spending time over. And I can swear on my knees that I shan't care a straw—in fact be rather relieved—if you, Duncan and Adrian agree.

Was I asked to dinner next Monday? If so, I should like to come.

V.W.

Berg

1431: TO R. C. TREVELYAN   *Hogarth House, Paradise Road, Richmond*

23rd Oct. [1923]

My dear Bob,

Leonard thinks that you once told us of a printer who prints poetry much more cheaply than the ordinary printers. If this is so, could you tell us whether you have seen his work, and what his address is? It would be very good of you. We want to go on printing poetry, but the prices are so high,

1. *Freshwater* was re-written and finally produced in January 1935.

that it becomes almost impossible, (unless we do it ourselves, and time is a great difficulty now).

Please come and see us some day—in a week or two better than now, as our manager is ill, and we have to work hard at the press.

Yours Ever
Virginia Woolf

Sussex

1432: TO JACQUES RAVERAT   *Hogarth House, Paradise Road,*
                                          Richmond
Nov. 4th 1923

My dear Jacques,

You were saying that you would like a little gossip about Maynard and Lydia. On Sept. 7th we went to stay with them at Studland—a ducal home,[1] in which they fared, rather uneasily I thought, because the dukes servants were in the pantry; and Lydia's habits, of course, are not ducal. I do not know how far I transgress the bounds of good taste, if I allude (oh it must be in a whisper, only in the presence of Gwen) to—well things called Sanitary Towels—you see blue bundles discreetly hidden beneath lace in the windows of small drapers. When used they should be burnt. Lydia, whose father was porter in a Petersburg hotel, and whose entire life has been spent hopping from foot to foot with the daughters of publicans, did not know this perhaps the most binding of all laws of female life (Ask any Darwin, excepting Mrs Litchfield[2]—they'll tell you) She put her weeks supply on the grate. The grate was filled with white shavings. Imagine the consequences. There she left them. The cook's husband, and Duke's valet, did the room. Soon the Cook herself requested to speak with the lady. There was such a scene, it is said, as shook the rafters,—rage, tears, despair, outrage, horror, retribution, reconciliation: and—if you knew Lydia you'll see how naturally it follows— lifelong friendship upon a basis of—well, bloody rags. Really, there is a curious feeling about that menage, as well may be with such a foundation. Lydia has the soul of a squirrel: anything nicer you cant conceive: she sits by the hour polishing the sides of her nose with her front paws. But, poor little wretch, trapped in Bloomsbury, what can she do but learn Shakespeare by heart? I assure you its tragic to see her sitting down to King Lear. Nobody can take her seriously: every nice young man kisses her. Then she flies into a rage and says she is like Vanessa, like Virginia, like Alix Sargent Florence [Strachey], or Ka Cox [Arnold-Forster]—a seerious wooman.

Ka Cox dined with us two nights ago. Is malice allowed? Is it deducted

1. The Knoll, the seaside retreat of the Duke of Hamilton. It became a hotel in 1931.
2. See p. 60, note 2.

76

from the good marks I have acquired or hope to acquire with the Raverat family? But then you've always known the worst of me—my incorrigible mendacity; my leering, sneering, undependable disposition. You take me as I am, and make allowances for the sake of old days. Well, then, Ka is *intolerably dull.* I am quoting my husband. I am not quite of that opinion myself: but why, I ask, condescend to the Woolfs? Why be so damned matronly? Why always talk about Will [Arnold-Forster]—that parched and pinched little hob goblin, whom I like very much but think an incorrigibly bad painter, as if he were Shelley, Mr Gladstone, Byron and Helen of Troy in one? I dont carry on about Leonard like that, nor yet Gwen about Jacques. What I suspect is that dear old Ka feels the waves of life withdraw, and there, perched high on her rock,[1] makes these frantic efforts to pretend, to make the Woolfs believe that she is still visited by the waters of the great sea.

Indeed, once upon a time, when we all swooned upon her in our love affairs and collapsed in our nervous breakdowns, she was. She was wetted punctually, and shone in her passive way, like some faintly coloured sea anemone, who never budges, never stings, never—but I am getting wrapped up in words.

Anyhow, both Leonard and I lost our tempers. We said nothing. We went to bed in the devil of a gloom. Are we like that? we said. Are we middle aged and content? Do we look like old cabbages? Is life entirely a matter of retrospect and county families and trying to impress people with ringing up men at the foreign office about French conscription of Natives in Africa? No, no, no. Let us change the subject.

Duncan has just been in to tea. I may tell you it is rather a fine November day, but dark by half-past four. Duncan was going on to Twickenham to see his mother to choose some silks for a chair cover—bright sunlight being essential. Its no good. One goes to the window and shows him the church all lit up. Off he wanders murmuring something about getting there by daybreak—Half his buttons seemed to be off; his braces are too long. He has always to be hitching himself together; and odd bits of shirt stick out. Anrep has done a mosaic which is said to be very good;[2] Segonzac has been admiring the London Group;[3] Sickert has surpassed himself;[4] Alix and James Strachey think we should go to war with France. Lytton is buying a house at Hungerford [Ham Spray].

What other news is there? Very little I think of interest, so far as facts go. And to convey feelings is too difficult. I try, but I invariably make enemies.

1. Eagle's Nest, Zennor, Cornwall.
2. Boris Anrep's mosaic pavement of 'The Blake Room' at the Tate Gallery.
3. André Dunoyer de Segonzac was in London for his own exhibition at the Independent Gallery.
4. Sickert's *The Bar-Parlour* (1922). The painting was purchased by Maynard Keynes.

I go to parties, very occasionally, and there get rather random headed, and *say too much.* I assure you its fatal—but I never can resist the desire for intimacy, or reconcile myself to the fact that all human relations are bound to be unsatisfactory. Are they? I rather expect Jacques, in his thick black beard, surveying the country from his motor car, knows all about it. I still play my game of making up Jacques and Gwen as I walk about London. No doubt I shall be picked off by a motor omnibus in the thick of it. After half an hours acute discomfort, should we settle down to the old relationship, whatever it was? Jacques I think was rather dictatorial; he called us silly women; he said the Oliviers[1] were *real*: but not most people. Gwen sat on the floor and said something very positive—being, poor woman, a Darwin to the backbone, and Virginia of course, shied and shilly-shallied, and—no, you must write Virginia's part, because she is oddly enough, the last woman I have any idea of. About coming, to Vence—this must be done somehow, and I aim at Easter, or later, or earlier. But we are tied by the navel string to the Nation; and—what awful, indecent things I keep thinking of this evening!

Please write someday soon; and explain what you think about, as you survey the world. And please think kindly of me. How I depend upon my friends! You wouldn't believe it, either of you.

Ever yrs
V.W.

Sussex

1433: To Gerald Brenan   *Monks House, Rodmell,*
Lewes [Sussex]

Dec. 1st 1923

My dear Gerald,

I am ashamed to say that I left a long unfinished letter to you behind at Richmond, and now have my doubts that I can accomplish, as I wish and have wished for long, a finished one. I am coming to the age when I sit staring at the fire and saying "I'm so busy: I'm so fearfully hard at work: I've not got a word to throw at a dog:" and so I do nothing. Oh, yes, I ought to be reading *4* manuscripts for the Hogarth Press, one by a young Frenchman, another by a paralysed girl, and a third by an astute and bold American [Theodora Bosanquet], who was Henry James' secretary, and a fourth by a Spaniard.

In the unfinished letter in the drawer of my Roman cabinet I went at some length into several points of disagreement between us. I disagreed entirely and with some heat in your estimate of Conrad: I repeated, with qualifications, my remark that he is a great, though limited, novelist: and

---

1. The four daughters (Margery, Brynhild, Daphne and Noel) of Sir Sydney Olivier, ex-Governor of Jamaica and a Fabian Socialist. Like Gwen Raverat, they had all been members of the "Neo-Pagans", a group of young intellectuals.

then I observed that Vanity Fair is inferior as a work of art to Wuthering Heights: and then I joked at you for taking me seriously when I was writing humorously (but humour never crosses the Channel) for your Aunt. Do you indeed accuse me of writing for money? Do you have the temerity to bid me forsake journalism? And in God's name, what do you mean by "working working working at my novel"?[1] How does one "work" at one's novel? Well, scribbling journalism is one way, and lunching with Lady Colefax to meet Hugh Walpole, is another. But do not let us quarrel over these misfits of meaning. Come to England and let us adjust them in hours of endless talk.

I saw Carrington two days ago, and we had a long long consultation, such as you can imagine, about Ralph, among other things. Since your advice, I have tried to be cordial; as to quarrel was none of our wish; indeed I always like him, but Carrington says, he suspects us—you're evidently right—he suspects all brain workers, who don't rampage about the purlieus of Soho chasing pretty powdered girls. I quite like seeing him do it: I don't bear the shadow of a grudge against him; but life is life. Surely that is a Spanish proverb? Interpreted it means, women of 41 can't be intimate with rowing blues of 28. Carrington was very sincere. She interests me more than he does. And don't think that your ruse was altogether successful. I suspected —but as you'll be seeing them, I shall drop this subject, as I don't want to be quoted, mentioned, or twisted like a figure of wax in front of your 6 eyes.[2]

Now we have a card to say you're in Morocco, and a picture of camels ploughing sandhills; so that my letter begins to evaporate. There it will be on the table over the braziers in your room among all the littered foolscap, and you'll never find it. Perhaps as you say, you'll marry a lady in a veil, and live among the palm trees like a sultan for ever.

That is not the life to make a good writer of you, however. I have a feeling that a street would put a backbone into your sentences, which, if you will excuse the frankness, I think they begin to want. For your story of Mr Unwin,[3] you should live in Birmingham, and have to eat in A.B.C. shops. Or, more boldly, live in Bloomsbury, and hear Clive Bell chattering. You asked me about him and Murry. Clive is a great source of pleasure to me, for one thing because he says outright what I spend my life in concealing. Never was there anyone so petty, conceited, open and good at bottom of heart. I always think of him as a mixture of Pepys and Boswell. Sometimes I imagine him the only one to survive of us all—for 50 years or so after his

1. Brenan's first published novel was *Jack Robinson*, 1933, under the pseudonym George Beaton.
2. Brenan had confessed to Ralph Partridge that he and Carrington were in love, which led to a temporary breach between the two men. However Carrington and Partridge stayed with Brenan on his return from Morocco on January 1924, and the friendship between the three of them was restored.
3. A story about lower middle-class life which Brenan began but never finished.

death. I should be more sure of this if he had not been slightly corrupted by Lytton. When I first knew him, he was perfection: a hunting squire who thought himself a Shelley. But he is always a delight to watch: and no one more annoys and outrages me: and also I am on perfectly friendly terms with him; and he pays my cabs, and stands me "Cold Snacks" at the Café Royal, where the waiter brings him the cold red beef to look at before he cuts it— but I can't trouble to go on with this account, or get it very like.

Please believe that I could write better if I took a little more time. But letter writing is now a mere tossing of omelettes to me: if they break and squash, can't be helped. Then, of course, you should know Roger, whose mind, far subtler and more richly stocked than Clives, never ceases for a second to glow, contract, expand, like some wonderful red-tinted sea anemone, which lives in the deepest water and sucks into itself every scrap of living matter within miles. He is close on sixty, and gets, so it seems to me, richer and suppler, richer and suppler—but they say his painting is very bad. As for Murry, I can no longer follow him even with amusement, much less with dislike. Eliot says he has unbuttoned his waistcoat and found his level. One might as well listen to a half starved clerk spouting religious revival on a tub at Hyde Park Corner. But you are right about him. His friend (he has one disciple left, Sydney Waterlow—a kind of spaniel who follows anybody who will beat him) his friend says that in the Adelphi he is purging his sins: and the process is holy to watch, and salutary to us, the unconverted, too. He is one of those Dostoevsky relics. He sees himself pulled asunder by the angels of darkness and light. As a matter of fact—but no: I can't go on with Murry either.

What about your defence of Joyce? Our press has its mouth wide gaping for *prose*. Did we tell you that Rylands, a young man at Cambridge, is coming in June to be our partner? So we shall be more capable of undertaking masterpieces. I rather agree that Joyce is underrated: but never did any book [*Ulysses*] so bore me. But then, as you think criticism is not my line (*meant humorously*) I will not go on to analyse. I will not send you my next book, which consists of criticism pure and simple. I will work work work—I wish I could laugh in person instead of trying to make my pen laugh. My ink pot is stood upon the hob; and the faint sizzling sound of boiling purple ink is now to be heard. We have been weeding onions in the light of a towering rose pink cloud, which, tugging a little at its anchor, moved very slowly across the sky, and over Mount Caburn, and so away. Indeed, I could spend my whole life describing clouds.

I am now going to read Greek.[1]

Ever yr.
V.W.

For Gods sake, send me your sonnets, and my Proust.

George Laʒarus

1. For her essay *On Not Knowing Greek* (*The Common Reader*, 1925).

1434: To Ethel Sands   *Hogarth House, Paradise Road,*
                                Richmond, Surrey
Tuesday [end of 1923?]

Dear Ethel,

I wonder whether you could possibly tell me the address of Miss Fass, at whose house concerts are given by the English quartet?[1] She sent me a programme, which I lost, and now I want one to give a friend, and would also like to try and come myself.

It is a shame to trouble you; but she is not on the telephone, and I think you go there. If not, please don't bother to answer. May I ever come and see you again? I should so much like to.

                                                Yours sincerely
                                                Virginia Woolf

Wendy Baron

1. Formed in 1902, the Quartet achieved a high reputation for chamber music under its leader Marjorie Hayward. Until its dissolution in 1925, it performed mainly in private houses, including the house in Bedford Gardens belonging to Marjorie Fass, the friend and patron of the composer Frank Bridge.

Letters 1435-1457 (January–mid-April 1924)

After searching for a London house in Chelsea, Maida Vale and Battersea, Virginia eventually found, in Bloomsbury, 52 Tavistock Square, which was to remain the Woolfs' London home until just before the Second War. It was a house too big for their needs, and the two central floors were occupied by a firm of solicitors. Virginia and Leonard lived on the upper floors, which Vanessa Bell and Duncan Grant decorated for them, and installed the Hogarth Press in the basement, a jumble of small rooms with a large room behind, where Virginia worked. Hogarth House was let to Saxon Sydney-Turner. The move was completed on 15 March, and Virginia was able to resume work on The Common Reader *and* Mrs Dalloway. *Among the first visitors to Tavistock Square was Vita Sackville-West, whom Virginia had not seen for nearly a year.*

1435: To George Rylands

Hogarth House, Paradise Road, Richmond

[early January 1924]

Dear Dadie,

We've just come back here, after suffering a good deal in the country. The poems have been returned; and another volume I've rejected on my own authority—hopeless drivel. We have now some Russian stories, which perhaps you'd like to see.

Will you be able to come here and stay the night, or weekend on your way to Cambridge?

There is a good deal to discuss. We have some new ideas about domestic arrangements.

Let me know.

Yr affte
V.W.

George Rylands

1436: To Molly MacCarthy

Hogarth House, Paradise Road, Richmond, Surrey

[early January 1924]

Dearest Molly,

I am searching for houses in London, in view of a possible move this spring or summer. Is Wellington Square[1] to be had still, and if so, at what rent, and for how long, and are there bedrooms, bathroom etc etc?

1. The MacCarthy's house in Chelsea, to which they returned after living for some time in Wiltshire.

I shoot from Maida Vale to Battersea—We are taking in a young man as partner [Rylands], and want to get him and the Press lodged near. The difficulties seem insuperable; so if you could write a line of information,—add a little friendship, so much the happier for me.

Shall you be in London soon?

Did I tell you how immensely I enjoyed the new instalment of your memoirs [in the *Nation*]? You have sickened me of fiction, which beside fact becomes more and more insipid, vapid, tedious, unprofitable. The least you can do is to find me a house.

Yrs V.W.

Mrs Michael MacCarthy

1437: To V. Sackville-West   *Hogarth House, Paradise Road,*
                               Richmond
Tuesday [8 January 1924]

My dear Vita

I'm afraid tomorrow is impossible for me. I'm in the thick of finding and moving houses. But wouldn't you and Lord Berners[1] dine here on Friday, 18th, 7.30—in the kitchen, without dressing? That would be much nicer than tea. Would you ask him from me?

Your aff
Virginia Woolf

Berg

1438: To Clive Bell   [*Hogarth House, Richmond*]
Postcard
[8 January 1924]

Can you possibly extend your already wide hospitality to a bed, on Saturday night—so that I needn't catch the steam train? But don't, if there's the least bother.

V.W.

Quentin Bell

1. Gerald Berners had first met Vita in Constantinople in 1911, when both he and Harold Nicolson were serving in the Embassy. He was an amateur musician and artist of great talent, and later wrote several novels and books of auto-biography.

Friday [11 January 1924]

Dearest,

I hear that Leonard has told you of my iniquities.

What has now happened is that we have asked Nelly [Boxall] to stay on as [cook] general, which, greatly to our relief, she has agreed to do. I then suggested that I should try to find Lottie a place in Gordon Sqre.[1] She said at once that she would be perfectly happy if she could be with you, either as cook or house maid—anything indeed except nurse. She has the makings of a very good cook I think, and Nelly says she would help her. I dont think her temper is a real objection, as I think it is mostly due to the fact that she and N. get very much on each others nerves alone here, and she would probably be much better in a bigger place. Anyhow, she is ready to do anything in order to be with you, and shes such a nice character that it is a pity she should be lost. She would go at the end of March.

Would you let me know if there is any chance of this, as I said I'd ask you before anyone else.

Will you be in to tea on Monday? I might come then.

Yr B.

Berg

1440: To Clive Bell   *Hogarth* [*House, Richmond*]

Wednesday [23 January 1924]

Dearest Clive,

I'm extremely sorry that Leonard's flue and my flux have prevented me from sitting by your side—or was I not asked? Communication by letter is far from satisfactory.

Old Miss Elwes[2] has just doddered in to borrow books for Major Grant. "But may we keep Pot boilers[3] rather longer? My family find it so fascinating—" but then there's madness in the family. *Dont* plume yourself on *that*. Old Randall [solicitor] on the telephone: "Mr Clive Bell's note might perhaps be thought a *trifle* strong"[4]—in short Clive Bell has been haunting the muggy damned damp January day; and here (my one little wizened,

1. The first plan was that Lottie Hope, the Woolfs' parlourmaid, should look after Vanessa at 46 Gordon Square. But in March Lottie went to Karin Stephen at 50 Gordon Square.
2. Companion to Duncan's mother.
3. Clive Bell's book of critical essays published in 1918.
4. There was a legal dispute about the lease of the flat at 50 Gordon Square which was let to Adrian and Karin Stephen. The Bells were their subtenants.

enfeebled attempt at a boast) is Lady Colefax (who's asked herself to tea) asking us to meet the Bibescos.[1] This great authoress sends Leonard a personal copy, dedicated, in a fluent flourishing foolish fist "to the author of the Village and the Jungle,[2] in deepest admiration"—or, translated, will he review Fir and Pine himself, favourably, at length in the Nation. And another lady, nearer home, but I'm too discreet to mention names, suggests that Mr Woolf shall send her novel to so and so, who has expressed fervent admiration for same. I'm not proud of our tribe, are you? This running and inarticulate style is the style natural to a Penkala [fountain pen]: they write of themselves: I'll give you one.

As for gossip, what? Lord Berners, Vita, Siegfried [Sassoon]: thats my style these last days: and oh dear for a carving knife to scrape the numbskulls a little sharper! Dear Vita has the body and brain of a Greek God; Berners is by all means admirable, and Siegfried the most delightful, and sensitive etc etc etc: but when it comes to sitting tight, 2 feet apart, over the fire from 8 to 11.30—more brain, O God, more brain! So Meredith cries, in a sonnet which in our youth we quoted:[3] and here, to solace myself, I've been reading a Maynard-Lytton 1906 correspondence, all about Hobbes and Duncan—oh so far away, and vivid, and bringing back, as charwomen say of hardboiled eggs, which "repeat". Again vulgarity, its Penkala's fault—(It's a red pen, with a *real* nib; gilt; but virile, none of that smooth mush the fountain pens have. I'll give you one. Remind me.)

And what else? Logan [Pearsall Smith] came to tea, a little censorious, mildly buggeristical, a young Spaniard having come to Chelsea all the way from his Estancia on the Steppe of Paraguay to translate Trivia. Its the American salt I dont relish, something coarse and briny in the blood.[4] Vita was well laughed at about P.E.N.,[5] but the poor girl has lost her way and dont know which light to turn on next. Would I introduce her to the Robert Lynds?[6] "Well, if you'll introduce me to Lord Lascelles."[7] "Why dont you

---

1. Prince Antoine Bibesco and his wife, formerly Elizabeth Asquith. Her latest novel was *The Fir and the Palm*, not *Fir and Pine* as Virginia gives it a few lines later.
2. Leonard's first novel (1913).
3. "More brain, O Lord, more brain!" (George Meredith, *Modern Love*, XLVIII).
4. When he was a young man, Logan Pearsall Smith's family emigrated from Pennsylvania to England, and he became a British subject in 1913.
5. See Letter 1375.
6. The essayist, who for many years contributed to the *New Statesman* under the pseudonym 'Y.Y.' He was also literary editor of the *Daily News*, which after 1930 became the *News Chronicle*.
7. The son of the 5th Earl of Harewood, whom he succeeded in 1929. He had been much in love with Vita in 1911-13, and in 1922 married Princess Mary, only daughter of George V.

contribute to the Queen's dolls House,[1] Virginia?" "Is there a W.C. in it, Vita?" "You're a bit hoity toity, Virginia." Well, I was educated in the old Cambridge School. "Ever heard of Moore?"[2] "George Moore the novelist?" "My dear Vita, we start at different ends". The poor girl looks divinely lovely, a little tousled, in a velvet jacket. But let us meet, for no more letter writing at my age; only a St Vitus' dance.

Love from the other invalid Leonard; who says that he was very glad of your note; he had meant to have one; his anger was roused; he didnt think you quite hit the first political point hard enough on the head, so he altered the first part, and made your original note into two.[3] Thats all.

V.W.

Quentin Bell

1441: TO ETHEL SANDS

The Hogarth Press, Hogarth House, Paradise Road, Richmond, Surrey

[end of January 1924]

My dear Ethel,

I must implore you to clear up the romances of your own drawing room.[4] Who is Virgilia? What is Shooter's Hill? Why am I represented in male costume with my head in the stars, accepting worship from a bowed x .. d woman? It is obscure; possibly improper. So you see what your plain duty as a hostess is.

How charming Arnold Bennett was![5] Never again will I say a word against his books. That's the worst of meeting authors—one is always at their feet.

Yours ever
Virginia Woolf

Wendy Baron

1. The doll's house, now at Windsor Castle, which Sir Edwin Lutyens designed for Queen Mary in 1922. Virginia had refused an invitation to contribute a miniature manuscript to its library, but Vita had accepted.
2. G. E. Moore, the Cambridge philosopher, and author of *Principia Ethica* (1903), which had much influenced the young men of Old Bloomsbury.
3. All these notes in the *Nation* were unsigned.
4. Boris Anrep had done a series of mosaics for Ethel Sands' house, in The Vale, Chelsea. Among the figures represented were Enid Bagnold (Virgilia) and Virginia.
5. Arnold Bennett was a fellow guest when Virginia dined with Ethel Sands.

86

1442: To Logan Pearsall Smith

Hogarth House, Paradise Road,
Richmond, Surrey

3rd Feb. 1924

Dear Logan,

It is a great pleasure to me that you should like anything I write, and it was very kind of you to tell me so.¹ I always feel myself such an ignorant chatterbox.

But this is the letter of a grasping publisher (its not your money this time, but your works.) We are very anxious to pounce upon you for a book.² Next autumn we shall be starting seriously, with Dadie's bread and butter to earn, and what we want to know is whether we can count upon you for anything—long, or short—and when?

Dont think us too much of a bore. We want to attract attention, and you would be a feather in our cap to brandish in the face of the public.

I will pursue Nickey to the death.³

Yours Ever
Virginia Woolf

Library of Congress

1443: To Margaret Llewelyn Davies

Hogarth House, Paradise Road,
Richmond

[February 1924]

Dearest Margaret,

Your woman [*unidentified*] is rather interesting—I've just had another article of hers sent me, with some remarks on the obscure Miss [Gertrude] Stein—who is a very rich, stout American lady, living in Paris, and buying modern pictures—a friend of Roger Fry's. I send you your's back—not that I suppose you want it.

Not this week alas: my whole day goes in stamping this 550

600 times, and folding 600 pages, and addressing 600 envelopes. It refers to Roger's new book⁴—we are in an awful rush and muddle. But all will be over next week; and then, I say, not another publishing season till we have the next beautiful young man [Rylands], Ralph's successor, to help.

1. Pearsall Smith had praised Virginia's review of *Essays of Montaigne*, which had appeared in the *TLS* for 31 January 1924.
2. Pearsall Smith did not publish another book with the Hogarth Press until 1927, but he did send Virginia and Leonard an article for the *Nation*. See Letter 1447.
3. Possibly Nicky Mariano, Bernard Berenson's secretary and constant companion. Berenson had married Logan's sister.
4. *Duncan Grant*, published by the Press this month.

But do ask me: don't let me become, as I fear Miss Tournier[1] has become, one of your suburban admirers.

Yr V.W.

Love from Leonard.

Sussex

1444: To Vanessa Bell   *Hogarth* [*House, Richmond*]
Friday, 22nd Feb. [1924]
Dearest,
    We should like you to do all the decorations[2] you estimate for, except Leonard's room. This you estimate at £7. So the cost of the whole would then be I suppose £20. 4.
    I hope to let you know about the sitting room in a few days, if it would still give you time. Its a question of selling some things here, and I don't know what they'll fetch. Needless to say, my aim is to get you and Duncan to paint it for £25. But would your paintings be detachable, or on the wall itself? This is a matter of some importance, as we may be turned out after 10 years, in which case your masterpieces would be destroyed, and I couldn't sell them to nourish my old age.
    Would you start work at once? We shall move in on the 13th.
    I'll come to tea on Monday, if I may—anyhow I shall be at 52 that afternoon—

Yr B.

We have decided to let the studio for £75. Would you tell Douglas Davidson[3] or anyone else? We want to let it by the year.

Berg

1445: To Vanessa Bell   [*Hogarth House, Richmond*]
[24 February 1924]
Dearest,

    We have decided that we should like you and Duncan to paint the sitting room for £25 as you estimate (I've no doubt you're charging only a 20th of the right price.) So would you start as soon as you can.

1. A former President of the Women's Co-operative Guild, of which Margaret Llewelyn Davies had been Secretary.
2. For 52 Tavistock Square.
3. The painter, and a friend of Lytton Strachey. In fact, the studio was not let, but was used as a store room for the Hogarth Press and Virginia wrote there.

Have you heard anything from D. Davidson? There are some other people who probably want to take the studio, and are coming to see it tomorrow. But I think we must give him the first choice, if he would let us know at once.

I'll come in to tea tomorrow.

Yr B.

I'd better give you the measurements of the bookcases: there will have to be two.

Berg

1446: To Theodora Bosanquet

The Hogarth Press, Hogarth House,
Paradise Road, Richmond,
Surrey

Typewritten
24th Feb. 1924

Dear Miss Bosanquet,

I have read your articles (which I send back separately—) with great interest. You are right in thinking that the article I had heard of was about Henry James' methods of work, dictation and so on. But we think your idea of combining the different articles a very good one. Would it be possible to begin by giving your personal memories, which would be of the highest value as there is no account I think of his methods during his later period, and go on with criticism of the novels themselves? About 10,000 words would be as much as we are able to manage. We should issue it as a pamphlet, and would give you 25% of the profits. I think it should make a most interesting little book.[1]

After March 13th our address will be 52, Tavistock Square, W.C.1.

Yours sincerely,
Virginia Woolf

Houghton Library, Harvard University

1. Published as *Henry James at Work* in November 1924, as Number 3 of *The Hogarth Essays*, First Series. Theodora Bosanquet was Henry James's secretary in the last period of his life, but she was not, as Virginia previously stated, herself an American.

1447: To LOGAN PEARSALL SMITH *Hogarth [House, Richmond]*

Monday [25 February 1924]

Dear Logan,

I'm very glad that I goaded you into writing your article, which is worth 25 dozen of that stupid Mr Beresford's[1]—I wont say how many of mine.

But now that you've started your hare you must go after her—You can't leave her on the mountains—more articles are required—but I rather agree with you that her breed is nobler than our beasts. There is much more to be said, though.

Yours very Sincerely
Virginia Woolf

I am in your debt for ever over Montaigne—altogether a different thing in French.

Library of Congress

1448: To LADY OTTOLINE MORRELL
*Hogarth House, Paradise Road,
Richmond, Surrey*

[February 1924]

Dearest Ottoline,

I have asked Mr Schiff[2] to let you know if he knows who the American secretary [of the Eliot fund] is:

Ezra Pound's address is 70 bis, Rue notre Dame des Champs, VI Paris—but where he is I dont know. Vivien [Eliot] would know (I don't like to ask Tom). I'm seeing her next week, and will send a card.

We are in the midst of confusion here—letting this house to Saxon,[3] measuring rooms, meeting builders, leading an amphibious life between this and 52 Tavistock Sqre, where we move next month, where you'll have to come and see us for all your malicious insinuations that we say the same thing over and over, and are morally spiritually intellectually and physically inferior to the refined spirits of Garsington. Now why do people who live in the country always give themselves such airs?

1. Pearsall Smith's article, *First Catch Your Hare*, was published in the *Nation* in answer to one on character creation in fiction by J. D. Beresford (1873-1947), the novelist and journalist.
2. Sydney Schiff. See p. 10, note 1.
3. Saxon Sydney-Turner took a lease of Hogarth House, where he lived with his mother.

I admit, I don't remember what London life is really like—The Bloomsbury Squares always intoxicate me with their beauty, and there used to be a great lady [Ottoline] once living in Bedford Square who managed to make life seem a little amusing and interesting and adventurous, so I used to think, when I was young and wore a blue dress, and Ottoline was like a Spanish galleon, hung with golden coins, and lovely silkin [*sic*] sails.

But I'm romancing; and must immediately ring up the Electric Light Company to instal us at once . .

I don't see any chance of any week end till after April 1st—but let us meet some time; and dont become too high and superb and proud and pure and like a poplar tree ever to notice the creeping creatures who race about so aimlessly in the grass.

Ever Yr
V.W.

Texas

1449: To Gerald Brenan 52 *Tavistock Square, London, W.C.*1

March 8th 1924

My dear Gerald,

This will be our address in three days time. So note it down, with a view to many envelopes. But I have to make the most appalling confession: I had read your letter once, your sonnets twice, when Lottie, thinking that—thinking heaven knows what—stuffed them into the fire!—For Gods sake send me a copy. It wasnt vanity only; it was something really venerable in me that was pleased by your praises. And I thought, at a first reading, that as poetry they were very interesting, were worth examining, were remarkable. A copy! a copy!

I can but reiterate and bark like a dog on the banks of a river, because we're distracted with moving: books on the floor, curtains down, linoleum to be valued—you cant think how these mosquitoes accumulate about one's head the last day or two. Saxon is coming here. Will Saxon buy our Turkey carpet and the electric light fittings? Ah well, its no use, I cant write.

Here is a letter that was mysteriously returned. And no news of Proust[1] I suppose?

I have heard that Ralph and Carrington are to be seen, Ralph getting tipsy at parties, and Carrington taking him home to bed. This is rumour, and you know more about Tidmarsh than I do.

We count on printing something of yours this summer or autumn.[2]

1. The copy Virginia had sent to Brenan and which had not arrived at Yegen.
2. The Hogarth Press never published anything by Brenan.

91

But good Lord! perhaps we shall see you! Before your letter vanished, I saw something about coming in April.

Now that will be a pleasure to your dusty old friends, who follow your mysterious career, with the greatest zest—often saying for example, Now what d'you think Gerald's up to? What d'you think Gerald'll write?—the last person to whom we said this being Bonamy Dobrée.[1]

Excuse bad writing

Ever yr V.W.

George Lazarus

1450: To Jacques Raverat   52 *Tavistock Square, W.C.*1

March 8th 1924

My dear Jacques,

This you see [her new address] is the reason why I havent written and cant write now and won't be able, so far as I can see to cross the channel this year—a new house, to which we move in a few days, which has had to be cleaned, scoured, painted and lighted, all in a hurry, leaving me a mere drudge, without a thought in my head, or, what is much worse, a penny in my purse. I dont therefore see how we can possibly take precedence of your better off friend. Let us creep into a cranny, if we can come. Otherwise assume we can't.

But thats no reason why our letters should languish. You don't want to hear about my new house, I know by experience. It has a basement for the Press and a large studio: 2 floors full of solicitors [Messrs Dolman & Pritchard], L. and I on top looking at all the glories of London, which are romantically, sentimentally, incredibly dear to me. The Imperial Hotel, all pink and blue, in Russell Square: St Pancras Church spire, carved from white plaster—do you know it? These are the things I love, better than olive trees and mountains, but not so much as Jacques and Gwen, after all.

You said very tactfully in your last letter, why did Adrian and Karin separate, or rather how did he stand that d—d American[2] all these years? I must say your language is a trifle strong. She is a good, honest woman: and in her place I'd have done the same, and in his too. Incompatible, is what they say: and this they've realised for 8 years, and ground their teeth over, while appearing in public the most love-locked of couples. We Stephen's are difficult, especially as the race tapers out, towards its finish—such cold

1. The literary critic (1891-1974). The Hogarth Press published three of his books in 1925, 1926, and 1932.
2. Karin Stephen could scarcely be described as an American. Her mother, Mary Costelloe (afterwards Berenson), was an American, but Karin's father Frank Costelloe was Anglo-Irish, and she herself was born and grew up in England.

fingers, so fastidious, so critical, such taste. My madness has saved me; but Adrian is sane—that's all the light I can throw.

I dare not go on, because my brain is in splinters—and my handwriting like drifts of wreckage. Do you remember Sydney-Turner? a phantom, gliding like a moonbeam through my Thursday evenings, and settling still on one chair for 6 hours on end? He's coming here with his old mother. I forget whom you like, and whom dislike. Dont you think you might write me your memories of all our friends? There are the Oliviers[1] now, whom I meet about, with their beautiful glass eyes, glazed and fixed and melancholy —Noel always enraptures me—she cries over Rupert's [Brooke] letters, she tells me; and really, I fall in love with her, being so sentimental, for doing it. Bryn has been divorced—that you know. Poor Hugh, so I'm told, spent his Sundays making wooden beds, for Sherrard to step into on Monday when he'd gone:[2] he was always making things—Ka [Arnold-Forster] is watching the spring, and Will has written a little book which we are printing.[3] Now, why dont you and Gwen write us a pamphlet about art? or life? *This is serious*. Something profound yet sparkling.

I'll write again: so do you

Ever V.W.

Sussex

1451: To V. Sackville-West   *Hogarth House, Richmond*

Tuesday [11 March 1924]

My dear Vita,

It is extraordinarily kind of you to offer your motor, but all is now in the hands of professionals, and we shall be lifted off bodily on Thursday.

I'm all right again, and very much want to hear your first hand account of Ottoline—but Heaven knows when or how.

But please come and baptise our rooms for us as soon as you can.

Your affectionate dirty illiterate
V.W.

Berg

1. See p. 78, note 1.
2. Hugh Popham divorced his wife Brynhild (*née* Olivier), citing as co-respondent F. R. G. N. Sherrard, who later married her. He had been in the Agricultural Economics Research Institute at Oxford, from which he was obliged to resign, and then became a farmer.
3. The Hogarth Press published no pamphlet by Will Arnold-Forster until March 1926, when *The Victory of Reason* appeared.

1452: To Violet Dickinson   52 *Tavistock Sqre.* [*W.C.*1]
[13 March 1924]

My Violet,
    I was just thinking of you, and of your house, and wanting to see you—
We're on the wing this moment—workmen spit and swear in every
room. So this is only a desperate wag of my tail. But come and see your
Sp[arroy]: and Leonard, who is one of your most faithful admirers.
    Don't tell me you're leaving 21¹ and the Graveyard, looking at which I've
had so many happy hours.
    You must see our printing works in the basement, and do, do, do, as you
love me, write me something about Miss Eden for the press.²
                                                            Yr
                                                                Sp:
Berg

1453: To V. Sackville-West
                        [52 *Tavistock Square, London, W.C.*1]
Postcard
Tuesday [18 March 1924]

We hope to see you tomorrow at 1—but prepare for a complete picnic,
among the ruins of books and legs of tables, dirt and dust and only fragments
of food.³
                                                            V.W.

Berg

1454: To Lytton Strachey   52 *Tavistock Square W.C.*1
March 21st 1924

Dearest Lytton,
    I am greatly distressed to hear that you are still plagued by diseases of all
kinds—just as I was snatching a few moments to read Books & Characters
too.⁴ Why do I always fly to your works when the electricians are in the
hall, the gasmen in the basement, and the telephone ringing with Tom's
[Eliot] sepulchral voice? It's a very queer fact, but in moments of crisis, I
always turn to you but supply me with another book soon. I open at page

1. Violet's house in Manchester Street, London, W.1.
2. In 1919 Violet had edited her great aunt Emily Eden's letters.
3. Vita wrote to Harold Nicolson after this visit: "It was the first time, I think,
   that I'd been alone with her for long. I went on . . . my head swimming with
   Virginia."
4. *Books and Characters, French and English*, published by Lytton in 1922.

173, and say Oh but I know this by heart; and it will soon be the case with all the pages: and this is no exaggeration; and I daresay no particular praise either; only one of your peculiarities as an author. Another is to beget Nicolsons. But the mixture is not appetising to me, for all the praises of Clive and Desmond, who have drunk too many glasses of his [Harold Nicolson's] champagne to be trusted. But then Byron seems to me tawdry and melodramatic.[1] And Claire and Trelawny[2] and so and so on—I conceive them like a cave at some Earl's Court Exhibition—a grotto I mean lined with distorting mirrors and plastered with oyster shells. Do not trouble to unwind this metaphor.

I am jangled and splintered by the move, and only hook together words by the force of affection: Say one word, and I will come down, and talk in a gentle and soothing voice about—well, did you hear how I rushed into Murry's arms at the Nation dinner the other night? *He* forced himself upon me. He has rolling and oleaginous eyes. I said we were enemies. He said we were in different camps. He said one must write with one's instincts. I said one must write with one's mind. He said Bloomsbury was a tangle of exquisite sensibilities. I said come and see me there. He said no. I said very well. He said I like you. I said come and see me then. He said no. So I got up and flounced out of the room, saying Not for ten years—Undoubtedly, he has been rolling in dung, and smells impure.

We live largely in the basement—The confusion is still confounded—busts of my mother standing upon rolls of carpet, chamber pots stuffed full of book binding tools, and my unfortunate books—oh never let the undertakers pack your books when you move—I haven't a single volume left whole. In compensation, Nessa and Duncan have painted me a room, where you *must* come instantly and sit and talk and talk and talk, and never have to catch a taxi, and so by degrees get delivered of that vast mass of communication which I assure you has been hoarding up within me, and so perhaps in you, these ten years. We will sit in the Square and let Dadie [Rylands] play tennis before us. This will be in the summer, with the leaves out, and exquisite ladies—but your taste doesn't lie that way.

I will write more coherently later.

Ask Carrington to let me hear how you are.

Yr.
V.W.

Frances Hooper

1. Virginia had already abused Harold Nicolson's *Tennyson*, accusing him of imitating Lytton. She now applied the same strictures to Nicolson's *Byron: The Last Journey*, published in 1924.
2. Claire Clairmont and Edward Trelawny, who figure in the biography.

1455: To Katherine Arnold-Forster

52 *Tavistock Square, W.C.*1

Saturday [12 April 1924]

Dearest Ka,

Its not lack of affection, but the usual interruptions, that make me so long in writing. Really we've had the devil of a time—Angelica being knocked over by a motor, and taken to hospital and thought very badly hurt last Sunday. Mercifully, it was a false alarm: nothing serious happened, except the shock; but it was a miserable and indeed utterly abominable time. Young doctors giving the worst possible news to parents without any warrant should be exterminated.[1] But this is all over now. I'm going to see Will's [Arnold-Forster] show if I die in the attempt! London is incredibly beautiful—not with the soft suburban beauty of Richmond: I find Blooms-bury fierce and scornful and stony hearted, but as I say, so adorably lovely that I look out of my window all day long. Theres St Pancras Church tower: omnibuses; wet pavements; and we lock ourselves in, and Ottoline is heard raging like a winter storm in vain.

We are off on Thursday to Rodmell for 10 days: then back to a furious season of publishing; and if you could snatch Leonard off to Cornwall, away from proofs, and labour party, I should be delighted.

There are a great many of your old friends prowling about—Kennedy[2] among them. Please remember me to him. I have a dream that he is to build me a house in the country, all sunshine and hot water.

The press expands: happily in the basement. There young Mr Rylands of Kings, and young Mrs Joad of Hampstead will brew over the books, while we descend now and then—its all a great joke, I must say, though we end in bankruptcy.

When you come, let me know, and the door shall be opened to let old Bruin oar her way in.

Yr
V.W.

Mark Arnold-Forster

1456: To Janet Case

52 *Tavistock Square, W.C.*1

[12 April 1924]

My dear Janet,

I have been a disgrace not to write until your daffodils, which were the

1. A doctor at the Middlesex Hospital had told Vanessa and Duncan that Angelica was very badly hurt and her case was hopeless.
2. George Kennedy, the architect (1882-1954). He had a house in Cornwall, and his wife's parents had owned Talland House, St Ives, where Virginia spent her childhood holidays.

crown of my new painted room, have had to be thrown away. Its not lack of affection—We've been a good deal agitated by an accident to Vanessa's little girl, who was thought to be very badly hurt in a motor car accident—She and her nurse were knocked down as they walked on the pavement. Happily, nothing was damaged; but for 2 or 3 days the doctors were as gloomy as could be, and poor old Nessa had the very devil of a time. Now Angelica is off to the country.

Olwen Ward Campbell,[1] to answer your questions as I'm in a hurry and cant write sense, and Janet must have her gossip, is a barefoot young woman, daughter of Sir James Ward of Cambridge, who walked in on me and Rupert Brooke at Granchester in 1911 and said she was engaged to another pagan spirit who was fetched from the gooseberry bushes. They were sandy, upright, then—but its 13 or 14 years ago. She must be aged now. They say her book is "not really good." Does this mean anything? The same man says Joan of Arc[2] is not good either: Francis Birrell says it *is* good; but, he says, Miss Thorndike is atrocious. Since you read every word of the papers, why ask me for news?

We are off to Rodmell for Easter. I love London. It is far more beautiful than Richmond, and then the mercy of sitting quietly down to read, and not rushing to catch the last train home. L. gets back to lunch from the office. We are both very well, and up to our eyes, like all elderly people, in business. When its not writing, its reading manuscripts, or printing. We have our shop in the basement; then Mr Pritchard the solicitor; then the Woolves on top. People swarm, but we lock the door. We say not at home. This is my doing as well as Leonards. But I do enjoy a good gossip still. My rooms are all vast panels of moonrises and prima donna's bouquets—the work of Vanessa and Duncan Grant.

Shall you come and see us? I'm ashamed to scribble; but must, or you would still wait for these very valuable and highly pondered remarks of mine.

Ever yr V.W.
Love to Miss Emphie Case [Janet's sister]

Sussex

1457: To George Rylands   52 *Tavistock Square, W.C.*1

[14 April 1924]

Dearest Dadie,

This is no more than a scrawl to say we hope you'll suggest any time to come when you're in London—we're very anxious to show you everything and so on. Have you taken the Torrington Sqre house?

1. The literary critic, whose *Shelley and the Unromantics* was published this year.
2. George Bernard Shaw's *Saint Joan*, which he wrote for Sybil Thorndike. It was her most famous role.

Why am I in such a hurry? Raymond[1] is arriving. Ha-ha!
We can manage meals, so come to one.

Ever yr
V.W.

Did you get a MS poem by a Trinity or Kings man called Thompson,[2] sent
for your opinion to Kings about a week ago? *Answer* this

George Rylands

1. Raymond Mortimer, the critic, was then 24 years old.
2. Edward Thompson's *The Other Side of the Medal* was published by the Hogarth
Press in November 1925.

Letters 1458-1488 (mid-April–July 1924)

To recover from the effort of moving house to Tavistock Square, the Woolfs spent ten days at Rodmell over Easter. Virginia worked on the revision of an article on modern fiction which she had already published, and turned it into the famous lecture (later to be published as Mr Bennett and Mrs Brown) *which she delivered to an undergraduate society in Cambridge on 18 May. There were visits to Lytton Strachey in May, to Garsington in June, and to Vita at Knole and Long Barn in July. Back in London, Virginia plunged into an intensive publishing season, now with the help of George Rylands, who joined Mrs Joad in the Tavistock Square basement on 2 July.*

1458: TO MRS B. GRANT   *Monk's House, Rodmell,*
                                          Lewes, Sussex

[17? April 1924]

My dear Mrs Grant,

    I hope you won't mind my writing one line to say how sorry I am for you, and how glad that I saw Major Grant that time.[1] He was always so charming, and one felt so much at home with him—but this is not to be answered of course. We hope, if you ever feel like it, you will come and see us.

                               Your affectionate
                               Virginia Woolf

Leonard wants if he may to send his love to you, and to say how sorry he is.

George Spater

1459: TO DAVID GARNETT   *Monk's House, Rodmell,*
                                          Lewes, Sussex

Sunday [20 April 1924]

My dear Bunny,

    I must thank you for 2 hours of pure delight last night. I like the Man better than the Fox,[2] on the whole—though its clumsier and less accom-

---

1. Major Bartle Grant, Duncan's father, died on 16 April 1924. Virginia had last seen him at his house in Twickenham on 6 January.
2. David Garnett's two books were *A Man in the Zoo* (1924) and *Lady Into Fox* (1922).

plished, I think there's more to it; and how you come by these magnificent, staring, apparently simple ideas, staggers me—But I refuse to own that I'm envious. You make me laugh aloud with the unexpectedness of your touches. Wollop of Wollop Bottom for example. Your humans are a little stiff I think. Also, being crabbed and verdigrinous myself, I should have liked more grimness, and a violent, sad, altogether miserable ending: But the idea is sheer genius—You twitch the world round and give me another side to look at. Excuse this scribble: I'm half asleep with the sun, write 20 more books, at once, I beseech.

Yr
V.W.

Berg

1460: To Ethel Sands
Monk's House, Rodmell,
Lewes, Sussex
52 Tavistock Sqre (after Monday)

April 24th [1924]

My dear Ethel,

I only wish your letters were longer, and contained fuller details of everything. For instance your new hat—you cut me off with a word, and yet I swear I can describe every hat I've ever seen you wear—last, the lovely black-white Hoopoe arrangement you wore at Tavistock the other day, when I felt that some airy and elegant bird had alighted. (The hoopoe is a bird)

But of course I've not bought a hat, or met a Princess, or had tea with anybody in particular. True, Ottoline threatened to come to tea, but I evaded her, and now we have to choose one of 12 weekends to go to Garsington. But you and I are the old and faithful guardians of Ottoline's friendship, and if we begin cracking jokes, she will be exposed to the jackels and hyenas, so I refrain. We've been here alone for a week, and every leaf has grown six inches under our eyes; but I believe you don't care for nature. This is said rather artfully to throw you into a paroxysm of rage, as it would me, and so make you write another letter. I have been writing and reading ferociously every day, fearing that I shan't get the chance in London. You say you hate your friends' novels, or dread them. I agree entirely. Facts are what I like; but fiction is like praying, nobody should listen; it relieves the soul. I will not ask you to hear my prayers, I swear: but vanity will get the better of me I know. I have to read Riceyman Steps [Arnold Bennett] in order to consolidate a speech which I have to make;[1] and I'm drowned in despair already. Such dishwater! pale thin fluid in which (perhaps, but I

1. The lecture which Virginia later published as *Mr Bennett and Mrs Brown*. See page 106, note 2.

doubt it) once a leg of mutton swam. On the other hand, I can't swallow quick enough Ariel by your friend Maurois.[1] I think he must be your friend. (It is part of my dream of you to imagine you, even now at this moment in some French drawing room with lilacs and polished floor, wood fires and witty Frenchmen) It amuses me infinitely more than all the works of Leo Myers, Percy Lubbock, Arnold Bennett and Virginia Woolf. So now write and defend your friends.

You gave me no address. And I take it that you wish for no answer! Well, it's quite true I've no news to send you.

Yours affect (certainly—it gave me such pleasure)

Virginia

Wendy Baron

1461: To Vanessa Bell

Monk's House, Rodmell, Lewes, Sussex

Friday [25 April 1924]

Dearest,

I've just had a letter from Clive telling me of Angelica's illness.[2] He says she's better, but evidently she must have been bad, though I don't quite gather what happened—he says septic poisoning. I shall go to Charleston tomorrow, and hear more. Oh dear, oh dear, what a wretched time you must have been having; and I do hope to goodness its all going well now. Still Seend [Clive's parents' house] must be the devil.

Its been almost too fine to be true here; and nothing has happened, except that Maynard and Lydia came over in their car, obviously unable to face even one whole day alone. "Politics are so interesting" Lydia remarked, but gossiped to me all the time about the Courtaulds[3] and such like. The problem of one's friends marriages is indeed insoluble. A rare bird would really suit Maynard better, I can't help thinking. However she caught a frog and was very charming about the crows which she rhymes to Cows, and her armpits, which are called mouseholes in Russian; and I see I should rather like her for a mistress myself. Its age and familiarity that would entirely crush. This is poor gossip, but I feel so miserable (this is really true: its spoilt the day) about Angelica being ill. You get no holiday; however, you can console yourself with the reflection that I'm madly envious of your children, and spent all night dreaming of Angelica, and often treasure up some bright idea for Quentin. An aunts affections must be wasted. Think of our Aunts: even the Quaker [Caroline Emelia Stephen] was no better

1. André Maurois' biography of Shelley (1923).
2. Angelica's neck glands were swollen and her gums bled following the extraction of some teeth. Her temperature fluctuated for several days.
3. Samuel Courtauld (1876-1947), the textile industrialist, and a great patron of the arts.

than a chest of drawers; tho' I remember your saying you wished on the whole she hadn't died.

Maynard and Lydia came over again to take me to Brighton, but they were so late, I went off to Lewes instead, and so did not enliven their second day together. Lydia was rather pathetic about going to Paris alone. Maynard's an odd fish: weighs 13 stone he says, and is somehow respectable.

We go back to Tavistock [Square] on Monday—Well, I hope I shall hear about you—dont bother to write.

This is only a kiss from all your darling singes[1] who adore you.

Love to Mr Bell [Clive's father].

(for a joke)

Yr B.

Let me know if I can do anything in London—with Julian, or anyone.

Berg

1462: To Vanessa Bell   *Monk's House, Rodmell,*
                                 Lewes, Sussex

Sunday [27 April 1924]

Dearest,

I found your letter on getting back from Charleston last night, and I must say that Angelica's teeth have their good side—at least I get the longest letter I've had from you this ten years, stuffed with tit bits such as I most relish. Oh how fascinating facts are—the Maggs, the magazine Club, the lamp with deers feet, which I remember, and also the ink pot made from a hoof.[2] So if you have any spare time, please give a literal account, no make up, of every instant of the day. I feel that we're mere butterflies in the sun; while the Bells remain for ever. The image is not fitting to the moment. Its raining hard. We've been to the post, seen the head of Shanks[3] through the window, had tea, and shall soon draw the blinds. All your family appeared yesterday. Duncan was rambling the passages with a rag; most sympathetically—which indeed is his outstanding quality—he brushed me, and put my shoes to dry, as I had bicycled into the middle of a ploughed field, there fallen off, and had clods hanging to my hair: What a spectacle for Clive! But Clive has entirely come round to the Nation, indeed recants all he said, which I think was Leonard's craft, who took it for granted that Mary was also hostile, whereas Flinders [Mary Hutchinson] wishes to write, and

1. The childhood nickname ('Apes'), by which Virginia referred to herself in writing to Vanessa.
2. Vanessa's letter had mockingly described the Bells' library at Cleeve House and the social life at Seend.
3. Edward Shanks, the poet, who owned a house at Rodmell.

Clive thinks her articles most amusing—Mary [Molly] MacCarthy's he finds
really too thin:
  So there you have it in a nut shell. I suspect I shall be in hot water this
summer over Mary (Hutch). My attitude will be dignified and unreproachful.
How can I talk at my ease, I shall say, when Lord Berners will be repeating
it, via Mary via Clive, to Lady Colefax on Tuesday? But such is life, I shall
say: the way of the world, I shall say; and I shall keep my friendship unbroken, but unrenewed. What do you think? Then we had tea; Clive at the
head, Duncan at the bottom; Duncan as fresh as a bride—I've never seen
him look handsomer, or appear more freakish (which reminds me, do the
Bells suspect a different strain?) Julian was rather Byronic, Quentin winking
and stuffing masses of sugar cake which I brought in a fish basket tied up in
note paper. After tea we had a gossip, we old ones, over the fire, chiefly
about Gumbo [Marjorie Strachey], and some boasting on my and Clive's
part about our articles, but this bored Duncan; poor devils, how you
painters must be bored by all our talk about "articles". It was a windy day,
but lots of vegetables out in your garden,—Duncan says the terrace is very
like the terrace at Blenheim, except that some of last years cabbages are
growing in the middle. Then we went: then Duncan went to Firle with us,
and told me all about the funeral,[1] which he has a wonderful gift for acting
the clergyman shaking hands, and old Mr Dince the undertaker, and Pippa[2]
in black and the urn which is to be taken to Rothiemurchus[3] in a portmanteau
—in short you can imagine all that. As we got into Firle, there came by
motor, with a veiled lady flashing her eyes at us, and waving—the impassioned Bobo, who thereupon took against ruddy Robin,[4] and no wonder. I
saw their miserable tea on the table as I passed—cut bread and butter, and a
plate of cress. So home: where I had your letter, cooked 4 sausages, and to
bed.
  That is all the news I can think of. Ottoline has written asking us to stay,
and I must now fabricate some answer; and Tom [Eliot] has written, asking
for news of Angelica; he has a good heart; I wish I were in touch with Elena,
whose beauty (at a distance) never fails to fascinate: I saw her, Mrs Rathbone,
old Lady de Vesci, and Marny all in a bunch at a concert the other night![5]
What a haul! Marny has the head of a fish gnawn cabhorse, grey, white lace
collar, with some dismal female, called Davies I think, of Kensington Sqre:

1. Of Duncan's father.
2. Philippa Strachey, Lytton's elder sister, was Duncan's cousin.
3. In Inverness-shire, where the Grant family originated, and still remain.
4. Robin Mayor and his wife Beatrice (Meinertzhagen), who had leased Little
   Talland House at Firle, where Virginia lived for a short time before her marriage.
5. Elena was the wife of Bruce Richmond, editor of the *Times Literary Supplement*. Mrs Rathbone was her mother. Lady de Vesci was the widow of the 4th
   Viscount de Vesci, whom Virginia had known in her youth. 'Marny' was
   Margaret Vaughan, Virginia's cousin.

but I had no talk with any of them. I was with [Raymond] Mortimer. He said to me with some penetration; "There's a friend of your past" pointing to Mrs Rathbone. She is still chewing her cud; wasn't Mr Rathbone in love with some body? —bitter straw; canker to her worm; thats her expression, and Elena sitting beside her, monumental, innocent, beneath mounds of fur. Its odd that you and I have never had what you might call a good piece of fur all our lives—never shall have now. Perhaps Angelica will have a good piece of fur (anyhow write a line to Tavistock to say how she is.)

I went to Hammonds, and got the very thing—a piece of matting large enough to cover the whole studio for £2. So thats a good foundation: Then I shall buy a rug; some artificial flowers, which you'll sell cheap, hang a canvas or two, lent me, by poor strugglers, arrange my books, and so have a superb meeting ground for the most advanced spirits of Bloomsbury. Its odd to be going back there, not to Richmond. I feel as if I were going on with a story which I began in the year 1904:[1] then a little insanity, and so back.

We have Rose Bartholomew[2] for the week end—I wish my name were Bartholomew. She has been mad, squints, and is singularly pure of soul. Nelly has gone back to clean the flat. R. B. is doing for us. [Edward] Shanks is packing his linen, and leaving for ever. Mr Hogg has run away, owing Hammond[3] £40 for furniture, and £4 to the village shop. Our reputation stands immensely high; and really, Rodmell is so lovely that I shan't buy another house just yet.

We go tomorrow.

Poor darling Dolphin, what a life she has, but all is made up to her by her singe troop, who are as gay as they are lovely, and as chaste as they are proud.

Leonard sends his love, and says do for Gods sake write him an article, or he'll have to ask Flinders [Mary Hutchinson].

Yr B.

Berg

1463: To Lady Ottoline Morrell   *Monk's House, Rodmell,*
                                   Lewes, Sussex

[27 April 1924]

Dearest Ottoline,

I was so sorry not to see you. I want someday to show you my painted room—which perhaps you won't like, though. We had a very agitating

1. In the summer of 1904, following her father's death in February, Virginia had a severe mental breakdown. It was after her recovery that the Stephens first moved to Bloomsbury.
2. A woman from Rodmell who occasionally worked at Monk's House.
3. A furniture shop and store in Lewes.

time with Vanessa's little girl, who was run over—but I expect you've heard all this.

We would like very much to come, if June, the middle or end, is not too late for you. May is all in a muddle—but let us come like humdrum old people, without the brilliant youth this time—though that was very amusing too.

We go back to London tomorrow.

Your affate
Virginia Woolf

Texas

1464: To Vanessa Bell   52 *Tavistock [Square, W.C.*1]

Tuesday [29 April 1924]

Dearest,

I got your telegram [about Angelica] so I hope things are really rather better. Clive has just been, and I showed it him. I couldn't get pink wincey, altogether pink; so I hope the striped, which was the pinkest, will do.

I'm afraid its quite damnable for you—it struck me I might be a short diversion—however, Clive says he's going for the week end anyhow.

But make your apes useful if you can. I had a visit from Lytton this morning, very affable and easy, and greatly excited, I think, about his house [Ham Spray], which is being drained, and has a studio for Carrington, a workshop for Ralph, and several gigantic beech trees. Also he seems to think he's got an idea for a book[1]—The rumour which has been circulating Tavistock Sqre that Carrington is with child is false—It is merely her mother's cloak. Karin [Stephen] has fled to Italy to escape the house painters; so Lottie lives with us, poisoned by paint and tinned salmon. Leonard lunched with Sydney Waterlow[2] today, ostensibly to discuss the Far East; but they ended heart to heart, discussing Sydney's change, and our inalterable vileness, which, Sydney says, is shown up in Molly's articles—supreme works of art, but entirely cut off from the heart—Lord what rubbish! But he is coming to exhibit his entrails further. I shall ask you to meet him. I sent Angelica some beads to make chains of—and have another small box of sewing things which I'll send tomorrow.

Leonard sends his love, and wishes to do anything for you, whom he adores.

Yr B.

Berg

1. Lytton Strachey published no new book until *Elizabeth and Essex* in 1928.
2. Sydney Waterlow was at this period Director of the Foreign Division of the Department of Overseas Trade. He had been a friend of several members of Old Bloomsbury, and had proposed marriage to Virginia, but for many years his relationship with them had been cooling.

1465: To Lytton Strachey   52 *Tavistock Sqre W.C.*

[2 May 1924]

Could you conceivably have us on the Friday [at Tidmarsh], till Sunday,
and could you conceivably motor, or convey Leonard, on Sunday afternoon
to Sutton [Surrey], where he has to make a speech?
Otherwise, he's afraid he can't get out of the speech,—can't come.
But this may well be impracticable.
I dream at night of your beech trees [at Ham Spray].
Just off to meet Walter Lamb[1] at the Royal Academy private view.

Yr V.W.

L says that he could come and leave on Saturday night.

Strachey Trust

1466: To T. S. Eliot   52 *Tavistock Square, W.C.*1

May 5th 1924

My dear Tom,

I am greatly flattered that you should wish to have anything of mine for
the Criterion, where, apart from your noble terms [£20], I would rather
appear than anywhere else. But the novel is getting too interwoven for a
chapter broken off to be intelligible; and I swear that I won't start other
critical adventures until I have collected my essays. The only thing I have is
the lecture I spoke of, a development of a Nation article, called Mr Bennett
and Mrs Brown.[2] This I could let you have; but the drawbacks are that it is
elementary and loquacious, being meant for undergraduates; that it is 5,000
words full; and that we are going to print it next autumn (when, is not
entirely fixed). If these can be overcome, I will send it you next month. But
in six months I hope to have much more time. It was a very good number, I
thought; and I am going to make another attempt, after a complete failure,
to see what Murry means. He implored me to write no more books like
Jacob's Room—indeed, said that it couldn't be done; so I look forward to

1. Walter Lamb had been the Secretary of the Royal Academy since 1913.
2. Virginia's criticism of the modern novel, *Mr Bennett and Mrs Brown*, appeared
   in its original form in the *Nation and Athenaeum* of 1 December 1923. She
   then rewrote it as a lecture, which she delivered to the Heretics at Cambridge
   on 18 May 1924. It was published in the *Criterion* (July 1924) as *Character in
   Fiction* and by the Hogarth Press as *Mr Bennett and Mrs Brown* in October
   1924.

reading your verdict[1]—alas, that I have laid another straw on your back in addition to no coal, no water, and the delights of the country.

I am subterraneously trying to get you and Vivien to come back to London—but the country at Easter was all they say it should be. [Edward] Shanks has gone,—was seen counting his blankets for the last time; so that the blot is removed. The Hoggs have absconded, and Mr Wilkinson of The Challenge has been appointed to a post which needs his constant presence in London. We remain in solitude with the clergy, which is as it should be.

Please begin to set aside your 19½ hours for Rodmell in September, and dont forget your essays;[2] and write another poem; (6 Waste Land ordered yesterday;) and give my love to Vivien, and come and see us soon.

Yr affly
V.W.

Sussex [copy]

1467: To R. C. Trevelyan   *The Hogarth Press,*
                                        *52 Tavistock Square, W.C.*1
May 6th [1924]

My dear Bob,

This is just a line to say how greatly I admired your poem in the New Statesman last week.[3] It seemed to me very beautiful and moving and perfectly done—

I rather think you are abroad. But anyhow this needs no answer.

Do you admire our new yellow paper?

Yours ever,
Virginia Woolf

I hope you're writing more poems—short ones, soon to be published, I mean.

Sussex

1. Eliot's article on the contemporary English novel appeared in the *Nouvelle Revue Française*. He had written to Virginia on 1 May 1924: "You do not make it easy for critics: one feels that a superhuman cleverness is called for, or disaster is inevitable" (*Sussex*). In the *Nation* of 10 March 1923 Middleton Murry had said that Proust, Joyce, and Virginia Woolf had "no use for a story. It is a kind of nursery-game for them. . . . The consequence is that the novel has reached a kind of *impasse*."
2. T. S. Eliot's *Homage to John Dryden: Three Essays on Poetry in the Seventeenth Century* was published by the Hogarth Press in November 1924.
3. "Happiness" (*New Statesman*, 3 May 1924). It was republished by the Hogarth Press in April 1925 in *Poems and Fables*.

1468: To T. S. Eliot   52 *Tavistock Square, W.C.*1

May 11th 1924

My dear Tom,
    What an enchanting letter you wrote me! I think one of your good
resolutions should be to write to me every Sunday night. But to business.
I am now furbishing up my lecture, which I have to deliver next Sunday at
Cambridge. I will send it you without fail the following week. But the final
condition is that you are to suspend judgment till you read it. It wasn't
written for an article, and I doubt that it does for one.
    Your oracles and counsels, Virginia, Leonard and Clive are fallible
mortals: we, that is L. and I, thought that you referred to Murry and the
sneer at Murry in the Criterion, and never, till you wrote, connected the
pseudo-Proust with Schiff. Most people will be in our condition, and this
ought to exonerate us, and appease Mr Schiff, and so, incidentally, save your
bones.[1] I still think it a very good number, though I have not read Murry,
lacking that just mind and steadfast purpose which are necessary, because
everyone—that is Lytton, Osbert Sitwell, Mary Hutchinson is claiming to
be an Ape of God[2] and identifying the rest of the pack.
    I send this to Clarence Gate: and hope if you're there that you'll come
round and dine with us, only let us know first, for our maid is frightened of
gentlemen, and prefers not to open the door.
                                                           Yours ever
                                                              V.W.

Mrs T. S. Eliot

1469: To Lady Ottoline Morrell
                             52 *Tavistock Square, London, W.C.*1
[20 May 1924]

Dearest Ottoline
    Forgive me for being so slow. We have been away, and I left your letter
here. We will come on June 28th with great pleasure, if we have to leave on
Sunday night.

---

1. Wyndham Lewis had published an article in the *Criterion* (April 1924) attacking
   'pseudo-Bohemian' writers. When some of his victims protested, Eliot wrote
   to Virginia claiming that she, Leonard and Clive had encouraged him "in the
   best tradition of British journalism to let one contributor say what he likes
   about another" (T.S.E. to V.W. 7 May 1924. *Sussex*, copy).
2. In the February number of the *Criterion*, Wyndham Lewis had satirised Lytton
   Strachey and the Sitwells in *Apes of God*, which he expanded and published in
   book form in 1930.

108

I have just met one million undergraduates,[1] and feel it a slight relief not to meet another million at Garsington—though the Oxford one is very different from the Cambridge.

Ever Your
V.W.

Texas

1470: To T. S. Eliot
The Hogarth Press, 52 Tavistock Square, W.C.1
May 21st 1924

My dear Tom,

Here is the article [*Character in Fiction*], in rather a dilapidated state. Leonard says "with regard to the Hogarth Press business, would you be good enough to ask the printer to give us an estimate for printing off one thousand copies[2] in sheets including a title page, copy of which we would supply, so that the whole could be bound up in a pamphlet. If the printer could also give us an estimate for printing a plain coloured stiff paper cover and binding up 500 copies, it would also simplify matters, but we would like the two estimates to be kept separate. Perhaps it would be best for him to send the estimates direct to the Hogarth Press. Would he also in giving the estimate inform us of the number of pages it will run to."

I find that a copy of Waste Land was sent to the Nouvelle Revue, when the book came out [in September 1923]. We have sent another, but it might be as well to find out if it has arrived safely, considering our experience with French posts. Perhaps, if you are in communication, you would do this.

Yours ever
Virginia Woolf

Sussex [copy]

1471: To V. Sackville-West
52 Tavistock Square, London, W.C.1
21st May [1924]

My dear Vita,

My letter has just been returned—owing to idiocy I put Sussex instead of Kent.[3] I do hope that I haven't again bothered you by this idiotic delay.

1. The Woolfs had stayed at Cambridge from 17 to 19 May, when Virginia gave her lecture to the Heretics, an undergraduate literary society.
2. Of the article, retitled *Mr Bennett and Mrs Brown*.
3. Vita and Harold Nicolson then lived at Long Barn, near Sevenoaks, Kent, two miles from Knole.

We are going away again this week end, and I was proposing that perhaps you might ask us later, in July, when we shall be freer. We should like to come, if only for a night.

But I was hoping to see you here, partly for your own sake, partly for the sake of the Hogarth Press, which is very anxious to know if there is any serious chance that you will let it have a book. If so, what and when? Could it be this autumn?

Forgive me for bothering you. We are trying to start young Mr Rylands on his career as a publisher[1] with some good books, and so I am taking the liberty of asking you.

He is very keen, and would do his best, and so would you. But come and see my bare studio in the basement, very nice to sit in this hot weather, with one chair, one table, one bed, one bookcase.

Ever Your
Virginia Woolf

Berg

1472: To T. S. Eliot   52 *Tavistock Square, W.C.*1

Friday [23 May 1924]

My dear Tom,

I am very glad that my paper does not seem to you superficial and flippant, as it did to me on re-reading. I suppose they will send me galley proofs, with a view to corrections. But is there any danger that the Criterion is dying?[2] I hope not.

I'm sending on your doctor's address to Roger, who seems to have come to grief again.[3] If we try again to get my temperature to normal, I will certainly go to him, but I feel so well, it hardly seems worth while. Many thanks.

Come again, and don't attract so many of your admirers next time, which we leave it to you to suggest.

Just off to Rodmell, so forgive the scrawl.

Yours ever,
Virginia Woolf

Mrs T. S. Eliot

1. George Rylands joined the Hogarth Press on 2 July.
2. In his letter to Virginia of 22 May (*Sussex*, copy) Eliot had referred to the possibility that the *Criterion* "might be extinguished". But only one issue (Autumn 1925) failed to appear.
3. A Frenchwoman, Josette Coatmellec, who was in love with Roger, had shot herself in late March. The doctor was a German, Dr Marten, who had treated Vivien Eliot and was now visiting London. It was not until June that Virginia heard the whole story.

1473: To Theodora Bosanquet   52 *Tavistock Square, W.C.*1

27 May 1924

Dear Miss Bosanquet,

I am very much interested to hear that you have done the Henry James article,[1] and look forward greatly to reading it.

As to America we have already had overtures from an American firm [Doubleday, Doran], with regard to the series of pamphlets. We should like to have an opportunity of dealing with the American rights of such pamphlets as we publish in this series. Would you have any objection to our doing so in your case, and we suggest that if we dispose of them we should take an agents fee of 15% of any sum realised, and that you should give us three months in which to try and sell the rights.

If you agree to this, could you send us the manuscript in duplicate. There is no great hurry, as we could not bring it out before the autumn, but if we are to try and dispose of it in America, it would be advisable to give us plenty of time to do so.

I have been away, or I would have written before.

Yours sincerely,
Virginia Woolf

Houghton Library, Harvard University

1474: To Ethel Sands   [52 *Tavistock Square, W.C.*1]

May 28th 1924

My dear Ethel,

It was a great pleasure to get a letter from you and it came one night when Mary Hutchinson and Osbert Sitwell were dining here, and looked very distinguished with its French stamp, and filled me with envy. To be able to understand cookery, to be so much mistress of the graces—fills me with envy. But in a subtle and inexplicable way which I will leave to describe until October next. Really, this room is getting very livable in; and as for the beauty of London at all hours, and its oddity and character and quality and romance, never mention Richmond to me again, to compare with it. Richmond is all very well for Americans—which reminds me that Logan came to tea, very magisterial and judicial; Bob [Trevelyan] haunts our basement with yards and yards of poetry; and we have roused about us all the persistent downtrodden grub that hack in London.

There's a poor woman who has written a satire upon Christ, with special reference to his relations with John. This she brings in her woollen gloves on a hot afternoon, and foams, literally, disgustingly, foams at the

1. See p. 89, note 1.

III

mouth, in her rage and ardour. "Aren't people interested in Christ? There must be thousands who would buy my work—if only it were printed". But how are we to print her work; and dear old Bob's just the same; and so am I; and so is Roger, and so is Logan: all convinced that we must be read and seen and heard. You alone dwell behind a veil of opaque modesty. I've been lecturing at Cambridge on your beloved Arnold Bennett, and not a single young man or woman in the place has a good word to say for him! This has left me so scatterbrained and loose lipped—you can't think how sick one gets of one's own phrases, and how passionately I long to be transformed into someone marmorial and mute, like Elsie Myers,[1] that I'm ashamed to chatter out letters to you. Clive is in Paris; but has made the acquaintance of a Countess; (this I know, because we have to send her his poems): Mary Hutchinson is now crossing the channel to him. London remains full, however; but rather frightening—so decorative, so vociferative, so smart too. That wouldn't frighten you as it does me. I slink off into my own haunts, and feel refreshed by Bloomsbury and paralysed by Bond Street. We have very small, very cheap parties. Nothing much to eat, nothing clever said, for I think it time to have done with the pomps and ceremonies, and reduce everything to perfect innocence and ease, what do you think? Won't you come and lend your distinction to our barbarity?

I was forgetting the great news; Murry's marriage to Violet le Maistre,[2] an unknown disciple of his; I met him twice, and we skirmished, and were bored and disillusioned, and found each other terribly gone to seed. But I can't help feeling that you have withdrawn into rarer air where all this chatter is as the chafing of gnats. Please write and describe what you are doing and forgive my scribble.

Yours affect
Virginia Woolf

Wendy Baron

1475: To Margaret Llewelyn Davies
52 Tavistock Square, W.C.1
Thursday [29 May 1924]

Dearest Margaret,

Is there any chance that you would dine with us next Tuesday, 3rd, at 7.30—needless to say without changing?

I think perhaps Charlie Sanger[3] is coming, and it would be very nice to see you again, now we are really settled in life.

1. The wife of L. H. Myers, the novelist.
2. After her marriage, Violet le Maistre published short stories under the pseudonym of Mary Arden. She died from tuberculosis in 1931.
3. Charles P. Sanger (1871-1930), the barrister and editor of the standard work on wills. He had known Virginia since her youth.

Leonard says "We are going away on Thursday and unless you will come on Tuesday, he won't be able to see you for at least another fortnight, though in any case he'll come up and see you when we come back, after Whitsun."

Don't make this an excuse though for not dining here: as Leonard is a shifty character, entirely given up to Colonial Office, India Office, Labour party etc etc etc.[1]

Yrs
V.W.

Sussex

1476: To Gerald Brenan   52 *Tavistock Square, W.C.*1

Thursday [29 May 1924]

My dear Gerald,

You have vanished into a street without a number.[2] Moreover I cant remember whether you're with Sedge or Vetch. So this must go via Carrington—only to ask you to step in next Tuesday night anytime after 8, when you'll find the old Woolves, and old Mr [C. P.] Sanger, and perhaps some young lady.[3]

Do if you can.

Your Virginia Woolf

George Lazarus

1477: To Lady Ottoline Morrell

[52 *Tavistock Square, W.C.*1]

Postcard

[30 May 1924]

I think the 28th June is the best week end for us, and we'll do our best to stay 2 nights; its not for want of wishing, only the difficulties of life.

V.W.

Texas

1. For nearly thirty years Leonard was the Secretary of the Labour Party's Advisory Committees on Imperial and International Affairs.
2. Brenan had come to England to work on a biography of St Teresa, and was living in one room at 10 Millman Street, W.C.1. His landlady there was Mrs Veitch.
3. In fact, Virginia had invited Margaret Llewelyn Davies, who was 63.

1478: To V. Sackville-West   *Monks House, Rodmell,*
                                  Lewes [Sussex]
June 7th [1924]

My dear Vita,

It is very generous of you to think of giving us any of your work, and we are all very much delighted at the prospect. Is there any chance we could bring it out this autumn? But do whatever suits you, of course.

Here we are for Whitsun—Your friend Mr Shanks has left the village, and we are entirely given up to rusticity, which I prefer.

We want to come and stay very much—there was a rush of week ends on top of each other: now only Garsington, I think, in prospect. Ottoline turned up the other night, dropping powder, and protesting against women who make up.

                                              Yr VW.
Berg

1479: To Jacques Raverat   *Monks House, Rodmell,*
                                  Lewes [Sussex]
June 8th 1924

My dear Jacques,

I have left your last long and delicious letter—between you, you write damned good letters, whichever has the credit, the good Darwin or the bad Frog[1]—in my box at home and so I can't answer your questions. What were they? Perhaps only a general desire to know if I'd seen Eily[2] lately, or [Ka] Cox, or any of our old flames. I was never in love with Eily. For a time Bernard took my fancy, until I stayed with them, and he talked too much golf—but he writes very well; like Jorrocks, only Englishmen can write like that; so dont you go and try. Will A. F. [Arnold-Forster] had another show, and I never went. Isn't it awful? Can one ignore the whole of one side of ones friends' lives, and yet keep on terms of any interest with them? I rather fancy that we're drifting apart—after all, its incredibly difficult to run down to the Lands End, and when Cox is in London, what with she impressing me with her politics, and I her with my literature, we don't get much forrader. Two weeks ago I was in Cambridge, lecturing the Heretics upon Modern Fiction. Do you feel kindly towards Cambridge? It was, as Lytton would say,

1. Jacques Raverat was dying slowly from multiple sclerosis, and was incapable of writing his own letters, which he dictated to his wife Gwen.
2. Elinor Monsell, who married Gwen's cousin, Bernard Darwin, the writer on golf.

rather 'hectic'; young men going in for their triposes; flowering trees on the backs; canoes, fellows' gardens; wading in a slightly unreal beauty; dinners, teas, suppers; a sense, on my part, of extreme age, and tenderness and regret; and so on and so on. We had a good hard headed argument, and I respect the atmosphere, and I'm glad to be out of it. Maynard is very heavy and rather portentous; Maynard is passionately and pathetically in love, because he sees very well that he's dished if he marries her, and she has him by the snout. You can't argue solidly when Lydia's there, and as we set now to the decline, and prefer reason to any amount of high spirits, Lydia's pranks put us all on edge; and Bloomsbury steals off to its dens, leaving Maynard with Lydia on his knee, a sublime but heartrending spectacle.

Please do not repeat this gossip. Lydia came over here the other day and said "Please Leonard tell me about Mr Ramsay Macdonald. I am seerious—very seerious." However then she caught a frog and put it in an apple tree; and thats whats so enchanting about her; but can one go through life catching frogs? You should hear Vanessa and Duncan on the subject.

I have had two bloody painful encounters with Middleton Murry; we stuck together at parties like two copulating dogs; but after the first ecstasy, it was boring, disillusioning, flat. The long and short of him is that he's a coward. First he fawns up to me, then when I attack him he plants his dart and runs away. He says we (Bloomsbury) deny our instincts: but why, after all, does writing badly prove that one is morally good? Answer me that, my dear Jacques: for I have no room to develop my own arguments. Now he's married a contributor to the Adelphi, and is breeding.[1]

Ottoline—was Ottoline ever a figure of any sort to you? She flaunts about London, not without a certain grandeur, as of a ship with its sails rat-eaten, and its masts mouldy, and green sea serpents on the decks. But no image will convey her mixture of humbleness and splendour and hypocrisy. She was shaking powder onto the floor and saying, "Virginia, why *do* women make up?"

We go back to London tomorrow. Whom do you wish me to see in particular? Do you remember Justin Brooke ?A sister of his lived in our house: Morgan Forster's novel [*A Passage to India*] is just out. Do you read him? And what do you think about?

Ever Yrs
V.W.

Why not some day send me the family portraits? children, and all.

Sussex

1. Murry and his second wife, Violet le Maistre, had a son and a daughter.

1480: To V. Sackville-West   52 *Tavistock Sqre, W.C.*1
[June 1924]

My dear Vita,
    A friend, Miss Ll. Davies, has asked me to send you on these papers,
about a [Russian] society which she hopes may have your sympathy. It has
mine and Leonards, but don't blame me if it bores you to death.

                                            Ever Yours
                                            Virginia Woolf.
We think you're first rate on Mr Symons.[1]

Berg

1481: To V. Sackville-West
                                    52 *Tavistock Square, London, W.C.*1
Sunday [29? June 1924]

My dear Vita,
    I think what the Russian society wants is that you should become a
member, which either costs you 5/- or nothing or £1-1.—I can't remember.
They are in a struggling state, starting; and names are very important to them.
    Weekends have become hopeless for Leonard—all his work is done in
them, but if you would have me alone, might I come for a night in the week,
rather than week end, before you go abroad? 2nd, 3rd, 4th—I would keep
which ever suited you.
    We go to Rodmell at the end of July. It is very good news that your
story may be ready then or is it a poem?[2]
    Oh how I envy you, finishing books straight off.

                                            Yours ever
                                            Virginia Woolf
Berg

1482: To Lady Ottoline Morrell   52 *Tavistock Sqre, W.C.*
[early July 1924]

Dearest Ottoline;
    This is a miserable belated letter to thank you for our 21 hours of
enjoyment.[3] However, it was all crammed with a variety of pleasures.

1. Vita's review in the *Nation* of Arthur Symon's *Collected Works* (28 June 1924).
2. Vita wrote the larger part of her long short-story *Seducers in Ecuador* while
   she and Harold were walking in the Dolomites from 8 to 21 July. It was
   published by the Hogarth Press in November 1924.
3. The Woolfs had stayed at Garsington 28-29 June. T. S. Eliot was a fellow
   guest.

Directly we got back we had to begin drudgery here, as Mrs Joad is ill, and Dadie has arrived [on 2 July], very charming, but with no knowledge, naturally, of how to write a bill.

I tried to remember the true nature of Mary Hutchinson last night, as defined by you and Tom [Eliot], but was bamboozled as usual. I expect. I think it is her lovely grey clothes with pearl buttons, and three red carnations at the breast.

Shall I buy you a house straight off?[1]

Leonard sends his love.

Your aff^{ate}
Virginia Woolf

Texas

1483: To Violet Dickinson   52 *Tavistock Sqre, W.C.*1

[July? 1924]

My Violet.

You are a wretched devil to go off without coming to see us. What I want to know now is what about your Great Aunt?[2] Is she coming to birth? When may I read her? This is a matter of very great importance, so please answer. The Press feels that it owes you an undying debt (if thats what its called) for buying it so loyally all these years—In future, you won't be worried so much. But our last batch is doing rather well—particularly the Rector's daughter, whose author, being the plainest woman in Europe, is appearing in Vogue.[3]

Did you let Manchester Street [Violet's house] to the woman?

Shall you ever come and see us again?

Your
V.W.

Berg

1484: To V. Sackville-West
52 *Tavistock Square, London, W.C.*1

July 6th [1924]

My dear Vita,

I have paralysed my own pen by telling you that you dont write intimate letters—which however you are going to reform in the Dolomites.

1. Ottoline did not acquire a London house again until 1927.
2. See p. 94, note 2.
3. *The Rector's Daughter*, by F. M. Mayor (Hogarth Press, May 1924).

But I have only to say that I was enchanted and made envious by my visit—and what can hostess do more?[1]

Knole almost crushed me—for I detest being unable to express anything of what I feel, and certainly couldn't. Then there was the [Long] Barn, which has led us to think of rebuilding our own cottage.

So you see, I was thoroughly happy and very miserable. In fact, I'm only now beginning to recover my normal spirits. Leonard says that if there is any decent book in he will send it tomorrow. Thank you for letting me come.

Yours Ever
Virginia Woolf

Berg

1485: To Violet Dickinson

The Hogarth Press, 52 Tavistock Square,
London, W.C.1

Typewritten
17th July, 1924

My Violet,
(excuse typewriter).

The Press is charmed by your great aunt [Emily Eden]; but thinks her rather too slight and scattered for publishing as a book. We feel that there ought to be a good deal more of you or a longer and more connected series of her letters. It is very tantalising, as the little that there is of each of you is so fascinating.

What we want, not as publishers, but as editor of the Nation to suggest is that you should allow Leonard to make up an article out of the Indian letters for the Nation. I enclose a sample of the sort of thing that he would like to use, if you approved. He wants me to say that he could not give a definite date of publication, as he is very crowded at the moment. But he would very much like to use the enclosed, if you would read it, make any alterations, and send it back. They pay, he says, about five guineas.

We are sending back the MS.

I am being brutally frank as you asked: I think it is a most delightful thing myself; it is only the slightness that makes the difficulty.

Ever Yr
Sp[arroy]

Berg

1. Virginia had driven down to Kent on the previous day and lunched at Knole with Vita and Lord Sackville. In the afternoon Vita took her to Long Barn for her first visit.

Typewritten
[20? July 1924]

My dear Marjorie,
You insist upon my using a typewriter, and see with what result—really, my own hand would be clearer in the end—I've been meaning every day to write to you, but we live in a gale of wind and every feather on my head is upright. That is the only description I can give of our life at the moment: Higgs, B. Higgs,[1] is driving us frantic with her cheery conversation; all the psycho-analyst books[2] have been dumped in a fortress the size of Windsor castle in ruins upon the floor; Higgs' head appears undaunted and garrulous above the battlements; Leonard's in his shirt sleeves; Dadie has run out to re-fresh his head by a walk round the square; Grizzle [dog] is making darts for peoples legs; the hamper has arrived from Rodmell and I have just counted out a ream of paper and found large hoof marks half way through. Then you think I can write a novel!

We hope to come up and see you one day this week; and we hope to find you up; and ready to go on your holiday, and we hope you'll never get pneumonia again; but lead the life of a grub burrowing placidly through mounds of manuscript without another thought in your head than the profit and glory of the Hogarth Press. What is love compared with that, what youth, friendship, society, drink, eating, and the delights of fine weather? You are expected to answer in the negative. Do you know what has set me off writing in this incoherent way? Mrs Berta Ruck.[3] I fell into her arms—which are wide and brawny—at Maynard's party the other night; and a whole room full stood agaze to see the lady novelists embrace. She said Oh if I were Virginia Woolf! I said Oh Berta, if I were you! And for Gods sake, I said, tell me how you do it, and what you get for it, whereupon Berta, rolling her fine eyes about, replied, "Would you believe me Mrs Woolf I abominate my own books more than I can say, and they only bring me in £400 a piece, and I have to write two every year so long as I and my husband and our boys do live, and its almost impossible to find another plot. I took Romeo and Juliet last time; and its going to be Don Quixote next; for there are only ten plots in the world; and Ethel Dell is my only rival; but

---

1. Miss Higgs, temporary employee of the Hogarth Press.
2. Early in 1924 James Strachey, who had studied with Freud in Vienna, suggested to Leonard that the Hogarth Press should take over from the London Institute of Psycho-Analysis the *International Psycho-Analytical Library*, which included the two volumes of Freud's *Collected Papers*. The Hogarth Press continued with the *Library* for over 40 years, and still publish Freud's *Collected Works*.
3. Mrs Oliver Onions, the popular novelist whom Virginia had met in 1922 when she used her name inadvertently in *Jacob's Room*.

since the war we dont make what we used to make; and do believe me, Mrs Woolf, I'm a cultivated woman. I read the classics, I know French; and if only I could write a paragraph—one paragraph—like Mr Lytton Strachey, I'd retire tomorrow; but what can you do, Mrs Woolf, when you've two darling boys and I want them to have the best of everything—Eton, sports; you should see them Mrs Woolf; for you have written in Jacobs room such a description of the beauty of young manhood" . . . (here we embraced once more) and with tears in my eyes I swore to come down to a rosy bower on the river, where they live 'like anybody else' she said; but I doubt it.

It was great fun at the party, enchanting, lyrical, Shakespeare with not a coarse word; and chaste conversation everywhere; dancing; the Davidsons, three of them, hung with chandeliers and stately as caryatids—(poor Berta was overcome): in a ballet designed by Duncan.[1] Lydia danced; we had a little fine champagne. However, I dont want any more parties for an age, but to live like a caterpillar on a leaf. Mayor is still selling[2]—Boots have just taken twenty; everything is selling a little; and we have a Russian manuscript from Jane Harrison and Hope Mirrlees;[3] another play from Mr Barber; a novel unsolicited; a novel from a lower class sturdy looking man in Putney who came in yesterday, and seemed, on first sight, to have every merit except literary merit—but how can you tell? He may be Keats: one must be sanguine. My partners are inclined to take acid views of these poor old duffers, so that I expand, as you can well imagine, into effusions of optimism.

I met that surly devil Bunny Garnett; and really, his fame has congested him. He is rigid with self importance and arrogantly told me that Mrs Mitchison[4] would go to another and a better publisher, as we didnt take her plays and had missed for the second time the chance of a life. Whereupon I said, Ah but we dont publish Weekend books, do we?; which struck him in the ribs, and he rolled over like a sulky bear. This I never did say except late that morning when in a desperate mood I was thinking over all the things I might have said.

Here's Leonard. Times book club wants the last twelve copies of Mayor this afternoon. That leaves us without a copy in the house. Others ordered, but dont come till this afternoon. Crisis! Catastrophe!

He sends his love. We will try and come up, but now I must dash into

1. In this transvestite ballet (*Don't be Frightened* or *Pippington Park*) the three 'chorus girls' were Angus and Douglas Davidson and George Rylands. The 'male' members of the chorus were Barbara Bagenal, Frances Marshall, and Bea Howe (later Lubbock).
2. F. M. Mayor's *The Rector's Daughter* published in May.
3. *The Life of the Archpriest Avvakum by Himself,* translated by Harrison and Mirrlees, was published by the Hogarth Press in November 1924.
4. Naomi Mitchison published her first novel in 1923, but the Hogarth Press did not publish any books by her until 1937.

the ruins of Windsor and Higgs and the triumph of Fanny Mayor. She'll be
the death of me.

Your affectionate,

Virginia Woolf

T. H. Marshall

1487: To Barbara Bagenal

52 *Tavistock Square, London. W.C.*

Typewritten

25th July 1924

My dear Barbara,

I am desolated to hear of your disease, and write, if only by typewriter,
to express my sympathy, and add my curse. For why should the limbs of a
nit be tortured? Is it rheumatism? Is it mere distaste (I can't spell, or keep to
grammar, but my hand is so tired with handwriting that I must use this) for
life? I have been to a funeral service myself,[1] and every one seems in a falling
way, mildewed, cankered, and slightly corrupt.

This always cheers one in bed—to think on the vices and diseases of
others. Our Mrs Joad, God damn her, has been away with pneumonia these
four weeks, and will take another six before she is back: with the result that
we all run about the basement, distracted, henlike, with wisps of string, labels,
brown paper, now answering the door—Please come in. Yes I'm the
advertising manager. Yes we give you 33½% on numbers over twelve—No;
we dont keep Songs of Sunrise (they come to us all day long, the wretched
bagmen [booksellers], to ask for books we dont sell) and so on and so on.
The Press has suddenly become monstrous, kicking and sprawling. We
have a drawer full of manuscripts which the authors deposit and the seediest
old bankrupts arrive who won't go away till Leonard, whose heart is of
gold, gives them five pounds, which they lavish on drink, but, as he says, we
shall all come to it one of these days. I dwell on these glories to make you
regret your marriage.

The news of Bloomsbury reaches you quicker than it does me, I'm sure.
You heard rumours no doubt of Maynards great party; and Duncans ballet,[2]
and how not a coarse word was said, or indeed thought, by some people. It
is coarseness that is the downfall of Bloomsbury. Dora Sanger left our last
affair in dudgeon; and was heard to say that she hadn't felt so ravaged since
Charlie—. . . . but Charlie has spread the rumour, which has reached
Malling[3] long since, that Dora's dudgeon was the result of drink. That

1. Of Virginia's cousin, Katharine Stephen (1856-1924), on 22 July.
2. See previous letter.
3. Barbara's husband Nick worked as a horticulturist at the East Malling Research
   Station in Kent.

explains much in Dora's conduct. I found myself looking at Saxon, at this same party, and saying That very distinguished man was once my friend. He has taken on a diplomatic refined twisted up and fastidious air which delights my heart; estranged though we be. It's all the roof in the best bedroom at Hogarth,[1] which falls and falls and covers all with gravel, so they say. Then the beetles have been very tactless; and Saxon says (but what a faery way he has with him—such things never happened to me) Saxon says a lark has nested in the kitchen boiler; naturally this upsets the cook. The lark soars to the ceiling and rains out its song as she comes down in the morning.

I see a great many people off and on; but only hear this sort of gossip— Lytton is moving [to Ham Spray], Ralph flirts,[2] Carrington is happy today, very unhappy tomorrow; Gerald teaches Lady Colefax's son Spanish;[3] Leonard has been put on a Government commission; Nessa never enjoyed any party so much as Kate Stephens funeral; we are all off to Sussex on Wednesday, which I have never wanted so much, since London makes one dry, brittle, febrile, and the country makes one sodden, rheumatic, and affectionate.

Please write again, and I will stick spurs to my typewriter; and get well, and come in your car to Rodmell with a melon.

Yr
V.W.

Berg

1488: TO ROGER FRY   52 *Tavistock Square* [*W.C.*1]
July 28th [1924]
My dear Roger,
      But I did write to you sheets and sheets,[4] and posted them 10 days ago— and you've never got it, and so accuse your old and devoted friend—However, this won't reach you either, so whats the use of writing? I addressed

---

1. Saxon and his mother were now living at Hogarth House, which they had leased from the Woolfs.
2. Primarily with Frances Marshall, whom he had met in the previous summer when she was working in the London bookshop run by David Garnett and Francis Birrell, and whom he married after Carrington's death in 1932. Carrington and Brenan were still very much in love.
3. Brenan never tutored Michael Colefax, but at this time he did teach English and French to the children of Boris and Helen Anrep.
4. Roger Fry had written to Virginia on 2 July from Souillac: "As I very much want a letter from you, I suppose the only way is to write to you" (*Letters of Roger Fry*, Vol. II, ed. Denys Sutton, 1972, p. 554).

Savillac, Lot:, or Serillac, Lot: I now find you are Souillac: but the fault was yours—so I'm cleared anyhow.

But there—

Desmond			Roger		
Lytton		pro Shaw	Francis Birrell		Contra
Leonard			R. Mortimer		
Clive					

Hedge

Virginia

who hasn't read or seen it [*Saint Joan*]

But come over to Rodmell.

Yrs
V.W.

Sussex

Letters 1489-1522 (August-December 1924)

For August and September the Woolfs moved to Monk's House, which was infested by rats and still lacked a bath and w.cs., but these drawbacks did not deter many summer visitors, including Vita, who went there for her first visit on 13 September. The Hogarth Press published her long story Seducers in Ecuador *in November. Virginia was slowly finishing* The Common Reader *and Mrs Dalloway—she described 300 words a day as 'a lot'—but she refused to discuss either book with her friends, even with Jacques Raverat, to whom she wrote her most intimate letters at this period, as he lay dying. The autumn saw the usual flurry of activity at the Press (the works of Freud were now added to their current list of smaller books), and George Rylands was succeeded by Angus Davidson towards the end of the year. Virginia was still concerned with the T. S. Eliot Fund, which was not finally wound up till 1927.*

1489: To Violet Dickinson
         Monks House, Rodmell,
         Lewes, Sussex

1st August 1924

My Violet,

  I imagine that A. B. W. is Mr Walkley, the Times Dramatic Critic—in fact I'm certain. But the poor old man seems to have got it all wrong—Mr [Arnold] Bennett has never agreed with me about anything.[1]

  Here we are, thank goodness, picking raspberries and clipping the yew. I wish you'd look in some time, and give us a few wrinkles. Leonard has just taken the tremendous step of dismissing one gardener and taking on another, but they're all robbers and all heavenly to talk to, and we never get our gooseberries, and all the lettuces are let run to seed—Still, its very nice here, all the same. I had the shock of my life last week running in to George and Gerald[2] at Katherine Stephen's funeral. George cant speak, and totters like an aspen: What has happened? Has he no teeth? And he seems already far gone in senile decay of every sort. Gerald is comparatively spry; but it was a grubby and dingy gathering of old fogies, and when you die, please be burnt to cinders and put on the path without any hanky panky ceremonies.

---

1. In *The Times* of 30 July, 'A. B. W.' criticised Virginia's *Character in Fiction*, published in the current issue of the *Criterion*.
2. George and Gerald Duckworth, Virginia's half-brothers, were then respectively 56 and 54. In this year George became Chairman of the Irish Land Trust for the re-settlement of ex-servicemen. Gerald had founded Duckworth Ltd., the publishers.

We had crucifixes and choir boys and the most woolly and thin blooded hymns. Nessa disgraced herself by treating it all as an afternoon party.

Come when you're back and have tea in the basement.

Your
V.W.

After 12 years of marriage, why should I bloom a maiden once more?

Berg

1490: To Dorothy Bussy   *Monks House, Rodmell,*
                                       Lewes [Sussex]
[13 August 1924]

My dear Dorothy,[1]

I'm afraid it is not much use our thinking of the translation, though I am sure it is first rate, and I admire the dialogue greatly. At present we have more work on hand than our present staff can manage, and we feel we had better not launch out into translations—The pamphlet public also imagines, wrongly I daresay, that it can read French literature, in the original. We are trying it with a translation of an aesthetic essay—but, even so, expect to lose.

Well: it is sad how seldom I see you. But you keep your glamour, which is the main thing, and next June we will have a really good tea party, ices, I think, in a shop.

Yours affly
V.W.

Texas

1491: To V. Sackville-West   *Monk's House, Rodmell,*
                                       Lewes, Sussex
19th August [1924]

My dear Vita,

Have you come back, and have you finished your book [*Seducers in Ecuador*]—when will you let us have it? Here I am, being a nuisance, with all these questions.

I enjoyed your intimate letter from the Dolomites. It gave me a great deal of pain—which is I've no doubt the first stage of intimacy—no friends, no heart, only an indifferent head.[2] Never mind: I enjoyed your abuse very much.

1. Elder sister of Lytton Strachey. She married Simon Bussy, the French painter, and was the author of *Olivia* (1949) and a translator of French fiction, particularly of Gide.
2. See Letter 1502, where she quotes Vita's exact words.

How could I think mountains and climbing romantic? Wasn't I brought up with alpenstocks in my nursery, and a raised map of the Alps, showing every peak my father had climbed? Of course, London and the marshes are the places I like best.

But I will not go on else I should write you a really intimate letter, and then you would dislike me, more, even more, than you do.

But please let me know about the book.

Yr V.W.

Berg

1492: To Pernel Strachey

Monk's House, Rodmell, Lewes [Sussex]

24th Aug. [1924]

My dear Pernel,

I suppose there is no chance of your coming here this summer? It would be very nice to see you again—I can't bear only meeting on the pavement in horrible dreary dusty surroundings. How I hate funeral services! and can't feel anything at them—either for Katherine or myself, or any one else. I wish I had seen her again. Never shall I forget her at Newnham,[1] hundreds of years ago, and sitting in that queer grim room with her talking—what a satisfactory and altogether charming human being she was!

Here I am writing in my garden room, which you have never seen, spreading first my left hand and then my right over an oil stove, to dry the excessive damp. In an hours time, perhaps, I shall see Clive appearing over the hill. On the other hand, if it goes on raining, Leonard and I will lunch together off roast (I think) mutton; I shall tell him how I woke up in the night and thought of writing a letter to you; and also of all kinds of catastrophes which may befall us in the coming year. We have now undertaken so many responsibilities—Dadie Rylands, a corncoloured youth, is one of them; and another is Mrs Joad. Both sit in the basement at Tavistock addressing envelopes, and cheered by occasional visits from me. We discuss literature. Mudies send for 20 Rector's daughter, by Miss Mayor, who may well be a friend of yours. She has the profile of a gorilla and once acted Ophelia—does that convey anything to you? Where ordinary women have hair, she has a brown sea weed—Lytton once had tea with her, and she hated us all, until I wrote to her in praise of her novel, when she whipped round the other way, and now steps the world (it is said) like a stallion in the sun.

I am writing great rubbish—do not blame me; for unless I *do* write something, Pernel will let the end of her line drop, and me go, for ever.

1. Katharine Stephen was Principal of Newnham College, Cambridge, 1911-20, the position which Pernel Strachey now held.

Isn't that true? Have you a word to urge in defence of your conduct? True, you're a great swell; at the top of your tree; magnificent, adored; and all the rest of it; but look down, my dear Pernel, into the grass, among the funguses, and see the lesser creatures who there abound. Myself among them.

I saw Hope [Mirrlees] the other day; but I shan't tell you what I think of her novel [*The Counterplot*] unless you write to me. I shan't tell you what I'm reading, writing, thinking, supposing, and inventing about my friends unless you write to me. Or it would be better still to come; but how can I suggest that? Years ago Pernel said she didn't visit where there weren't baths kept.

Leonard sends his love.

Yrs aff.
V.W.

Strachey Trust

1493: TO V. SACKVILLE-WEST   *Monk's House, Rodmell,*
                                 Lewes [Sussex]
Aug. 26th [1924]

My dear Vita

The position about your story is this: if you could let us have it by Sept. 14th, we should make an effort to bring it out this autumn; if later, it is highly improbable that we could bring it out before early next year. For ourselves, we should prefer to have it this autumn, so if you can do it, without overwork, cursing us, or spoiling the book, let us say Sept. 14th. But of course this is entirely for you to settle. Only might we know which?

Perhaps you will be this way again and will look in, which would be very nice indeed, if you dont mind—but I'll know you'll say you dont mind —discomfort, and all the rest of it—etc. We would offer you what Leonard says I must confess to be the most uncomfortable bed in the smallest room in Sussex. There was a young man [Rylands?] here the other Sunday who was saying he wished nothing more than to meet you—And you might have come in.

But really and truly you did say—I cant remember exactly what, but to the effect that I made copy out of all my friends, and cared with the head, not with the heart. As I say, I forget; and so we'll consider it cancelled.

I haven't time to inflict on you 20 reams to explain why I am so outraged at being taken for a writer. It is getting darker and darker and we are nursing a wood fire.

Yr Aff
V.W.

Berg

127

1494: To V. Sackville-West   *Monks House, Rodmell,*
                                     Lewes, Sussex
Sunday [31 August 1924]

My dear Vita,
   It is very good news about your book. We are now making out a list of
our autumn books, and could you tell us what yours will be called; about
how long it will be*; and say something to give a notion what it is about,
which we could quote.
   I'm sorry to be such a bore.
   The other thing is, could you come on Saturday 13th, not Sunday 14th,
as Leonard has to disappear [to Yorkshire] on Monday at dawn, and therefore wouldn't see you at all.
   I ought to warn you of the inconveniences and discomforts of this house,
especially when it rains, but they are too many to begin on. Anyhow, we
shall enjoy seeing you.
                                          Yours ever
                                          Virginia Woolf

* whether, in particular, it should be called a story or a novel.[1]

Berg

1495: To T. S. Eliot   *Monks House, Rodmell,*
                                     Lewes [*Sussex*]
Typewritten
3rd Sept. 1924

My dear Tom,
   It is a dreadful pity the Prince of Bores[2] can't come to keep his reputation
on the boil. Who knows? This time next year I may have found someone
more princely and more boring, and where will you be then? However . . .
Come by dromedary (this leaves me quite mystified)[3] rather than not at all;
and make Vivien come.
   The serious answers to questions must now begin. We want your
defective compositions as soon as we can have them.[4] We should have them
suitably printed, and produce after Christmas. Dont think that this allows

1. *Seducers in Ecuador* was only 74 pages long.
2. The term which Eliot applied to himself when writing to Virginia on 27 August
   (*Sussex*, copy).
3. Eliot had written: "Should I come to Eastbourne, we might visit you by
   dromedary for tea."
4. See p. 107, note 2. 'Defective compositions' was Eliot's own description of his
   essays.

you plenty of time; it does not. Send as soon as you have done your preface. I dont like paying fellow authors compliments, because I like there to be one cake of praise which is reserved entirely for me, but visiting Charleston the other day (my sister's) I there picked up The Sacred Wood[1] and came home and burnt every one of my own leading articles in the Supplement. Why are you the only man who ever says anything interesting about literature? There are we all pouring out gallons of ink weekly, and never a drop of it stays. However, I admire your work too much. It can't be as good as all that. But your brain seems to work.

Yes I am in the depth of modesty; cant bear my own writing; and wish I had been born with a gift for sewing instead.

But send us your manuscripts. The Criterion is praised on all sides. Clive, Mary etc etc.

Yrs V.W.

Mrs T. S. Eliot

1496: To Jacques Raverat

Monks House, Rodmell,
Lewes [Sussex]

Sept 4th 1924

My dear Jacques,

Well, as you say I don't answer your questions, so I will sit down with your letter before me and take them, one, two, three.

1) Why will Maynard be dished if he marries her [Lydia Lopokova]?

Because she has the nicest nature in the world and a very limited head-piece. She came to tea on Sunday with your brother-in-law Geoffrey,[2] and really I had the hardest time in the world. Her contribution is one shriek, two dances; then silence, like a submissive child, with her hands crossed. At 30 this is pathetic. Soon she will be plaintive. And they say you can only talk to Maynard now in words of one syllable. This he will tire of. She will cry, and the great ladies wont ask her to their parties: you old married people can fill it in at your leisure. (I get this largely from other sources).

2) Why should he marry her? She wants to send her sons to Eton.

3) I agree that Maynard's fallability endears him to me.

4) What is the *real* relation between Lytton, Carrington and Mr P[artridge]?

Now that's asking, as they say (unless I have got it wrong) God knows. I imagine a bed has two pillows though, and—but here again I'm quite ignorant, for at our time of life we ignore each other's private relations, and find them boring—Partridge is a bit of a bore; but then what muscles! How he cuts wood, breeds hens, and answers the bell! Carrington is worth twice

1. Eliot's volume of critical essays, 1922.
2. Geoffrey Keynes; Maynard's brother, married Margaret Darwin, Gwen Raverat's sister. Keynes is a surgeon, and an eminent bibliographer and biographer.

his salt—but he's a seemly pink firm-fleshed young man, without a doubt. And Lytton of course does not supply *every*thing. I leave this too, to be spelt out.

5) What am I writing? I dont think I shall tell you, because, as you know perfectly well, you don't care a straw what I write; and, like you and Gwen for the matter of that, I'm terrifically egotistic about my writing, think practically of nothing else, and so, partly from conceit, partly shyness, sensitiveness, what you choose, never mention it, unless someone draws it out with red hot pincers, or like Forster, really takes an interest in my adventures.

(however, I've almost finished 2 books)[1]

6) What do I read? On my table are: Yeats poems. Le Bal du Comte d'Orgel:[2] (which I think very interesting); Susanne et le Pacifique: (also interesting); the Adelphi; Chaucer; Lord Willoughby de Broke's auto-biography (sporting); a good many Elizabethan plays which I'm going to write about and—mere daily trash: *Joan of Arc* [*Saint Joan*]: I can't see why people are moved by this: interested, instructed—yes; but I cant squeeze a tear. I like Shaw as a figure: he seems to me lean, lively, destructive and combative. But Lord! leave me on a desert island with his plays, and I'd rather scale monkey puzzles. But this I've always suffered from. I dont quite trust myself.

7) What is my husband like?

A Jew: very long nosed and thin; immensely energetic; But why I don't talk about *him* is that really you are Anti-Semitic, or used to be, when I was in the sensitive stage of engagement; so that it was then impressed upon me not to mention him. I think this was so. And then Gwen, to take up old scandals, said it was high time at my age, I married, and as I was only 3 years older than she, I was hurt, profoundly, and thought you both con-descending, flippant, and oh dear, how the Neo-paganism at that stage of my life annoyed me—Every street in Bloomsbury seems now branded with my miseries, but I was more than a little mad. I will send you a picture of me done for a vulgar paper called Vogue when I get back.

You see, I'm very famous in some circles, *rather* famous, I mean: Americans want to buy my manuscripts. I should like you to have a high opinion of me in this way, and yet—how interesting one's own psychology is—won't talk to you about my writing.

I dont think this is a very nice letter, my dear Jacques, but then you brought it on yourself by asking all those questions; and my style is not good at questions:

1. *Mrs Dalloway* and *The Common Reader*.
2. A novel by Raymond Radiguet (1924). Jean Giraudoux published *Suzanne et le Pacifique* in 1921. Lord Willoughby de Broke's autobiography was *The Sport of our Ancestors* (1921).

By the way, I like your daughter's poems.[1] I don't know how much it is their being French. Everything French has a perfection in my eyes. Anyhow I think them very lovely, very enchanting. May I keep them?

And I don't like my own letters. I don't like the falsity of the relationship —one has to spray an atmosphere round one; yet I *do* like yours and seem to be able to pierce through your spray, so may you through mine.

Please write soon again. But could you tell me about your painting now? And isn't it the nut, core, kernel (as my Quaker aunt used to call it) of your soul! Gwen don't count compared with your smudges—(excuse what is only literary) does she?

What do you think of Duncan and Vanessa as painters? I should like to know.

Yrs
V.W.

Sussex

1497: To V. Sackville-West   *Monk's House, Rodmell,*
Lewes [Sussex]

Monday [15 September 1924]

My dear Vita,

I like the story [*Seducers in Ecuador*] very very much—in fact, I began reading it after you left,[2] was interrupted by Clive, went out for a walk, thinking of it all the time, and came back and finished it, being full of a particular kind of interest which I daresay has something to do with its being the sort of thing I should like to write myself. I don't know whether this fact should make you discount my praises, but I'm certain that you have done something much more interesting (to me at least) than you've yet done. It is not, of course, altogether thrust through; I think it could be tightened up, and aimed straighter, but there is nothing to spoil it in this. I like its texture—the sense of all the fine things you have dropped in to it, so that it is full of beauty in itself when nothing is happening—nevertheless such interesting things do happen, so suddenly—barely too; and I like its obscurity so that we can play about with it—interpret it different ways, and the beauty and fantasicallity of the details—the butterflies and the negress, for instance. This is all quite sincere, though not well expressed.

I am very glad we are going to publish it, and extremely proud and indeed touched, with my childlike dazzled affection for you, that you should dedicate it to me. We sent it to the printers this morning.

1. Elizabeth Raverat, who was then only 8 years old.
2. Vita spent the night of 13 September with Virginia and Leonard, her first visit to Monk's House.

Clive came over, and had to be broken the news to;[1] we ate your figs, sat on the mill stones and said—oh things you wouldn't believe, I daresay.

Leonard is sending Mr. Nicolson a copy of my pamphlet [*Mr Bennett and Mrs Brown*], in order that the cover may seduce him in to letting us have his Byron;[2] but Byron can be longer or shorter than Mrs Brown—whatever he chooses; so that he lets us have it.

I felt rather spirited up by your story, and wrote a lot—300 words—perhaps, this morning, and have a comfortable feeling that I am going to enjoy reading you again—so I can't help thinking it must be a good story, for God knows there are very few people I ever feel that about, even the ones I admire. By the way, you must let me have a list of people to send circulars to—as many as you can. And to do this you must come and see me in London for you should have heard Leonard and me sitting over our wood fire last night and saying what we don't generally say when our guests leave us, about the extreme niceness etc etc and (I'm now shy—and so will cease.)

                                                            Yrs Ever
                                                            V.W.
Berg

1498: To Roger Fry   *Monks House, Rodmell,*
                                       Lewes [*Sussex*]
Sept 22nd [1924]

My dear Roger,

I have just finished your pamphlet,[3] so I must write off at once and say how it fills me with admiration and stirs up in me, as you alone do, all sorts of bats and tadpoles—ideas, I mean, which have clung to my roof and lodged in my mind, and now I'm all alive with pleasure. At the same time, I'm much annoyed about Clive.[4] The truth is, one forgets Clive so quickly even at his most vivacious, that though I read him in the Nation, he has left no impression on me—except as a mere snap shot of your argument; and I dont think for a moment any reader of yours will confuse the two. It was a pity Leonard didn't send it him back; but it has become a joke almost—Clive's cribbing—here was Maynard yesterday saying the same thing. I wish (not merely from my usual malice) that you would yourself say

1. That he had missed Vita.
2. After Harold Nicolson's *Byron: The Last Journey*, published by Constables earlier this year, he published no other work on Byron until 1943.
3. *The Artist and Psycho-Analysis*, published by The Hogarth Press in November of this year.
4. His article in the *Nation and Athenaeum* (6 September 1922) on the same subject, *Dr Freud on Art*.

something to him about it. However, the main point is your article, which is far far beyond his or anybodies reach: which you know is my sincere opinion, and not merely the flattery of a publisher. I'm puzzling, in my weak witted way, over some of your problems: about 'form' in literature. I've been writing about Percy Lubbock's book,[1] and trying to make out what I mean by form in fiction. I say it is emotion put into the right relations; and has nothing to do with form as used of painting. But this you must tidy up for me when we meet, which must be soon and often. If you ever go to the mythical post office of Serillac, you will find all my reasons for wishing to see you couched with a fervour of expression which I shall never reach again.

We go back to London about the first. We have been seeing a few people, hearing Nessa grumble about Mary and the Tiltonians,[2] as she calls them, which always amuses me—she is so damned uncompromising—now I lick any hand thats held out, and was very much charmed by Mary, chiefly because she has such pretty legs. Of her head I cant say much, nor of dear Lydia's either. All the intervals of talk we fill in most desperately full with reading and writing. I've almost done my novel [*Mrs Dalloway*], which I hope to God you'll like; and sent 800 circulars to the Royal Academy Exhibitors who have bought 4 copies of Duncan.[3]—not wildly encouraging, but better than nothing. And I'm rather alarmed at the productivity of the Hogarth press this autumn—having laid out £800 in the works of Freud, which will sell they say because he has cancer; but I doubt any book selling that isnt by Berta Ruck. You are rather hard on "lady novelists": or perhaps my corns are tender. This is not to excuse you from writing—so dont think it. The best sellers are gentlemen, like Hugh Walpole, and Compton Mackenzie, of a peculiarly poisonous breed. The Rucks do it to send their sons to Eton, which, though not my ambition in life, is comparatively harmless.

This is dull: but as a matter of fact, a little talk is what I want: you painters I suppose never come to detest the sound of your own voices; as I do mine. I wish I could write anybody elses style for a change. Whereas, of course, one gets more steeped in it as one ages. Would you send back your proof [of *The Artist and Psycho-Analysis*] at once, and forgive the poor Woolves your devoted admirers

V.W.

Sussex

---

1. *The Craft of Fiction* (1921). Virginia dealt with the same subject in *Modern Fiction*, which appeared in *The Common Reader*.
2. Maynard Keynes and Lydia Lopokova, who lived at Tilton, a mile from Charleston.
3. Fry's book, *Duncan Grant*, published by the Press in February 1924.

Monk's House [Rodmell,
                                                   Sussex]
Sunday [28 September 1924]

Dearest Clive,
     I am going to ask what you must not hesitate to refuse—Marjorie Joad
has left [Prof. C.E.M.] Joad, (this is supposed to be a secret). She can't go
back to Hampstead, has to look for rooms; has nowhere to stay in London,
and is penniless, except for our pay. Could you let her use one of your
bedrooms for a few nights while she looks about? She is going up on
Thursday. Thus if you can manage it, would you write to her at
                              Courtlands
                            South Water
                              Horsham
                              Sussex—
She would only want a bedroom, and would be out all day and arrange for
herself about meals. Naturally, this mayn't be possible, and I rely on your
saying so. Her having been ill rather complicates things.
     I am sunk in the depths of sleep, having Karin, Ann, and Daisy [nurse]
on my shoulders, and just back from Bunny [Garnett], Saxon, Barbara,
Maynard and Lydia at Charleston.
     Love to the yellow Parrokeet [Mary Hutchinson] whose letter I shall
answer when circumstances grow more favourable.
     I am telling Marjorie Joad that I have asked you, but am extremely
doubtful if you can manage it.
                                                        Yrs V.W.

Quentin Bell

Monk's House, Rodmell
                                                   [Sussex]
Oct. 2nd [1924]

Dearest Molly,
     I don't think I can absorb French history at my time of life (I don't mean
you to infer by this that I'm at the funny time). Couldn't it be French
language instead—which I'm pining to speak? F.B. [Francis Birrell] might
take an elementary class in grammar first.
     We go back—Leonard's already gone back—on Saturday. I wither on
like a last leaf.
     Wouldn't it be possible to meet some time without making the
Carlovingians and Charlemagne an excuse? Though I admit there's a special
sweetness in flirting in school. I shall be plunged in publishing affairs at
once; we are publishing all Dr Freud, and I glance at the proof and read how

Mr A. B. threw a bottle of red ink on to the sheets of his marriage bed to excuse his impotence to the housemaid, but threw it in the wrong place, which unhinged his wife's mind,—and to this day she pours claret on the dinner table. We could all go on like that for hours; and yet these Germans think it proves something—besides their own gull-like imbecility.

I'm sitting over my fire, and wish for a companion. You should be wafted to me. By the way, I've been reading your childhood over again with envy and delight, and even scribbled a wretched review for The Times.[1] I thought I'd better make a breast of it; (clean breast it should be). I did it in a frightful hurry; and missed out all I wanted to put in, and did not convey in the least my envy and delight. Now you will be squirming with horror, like a toad one's half trodden on in the dark. But I detect in your tone a slight audacity which I take to mean that you have been considerably complimented, and find it rather refreshing. I thought old [A.C.] Benson rather good, considering what a foggy dew the poor man's mind is.

Shall I be raped, sleeping alone in the house to-night? Rose [Bartholomew], the Char, has just been in to ask, I say, I'm past raping.

We've had a spasmodic gay summer—all sorts of odds and ends dropping in—Maynard and Lydia, with roses twisted in her top knot, and Vita Nicolson, more than ever like a Guards officer in bearskin and breeches. Very Elizabethan too. And Clive and Mary and so on and so on.

But I must stop, and thank you once more, my dearest Molly, for writing such a charming—hush! hush! She's squirming!

V.W.

Mrs Michael MacCarthy

1501: To Jacques Raverat   *Monks House, Rodmell*
                                          [Sussex]
Oct. 3rd 1924

My dear Jacques,

Certainly the painters have a great gift of expression. A highly intelligent account you seem to me to give of the processes of your own mind when I throw Neo Paganism in. In fact I rather think you've broached some of the problems of the writer's too, who are trying to catch and consolidate and consummate (whatever the word is for making literature) those splashes of yours; for the falsity of the past (by which I mean Bennett, Galsworthy and so on) is precisely I think that they adhere to a formal railway line of sentence,

---

1. *The Schoolroom Floor*, a review of Molly's memoirs, *A Nineteenth Century Childhood* (*TLS*, 2 October 1924).

for its convenience, never reflecting that people don't and never did feel or think or dream for a second in that way; but all over the place, in your way.[1]

I'm writing now, partly because I was so much intrigued by your letter, and felt more in touch, partly because this is my last evening of peace. I go back to London tomorrow. Then there'll be people upon people; and I shall dash in and out, and go to concerts, and make engagements, and regret making engagements. The difficulty of writing letters is, for one thing, that one has to simplify so much, and hasn't the courage to dwell on the small catastrophes which are of such huge interest to oneself; and thus has to put on a kind of unreal personality; which, when I write to you for example, whom I've not seen these 11 years, becomes inevitably jocular. I suppose joviality is a convenient mask; and then, being a writer, masks irk me; I want, in my old age, to have done with all superfluities, and form words precisely on top of the waves of my mind—a formidable undertaking.

About your letter, however; I didn't mean that private relations bore me: which is indeed an intolerable perversion of my real meaning, who find relations of all kinds more and more engrossing, and (in spite of being made a fool of so often by one's impulse to surrender everything—dignity and propriety—to intimacy) final, in some way; enduring: gigantic; and beautiful. Indeed, I find all this in my relations with people, and what I can guess of theirs. What I meant was that *sexual* relations bore me more than they used: am I a prude? Am I feminine? Anyhow for two years past, I have been a spectator of I daresay a dozen affairs of the heart—violent and crucial; and come to the conclusion that love is a disease; a frenzy; an epidemic; oh but how dull, how monotonous, and reducing its young men and women to what abysses of mediocrity! Its true that all my lovers were of the simplest type; and could only flush and fade crudely like sea anemones bathed now blue, now red. Thats what I meant, I think.

Our loves, yours and mine and that granite monolithic Gwens—(until she writes to me, I shall say what I like in abuse of her to her husband) were of a very different kind. But then we were creatures of temperament. No: your admiration of me was not apparent; but then I was alarmed of your big nose, your bright eyes, your talking French, and your having such a quick easy way with you, as if you had solved the problems of life,—gone straight into the middle of the honeycomb without one miss. Yes—thats how I figure you: thats still (vaguely now) the image I have of my dear and adorable Jacques—but I should never have dared call him so to his face. And then, (this is a secret) for some reason, your and Gwen's engagement, being in love, took on for me a symbolical character; which I even tried to put

1. Jacques had written to Virginia about the problems of writing and painting, suggesting that a word like 'Neo-Pagan' aroused many associations, like throwing a pebble into a pond: "There are splashes in the outer air in every direction, and under the surface waves that follow one another into dark and forgotten corners." See Quentin Bell, *Virginia Woolf* II, p. 106.

down in writing. All very absurd I suppose: still you were very much in love, and it had an ecstatic quality. Indeed, you will laugh, but I used to think of you, in a purely literary way, as the two people who represented that passion in my mind: and still, when I think of you, I take out my brush, and paint both of your faces a divine sunset red. How oddly composed are one's feelings! You would never have guessed, I daresay, that Jacques and Gwen always appear to Virginia in a sunset glow?

As for gossip, I hope to collect some in the great world.

Vanessa is getting a little querulous about Maynard and Lydia, and will have, she says, to turn out.[1] Our Mrs Joad has left her Mr Joad. Our Dadie is a very nice boy. Our Karin Stephen sent me to bed with a violent headache last week, and ruined the last pages of my novel (Oh yes, I'll write another letter and tell you about my writing—anything you want to know). She descended on us, and God knows I like her; but there's a deafness of the spirit about her, which exhausts more than dragging a ton of coal upstairs. So hearty she is, good humoured, and right minded. The poor devil interests me for having tried to live with Adrian, and for being inarticulately aware of her own obtuseness. She can't feel; she cant enjoy; she cant be intimate: she cares for nothing. Yet she has the most perfect apparatus for life in body and head and wealth and freedom. To cure herself she pays £1 daily to a psychoanalyst; and would, she told me, prefer to be entirely destitute could she only feel things, instead of being as she is now non-feeling. But this may convey nothing to you.

However, I'm awfully shy of saying how really and truly I would do a great deal to please you and can only very very dimly murmur a kind of faint sympathy and love.

Yrs
V.W.

I've been trying to buy Valéry in London, and am told he is out of print. Can you tell me how I could get his dialogues?[2]

Sussex

1502: To V. Sackville-West   52 *Tavistock Sqre, W.C.*1

[4 October 1924]

Dear Vita
    An elderly lady [Duncan's aunt Daisy] whose life centres entirely in her

1. Exasperated by the proximity of Maynard Keynes and Lydia Lopokova, Vanessa went to Norfolk in mid-October to look for a new house, but she gave up the plan.
2. Paul Valéry's *L'Âme et la danse* and *Eupalinos ou l'Architecte* (1923), essays in the Socratic manner.

yacht has asked me to try and get passengers for her. If she doesnt, the yacht will have to be sold, and the centre of her life will be in ruins. So should you be able to send somebody off—its said to be an extremely good holiday and very comfortable—it would be very good of you.

We are just back; what did I find on the drawing room table, but a letter from which (to justify myself and utterly shame you) I make this quotation: "Look on it, if you like, as copy,—as I believe you look upon every-thing, human relationships included. Oh yes, you like people through the brain, rather than through the heart" etc:[1] So there. Come and be forgiven. Seducers in Ecuador looks very pretty, rather like a lady bird.[2] The title however slightly alarms the old gentlemen in Bumpuses [booksellers].

Yrs ever V.W.

Berg

1503: To Dora Carrington   52 *Tavistock Sqre, W.C.*

[October 1924?]

My dear Carrington

Would you answer these 3 questions:
1. Where do you get your tea, what is it called, and what price?
2. Where do you get the marbled end papers?[3]
3. —I can't remember what: but when are you coming to see the Loups? I'm having French lessons and have acquired this word.

Yr V.W.

—My books are being disposed of, and I hope to have a little money for binding soon: tell Ralph.

Robert H. Taylor

1504: To Dorothy Bussy   52 *Tavistock Square, W.C.*1

Oct. 10th 1924

My dear Dorothy,

I know I am breaking the rule of our friendship in writing to you—as we ought not to speak till next June. But forgive this. What I write to ask is, if

1. This is a quotation from Vita's letter to Virginia, written from the Dolomites on 16 July 1924 (*Berg*).
2. The book had a marbled red and black cover.
3. Virginia and Leonard had visited Lytton and the Partridges at Ham Spray, Hungerford, on 8 October. Ralph Partridge had taken up book-binding as a part-time occupation.

138

there is any chance that Janie[1] would like to translate my book *Jacob's Room* into French. The editor of *Europe*, a monthly magazine, has said that he would like to publish it, if I can get a *good* translation made. Naturally I thought of Janie. I'm afraid the pay is very small—only a few francs a page; but if she thought it possible, I would find out more. We are just settling in to be very busy.

However, as I say, I must not anticipate June 16th when you are coming to tea with me.

Your aff.
Virginia Woolf

Texas

1505: To Hugh Walpole   52 *Tavistock Square, W.C.*1

11 Oct 1924

Dear Mr Walpole,

I am reading your book [*The Old Ladies*] with great pleasure, and need not say how much it pleases me to have it as a present from you.

With many thanks,

Yours sincerely,
Virginia Woolf

Texas ·

1506: To Richard Aldington   52 *Tavistock Square, W.C.*1

[early November 1924]

Dear Mr Aldington,

I'm so glad you can come on Wednesday 13th.

You did not send me the signed promises to pay [for the Eliot Fund]. They would be useful, I think, as the question now is whether to return the money or what to do with it—Tom says he wont keep it. I dont know who the subscribers are.

Yours sincerely,
Virginia Woolf

Texas

1. Simon and Dorothy Bussy's daughter Jane.

Typewritten
[early November 1924]

Dear Mr Aldington,

If you are staying in London won't you dine with us on Wednesday (I agree it is the 12th) at 7.45 instead of lunching? That would be much nicer. But come to lunch if you can't manage dinner, of course.

I heard from the Bank about Mr Pearsall Smiths ten pounds and gave my consent to his taking it back; but they wanted yours too.

As far as I remember we offered Tom £50, and he left it untouched; but I'll find out. Difficulties arise at once. Tom wants the money handed on to another deserving case—but which? And will people ever agree? However we will thrash this out when we meet.

Would you let me know about dinner?

Yours sincerely
Virginia Woolf

Texas

1508: To V. Sackville-West   52 *Tavistock Sqre, W.C.*1

Sunday [9 November 1924]

My dear Vita,

You have added to your sins by coming here without telephoning—I was only rambling the streets to get a breath of air—could easily have stayed in, wanted very much to see you. Next time remember, 2621 Museum: if no answer, 3488 Museum: only keep this last secret, as we have our hiding places.

Leonard is giving you official particulars of Seducers, which is being rebound—very good, since not a review of any importance has yet appeared. I hope Raymond Mortimer will do it somewhere. I sent off the circulars. I will sign as many books as Lady Sackville [Vita's mother] wants. No: I will not forgive you. Wont you be coming up for a day later, and won't you let me know beforehand?

There are several matters that require going into at length.

What about your long poem?[1]

Yours Ever
Virginia Woolf

I have met Mrs Thomas Hardy, Charlotte Mew, (the greatest living poetess),[2]

1. *The Land*, which Vita had begun to write in the autumn of 1923.
2. In the opinion of Thomas Hardy.

Siegfried Sassoon, Nancy Cunard,[1] and rather expect in the course of the next ten days, to meet Percy Lubbock, so you see I'm exploring our profession thoroughly.

Berg

1509: TO LYTTON STRACHEY   52 *Tavistock Square, W.C.*1
Typewritten
11.11.24.

		£.	s.	d.	
To a/c rendered		1	7	0	
„ 1 West's Seducers @ 4/6			4	6	
„ 1 Avvakum @ 6/-			6	0	
„ 1 Ransom's Grace @ 4/6			4	6	
„ 3 Pamphlets @ 2/6			7	6	
„ 1 do @ 3/6			3	6	
		£2	14	0	[*sic*]
to 1 Kenya @ 15/- net			15	0	
		£3	4	0	[*sic*]

[in V.W.'s handwriting:]

Lytton Strachey Esq.,   Your attention is particularly called to the above
Ham Spray House,   account outstanding since May,—causing the devil
Hungerford,   of a bother in our Books; which won't balance till
Berks.   you pay; as an Englishman, on Armistice day, we
                        implore.
                        Signed: 2 Woolves
                                1 Dadie
                                1 Mrs Joad
                                in love and reverence

Strachey Trust

1510: TO ETHEL SANDS   52 *T*[*avistock*] *S*[*quare, W.C.*1]
[November 1924]

I'm *not* faithless; only got decoyed last Wednesday into sitting up late talking and so was stupid as an owl and no ornament to a tea party next

1. Daughter of Maud Emerald Cunard, and founder of the Hours Press.

day; this Thursday, Lady Colefax has seized on these 3 weeks, but if she goes, I will rush to you; and anyhow the Thursday after I shall come without fail, bringing Dadie, if I may.

Bosanquet was despatched today.

Wendy Baron

1511: To Richard Aldington   52 *Tavistock Square, W.C.*1

[mid-November 1924]

Dear Mr Aldington,

Please dont apologise for a second about not coming. I have great sympathy with people who dont keep engagements and live in a rush—it constantly happens to me. But I hope you'll come one day and see us, not on business, which is dreary enough.

I quite agree with you that it is best to send the donors back their money. The Morrells did not want to take theirs, and two other subscribers were of the same mind—but they all had different people they wanted to give it to: and as this would obviously be the case with most of them, it is much simpler to return it, and let them do as they like.

I cant remember any slips, and feel sure they were not sent to me. So I have written to the Bank for a list of names, which they should have, and will write to each an explanation as soon as I can. I hope it wont be necessary to bother you again.

Yours sincerely,
Virginia Woolf

Texas

1512: To Harcourt, Brace (*New York*)

52 *Tavistock Square, W.C.*1

Nov. 15th 1924

Dear Mr Brace,

I was on the point of writing to you when your letter came. I am hoping to send you my book of collected essays, which I am calling "The Common Reader" and a novel, "Mrs Dalloway", about March. We are bringing them both out in the spring—the essays probably in March, the novel at the end of April. I should prefer the essays to come out before the novel —but, if you wish to publish them, that is a matter which we could arrange later.¹ We were sorry not to see you here last summer, and hope to have the pleasure this year.

Yours sincerely,
Virginia Woolf

Lilly Library, Indiana University

1513: To Molly MacCarthy   52 *T[avistock] S[quare, W.C.*1]

Saturday [22nd November 1924]

Dearest Molly,

We were visiting the Zoo this afternoon and so missed you—but I intend to miss you, in order that you may go on writing letters. Suppose we live in London till we're 80, never meet, but correspond: what an interesting situation, and we might meet once, very very old, in the Kings Road by chance.²

I don't in the least agree about your dress: I thought it a mixture of snowdrop and viper: a green viper. Scintillating as the snow, and very effective and chaste; compared with which I felt Dora Sangerish mixed with Melian Stawellish.³ So don't go and change it. Don't be downed by those pert misses, the [Elizabeth] Ponsonby, [Viola] Tree, Diana Manners⁴ group, who have shaved themselves to resemble nothing so much as tubes of piping. I was bitterly disappointed in them all, and turned to you in your white dress as some consolation.

As for the Clive-Mary affair, I've so often suffered in the same way myself that I advise you, as one matron to another, to let him be. He *will* say disagreeable things—and you were undoubtedly passionate and indiscreet (so I imagine) and he has a kind of tiresome chivalry about Mary which almost drives Leonard and me mad with irritation—always insisting that we should all be praising her; but it has its good side too, that is to say he is in his way faithful to her; and to you into the bargain; so that if you take no steps and in fact withdraw rather than advance, he will be consoled in a year's time. However I daresay this wisdom is coals to Newcastle; and my pen is so spindle shanked that I can't write a line.

But take out your goose quill, and let us correspond.

Yr V.W.

Mrs Michael MacCarthy

1. On the original of this letter Donald Brace has noted "advance £30 on novel, £20 on essays".
2. The MacCarthys had moved back to their former house in Wellington Square, Chelsea, from Oare in Wiltshire.
3. Florence Melian Stawell (1889-1938) was a classical scholar at Newnham College, Cambridge, and a friend of Roger Fry.
4. She had married Duff Cooper in 1919.

Nov. 29th 1924

My dear Dorothy,

I ought to have written before, but there have been various delays. Now the Revue Française have written to me to say they want to publish a translation of Jacob's Room, and apparently they provide their own translator. So I'm trying to come to terms with them—and I think, myself, Janie is well out of it. Colin (of Europe) talks of doing another of my books; but the pay is so little, that I don't believe it would be worth Janie's while—also his plans are vague.

As to the translation of Gide, we should like to see it, but the trouble is that it is hardly possible to make translations from the French pay. Our sort of public reads French, or pretends that it does, and the printing costs leave very little chance of covering expenses.

These dismal affairs being discharged, there remains nothing to be said till June 20th when you are engaged to tea with me at Rumpelmayer's—Did you know it? I had a visit from Gwen the other day, very tragic I thought,[1] and I half intend to go and see them, in which case I shall sponge a tea off you. Last night Pippa [Strachey] looked in, entirely resembling a nice small dancing bear. She danced once round the room on her hind legs and went off to the ballet. Marjorie [Strachey] continues to develop the soundest and ripest character in Bloomsbury; in short, all Stracheys are doing well. Adrian and Karin are still separate; Leonard and I continue married.

That is all

Yrs V.W.

Texas

Nov 29th 1924

My dear Jacques,

I am much distressed, not figuratively but genuinely, to hear what a horror of a time you have been having. It was tantalising to see old Gwen for such a second, but the best of these Darwins is that they are cut out of the rock, and three taps is enough to convince one how immense is their solidity (to which Gwen has added, I thought, some vein of wisdom, and sweetness of temper which I rather envy her—I like seeing women weather the world so well).

But what am I to do with your copy of the Revue Française? I don't like to trust it to the post, which has lost me my Proust memorial volume

1. Jacques Raverat was nearing his death.

this year. Who is going out to you next? Tell me, and I'll send it. I hope to read Valéry again. My first reading rather baffled: I felt an odd emptiness, conformity of some kind, triteness, I even go so far as to add, beneath the beauty and brilliancy of the surface. I felt I'd read it before, not so well set out. But I don't trust myself reading French: lately I've had one or two disappointments, expecting more from the manner than I got in the end; so I must read this again. You French are fundamentally so damned logical, and this freezes the soul in one or two of its veins.

What were the questions I had to answer? About the young man in the basement, George Rylands. Alas, he will soon cease to be in the basement, King's College requiring him to work harder at his dissertation, and so he will be going after Xmas to write upon Diction in Poetry, and so win a fellowship, and live at Cambridge and teach, which they now insist on—rather a nuisance for us. It makes it necessary to reorganise our staff, take in a new partner, engage a new secretary and so on: but I wont bore you with domestic details. Hours and hours of our time go in discussions and interviews. He is a semi-Neo Pagan perhaps. At King's they are all reminded of Rupert—partly his yellow hair, partly his poetry, which is not so good as Rupert's. He is a very charming spoilt boy, sprung of the rich who have no money, and so rather dazzled by London and parties, and perhaps he scents himself; but at heart he is uncorrupted, (so I think— others disagree) and all young and oldish men, like Eddie Marsh and so on, fall in love with him, and he dines out every night, and treats his lovers abominably. However, if he don't get his fellowship, he will come back here, if possible. A life at Cambridge teaching seems to me a skeleton life; but then, it has to be.

Once reflection occurred to me, dealing with our Mrs Joad, the other basement dweller—how much nicer young women are than young men. I hope to get a rise out of you. Nicer, I say, humaner, less conceited, more sensitive,—not cleverer. But a man has to be very clever to balance what my dear Jacques I can only call his damned offensive good opinion of himself—of his sex.

Now please tell me about your autobiography,[1] which so whets my curiosity that I must entreat you to let me see it. If I translated it, couldn't we publish it?

Please write it with a view to this, and let it be the waste paper basket, conduit pipe, cesspool, treasure house, and larder and pantry and drawing and dining bed room of your existence. Write about everything, without order, or care. Being a Frog, you won't of course: you will organise and compose. Still, let me see it, and get on with it.

It is awful how business runs away with one's time. Soon I shall have to describe a fresh set of people to you—a man called Angus Davidson,

1. Raverat died before he completed his autobiography.

who thinks of coming to us.[1] Then, socially, what about Lady Colefax? Being the most successful, hardest mouthed hostess in London, she retains spots about the size of a sixpenny piece of astonishing sensibility on her person. Having left her umbrella here, I, in malice or sport, proceeded to describe it, glowing and gleaming among my old gamps. Whereupon this hard bitten old hostess of 50 flushed quite red, and said "Mrs Woolf, I know what you think of my umbrella—a cheap, stubby, vulgar umbrella, you think my umbrella: and you think I have a bag like it—a cheap flashy bag covered with bad embroidery". And it was too true. Only, if she saw it, must there not be depths in Lady Colefax? Think this out, and let me know.

Please write and say how you are.

Yrs
V.W.

Sussex

1516: To Violet Dickinson

52 *Tavistock Square, London, W.C.*1

30th Nov. [1924]

My Violet,

It was charming to get a letter from you, in your well known style—but I didn't mean you to bother—only to listen to my affectionate chatter. I envy you, going to Brighton. It is the most beautiful town in the whole world. Its chief blot is that once the Fisher family lived there—do you remember Aunt [Mary] Fisher? She was blown against a motor car one day and annihilated [in 1916]. Herbert, on the contrary is safely lodged at New College[2]—Either one goes up in the world or down. The up goers are always detestable—thats one comfort, keep butlers, condescend to me. George [Duckworth] for example, what a loathsome type that is, and Lady Margaret [his wife], gone lame I'm told, and highly religious. Do you think, if we'd taken our opportunity and gone to Devonshire House, we should have married better? Thats a question Nessa and I often ask, sitting so shabby as we do, without a set of furs between us, and the family jewels up the spout.

On Sunday I met an old friend of yours, the valiant [Janet] Case. D'you remember her? She had tea with you once, wearing a pair of new white kid gloves, you said, and spitting slightly, owing to the conformation of her jaw. All her teeth are out now: her hair is bobbed—She has Grave's disease (which I confuse with a Zebra of that name) and lives in the New

1. Angus Davidson joined the Hogarth Press on 10 December.
2. H. A. L. Fisher became Warden of New College, Oxford, early in 1925, while retaining his seat in the House of Commons until 1926.

Forest—The old age of Greek teachers fills me to the brim with admiration. Having £200 a year, she has built a Cottage, observes nature, has no water laid on, reads Blake, never pines a moment, and comes up—for what d'you think? to see Tchekov at Barnes. Now if I die like that, I shall expect something like a general conflagration in the sky. Then we lunched with Irene Noel[1] yesterday, married to an admirable worthy good simple hearted man who runs—called Baker. Perhaps we shall go to Greece this spring.

I have just finished a novel—all except copying out the last chapter. Shall you like it? Shall I write another book of essays? or a play? or a biography? or a philosophy? I want to do them all instantly, and your advice will be greatly prized. Someday please show me all your letters and let us put our heads together and write a memoir of our own Times. At Brighton you might begin.

Yr
VW.

No answer required. Leonard sends his love and best respects.

Berg

1517: To Lady Cecil[2]   52 *Tavistock Square, W.C.*1
[mid-December 1924]

My dear Nelly,

I suppose you would not come here? This is not pure laziness on my part—but, first, I have to be here, in the press, till 4.30, as we are short-handed; second, I want you to see our decorations: third, I'm dining out both Wednesdays, so should have rather a rush from Grosvenor Sqre. But rather than not see you, or if its at all inconvenient, I'll certainly come. Shall we say this Wednesday 17th?

Only let me know which its to be. No, of course the Nation can't review its editor's wife's books. For the first time in my life, I'm making money out of them.[3]

Yours ever,
V.W.

Hatfield

1. Whose family Virginia had visited in Euboea, Greece, in 1906, while on a Greek tour with Violet. In 1915 she married Philip Baker, who had been an Olympic medallist, and after working with Lord Cecil at the League of Nations, entered Parliament in 1929.
2. Lord Robert Cecil was created Viscount Cecil of Chelwood at the end of 1923.
3. In 1924 her total income from her books was £37. See Leonard Woolf, *Downhill All the Way* (1968), p. 143. But Harper's had just offered her £50 for an article.

52 *Tavistock Sqre. W.C.*
[22 December 1924]

Dearest Margaret,

I am greatly excited to hear of the house,[1] but don't much expect ever to see it. We have been reorganising our Press, which takes ages. We have now a very steady young man [Angus Davidson], who will let us come and see you sometimes I hope.

This is not even an attempt at a letter: only a line of abuse for your many sins and admiration of your many virtues.

I will come and bring Leonard to the next Russian debauch[2] if you'll let us know. Rab (the Russian) has been very friendly and given us names from your list.

Please don't drop your dirty friends, now you've a house of your own.

Yrs
V.W.

I'm glad to say L. has given up *part* of the Nation and will I hope give up more.[3]

Sussex

1519:   To Vanessa Bell
        From Leonard and Virginia Woolf
                              Monk's House [*Rodmell,
                              Sussex*]
Typewritten
25/12/24

My dear Vanessa,

You have thrown the most beautiful but dangerous apple of discord into the domestic bliss of Tavistock Square, and V and I wrangle at intervals over who shall have your picture. We both like it so enormously—which I know is no compliment in your austere eyes—and I claim to have it in my room as it was addressed to me. V claims it for the dining room. I hope you will support me particularly as I nearly always support you in discussions. We both feel however that your present is too handsome for Christmas.

1. At 26 Well Walk, Hampstead, N.W.3.
2. See Letter 1480.
3. He remained Literary Editor of the *Nation and Athenaeum* until 1930.

We may descend upon you before you get this if the weather keeps to its today's behaviour.

Yours
Leonard Woolf

[in Virginia's handwriting:]
I hope you will take my side in the dispute. I think it is one of the most interesting examples of your art, owing to the entirely new vein disclosed—Angus agrees.

Angus sends love—so does Grizzle. Really you ought not to give us such a superb present.

Berg

1520: To Jacques Raverat   *Monk's House, Rodmell*
                                            [Sussex]
Dec. 26th 1924

My dear Jacques,
    Do not expect wit or sense in this letter, only the affection of a drugged and torpid mind. Oh an English Christmas! We are not Christians; we are not social; we have no part in the fabric of the world, but all the same, Christmas flattens us out like a steam roller; turkey, pudding, tips, waits, holly, good wishes, presents, sweets; so here we sit, on Boxing day, at Rodmell, over a wood fire, and I can only rouse myself by thinking of you. In particular, I want to know 1. how you are. 2. Whether you are getting on with your autobiography; 3. What you are thinking; 4. what feeling; 5. what imagining, criticising, seeing—do catch that wild woman Gwen and stick a pen in her paw.
    All that I predicted about Maynard and Lydia is coming to pass. They dined with us 2 nights ago: and my God! the poor sparrow is already turning into a discreet, silent, serious, motherly, respectable, fowl, with eggs, feathers, cluck cluck clucking all complete. A melancholy sight indeed, and I foresee the day when she dislikes any reference to dancing. Maynard is—But enough of the Keynes', as they are called in Bloomsbury. "Mr Keynes has very bad taste," my cook said to me, after the dinner. "Madame laughs, and he is so serious". Soon Vanessa is escorting her to the divorce court. Once divorced, she will give up dancing.[1] But enough of the Keynes.
    Now who shall we pitch on? Casting a shadow over my paper at the present moment, is the fine oriental head of Angus Davidson. He is staying here to know us and be known (he is our partner now) and, despite his brother's [Douglas] neck, I like him very much; and think him likely to

1. Lydia Lopokova was separated from her first husband, who was living in America.

be our salvation—gentle, considerate, cautious, kind, with a mind smooth and sensitive as the thickest cream. Do you know that quality in young well-bred Englishmen? Slightly hesitating, diffident, and unselfconscious. He is working in cross stitch at a design by Duncan for a chair; Leonard is ordering onions from a catalogue. Who should come in, the other day, but our Will [Arnold-Forster]; more stretched, pinched, parchmenty than ever: squeaking with goodness; and as nice as can be, but why will Ka always introduce him in a letter calling attention to the wildness and ferocity of his genius: whereupon one hears a squeak on the stairs and in runs Will. "Little Wully's by way of being a painter" he said at tea, I urging him, with my notorious lack of consideration, to write books, either about roses, or about the League of Nations, which to tell the truth is far more his line than perpetually worrying the finest crow quills over the Appenines or whatever that eternal picture of his may be. But enough of the Coxes.

Who is there next? Well, only a high aristocrat called Vita Sackville-West, daughter of Lord Sackville, daughter of Knole, wife of Harold Nicolson, and novelist, but her real claim to consideration, is, if I may be so coarse, her legs. Oh they are exquisite—running like slender pillars up into her trunk, which is that of a breastless cuirassier (yet she has 2 children) but all about her is virginal, savage, patrician; and why she writes, which she does with complete competency, and a pen of brass, is a puzzle to me. If I were she, I should merely stride, with 11 Elk hounds, behind me, through my ancestral woods. She descends from Dorset, Buckingham, Sir Philip Sidney, and the whole of English history, which she keeps, stretched in coffins, one after another, from 1300 to the present day, under her dining room floor. But you, poor Frog, care nothing for all this.

Roger Fry is getting a little grumpy. He is not, you see, (or I imagine you see) a born painter, and this impediment seems to obstruct the run of his sympathies, so that he makes no allowances, but judges the imperfect and frail purely as if he were still an impeccable undergraduate, an incorruptible Apostle: whereas for my part I grow more mellow every day.

There!

I think I will leave off with that tribute to myself.

Love from everybody in the room.

Yours aff.
V.W.

It is said that the Adelphi is coming to an end.[1]
We go back to London next Saturday.

Sussex

---

1. Middleton Murry continued to control the *Adelphi* until 1948.

1521: To V. Sackville-West   *Monk's House, Rodmell,*
                                     Lewes [Sussex]
Dec. 26th 1924

My dear Vita,
    It is sad that you should be determined to undermine my virtue.[1] Never have I been so happy as I was two nights ago, though we had the dullest possible party. (a purely business conversation) Still I sipped my glass, I became more and more genial, more and more condescending, affable and intimate, till the company was suspicious. But really you ought to keep these treats for my visits to you. Home tippling will be my ruin.
    We are badly in want of a drop here, in this watery and teetotal house, where the turkey and cold sausages are never finished.
    We are sitting over the fire—at 6 o'clock on Xmas Eve, as we were packing to come here, arrived an order from America for 25 Seducers. Off we went to the post in the rain—then I had a sip to warm me. 899 Seducers sold.
    A thousand thanks for the bottle—and please come and see us again soon—
                                     Yr V.W.
I hope you are better.

Berg

1522: To Vanessa Bell   *Monks House, Rodmell*
                                     [Sussex]
Wednesday [31 December 1924]

Dearest,
    I'm much distressed that our presents came so late. They were sent off on the 23rd—but I see from the papers this happened everywhere. Its never too late to spill milk as you would say. Did Angelica get bricks as well as stencil? I only ask, not to cadge for thanks, but because I had my doubts of the shop sending them both.
    We are completely cut off from crossing Southease Bridge, as the river has overflowed and the road is 18 inches under water. Angus had to wade back on coming home from you on Sunday.
    If its fine, we shall try to come on Friday, lunch, but God knows: I don't suppose theres any chance; but on a bicycle perhaps one might swim through.
    The state of mud here is indescribable, added to which enormous rats join the family every evening and make conversation difficult.

1. Vita had given Virginia a bottle of Spanish wine as a Christmas present.

Angus told you about the American covers—its now likely that the Common Reader will be a larger book than we thought.[1] Can you enlarge your design? I will send you the exact size from London.

Tell Julian I think his paper very remarkable, and oddly enough his arguments are used in a French book I'm reading. His style reminds me very much of Thobys—in fact I was greatly impressed.

Can we make up a party to go to Islington Fair?

Was the Dunciad a success?[2]

I have some ideas for a new one, tell Quentin.

We return on Saturday

Yr VW

Berg

1. In fact the American edition was the same size as the English.
2. The Dunciad was a 'Life' of Duncan Grant, written by Virginia and illustrated by Quentin, for Christmas 1924.

Letters 1523-1544 (January–March 1925)

When Virginia wrote on 8 October 1924 that she had 'finished' Mrs Dalloway, she meant the first, second or third draft. A long process of further revision and retyping followed, and it was not until January that the novel had its first reader, Leonard. The second was Jacques Raverat, to whom she sent the proofs on 6 February, but he managed to read (or have read to him by his wife Gwen) only part of it before he died in great pain on 7 March. Virginia felt his loss dreadfully, for although they had not met for some eleven years, his 'hard truculent mind' had remained a stimulus to her own, and after his death she continued the correspondence with his widow. Virginia herself was ill with flu and subsequent headaches from mid-January to mid-February, but her illness gave her the excuse to miss on 4 February the party which she had arranged jointly with her sister-in-law Karin Stephen. There were further changes at the Hogarth Press: Mrs Joad left in February, and a temporary, Bernadette Murphy, joined Angus Davidson as assistants to Leonard.

1523: To David Garnett *52 Tavistock Square, London, W.C.1*

Jan 4th 1925

Dear Bunny

I love fossils, and have a passion for Trents Last Case,[1] but I can't come, much though I should like to be wished the health of by you. I have got horribly late with a book I am trying to finish and even to rub up a few facts about Fielding is beyond me.

Why not try Vita Nicolson? She is now, I think, in London; anyhow Long Barn, Sevenoaks, Weald, Kent, finds her, and she is of ravishing beauty, and commanding presence, which I'm sure is what the Square Club[2] wants: not Fielding, but woman. But many thanks for asking me.

When we're at Cambridge, we shall look in for tea. Leonard is rather anxious about your fruit trees, put in in this weather.

We came back from Rodmell last night, flooded out.

Yr affec
V.W.

Berg

1. The detective story by E. C. Bentley (1913).
2. A dining-club (named after the character in Fielding's *Tom Jones*) which met monthly to hear a literary address.

153

1524: To Jacques Raverat   52 *Tavistock Sqre., London*
Jan 24th 1925

My dear Jacques,

As I was eating my muffin in bed this morning in came an exquisite crate from the South of France filled with flowers of every colour and smell, which I frantically tumbled on the bed to see who could have sent them, and there was your card![1] I assure you it brought the tears to these hardened eyes of mine, that *you* should have thought of me. And I was just writing to you (a thing I enjoy doing thoroughly, for I write to no one else now) to say that if you'd really like it, I'll send out the proofs of my novel [*Mrs Dalloway*], which has just arrived, on condition you don't bother to write to me about it, or even read it; and *don't mention* it to anyone, for fear we should be asked for it, and it wont be out till May. For no other human being in the world would I do this—why, I dont know. But I'm a little morbid about people reading my books.

I was seeing Roger Fry last night, and he said, talking of you, that he thought your work getting more and more interesting, and wanted to see it, and wished me to tell you this, and would like to write to you about it himself, but perhaps he won't, so I do instead. What he said was that he thought it extraordinary how you had put aside the things likely to lead to success, and gone on your own lines, so that he thought your last work infinitely better than your early. His praise about painting always seems to me the best worth having, not that one agrees with him, but that his honesty is so incorruptible, and his perceptions so fine. Tell me if there is anything more particular I can ask him. When people praise my writing I want to know why. Anyhow he praised your painting very highly.

I've been engaged in a great wrangle with an old American called Pearsall Smith on the ethics of writing articles at high rates for fashion papers like Vogue. He says it demeans one. He says one must write only for the Lit. Supplement and the Nation and Robert Bridges and prestige and posterity and to set a high example. I say Bunkum. Ladies' clothes and aristocrats playing golf don't affect my style; and they would do his a world of good. Oh these Americans! How they always muddle everything up! What he wants is prestige: what I want, money. Now my dear sharp pointed and Gallic Jacques, please decide between us.[2]

Then I have seen our Ka, in her mother-in-laws grey suit and set of furs, a perfect specimen of solid county life, outwardly; but inwardly, much

1. On 25 January Virginia was 43.
2. In an autobiographical summary of his correspondence with Virginia, now in the Library of Congress, Logan Pearsall Smith wrote: "I happened to express the opinion that journalism of this kind might be detrimental to authors of promise, who, if they habitually wrote for trashy people, would very likely end by writing trash themselves."

as usual; that is rather flustered and affectionate, and troubled, it seems to me, about her past; and life's discrepancies, very wise in her own way, which is not *our* way. She has no feeling whatever for the arts. This is the greatest barrier of all, I believe. You and I can chatter like a whole parrot house of cockatoos (such is my feeling) because we have the same language at heart: but with Ka, one looks across a wall. Whether what one says reaches her I doubt. But these barriers have their fascination. Only for living with, they're impossible.

You ask me about Mrs Joad—truth to tell, she is rather a problem. The younger generation, I suppose one ought to say; but I don't much believe in these distinctions. She is a tall, straight shingled woman of 25. Came to London, School of Economics, read Shaw, thought she ought to live with a man; did; took up with a clever little bounder called Joad; lived with him; married him; found a letter from a woman in a drawer; left him; now has a room of her own, and walks out with various Cambridge young men, who are not entirely devoted to the fashionable foible of loving their own sex. Now comes the point. Being thus, one would have thought emancipated to the verge of dissolution, she won't let Joad divorce her. Him she wishes to divorce. But why does respect for convention suddenly assert itself here? Anyhow, she is without illusions, and faithful as these young women are; fiery; on her dignity, and quite capable of biting the end of Angus' [Davidson] nose off, if he should put upon her which God knows, Angus is the last man to do. She quarrelled all day with Dadie (the fair young man Gwen saw in the basement) but has, I think, affection and respect for the old Woolves—the male wolf anyhow.

Have you any views on loving one's own sex? All the young men are so inclined, and I can't help finding it mildly foolish; though I have no particular reason. For one thing, all the young men tend to the pretty and ladylike, for some reason, at the moment. They paint and powder, which wasn't the style in our day at Cambridge. I think it does imply some clingingness—a tiny lap dog, called Sackville West, came to see me the other day (a cousin of my aristocrat and will inherit Knole) and my cook said, Who was the lady in the drawing room? He has a voice like a girls, and a face like a persian cats, all white and serious, with large violet eyes and fluffy cheeks. Well, you can't respect the amours of a creature like *that*. Then the ladies, either in self protection, or imitation or genuinely, are given to their sex too. My aristocrat (oh, but I have now 2 or 3, whom I'll tell you about—they interest me) is violently Sapphic, and contracted such a passion for a woman cousin, that they fled to the Tyrol, or some mountainous retreat together, to be followed in an aeroplane by a brace of husbands.[1] The mothers of girls are said to take it to heart. I can't take

1. Virginia gives a slightly distorted version of Vita's elopement with Violet Trefusis, who was not a cousin but a friend since childhood. In February 1920

155

either of these aberrations seriously. To tell you a secret, I want to incite my lady to elope with me next. Then I'll drop down on you and tell you all about it.

Karin Stephen is giving a party with me; so on the 4th of Feb. think of me with commiseration and affection. For its all my damned sentimental desire to be of use to the afflicted thats to blame. I've just been involved in another affair of the kind with the poet Eliot, and Leonard says it is positively disgusting—this trait in me—pure vanity. Now is it? She is imprisoned in a kind of fastness of callousness; cant feel or hate, or enjoy; and has a purely fictitious idea that if only she could see people, in crowds, constantly but never alone, for she dreads intimacy, she would be cheered and made like other people. So once a month there is to be a party—and each party is to be mothered by Karin and one other lady—and each will be a ghastly failure, and she will fling herself on her bed in tears. Halfway through every evening, the vanity of life dawns upon her; and she despairs. It is a curious case, and she suffers, I believe, tortures.

Well, this is all very rambling; merely a gossip and I don't suppose you realise in the least how the flowers coming from you, on the eve of my birthday too, pleased me. There they are, against my painted walls, great bouquets of yellow and red and pink. They rather remind me of all your quips and cranks, and sitting by the river at the Grange, when you made me smoke one of Sir George's[1] cigars—and I so much wanted you to admire me, and thought I was a desolate old stick compared with the younger generation. But now we are back at the Neo Pagans; and then there's a great deal to be said, which I shall continue in a few days.

Let me see your memoirs, and send any scrap of a letter you like to dictate to that dear old creature Gwen.

Yrs. aff.
V.W.

Sussex

1525: To Logan Pearsall Smith

52 *Tavistock Sqre.* [*W.C.*1]

Postcard
[25 January 1925]

I was too shy yesterday to put to you a question which interests me deeply.

---

they ran away, intending to spend the rest of their lives together, but only got as far as Amiens in France, where their husbands, Harold Nicolson and Denys Trefusis, caught up with them and persuaded them to separate and return.
1. Sir George Darwin, Gwen Raverat's father, a professor of astronomy and physics, who lived at Newnham Grange, Cambridge.

Did you read my article in Vogue—"Indiscretions"[1]; and if so did you think, as an impartial critic, that it was inferior to/or in any way differed from articles that I write for The Nation?

Much depends upon your answer.

Virginia Woolf

Library of Congress

1526: To V. SACKVILLE-WEST

52 *Tavistock Square, London, W.C.*1

Tuesday [27 January 1925]

My dear Vita,

I was just writing to ask you to dine, when the devil of influenza and headache returned, and I have had to promise to lead the life of a hermit for a fortnight.

But if you would come and drink a mild tea cup with me on Friday it would be angelic and charitable and very very dull (for you).

I say ¼ to 5 because I have only one maid; she may be out: then you couldn't get in.

This sort of thing doesn't strike d—d aristocrats. It's one of their drawbacks—the others I will recount on Friday.

Ever Yr

V.W.

Berg

1527: To LOGAN PEARSALL SMITH

52 *Tavistock Square, London, W.C.*1

Wednesday [28 January 1925]

Dear Logan,

It is very good of you to send me the books, and to bother to make enquiries. It will be a great help to me, as I am completely at sea about Modern American Literature.[2]

I am sorry your visit was so disagreeable to you—one ought to leave a tea party happier not more miserable. But you have the laugh of me. I had planned such a trap for you—I did send one article to Vogue, but it was intended for The Nation, and just about to be printed, when Todd[3]

1. *Vogue*, late November 1924.
2. Virginia published *American Fiction* in the *Saturday Review of Literature*, 1 August 1925.
3. Dorothy Todd, editor of the British *Vogue*, 1922-6. She commissioned several Bloomsbury writers to contribute to the magazine, in order to expand its scope beyond fashion articles.

became clamorous, and rather than write specially for her, I snatched it from Leonard, to his fury. And I hoped you would detect signs of Todd and Vogue in every word.

I am in bed with the influenza, (which I hope I did not give you—perhaps that accounts for my disagreeableness the other day) and have been ruminating the whole question of Vogue and Lit. Sup. and Robert Bridges and respectability and Mayfair. On top of my ruminations comes a letter from a young man, who writes for The Lit. Sup., complaining that they have cut a very mildly irreverent story from his last review. That sort of thing does seem to me bad for young writers—perhaps worse than the vulgarity, which is open and shameless, of Vogue. Anyhow, the young would say, Todd lets you write what you like, and its your own fault if you conform to the stays and the petticoats. Then, Duncan says he is perfectly ready to paint covers for her, or ball rooms for Lady Cunard—who doesnt know one picture from another, and has a drawing room filled with the riff raff of London (I hope this does not hurt your feelings) Duncans argument is that if Bloomsbury has real pearls, they can be scattered anywhere without harm.

Perhaps we aren't quite sure of our pearls—I don't know. It is all very complicated. One thing emerges however—except for a few stars, whom she pays what they ask, Todd's prices are exactly the same as The Nation's.

Forgive this tedious and influenza letter, and do not allow my perversities to prevent you from coming again.

Yours very Sincerely
Virginia Woolf

Library of Congress

1528: To Ethel Sands   52 *Tavistock Square, W.C.*1

Wednesday [28 January 1925]

Dear Ethel,

Leonard is dining out in Chelsea on the 9th; shall I come alone (but what time?) and might Leonard fetch me later, if you don't mind his not dressing. The 6th we are engaged.

I've been in bed with a slight attack of the influenza, and as I have a little temperature still, I suppose I shan't get to you tomorrow.

What a bore! But don't you think you might come and see me—Would Sunday be possible? tea? It would be a great treat to see you, and I don't think there's the least risk of infection. I often get these temperatures and nobody catches them.

My party weighs me down with horror. Will you be an angel, and merely exert your genius as a hostess. Think only of others—expect no pleasure for yourself—you will be rewarded one of these days, but not on Wednesday 4th.

No wine, no food, nothing. But I count on you.

Yrs affect
V.W.

Wendy Baron

1529: To V. Sackville-West

52 *T.[avistock] S.[quare, London, W.C.*1]

Thursday [29 January 1925]

My dear Vita,

I ought to take up Rebecca Wests line when you offered her a lift in a Rolls-Royce—but being of a humbler nature, I accept peaches, kummel, everything, with complete gratitude and delight. Leonard and I sat down very critically to your peaches last night, doubting if they could be what they looked. And they were—heavenly, delicious.

I did not really deserve them either, as I got up yesterday, and consider myself quit of the disease. In honesty I have to admit a *slight* temperature still, in case you think it wiser not to come, but I often get this when I'm well, and never infect anyone, so I hope you will come—tomorrow, a quarter to five. We are making money very comfortably out of Seducers. I am very pleased, not only commercially, but I think it to people's credit, considering how out of the way it is, in size and price and meaning and everything.

I'm fishing for your poem [*The Land*]—thats what I'm after. Do you see my line? I've been engaged (in fact it gave me the influenza) violently arguing with Logan Pearsall Smith the morality of writing for Vogue and Heinemann, as against the Times Lit. Sup. and the Hogarth Press. Do you write differently for different people? Does Todd pay you immense sums? Does the Editor of the Lit. Sup. cut out your improper stories? Do you feel sanctified by Leonard's character when you write for him?

All these questions I will ask you tomorrow. I wish I had been able to come to your cousin's [Eddy S.W.] party—I've had very bad luck lately.

(By the way, if you meet Lady Colefax do *not* say that you are coming here tomorrow, as I have put her off.)

One thing more, and I have done—Mrs Candy's [Vita's typist] present address. She said she was moving: and I want her to type some things quickly.

Now with a thousand thanks, dear Mrs Nicolson, for the lovely peaches, which I will *not* throw at your head,

> Your affate
> V.W.

We are giving an awful, awful, awful party (I'll tell you about it) but you and Mr Nicolson MUST come.

No peaches will avail if you dont.

Berg

1530: TO LYTTON STRACHEY   52 *Tavistock Sqre*

[31 January 1925]

An appalling party is being given by Woolves and Stephens at No 50 Gordon Sqre. on Wednesday next—9.30.

No wine; no food; nothing (except indeed Philip Ritchie).[1]

If you like to come, we shall be enchanted.

I'm in bed with the influenza: but recovering.

> Yr. V.W.

A letter would be comforting.

Strachey Trust

1531: TO ETHEL SANDS   52 *Tavistock Square, W.C.1*

Saturday [31 January 1925]

Dear Ethel,

Alas—Monday is no good. To make it worse, I'm afraid I shan't be able to come on the 9th. I've had to retire to bed again, and Leonard, who is a terrible fuss, insists upon my going down to Rodmell, after the horrors of the party are over.

I feel I am behaving in a most tiresome way—all the more so because I mistook your invitation in the first place—thought the maid said 'Mr *or* Mrs Woolf' and so thrust myself singly upon you, when, so she now tells me, you wanted both or neither.

Forgive and forget, and come and see me, and ask both or neither again.

> Yrs affect
> V.W.

Wendy Baron

1. The eldest son of Lord Ritchie of Dundee. Lytton Strachey had met him and fallen in love with him while Ritchie was still an undergraduate. He became a barrister, but died young in 1928.

1532: To R. C. Trevelyan   52 *Tavistock Square, W.C.*1

Typewritten
[January 1925]

My dear Bob,

We would like to print your poems [*Poems and Fables*], and think we ought to keep it a small book, which we could print ourselves. Thus, it would be better to leave out the Prelude to the long poem. I think you said there was another poem, which Desmond is printing [in the *New Statesman*]. Perhaps you would send us that, when convenient. The poems you left with me would make about the right length for printing ourselves; anything longer would mean waiting a considerable time.

As it is, of course we can't bind ourselves to have it done by any particular time. But this is only to say that we should like to do it, and details can wait. I cannot write on a typewriter, but I hope enough emerges to make my meaning plain.

Yours ever,
Virginia Woolf

Sussex

1533: To Marjorie Joad   52 *Tavistock Sqre, W.C.*

Monday [2 February 1925]

My dear Marjorie,

Your letter is a great disappointment to us both. Leonard will write to you, this is merely privately, not from the Press. I'm very worried to think that the work may have been too much for you, and that we, perhaps, could have made things easier than we did. If the doctor advises you not to go on, of course there is nothing else to be said. But we both feel that we shall miss having you much more than you probably realise. I don't think anybody could have been nicer to us both, and for my own part I feel that I shan't find anybody I like so much working with. But we must see you, and not settle anything in a hurry.

It would be very good of you if you could send a line, or get someone else to, to say how you are.

I had to retire to bed again on Friday, and am still there and shan't be able to go to the party after all. Leonard is going to give it for me. I got a violent headache—temperature again, and rather doubt that I shall be up before Wednesday or Thursday and then we shall try to get a few days at Rodmell. Angus seemed to be sickening, but has recovered today. What a world! My only gratification is that I don't think I can have given you the flu, or you would have started it before.

Rumours of the world reach me, rather obscurely—Vita arrived with an enormous dog on a chain: a pure bred spaniel, which is to have a puppy, for our benefit; but can I live up to a Sackville Hound? Then the police arrived, to say her motor had no lights: then old Mr Pritchard[1] appeared and offered to bail her out. Then at 10 this morning, a strong smell of burning issued from the water closet: Nelly flew into a panic; Leonard went for the fireman: I sat up in bed and advised Nelly to watch the smoke with a bucket of water in case of flames—which she did. Firemen arrived, and said they must take up the stairs. Smoke still issued. At last the man next door owned to having lit a fire in his flue. Leonard lost his temper. Nelly banged my door. The handle flew off. Everyone went out. I found myself locked in: and now, at 4.30, have only just been let out. Its odd how life assumes a melodramatic quality directly one's ill in bed. I daresay your ceiling will fall in the night. Ring me up if so, and I will offer consolation.

But you must be dying to hear about the servants party. It transpires that Mr Harland [Keynes's servant] had hired two suits—one for Mrs Harland as Cupid; one for himself as Napoleon—which would have suited him very well. Then "that little word Mister", as he put it, being omitted on the card, he flew into a rage, took the Cupid and Napoleon back at once, and was seen scowling at the area when the dance was at its height. Nelly was panic struck; happily George, the greengrocer's boy who is walking out with Daisy was there, and no violence ensued. But you can imagine what a state of frantic excitement Bloomsbury is in today.

I can't think of any other news. I am reading Mansfield Park, two words at a time. Lady Colefax has invited me to tea. Lord Berners has asked me to dine, and I don't think anybody else has shown the slightest interest in me.

I ought to be working at those damnable essays [*The Common Reader*]; but can't imagine anyone wishing to read them, so why bother?

Besides half my pleasure in writing my books will be gone, now you have taken up with Heinemanns, and will be riding in your coach.

Shall you ask me to come and see you? Don't be proud, and forget your basement days.

Oh God! how I shall hate not having you to tease, and not having you to boast to, and not having you to look at in your handsome new jersey which was a base imitation of mine. Tears would have visited even your strong eyes could you have heard me read your letter, and how Leonard said he thought you always came out of everything so extraordinarily well, to which I replied Yes. But then she has an extraordinary nice nature. Well, I've always said so, said Leonard. This is an accurate verbatim account, and in the highest degree complimentary.

Now I must stop, for my head is not capable of much amusement.

1. The solicitor, whose firm had two floors of 52 Tavistock Square.

Also I must look to see if the house is on fire again. If so, Angus is to fetch the Brigade, Nelly having gone round to 50 to discuss Mr Harlands behaviour with the others.

Please be very careful, and consider whether it would not be a good thing to go down to Rodmell with a friend for a change.

Your affte
V.W.

T. W. Marshall

1534: To Jacques Raverat   *52 Tavistock Square* [*W.C.*1]

Feb: 5th 1925

My dear Jacques,

I was struck down with influenza the very day I wrote to you, and am still in bed. Otherwise, I should have sent off my proofs [of *Mrs Dalloway*] before, but they were muddled up, and influenza makes me like a wet dish cloth—even to sort them was beyond me. I have left them uncorrected. Much has been re-written. Do a little re-writing on my behalf. Anyhow, don't cast me from you; and say nothing, or anything, as you like. (It will be sent tomorrow, 6th.)

Being bedridden, my view of the world has had a great thumb put over it. I can't think how you keep so sharp and clear. I have seen Clive Bell, who gave me another headache; he is a good fellow, however. I was so rash as to tell him he praised his Polly Flinders too much—his pretty Poll —his paramour—his Mary Hutch I mean. (I forget if you are aware of that highly respectable alliance, which is far more lasting and punctiliously observed than any marriage). I said he should not be praising her legs in company, or cracking up her little witticisms, or even repeating the tributes of other gentlemen. But, he said, he did it to show Vanessa that she is a serious human being. He said, just because Mary dresses well, and you and Nessa badly, you think her dull: so I must prove how silly you both are.

Clive is now shaped like a spade and thick as an oak tree. He wears bright blue socks, which he is forever hitching up, and his trousers, for some reason which a man may know, are always above his knees. But how good hearted he is—bunches of grapes arrive for me; and yet I never do anything but bite his nose off when I see him, and laugh at him behind his back. I have an idea you and Gwen hated him. Let me assure you, you were wrong. Not that I claim for him any of the heroic virtues. Being bred a Puritan, (in the main—but I had a French great grandmother to muddle me) I warm my hands at these red-hot-coal men. I often wish I had married a foxhunter. It is partly the desire to share in life somehow, which is denied to us writers. Is it to you painters? Ever since I was a child I have envied

163

people who did things—but even influenza shall not mislead me into egoistical autobiographical revelations—Of course, I long to talk to you about myself, my character, my writings, but am withheld—by what?

Karin's party came off last night, and I lay in bed and imagined it all very brilliant. Leonard put on his deceased brother-in-law's (who died in a Bath at Eastbourne) dress clothes, and went off to brew the punch. Hope Mirrlees arrived half an hour early (do you admire her novels?—I can't get an ounce of joy from them, but we like seeing her and Jane [Harrison] billing and cooing together). Then came 40 young Oxford men, and three very pretty girls; Vanessa, Mary Hutch, Clive and Lytton—Lytton gravitated to the 40 young men, and was heard booming and humming from flower to flower. Vanessa, who had not dressed, sat commandingly on a sofa, talking to a sculptor called Tomlin,[1] and to no one else, for she is beyond the pale now, makes no attempt to conciliate society, and often shocks me by her complete indifference to all my floating loves and jealousies, but with such a life, packed like a cabinet of drawers, Duncan, children, painting, Roger—how can she budge an inch or find a cranny of room for anyone? Clive came in late, having been dining with Mary at her new house in Regent's Park. She has a ship's steward to serve at table, and whether for this reason or another provides the most spicy liquors, foods, cocktails and so on—for example an enormous earthenware dish, last time I was there, garnished with every vegetable, in January—peas, greens, mushrooms, potatoes; and in the middle the tenderest cutlets, all brewed in a sweet stinging aphrodisiac sauce. I tell you, I could hardly waddle home, or compose my sentiments. So Clive gets a little warm, and very red about the gills towards midnight.

Then Karin, who felt the approach of disillusionment about eleven, ran down to the kitchen and borrowed the housemaid's gramophone. The 40 young men began waltzing, and the three lovely girls sat together flirting in corners. Isn't it an odd thing that Bloomsbury parties are always thus composed—40 young men; all from Oxford too, and three girls, who are admitted on condition that they either dress exquisitely, or are some man's mistress, or love each other. Much preferring my own sex, as I do, or at any rate, finding the monotony of young mens' conversation considerable, and resenting the eternal pressure which they put, if you're a woman, on one string, find the disproportion excessive, and intend to cultivate women's society entirely in future. Men are all in the light always: with women you swim at once into the silent dusk. But to return. They danced. Leonard got horribly bored. He was set upon by little Eddie Sackville West, who is as appealing as a kitten, a stray, a mangy, unloved kitten; and this poor

1. Stephen Tomlin, then aged 24. He later sculpted the bust of Virginia now in The National Portrait Gallery.

164

boy, after pouring forth his woes (all men confide in Leonard—especially such as love their own sex) sat by mistake down on the best tea cups. Being an aristocrat out of his element, he was considerably discomposed. Sweets and jams stuck to his behind, and Leonard had to dust him, and pat him, and finally leave him; trying I believe, to smoke a pipe in full evening dress, and white waistcoat. They work very hard, the aristocracy. Karin was heard to say, between the waltzes, Isn't this jolly?—On being assured it was, she plucked up heart, and means to give another party, with another hostess, next month.

Really, you have done me good. This is the first time I have cantered out on paper this fortnight. I find a great pleasure in waking all the doves in their dovecots—in stirring my words again. But this I can never explain to a painter, I suppose; how words live in companies, never used, except when one writes.

What about the autobiography? You jeered at me for saying I would print it. But I swear I will. I can see the very book it shall be and if you don't look out, I shall add to it some of your pictures, with a description of them from my own pen. (This is a threat, because writers can't write about anything except writing).

So now I must stop, and do a little cross stitch, and I shall dwell upon you, as indeed I have been doing a great deal, lying here—and though you'll snap my nose off for saying so—with considerable admiration as well as affection.

Yours,
Sussex   V.W.

1535: To Gerald Brenan   52 *T.*[avistock] *S.*[quare, *W.C.*1]
Thursday [5 February 1925]

My dear Gerald,
    I am ashamed not to have written to thank you for the flowers, but I have been very headachy and stupid as an ox.

How did you know that I have a sentimental passion for the coloured anemones? and these are the first I have seen. It was a stroke of genius on your part, and promises well for your book [on St Teresa], which I hope shortly to read.

We go to Rodmell tomorrow, and I hope to see you when we get back.

Yours
Virginia Woolf
George Lazarus

1536: To Margaret Llewelyn Davies

Monks House, Rodmell
[Sussex]

Typewritten
Feb 9th [1925]

Dearest Margaret,
   This is a great deal clearer than my handwriting, you must admit, though it spells badly. I left your letter at home, so I know I shall forget to answer some of the questions. However, first; Leonard says he "will be glad to consider any manuscript" you choose to send him; this refers to Mrs Layton.[1] Second, the best time for Mr [William] Nicholson to come and see the decorations alone (in which I much sympathise) is any afternoon between two and three. Later, there is no one to let him in. We are in the basement. Dickens next. I used to think David Copperfield a masterpiece; but having read Hard Times lately, I was disgusted and disappointed. It seemed to me mere sentiment and melodrama, and your boasted zest for life, nothing but rant and rage. No doubt it is a bad one; and I shall try another. If you want a modern with a zest, why not try Proust? He has as much of it as Dickens, and his life is (to me) of a far more interesting kind. Ten volumes however, difficult French; I've only read three. I transacted influenza in the drawing room, and if it had not been for one of my old familiar headaches, should have got off lightly. Many thanks for the Favil press notice; I think we shall try them, if they do small jobs, for ordinary printers fail lamentably. But when are you coming to see our works?
   Once more we are reorganising—Mrs Joad having finally retired with slight pneumonia; and Miss Bernadette Murphy having taken her place. The difficulty of business is not the work, but the subordinates—witness Lilian.[2] If only they were dumb, wooden, enduring! Leonard went back last night; I return tomorrow. This I shall venture to address, probably wrongly. My mother once lived at Well Walk [Hampstead], in a lovely house. One of these days I hope we may meet, and Monks House is always a little hurt by your indifference.

                                        Yrs
                                        V.W.

Sussex

1. A member of the Women's Co-operative Guild, who contributed a long autobiographical essay to *Life As We Have Known It*, edited by Margaret Llewelyn Davies, introduced by Virginia, and published by the Hogarth Press in 1931.
2. Lilian Harris was Assistant Secretary of the Women's Co-operative Guild, when Margaret Llewelyn Davies was Secretary.

1537: To Marjorie Joad   52 *Tavistock Square* [*W.C.*1]
Typewritten
Sunday [15 February 1925]

My dear Marjorie, or rather foolish, wild, unpractical woman—why should you torment yourself with thinking you are hated and despised and forgotten—that people slander you, and the Woolves revile you? Is it the effect of lying in bed? One moments thought (as people say) should have told you, what is true—I only got back from Rodmell on Tuesday night; since when, what with a headache and Murphy[1] and the Press, I have scarcely been out, and written only the completely idiotic trash which I have to do for my abominable books. All is forgiven to influenza though. Moreover, I peered in at your gratings in a hail storm on Saturday and fancied rows of blizzard-bitten women recumbent, coughing, spitting, swearing. However, I also figure Marjorie Joad perpetually attended by troops of Knights, who alight from their horses with bouquets. The old Woolves are not acceptable visitors compared with young Knights. You must admit the force of that—even in your craziest, crankiest mood. Both are old; both shabby; moreover, their dog has the mange.

That is what you invalids make no allowance for—the mange; the Murphys. Grizzle has a pink hole in her back; Murphy has mushrooms for fingers. Oh how my back aches with stooping over those infernal trays and tossing 'u's into t boxes and 'y's into 'j's. Despair has set in. Leonard has devised a spring list which combines three founts and five different sizes. The Cambridge Press has done it—why not the Hogarth? And Angus (who has a touch of enteric) and Murphy (who has fungus on the finger) are set to help me. You will wish for a complete account of Murphy; you would rather like it to be very very acid (which I can be when I like). The truth is I have only done two days work with her, and except for this brilliant comparison—she is a mushroom—have scarcely a word to throw at the poor dog. All powder, paint, walking sticks whose handles come off in the street, yellow shoes, shingled hair, officers riding up on chargers, scented sonnets dropped into the pillar box—all *that* kind of thing which we used to know once upon a time in our palmy days is now a thing of the past. We have sunk twenty five degrees in fashion; 100 in looks; mushrooms wear waterproofs and black slippers down at heel. For their other qualities, you must ask Leonard. For my own part, a little beauty is what I crave; anybody can be good; wits I have myself.

There! Very cleverly I end on an agreeable note. But what news is there? Leonard has just written the most intemperate abusive letter to

---

1. Bernadette Murphy stayed as an assistant at the Press only from February until June 1925.

Austin Johnson[1] I ever saw. Austin culminated by asking Angus not to call him a liar to his face. Leonard replies, Your insolence to Mrs Joad and Mr Rylands was enough; this is superfluous. Ask any man woman or dog in Cambridge to explain the Freud prospectus (he is still asking, do we give a reduction, which books are out etc etc). But let us never be troubled by such a surly vindictive lying brute as A.J. again. This is not exaggerated. So if you hear of an elderly corpse floating in the Cam, swollen to a disgusting size, and purple about the gills, that will be your old friend who has taken himself off in a hurry. But no; he will survive to crawl over our corpses yet.

My party was absolutely heavenly. I lay in bed and imagined it. Never shall I go to a party any other way. One is so brilliant; so happy; so beautiful. What really happened was a solid mix of incompatibles. Vanessa Bell behaved disgracefully; science scowled at art; letters meandered. There was Lytton Strachey held down by the widow of a Professor Malthus. His anguish penetrated even to me. Mrs [Naomi] Mitchison fastened herself upon the heir to Knole, who only likes boys; he, too, sobbed aloud. Then Leonard went the rounds with large (but alas, broken) cups, the crockery having given out, full of what would have been punch if they had not forgotten the rum. Roger Fry enjoyed it immensely, because he met a more or less negro lady, one of Corkies friends who had got in by mistake. And so on and so on.

You and I will give a party in the summer, for compatibles only, in the studio. I insist upon a sufficiency of young women. Oh the unnumerable dull young men I know! I forget why I am so cross about this at the moment; but whereever I go, there springs out some young man who writes, and is shameless. Oh for beauty, oh for modesty! Really, they are more interesting now—the modest and chaste, I mean. But *you*—that hardly applies to you.

[*in Virginia's handwriting:*]
There! I have left off upon an agreeable note again: We have just had tea—Leonard has discovered 8 fleas on Grizzle: Bob Trevelyan is done: He [Leonard] has gone down to start Nancy.[2] Lottie is spending Sunday with us; they are making marmalade, and I modelled the head of a dog in pastry for our Plum Tart today. These, you see, are the facts of life; not your vain imaginings.

Let us know when you would like to see us, which you would like to see, how you are, when you emerge, and any other sense or nonsense that comes into your head.

1. A bookseller's representative, or 'bagman', from Cambridge.
2. In April of this year the Hogarth Press printed and published R. C. Trevelyan's *Poems and Fables* and Nancy Cunard's *Parallax*.

168

But do not impute base, selfish, dishonourable thoughts to your old, attached, and quite submissive friends,

L. and V. Woolf, Hogarth Press, Tavistock Square.

etc etc etc

T. H. Marshall

1538: To Richard Aldington   52 *Tavistock Square, W.C.*1

Typewritten
16th Feb. [1925]

Dear Mr Aldington,

I have now heard from Tom [Eliot], who says that he is writing to me, I suppose on this matter, tomorrow. Therefore I will postpone further discussion until I have heard what he says, and will then write to you.

I will only say now that your account of conditions at the Bank is quite new to me. It is entirely different from what we had gathered from Tom or Vivien. She definitely told me, that if it were not for her she thought Tom would be happier in the Bank than as literary editor of the Nation.[1] In talking to us, Tom has always laid great stress upon the extraordinary kindness which the Bank has shown him. This was one of his stock arguments against leaving. And in our last talk on the subject—about a year ago—he said not a word of complaint of his work or his treatment and led us to think that he had been given promotion, and had every reason to be grateful to them. He certainly said that he was thankful he had stayed on at the Bank. The truth is I expect that he takes different views at different times and to different people. He knows that we urged him to accept the Nation and is naturally anxious to justify himself to us. But of course what you say he tells you is very important and makes a great deal of difference. We are in the position of having urged him to leave the bank and to take up journalism; and his arguments against doing both are deeply impressed upon us.

May I say that I dont think you realise the force of what we say of his utter misery over the Nation and his incapacity to take the plunge? He told us then that he was desperate; the offer was good; we urged it; and yet it was effort and misery thrown away. My husband says he would give you his reasons for thinking Tom should not leave the Bank if you liked to see him on Monday or Tuesday at the office. Tom always consults us jointly.

1. T. S. Eliot had been offered the literary editorship of the *Nation* in February 1923. He declined it, and remained at Lloyd's Bank until the autumn of 1925, when, with Lady Rothermere's support, he was able to devote himself exclusively to writing, and to editing the *Criterion*.

I would not have suggested approaching the Bank directors if it had not been that Lady R[othermere] has already done so, presumably with Tom's knowledge, and certainly with complete success. Naturally I shall not take such a step off my own bat. Yes: the cottage is another "mere palliative" but every letter I have had from Tom or Vivien lately has reiterated their desire to have a country cottage and his belief that most of their ill health is due to their not having one.

Please dont think it necessary to apologise for differing from me and saying so outright. I feel that we are groping in the dark, and the only chance of seeing light is to say whatever one has in ones head—as I do herewith!

Yours very sincerely,
Virginia Woolf

Texas

1539: To V. Sackville-West
52 Tavistock Square, London, W.C.1

Tuesday [17 February? 1925]

My dear Vita,

We would like very much to come, but do you think that Lady Gerald[1] would ask us another night?

I'm being bothered by a beast of a headache, and have to keep very quiet and not dine out till I've got rid of it—which I hope to do completely next week.

Please thank Lady Gerald, and please come and see us yourself.

Seducers [in Ecuador] still selling.

Yr VW.

Berg

1540: To W. J. H. Sprott   52 *Tavistock Square, W.C.*1

Typewritten
18th Feb [1925]

Dear Sebastian,

I look forward to reading your novel;[2] but it has not yet come. I'm afraid that it may be some little time before I am able to read it, as I have been having a relapse from influenza and have to be very quiet for a bit.

1. Dorothy Wellesley, the poet. In 1914 she married Lord Gerald Wellesley (afterwards 7th Duke of Wellington), from whom she separated in the mid-1920s. She was an intimate friend of Vita.
2. This novel was never published.

This also makes it rather doubtful whether we can come to Cambridge as you suggest—much though we should both like to.

We have not yet settled, but we are thinking of going away for a holiday about then. So you must make arrangements independently of us.

I think we could get rooms always if we came.

Many thanks for asking us.

Leonard wants me to add that he was not able to send you the books yesterday, but if he possibly can, will send them later. It is a question of space, as usual.

Yours
Virginia Woolf

King's

1541: To Gwen Raverat   52 *Tavistock Square, W.C.*1
11th March [1925]

Dearest Gwen,

Your and Jacques' letter came yesterday, and I go about thinking of you both in starts, and almost constantly underneath everything, and I don't know what to say.[1] The thing that comes over and over is the strange wish I have to go on telling Jacques things. This is for Jacques, I say to myself; I want to write to him about happiness, about Rupert [Brooke], and love. It had become to me a sort of private life, and I believe I told him more than anyone, except Leonard; I become mystical as I grow older and feel an alliance with you and Jacques which is eternal, not interrupted, or hurt by never meeting. Then of course, I have now for you—how can I put it?—I mean the feeling that one must reverence?—is that the word— feel shy of, so tremendous an experience; for I cannot conceive what you have suffered. It seems to me that if we met, one would have to chatter about every sort of little trifle, because there is nothing to be said.

And then, being, as you know, so fundamentally an optimist, I want to make you enjoy life. Forgive me, for writing what comes into my head. I think I feel that I would give a great deal to share with you the daily happiness. But you know that if there is anything I could ever give you, I would give it, but perhaps the only thing to give is to be oneself with people. One could say anything to Jacques. And that will always be the same with you and me. But oh, dearest Gwen, to think of you is making me cry—why should you and Jacques have had to go through this? As I told him, it is your love that has forever been love to me—all those years ago, when you used to come to Fitzroy Square, I was so angry and you

---

1. Jacques Raverat died at Vence, in southern France, on 7 March. Before his death he dictated a letter to Virginia about *Mrs Dalloway*, which she had sent him in proof.

were so furious, and Jacques wrote me a sensible manly letter, which I answered, sitting at my table in the window. Perhaps I was frightfully jealous of you both, being at war with the whole world at the moment. Still, the vision has become to me a source of wonder—the vision of your face; which if I were painting I should cover with flames, and put you on a hill top. Then, I don't think you would believe how it moves me that you and Jacques should have been reading Mrs Dalloway, and liking it. I'm awfully vain I know; and I was on pins and needles about sending it to Jacques; and now I feel exquisitely relieved; not flattered: but one does want that side of one to be acceptable—I was going to have written to Jacques about his children, and about my having none—I mean, these efforts of mine to communicate with people are partly childlessness, and the horror that sometimes overcomes me.

There is very little use in writing this. One feels so ignorant, so trivial, and like a child, just teasing you. But it is only that one keeps thinking of you, with a sort of reverence, and of that adorable man, whom I loved.

Yours,
V.W.

Sussex

1542: To Gwen Raverat   52 *Tavistock Square, W.C.*

Sunday, March 22nd [1925]

Dearest Gwen,

It was a great relief to get your letter. I had been feeling that perhaps I had said something idiotically foolish, to hurt you more. Not that one is hurt by foolish things however. But this is a practical letter. We are going on the 26th to Hotel Cendrillon, Cassis for 10 days. That is all the time we can get off, owing to our books; but if you could come and stay a night, do. I'm afraid you will be in Italy then. I don't see any chance of going abroad later—we have a new man [Angus Davidson] come to work, and he is anxious about being left alone. But write later, and suggest meeting somehow else.

Yes, I will tell you the whole of my life history one day, but I think it was my affair with Clive and Nessa[1] I was thinking of when I said I envied you and Jacques at Fitzroy square. For some reason that turned more of a knife in me than anything else has ever done.

What about the thing [his autobiography] Jacques was writing? Can I see it? Also, have you a snapshot or any photograph of him?

1. The flirtation between Virginia and Clive Bell, which began in Cornwall in the spring of 1908, little more than a year after Vanessa and Clive had married.

172

I go on making things up to tell him; and shall have to go on writing to you I believe.

But not now. Molly MacCarthy has been in, like a dreaming moth to give me a copy of Shakespeare, and now we have to dine with Clive: I'm quite well again, but had to put my head under my wing and sleep for a month.

Write if you would ever care to; for I should like nothing better.

Yours
V.W.

We shall be at Cassis till Monday 6th

Sussex

1543: To Molly MacCarthy   52 *Tavistock Square* [*W.C.*1]

[25 March 1925]

Dearest Moll,
    The Eliots address is
        9 Clarence Gate Gardens, N.W.1
    Write to him, as she is ill.

I think it would be a godsend to them to have a cottage for a time, as they seem in a desperate state of health and misery altogether.

Oh damn you for giving me Shakespeare. Why will the MacCarthys outdo us all in every way?

Off to France tomorrow but back in two weeks, when we may meet at the Club which I hear you're starting.

Ever your dear old friend

V.W.

Mrs Michael MacCarthy

1544: To W. J. H. Sprott   52 *Tavistock Square, W.C.*1

Typewritten

25th March 1925

Dear Sebastian,
    Your book has interested me very much, but on the whole we dont think we can publish it; though we are extremely sorry not to. My feeling is that you dont get going till rather late—it seems as if your theme interested you, and not the people; so that in spite of the fact that the end gets an emotion which is quite genuine, it is too late to tell; and as a whole the book is not pulled off. I only give you these criticisms as you asked me; honestly,

I dont trust myself on other peoples novels, simply because, as I write them myself, I get my eye out. I feel that you ought to stand more on your own feet, and that at present you accept too brilliantly what other people tell you and are afraid of your own observations. But this may well be nonsense. The other point is that the public won't like the theme or understand it, which of course makes it risky from the publishing point of view. But it will be very interesting to see what you write next, though after this plain speaking we have no right to ask you to let us see it.

Would you send Angus [Davidson] a card to say where you would like the MS sent?

I suppose you are no longer at Cambridge.

Yours
Virginia Woolf

King's

Letters 1545-1570 (April–July 1925)

The Common Reader was published on 23 April, and Mrs Dalloway on 14 May. Both had a generally good reception from the critics: Morgan Forster liked the novel; Lytton Strachey didn't. Inevitably the 'common reader' contrasted the intelligibility of Virginia's critical writing with the difficulty of her experimental novels, and she was patient in replying to her slightly bewildered correspondents, except Violet Dickinson, whom she advised to give up reading her books. She immediately embarked on a series of short stories, and then began to think out To the Lighthouse, which had been at the back of her mind for at least two years. There was a break of twelve days at Cassis in the south of France (26 March to 7 April), which she enjoyed in spite of the 'Bugger Bloomsbury' young men whom she found there. Her London social life expanded with her growing fame, and she was now in much demand, both in England and the United States, for contributions to periodicals. She accepted invitations from Lady Colefax as readily as she wrote for Vogue.

1545: To Vanessa Bell　　　　　　　　[*Hotel Cendrillon, Cassis, France*]

Postcard
[31 March 1925]

We sailed into this bay[1] yesterday, and thought of the Dolphin tribe. Perfectly happy here—hot, bright, omelettes, coffee in garden. Roger's pictures on every side, met Douglas Davidson [Angus's brother], Penrose[2] and mixed company of overdressed Greeks, L. refused to be introduced, lady novelist [Miss Toogood] still here, also gent [Mr Howard]. Much literary discussion, we sit out and walk Just off to Toulon.

　　　　　　　　　　　　　　　　　　　　　　　　　　V.W.

Berg

1546: To Vanessa Bell　　　　　　　　*Hotel Cendrillon, Cassis*
　　　　　　　　　　　　　　　　　　　　　　　[*France*]
Friday. April 3rd. [1925]

Dearest.
　　You don't deserve a letter, whereas Mary [Hutchinson] does. She has

1. Cassis is on the coast between Marseilles and Toulon.
2. Possibly Roland Penrose, then aged 24, later founder of the Institute of Contemporary Arts.

175

just written me 6 bright blue sheets full of gossip. Dolphin never writes, nor is it much consolation to me to be given your love by a stalwart bugger called [Hugh] Anderson last night—indeed, I was a good deal shocked to hear you called Vanessa familiarly by two such chattering long-winded wrynecked dry boned duffers as Tomlin[1] and Anderson. Lord lord for a little charm—an ounce of sympathy! For both of these I have to depend upon the New Zealand novelist Miss Toogood, whose health is positively collapsing under the strain of finishing her novel, which ought to have been out last autumn, and now won't be till next, though she sees the end in front of her, but can't drive herself an inch further. Mr Howard has practically finished his, and Miss Betsy Kingsford[2] thinks it one of the most beautifully moving touching books she has ever read—This is about all the news there is—except that Mrs —— from Australia has gone to Toulon to meet her daughter.

I wish to God that the Tomlins, Penroses, and Andersons had never left Bloomsbury. The rooms ring with their bright Bugger-Bloomsbury up to date bragging—all about Vanessa and Clive, and how Duncan looked out of the back window and told Clifford Sharp[3] his taxi was there; and dear good Angus reproved him; but Duncan, being very drunk,—and then Lady Colefax comes in, and how Vanessa and Sybil embraced. Can this be true? Have you really promised to give a party at Argyll House?[4] Oh dolphin, dolphin!

This place has every merit (except the prevalence of that species whom Duncan loves) food delicious; harbour divine, hot; sun; vineyards; olives; etc. etc. Old Gwen writes that she was greatly touched by Duncan's letter. We shall just miss her; and shall have to start back on Tuesday. We sit out all the morning; go for walks; go to Marseilles and Toulon, which is a lovely town, and altogether are very very happy and good and well disposed to the whole world, though I don't like hearing Dolphin called Vanessa in the public dining room. Modesty is my sin—after all.

Nobody writes to me, except Mary, and her letter is chiefly a quotation from Anatole France in French, with all the accents—I gather that the Raymonds and the Sebastians[5] and Max Beerbohm, Philip Ritchie and Ly Colefax all continue much as usual, but no-one has penetrated the cave where Dolphin lies couched, like some proud sea monster. We sailed round the coast the other day; we motored where a man had just driven over a precipice; then we had coffee in an Inn, and I bought a cake, and then Miss Toogood came, and told us about the blue gum trees in N. Zealand.

1. Stephen Tomlin's brother Garrow, who was killed flying in 1932.
2. A fellow guest at the hotel, whom Virginia calls 'Betsy Roberts' in her diary.
3. The editor of the *New Statesman* from its foundation in 1913 until 1931.
4. Lady Colefax's house in Chelsea.
5. Raymond Mortimer and W. J. H. ('Sebastian') Sprott.

A man called Tissamond says he will send me pictures for 10/- in a portfolio on hire.

Is this a good plan?

Yr B.

Leonard sends his love and kisses

× × ×

Berg

1547: To Gwen Raverat   52 *Tavistock Sqre.*

April 8th 1925

Dearest Gwen,

  After all, we had to come back a day earlier than we meant, as the hotel became crowded. But we had snuffed up every moment—it was fine incessantly, and I now see why you and Jacques pitched on the borders of that sea. But I was going, inconsistently, to beg you to live in London. Trust me to find you a house. Then I would flirt with your daughters, and talk the sun out of the sky with you. Paris is a hostile brilliant alien city. Nancy Cunard and Hope Mirrlees and myriads of the ineffective English live there, or rather hop from rock to rock. Here we grow slowly and sedately in our own soil. Coming back last night was like stepping into some grave twilit room, very spacious and quiet, with a few lights and the great misty squares, and everything very mute and muffled, and out at elbows.

  I cannot think what I was going to write to Jacques about love. I constantly thought of him at Cassis. I thought of him lying among those terraces and vineyards, where it is all so clear cut, and logical and intense, and it struck me that, from not having seen him all these years, I have no difficulty in thinking him still alive. That is what I should like for myself, that there should be no breach, no submission to death, but merely a break in the talk. I liked that uncompromising reality of him: no sentimentality, and no beating about the bush. This is all very ill written, chopped and jerky, when I should like to write even the racketiest letter to Gwen beautifully, but I went out early this morning to see Nessa's new house [37 Gordon Square], and saw a woman killed by a motor car. This pitches one at once into a region where there is no certainty and one feels somehow, abject and cowed—exalted. I want so much to understand my own feelings about everything, to unravel and re-christen and not go dreaming my time away. Jacques' death will probably make you, because it will so intensify everything, a very interesting woman to me. But as I said before, I cannot conceive such an experience, not at your age.

177

I feel that Jacques was thinking a great deal of Rupert at the end. Rupert was a little mythical to me when he died. He was very rude to Nessa once, and Leonard, I think, rather disliked him; in fact Bloomsbury was against him, and he against them. Meanwhile, I had a private version of him which I stuck to when they all cried him down, and shall preserve somewhere infinitely far away—but how these feelings last, how they come over one, oddly, at unexpected moments—based on my week at Grant-chester [in 1911], when he was all that could be kind and interesting and substantial and goodhearted (I choose these words without thinking whether they correspond to what he was to you or anybody). He was, I thought, the ablest of all the young men; I did not then think much of his poetry, which he read aloud on the lawn; but I thought he would be Prime Minister, because he had such a gift with people, and such sanity, and force; I remember a weakly pair of lovers meandering in one day, just engaged, very floppy (A. Y. Campbell[1] and his bride who now writes on Shelley). You know how intense and silly or offhand in a self-conscious kind of way the Cambridge young then were about their loves—Rupert simplified them, and broadened them—humanised them—and then he rode off on a bicycle about a railway strike. Jacques says he thinks Rupert's poetry was poetry. I must read it again. I had come to think it mere barrel organ music, but this refers to the patriotic poems, and perhaps is unfair: but the early ones were all adjectives and contortions—weren't they? My idea was that he was to be Member of Parliament and edit the Classics, a very powerful, ambitious man, but not a poet. Still all this is no doubt wholly and completely wrong.

This morning to hearten myself, I read Jacques letter about Mrs Dalloway again.[2] I was afraid and indeed half sure, he wouldn't like it, as I meant to have asked him to let me dedicate to him. When you have time one day, do tell me why you liked it—or anything about it. This is partly author's vanity and that consuming interest in one's own work which is not entirely vanity—partly it springs from my own feeling that to be brought before you and Jacques was a tremendous ordeal, at that time, and the impression it made on you would mean more to me that what other people could say of it. But forgive this importunity, I am off for Easter to Rodmell—a place you'll have to visit. But when are you coming over? I can't tell you how that 10 days at Cassis has burnt truly upon my mind's eye the beauty and our happiness, and you and Jacques. Well, I am interrupted by an author, who rings up and says he or she must deliver a manuscript into my own hands. What about Jacques' autobiography?

1. Professor of Greek at the University of Liverpool, 1920-50. In 1912 he married Olwen Ward, author of *Shelley and the Unromantics*.
2. In her diary on 8 April, Virginia wrote that Jacques' letter "gave me one of the happiest days of my life".

This is a scrap—but only in meaning, for it is too long. I am too harried to write a nice letter, and yet I don't think you mind whether one writes a nice letter or not, so I shall send it. And I will certainly keep up the habit of garrulity, to which Jacques induced me. I never write a word to anybody nowadays—except for him, I don't think I wrote a letter in 8 weeks.

Tell me about your children.

Does the little creature [Gwen's daughter] write more poems?

Yours,
V.W.

Sussex

1548: To Lady Colefax   52 *Tavistock Square, W.C.*1

Typewritten

17th April, 1925

The Hogarth Press presents its compliments to Lady Colefax, and much regrets to inform her that after trying, for some hours, to interpret the following word

they are unable to do so, and thus cannot follow out Lady Colefax's wishes. Directly they are informed what the word is, they will send her whatever it may be. The betting is equally divided between Garnet and James. Mrs Woolf denies having anything to do with either. Mrs Woolf much looks forward to seeing Lady Colefax, and the novel [*Mrs Dalloway*] will be sent when out—next month.

We have the honour to remain, Lady Colefax's obliged, obedient, and slightly mystified humble servants,

The Hogarth Press

Michael Colefax

1549: To Lady Colefax   52 *Tavistock Square, W.C.*1

Typewritten

April 20th 1925

But the Hogarth Press must point out to her Ladyship that the Hogarth Press never did and never will publish any work by the distinguished writer called Garnett; if they did they would only be too pleased to carry out her ladyship's commands; as it is they can only regret and apologise and suggest that her Ladyship should apply to Messrs Chatto and Windus who publish Mr Garnetts works.

At the same time, Lady Colefax may like to know that Mrs Woolf has won her bet of two and six. She said it was Garnet not James, and guessing what Lady Colefax means is one of presses most enjoyable occupations, let alone the profit to the successful.

Michael Colefax

1550: To Gwen Raverat   52 *Tavistock Square* [*W.C.*1]

1st May [1925]

My dear Gwen,

It comes into my head to write to you, because I ought to be doing so many other things, and have refused to go to the Private View of the Royal Academy to do them; and now sit down and write to you, instead. I wish you didn't feel dumb: but, I reflect, you're a square-tipped painter; (and painters fingers are square); and I always connect this with some impermeability. You all live in the depths of the sea; except indeed Jacques, who was half chatterbox, as I am wholly chatterbox. Even now, I've so much to say to you, I can't begin. I wish you had someone to talk to. I wish I could be in reach of you. I believe somehow we should set up communication. You should paint, and I should walk about talking. Now and again you would take the brush from your lips and make some sagacious remark. That is the devil of these deaths—Thoby's[1] and Jacques: they leave life duller; and that is what one resents. Not the horror of the moment; but the flatness afterwards. But don't let it—let us polish off that demon. Indeed, my respect and belief in you is such that I can believe you will be a superb character, after my own heart. For, to tell you the truth, I have so little faith in myself, that I glorify some of my friends. Then you're younger than I am; and I feel bidden to stand in the relation to you of elder and wiser. Did you ever think of that? Do you remember an evening at the Grange, and the poplar trees, and Margaret[2] talking about Pragmatism? It comes back to me, half visually, the lawn and the poplars. What you say about Mrs Dalloway is exactly what I was after. I had a sort of terror that I had inflicted something on you, sending you that book at that moment. I will look at the scenes you mention.[3] It was a subject that I have kept cooling in my mind until I felt I could touch it without bursting into flame all over. You can't think what a raging furnace it is still to me—madness and doctors and being forced. But let's change the subject.

1. Thoby Stephen, Virginia's brother, who died of typhoid in 1906 at the age of 26.
2. Margaret Darwin, Gwen's sister, who married Geoffrey Keynes, Maynard's brother.
3. The madness and suicide of Septimus Warren Smith.

Let me have anything you will of Jacques'. I miss him so queerly. It is that obstinate life of his that would never be submissive that I find myself wanting; his hard, truculent mind. And reading his letters again I find he says I knew very little of him really. Tell me more one of these days. I like making him up as I walk about London—now to buy a cup of coffee, now to take tea with Lady Colefax, who interests me, as you would be interested by a shiny cupboard carved with acanthus leaves, to hold whisky—so hard and shiny and bright is she; and collects all the intellects about her, as a parrot picks up beads, without knowing Lord Balfour from Duncan Grant. Now I want to discuss your view, or Rupert's view of Bloomsbury but have no time. After all, I always wind up, if six people, with no special start except what their wits give them, can so dominate, there must be some reason in it. And what Rupert never allowed for was that half of them were every bit as lacerated and sceptical and unhappy as he was. Where they seem to me to triumph is in having worked out a view of life which was not by any means corrupt or sinister or merely intellectual; rather ascetic and austere indeed; which still holds, and keeps them dining together, and staying together, after 20 years; and no amount of quarrelling or success, or failure has altered this. Now I do think this rather creditable. But tell me, who *is* Bloomsbury in your mind? Tell me too what you are painting. I like the poems[1]—but how is she being taught? Does she read? They are like a child singing—very pure and lovely.

Is Ka [Arnold-Forster] vain? And what is Eily [Darwin] like? Eily is on my conscience at the moment.

I am going to Cambridge this weekend, and will write to you—tell you what odds and ends I pick up. And do believe that I wish to understand you; I know, one can't; but it is a genuine thing in my life—your going on alone.

And you must forgive me for all sorts of follies in my letters, my dear Gwen.

V.W.

Sussex

1551: To Vanessa Bell   52 *Tavistock Square, London, W.C.*1

Tuesday May 5th [1925]

Dearest,

We went off to Cambridge for the week end, so I thought I should not see you at Cambridge, Newnham rather, where I prosecuted my search for the young and lovely, I met Helen Palmer, an old friend of yours—was Helen Lamb: married a schoolmaster; who died, and will always think

1. By Gwen's daughter Elizabeth.

181

of you with gratitude. I couldnt say the same of her brothers.[1] Glyn Philpotts has painted an enormous portrait of Kate[2] in grey, which is said to be very subtle, but unfortunately can't be seen because of the glass catching the light.

I saw an enchanting paralytic man. Also Maynard, not enchanting, rather cross. On Saturday I go to the Greek play with Lydia [Lopokova] and Berta Ruck. The male parrokeet [Clive] came to tea, very glum indeed —why? Isn't he taking the female [Mary Hutchinson] abroad? I didn't like to ask. Lytton est amoureux d'Angus je trouve—c'est bien amusant, mais un peu fatigant—toujours il prend les gens du [Hogarth] Press. Dadie [Rylands] and Douglas [Davidson] came in today, much pleased with their rooms. Lytton has been having flu, but paid us 2 visits, and I hope to make Mary jealous. Desmond [MacCarthy] has been having flu in Venice, but returns today. [Raymond] Mortimer has measles in Paris, and has probably infected Nancy's [Cunard] flat. This is all the news I can think of, and its very good of me to send it. The Star has a whole column about your decorations of the Common R:[3] and says I try to live up to them by being as revolutionary and nonsensical—a very good advertisement.

All your apes kiss you, and Duncan.

B.

Berg

1552: To G. Lowes Dickinson   52 *Tavistock Square, W.C.*1
[9? May 1925]

Dear Goldie, (if I may call you so)
    It was extraordinarily nice of you to write to me, and your letter gave me great pleasure.[4] I was very nervous as to what people like you might think, as I have so little education, and I thought that much of that book was great nonsense. However, if you like it, it gives me great encouragement to go on.
    Won't you ever come and see us, if you are in London?

Yours
Virginia Woolf

Sussex

1. Helen Lamb was the sister of Henry Lamb, the painter, and Walter Lamb the Secretary of the Royal Academy.
2. Katharine Stephen, Principal of Newnham, 1911-20. Glyn Philpot (1884-1937) was a portrait painter and sculptor.
3. *The Common Reader* was published on 23 April, with a jacket by Vanessa.
4. Lowes Dickinson had written about *The Common Reader*: "This is the best criticism in English—humorous, witty and profound."

1553: To Desmond MacCarthy   52 *Tavistock Square, W.C.*1

[17 May 1925]

My dear Desmond,
    I'm almost through this morning's batch, so please send along another as soon as you can.¹ Remember your Empire Review article on Conrad. It is panning out very well I think: what I want now is to get an idea of the whole, so as to make my decisions final.
    It amuses me enormously to do, and I warrant you it is going to make a fascinating book. A few more on *life* are desirable. But send a heap of all kinds.

                                                    Yr Affte
                                                       V.W.

The dinner was great fun last night, but I find Waley² a little demure and discreet, and wish you could have juggled your other invitation and come. Are you at Ottoline's tonight? I'm not. Mrs Dalloway is being sent to the E.R. [*Empire Review*].³

Mrs Michael MacCarthy

1554: To C. P. Sanger   52 *Tavistock Square, W.C.*1

26th May [1925]

Dear Charlie,
    It is extremely good of you to write and tell me what you think of Mrs Dalloway and your views interest me enormously.⁴ I expect you are right about the lack of sympathy, but in self-defence I must remark that I think the queerness of the method is partly responsible for your feeling this. I think, at least, that at first go off it is much easier to feel the technical qualities of an experiment than to get any emotion from it. I quite agree with what you say about Tchekhov—but then the Russians start with an enormous advantage over us in having no literature behind them, and after all, a very much simpler society to describe.

1. The Hogarth Press were considering the publication of a selection of Desmond MacCarthy's articles and reviews, but the idea came to nothing.
2. Arthur Waley, the orientalist and translator from the Chinese. The dinner party was given by Edith Sitwell.
3. Virginia's novel was published on 14 May.
4. In his letter of 24 May Sanger had said that he found Virginia's drawing of characters in *Mrs Dalloway* "too analytic and not sufficiently sympathetic. . . . You do not make me interested in their fate." He compared Tchekhov to Dostoevski, finding Tchekhov "so vastly greater just because he is not an obviously literary man. . . . Could you in your next book get a little of Tchekhov?" (*Sussex*).

183

But these are excuses, and dont do away with the fact that I feel that there is a great deal of truth in your criticism. Indeed, the reason why I inflict these experiments upon you is that I can't lie down in peace until I have found some way of liberating my sympathies, instead of giving effect to my analytic brain. But the conditions make it very hard for a novelist to do this now—in England at any rate.

But come and see us, and let us argue the question by word of mouth.

Anyhow, your letter gave me great pleasure, and it was very good of you to write it.

Your affte
Virginia Woolf

Daphne Sanger

1555: To Daphne Sanger   52 *Tavistock Square, W.C.*1
[27 May 1925]

Dear Daphne—I wish you would call me Virginia, or I shall have to call you Miss Sanger[1] —

I am as much surprised as you are that you liked Mrs Dalloway, and also very pleased. I expected you to be bored to death.

I never expect anyone to agree with me in liking the books I like, because I rather want novels to depress me, and I don't much mind whether I like the people in them or not. So I expect the books I write to be depressing and full of horrid monsters. About omnibuses—I suppose if I write it in full it is because "buses" sounds to me like "booses", and not "busses"— but I will see to it next time. Next time I will write a book all from the inside outwards, and it will be more depressing than ever, and Mr Sanger will tear his hair.

I think your first letter to an author is a great success, and shall count upon one every time I write a book if it is only a shriek of horror.

But you must come and see us. Are you always at the Opera? I hope to go on Friday.

Yours
Virginia Woolf

Daphne Sanger

1556: To V. Sackville-West
52 *Tavistock Square, London, W.C.*1
Wednesday [27 May 1925]

My dear Vita,
Hah ha! I thought you wouldn't like Mrs Dalloway.

1. Daphne was the daughter of Charles and Dora Sanger. She was then 19.

On the other hand, I thought you might like The Common Reader, and I'm very glad that you do[1]—all the more that its just been conveyed to me that Logan P. Smith thinks it very disappointing. But oh, how one's friends bewilder one!—partly, I suppose, the result of bringing out two books at the same time. I'm trying to bury my head in the sand, or play a game of racing my novel against my criticism according to the opinions of my friends. Sometimes Mrs D. gets ahead, sometimes the C. R.—

I will certainly come—towards the end of June? Might we perhaps call in for a bed after a walk? We have got into the habit of going for country outings, and perhaps you could tell us a good walk ending at Long Barn. I was amazed at the beauty of Kent, seeing it the other day from the train. I dont want at the moment to meet *anyone*. In the past 3 days I've met Osbert, Sachy and Edith Sitwell, an American, an Indian, Ottoline, Philip and Julian Morrell, a Gathorne Hardy,[2] Desmond, and am to meet a new poetess called Warner tonight,[3] and the Princess Bibesco has rung her bell and summoned me to her bedside.

Why can't you write? I cant stop writing. I'm ashamed to think how many stories I've written this month, and can hardly bear to keep my fingers off a new novel, but swear I won't start till August. Do chickens pay? Leonard wants to buy up the late poet Shanks' cottage at Rodmell and run a chicken farm there.

I suppose theres no chance you would dine with us next Wednesday to meet Morgan Forster, who wants to know you.

No; I dont like Geoffrey Scotts book:[4] I'm sure I'm right, though I've not finished it.

Please forgive this disjointed letter. I ought to be washing to dine with Miss Warner, but it does please me enormously that you should like The Common Reader

Yours Ever
Virginia Woolf

Berg

1. Vita had written to Virginia (26 May): "The Common Reader grows into a guide, philosopher, and friend, while Mrs Dalloway remains a will-of-the-wisp, a dazzling and lovely acquaintance" (*Berg*).
2. Robert Gathorne-Hardy had met Lady Ottoline Morrell as an Oxford undergraduate, and was later to edit her *Memoirs* in two volumes.
3. Sylvia Townsend Warner, whose first book, *The Espalier*, was published in this year.
4. *Portrait of Zélide*. Scott lived in Florence, and had previously published *The Architecture of Humanism*.

52 *Tavistock Square* [*W.C.*1]

May 31st [1925]

My dear Saxon,

I don't see what I am to do about Ann Whiteside's demise; the Crombies have long been lost to me; but it was a thoughtful act on your part to forward the letter.

I have been to the Walküre, and to Lords: at both places I looked for you in vain. I saw Hearne make 56, by which time we were so cold, we went home. Walküre completely triumphed, I thought; except for some boredom —I can't ever enjoy those long arguments in music—when it is obviously mere conversation upon business matters between Wotan and Brunhilde: however, the rest was superb. The fire is terrible: I saw at once that it was made of red silk, and that used to be done quite satisfactorily. Also I missed the ride of the horses. Still, when all is said, we were completely exhausted, and had to go to bed early last night to recover.

I daresay you are out walking somewhere, and we are going to see the Bird Sanctuary this afternoon, which I hear is the one place which birds abhor, as they burn weeds there. But our main object is to get a little air.

Do you think there is any sense in my remarks on Greek in the Common Reader? What about you great grandfather's memoir? We have a little memoir of Angus's great great grandmother.[1] Perhaps, joined together, they might make one book.

Leonard is in a great state of fuss about a certain meeting which I dare not name even on a sheet directly to be consumed by the flames. You know what a price all A——s set on secrecy: well, Sir Fred Pollocks secretary rang me up to ask what were the aims and objects of the C——d C——e S——y[2] in order that he might compose Sir Fred's speech at same. The infamy of this almost made me faint. I shall not be there, but hope to see you in less august surroundings soon.

I saw Barbara's [Bagenal] child last Sunday, and named her straight off without warning. I never saw such a complete balance between Nick and Barbara. I walked over [to Charleston] from Rodmell, and had the misfortune to lose a good many of my underclothes on the top of the downs. Marjorie [Strachey] was reading an Arabic grammar in the drawing room, —which all seemed very familiar.

1. Dorothy Snell's letters (1735-46) to her husband. Though they gave an interesting picture of rural life, Virginia decided they did not merit publication. For Saxon's great-grandfather, see p. 286, note 1.
2. 'The Cambridge Conversazione Society' (in spite of Virginia's C——d), otherwise known as the 'Apostles'. Sir Frederick Pollock, who at this date was 79 years old, was an eminent jurist and Editor-in-Chief of the *Law Reports*. The annual dinner was being held on 16 June, and Leonard had been chosen to preside.

I'm glad you got more pleasure from Mrs D than from Js R [*Jacob's Room*]. I enjoyed the writing of it much better.

No more news.

Yours

V.W.

Sussex

1558: To Ethel Sands   52 *Tavistock Square, W.C.*

May 31st [1925]

My dear Ethel,

It was a great pleasure to get your letter, not so much for its news, as for making me think that you're not a heartless siren, who dives into the depths of the sea, and forgets all her human friends, till she rises up again about October the 10th.

You are greatly missed. The hostesses of Chelsea are all singing their loudest, but I miss the peculiar melody of Ethel's hostessry. Ottoline turned up two nights ago, and I was rather overcome by her ravaged beauty, and desperation, and humility. Not a single party has Julian [Morrell] been asked to, though they put a notice in the Morning Post. The truth is that Julian can't cut a dash in London; she is a little thick and stumpy—countrified, and likes simple talk about dogs better than anything. But Leonard liked her.

I have seen too many people lately, and cant stop writing stories all the time.[1] I admit that writing stories and publishing books are difficult to combine. I get so worried by all the old gentlemen telling me I'm a born critic and not a novelist, and all the young gentlemen telling me I'm a born novelist and not a critic. However, we are making some money this time, which is great fun, and if the Common Reader and Mrs Dalloway keep it up, we are going to build a W.C. and a bathroom at Rodmell, and then you'll have to come and stay with us.

Clive is away, and it is said that the squares of Bloomsbury are so quiet you can hear a pin drop. It is also said that he was seen in the company of a lady—which is thought not improbable; but does her name begin with an M or a J?[2] That is the question. Nessa says it don't matter which. But Nessa and Duncan are too august and austere, and as for Roger, his manners are so unaccommodating, indeed he's grown so surly and incorruptible, biting aristocrats at sight, that I can only have him here with the greatest pre-

1. On 14 June Virginia wrote in her diary: "I've written 6 little stories, scrambled them down untidily and have thought out, perhaps too clearly, To the Lighthouse." These stories were collected by Stella McNichol under the title of *Mrs Dalloway's Party* (1973).
2. Mary Hutchinson or Juanita Guanderillas.

187

cautions. He was utterly disillusioned in Paris by meeting the Princesse Marthe,[1] and realising that her blood is blue, he at once perceived that she is also the silliest, foolishest, vulgarest of women, and her friends mere boobies.

Life must be very simple for painters. There's Sibyl Colefax pining for one real Bloomsbury party—she thinks we eat off the floor and spit into large pots of common bedroom china. Well, I can't get a single friend of mine to meet her; no painter at any rate; because they know, a thousand miles off, that she is tainted, tarred, corrupt, or whatever they call it. But I like a little high meat—in proof of which, I have to go and see Elizabeth Bibesco who is in a nursing home, having had the organ of her passions removed, so Ottoline says, and I am to be the bait they try her with. Having dropped Philip Ritchie, will she bite at me?

I dont know your address [Auppegard, near Dieppe]. Send me a picture post-card so that I may imagine your house.

Yours affect
V.W.

Wendy Baron

1559: TO LADY COLEFAX 52 *Tavistock Sq.* [*W.C.*1]

Tuesday [May? 1925]

My dear Sibyl,

I have actually made out every word of your letter, an author's vanity, I suppose, lending me a kind of inspiration. I did not expect you to read the masses of me which have been coming out. But your courage and kindness are equal to anything. Perhaps that is why I am far more terrified of you than you are of me. I shake whenever I think I see you far off at a concert.

Leonard hopes to come to your party—if I can get away from a dinner, I do too, but don't expect anything but shakes and shivers and tremors from your obliged obedient devoted humble servant

Virginia Woolf

Michael Colefax

1560: TO GERALD BRENAN 52 *Tavistock Square, W.C.*1

[14 June 1925]

My dear Gerald,

It was very good of you to write. But I shan't answer your criticisms

1. Princesse Marthe Bibesco, the French writer, and a cousin by marriage of Antoine and Elizabeth Bibesco. Virginia's comments are based on Roger Fry's letter of 5 May to Leonard, see *Letters of Roger Fry*, Vol. II ed. Denys Sutton (1972).

(and I daresay you don't want me to) because at the moment I can only pit them against other peoples' criticisms, and cannot make them refer to Mrs Dalloway itself. This is partly, I suppose, that I have just had a long talk with Roger, and he gave me an entirely different view of Mrs D from yours—in fact I think you and he contradict each other on practically every point of importance (the two I now remember being Septimus: to him the most essential part of Mrs D: And this I certainly did mean—that Septimus and Mrs Dalloway should be entirely dependent upon each other —if as you say he "has no function in the book" then of course it is a failure. And fate—no book to him more full of fate). Meanwhile, as I finished it 8 months ago, and am now at work on something different [*To the Lighthouse*], I feel very far away, and as if I saw you and Roger turning a little wax model this way and that—something that I have, at the moment, very little connection with.

Perhaps it is this lack of criticism, or rather the fact that I affect different people so differently, that makes it so difficult for me to write a good book. I always feel that nobody, except perhaps Morgan Forster, lays hold of the thing I have done: they meet in conflict up in the air; and so I have to create the whole thing afresh for myself each time. Probably all writers now are in the same boat. It is the penalty we pay for breaking with tradition, and the solitude makes the writing more exciting though the being read less so. One ought to sink to the bottom of the sea, probably, and live alone with ones words. But this is not quite sincere, for it is a great stimulus to be discussed and praised and blamed; I shall keep your letter and read it very carefully in a few months time. At the moment, I am letting the different opinions (here are two letters, from highly intelligent people—one [from Lytton] to say that Mrs D herself is a failure, the whole interest centering in Septimus and Rezia—another [from Sanger] imploring me to write more like Tchekhov, and lamenting the fact that I "contemplate the lives of the idle rich")—I say, I am letting these opinions accumulate, and then, when all is quiet, I shall creep out of my hole, and piece them together.

I'm out of temper and in disgrace tonight, having gone to Ottolines and spent the evening talking to Mrs Anrep,[1] because I like talking to Mrs Anrep, and now Ottoline accuses me of spoiling her evening because I ought to have talked to 20 brilliant young men, who bore me to death; but one can't rend Ottoline, any more than stab a pillow to the heart— So I must suppress my rage. But Mrs Anrep is worth 20 dozen Philip Ritchies, W. J. Turners,[2] and Kitchins[3] into the bargain; thats my opinion. She has lovely eyes and womanly hands. What odd things one likes people

1. Helen Anrep, wife of Boris Anrep, the Russian mosaicist.
2. Poet, dramatic critic of the *London Mercury*, literary editor of the *Daily Herald*, and music critic of the *New Statesman*.
3. Clifford Kitchin, writer and barrister, author of *Streamers Waving* (Hogarth Press, 1925) and the famous detective novel, *Death of My Aunt* (1929).

for! But I find I can't be bothered any longer to like the people I ought to like.

Come and see us when you're back. And how do you lodge with a Jewess on the Wiltshire downs?[1] Are you getting on? I find it almost impossible to concentrate in this weather: my mind feels like a large balloon, which goes floating away, and though I've 2 books in my head, I cannot write more than 20 words a morning. How many words do you write?

Put this letter, where it deserves to be, in Mrs Levey's earth closet; I would not send it, if I could write a better, but it is not possible, not in this perfectly divine heat. I'm reading Waley's Japanese novel[2] and David Copperfield.

Yours
V.W.

George Laʒarus

1561: To Lady Ottoline Morrell
52 Tavistock Square, W.C.1

[14? June 1925]

Dearest Ottoline

Yes, I was acutely conscious that I was in disgrace.

But why? Mayn't I talk to Mrs Anrep? I never see her, and I find her very sympathetic.

We both feel terrified at what you may expect of us in the way of social behaviour,—nevertheless, it will give us great pleasure to dine with you on Wednesday 24th at 8.15.

Then you must tell me what I said that was unkind. I can't remember a thing.

But do what you will, invent what you will, expect what you will, exact what you will, never, never, will you quarrel

with
your
devoted
humble
admirer and
disciple
Virginia
Micawber
Woolf

Texas

1. Brenan had taken lodgings with Mrs Levy near Hungerford, where he was close to Carrington at Ham Spray.
2. Virginia reviewed *The Tale of the Genji*, Vol. I, by Lady Murasaki (translated from the Japanese by Arthur Waley), in *Vogue*, late July 1925.

1562: To Violet Dickinson
52 *Tavistock Square, London, W.C.1*
[23 June 1925]

My Violet,
It was very nice to get one of your scraps—which, by the way, I'm going to publish, bound in white, after your demise.

Don't go on reading my works. Give it up.

I see you're hopelessly stuck and it is only the dogged courage of your race that eggs you on.

One of these days I hope to see you again; and then we can discuss George [Duckworth], better than on paper.

Your
Sp:
L's love.

Berg

1563: To Janet Case
52 *Tavistock Square, W.C.1*
[23 June 1925]

My dear Janet,
I am very glad you like the Common Reader. I was rather nervous lest you should curse my impertinence for writing about Greek [*On Not Knowing Greek*], when you are quite aware of my complete ignorance. I wonder if you think that I said anything to the point about Greek? I am in a state of complete bewilderment, as everyone seems to prefer either Mrs Dalloway to the C.R. or the other way about, and implore me to write *only* novels or *only* criticism, and I want to do both.

I look forward to Wednesday, when we communicate via the Manchester Guardian.[1] I can't think how you write with such authority about every kind of plant, considering you're a mere Cockney. But I enjoy it very much, and wish it were 2 or 3 inches longer. Are you trustworthy?

I'm sorry about your League of Nations review. The book[2] is selling in quantities, for some reason, and we expect to make our fortunes.

Everybody in London is going to hear Pirandello,[3] and I have actually

1. Janet contributed a 'Country Diary' weekly to the *Manchester Guardian* from February 1925 to June 1937.
2. *The Story of the League of Nations Told for Young People*, by Kathleen E. Innes, was published by the Hogarth Press in April 1925.
3. The New Oxford Theatre was having a Pirandello Season.

stumbled through a play in Italian. Everybody is giving parties, and Leonard and I have to dine with Ottoline tomorrow, which makes him melancholy mad. I am beginning to look forward to 2 months at Rodmell, when I shall hope to get a letter from you.

Give my love to Emphie [Janet's sister], and beg her not to forget me, though I agree that trees are better than people.

That is your philosophy isn't it?

Yours affte
V.W.

Sussex

1564: To Ralph Partridge   52 *Tavistock Square, W.C.*1

[29 June 1925]

My dear Ralph,

I could not catch you the other night to ask you to send me a list of your terms for binding books. I want some done—so please send this. Would you ask Lytton to be so good as to tell me what is the best edition of Madame de Sévigné? Also give my love to Carrington and come and see the poor old Wolves some day.

Yours ever
V.W.

Frances Partridge

1565: To Edward Sackville West
52 *Tavistock Square, London, W.C.*1

Sunday [5 July 1925]

Dear Mr Sackville West,

We should like it so much if you could dine with us at 7.45 on Tuesday 14th.

Of course, we don't dress. I have a book of yours The Inheritance,[1] which I read now and then with great pleasure, but will return honestly if you come.

Yours sincreely
Virginia Woolf

Berg

1. By Susan Ferrier (1824), a humorous novel of Scottish life.

1566: To H. G. Leach   52 *Tavistock Square, W.C.*1
Typewritten
5th July, 1925

Dear Mr Leach,
    I am just finishing a story of about three thousand words, and should
be glad for *the Forum* to have it as you suggest.
    Perhaps you would let me know what fee you propose to pay,[1] and I
will let you have an answer without delay.
    My address, as you will see, is now as above.

                                        Yours sincerely,
                                        Virginia Woolf
                                        (Mrs Woolf)
Harvard University Library

1567: To J. D. Hayward   52 *Tavistock Square, W.C.*1
Typewritten
18th July 1925

Dear Mr Hayward,[2]
    When we saw you at Cambridge you said something about a book—
Restoration, I think—which deserved reprinting. We are very anxious to
try something of the kind, and I wondered whether you would like to
consider doing it. What we should like would be something fairly short,
which did not mean a great deal of work, so that the risk for everyone
would be small. Forgive me for being so vague and troubling you perhaps
unnecessarily.

                                        Yours sincerely
                                        Virginia Woolf
King's

1. The *Forum* (New York) offered her $250 for a story, and she sent them *The
   New Dress*. Mr Leach at first rejected it (see Letter 1592), but eventually
   published it in May 1927.
2. John Davy Hayward (1905-65), the bibliographer and anthologist, was then
   an undergraduate at King's College, Cambridge. In 1926 he published the
   collected works of the Earl of Rochester (1647-80), but nothing for the Hogarth
   Press.

1568: To George Rylands   52 *Tavistock Square, W.C.*1

Monday [20 July 1925]

My dear Dadie,

Of course it will give me enormous pleasure to have your poem[1] dedicated to me, and Old Woolf himself can find no objection to it. So we shall do it.

But I think you are exaggerating—our kindness, and so on. Didn't we shut you up in the basement with the passionate Higgs?[2] Aren't you one of the people we both like best, and don't we look forward to seeing you eminent, beloved and triumphant? Of course we do, and if I weren't overcome by that bashful timidity which is a mark of my nature (and one of the reasons why I'm such a nice woman in spite of all you can say to the contrary) I should fling my arms round you and tell you so. Yes; it gives me enormous pleasure.

[Bernadette] Murphy was took ill this morning, and had to be laid on the floor while Angus [Davidson] went for a taxi: Maynard has jumped a pamphlet on us, which has to be printed, reviewed, circulated in one week —10 thousand copies:[3] Ottoline made me dizzy last night with her scent and so you see I am not capable of writing a letter.

I saw you had got your money renewed. I don't feel the least doubt that you'll get your fellowship.

So good bye my dear Dadie, and write to us sometimes; on the late Master's paper,[4] and I'm very much pleased.

Your affte
V.W.

But I think it is a poem full of promise.

George Rylands

1569: To Philip Morrell   52 *Tavistock Square, W.C.*1

Monday [27 July 1925]

Dear Philip,

You are very ignorant of authors if you think that praise is ever indifferent to them. Your letter [about *Mrs Dalloway*] gives me great pleasure

1. *Russet and Taffeta*, published by the Hogarth Press in December 1925.
2. A temporary woman assistant at the Press while Rylands worked there.
3. John Maynard Keynes' *The Economic Consequences of Mr Churchill*. Seven thousand copies were published by the Press this month.
4. A. C. Benson, Master of Magdalene College, Cambridge, since 1915. He died on 17 June 1925, and Rylands had written to Virginia a letter on his notepaper (*Sussex*).

and encouragement. I get a good deal of abuse, and sometimes feel so bewildered by what people say that I find it difficult to go on. Now, after your letter (which I think you were very kind to write) I shall start again refreshed.

One thing interests me very much—that you should think yourself the dullest man in the book[1]—I wonder what extraordinary complex this springs from? There is not the least foundation in fact for it. First, my idea of you doesn't in the least correspond with my idea of Hugh Whitbread or Richard Dalloway: secondly, my friends are quite safe from me, because I cant write about people I am in the habit of seeing, anymore than I can describe places until I have practically forgotten them. It's not humour; its simply the way my mind works.

There were originals for some of the people in Mrs Dalloway: but very far away—people I last saw 10 years ago and even then, did not know well. Those are the people I like to write about.

But I'm so much interested by this revelation of what you think I think of you that perhaps one of these days I shall be tempted to break my rules and try to do you—

But no—I couldn't.

By the way, I meant Richard Dalloway to be liked. Hugh Whitbread to be hated. You hate them both I gather.

Anyhow many thanks for writing.

Yours Ever
Virginia Woolf

Texas

1570: To Edward Sackville West

52 Tavistock Square, W.C.1

Tuesday [28 July 1925]

Dear Mr Sackville West,

It is disgraceful of me not to have written before—We have been in a turmoil publishing Maynard Keynes' pamphlet. But the piano arrived safely, and has already given a 2 hour concert, when one of Angus Davidons's brothers sang, and it was the greatest success.

I hope to give many more concerts of this kind in the autumn, and we shall consider you our patron. All the thanks are on our side.—which reminds me that Chappell must, of course, send me their bill for tuning, if you would be so good as to tell them to come regularly.

---

1. Philip Morrell wrote to Virginia on 22 July: "When I read any of your books I always feel myself to be the sort of model of all the dullest characters—a kind of combination of Hugh Whitbread and Richard Dalloway" (*Sussex*).

The studio makes a very good concert room—but you must remember to come and hear, when you are in London.

Again many thanks,

Yours ever

Virginia Woolf

Is there any chance that your pamphlet will be ready about the end of August?[1]

Don't bother to answer if there is none; but I hope there may be.

Berg

1. The only pamphlet by Edward Sackville West which the Hogarth Press published was *The Apology of Arthur Rimbaud: A Dialogue* (March 1927).

Letters 1571-1601 (August–November 1925)

Virginia went to Monk's House in early August, foreseeing with pleasure two uninterrupted months of work on To the Lighthouse. *Her plan was ruined by a sudden fainting fit at a Charleston party on* 19 *August, and she was in bed, on and off, for the next four months, at first in the country, then in London. She did manage, however, to make "a very quick and flourishing attack" on her new novel (her diary of* 5 *September), and wrote, beside many letters, her essay* On Being Ill. *Leonard's relaxation at Monk's House was gardening, and Virginia's wool-work. She read a great many manuscripts forwarded from the Press, but on returning to London she attempted too soon to resume the manual work, and again succumbed to illness.*

1571: To Lady Ottoline Morrell   *Monk's House, Rodmell,*
                                          Lewes, Sussex
[August 1925]

Dearest Ottoline,

I'm so sorry about Monday, but we have promised to spend the day at Bexhill with Leonard's mother, who is only there for a few days, and as we don't often go would be hurt, I'm afraid, if we put her off.

But you wont miss much—I should be ashamed to set you down to the eternal gooseberries and water which our local lady produces. However, I wish it could have been differently arranged.

Excuse scrawling—the post is just off.

                                          Your
                                          V.W.

I've not heard a thing from Vanessa—
      Charleston
          Firle
              is the address: but she may be at Seend.
      Texas

1572: To V. Sackville-West   *Monks House, Rodmell*
                                     [Sussex]
Monday [24 August 1925]

My dear Vita,

How nice it would be to get a letter from you!
But then you don't write letters unasked.

197

So I will put my plea before you that I'm in bed, and its raining, and Leonard's in London; Will that do it?

We went to a great birthday and bridal party at Charleston the other day. The noise and heat were such that I could do nothing but fall prostate to the floor in a faint, and have been in bed ever since, with a headache[1]——But not as bad as sciatica, I daresay.

I have a perfectly romantic and no doubt untrue vision of you in my mind—stamping out the hops in a great vat in Kent—stark naked, brown as a satyr, and very beautiful. Don't tell me this is all illusion. We came away from London so parched and cynical that all we wanted was to sit in the damp and observe insects. Naturally, this being so, telegrams pursued us, and the Morrells would have been on us, Ottoline and Philip, demanding beds, and weaving the whole smoke cloud over us again, had it not been for some valiant lying on my part. One can't tell the Truth to Ottoline. She found it out,—as indeed a babe in arms could; but showed it. Now dont you, as a born aristocrat (which is said to annoy) call this damned bad manners? I do. So we are under a ban. If I say that I have to meet my mother in law in Bexhill, you ought to believe it. Still—no doubt this bores you.

Otherwise, what has happened, and at what stage did we last meet? At the Morrells, I believe, and broke off wedged in the midst of a terrific argument which someone, a week later, told me seemed to him one of the most exciting he had ever heard. But who? Everything is now obscure.

I am weighed down by innumerable manuscripts. Edith Sitwell; 20 dozen poets; one man on birth control; another on religion in Leeds; and the whole of Gertrude Stein, which I flutter with the tips of my little fingers, but dont open. I think her dodge is to repeat the same word 100 times over in different connections, until at last you feel the force of it.

But please tell me about your poem [*The Land*]. Are you writing it? Is it very beautiful? I rather think I shall like it: but I am very old fashioned in my poetry, and like reading Crabbe. What I wish is that you would deal seriously with facts. I dont want anymore accurate descriptions of buttercups, and how they're polished on one side and not on the other. What I want is the habits of earthworms; the diet given in the workhouse: anything exact about a matter of fact—milk, for instance—the hours of cooling, milking etc. From that, proceed to sunsets and transparent leaves and all the rest, which, with my mind rooted upon facts, I shall then embrace with tremendous joy. Do you think there is any truth in this? Now, as you

---

1. The party was held at Charleston on 19 August to celebrate Quentin's birthday and the marriage of Maynard Keynes and Lydia Lopokova, which had taken place on 4 August. In the middle of the party Virginia collapsed, and for many months thereafter she suffered intermittently from headaches and exhaustion.

were once a farmer, surely it is all in your head ready. Tennyson, you see, was never a farmer: Crabbe was a parson, which does as well. But I must stop. I shall get up tomorrow; and be quite well next day I hope. How is sciatica?

Your joke made me roar.

Yr VW.

Berg

1573: To V. Sackville-West   *Monks House, Rodmell*
                                              [Sussex]

Tuesday [1 September 1925]

My dear Vita,

How nice it would be to get another letter from you—still better, to see you. I haven't suggested it since the headache has been an awful nuisance this time, and I have had another week in bed. Now, however, even Leonard admits that I'm better.

My notion is that you may be motoring past and drop in and have tea, dinner, whatever you will, and a little conversation. One day next week? I'm going to be awfully quiet, and don't dare suggest what I long for—a drive to Amberley [West Sussex]. But when I'm in robust health, as I shall be, could it really be achieved? Ottoline took me motoring one midnight in London; and the effect was stupendous—St Pauls, Tower Bridge, moonlight, river, Ottoline in full dress and paint, white and gaudy as a painted tombstone erect on Tower Bridge in the midst of all the hoppers and bargees coming home drunk on Bank Holiday.

In bed I have been fuming over your assumption that my liking for the poet Crabbe is avowed. I assure you I bought a copy out of my own pocket money before you were weaned. What's more, I have read Peter Grimes I daresay 6 times in 10 years; "But he has no compassion in his grave"—That is where that comes from. There is also a magnificent description of wind among bulrushes which I will show you if you will come here. But I find to my surprise that Crabbe is almost wholly about people. One test of poetry—do you agree?—is that without saying things, indeed saying the opposite, it conveys things: thus I always think of fens, marshes, shingle, the East Coast, rivers with a few ships, coarse smelling weeds, men in blue jerseys catching crabs, a whole landscape in short, as if I had read it all there: but open Crabbe and there is nothing of the sort. One word of description here and there—that is all. The rest is how Lucy got engaged to Edward Shore. So if your poem [*The Land*] is as you say all about the woolly aphis, I may come away from it dreaming of the stars and the South Seas. But hurry up, and write it.

199

Well, you may think my life a complete failure—what with one thing and another. All I say is that if it comes to giving people pleasure (and I'm not here fishing in your stagnant pool for a compliment) I'm sure my printing Mr Palmers poems,[1] as I did this summer, gave him a more intense pleasure than all the Common Readers and Mrs Dalloways I shall ever write gave the rest of the world. And whats the objection to whoring after Todd [Editor of *Vogue*]? Better whore, I think, than honestly and timidly and coolly and respectably copulate with the Times Lit. Sup.

But you see you must write a long letter.

And don't go striding above my head in the moonlight, exquisitely beautiful though the vision is.

I must stop: or I would now explain why its all right for me to have visions but you must be exact. I write prose; you poetry. Now poetry being the simpler, cruder, more elementary of the two, furnished also with an adventitious charm, in rhyme and metre, can't carry beauty as prose can. Very little goes to its head. You will say, define beauty—

But no: I am going to sleep.

Your V.W.

Berg

1574: To Lady Cecil   *Monk's House, Rodmell*
                                       [Sussex]
Sept 1st [1925]

My dear Nelly,

I've copied out your praises,[2] and sent them to Hope Mirrlees, as they will give her such pleasure.

She's the daughter of a very rich sugar merchant. Her mother was (is, I mean) a Scotch lady—Moncrieff, I think her name was. As a family they are a typical English family, devoted, entirely uncultured, owning motor cars, living in a large house near Cambridge in order to be near Hope when she went to Newnham. She is her own heroine—capricious, exacting, exquisite, very learned, and beautifully dressed. She has a passion for Jane Harrison, the scholar: indeed they practically live together, and go to Paris to learn Russian. Hope knows Russian and Greek like her native tongue.

She took some years to write Madeleine, and it was refused by six or seven publishers. Then she fell into despair; Collins suddenly gave her £50 for it: I was asked to review it, and of course found it an awful burden, and didn't like the book as much as I should have done, and when my review came out, Hope was very much disappointed: however, we've made

1. Herbert E. Palmer, *Songs of Salvation Sin & Satire*, printed by the Press and published in October 1925.
2. Of Hope Mirrlees' novel *Madeleine*, 1919.

200

it up now. That's about all I know of her—I like her very much, but also find her as indeed I find her writing so full of affectations and precocities, that I lose my temper. But these things are mainly caused by being a spoilt prodigy, and also she has some disease, which is always making her ill. Her brother is a soldier: her sister married to one; and her father gives her motor cars for her birthday. Will you come and meet her when she's next in London? I imagine that she sees an odd mixture of rich conventional people, and highly sophisticated French poets and scholars. She can never make up her mind which she prefers. She is devoted to her family anyhow.

It was a great pleasure to see you here, and we hope you'll come again, and spend the night, when we have a bathroom. I have just bought a Greek statue for 2/6.

Yours afft
V.W.

I have written this account of Hope in a hurry, and I daresay not a word of it, save the facts, is true.

Hatfield

1575: To Janet Case   *Monks House [Rodmell,*
                                        Sussex]
Tuesday [1 September 1925]

My dear Janet,
I should have answered you before, but have been rather afflicted with headaches and spending most of my time in bed.

I'm so glad you like the Common Reader. It's very odd—that and Mrs Dalloway coming out at the same time. Everyone over 40 prefers the C.R: everyone under 40 Mrs D. I find myself torn between the two—my only wish being, as you may remember—to get the maximum of praise for both books. But Mrs D: is at present leading, in praise and sales, (in fact we're reprinting her)[1] so I'm glad of a good word for C.R.

But dont, I beg of you, father on me that doctrine of yours about the way things are written mattering and not the things: how can you accuse me of believing that? I don't believe you can possibly separate expression from thought in an imaginative work. The better a thing is expressed, the more completely it is thought. To me, Stevenson is a poor writer, because his thought is poor, and therefore, fidget though he may, his style is obnoxious. And I don't see how you can enjoy technique apart from the matter—but perhaps I'm misrepresenting you. I don't see what you mean.

But how difficult criticism is! Not a single word has the same meaning

1. By 20 July *Mrs Dalloway* had sold about 1550 copies.

for two people. As for being helped in one's own work, I have given up all hopes of it. Blame is unpleasant, and praise pleasant, but neither has any bearing on what one is doing—However, as I always maintain, it is the pleasure one has oneself that is the only guide, and that is leading me at present to plan four more books.

Our garden is the envy of Sussex. We have discovered a colchicum, like a little purple tulip, which you plant one week and it comes up the next. Needless to say, this is all Leonard's doing: he works like a navvy, and also climbs to the top of pear trees like a monkey. Now, wasn't I right to marry a man like that? I offer my admiration, but am seldom allowed an active part—Really, I don't believe anything is so lovely as a garden on a hot day. In one's middle age one says these simple and commonplace things with profound conviction.

Now I've got to defend myself from a woman (aged 33) who tells me that I sell my soul by writing criticism, and wishes all my energies devoted forever to writing novels. Oh you readers!

Well, I suppose this is all very egotistical as usual, *my* books, *my* garden, *my* husband. So go and revenge yourself telling me of *your* books, *your* garden, *your* sister.

I don't believe we shall ever get to the New Forest—it isn't my fault—it's Leonards. Once we get into the web at Tavistock Sqre., he has his Labour party,—his Nation, and his great work[1] (which is ever so much more important than any I shall ever write, but then he's modest, which I never was): and so, though Thomas Hardy has asked us to come and see him (this is a boast) we don't do it; and I'd rather see Janet, as I hate great men.

However, the penny halfpenny post still remains.

Your aff
V.W.

Sussex

1576: To Vanessa Bell   [*Monk's House, Rodmell, Sussex*]

Thursday [3 September 1925]

Dearest,

Would you have the great kindness to accept a small commission from me—to wit £1. 1.—and do me a design for a chair cushion?

We have got some new dining room chairs, and I find embroidery so soothing to the head that I want to work a cushion while I am here.

---

1. *After the Deluge: A Study of Communal Psychology.* Leonard worked at this study from 1920 onwards. The first volume was published in 1931, the second in 1939, and the third (which he entitled *Principia Politica*) in 1953.

The measurements are

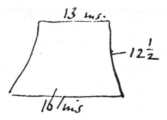

(I hope this is plain)

I should like a large mesh, so that I can hope to finish within a lifetime. The chairs are ordinary dark brown.

Design, colour, everything, is left to you—my only desire is that you will be quick, as I want to start.

I am practically recovered. Who do you think descends on us tomorrow —Bruce Richmond [Editor of the *TLS*] and Elena!

I am frantically trying to look more like a gentleman's house, but it is impossible.

I shall hope to see you shortly; tell Quentin I shall arrange the walk before he goes.

Yr B.

Berg

1577: To T. S. ELIOT   *Monks House, Rodmell*
                                        [*Sussex*]
Sept 3rd [1925]

My dear Tom,

I was very glad to see your pencil again—Yes, the country is lovely, and when are you coming to see it? I've been spending the last two weeks in bed though—a chill, a headache, and so on, but am practically recovered now, and looking at the evening sky sitting upright. And I wish you were opposite me.

Of course I should think it an honour to figure in your first number (by the way, what's the name? Criterion Junior—waiting for the demise of Criterion Senior?) but you'll have to let me know when you want it, and how long, and what is your publication date.[1] I've two or three things promised to America during the next months—a story, an article on some-

---

1. Virginia published *On Being Ill* in Eliot's *New Criterion* for January 1926. She later published the article in the *Forum* (New York, April 1926).

thing like Painting and Writing, and another undecided[1]—but I should have to say soon if you wanted to print here.

I wonder whether you ever cornered the Countess—Is she only a Baroness?[2] and whether she cut up rough, as I suspect. Otherwise, why have you 2 magazines on your shoulders? What a life, to be sure! On the whole, dealing with authors steadily decreases my opinion of the human race. I won't say who this applies to—not you. Bumpus says we *must* reprint *Waste Land.*[3] People worry his life out for copies—so think sometimes, among all your glories and horrors, of that rapacious animal the Hogarth Press.

Really, there are so many things to discuss you'll have to come here. I can't begin even in a letter.

Love to Vivien. I'm very glad about the Stoppers.[4] They have changed my life too.

Yrs
V.W.

Mrs T. S. Eliot

1578: To V. Sackville-West

Monk's House, Rodmell
[Sussex]

Monday [7 September 1925]

My dear Vita,

Well, I dont see why you don't write to me, but perhaps it is my turn, only you are better situated for writing letters than I am. There are two people in your room, whom you can hear talking.[5] There is one dog in my room, and nothing else but books, papers and pillows and glasses of milk and quilts that have fallen off my bed and so on. This has bred in me such a longing to hear what your two people are saying that I must implore you to tell me. Who are they? Elizabeth Bibesco and Geoffrey Scott? John Drinkwater[6] and Rebecca West? The King and Queen? I give it up. Only for me they are brilliant, mysterious, intensely desirable. Tell me who you've been seeing; even if I have never heard of them—that will be all the better. I try to invent you for myself, but find I really have only 2 twigs and 3 straws to do it with. I can get the sensation of seeing you— hair, lips, colour, height, even, now and then, the eyes and hands, but I

1. *Cinema*, published in *Arts* (New York, June 1926).
2. The Viscountess Rothermere had offered to finance Eliot as editor of a new magazine.
3. In fact, the second edition of *The Waste Land* was published at the end of 1925 by Faber and Gwyer, whom Eliot had joined in November.
4. Probably 'ear-stoppers' to help her sleep at nights.
5. A phrase extracted from Vita's latest letter.
6. The playwright, poet and actor (1882-1937).

find you going off, to walk in the garden, to play tennis, to dig, to sit smoking and talking, and then I cant invent a thing you say—This proves, what I could write reams about—how little we know anyone, only movements and gestures, nothing connected, continuous, profound. But give me a hint I implore.

It would be better to talk—much better. But I cant talk yet without getting these infernal pains in my head, or astonishingly incongruous dreams. Two dull people come to tea, and I dream of precipices and horrors at night, as if—can they keep horrors and precipices concealed in them, I wonder? Then if you came, I should perhaps dream the other way about —of bumble bees and suet pudding. Read this over, you will see that a compliment is implied.

I'm really better, and only waiting for Leonard to say the word to ask you once more if you can't come here. "Avowed" should be simple;[1] but has now taken the meaning "protested insincerity"; for me at least, who am, I suppose, grown hoary in sin, and impute meanings to good English words which, I agree, they dont bear. But write to your affectionate villain all the same.

Yr V.W.

What a scrawl! I cannot write at this angle with this pen.

Berg

1579: To Vanessa Bell   [*Monk's House, Rodmell,*
                                     Sussex]
Postcard

[8 September 1925]
Very well—if you prefer to be an Aunt Mary Fisher or Creeping Jesus—
I suppose I may offer to pay for wool and canvas?[2]
If so, will you buy both, and transmit.
Creeping Jesus is a good phrase.
No sooner had you gone, than Maynard and Lydia arrived.

VW.

We expect Clive on Friday.

Berg

1. A reference to Virginia's comments on Crabbe (see Letter 1573). Vita suspected that Virginia did not know what 'avowed' meant.
2. For the chair-cover design. Vanessa had refused to accept payment.

205

1580: To LYTTON STRACHEY   *Monk's House, Rodmell*
                                               [Sussex]

Sept 8th [1925]

Dearest Lytton,

Do you remember one of Leslie Stephen's daughters, the younger, I think, called Virginia? She married a chap called Woolf in the Indian, or Ceylon, Civil Service. Well, they write. Indeed she wrote a book, essays and so on; and wants to know if you could help her to correct a misprint or so—that is, if you remember her—a tall girl, she was, rather badly dressed, parted her hair in the middle.

Does this form of address wring your withers? No; But all the same you might tell me what the misprint in the Common Reader was that you snarled out at Leonard once in Gordon Sqre. We hope to reprint, and I'm collecting the more obvious and glaring howlers with which, I'm told, the book pullulates.

I don't much think we shall see you this summer. But we shan't be hurt; we shan't think the better of your taste to hear that you're at Maynards, but, I repeat, we shall love you all the same—and the beds here are damnably uncomfortable.

I have been spending 10 days there, blasted by dissipation and headache. When I was at my worst, Leonard made me eat an entire cold duck, and, for the first and only time in my life, I was sick! What a hideous and awful experience! And you are sick every Monday, I'm told: after that, we can forgive much.

Find me a house where no one can ever come.

I like talking to you, but to no one else in the whole world.

Your old, rake, and fireside hag,

                                                    V.

Strachey Trust

1581: To VANESSA BELL   *[Monk's House, Rodmell,*
                                               Sussex]

Postcard

[September 1925]

Yes, I'll come in by the 4.15 and have tea (only who's going to pay for it?—) I will postpone my visit till the following Sunday, if it suits, as L. thinks the society of C. J. [Creeping Jesus—Vanessa] and her parasites might prove too stimulating

Berg

206

Monks House, Rodmell
                                              [Sussex]
Tuesday [15 September 1925]

Oh you scandalous ruffian! To come as far as this house and make off! When the Cook came up to me with your letter, and your flowers and your garden,[1] with the story that a lady had stopped a little boy in the village and given him them I was so furious I almost sprang after you in my nightgown. Ten minutes talking wouldn't have hurt me, and it would have been such fun. As for the garden and the flowers, words fail me: in fact I cant bear writing when I might have been talking. The garden has had a jug of water carefully poured over it. The flowers are in a broken pot. But beware how you give me things—woolwork is my passion. Another present from you, and a tea cosy worked with parrots and tulips will arrive, and what will you do then? No: write to me; or better, come and see me; but I will let Leonard decide. All I insist on is one day before we go back.

Did I write you—I'm afraid I must have—a dismal complaining down-trodden letter? There was no reason for it, only just as one recovers, one always curses—it is a sign of health. Here I am, very comfortable, sitting in the sun in the garden, with your fascinating creation, which reminds me of a Chinese mountain, by my side, and my woolwork, and, as you guess, masses of books. (By the way, why not let me read and criticise your poem? Will you?) This morning the thickest manuscript you ever saw arrived from an inspired grocer's boy at Islington, who, being inspired, has not had it typed, and says he will give up grocery for literature if we encourage, or even if we dont: but read it, every word, we must: while Miss Somebody,[2] of Nicosia Road Wandsworth writes at the same time to say she divines a human heart in me, and will I tell her how, without insincerity she can so titivate her heroine's character that it will win popularity with a large number of readers, since she has not a penny in the world, has two or three old mothers to support, and nothing will induce her to give up literature. You must admit that this passion for writing novels in the remoter suburbs is all much to their credit, and worth 20 Mrs Dalloways at least. I'm *not* fishing for a compliment but you certainly didn't like Mrs D. when you read her—and small blame to you!

I suppose that spaniel is the dog—may one say bitch?—that I so much respected at Tavistock Square one day.

Leonard says 7 puppies are too many. Leonard is very anxious to get your article.[3] I wish you could explain exactly what they're doing to the downs at this moment; men, horses, old women—all seem to be creeping

1. A miniature garden, constructed in an earthenware pot filled with soil and stones.
2. Doris Daglish. See Letter 1588.
3. *The Garden and the Oast* (*Nation*, 10 October 1925).

and crawling; setting fire to weeds; and indeed by walking to my garden gate and looking over I can see—I long to describe it, but you would be bored, and perhaps one ought to say nothing about these matters, which are so important, but so hopelessly remote from conversation. Why do you spoil me so with your Chinese mountains?

VW.

Berg

1583: TO ROGER FRY   *Monk's House, Rodmell, Sussex*

Sept. 16th 1925

It must have been a movement, my dear Roger, of that sympathy which in spite of all you can say to the contrary, still unites us that made you write to me, the very same moment, I daresay, that sitting on my lawn I was saying to Leonard, Well, if I wrote to anybody, it would be to Roger (or Crusty, as I call you, to those who, knowing your worth, yet find a certain truth in that description). Now I actually will write to you. Indeed, you would have liked a verbatim report of that conversation on the lawn, for I said you were also about the only person in the world I wished to see. I've been spending practically all the time here comatose with headaches. Cant write (with a whole novel[1] in my head too—its damnable) can only read oceans and floods of trash: and would like a good gossip with you better than anything. However, I am much better, and only swear to forego aristocratic society in future; which I'm sure is my undoing. Its being stupid thats so tiring—not being clever: trying to see whats to be said for Lady Colefax, and gently unthreading the intricacies of that corrupt and tangled mass, Ottoline's soul. Crusty never tries any of these things, so its no good appealing to him for sympathy.

Your discussions on the novel sound fascinating and incredible[2]— incredible here, I mean, where the whole thing would turn into a summer school, and politics and virtue and plain living and ideals and female ugliness and male stalwartness of the most depressing type would inevitably creep in. (By the way, of course we will do Maurois as a pamphlet if we can get hold of him).[3] But then—however, you know my arguments in favour of English literature at any rate, and English eccentricity and quality—of which by the way, you're a prime specimen yourself, for there's no one I think of with greater relish than of you, deny it as you may. For example who

1. *To the Lighthouse.*
2. Roger had been attending a literary conference at Pontigny in France.
3. One of the papers read at Pontigny was on 'The Nature of Literary Honesty', by André Maurois. The Hogarth Press did not publish it.

but you would sit up in the corner of an express train and translate mediaeval French with such vitality? I think they're very good judging without the originals.[1] Anyhow they have colour and character—how do you do it, in a train or at a table, I can't conceive. It makes me return to my old charge —that you *must* write more, and about literature. Let the idea simmer in your brain: one morning you'll toss it over, a perfect omelette. Think of the long dusky dampish evenings at Dalmeney,[2] with the lumbago on you, and one colour much the same as another: however, I shall be at hand then, and I consider it one of my functions, as they say, to be a gadfly in your flanks. I will have a book out of you for next autumn season.

This reminds me—if you are in Paris, please ferret out some little man who sells printing paper. All the new French reprints are on a yellowish thinnish paper which is said to be immensely cheaper than anything English. We are making an effort to cut down our prices: and they all centre upon paper. We are lying crushed under an immense manuscript of Gertrude Stein's.[3] I cannot brisk myself up to deal with it—whether her contortions are genuine and fruitful, or only such spasms as we might all go through in sheer impatience at having to deal with English prose. Edith Sitwell says she's gigantic, (meaning not the flesh but the spirit). For my own part I wish we could skip a generation—skip Edith and Gertrude and Tom and Joyce and Virginia and come out in the open again, when everything has been restarted, and runs full tilt, instead of trickling and teasing in this irritating way. I think its bad for the character too, to live in a bye stream, and have to consort with eccentricities—witness our poor Tom, who is behaving (I can't go into details—I don't suppose you need them) more like an infuriated hen, or an old maid who has been kissed by the butler than ever.

When you withdraw into these altitudes of yours, Cassis, I mean— heat and light and colour and real sea and real sky and real food instead of the wishywashy watery brash we get here—then you become exalted above gossip. You don't want human beings. It's one of your peculiarities. (Do you perceive that I'm writing a character of you?—I must put you into a book one of these days). That is why you painters are, as a rule, such exemplary characters; why calm and well being exhale from you. Certainly this is true of Bell and Grant: I never saw two people humming with heat and happiness like sunflowers on a hot day more than those two. But you have a dash of the dragon fly about you.

As for my gossip I haven't any—except that I have beat off a most persistent attack on the part of Ott. and Philip, who proposed to stay here,

1. Fry's letter to Virginia of 12 September (*Sussex*) was written in a French train, and he enclosed some of his translations of Ronsard's sonnets.
2. Roger's house, 7 Dalmeny Avenue, London N.7.
3. In November 1926 the Hogarth Press published Stein's *Composition as Explanation*. It was only 59 pages of print.

and if not stay, then feed here, at which my spirit sank so low that I furbished up the feeblest lie—about going to Bexhill—and was seen through by Ott: who replied with the dismal frigidity of a funeral horse—so that's the end of that.

However, I must stop. Not that I haven't millions of things to say; but you must write another letter. That's decided.

Give my love to Miss Toogood, the Howards and Miss Robinson:[1] they were at Cassis in April: but I'm sure they're at Cassis in September. Miss Toogood is an Australian who writes novels: Mr Howard is an archaeologist. Miss Toogood has stuck in the last chapter.

Leonard has not yet read your sonnets, but will.

Yrs ever
V.W.

Sussex

1584: To Vanessa Bell   *Monks House [Rodmell,*
                                  Sussex]
Thursday [17 September 1925]

Dearest Dolph:

A thousand thanks for the various objects which I am fascinated by. However, my disabilities as a needlewoman are such that I shall never do you credit. I can't tear myself from it and am in the heart of the Rose at the moment. I came back to find a stout budget from Roger, who had been stricken at dawn in a French train with the desire to translate obscure mediaeval French poetry, and had of course reeled off about 10 difficult sonnets into perfect English: also a budget from Saxon who thought I might like to know that he was reading Frontinus' De Legibus in a Café in Vichy where, he made bold to say, Frontinus had never been read before —And then we claim to be normal human beings! Anyhow Dolphin is the bell wether of the eccentrics—never did I see such a sight as Dolphin in a needlework shop trying to conceal her picture under the counter which promptly fell flat on the floor to the horror of ten spinster women buying post cards.

Tell Clive—this won't interest you—that a lady in a large blue motor car stopped a small boy in Rodmell village two days ago, and gave him a large bunch of roses, an earthenware pan containing several rocks and small alpine plants, and a letter, telling him to give them to Mrs Woolf with her love, and then drove off—This was our (Clive's and my) Vita.

Leonard is coming to see you. I am kept very short of pleasures still, but submit, like the sweet hearted innocent I am. Tell Angus: that I'm in

1. Virginia had previously called this woman 'Betsy Kingsford' and 'Betsy Roberts'.

daily touch with Doris [Daglish] of Nicosia Road Wandsworth, and find
it a clammy proceeding. She perspires—she is without charm.
Tell Duncan I wish to God he would come and see me.

VW.

Berg

1585: To Janet Case

Monk's House, Rodmell
[Sussex]

Friday [18 September 1925]

No, my dear Janet, it can't be done. I see your kindly wish to praise me;
but it won't do, what you say, in the least. I can assure you, being an expert
on these matters, that you can't get any pleasure—not real pleasure, worth
having—from things being pulled off, and technique being clever, and
words magical, and all so beautiful—that's precisely my point about
Stevenson. One can always separate his technique from his matter, and the
pleasure is so thin that I, for one, can't read a single thing of his (except
some of the poems perhaps) a second time.[1] But try Lamb. I defy you to
say of him what you say of Mrs D.—its all perfectly shallow and uninterest-
ing and unreal in matter but its so lovely and clever and dashing and brilliant
in style that one cant help reading every word. I assure you, not one of
his essays, which are, of course, technically perfect, can be split into two
like that. The difference is really rather an interesting and important one I
think. I have to lecture a girls school on it[2]—that is, on the right way of
reading novels—so that is why I am cheerfully sacrificing Mrs D. to higher
objects—your complete rout and reversal—you admit I've done it. But
you're extremely kind—I don't deny that.

I am still a good deal bothered with the infernal headache, so have to
think about writing, instead of writing, and find all these problems awfully
difficult. What is form? What is character? What is a novel? Think them
out for me. The truth is of course that no one for 100 years has given a
thought to novels, as they have done to poetry: and now we wake up,
suffocated, to find ourselves completely in the dark. But its an interesting
age, you'll admit. Only, for a novelist, confusing. I don't think you settle
the matter by labelling the elderly Victorians and the young Georgians.
This all proves that I must come to the spare room and sit up till dawn
arguing. Love to Emphie.

Yrs
V.W.

Sussex

1. See Letter 1575.
2. At Hayes Common on 30 January 1926. The lecture was published as *How
Should One Read a Book* (*Yale Review*, October 1926).

1586: To Saxon Sydney-Turner   *Monk's House [Rodmell,*
                                    Sussex]
20th Sept [1925]

My dear Saxon,
    None of your friends has ever shown greater proof of devotion than I,
in writing this.
    Writing has become a frivolity and a weariness—indeed, for 5 weeks I
have lain like a log, chiefly in bed, and when out, unvisited by ideas—except
that it is hot (more likely cold) cloudy, likely to blow a gale, and so on.
    I am now however moved by your cheque, and that picture of you
reading Frontinus at Table d'hôte which you knew I should like, to write,
if only one page.
    Nothing can be said to have happened—a visit from Clive, very portly
and prosperous, a visit from Lydia, who rode a bicycle against Maynard's
wish, and so very rightly fell off and cut her knee, a visit from Angus:
but nothing said half so clever, I daresay, as what you said to Wittgenstein
—the fame of that interview has gone round the world. How you talked
without ceasing, some say in an obscure Austrian dialect, of the soul, and
matter, till W. was moved to offer himself to you as bootboy at Hogarth
House, in order to hear you still talk. I have always been one of those who
maintained that the flowering of the aloe, once in a hundred years, was
worth waiting for. I have compared it to snow falling by moonlight. The
extreme rarity, I have said, of the loveliest things is part of their charm.
And this had reference to you.
    But then, too, I have always liked the frozen water and the closed buds.
In fact, if I had to write an obituary of any of my friends, for sheer pleasure
give me, either yours or Rogers, I don't know which. This refers to the
fact that by the same post as your letter, Roger wrote saying how he was
sitting up in a railway carriage as dawn broke over the Pyrenees translating
Ronsard. A pair of you! I like to think of the wilderness of France salted
with such as you.
    Of other news (this must count as news, and I daresay, except when
you are shaving you never give yourself a thought—it is in my brain that
you chiefly live—a terrible and indeed overwhelming thought, considering how very crack brained I am, and how easily the image may be
shivered)—except for news of you and Roger I have little. Bunny I see
has brought out a book about a prize fighter and a negress:[1] but—You
may interpret that to mean that I have my doubts. You will say I am jealous;
hypercritical, ungenerous: I reply, no, I am willing to be pleased, but doubt,
I think, his brain power. What I mean is, the train is laid, carefully, con-
scientiously, for satire: and then, the brain fails, and the train remains—but

1. *The Sailor's Return* (1925), by David Garnett.

I mean pattern, design, story, rather, laid as carefully as ever: I am growing old, and want more mustard to my meat.

Talking of the aged, Lytton is said to come this way, to Maynard, I think, tomorrow. I daresay I shall see him, and we shall fall into disagreement, but amicably, about everything under the sun; love, and beauty, and prose, and poetry. Then we shall disintegrate happily in mere gossip, of an entirely frivolous nature: you, for example.

We go back in 10 days or so. What a miracle I am! I have written 4 pages in little over 15 minutes. The bells are ringing for harvest festival; it simply pours, which I can't help admiring—so my dear Dr Johnson would have behaved if silly donkeys offered him vegetable marrows and purple asters after a summer like this. Leonard has just ridden off to take train to London. Grizzle is asleep in his chair. I think that is probably a rat in the wainscot—I dont know, as you would say, it may be a mouse. Come and see us and don't forget—I have no room to say what.

Yr
V.W.

I wrote this 10 days ago, and it got put away. So now I daresay you're at Hogarth again. We are in London. (2nd Oct)

Sussex

1587: To Vanessa Bell   *Monks House, Rodmell*
                                          [Sussex]
Wednesday [23 September 1925]

I enclose the only one of L's signatures I can find.

But if you want his full name, I daresay I could get it.

I am sending you a book by a brother brush by the way, for the sake of the pictures—never return it. The Keynes' are back,[1] entirely rigged out in Russian shirts, boots, hats etc and are on us this afternoon. Tilton is too near.

If you and Duncan were to come over, of course we should be delighted, but I dont expect you can.

Oh thanks for the Venison—delicious.

Its awful to be going back so soon.

I've bought a lot more wools, and work hard, but not hopefully.

Berg

1. From Russia, where they had spent their honeymoon.

Monks House [Rodmell, Sussex]

Wednesday [23 September 1925]

My dear Vita,

Do keep it up—your belief that I achieve things.[1] I assure you, I have need of all your illusions after 6 weeks of lying in bed, drinking milk, now and then turning over and answering a letter. We go back on Friday; what have I achieved? Nothing. Hardly a word written, masses of complete trash read, you not seen, but what was the good of asking you to come for half an hour, and then being furious to see you go? The blessed headache goes—I catch a cold or argue violently and it comes back. But now it has gone longer than ever before, so if I can resist the delights of chatter, I shall be robust for ever. But what I was going to say was to beg for more illusions. I can assure you, if you'll make me up, I'll make you.

The grocer[2] had to go back—What a weight I found him to carry to the post! Inconceivable trash—conceive a boy, after ladling sugar and rice all day, sitting down to copy out in a firm beautiful hand, with large black capitals, 600 pages of moonshine raptures about the violet lids of ladies, and Lord Eustace in a motor car! The Lady at Wandsworth [Doris Daglish] says she must see me; has no money: feels the romance of virginity in her bones: So I've told her to write it out of them in her own proper name— Why these cloaks and disguises? The idea had never struck her that her one novel, with ten different names, is all about herself. She thinks the idea bold and fascinating. So do I. There is an odd mixture of desperation and futility about her, but she'll come, and spend an hour, and oh how I shall squirm at the end of the line! But then, you see, providence has so arranged it that other peoples lives—I'm thinking of yours not hers—are romantic; and so by creating and being created one swims along, never knowing the truth about anything. It is providence after all—that you should have illusions I mean.

This is miserable scribbling, the effervescence of idleness. (I'm waiting for luncheon) but I shall rouse up in London. However, I'm going to live the life of a badger, nocturnal, secretive, no dinings out, or gallivantings, but alone in my burrow at the back. And you will come and see me there— please say you will: if you're in London, let me know. A little quiet talk in the basement—what fun! And then I'm going this winter to have one great gala night a month: The studio will be candle lit, rows of pink, green, and blue candles, and a long table laid with jugs of chocolate and buns.

1. Vita had written on 18 September: "You are one perpetual achievement, yet you give the impression of having infinite leisure. . . . How is it done? I can only suppose you don't fritter." (*Berg*)
2. See Letter 1582.

Everybody will be discharged into this room, unmixed, undressed, unpowdered. You will emerge like a lighthouse, fitful, sudden, remote (Now that is rather like you) This way of seeing people might be gigantically successful, and then your cousin [Eddy] has lent me his piano, and I intend to break up the horror of human intercourse with music. It struck me on my snails walk to the river this afternoon (I have now had tea and lit the fire, unsuccessfully) that the fear and shock and torture of meeting one's kind come from the conditions—being clasped to each other unmitigatedly, on a sofa—pure, neat, entire (I cant think of the word I want). Now if we could be dispersed a little—could we visit St Pauls, or the Tower or Ken Wood, where the scenery or the noble buildings would intervene between us, then we should sail gradually and calmly into latitudes of intimacy which in drawing rooms are never reached. Do you agree? Every Wednesday I shall take a trip in an omnibus with someone to mitigate the shock of human intercourse.

But I was going to write about Hamlet, which I read last night, but have no time. What a bore! Directly one begins a letter one has to stop. I was going to say, too, something so interesting. But, anyhow, when is your poem coming? Now I feel afraid of having asked for it, as I cannot criticise poetry, only buzz outside like an old intoxicated frantic bee: whereas you go about your business calmly within. How I envy you!

By the way, the great excitement of my life, responsibility, and in a sense burden, because Leonard is furiously jealous, is your garden. The cook shouts "Oh ma'am, a crocus is coming up". Then "A mouse has nibbled the crocus, ma'am!" I spring up, accuse Leonard; find its a false alarm. But you have complicated my relations for life.

Your V.W.

Berg

1589: To V. Sackville-West   *Monk's House, Rodmell*
                                   [Sussex]
Sunday [September 1925?]

My dear Vita,
    For a famous novelist, I don't think you show much acumen in dealing with the awful situation of Friday.
    I may state categorically in your own alphabetical system that
    (a) neither of the Wolves suspected you for a moment of wishing to put them off
    (b) far from being officious, they thought the offer the natural instinct of a generous heart which
    (c) they would certainly have accepted if
        (1) it had been a fine day
        (2) or Mr Woolf had been unable to go by train.

In conclusion I'm afraid you must think (1) me an appalling vile valetudianian [*sic*], (2) Leonard an awful fuss. But the truth is that (3) headaches can be the devil, so that (4) Mr Woolf gets alarmed, loses his head, accepts offers, (5) Mrs Woolf wakes up better, (6) he repents of dragging Vita out, (7) she rings up, (8) Wolves incline to train, (9) Vita obstinate but (10) succumbs—and there you are.

As to going home, I can't be sure which day, so come to Tavistock instead (I shall be back Tuesday or Wednesday) and (11) dont put me off and (12) many thanks from us both and (13) much affection from Virginia Woolf who thinks (15) Mrs Nicolson one of the nicest women she (16) has ever met.

Do you think this style is clearer than the other? I'm not sure. Anyhow I cannot write a legible word, tonight, and am ever so much better.

yr
V.W.

Berg

1590: To Vanessa Bell   [*Monk's House, Rodmell, Sussex*]

Tuesday [29 September 1925]

Dearest Dolph:

We go on Friday, at cockcrow, so come before then if you can.

Leonard saw Lottie yesterday, and Karin does seem to be very bad[1]— in fact it sounds ghastly, but they hope it may improve—She's had to give up going to America.

As for Lottie Elle est amoureuse de l'homme qui mène les vaches à Thorpe, et il répond passionement. C'est bien ennuyant, mais que voulez-vous? L'Amour est le tout puissant dieu des mortels, et l'homme, qui s'appelle Claud Crisp, est vraiment beau, et habite, avec sa vielle mère, une petite maison bien commode, dans laquelle le grand docteur, William Gull, naquit il y a plusieurs anneés. *This is a deadly secret*—even about Sir William Gull.

Give my love to old convolvulus bed [Duncan]—what a perfect image of his voluptuous creamy grace that was to be sure—and then the snakes, no thicker than a whip, but deadly. Roger has fallen over a public shelter at Cassis by night and knocked out all his front teeth.

---

1. During an operation on Karin Stephen to relieve her deafness, the surgeon cut a nerve in her face, which half-paralysed it and rendered her temporarily speechless.

Sussex is becoming nothing but an annexe to Chelsea—we only missed
by the skin of our teeth—whom do you think?—Herbert Fisher!
I'm for the Isles of Stornoway [Outer Hebrides].

B.

Berg

1591: To V. Sackville-West   52 *Tavistock Square, W.C.*1

Tuesday [13 October 1925]

My dear Vita,
      But for how long?[1]
      For ever?
      I am filled with envy and despair. Think of seeing Persia—think of
never seeing you again.
      The Dr has sent me to bed: all writing forbidden. So this is my swan
song. But come and see me.

Yr V.W.

Do let me hear. I hope the tooth is better

Berg

1592: To H. G. Leach   52 *Tavistock Square, W.C.*1

Typewritten
Oct 14th 1925

Dear Mr Leach,[2]
      My husband has told me of his talk with you, and I have now had a
letter from the Forum office. It is very good of you to ask me to submit
another story for your consideration, but I feel that it would only be a
waste of your time. The stories I have at present are much in the same
style as The New Dress and are open to the same objections. But if at any
time I should write anything which appears more likely to suit you, I shall
have great pleasure in submitting it. I much regret that illness prevented
me from seeing you.

Yours sincerely
Virginia Woolf

Houghton Library, Harvard University

1. Harold Nicolson was told by the Foreign Office that he had been posted to
   the British Legation in Teheran. He left England on 4 November, and in reply
   to this letter from Virginia, Vita told her that she intended to visit him in
   Persia from January to May 1926, and again in October of that year, but not
   to remain there.
2. Editor of the *Forum* (New York). See Letter 1566.

1593: To V. SACKVILLE-WEST   [52 *Tavistock Square, W.C.*1]

Wednesday [14? October 1925]

I'm hoping to get Leonard to ask you to come and see me tomorrow. Nessa I think comes Friday. It's frightfully selfish as I'm too stupid to talk. But I should so like it, if it isn't difficult for you. I'm much better. I had rather sharp pain for two days, and so feel rather done up, but I've slept almost all day for 3 days, not thought or read, and there's nothing to worry about. I'm very comfortable.

The flowers are quite divine. How good you are to me!

Don't come if its the least bother.

Berg

1594: To V. SACKVILLE-WEST   52 *Tavistock Square, W.C.*1

[26? October 1925]

My dear Vita—only it ought to be all execration—

I asked you to LEND me M.B¹—Now you GIVE him. Very well—I'll never ask you for so much as the loan of a boot button again.

Nevertheless, your present was perfectly timed—All Friday [23 October] I was sick without stopping (my own fault—I refused to believe the doctor who said it would stop if I ate a mutton chop—when I did I was cured instantly) but by 6 p.m. I was almost extinct with the horror and then your present came: I ate my chop, revived, and read till I fell asleep. Nothing could have suited better. Indeed, I think he's very good—so demure, so sprightly.

Only your character remains irretrievably damned.

I agree about the horror of one hours talk²—3 would be far less tiring, as half an hours writing is more effort than 2.

Still, at present its all I can get. As for coming to you, I should really like it—this is the greatest compliment I can pay and it is very good of you to think of it. Only at present I can't make the Dr. say when I can get up, when go away, or anything.

So may I leave it? Only you must plan independently.

L. likes your poem, and is printing it.³ I like it—I'll tell you why, if you can face another hours torture. You did not tire me: it was enchanting: and next time I would arrange for some silence for you—

1. Maurice Baring, the poet and man of letters. Vita had sent Virginia a copy of *The Puppet Show of Memory*, his autobiography, published in 1922.
2. Vita had tea with Virginia on 19 October.
3. *On the Lake* (*Nation & Athenaeum*, December 1925).

My love to Harold. Beg him not to drop me when he becomes an
Ambassador.

Yr
VW.

I hope I didn't give you your cold—how bloody the body is

Berg

1595: To Gerald Brenan   *52 Tavistock Square, W.C.*1

[4 November 1925]

Dear Gerald,

I won't deny that your flowers came at the very nick of time, and are
showering above me in such beauty that I can't keep my eyes off them—
but still it pains me to see you so extravagant. Please dont ever give me such
splendid things again.

I wish I could ask you to come and see me—when we could go into the
question of your character at greater length—but I'm kept very low in
the matter of visitors at the moment. Perhaps too, you, very reasonably,
hate sick visiting. But next week I hope you'll come, if I can square the
doctors.

Meanwhile, as I say, don't be so fantastically generous any more.

Yrs
V.W.

George Laʒarus

1596: To V. Sackville-West   *52 Tavistock Square, W.C.*1

Wednesday [early November? 1925]

My dear Vita

This is the only paper I can find. I cannot remember where we had got
to: cruelty? I was cruel, you said. I say, no, not cruel, only being ten years
(I suppose—b.1882) older than you, thus in another climate altogether,
honesty was so important that all my spies had to be forever watching
what came in with a view to imposters. I will explain one day.

I am alone, too. Leonard speaking at a meeting, then going to a party,
where a poor widow [Gwen Raverat], whose husband died by inches,
throughout his youth, of paralysis, is trying to fan a sort of ghastly flame
alive again.

She tells me awful things—But no matter: Don't lets go into death

219

and disillusionment. Aren't you one of the nicest and magnanimous of women? I think so. "Esteem" is a damned cold word—(yours for me) Still I accept it, like the humble spaniel I am.

We then come to what?—Not much news here. I wish you were in the chair opposite. Yes, I am actually sitting up, after dinner; and no pain.

Yes, I am very fond of you: but the poor spaniel will have its nose rapped if it says anything more.

I have to write a lecture, for school girls: "how should one read a Book?"[1] and this, by a merciful dispensation, seems to me a matter of dazzling importance and breathless excitement.

But I have been trying to prove to Raymond Mortimer that this is not vanity; No; I am not much impressed by what I do; only intoxicated by what is something like your night, your solitude, in which, as I maintain we writers—oh but I cannot find the image. So come and catch it. Its a question of being alone, in writing.

Yr VW.

Berg

1597: To T. S. Eliot   52 *Tavistock Square, W.C.*1

13th Nov: 1925

Dear Sir,
    I am sending my essay tomorrow,[2] Saturday morning, so that I hope it will reach you in time.
    I am sorry to have delayed, but I have been working under difficulties.

Yours sincerely
Virginia Woolf

Mrs T. S. Eliot

1598: To Janet Vaughan   52 *Tavistock Square, W.C.*1

Sunday [15? November 1925]

My dear Janet,
    I hope you won't mind my writing to you. I have thought so much of you, since Madge's death.[3] She was such a part of our childhood—I cant

1. See p. 211, note 2.
2. *On Being Ill* (*New Criterion*, January 1926).
3. Margaret Symonds, who married Virginia's cousin William Wyamar Vaughan, had been an intimate friend in her youth, and was the original of Sally Seton in *Mrs Dalloway*. Since then, they had seldom met. Madge died on 7 November 1925. Janet, her daughter, was 26 years old and a student of medicine. In 1945 she became Principal of Somerville College, Oxford.

describe to you what she was like when she used to stay with us at St Ives, and how we worshipped her. I had a long letter from her last summer, which was full of you, and the pleasure you gave her. She seemed so happy with you. She said then she wanted to come and see us in October, but I have been in bed ever since we got back, and so could not suggest anything. But if you ever liked to come and see me, it would be a great pleasure.

But please don't answer this. It is really selfish to write—but one can't help it.

Your affte
Virginia Woolf

Dame Janet Vaughan

1599: To V. Sackville-West   52 *Tavistock Square, W.C.*1
Monday [16 November 1925]

My dear Vita,

Its perfectly enchanting and has lasted me two whole days—your picture: the chauffeur, the secretary your mother the night.[1] There are at least 3 novels in it. Send me some more: If only all novels were that—balls of string for one to pull out endlessly at leisure.

I want you to invent a name by the way which I can use instead of 'novel'. Thinking it over, I see I cannot, never could, never shall, write a novel. What, then, to call it?

I've flashed to the top of Hampstead Heath in a motor car, sat on a bench and seen three fir trees in the fog; flashed back and seen Nancy Cunard, whose father has left her, to be kept perpetually, an entire fox of solid silver. And why dont I see you?

Owing to standing or sitting 3 minutes too long in the Press I am put back into bed—all the blame now falling on the Hogarth Press. But this is nothing very bad—I feel as if a vulture sat on a bough above my head, threatening to descend and peck at my spine, but by blandishments I turn him into a kind red cock.

I am very sorry for you—really—how I should hate Leonard to be in Persia! But then, in all London, you and I alone like being married.

And where's your poem [*The Land*]?

Yr VW.

Berg

1. Vita had just spent four days with her mother, Lady Sackville, in her house at Brighton, and had described the visit in a letter to Virginia.

1600: To Edward Sackville West
52 *Tavistock Square, London, W.C.*1
[November 1925]

Dear Mr Sackville West

It was very good of you to write.

I am still kept strictly in bed and visitors rationed, but if you should be in London, I hope you will come and see me, only its better to ring up first.

This explains why the piano has remained dumb. I make do with an algraphone,[1] as I can't get down to my studio.

Your
Virginia Woolf.

Are you writing de Quincey?[2]

Berg

1601: To Edward Sackville West
52 *Tavistock Square, London, W.C.*1
Nov 30th [1925]

Dear Mr Sackville West,

Please send me a line anytime either to me or to Angus Davidson, and the piano will be given up. It has been bad luck that I have not made more use of it; but it was very good of you to lend it.

My plans are very vague at present, but I hope if you are in London there may be a chance of seeing you. The dr. lets me read and write, but is very strict still about the pleasures of society.

Yrs Sincerely
Virginia Woolf

Berg

1. Joke-word for a gramophone in a sick-room.
2. Edward Sackville West's book on de Quincey, *A Flame in Sunlight,* was not published until 1936,

Letters 1602-1612 (December 1925–mid-January 1926)

On 17 December Virginia went to stay with Vita at Long Barn for three nights. It was the beginning of their love-affair. "A peaceful evening", wrote Vita in her discreet diary on the 17th. But on the 18th: "Talked to her till 3 am. Not a peaceful evening." They met another six times before Vita left for Persia on 20 January, and although their correspondence contains veiled references to what happened at Long Barn, Vita did not for the moment tell Harold Nicolson, and denied it hotly when challenged by Clive Bell.

1602: To V. Sackville-West   [52 Tavistock Square, W.C.1]

Wednesday [9 December 1925]

My dear Vita,
    The dr. says I may go away. Would you like me to come to you for a day or two, if you are alone, before the 20th? I expect this is too late and too difficult; I only suggest it on the off chance, and the understanding that you will say *honestly*.
    Or would after Christmas be better?
    I am perfectly well, but they would not say so until last week.
                                        Yours ever,
                                        V.W.

Could you let me have a line, as I have various arrangements to make.

Berg

1603: To V. Sackville-West   52 Tavistock Sqre, WC

Thursday [10 December 1925]

My dear Vita,
    That will be enchanting—its awfully good of you.[1]
    Would Tuesday afternoon suit you?

1. Vita's letter of 8 December had crossed with Virginia's. The eventual arrangement was that Vita met Virginia in London on the 17th and brought her down by car to Long Barn, where she stayed for three nights, Leonard joining them for the night of the 19th.

Should I stay till Friday or Saturday?
Should Leonard come and fetch me back?
Should you mind if I only brought one dressing gown?
Should I be a nuisance if I had breakfast in bed?
As for your mysteries, I will leave them till I see you, and can investigate at leisure.[1]

But I only put these questions on the understanding that you explain your wishes frankly.

No, I can't go into the question of Raymond and Syria:[2] but beware —all this romantic travelling soon becomes monstrous absurd. I am jealous.

Yr
V.W.

Berg

1604: To V. Sackville-West   52 *Tavistock Square, W.C.*1

Tuesday, Dec. 22nd [1925]

My dear Mrs Nicolson—ah hah!—this is only to say what in the scramble I had not time to say yesterday, that my address is Charleston, Firle, Lewes, till Monday next, and hope for a letter from you. Also that I woke trembling in the night—what at? At the thought that I had been grossly inhospitable about lunch on Sunday. There it was smoking on the table—chicken and apple tart, cream, and coffee: and you, after motoring, spoiling, caring cossetting the Wolf kind for 3 days, sent empty along the pavement. Good God—how the memory of these things bites like serpents in the night! But the bite was assuaged by the pleasures.

I am dashing off to buy, a pair of gloves. I am sitting up in bed: I am very very charming; and Vita is a dear old rough coated sheep dog: or alternatively, hung with grapes, pink with pearls, lustrous, candle lit, in the door of a Sevenoaks draper. I'll ask Nessa whether Saturday or Sunday [at Charleston] and write to Knole. But do not snuff the stinking tallow out of your heart—poor Virginia to wit, and Dog Grizzle (who is scratching under my bed) Now for a Bus down Southampton Row.

Ah, but I like being with Vita.

VW

Berg

1. Vita had written: "I have been doing something so odd, so queer . . . entirely connected with you, and wild horses won't drag from me what it was" (*Berg*). The 'mystery' still defies detection.
2. Raymond Mortimer joined Vita and Harold in Persia (not Syria) in the spring of 1926.

1605: TO V. SACKVILLE-WEST   *Charleston, Firle,*
                                               Lewes [*Sussex*]
[23 December 1925]

Dictated by Clive

Dearest Vita,

It is the universal wish of the house that you should *come*, and we
hope to see you any time on Saturday morning, to stay to lunch, tea dinner
—anything.[1]

I am sorry to say that my dear old friend Crusty Roger [Fry] who has
been talking of the Gulf Stream, Rembrandt, instinct, sex in chickens,
since Dawn, will *not* be here. But my sister Fusty Vanessa, whose beauty
burns through her rags (dictated by Vanessa) is in great spiritual vigour:
oaths and tropes roll and rollick from her lips; she is entirely loveable,
cuddlable and delightful. As for my dear (dictated by Virginia) Clive,
whose heart is turning to honey, in which the yellow bee *blooms*, he has
provided a stuffed Turkey, lozenged with truffles: he is as ripe as can be;
vigorous, virile, virtuous, and now we walk through the clods together
talking, first one and then another, of Vita Vita Vita as the new moon rises
and the lambs huddle on the downs.

Berg

1606: TO SAXON SYDNEY-TURNER
                                           52 *Tavistock Square, W.C.*1
Dec 29th [1925]
Dear Saxon,

Many thanks for the cheque, which I got at Charleston, but could not
acknowledge, as my ink gave out, and the house was dry of ink.

We had a very amusing Christmas. Your sweets were appreciated. We
drank audit ale. It was very wet—I am glad to be back. I hope you will
come and see me. Whats the use of reading my books when you never
give tongue to your probably infallible criticism?

                                                        Yours V.W.
Sussex

1607: TO V. SACKVILLE-WEST   [52 *Tavistock Square, W.C.*1]

Tuesday [5 January 1926]

Yes, my dear Creature, do come tomorrow, as early as possible—I'm

1. Vita lunched at Charleston on 26 December.

225

threatened with Robert Graves, Mrs R., and Nancy Gottshalk,[1] so come early and we'll stick stamps or see fish—But I want to know *why* you were perturbed, and wrote in such a whirl, and *what* your fire talk was about— oh and crowds of things.

But I'm in a rush—have just taken Grizzle to a vet. in the Grays Inn Rd. and now must dash off—Ah, if you want my love for ever and ever you must break out into spots on your back. And you won't; for if ever a woman was a lighted candlestick, a glow, an illumination which will cross the desert [to Persia] and leave me—it was Vita: and thats the truth of it: and she has nothing, nor will ever have, in common with dog Grizzle who stands before me, raw, greasy, mudstained—

But, as I say, come early
I can't form a word

VW.

Berg

1608: To V. Sackville-West   [52 *Tavistock Square, W.C.1*]

Thursday [7 January 1926]

This is simply to ask how you are—temperature 101, 102, 103? Feeling very miserable, half asleep, taking a little tea and toast, and then, I daresay, towards evening becoming rather luminous and remote, and irresponsible.[2] All this takes place in a room in the middle of Knole—What takes place in all those galleries and ballrooms, I wonder? And then, what goes on in Vita's head, lying under her arras somewhere, like a tiny kernel in a vast nut?

Nothing has happened to me: but Leonard is lunching with Tom Eliot, and Nancy (*Cunard*) who telephoned the moment you left, is coming to tea—oh, and I had an interview with the devastation of all hearts, Stephen Tomlin, who is flying, like Daphne, was it, pursued by his lovers, to a refuge in the outskirts of London, where no one shall follow him, for really he says he is now half crazy: wishing to love, and to give, accepting every invitation, and then finding, what appals him, that people love him in return. I found him rather an interesting object, for one reason in that he resembles me (what other is so attaching?) in this myriad minded innumerable curiosity about others—But, whereas they return his interest, no one returns mine. So he is gone to his retreat. After that—what? I read

1. Robert Graves, the poet, was then married to Nancy, daughter of William Nicholson, the painter. 'Nancy Gottshalk' was the American poet Laura Gottschalk, who later called herself Laura Riding. She collaborated with Robert Graves on *A Survey of Modernist Poetry* (1927).
2. Vita had been inoculated in preparation for her Persian journey.

some of the Tempest, to compare with Defoe.[1] But oh my dear Vita, what a rush of delight and relief it is to read poetry after prose!

So continue your poem: and one day I will explain the torrent of my own emotions about Shakespeare—compared with Defoe. For many years I have not dared to say anything about poetry. These professors hem one down in their hen-coops. What is poetry and so on: their replies to questions have kept me dumb. Shall we write a little book on poetry together? But I must have my luncheon: veal, I think, an orange, and a new kind of cake, made white red and orange; then print: then Nancy. But tell me what you are feeling? Are you aching? And if you were asked, do you like Canute [Vita's elk-hound], Canute's wife, or Virginia best, what would you say?

I left a rain coat, a crystal ruler, a diary for the year 1905,[2] a brooch, and a hot water bottle somewhere—Either Long Barn or Charleston—and so contemplate complete nudity by the end of the year.

Yr
VW

Berg

1609: To V. Sackville-West   52 *Tavistock Square, W.C.*1

Saturday [9 January 1926]

Isn't it damned? Here I am in bed with the flu, caught the moment I'd written to you about the delights of fever. Hot and sticky describes it. But what I'm writing about is Tuesday. I hope to be perfectly well, but infection? Shan't I give it you again? I think you'd better ring up on Tuesday morning. You see, if you came, I should let you in without fail, whatever the risk for you—I do want so much to see you. And it'll be 5 days by then and so I dont think there can be any risks: its only conscience.

No: I'm not susceptible to the mind: only the body (I think) and Tommie [Stephen Tomlin], tho' sprightly as an elf, is misshapen as a woodpecker—Whereas Vita—beech trees, waterfalls and cascades of blue black paper—all so cool and fruitful and delicious, especially when one's got a little temperature. I'm so furious: I was to begin that wretched novel [*To the Lighthouse*] today, and now bed and tea and toast and the usual insipidity. Oh damn the body.

But it is a great comfort to think of you when I'm not well—I wonder why. Still nicer—better to see you. So I hope for Tuesday.

1. *Robinson Crusoe* (*Nation & Athenaeum*, 6 February 1926).
2. In a paper read to the Memoir Club (which Quentin Bell dates 'about 1922'), Virginia said: "For some months in the winter of 1904-5 I kept a diary...." It survives in the Berg Collection.

(I'm not at all bad)
No news of Clive

Yr V.W.

A very nice dumb letter from you this morning. Tell me about the Boy Scouts?[1]

Berg

1610: To V. SACKVILLE-WEST
52 *Tavistock Square, London, W.C.*1
Monday [11 January 1926]

I am much better. The Dr.[2] says that I had a rash which may have been German Measles. It went almost at once, and I have had no temp. all day today. She thinks there is no risk of infection now whether it was German Measles or influenza. But if you've the least doubt about it, for God's sake don't come, for to start the journey with any kind of disease would be madness.

Of course I *want* you to come: enormously: its only conscience, and you must be extra cautious

Anyhow, I shall be in bed here alone all day tomorrow. If you come, stay as long as you can spare: I feel perfectly well, and I'll tell you all my views on the entire world: and it would be so nice.

Yr VW.

6 PM. Temp. normal—so thats 24 hours normal now—I think must be all right.

Berg

1611: To V. SACKVILLE-WEST   [52 *Tavistock Square, W.C.*1]
Friday [15 January 1926]

Dearest Creature,
    I saw Clive yesterday, who says will you and Leonard and I dine with him on Monday at the Ivy? If you cant, (as I fear) come to his rooms as soon as you can—We will come at 10.30, but I suppose I shan't be allowed to stay late.

1. A jamboree at Knole, where Vita was staying for several days.
2. Elinor Rendel, who was the daughter of Lytton Strachey's eldest sister.

228

Would you write a line (50,000 lines) to me on the matter, and I'll let him know.

Now, he is a damned good fellow isn't he? He was as red as a lion and as sweet as honey yesterday, and so raved, with such warmth and emotion, about you, that my heart was touched.* Oddly enough, he bagged one of my phrases for you—said you "glowed"—"a brilliant human being", "after Mary and Virginia the woman he would miss most". This brought us to the following petition: that you shall not go back to Persia in the autumn. For it can be proved to cause more pain than pleasure. As a poet you'll have sucked all that Persia has to give: whats six weeks with Harold to him compared with 4 months without you to us? And so on.

I got up and went out yesterday into the loveliest spectral world, all white, and with one or two lights. Then, round the Square came an eternal procession of funerals (so it seemed) walking, covered with white flowers. Only the burial of a Churchwarden I suppose, but more august than I can say. The Dr says I'm ever so much better than before Christmas. Did I have a thorough rest when I was away? So I said it was Long Barn; Early hours: lack of exciting conversation: Staying with the aristocracy in short. "Ah I see: good food and no mental or physical strain."

What else is there? I must stop and try to polish off my lecture [*How Should One Read a Book?*]; and tomorrow begin the novel, and send my bed back and resume my struggle with the world—Oh and Vita won't be here next week to adulterate it—you know what I mean—Its a word I can't find at the moment.

The party went off. Lady [Margot] Oxford was refused admittance by Molly MacCarthy. I like the barbarous incivility and independence of Bloomsbury manners. Mrs Courthauld[1] was also outed. So they kept themselves to themselves; and got tipsy.

Here's Roger ringing up to ask me to go to the Sargent show: Doris Daglish[2] wanting to see us: "a little work would keep me from using my writing in a degrading way" and so on.

But I'm rather spoilt, and want Vita; and not Roger: and not Doris: and not Mary: and not nobody else.

What time will you come on Monday? dearest Creature?

Now though this has been written, by the glare of the snow, sitting up

* He gave me his version of the conversation at Sherclos: [?][3]

1. Elizabeth Courtauld, wife of Samuel, the industrialist and patron of the arts.
2. See Letter 1588.
3. This was Sherfield Court, near Basingstoke, Hampshire, Dorothy Wellesley's country house. Vita had spent New Year there, with Clive as a fellow guest. He asked Vita whether she had slept with Virginia, and Vita hotly denied it.

in bed, in precisely 10 minutes for the cook to post when she goes to buy a dish of meat, it is not a dumb letter. Dogs letters are.

Yr VW.

Berg

1612: To V. Sackville-West   [52 *Tavistock Square, W.C.*1]

Saturday [16 January 1926]

Dearest Creature,

I'm perfectly well again—only made a fuss because I was so damned angry to spoil a day's writing.

Of course you shall come on Monday—don't you get through measles? Call her Vanessa. I'm amused at this advance on her part. Now I'm jealous.

Sales and reviews go on well.

Yr VW.

I do want to see you.

Berg

Letters 1613-1637 (mid-January–mid-May 1926)

Vita was away for four months, six weeks of which were taken up by her outward journey to Persia through the Mediterranean, Egypt, India, the Persian Gulf and Iraq, and ten days by the homeward journey through Russia and Poland. Virginia missed her dreadfully. At first she was consoled by the good progress she made with To the Lighthouse *("I have never written so fast"), but her elation was dimmed by German measles, Vita's long absence, the demands of the Press and the* Nation *(both of which Leonard considered giving up), constant social interruptions, servant trouble, and finally by the General Strike in early May, when Virginia and Leonard instinctively took the strikers' side. She enjoyed visits to two of Leonard's brothers in the country, and a longer trip to Dorset in April.*

1613: To V. Sackville-West   52 *Tavistock Sqre* [*W.C.*1]
Tuesday, January 26th, 1926

Your letter from Trieste came this morning—But why do you think I don't feel, or that I make phrases? "Lovely phrases" you say which rob things of reality. Just the opposite. Always, always, always I try to say what I feel. Will you then believe that after you went last Tuesday—exactly a week ago—out I went into the slums of Bloomsbury, to find a barrel organ. But it did not make me cheerful. Also I bought the Daily Mail—but the picture is not very helpful. And ever since, nothing important has happened—Somehow its dull and damp. I have been dull; I have missed you. I do miss you. I shall miss you. And if you don't believe it, your a longeared owl and ass. Lovely phrases?

You were sitting on the floor this time last week, where Grizzle is now. Somehow, as you get further away, I become less able to visualize you; and think of you with backgrounds of camels and pyramids which make me a little shy. Then you will be on board ship: Captains and gold lace: portholes, planks—Then Bombay where I must have had many cousins and uncles. Then Gertrude Bell—Baghdad. But we'll leave that, and concentrate upon the present. What have I done? Imagine a poor wretch sent back to school. I have been very industrious, no oranges picked off the top of a Christmas tree; no glittering bulbs. For one thing, you must have disorganised my domesticity, so that directly you went, a torrent of duties discharged themselves on top of me: you cant think how many mattresses

231

and blankets new sheets pillowcases, petticoats and dustpans I haven't had to buy. People say one can run out to Heals and buy a mattress: I tell you it ruins a day; 2 days: 3 days—Every time I get inside a shop all the dust in my soul rises, and how can I write next day? Moreover, somehow my incompetence, and shopkeepers not believing in me, harasses me into a nagging harpy. At last, at last,—but why should I go through it again? I sold 4 mattresses for 16 shillings; and have written I think 20 pages. To tell you the truth, I have been very excited, writing. I have never written so fast [*To the Lighthouse*]. Give me no illness for a year, 2 years, and I would write 3 novels straight off. It may be illusion, but (here I am rung up: Grizzle barks: settles in again—it is a soft blue evening and the lights are being lit in Southampton Row: I may tell you that when I saw crocuses in the Sqre yesterday, I thought May: Vita.[1]) What was I saying? Oh only that I think I can write now, never before—an illusion which attends me always for 50 pages. But its true I write quick—all in a splash; then feel, thank God, thats over. But one thing—I will not let you make me such an egoist. After all, why don't we talk about *your* writing? Why always mine, mine, mine? For this reason, I expect—that after all you're abundant in so many ways, and I a mere pea tied to a stick.

(Do you see how closely I am writing? That is because I want to say a great many things, yet not to bore you, and I think, if I write very close, Vita won't see how long this letter is, and she won't be bored) Have I seen anyone? Yes, a great many people, but by way of business mostly— Oh the grind of the Press has been rather roaring in my ears. So many manuscripts to read, poems to set up, and letters to write, and Doris Daglish to tea—A poor little shifty shabby shuffling housemaid, who ate a hunk of cake, and had the incredible defiance and self confidence which is partly lack of Education; partly what she thinks genius, and I a very respectable vivacious vulgar brain. "But Mrs Woolf, what I want to ask you is—have I in your opinion enough talent to devote my life entirely to literature?" Then it comes out she has an invalid father to keep, and not a halfpenny in the world. Leonard, after an hour of this, advised her, in his most decided voice, to become a Cook. That set her off upon genius and fiction and hope and ambition and sending novels to Tom Eliot and so— and so. Off she went, to Wandsworth; and we are to read her essay on Pope. Raymond I've seen: Clive and Mary. Siegfried Sassoon, Dadie and my French widow [Gwen Raverat].

Now Vita's getting bored in Bombay; but its a bald prosaic place, full of apes and rocks, I think: please tell me; you cant think how, being a clever woman, as we admit, I make every fragment you tell me bloom and blossom in my mind.

As for the people I've seen, I've fallen in love with none—but thats

1. She returned from Persia on 16 May.

not exactly my line. Did you guess that? I'm not cold; not a humbug; not weakly; not sentimental. What I am; I want you to tell me. Write, dearest Vita, the letters you make up in the train. I will answer everything.

I'm going to have a little dramatic society—I mean a flashy actress came to see me,[1] who having had her heart blighted, completely, entirely, irretrievably, has most unexpectedly got work, and says will I come and see her behind the scenes—I like the astonishing profusion of these poor creatures—all painted, glittering and unreal; with the minds of penny whistles; all desperate, what with being out of work, or in love: some have illegitimate children; one died on Sunday, and another is ill with typhoid. They think me a grotesque, semi-human gargoyle; screwed up like a devil in a Cathedral; and then we have tea, in some horrid purlieus of Soho, and they think this frightfully exciting—my unscrewing my legs and talking like a book. But it won't do for long. Its a snobbery of mine to adorn every society except my own.

Now I must finish, for I have to do my lecture for the school at Hayes Common on Saturday. Mary offers to lend me her motor: but no; I wont. I want Vita's motor; I want to be nicely treated by her; and I shant be.

Couldn't you write me lots more letters and post them at odd stations as you pass through?

But of course (to return to your letter) I always knew about your standoffishness. Only I said to myself, I insist upon kindness. With this aim in view, I came to Long Barn. Open the top button of your jersey and you will see, nestling inside, a lively squirrel, with the most inquisitive habits, but a dear creature all the same—

Your Virginia

Are you perfectly well? Tell me.

Berg

1614: To Richard Aldington   52 *Tavistock Square, W.C.*1

Jan 26th 1926

Dear Mr Aldington,

I am much flattered that you should ask me to write an introduction,[2] but I'm afraid I must refuse. I have so much work on hand that I don't know when I should find time to do it, and I am entirely ignorant of French 18th century memoirs: in fact I have never read Mme de Stael-Delannay.

Lytton Strachey is in the country, so I am writing him a line. I think

1. Hilda Trevelyan, (1877-1959), who acted under the stage name of Hilda Blow, and was the original 'Wendy' in Barrie's *Peter Pan* (1904).
2. To a new translation of *La Vie Privée du Maréchal Duc de Richelieu*.

233

if you wrote straight to him it would be best. His address is, Ham Spray House, Hungerford, Berks.

Yours sincerely,
Virginia Woolf

Texas

1615: To Lytton Strachey   52 *Tavistock Square W.C.*1

Jan 26th [1926]

Dearest Lytton,

Read the enclosed letter, but don't blame me for it. I have told Aldington that he may write straight to you. And I don't want it back—nevertheless you might write to me. I hear of you fascinating rabbits at parties. Also it is said that you are getting up a subscription to give Edmund Gosse gold sleevelinks on his 100th birthday. Poor old Angus has just stopped the rollers with paraffin, and the question, as put by Leonard with some force, is, "Is he a congenital idiot or not." I say "Congenital certainly."

I have had chickenpox whooping cough influenza and cowpox. I lead the life of a widow of 90, whose sons all perished in the Indian Mutiny or Crimean war, I forget which. This venerable lady finds her chief consolation in the works of Shakespeare and Lytton Strachey. And Mrs Smith of Cheltenham writes that she loves L.S. for having dedicated Q.V. [*Queen Victoria*] to V.W. So we are brought together mysteriously. Did you hear that Ottoline is at Chirk Castle having been exposed in every organ, to the Xrays and proved to be full of nothing but stale milk? All her injections for the past 5 yrs. at the hands of Dr Martin of Freiburg, were nothing but that.[1] Milk you know permeates, congeals and sours the most intimate organ.

Do tell Carrington to come and see me.

Yr. V.W.

Frances Hooper

1616: To Richard Aldington
                The Hogarth Press, 52 *Tavistock Square, W.C.*1

Typewritten

31st Jan [1926]

Dear Mr Aldington,

I happened to meet Lytton Strachey two days ago, and told him about

1. Ottoline Morrell was undergoing a cure at Chirk Castle, North Wales (since 1595 the property of the Myddelton family). Dr Marten had given her a fluid with which to inject herself. She passed on some of it to Siegfried Sassoon, who had it analysed. It turned out to be pure milk.

the introduction. I am afraid he is too much bothered with a new book he is trying to start to take on anything else, but no doubt he will write to you himself. I did my best.

I wish I could myself write the introduction you suggest—it is not that I dont want to do it. But after having been ill off and on for four months, and so having to put aside a new novel, I am now just beginning it again, and feel I must work straight ahead, and undertake as little outside that at present as possible. But it was very good of you to ask me, and I should have liked very much to do it, if I had not been in difficulties.

Yours sincerely
Virginia Woolf

Texas

1617: To V. Sackville-West

*The Hogarth Press, 52 Tavistock Square, W.C.*1

Sunday, Jan. 31st 1926

Look, I have stolen a piece of the press notepaper to write on, and it is Sunday morning about half past eleven, and I have written all I am going to write this morning. Now where are you? With Miss Gertrude Bell,[1] I suppose. I suppose you are very happy, seeing things—lovely things. I dont know what Baghdad is like, so I won't tell you. Miss Bell has a very long nose: she is like an Aberdeen terrier; she is a masterful woman, has everyone under her thumb, and makes you feel a little inefficient. Still, she is extremely kind, and asks so and so to meet you, and you are very grateful to her—Enough of Gertrude Bell; now for Virginia. Shall I write the letter I made up in bed this morning? It was all about myself. I was wondering if I could explain how miserable I have been the past 4 days, and why I have been miserable. Thought about, one can gloss things over, bridge them, explain, excuse. Writing them down, they become more separate and disproportioned and so a little unreal—Only I found I had to write the lecture for the girl's school, and so had to stop writing To the Lighthouse. That began my misery; all my life seemed to be thwarted instantly: It was all sand and gravel; and yet I said, this is the truth, this guilty misery, and the other an illusion; and then, dearest, people began ringing me up to go to lunch and tea—I was asked to meet a Spaniard in Holloway, a Frenchman in Chelsea, and see an Italian dance in Soho. Why did this make me desperate? I said, I must go and meet Jacques Blanche,[2]

1. Vita visited Gertrude Bell in Baghdad on 27 February and stayed with her a few days. She was then Oriental secretary to Sir Percy Cox, British High Commissioner in Iraq, and Director of Antiquities. She died a few months later on 12 July 1926.
2. Jacques-Emile Blanche, the French portrait painter, whom Virginia met through Ethel Sands.

because he will tell me about Proust; and also Hilda Trevelyan [Blow] has left me no loophole of escape; but now I must buy a hat. And last week I sold 4 mattresses, and bought the cook new bedroom curtains. Now I must waste a whole afternoon and suffer sheer agony in shops again buying a hat. And then, there being no illusion in my soul, no water under my keel, I had to dine with Dadie [Rylands], and undergo a large vociferous Bloomsbury party—sitting outside, with glass between me and everybody; hearing them laugh; and seeing, as through a telescope, (she looked so remote and washed up on a rock,) poor Edith Sitwell in her brocade dress, sitting silent.

I cant tell you how intense my unhappiness has been, starting up in the night, and clenching my hands, all over going out to dinner, and buying a hat, and meeting Jacques Blanche! And I had to take a sleeping draught. Then, in the middle of these 4 days, I went to hear Tolstois daughter lecture on him and her mother. And Lytton came up and praised my article in the Criterion [*On Being Ill*] tremendously, which, as we never praise each other's writing now, did for the moment illumine me: and Desmond came up and praised it, and this did not much please me, for his mind is all torn up sheets of paper now—such a ragbag; and then Countess Tatiana spoke, and I hated us all, for being prosperous and comfortable; and wished to be a working woman, and wished to be able to excuse my life to Tolstoi. Not that it was a good lecture. It was quite dull. But seeing his daughter, a shabby little black old woman, a perfect lady, with his little eyes, excited me; and made the whole world inside my head spin round, and the tears come to my eyes—but this is what always happens to me when the disgusting and foetid story of the Tolstois married life is told me and by their daughter too. And also, in Hill Street, Berkeley Square to an audience which seemed to have cheeks of paté de foie gras and sables on their backs and nothing nothing left of humanity or emotion at all. "The ladies will know what it means to nurse 13 children" said Tatiana: but I felt the ladies did not even know what it is to have monthly periods.

So I went off—with Mary in a taxi, as it happened. And Raymond came to dinner, and wanted me to meet Mrs Craigie,[1] and I said I didn't want to meet the upper classes: I wanted to meet washerwomen, and shopkeepers. Of course, how was Raymond to know I had been spun round by Tolstoi? I seemed to him merely waspish and plaguy, making excuses, and sneering and laughing at his ladies. And what was at the back of it all was simply my not being able to get away off into my novel; my being pinned down tight to my lecture. I gave this at Hayes Common yesterday.

Do you by any chance remember Kent? After all, I did go down in Mary's [Hutchinson] motor, with Nessa and Duncan. It struck me then

1. Marjorie Craigie, who for some time had worked in Paris as a *vendeuse* for one of the great fashion houses. She was a woman of outstanding elegance and charm.

that part of my misery is not having you. Yes, I miss you, I miss you. I dare not expatiate, because you will say I am not stark, and cannot feel the things dumb people feel. You know that is rather rotten rot, my dear Vita. After all, what is a lovely phrase? One that has mopped up as much Truth as it can hold.

But this analysing reminds me of my lecture, which I am infinitely sick of—To explain different kinds of novels to children—to make little anecdotes out of it—that took me more time and trouble than to write 6 Times leaders. But it was all right—60 nice children: a large Georgian country house; immense cedars; angular open minded school mistresses: a drive home in the dark with Nessa and Duncan, who pour out pure gaiety and pleasure in life, not brilliantly or sparklingly, but freely quietly luminously. And as we drove, I kept seeing the streets you drove me through: and thinking about you, and thinking how shy I had been of you; and then, when I rushed you, how you at once stepped out of that focus into another; and what distance shall we be at on Monday the 10th May [Vita's return]?

Tuesday, Feb. 2nd. Now I must end this. And I haven't said anything very much, or given you any notion of the terrific high waves, and the infernal deep gulfs, on which I mount and toss in a few days. So does everyone. Up and down we go, violently, incessantly; and I'm half ashamed, now I try to write it, to see what pigmy egotisms are at the root of it, with me anyhow—that I can't write my novel, must go out to tea, should buy a hat. Oh but there's Vita too—thats not a pigmy egotism—wanting her.

D'you know—I had a real shock of disappointment this morning? I was certain I had a letter from you—tore it open—found, instead, a letter from a woman [Ethel Pye] who sat opposite me in a blue bus 10 years ago, and wants now to come and do a bust of my head—But the flattery of this made me so angry that I've been again cursing—no privacy, always people coming, and *no letter from you.* Why not? Only a scrap from Dover, and a wild melancholy adorable moan from Trieste.[1]

No photograph either.

Goodbye, dearest shaggy creature.

Yr V.W.

Berg

1618: To V. Sackville-West   52 *Tavistock Square, W.C.1*

Feb. 3rd 1926

Heres a letter from Cairo, I mean from the shores of Greece [Crete],

1. "It is incredible how essential to me you have become. . . . Damn you, spoiled creature; I shan't make you love me any the more by giving myself away like this." (Vita to Virginia, 21 January 1926, from Trieste. *Berg*)

come this morning, a dumb letter; but I'm getting good at reading them. I did like it. And I wrote to you yesterday, to Baghdad, and see that I must write now to catch the mail, to Teheran; so theres no news—Also, you'll be so excited, happy, and all that. You'll have forgotten me, the room, the crane. We cut a very poor show against Teheran. Grizzle is in hospital, with mange; and I'm alone—oh Thank God—Morgan Forster and a wretched Frenchman, who talked without stopping, having this moment gone. How difficult it is to imagine any word of this reaching to you at Teheran! Have you got through safe and well? Are you happy? What do you see when you look over this paper? Rose pink hill, and little tufts of red flowers, I imagine.

I'm too dissipated to write. Morgan has been staying with old Hardy —The film company rings up and says "will you arrange for us to film the great novelist at work? For we hear he can't live long." Mrs Hardy came in to tell Morgan this, much distressed, for old Hardy hadn't been well. Then she says, "Who do you think should write my husbands life?" In order to feel the ground, Morgan says, "Well, Middleton Murry's a great admirer"—Whereupon Mrs Hardy flames out (to all our joy) "No, no, Mr Forster, We should not like that at all"—in spite of the devotion of that worm, who took his wife to be delivered of a son, to be called Thomas, in Dorchester, but she was delivered, of a daughter, 50 miles away. Murry, by the way has arraigned your poor Virginia, and Virginia's poor Tom Eliot, and all their works, in the Adelphi, and condemned them to death.[1]

On Friday (but this will have happened weeks ago) we go to Rodmell. Dearest, how nice to have you there, in a month or two. I made £20 unexpectedly yesterday, and vowed to spend it perfecting the water closet on your behalf. But Teheran is exciting me too much. I believe, at this moment, more in Teheran than in Tavistock Square. I see you, somehow in long coat and trousers, like an Abyssinian Empress, stalking over those barren hills. But really what I want to know is how the journey went, the 4 days through the snow, the caravan. Shall you write and tell me? And the affectionate letter—whens that coming?

I am back again in the thick of my novel, and things are crowding into my head: millions of things I might put in—all sorts of incongruities, which I make up walking the streets, gazing into the gas fire. Then I struggle with them, from 10 to 1: then lie on the sofa, and watch the sun behind the chimneys: and think of more things: then set up a page of poetry in the basement, and so up to tea and Morgan Forster. I've shirked 2 parties, and another Frenchman, and buying a hat, and going to tea with Hilda Trevelyan: for I really can't combine all this with keeping my imaginary people going.

1. In this month's *Adelphi* Murry asserted that both *Jacob's Room* and *The Waste Land* were 'failures' and would not be read in fifty years' time.

Not that they are people: what one imagines, in a novel, is a world. Then, when one has imagined this world, suddenly people come in—but I don't know why one does it, or why it should alleviate the misery of life, and yet not make one exactly happy; for the strain is too great. Oh, to have done it, and be free.

Wandering into the basement, where someone is always walking up and down talking it seems to me, I ran into Bob Trevelyan, who started off about you and Dotty: how he had read a poem of hers: thought you had a real literary gift; liked your Hops article [*Nation*, 10 October 1925]: and then, of course, he dwindled off on to his own poetry, and how to finish 3 plays and 4 epics, he must retire to Italy. Here the door opens and Mr [Hubert] Waley sends poems by Camilla Doyle[1] for Mrs Woolf to read. Mrs Woolf has 2 long novels to read; and should be at it now, instead of scribbling to Vita, who's much too happy and excited to attend, and looking divinely beautiful too (I say, what do you wear—the purple dogs hair dress?) So I will end, being exacting by nature, and hating the sort of divided attention which is all I can get now.

But I'm faithful, and loving: and have met no one a patch on you—no one so comforting to be with.

Remember me, is that the phrase?—to Harold.

Yr VW.

Berg

1619: To EDWARD SACKVILLE WEST   *Monks House, Rodmell,*
                                   Lewes [Sussex]
Saturday [6 February 1926]

Dear Eddy,

Would you perhaps dine with us on Friday 12th, and invite the party who was to dine at the Ivy round to 52 Tavistock Square after dinner instead?

I suggest this compromise, as I'm already surpassing what I am allowed in the matter of dinners out.

If this is impossible, I'll try to get round the law. But I think Lytton is dining with us.

Please invite anyone you like

Yours ever
Virginia Woolf

I am very glad you liked my article [*On Being Ill*]—I was afraid that,

1. She published three books of poetry between 1923 and 1937.

239

writing in bed, and forced to write quickly by the inexorable Tom Eliot
I had used too many words.
I've found out a little about de Quincey.
We go back to London on Monday
I think you ought to take your piano away as soon as possible—the damp
is something awful.

Berg

1620: To Edward Sackville West
                            52 *Tavistock Square, London, W.C.*1
Sunday [14 February? 1926]

Dear Eddy
      Leonard has measured the piano. The measurements are length—6' 1"
breadth at keys—2' 8½"
depth from top to
where legs begin—1' 6"
      Let me know when you want it sent
      I've been looking at de Quincey, but am in bed at the moment with
a chill or something which makes me so heavy-headed that I'll write later.
      I do hope you are better—what a ghastly time you've had!

                                          Yr
                                    Virginia Woolf
Berg

1621: To V. Sackville-West   52 *Tavistock Sqre. [W.C.*1]
Feb. 17th 1926

      You are a crafty fox to write an alphabet letter, and so think you have
solved the problem of dumbness.[1] Well, I shall write a news letter—
Princess Mary has a cold. Oulton Hall[2] has been burnt down with the loss
of much valuable plate. Sidney Waterlow has been removed, some say
forcibly, to Siam,[3] where it is thought he will impress the natives.
      What else has happened in the great world of politics and society? I
have been considering the question of snobbery. Eddy very kindly gave

1. Vita had written from Luxor, Egypt, on 29 January a letter which began,
   "Amon, Americans, alabaster, Arabs; bromides, buffaloes, beggars, Bronx",
   and ended, "zest (my own)." (*Berg*)
2. In Cheshire. It was a country house built for the Egerton family in the grandest
   style of 1715.
3. Sydney Waterlow was British Minister in Bangkok, 1926-28.

me dinner at the Ivy. (D'you remember the Ivy?) Of course I said, driving home, Now I'll pay the cab. Eddy said nonsense. I said you're a damned aristocrat, and I *will* pay the cab. Which I did, and gave him not only my well known lecture upon Russells and Herberts but a new chapter, added for his benefit, called, How no aristocrat can write a book. So we quarrelled over this for a bit, and next day, oddly enough, I had to defend him— against someone who shall be nameless—from the charge of being an *arriviste*. What motive can he have in coming to Bloomsbury etc? Well, I said, it shows his intelligence. But, they said, with that name and appearance, he can't be intelligent. Damn you, I said, thats Russells and Herberts the other way round all over again. So it is. And which is worse—Mayfair snobbery, or Bloomsbury? I've been awfully worried by elderly relations. Three old gentlemen,[1] round about 60, have discovered that Vanessa is living in sin with Duncan Grant, and that I have written Mrs Dalloway —which equals living in sin. Their method of showing their loathing is to come to call, to ask Vanessa if she ever sells a picture, me if I've been in a lunatic asylum lately. Then they intimate how they live in Berkley Sqre or the Athenaeum and dine with—I don't know whom: and so take them-selves off. Would this make you angry? And why philosophically speaking as Koteliansky the Russian used to say, do 20 years in time make this gulf between us?

Then there was Rodmell. Now that was a joy—I cant tell you how lovely,—the water meadows soaking wet, but now and then the sun coming out and stroking the downs. D'you remember how they turn from green to blue, like opals? I don't think you ever walk. You are always charging at the head of an army—but I walk, nosing along, making up phrases, and I'm ashamed to say how wrapped up I get in my novel. Really, I am a little alarmed at being so absorbed—Why should one engross oneself thus for so many months? and it may well be a mirage—I read it over, and think it is a mirage: but I can scarcely do any thing else. I got up on to the Downs though, where you went plunging in the motor, and then came down to tea, and sat over a wood fire, and read some poetry, and a manuscript, (thinking still of my own novel) then cooked an omelette, some good coffee; and wanted a little drop of wine, with you. (Have you been tipsy often? Do you know it was 4 weeks yesterday that you went?) Yes, I often think of you, instead of my novel; I want to take you over the water meadows in the summer on foot, I have thought of many million things to tell you. Devil that you are, to vanish to Persia and leave me here! —dabbling in wet type, which makes my fingers frozen; and setting up the poems of Mrs Manning Sanders,[2] which the more I set them, the less I like. And, dearest Vita, we are having *two* waterclosets made, one paid

1. Possibly three of her Duckworth relations.
2. Ruth Manning-Sanders' *Martha Wish-You-Ill* was published by the Press in July.

for by Mrs Dalloway, the other by The Common Reader: both dedicated to you.

Then I lunched with Lytton at Kettners. First I was so dazzled by the gilt and the warmth that in my humility I felt ready to abase myself at the feet of all the women and all the waiters; and really humbled at the incredible splendour of life. Halfway through lunch, reason triumphed; I said this is dross; I had a great argument with Lytton—about our methods of writing, about Edmund Gosse, about our friendship; and age and time and death and all the rest of it. I was forgetting Queen Elizabeth—He is writing about her.[1] He says that she wrote to an ambassador "Had I been crested and not cloven you would not have dared to write to me thus." "Thats style!" I cried. "It refers to the male and female parts" he said. Gosse told him this, adding that of course, it could not be quoted. "You need some excuse for lunching with Gosse," I said. But Lytton thinks me narrow minded about Gosse. I say I know a mean skunk when I see one, or rather smell one, for its his writing I abominate. And, Vita, answer me this: why are all professors of English literature ashamed of English literature? Walter Raleigh[2] calls Shakespeare "Billy Shaxs"—Blake, "Bill"—a good poem "a bit of all right." This shocks me. I've been reading his letters. But dear old Lytton—he was infinitely charming, and we fitted like gloves, and I was very happy, we nosed about the book shops together, and remarked upon the marvellous extent of our own reading. "What haven't we read?" said Lytton. "Its a question of life, my dear Lytton" I said, sinking into an arm chair: And so it all began over again.

What bosh letters are, to be sure! I dont think this gives you much idea of what I have done for the last fortnight. There are immense tracts unnamed. I daresay the dumb letters are best. Ethel Sands has just been to tea. We have been sitting over the gas fire; the crane still goes on lifting. She says I am very attractive and asks me to stay with her. (I put that in to make you jealous—) But no, you wont be jealous, not in Persia, where the air is rose-coloured, and this—what you call Gloomsbury—is so infinitely remote and mean. You may have discovered entire new countries in your own soul. Your soul may be highly prominent at the moment. But what I was going to say was that none of this letter is really very true, because I have been a great deal alone, two days, not able to write rather tired (but not ill—very well for the most part); and the rest of the time the usual muddle of thoughts and spasms of feeling. None of this does one ever explain:

But oh yes—I should awfully like to see you.

Yr VW.

Berg

1. *Elizabeth and Essex*, 1928.
2. Sir Walter Raleigh, Professor of English literature at Oxford, died in 1922. His letters, edited by his widow, were published in two volumes in 1926.

March 1st, 1926

Yes, dearest Towzer, it is all very well about Bloomsbury being a rotten biscuit, and me a weevil, and Persia being a rose and you an Emperor moth—I quite agree: but you are missing the loveliest spring there has ever been in England. We were motored all through Oxfordshire two days ago. Sometimes we got out and looked at a little manor house under a hill. Then we got right up up up on top of the world; and there was an old farm house, and a walled garden; flagged path; turf; a woman walking reading a book. Meanwhile, as I assure you, it was so incredibly lovely— the woods, the hill sides, the river, that, though I was thinking of you all the time motoring too, through the desert, I could not think it was lovelier, or stranger. This spring, I may tell you, is not ordinary; for there is nothing out, no leaves; yet it is as hot as June, but much more delicate and distinguished; and so empty that everything seems august. Russell Sqre:; the plane trees;—I dont know how to describe it: and no doubt my dear Towzer is bored.

The people who took us were Leonards brother and his wife.[1] I promptly fell in love, not with him or her, but with being stock brokers, with never having read a book (except Robert Hitchens)[2] with not having heard of Roger, or Clive, or Duncan, or Lytton. Oh this is life, I kept saying to myself; and what is Bloomsbury, or Long Barn either, but a contortion, a temporary knot; and why do I pity and deride the human race, when its lot is profoundly peaceful and happy? They have nothing to wish for. They are entirely simple and sane. She has her big dog. They turn on the Loud Speaker. When they take a holiday they go to the Spring of the Thames where it is as big as a man's arm, not big enough for a boat; and they carry their boat till they can put it in, and then they skull all the way down to Marlow. Sometimes, she said the river is level with the banks; and it is perfectly deserted. Then she said to me suddenly, as we were looking down at the wood from her window "Thats where the poet Shelley wrote Islam. He tied his boat to the tree there. My grandfather had a walking stick cut from that tree." You always run up against poetry in England; and I like this dumb poetry; and I wish I could be like that. She will live to be a hundred; she knows exactly what she enjoys; her life seems to me incredibly happy. She is very plain; but entirely unvexed, unambitious; and I believe, entirely right. Yes; that what I've fallen in love with—being a stockbroker.

1. Herbert and Freda Woolf, who lived at Cookham, Berkshire.
2. Robert Hichens (1864-1950), the popular novelist, whose best known book was *Garden of Allah* (1904).

Tuesday [2 March]

There have been masses of parties. But I cried off, after one at Clives with Lord Berners and Raymond; and one, a very quiet one, at Nessas. I shall never dine out again, I thought, in the middle of drinking Clive's champagne—because one always says the same things; well, that was the champagne, perhaps. One talks about Sybil [Colefax] and the Sitwells; Chrissie,[1] and Eddie Marsh. Clive would parade a new affair of his. "I've been dealt a new hand" he kept saying: "It takes me, I'm glad to say, into the lower walks of society." Absurd little cockatoo! However there was lots of champagne—slabs of salmon—I don't know what; and your poor Weevil—if thats to be her new name—was as excited as usual.

But to write a novel in the heart of London is next to an impossibility. I feel as if I were nailing a flag to the top of a mast in a raging gale. What is so perplexing is the change of perspective: here I'm sitting thinking how to manage the passage of ten years, up in the Hebrides:[2] then the telephone rings; then a charming bony pink cheeked Don called Lucas[3] comes to tea: well, am I here, asking him about the Life of Webster, which he's editing, or in a bedroom up in the Hebrides? I know which I like best— the Hebrides. I should like to be with you in the Hebrides at this moment.

I've arranged our French motoring so that we shall be back by May 10th. So please see to it that you land that day. A lovely dumb letter from you came on Saturday, written on board ship. I extract by degrees a great deal from your letters. They might be longer; They might be more loving. But I see your point—life is too exciting. And don't go tempting and tantalising poor Weevils. Of course, of course, I want to see deserts and Arabias—I worried Leonard for an hour about taking a year off and seeing the world. We will go to Burma, I said: to the South Seas: We have only one life; we are growing old. And he has a passion for the East: so perhaps we shall. I read a bit of your poem the other night—it must be good, I think: one can break off crumbs and suck them. I wonder what you'll come to, as a writer (go on falling in love and being tipsy, as a woman: I like that in you.) But as a writer? I wish you'd not say 'profile' on the first page; its not right there: outline—something English would be better there.[4] Like a rich cake, I can break crumbs off your poem. I imagine it wants a little central transparency: Some sudden intensity: I'm not sure. Send me some-

1. Christabel Aberconway, who married the 2nd Lord Aberconway in 1910. She and her husband were patrons of the arts and had a distinguished salon in Mayfair.
2. *Time Passes*, the second section of *To the Lighthouse*.
3. F. L. Lucas, the critic, novelist, poet, and Fellow of King's College, Cambridge.
4. Virginia had been reading a typescript of *The Land*. Vita took her advice, and altered the lines to read:
   "And still their outlines on our tenderer sky
   Simple and classic rear their grave design."

thing you've written. What I mean by a sudden intensity may be nonsense, on reflection—But what is the use of reflecting? I've sat with my pen in the air these ten minutes, thinking about your poem; but I cannot send it to Persia: Ones thoughts are too transitory—If you were in the arm chair opposite, you could just catch them before they fall.

Another break. Now its the next day. I'm so orderly am I? I wish you could live in my brain for a week. It is washed with the most violent waves of emotion. What about? I dont know. It begins on waking; and I never know which—shall I be happy? Shall I be miserable. I grant, I keep up some mechanical activity with my hands, setting type; ordering dinner. Without this, I should brood ceaselessly. And you think it all fixed and settled. Do we then know nobody?—only our own versions of them, which, as likely as not, are emanations from ourselves.

Again, interrupted. This letter is all breaks and starts. What was I saying? I was sitting over the fire and dreaming.

We're in the midst of our worst week. It always happens—here are all the books coming out, and our Staff collapses. Last year it was love: we abolished love [Mrs Joad], took an elderly widow instead;[1] and now its measles. One little girl has measles; the other probably mumps—May she go off? So we're left to deal with the bills, the parcels, the callers—a gentleman who has been in Armenia, wants to write a book, and discourses for an hour about Bishop Gore, Leonard thinking him to mean Ormsby Gore —Hence misunderstandings. Then theres our Viola[2]—thrown from a taxi and bruised her ribs, and must go to Brighton to recoup. Will we correct her proofs? And Lady Oxford has been at them, and scribbled over every margin, "Darling Viola, don't use the word "naturally" please—I hate it. Don't call Ribblesdale 'Rib'. All this is trash—ask Mrs Woolf—" What is the printer to make of it? There must be a revise—So thats held over. And our fortunes tremble. If the books don't sell, I warn you I shall apply for the place of black Baby[3] at Long Barn. Tomorrow I'm to meet Ottoline and Percy Lubbock: they say he has deserted Lady Sybil,[4] and retires to his own mat weaving at Sevenoaks. Whats the truth?

Thank God we get off to Rodmell on Saturday; and with luck I shall stay an extra day.

Please, dearest, a nice long letter: anything you like. I *dont* laugh at you. It's you who laugh at weevils.

Did I tell you how Grizzle is in hospital? No; I concealed it lest you

1. Mrs Cartwright, who had joined the Press in July 1925.
2. Viola Tree, whose book, *Castles in the Air: The Story of My Singing Days*, was published by Hogarth in April 1926.
3. Vita's elder son Benedict, who was then 11 years old.
4. Lady Sybil Scott, the wife of Geoffrey Scott, whom she divorced in 1926, following his love-affair with Vita. In this same year she married Percy Lubbock.

should be anxious: the mange: rainbow stripes have appeared across her back. But they are sanguine on the whole. And Raymond left today [for Persia]. And I envied him: And I want a little spoiling. No: I don't forget you—

Yr V.W.

Berg

1623: To Lady Sackville   52 *Tavistock Square, W.C.*1

7th March 1926

Dear Lady Sackville,[1]

It is most good of you to let me know about Vita. I have been wondering all these days whether she had arrived safely, and it is a great relief to have your news. Now I feel we may begin to think of her coming back—It must have been a great strain for you; but now I feel the worst of the journey is over.

Vita told me she was sending me the photograph she had taken for her passport—This has never come. I wonder if you would have the great kindness to send me a card with the photographer's name, that I may write to him myself? But not, of course, if it is the least trouble to you.

It is very good of you to say that I may come and see you. I should so much like to, if I am in Brighton.

Thank you again for thinking of writing to me.

Yours sincerely,
Virginia Woolf

Berg

1624: To V. Sackville-West

52 *Tavistock Square, London, W.C.*1

16th March 1926

I have been meaning every day to write something—such millions of things strike me to write to you about—and never did, and now have only scraps and splinters of time, damn it all—We are rather rushed—But, dearest Vita, why not take quinine, and sleep under mosquitoe nets? I could have told you about fever: do tell me if you are all right again (a vain question: time has spun a whole circle since you had fever off the Coast of Baluchistan) Much to my relief, Lady Sackville wrote and told me you had arrived: also she asks me to go and see her, to talk about you, I suppose. "I know you are very fond of Vita"; but I haven't the courage, without you.

1. Vita's mother.

Last Saturday night I found a letter from you in the box: then another: What luck! I thought; then a third; incredible!, I thought; then a fourth: But Vita is having a joke, I thought, profoundly distrusting you—Yet they were all genuine letters. I have spelt them out every word, four times, I daresay. They do yield more on suction; they are very curious in that way. Is it that I am, as Ly Sackville says, very fond of you: are you, like a good writer, a very careful picker of words? (Oh look here: your book of travels.[1] May we have it? Please say yes, for the autumn.) I like your letters I was saying, when overcome by the usual Hogarth Press spasm. And I would write a draft if I could, of my letters; and so tidy them and compact them; and ten years ago I did write drafts, when I was in my letter writing days, but now, never. Indeed, these are the first letters I have written since I was married. As for the *mot juste*, you are quite wrong. Style is a very simple matter; it is all rhythm. Once you get that, you can't use the wrong words. But on the other hand here am I sitting after half the morning, crammed with ideas, and visions, and so on, and can't dislodge them, for lack of the right rhythm. Now this is very profound, what rhythm is, and goes far deeper than words. A sight, an emotion, creates this wave in the mind, long before it makes words to fit it; and in writing (such is my present belief) one has to recapture this, and set this working (which has nothing apparently to do with words) and then, as it breaks and tumbles in the mind, it makes words to fit it: But no doubt I shall think differently next year. Then there's my character (you see how egotistic I am, for I answer only questions that are about myself) I agree about the lack of jolly vulgarity. But then think how I was brought up! No school; mooning about alone among my father's books; never any chance to pick up all that goes on in schools—throwing balls; ragging: slang; vulgarity; scenes; jealousies—only rages with my half brothers, and being walked off my legs round the Serpentine by my father. This is an excuse: I am often conscious of the lack of jolly vulgarity but did Proust pass that way? Did you? Can you chaff a table of officers?

Do tell me scraps of the Lorraine's[2] talk: or what the woman says who has read Oscar Wilde. Then about the expeditions you make to find flowers. I must go and lunch. We have had lunch, off roast beef and Yorkshire pudding. Also a romantic pudding in which you find almonds lodged in cream. It is bitter cold; a black wind is blowing and scraping old newspapers along the street—a sound I connect with March in London.

But I was going to talk about Ottoline: and the ghastliness of that party at Ethels. It was a blizzard, thunder and snow; and Dadie fetched me, and we had to cross London to Chelsea. Well, by the time I got there, my poor old hat (I never bought a new one) was like a cabmans cape: and

1. *Passenger to Teheran* was published by the Hogarth Press in November 1926.
2. Sir Percy Loraine was British Minister in Teheran, 1921-6.

a piece of fur, hurriedly attached by a safety pin, flapping. And those damned people sitting smug round their urn, their fire, their tea table, thought O Lord, why cant Virginia look more of a lady: which so infuriated me, through vanity I own, and the consciousness of being better than them, with all their pearl necklaces and orange coloured clothes, that I could only arch my back like an infuriated tom cat. As for Ottoline, she is peeling off powder like flakes on a house; yet her skirts are above her knees: I cant describe the mingling of decrepitude and finery: and all the talk had to be brought back to her. There was Percy Lubbock. We were egged on to discuss the passions. He mumbled like an old nurse that *he* never had such nasty things: whereupon, in the vilest taste, I contradicted him, never thinking of Lady Sybil, and he bubbled and sizzled on his seat with discomfort, and said, please Mrs Woolf leave *me* alone. And I felt inclined to leave them all alone, for ever and ever, these tea parties, these Ottolines, these mumbling sodomitical old maids (Leigh Ashton[1] was there too.) Talk of the romance, the experience and upset and devastation of Persia! Come with me further and remoter (I doubt that this is English, though it may be the *mot juste*) to the living, unconcerned, contented, indifferent middle classes of England. I've lived in Persia half my life; but never been among the stockbrokers, till this spring. Last week it was Lord Rothschilds agent—that is another brother of Leonards [Philip Woolf],— at Waddesdon. There again I fell in love—But Eddy says this is snobbery: a belief in some glamour which is unreal. They are again, entirely direct, on the top of every object without a single inhibition or hesitation—When my sister in law showed me her hunter (for hunting is the passion of her life) I had the thrill in the thighs which, they say, is the sign of a work of art. Then she was so worn to the bone with living. Seven miles from a village: no servant will stay; weekend parties at the Great House; Princess Mary playing cross word puzzles after lunch, my sister in law stripping her one pair of shoes and skirt to ribbons hunting rabbits in the bushes by way of amusing Princess Mary; two babies; and so on. Well, I felt, nothing that I shall ever do all my life equals a single day of this. But Eddy says he knows about it: it is my snobbery. I like Eddy: I like the sharpness of his spine: his odd indivualities [*sic*], and angles. But the young are dangerous. They mind so much what one thinks of them. One has to be very careful what one says. That buzzing bluebottle Clive almost involved us in a row: but it is past; and I am dining with Clive tomorrow, to meet some mysterious admirer,[2] for Clive thinks me so vain I must always meet admirers, and drink the usual champagne.

1. Keeper of the Department of Textiles in the Victoria and Albert Museum, of which he became Director in 1945.
2. Lord Ivor Spencer Churchill, youngest son of the 9th Duke of Marlborough. He was then aged 28.

Sure enough—here is Clive ringing up to ask us to lunch to meet Sybil—yes, Sybil's back: here's a note to remind you of Sybil. Then I met Rose Macaulay and George Moore (d'you remember scolding me— one of your scoldings—for not meeting writers?) What I say about writers is that they are the salt of the earth (even if to say it I must unsay something of my rapture for the middle classes—the huntresses the stock brokers) With both of these people, Rose and George, one can tell the truth—a great advantage. Never did anyone talk such nonsense as George. "Do not tell me you admire Hardy, Mrs Woolf. My good friend, tell me if he has written a single sentence well? Not one. Is there a single scene in all those novels one remembers?" Whatever I said he poohpoohed; till at last (this was at Mary's with Jack [Hutchinson] in plum coloured velvet, like a tea cosy) I said "Mr Moore, when one is Mr Moore, that is enough" And we floated off to waterclosets and Paris; and he attacked Conrad and Henry James and Anatole France: but I cant tell you how urbane and sprightly the old poll parrot was; and, (this is what I think using the brain does for one) not a pocket, not a crevice, of pomp, humbug, respectability in him: he was fresh as a daisy.

Devil, you have never sent me your photograph. Angel, you wish to know about Grizzle: she has eczema, and a cough. Sometimes we peer into her throat and Leonard moves a bone.

The publishing season trembles: not a review of us so far. I have done up 19 parcels to China, via Siberia; which as you know, must not weigh over 4 lbs: each; and be open ended. Also, folded a myriad of these leaflets. Also rejected [Doris] Daglish on Pope. Also accepted Mary's stories.[1] And today began a new writing book, having filled the old, and written close on 40,000 words in 2 months—my record. Birds flap and fluster at my panes; but mostly the common sparrow, the domestic hen. Never mind. In the intervals of being leaden with despair, I am very excited. I say, *when* do you get back? *When* shall I stop writing to you? All our plans about holidays are in the fire again; God knows when we shall get off: but I dont want to be poking about in Provence when you're here.

Yes, dearest Vita: I do miss you; I think of you: I have a million things, not so much to say, as to sink into you.

Tell me how you are *and be very careful.*

Yr VW

Berg

1625: To Clive Bell   52 *Tavistock Square, W.C.*1
[mid-March 1926]

Dearest Clive,
    I shall be delighted to dine on the 19th; but can't possibly be well if

1. *Fugitive Pieces*, by Mary Hutchinson, appeared in June 1927.

249

its Ottoline, or any relation, even by marriage of Ottoline's, that I'm to meet—so I warn you. 5.30 Thursday would suit us: so shall hope to see you then.

Yrs
V.W

Quentin Bell

1626: To V. Sackville-West

The Hogarth Press, 52 Tavistock Square,
London, W.C.1

29th March 1926

No letter from you for over a fortnight, but that may be, I suppose, something to do with the Foreign Office. Now you must pretend to be interested in your friend's fortunes: but it will all seem so remote and silly to you: you have forgotten a paper called The Nation; Leonard was literary editor once: and since Wednesday he is no longer. We have resigned.[1] Thank God. What a mercy—no more going to the office and reading proofs and racking ones brains to think who to get to write. We shall have to make £500 a year; and I shall sell my soul to Todd; but this is the first step to being free, and foreign travel and dawdling about England in a motor car; and we feel 10 years younger, utterly irresponsible, and please, dearest Vita, do make Harold do the same thing. One walks into one's wifes room, carrying her tray, at 8.30, and says "By the way I'm going to give up the Nation today"—or the Foreign Office, as the case may be! Its over in 10 minutes. Seriously, giving up appointments (this is the 4th time since we married) is the only pleasure in the world. He will be there till October or July as a matter of fact. (So send articles)

I cannot think what it will interest you to be told of, now you are embedded in Persia. I see you always picking little bright red flowers high up on stony mountains. Raymond (give him my love) will be with you now; and so you will have heard all about London—how Clive is in love, and Lady Colefax, and all that. Do you infer from this that Sybil is in love? No, no. She has not been tainted by *that* passion: she has merely stayed with Coolidge, Esme Howard,[2] Doug [Fairbanks] and Mary [Pickford], Charlie Chaplin, been four thousand miles in a motor car; etc. etc. Does it matter what Sybil does? A coal mine, heaven, its all the same. She pants a little harder—that is all. Then there were Lord Ivor S. Churchill; Roger Fry and Virginia Woolf—and all very brilliant at Clives the other night;

1. Maynard Keynes persuaded Leonard to reconsider this decision, but Leonard stipulated that he would spend only two days a week in the office. He remained Literary Editor until early 1930.
2. The British Ambassador in Washington.

and Walter Sickert, Therese Lessore,[1] Leigh Ashton, all very silent at Vanessa's the other night; and a ghastly party at Rose Macaulays, where in the whirl of meaningless words I thought Mr O'donovan said Holy Ghost, whereas he said "The Whole Coast" and I asking "Where is the Holy Ghost?" got the reply "Where ever the sea is" "Am I mad, I thought, or is this wit?" "The Holy Ghost?" I repeated. "The Whole Coast" he shouted, and so we went on, in an atmosphere so repellent that it became, like the smell of bad cheese, repulsively fascinating: Robert Lynds, Gerald Goulds,[2] Rose Macaulays, all talking shop; and saying Masefield is as good as Chaucer, and the best novel of the year is Shining Domes by Mildred Peake; until Leonard shook all over, picked up what he took to be Mrs Gould's napkin, discovered it to be her sanitary towel and the foundations of this tenth rate literary respectability (all gentlemen in white waistcoats, ladies shingled, unsuccessfully) shook to its foundations. I kept saying "Vita would love this" Now would you?

Now it is Wednesday. I did get a letter from you—a nice dumb letter. When I went to Italy for the first time I too picked up a clod of earth. A very nice letter. I wish I could write one to match; but for 2 days we have had nothing but talk, interruptions, and the whole blessed thing—Press and Nation—in the frying pan. This is exciting, but harasses the mind. It would bore you to go into it: It is only a question whether we shan't give up the Press too, cut adrift, and make a bolt. Manuscripts shower; authors never cease coming: Viola's book again held up—in short the bother and the work have a little overcome us, for the moment—whether we can keep up with it, I mean. But it is also great fun. If you had come in yesterday you would have seen me with the floor all strewn with little squares of paper, like the learned pig, making an index for Viola.

Some items of news: Dadie has not got his fellowship.[3] Hilda Bewicke is a friend of Clives. Arnold Bennett is having a Baby.[4] Ethel [Sands] clothes are lovely—sleeves like pen and ink drawings—all one line. Nessa and Duncan are going to Italy. Princess Victoria has pneumonia. Francis Birrell may be offered Editorship.[5] Had I married Sydney Waterlow I should have gone to Bangkok. A letter from Raymond just come. Much enjoyed. Hot X Buns. etc etc.

Berg

1. The painter, and third wife of Walter Sickert.
2. The critic, journalist, and poet (1885-1936).
3. Later George Rylands was awarded a Fellowship at King's College, Cambridge.
4. Bennett had fallen in love with an English actress, Dorothy Cheston, and their child, a daughter, was born in 1926.
5. He edited for the publishers Gerald Howe a series of short books called *Representative Women*, to which Vita contributed *Aphra Behn* in 1927.

1627: To Clive Bell   52 *Tavistock Square, W.C.*1

[9 April 1926]

Dearest Clive,

I will bear M. Renoir[1] in mind. But I should think the higher walks of life were more profitable—Sybil, and so on. She is beaming with good will.

We are cowering over our gas fire, and cursing fate which drives us out to tea with Lotta Leaf.[2] Kitty is rather an exquisite nymph—that is the only consolation. Bank holiday we spent in the Basement, very happily: next day tramping Windsor Park with Gerald Brenan: and there have been the usual number of strays about—HOM[3] for example, brutally despatched by Leonard, without a cup of tea even, just as he was displaying those powers of conversation which used to hold me spell-bound. My only adventure has been connected with nibs. Did I tell you how the Penkala has failed: nobody in the whole world uses it except me: and when I went to get nibs I was told they had all been sold off to a hawker in the Farringdon Road. Off I went, as you can imagine, and beat up and down the Farringdon Road until I found him and bought 2 gross, which will last me, L. says, 6 years. On the way I ran into Mrs Clifford[4] and Turkey—a painful and curious encounter.

We go to Iwerne Minster[5] on Tuesday. It is a great risk. I shall retire upon Dorchester and Tom Hardy if it don't do. We shall come to Rodmell on or about the 23rd for 10 days or so. Shall you still be at Charleston? I hope so.

I am reading Mrs Sidney Webbs autobiography and find it enthralling. As for Walter Raleigh I find him disgusting.

Leonard sends his love. Kiss Vanessa for me. I wish she would write to me. I can't write much, as I don't want to waste my nibs. I dont know about Roger—whether I may kiss him or not. Please ask him.

Yrs V.W

Quentin Bell

1. Jean Renoir, the film director and son of the painter.
2. Charlotte Leaf, the daughter of John Addington Symonds and the sister of Madge Vaughan, had been a friend of Virginia in her youth. Kitty was Charlotte's daughter.
3. H. O. Meredith, a Fellow of King's College, Cambridge, and a Lecturer in economics.
4. Lucy Clifford, the novelist and playwright.
5. In Dorset, where Virginia and Leonard went for a short holiday.

13th April 1926

Here is a cheque.[1] See what you might have had if you had stuck to the old firm—cheques for £10 every other day perhaps; and distinction which, rightly has no price. But I'm in a rush, going off to Iwerne Minster today, throwing myself upon life practically naked. This means only that we shall range about Dorset for 5 days and neither read nor write.

I got a letter from you last night, and you say I am to write once more. This is an anticlimax; I had written my farewell. But I want particularly to impress upon you the need of care in travel. Remember your dog Grizzle and your Virginia, waiting you; both rather mangy; but what of that? These shabby mongrels are always the most loving, warm hearted creatures. Grizzle and Virginia will rush down to meet you—they will lick you all over. So then, when you are tempted to folly, tremble on the brink of a precipice, sleep out on the Steppes,[2] and so on (coming through Russia where Raymond hasn't been you can lie as much as you like) remember how desolated we shall both be should you lose a hair of your head, or scratch one scratch on those lovely pillar like legs. (The Greeks and Hebrews used "pillars" as a metaphor: I now see why often one catches up Greeks and Hebrews in living.) I am rather repentant at having criticised your poem, without really reading it through. I find reading in type script rather hard. Give me the proofs and let me furbish up a proper opinion. But I dont understand—are you still adding? Then when does it come out? I expect I only meant something about descriptive poetry needing a human focus in the middle. Vegetables become rather crushing. I expect though it is there; only a little obscured by detail (and that may be my slovenly reading.) Lets go through it carefully together before you send it to Byard.[3] Byard will smoke his big cigar, and eat his blood red chop. I, doing neither, dont print your poems. How odd it is—the effect geography has in the mind! I write to you differently now you're coming back. The pathos is melting. I felt it pathetic when you were going away; as if you were sinking below the verge. Now that you are rising, I'm jolly again.

But what news is there to bring you of the outer world? Precious little, of what Sybil Colefax calls news. No dinners, no parties—Everyone away, Sybil, Ethel, Clive, Mary, Vanessa—all in rural retreat. So I have been doing up parcels with Angus: standing at a table with string and paper and hearing scraps of interviews. Advertising touts, with tempting offers: Mr Besherman Editor of Youth; Mr Morrell, the printer. All this goes forward,

1. For *Seducers in Ecuador*, which the Hogarth Press had published.
2. Vita travelled back from Persia across the Caspian to Baku, and thence by train to Moscow.
3. Theodore Byard, Director of Heinemann's, who published *The Land* in the autumn of 1926.

as I tie, as I tie—(d'you remember "sweeping up leaves," the refrain in Hardy's poem?[1]) My mind is all awash with various thoughts; my novel; you; shall you take me for a drive to the sea?; the cinema; and so on; when the door opens and Dadie comes in. Desultory conversation goes forward: for I have to think what I'm doing, and not close the ends of parcels for abroad—perhaps my greatest sin as a packer. At last, I say I want tea. Dadie comes up for 5 minutes. Bell rings. Eddy comes. Telephone rings. Duncan is coming. We all have tea together. Make toast. Room frightfully untidy. Never mind. Eddy is very well and spruce. Duncan like an old bundle, which is coming undone in the middle. He perpetually hitches up his trousers as he talks. We all chatter hard, about music—Eddy explains about 19th Century music and rhetoric—Duncan attacks: but seldom uses the word he means: sometimes has to unbutton his waistcoat while endeavouring: very interesting: we compare movies and operas: I'm writing that for Todd:[2] rather brilliant. All, to me, highly congenial, and even a little exciting, in the spring light; hammers tapping outside; trees shaking green in the Square: suddenly we find its 7 and all jump up.

Oh I've no time—I can't write sense or sound, not to say grammar, with Leonard and Grizzle, and Chappells piano tuner all flourishing about, and saying are you ready, have you Mr Sackville Wests piano? and the general atmosphere of movement and departure. I had wanted to go into the matter of profound natural happiness; as revealed to me yesterday at a family party of an English Banker [Walter Leaf]; where the passion and joy of sons and daughters in their own society struck me almost to tears with self-pity and amazement. Nothing of that sort do we any of us know— profound emotions, which are yet natural and taken for granted, so that nothing inhibits or restrains—How deep these are, and unself conscious. There is a book called Father and Son [1907], by Gosse, which says that all the coast of England was fringed with little sea anemones and lovely tassels of seaweed and sprays of emerald moss and so on, from the beginning of time till Jan 1858, when, for some reason, hordes of clergy and spinsters in mushroom hats and goggles began collecting, and so scraped and rifled the coast that this accumulation was destroyed for ever—A parable this, of what we have done to the deposits of family happiness. But I'll flood you with all this when you come. When? And take care.

Also, I will tell you about Anna Karenina, and the predominance of sexual love in 19th Century fiction, and its growing unreality to us who

<hr>

1.   "Often I ponder how
                      Springtime deceives,—
              I, an old woman now,
                Raking up leaves."
              —Thomas Hardy, *Autumn in King's Hintock Park.*
2. *Cinema* was not published in *Vogue*, but in *Arts*, New York (June 1926).

have no real condemnation in our hearts any longer for adultery as such. But Tolstoy hoists all his book on that support. Take it away, say, no it doesn't offend me that AK. should copulate with Vronsky, and what remains?

Put to yourself that question on the Steppes with the owls hooting and a melancholy wolf slinking behind the everlasting birch trees.

Leonards⎫
Grizzles ⎬love.
Virginias⎭

Yr V.W.

Berg

1629: TO LADY OTTOLINE MORRELL

The Talbot Inn, Iwerne Minster,
Blandford [*Dorset*]
April 14th [1926]

Dearest Ottoline,

We are wandering about Dorsetshire for a few days holiday, or I would have written before. I'm afraid we can't manage the week ends you suggest, as we are going to France for a little tour, and to Rodmell. Our holiday is all being broken up into short rushes, and I don't quite know at what times—Perhaps we might come later?

It is so divine down here that I can't think how we are idiotic enough to live in London. No. You are quite right to decide against balls and streets. We are now going to Shaftesbury: then to Child Okeford—the names are enough to make one happy by themselves. I'm trying to end at Dorchester and see Thomas Hardy but doubt if we shall have time.

Love from us both to you and Philip and Julian

Your
V.W.

Texas

1630: TO VANESSA BELL   *The Talbot Inn, Iwerne Minster,*
Blandford, Dorset
Friday. April 16th [1926]

Dearest.

You are a scandal to sisterhood not to have written—Everything in the way of affection is always left to me. The time will come when exhausted nature sleeps. But, you will say, the pen is lost; but, I reply, my stack of pens will only last, with care, 6 years.

255

Anyhow it is a pouring wet day. Naturally, the weather broke the first morning, and we have only seen the country, which is nevertheless so divine that I could well describe it for pages, under a black cloud, which is not becoming. Now, as I say, it is pouring. Leonard refuses to leave the fire. We have just put our noses out, that is all. It is a perfect Inn—that is the only consolation: hot baths, big fires, good food, always the chance of cream; and yesterday roast chicken. Iwerne Minster is entirely controlled by Mr Ismay,[1] a millionaire, so that rare flowers burst out of every cranny in every cottage; the villagers wear specially knitted red waistcoats, if male; if female, red cloaks. You might well eat off the street. The shops are stocked with commodities—and all this, as I say, in the midst of downs, water meadows, trout streams, ancient bridges, stone houses, of which the most romantic to me is Stepleton House where the great hunter Beckford lived,[2] of whom you know nothing, so I say no more.

We have been twice to Shaftesbury; of which I say no more, because you have not read Jude the Obscure [Hardy]; a town on a hill, with a view, of which I say no more, because if there's one thing you can't nohow tolerate it is descriptions and yet as a painter, you do nothing but describe views—so now rationalise your contradictions, eh?

But you'll like to hear about the Leafs, I know. If there is any doubt anywhere about the perfect roundness and sweetness of English family life, I hereby denounce it. The Leafs are more than you could dream of. Of course Lotta is rather drowsy now; but then she is grown very fat; like a large chest of drawers covered in a black velvet pall. She dozes a little, but only with supreme content. And well she may. There is Walter benevolent as an ape, merry jocund, facetious; and his son Charles, 6 ft. 6. who, I assure you, picked Walter up in his arms, kissed him all over, blessed him, then rushed across the room, swept Kitty off her feet,—the whole atmosphere was so overpowering in its affection and humility that I quarrelled with Leonard all the evening about profound natural happiness: why we haven't got it; its beauty, and so on; which he said was sentimental; and one would find Lotta an awful bore. All the rooms are hung with Charles Furses[3]—now my recollection is he was a bold, voluptuous painter, with great gusts of red and yellow paint. Not a bit of it (it suddenly got fine here, so we went out, and have now lunched off cold chicken and tongue—this I mention in case you are motoring near, and advise you to stop your car at the Talbot) Charles Furse's pictures are the most pinched, wintry, effeminate things you can imagine. Lotta in black silk, singing: Lotta in a

1. James Ismay (1867-1930), one of the Ismay family who managed the White Star line.
2. Peter Beckford, author of *Thoughts on Hunting* (1780). The house was now owned by Sir Ronald Lindsay, the diplomatist.
3. Charles Furse died in 1904 at the age of 36, and was the husband of Katharine, Charlotte's sister.

large straw hat walking; Walter without any legs; but only a dash of acrid green chintz in the room—all the rest anaemic and sentimental to a degree, as you would say.

Not much light was thrown on the Cartwright mystery by Angus.—except that she had taken one of Leonard's jokes seriously—All he could say was that he had the impression she was dissatisfied.[1] I'm sure he really thought this; but it aint much to go on. Otherwise our conversation was rather inconclusive, and broken short; and we are to have another next week—On principle I believe its wrong to employ one's friends or be employed by them—It lends such exacerbity to every question. With old Cartwright it just blows over. However, we shall be coming down on Friday next, if Philcox [builder] is willing, and I propose to have a grand opening party at Monks, when the two plugs will be pulled and the hot water turned on in the bath for the first time. Perhaps you will come. Or we will come to you. I suppose, as I heard nothing, that Clive's electric light has been turned off.

We go back on Sunday, motoring in a bus through Poole to Bournemouth where we lunch and see the town, which will be very exciting—in short I'm all in favour of your plan of taking to the roads. Even in black horror like this one sees an immense number of curious things—nothing so odd as Dolphin though in her Dolphinry—Quentin, Julian, and Angelica to wit. Please give the children their old Aunt's love. A letter from Noel Vaughan Williams![2]

V.W.

Berg

1631: To Vanessa Bell   [52 *Tavistock Square, W.C.*1]

[21 April 1926]

Your letter; with its wildly unjust accusations,[3] just come.

With a loving heart I ask you and Duncan to dine with us at some pot house on Thursday.

You can ring up.

By mentioning the Club vaguely to Gerald [Brenan], I seem to have fulfilled all your wishes: viz: (ask Julian to explain the word) to give pain to the greatest possible number of people. Obviously, he has already done this: What more do you want?

---

1. Mrs Cartwright and Angus Davidson both resented Leonard's autocratic attitude, although they were fundamentally fond of him.
2. Ralph Vaughan Williams's second cousin. She died a spinster in the 1960s.
3. Vanessa had accused Virginia of betraying her plans to found a dining club, because people would be hurt if they were not invited to join.

But oh God, the Frys at Rodmell![1]
I leave Sussex for ever
Of course, nothing is ready at Rodmell [new bathroom], or will be ready; so here we bide.

Berg

1632: TO VANESSA BELL   52 T[avistock] S.[quare, W.C.1]
Tuesday [27 April 1926]

Dearest
Would it be possible for us to come to you for *Thursday 29th* for night? bringing Nelly, who would do everything for us. (that has all blown over:[2] she says it was the toothache!)
We should go to Rodmell on Friday. They cant get it cleaned until then. We would bring down a chicken or whatever we should be taking for our dinner, so don't get in anything extra.
Of course this may be difficult—so please say—so that I may know on Thursday morning.
It would be very nice to see you and Angelica—but perhaps you'll anyhow come over for a night to Rodmell and enjoy our baths and W Cs —about which I'm feeling grave doubts.
I expect the boys [Julian and Quentin] to tea

Yr V

Berg

1633: TO VANESSA BELL   52 Tavistock Square, London, W.C.1
[29 April 1926]

Dearest,
I was just telegraphing to say we could not come, when your letter came. At the last moment, of course, the well fell in at Monks House, and L. had to rush off yesterday to find that we can't possibly go there till Wednesday. Would you be able to come over and spend the night (if its feasible) on Thursday? That will be the only chance of seeing you, I'm afraid; but I'm afraid it looks unlikely for you. If our plans change again, I'll let you know. If you're at Charleston on Wednesday I might call in perhaps for tea: but the future is obscure—The worst of it is that I'm brimming with gossip:

1. Roger Fry and Helen Anrep considered taking a house a mile from Monk's House.
2. Nelly Boxall withdrew her notice, saying she could never be happy with anyone else.

258

Maynard, Lydia, and so on. Maynard is torn between the Provostry of Kings[1] and respectability; and Gordon Sqre and scalliwags. He says he has a very good chance. L. said Lydia was an ideal mistress; I, that you and Duncan couldn't possibly stay at the [Provost's] Lodge, owing to no dress clothes—This rather nettled him. I think he means to stand. We're having a talk with Angus tomorrow I think. Tonight we go to Ralphs and Frances's bridal party.[2] I shall try to make Carrington drunk.

However, I won't go on gossiping, or you wont come over. The boys were enchanting. We chattered incessantly. I can't believe theyre not my younger brothers. Also they laughed at you a great deal. "I have a great respect for old Nessa's brains" said Julian; "but she doesn't always use them"—very like Thoby. They caught their train.

V.

Nelly of course quite angelic, and everything once more settled for ever.

Berg

1634: To David Garnett   52 *Tavistock Square, W.C.*1

5th May [1926]

Dear Bunny,

I write from this doomed city and I have great doubts that this will reach you. We had arranged, before this horror [The General Strike], to stay with Dadie at Cambridge on the 21st—God knows what will have happened by then. But let us come later, if its possible. We very much want to.

There has been such confusion here (all helpers in the Press fled) that we couldn't send you Viola [Tree's *Castles in the Air*]; now parcels aren't taken. But we will send directly it is possible again:

Well—I like snakes: so far as human feelings are left me. After 2 days of worrying and doing nothing, and talking and listening in, one is scarcely a worm, let alone a bird. What happens to you in the country?

Yr
VW

Berg

1. Since 1924 Keynes, in addition to his many other activities, had been Bursar of King's College, Cambridge. He never became Provost.
2. Ralph Partridge and Frances Marshall had fallen in love during the autumn of 1925. They now agreed with Carrington, Ralph's wife, that Ralph and Frances should share a flat in London, but would often visit Carrington and Lytton Strachey at Ham Spray. After Carrington's death, Ralph and Frances married.

1635: To Vanessa Bell   52 *Tavistock Square, W.C.* 1
Wednesday 12th May 1926

Dearest,

We have just been told as a dead secret that the strike will be settled this afternoon. This comes from Laski,[1] but as nobody tells the truth, it may well be another maresnest. However, everybody agrees that something is happening—either there will be peace today or strike going on for several weeks. It beggars description. Recall the worst days of the war. Nobody can settle to anything—endless conversations go on—rumours fly —petitions to the Prime Minister are got up. The past 3 days Leonard and I have been getting signatures from writers and editors to the Archbishop of Canterburys proposals.[2] That is to say Miss Bulley[3] arrives at 9.30: Gerald Brenan with his bicycle at 11: Ralph Partridge, just out of a railway accident on the Cambridge line, at 11.15. Clive is in and out all day. The telephone rings 8 times in 20 minutes. I have to argue with Jack Squire at Aldershot. Desmond is expected. Francis Birrell begs us to come and see his father [Augustine]—or better still go to the Oval and talk to Hobbs.[4] Desmond arrives fresh from Asquith; has a whisky and soda. Maynard rings up from Cambridge—where he has been driven with Lydia in search of coal—to command us to print the Nation on the Hogarth Press. Leonard refuses twice, though several undergraduates have volunteered to motor up and act as compositors. Leonard is now employed by the Labour party to write articles; I have to take despatches to the House of Commons.

Meanwhile, there are no tubes and no buses and no taxis—except those run by special constables often with fatal results. They charge 3d a ride anywhere; but after going to Westminster by bus, with a policeman on the box, and boards up to protect us from stone throwers (the streets in the West End are perfectly peaceful, as a matter of fact) walking seems preferable. Suddenly Roger and Helen arrive—it is now tea time, carrying a market basket containing chocolate and melons, which nourish and provide drink, in case of bloodshed at Camden town, which is the most riotous part of London. Roger is wilder than ever, but agrees with me in thinking it all unutterably boring and quite unimportant and yet very upsetting—Between

1. Harold Laski, Professor of Political Science at the London School of Economics, from 1926 until his death in 1950.
2. For a compromise solution between employers, Government, and workers, which would not leave the latter embittered after the failure of the Strike. Leonard was invited to support the Archbishop (Randall Davidson) by collecting signatures from prominent writers and artists. See *Downhill All the Way*, pp. 217-18.
3. Margaret Bulley, the art historian, later Mrs G. W. Armitage.
4. J. B. Hobbs, the most famous cricketer of this period.

telephone calls from Arnold Bennett and Mr Garvin[1] and despairing interviews with Miss Bulley who has been insulted by Edmund Gosse—Roger explains that the Gower Street house is off, as the Bedford agent exacts complete respectability and no subletting except to members, by blood, of one's own family—which says Roger he can't guarantee: so he's now after a house in Bernard Street. He has tried, but failed, to get your show put off;[2] and then to have it broadcast. Well, with 3 weeks, I think its not so bad. (The press by the way carries on dismally—Mrs C[artwright]. arrives on Faith Henderson's bicycle, red with rust; she, too, red with exercise and fury at strikers. She and Leonard argue. But she is a monument of virtue and motherliness and at intervals I sob on her shoulder—for instance when Bob [Trevelyan] arrives having bicycled from Leith Hill, wanting cold meat at 3.30. and brings two poetic dramas for us to read—But now it is tea time, and Desmond suddenly assumes the rôle of Mussolini—marches off to see Lord Beaverbrook and the Editor of the Morning Post—which he does with great success, while Clive complains bitterly that if only we had got Mary's car, which we cant have, because Jack has tonsilitis, and refuses to let Mary or the car out of his sight, we might have tackled Winston Churchill himself.[3] Miss Bulley arrives for the 6th time—will not sit down —but would like 20 copies of the [Archbishop's] letter, which I proceed to type. It is now 7 o'clock, and Roger and Helen put on their boots and decide that it is time to start off for Dalmeny, with their melons, by a back road, to avoid rioters. Walking has almost cured Roger's disease. At last they go, as Desmond returns. We then argue a little about psycho-analysis and Swinburne, which is some relief—

Soon however, Hubert Henderson rings up to say that this is the gravest moment of the strike, and there is imminent danger of civil war in South Wales. Winston has tear gas bombs in readiness: armoured cars are convoying meat through Piccadilly; all the T.U. leaders in Birmingham have been arrested. The Roneo printers refuse to print L's article on the Constitution. Will L. come to the office at once? Now it is 7.30 and we have to dine with Eileen Power and Romer Wilson:[4] Desmond has to dine with the Asquiths: Clive is going to stand by in case he can get through to Manchester on the telephone—So we dine with Eileen Power who has

1. J. L. Garvin, Editor of the *Observer*. He refused to sign the Archbishop's appeal.
2. The London Artists' Association exhibition, which opened on 12 May.
3. During the Strike, Churchill edited the official Government newspaper, the *British Gazette*. He was then Chancellor of the Exchequer, and was the most resolute opponent of the strikers.
4. Eileen Power (Eileen Postan) was a Mediaeval historian and Professor of Economic History at the London School of Economics. Romer Wilson, the novelist, had won the Hawthornden Prize in 1921 with her book *The Death of Society*.

heard that there is no hope of a settlement for 3 weeks; and says at intervals "This is the death blow of Trades Unionism in England"—

So we go home at 11, to find Nelly hanging over the stairs to say that a man called Cook and a woman called Brown want us urgently and have been calling at intervals since 8 o'clock. As we talk, the bell rings, and Janet Vaughan appears, who says that Lord Haldane and a friend of hers are bringing out an emergency paper and will we give them our letter and list of names to be printed at once. She has a bicycle outside, and though she has just bicycled from Wandsworth where she has been acting to strikers,[1] she will bicycle with it to Fleet Street (all papers are about the size of foolscap, and mostly typewritten.) While this is being prepared, Brown or Haldane rings up to say it is now too late. At last we go to bed. At 9.30 this morning, as I began by saying, Laski rings up—and so we go on.

Strike settled 1 P.M. This has just been broadcast—as you'll probably have heard by now. Everyone is in the greatest spirits. Books at once begin to sell—I've spent the afternoon in wild discussions with Viola, who is beside herself to get her book floated—We are probably having 24 sandwichmen on Monday. I hope your show is now safe—Work begins tonight. Miners still have to settle terms finally wh. they do on Friday. The Nation is coming out—Maynard is up—In short everybody is jubilant and almost hysterical. You probably think this all nonsense—but the relief after all these days of misery with lights half out, nobody doing anything, and the only news coming at intervals in Nelly's bedroom from the wireless is terrific. We're going to have a strike dinner and drink champagne with Clive, the Frys, and other spirits.

Please write.

We shall now be rushed off our feet I hope with orders.

Yr B.

Berg

1636: To Edward Sackville West
The Hogarth Press, 52 Tavistock Square,
London, W.C.1

Saturday morning [15 May 1926]

Dear Eddy

I am awfully sorry, having just said I would go on Tuesday. Now I am overcome by the feeling that I can't—the truth is I am all over the place trying to do a difficult thing in my novel [the *Time Passes* section], also I was chattering horrible nonsense all last night, and feel positive I should

1. Janet Vaughan (Madge's daughter) and Hilda Matheson, Lady Astor's political secretary, were organising concerts for the strikers.

wreck your evening. This is not a pose; I would much rather you came and saw me, say tea, on Wednesday; and got somebody else to go to the concert.

Please forgive me; but you will understand the horror that comes over one of ones self and being engaged and making a mess of things.

Yours Ever
Virginia Woolf

I can't remember your telephone number.

Berg

1637: To Edward Sackville West

52 Tavistock Square, London, W.C.1

Monday [17 May 1926]

Dear Eddy

Yes, do come to tea here on Thursday, 5 o'clock. For a novelist you show a feeble and perverted psychology. Any thing less like my and Leonard's conversation I can't imagine. Did Leonard ever persuade me to accept an invitation? "Well, you're a damned fool if you do." thats his style:—mine is unprintable. but, in this case, flattering to you.

Your
Virginia Woolf.

It is really (now I come to think of it) extremely good and kind of you to ask me.

Berg

Letters 1638-1658 (mid-May–July 1926)

The Woolfs paid two short visits to Monk's House, now more comfortable with the addition of a bathroom and two w.c.s, but were otherwise in London, publishing their early-summer list. They spent a weekend at Garsington in June, from where they visited Robert Bridges at Boar's Hill, and in July Virginia was writing To the Lighthouse *quickly enough to foresee its end. In the same month they called on Thomas Hardy in Dorset.*

1638: To V. Sackville-West   52 *Tavistock Square, W.C.*1

Wednesday [19 May 1926]

Yes, yes, yes. Come at once.

Everybody is longing to see you. Grizzle in paroxysms. Lunch *here* at 1. Friday. Better still come to the basement at 12.30 and have a preliminary talk (must it be about the Polish rebellion?)[1] with me in my studio—then 6 or 7 hours upstairs. (unless you'll dine with me on *Thursday*, when I happen to be alone)

Ah-hah! Revolutions—Poland—enquiries—scrapes—what fun it'll be.

Yr VW.

Grizzle's mange *is* better—I know how anxious you must be.

Berg

1639: To Vanessa Bell   52 *Tavistock Sqre* [*W.C.*1]

May 19th [1926]

Dearest,

I have done your commissions so far as posting the letters go—not very arduous so far. You seem almost as maltreated as we are—it is a good deal colder than February, generally raining, and now and then a black fog. One came on as I was starting for your show—so I gave it up, and you must wait for criticism which will I know profoundly interest you. Meanwhile I hear that your still life is greatly admired; I hope, bought. probably you

1. Vita returned to England on 16 May, having had an adventurous journey from Moscow. Riots broke out in Warsaw, and she was forced to take a circuitous route through southern Poland into Germany.

have heard from better sources however. The only papers I have seen say nothing about Adeney[1] and compare Duncan to Fragonard—but this is the spiteful [Evening] Standard man.

We should be grateful if you could have some talk with Angus. I think you could make him see the sort of difficulty that arises better than we could —it is mainly the languor and slowness, I think; I can't help feeling sometimes that the irregularity of the Press and the strain of its being such a gamble (I suppose we are certain now to have a loss next year)[2] will always be more worrying to him than to most people. And that of course reacts upon us. But we leave it to your tactful nature.

We are having rather a grind at the moment to get Viola [Tree] going again. Twenty four sandwichmen are parading the West End today, and I have just travelled Kensington High Street—which almost made me vomit with hatred of the human race. Innumerable women of incredible mediocrity, drab as ditchwater, wash up and down like dirty papers against Barkers and Derry and Toms. One was actually being sick or fainting in the middle of the street. All our past—George Gerald Marny and Emma[3] —rose about me like the fumes of cabbage. And I had to sit next a man in the tube who picked his ears with a large pin—then stuck it in his coat again. Meanwhile you are in Venice—Rain or no rain, Duncan with a sore throat or not (I hope he's better—please give him my fondest love)—its better than this.

But to the Keynes'—Maynard has decided not to stand for the Provostry. He says he would always be called the Provost and not Keynes: he would become respectable; he would sink and disappear. Also the more you refuse, the more you are requested. So he is *not* lost to Bloomsbury. But as everyone agrees that he would almost certainly have failed, the arguments do not convince me. Leonard said he seemed greatly depressed. I have seen nothing of them. On the other hand I sat next Mrs Gilchrist of Cardiff last night at Figaro, and she told me that her husband had not a dram of ambition. Needless to say, she had known Saxon when he was in Eton collars. One could have told that far off to look at her. Also she asked me how many people Covent Garden seats. I said roughly 6,000; but advised her to ask the attendant. And there was Ralph and Frances [Marshall], connubial, furtive; James [Strachey] and Noel,[4] both grey as badgers and sleek as moles (I have just been to the Zoo, and noted these facts accurately.) And Adrian and Karin are inseparable; and are re-arranging the house, beds being now only one wall off—I mean, bedrooms next door. Morgan

1. Bernard Adeney (1878-1966), the painter and textile designer, and a founder member of the London Artists' Association.
2. In fact the Hogarth Press made a profit of £27 in 1926.
3. George and Gerald Duckworth; Margaret and Emma Vaughan.
4. Noel Olivier, who married a fellow doctor, Arthur Richards, in 1921.

[Forster] came to tea yesterday; but we argued about novel writing, which I will not fret your ears with—his mother is slowly dispatching him, I think—He is limp and damp and milder than the breath of a cow. Mr Brace came—the American publisher. He says they would most warmly welcome a children's story illustrated by Mrs Bell. Do for Gods sake bestir yourself. What other news? Mary has rung up to ask me to go and see her rooms, with the "lovely new decorations."[1] Shall I thrust her through with a few home truths?—I didn't go—couldn't face Jack on a sofa recovering from tonsilitis. And she joins the parrokeet in France soon, I gather.

I'm panting to pull up my [bath and lavatory] plugs at Rodmell, and when poor old Angus comes back, I suppose we shall at last get there for 5 days. God knows if we shall motor with Gwen—here's Hubert Waley—come to discuss his infernal pamphlet[2]—and you are safe at Venice; how happy you are—and you dont want anybody—and you don't have electric light at half cock, as we do since the strike. But then you never saw armoured cars convoying frozen meat along Oxford Street. I shall have lots of stories to tell you about that.

Love to Angus and D[uncan].

B.

Berg

1640: To V. Sackville-West   52 *Tavistock Square, W.C.*1

Saturday [22 May 1926]

We will get tickets for some entertainment (I can't be certain which) on Tuesday, So come, and it will be great fun. You'll find me here anytime after six. But I'm afraid I chattered too much yesterday, and meaning to let you in, Leonard did, which saddened me.

But to business. You said you were going to finish a book in Persia. Would you let us have it? The point is I don't want to press you, if you feel, as you may, that Heinemann's has a right, and is, as maybe too, more profitable.[3] At the same time I dont want these refinements of feeling to lose us a chance which would give a great fillip to our autumn season. So consider.

I did enjoy seeing you, and am wearing your necklace, and my exuberance after all is not my egotism, but your seduction. Is your garden good?

Yr VW.

1. Vanessa and Duncan had done the original decorations to the Hutchinson's River House, Hammersmith, in 1917. They had now moved to Regent's Park.
2. *The Revival of Aesthetics*, published by the Press in March 1926.
3. Vita broke her contract with Heinemann's to publish *Passenger to Teheran* with the Hogarth Press.

Excuse this handwriting—we are going to watch cricket at Lords and I must wash.

Berg

1641: To Edward Sackville West

52 *Tavistock Square, W.C.*1
Friday [1926?]

Dear Eddy,
No, it wasnt what I said to Clive at all. This is more like it (as far as I remember) that you had a passion for Wagner, were a fanatic, and thought Lawrence the best living English writer—(which were I think your very words,) all of which I repeated admiringly, and with agreement (not as to the fact, of course, but as to the spirit—my theme being that I liked your enthusiasm) This Clive, I suppose, cooked up at some lunch party, annoyingly, I agree, in the way you say: but I don't believe he was in the least malicious.
God knows what one is to do. He has a passion for being au fait with all goings on; and a little more.
My only shred of "mature wisdom" is that such things are the penalty one pays for the pleasure of talking freely. I've paid it dozens of times. At this moment, doubtless, Philip Ritchie is repeating what Eddy says Virginia says and next week it will come round to me—Such is life in Bloomsbury. But it is not done maliciously: though I agree with you, I can never help being angry at the distortion at the moment I hear of it. All I try now is *not* to hear it.
As for "drawing you out", please believe I don't do such things deliberately, with an object—Its only that I am, as a rule, far more interested in people than they are in me—But it makes me a nuisance, I know: only an innocent nuisance.
And a thousand apologies for thus causing you annoyance when I felt nothing but gratitude and expressed nothing but pleasure in seeing you to Clive, or anybody else

Yr
Virginia Woolf

Berg

1642: To V. Sackville-West   52 *Tavistock Square, W.C.*1
Tuesday [1 June 1926]

It is all infinitely good of you—what we thought of, for your travels, was to have large, numerous photographs.

267

At the same time, we are a little conscience (oh damn! I've been addressing envelopes all the afternoon, and cannot write a word) I was saying we feel a little guilty about taking you from the prosperous Heinemann. Lets talk it over in cold blood

Now about coming—I could come *alone* for the *night* on Friday: weekend impossible, owing to dining out Saturday. Or, Leonard says he could come and would like to come for Saturday night the week following —that is 12th (I mean, we could both come.) But then we were not asked then. So choose which you like. Only let me know. (I mean this *next* Friday, 4th, I could come:)

You are utterly wrong about Viola.[1] Why read memoirs as if they were poems? Don't you see her vulgarity is *not* vulgar, her irreticence is *not* unashamed: an aroma—she aims at that: life: fact: not the thing we go for—but I cant make you understand: try reading as if you were catching a swarm of bees; not hunting down one dart like dragon fly. Please, please, don't ask a soul [to Long Barn] ever. Aren't we suffocated with souls? The Sitwells, and Gertrude Stein tonight.

Yr VW.   Love to Pippin [Vita's dog]

Sybil [Colefax] writes: "I'm flung into writing to you as I actually dreamed last night that you'd gone to a theatre *twice* with Dottie—now to be called Dorothy—Wellesley! ! !"
Well: what is the interpretation?

Berg

1643: TO LADY OTTOLINE MORRELL

52 Tavistock Square, W.C.1

[early June 1926]

Dearest Ottoline,

I'm going to give up writing letters—I always say, or convey, the exact opposite of what I mean—in my last letter I fished for an invitation— surely you are not blind to my lines? However, this is to say that I shall be delighted to come the last week end which is the 26th if that suits you; and Leonard wants me to say that he would very much like to come, but may he leave it a little longer, as his Nation horrors have to be arranged? If this upsets your plans, of course don't bother,—and he will settle not to come. I'm afraid we must catch the usual Sunday evening train back.

1. "Dear, idolised Virginia that you are, how *could* you publish Viola? It makes me vomit. I don't like you to sell your soul." (Vita to Virginia, 29 May 1926, *Berg*.)

But anyhow that will be very nice. (I hope you see what simple language I'm using, so that there may be no mistake).

Do you mean you're settling in Bloomsbury?[1] Will all your glories be revived? Or is it only 3 months again? Is it number 4? Shall I be asked to tea?

Yr
V.W.

Texas

1644: To Vanessa Bell   52 *Tavistock Square, W.C.* 1

2nd June. 1926

Dearest,

Bloomsbury is ringing with two great excitements: 1: Julian Morrell is engaged to a son of old Vinogradov: 2: Miss Bulley—the stormy petrel of revolution—is engaged to her Cousin Armitage. You will be delighted to hear that Ottoline and Philip are behaving scandalously: refuse to consent; dislike the young man who is penniless; and ignore the whole affair Julian is behaving with great spirit, and it is said that Garsington presents a scene of unparalleled horror.[2] Needless to say, I am going to stay there. Bulley's climax is hailed with high joy. People, like Angus and Francis and Duncan, say she has been lumbering after them since 1910: daily growing more vociferous, as her natural charm decreased. But how, high and arid as she is, Armitage has succumbed, I know not. Further, Ottoline has taken, on long lease too, a house in Gower Street—She settles in next autumn. (But I meant to conceal this, as I tremble lest you should at once buy a Palazzo or a Canaletto: really, you'll be touched to hear, I pine for a cup of tea with you: I am starved; I wake in the night crying your name: I am jealous of Duncan) So you see what we're gossiping about in Bloomsbury.

We were at a party at Edith Sitwell's last night, where a good deal of misery was endured. Jews swarmed. It was in honour of Miss Gertrude Stein who was throned on a broken settee (all Ediths furniture is derelict, to make up for which she is stuck about with jewels like a drowned mermaiden.) This resolute old lady inflicted great damage on all the youth. According to Dadie, she contradicts all you say; insists that she is not only the most intelligible, but also the most popular of living writers; and in

1. Ottoline had decided to sell Garsington and move to London, where she bought the lease of 10 Gower Street.
2. Julian Morrell had fallen in love with Igor, son of Sir Paul Vinogradoff, Professor of Jurisprudence at Oxford from 1903 until his death in 1925. Ottoline and Philip opposed their engagement, and in 1928 Julian married Victor Goodman. After their divorce in 1942, she married her earlier love, Igor.

particular despises all of English birth. Leonard, being a Jew himself, got on very well with her. But it was an anxious exacerbating affair: Germans were introduced to me; Mr Ackerley; Isaacs; and at last a wizened wire-drawn excruciated little man, whose name, he said, I should never have heard: it was Squire,[1] or Squires: he said he is perhaps the worst living painter, admires you and Duncan hugely, and—that was about all—Of course I said he was only too modest. But what is one to say? He said Duncan as a boy used to be the most garrulous of company; laughed and talked without stopping—(This was in the year 1900). Now, he said, he is completely changed. But he may have been talking of some other Grant. Then I said, by way of a joke, how you had broken your watch, and could never come home any more. So he pointed out how there is a clock at St Marks [Venice]. By this time I was so morose that I flew to the bosom of Todd, and there reposed. I have asked her to write her life, but I gather that there are passages of an inconceivable squalor. (did I tell you how I made Todd tell me of a dressmaker, your Miss Fletcher reducing me to such a state of despair and fury that I was driven to a step which nothing, I thought, could have led me to: I am now going to get 3 10 guinea dresses a year.)

. . . . . *[Two lines omitted]* . . . . .

. . . .

Vita is back—that will bore you. Nor do you really want to hear my rhapsodies about Monk's House, where we were last week. It is not of course by any means ready; but the luxury of water running in torrents, boiling hot, for every purpose is inconceivable. Even Nelly had to admit she can cook perfectly there. But I shall want a great deal of advice, not to say help, from you—The drawing room, for example ... Here I check myself, well knowing from the experience of years, how my nose can be rapped. I meant to expostulate with you, by the way; is it really true that you think I have a bad temper? Some of the ravens of Bloomsbury, fowls of darkness, so aver; to which I reply, vain, egotistical, selfish, I may be— but my temper (as my husband will vouch) is angelic.

Then I went to your show. Angus will have told you about the sales: I hope your 4 pictures were £100 each. Bicknell [Director, Leicester Galleries] introduced himself, and said it was all a tremendous success: the first day 4 people were bidding at once for Grants Twickenham: the only question was, who could stick the ticket on first. But you brush all this aside. It is my opinion you want. What I think is this: there is a divinely lovely landscape of yours of Charleston: one of flashing brilliance, of sunlight crystallised, of diamond durability. This I consider your master-piece. I do not think the big picture of Angelica etc. in the garden quite succeeds. I expect the problem of empty spaces, and how to model them, has rather baffled you. There are flat passages, so that the design is not

1. Harold Squire, a member of Vanessa's Friday Club, and later of the London Group.

completely comprehended. Of the smaller works, I think the blue boat by the bridge is my favourite. Indeed, I am amazed, a little alarmed (for as you have the children, the fame by rights belongs to me) by your combination of pure artistic vision and brilliance of imagination. A mistress of the brush—you are now undoubtedly that; but still I think the problems of design on a large scale slightly baffle you. For example the Aunt Julia photograph. It seems to me that when you muffle the singing quality of your tone, and reduce the variety and innumerability of colour (The pigeon breast radiance in which you are so supreme that, before hot pokers, or the asters (?) my mind shivers with joy) to bone, where the frame of the design is prominent, then, now and again, you falter, or somehow flatten. But I was hugely impressed, and kept on saying that your genius as a painter, though rather greater than I like, does still shed a ray on mine. I mean, people will say, What a gifted couple! Well: it would have been nicer had they said: Virginia had all the gifts; dear old Nessa was a domestic character —Alas, alas, they'll never say that now. As for the meretricious loveliness of Grant, I need say nothing. Twickenham, I see, is what people call genius: I'm not sure I dont prefer the Wilmington landscape. I like the bareness of that: also of Bea [Howe]. (whose stories I'm just rejecting, very tenderly and encouragingly) I like its impure colour. I thought [Frederick] Porter's purple sea scape singularly enchanting: Dear old Roger. Suddenly pirouettes, round and round, in the manner of Duncan. And he sold that one too. No: I will not let you two bitches have the laugh of me any longer. Duncan is gibbering as he used in the year 1900. My dear Duncan, why did Squires make you laugh in the year 1900? I see why you laugh at me for writing about painting; but Squire was no laughing matter last night, I can assure you.

The Press is thinking of talking again, one day soon. Angus is charming; only very sleepy. We are now doing rather well.

Do come back soon. I borrowed a necklace of yours the other day

Yr B

I have paid your bills; I dont think they come to £7 quite. We were very much under-rated; absurdly; so I see no reason why your rates should have gone up half as much as ours.

Berg

1645: To V. Sackville-West   52 *Tavistock Square, W.C.*1

Monday [7 June 1926]

Next Saturday then, God willing. I'd have liked to come on Friday—but, another confession—I've had to take to the sofa with some kind of influenza

271

and if a germ remains or a headache or anything nothing will induce me to afflict you, much though I should like to. Shall Leonard ring you up?

Sybil did ask us on 15th: we refused: now, to meet you, I've accepted —Lord, how one does treat that woman, and seen privately alone at tea here, she's so nice: only glittering as a cheap cherry in her own house.

Not much news. Rather cross—Would like a letter. Would like a garden. Would like Vita. Would like 15 puppies with their tails chopped off,[1] 3 doves, and a little conversation. The Sitwells was a ghastly frost. I put it in to make you feel a bumpkin—and it did, and thus confirmed my view that other peoples parties have a mystery and glamour one's own are without. Are you writing poetry? If so, then tell me what is the difference between that emotion and the prose emotion? What drives you to one and not the other? I am trying to work this out; not for Vogue: so dont snub me. Last night I read some poetry of yours in an anthology and liked it: so let me have your Georgics [The Land] complete. My novel is very very bad: all my worst faults displayed so I daresay its as well I have to drop it for the time. Is Montaigne any good?—the one by the woman whose name I can't remember.[2] And are you so intensely, completely, happy that one drop more would make you spill? Is this solitude? I'm thinking of retiring to Rodmell too to try.

Yr VW.

Berg

1646: TO MOLLY MACCARTHY   52 *Tavistock Square* [*W.C.*1]

Wednesday [9 June 1926]

Dearest Molly,

I still write from bed, where [Dr] Elly [Rendel] keeps me, because I have had a dribbling little temperature and then a damnable what they call nerve exhaustion headache—One's back seems to be made of a membrane, like a bats wing: this should be stretched tight, in order to deal adequately with the flight of existence; but suddenly it flops, and becomes (I imagine) like a veil (do you remember the veils of our youth?) which has fallen into a cup of tea. So I am lying on the sofa, in my nightgown, picking at a book or two, and dropping them on to the floor. I see nobody partly because I have nothing to say except oh! Shall I ever have anything to say except oh!

Well—anyhow we hope to go to Rodmell on Saturday and there I shall look at downs and swans, and steep my faculties in cabbages and green grass. And then we shall come back; and do let us come and dine

1. Vita's two dogs, Pippin and Freya, had both had litters recently.
2. *Michel de Montaigne*, by Edith Sichel (1911).

with you. Only dinner is not the same as an old crones' crumpet tea. Please don't get out of that. And I want very much to see Michael [Molly's son] —so does Leonard. We have a great affection—inbred—I cant remember the right word for him; and I shall try to get him to dinner before he goes.

One moment: I have a request. Please attend. Leonard has a brother Philip who has a boy aged 4. He wants the boy to go to Eton. He writes to ask if we can tell him anything—who are the best housemasters? Could we write a word of introduction? Do you know anything about Eton now? Could you possibly advise? This is the only boy Woolf in existence[1] and the father would do anything in the world to advance him. So I feel I must take steps, but can only remember old Mr Luxmoore and Hester Alington when she was a carroty girl. Any help would be most gratefully received.[2]

Ever your dear old friend

Virginia

Mrs Michael MacCarthy

1647: TO VANESSA BELL

Monks House, Rodmell
[Sussex]

Sunday June 13th [1926]

Dearest,

We have been having an influenza epidemic, caused, it is thought, by Lottie [Hope] and the Stephen's dog, so have come down here for a few days, as it gave me a slight headache. But I'm practically all right again. I suppose there's no chance of your being at Charleston? If so, I might possibly see you—or even inveigle you over. I did not like to insinuate that your genius with the brush and the pot is badly required: but so it is; and I have purposely left several bare beams in the drawing rooms, should you feel inspired. I will say this: it has the makings of a most peculiar and I think comfortable, charming, characteristic, queer resort; but a paralysis attacks my vision when directed to practical details. What curtains? What chair covers? Would I be allowed some rather garish but vibrating and radiating green and red lustres on the mantelpiece? Showers of glass, shaped like long fingers in a bunch—you know my taste that way. Also I want to buy a ship in a glass bottle: also a mother of pearl and wooden platter. But I will wait for you.

1. Leonard's parents had nine children who grew to adulthood. All but one married, but five had no children, two others had girls only, and only one (Philip) a son, who was named Cecil. See family-tree, p. 522.
2. Molly was the daughter of Francis Warre-Cornish, Vice-Provost of Eton, 1893-1916. Henry Luxmoore was the senior assistant master, 1864-1904; and Hester (*née* Lyttelton) was the wife of Cyril Alington, the Head Master of Eton since 1917.

It was Francis [Birrell] who told us about Bulley. Other people agree that it is true—He says he has suspected it this 12 months. Ever since he lunched with Mr Armitage and Bull: and was positive from their enamoured ways; but said nothing, and it is now (he says) public: Armitage is charming, rich, fair haired and a cousin: Bull: is like a rich galleon at last afloat, all her banners streaming, and her caskets (what this may signify I know not) open to the air. I saw Sybil (my dear friend Sibyl Colefax I mean) who had met Ottoline nefariously engaged in trying to bring about an engagement between Julian and the Hon. Richard Smith, son of W. H. Smith [the book-seller], fabulously rich:

.   .   .   .

.   .   .   .

.   .   .   .

.   .   .   .   *[Seven lines omitted]*   .   .   .   .

.   .   .   .

.   .   .   .

.   .   .   .

Ott, is giving bi-weekly tea parties at 6 [10] Gower Street during the autumn (during 6 autumns, for they have a 6 year lease) one for intimacy, the other society "We will discuss *everything* in the whole *Universe*" she says. Really, her style is much like Madges [Vaughan].

Leonard wants me to begin by giving you his best love: to go on, by saying, in sorrow, not anger, that it is a little ungenerous of you, he can't help thinking, to plant him with a complete imbecile like Ede,[1] and then to complain of Ede's idiocy. The village cat could have written a better article than Ede. Ede now haunts him and demands more work: but why did you recommend Ede? Ede is your hatching; Ede is your brewing. Ede must now be despatched by you—you know how—"I am sorry to tell you etc etc." We had the first of our talks with Angus. He gave way on every point, as you said. He thinks he mistook what was wanted, and will try to take up a new attitude. Meanwhile, a man who has been with Arnold[2] for 12 years and has vast experience, wants to come. I expect for the sake of the Press we ought to take him; on the other hand, Angus is so charming, and might develop, and brisk up—anyhow, We are to talk again.

What could account for Duncan's habits except his genius? Of course Twickenham is a work of genius: all I say is, Duncan has genius: but Duncan has, what is much rarer—sanity. These two together fuse into blocks of solidity; the one shoots into spirals of volatility. I'm much amused you should cast a days thought after my criticism—considering how it was fired off with my feet on the fender in 6 seconds precisely.[3] I see I did not

1. H. S. Ede, who in 1926 published *Florentine Drawings of the Quattrocento.*
2. Edward Arnold, the publisher of Leonard's novels.
3. See Letter 1644.

express my enormous admiration of both your gifts: which was even more direct and ardent than usual. No pictures now painted give me so much pleasure.

Vita is now arriving to spend 2 nights alone with me—L. is going back. I say no more; as you are bored by Vita, bored by love, bored by me, and everything to do with me, except Quentin and Angelica; but such has long been my fate, and it is better to meet it open eyed. Still, the June nights are long and warm; the roses flowering; and the garden full of lust and bees, mingling in the asparagus beds. I must go in and tidy up.

V.W.

Berg

1648: To Leonard Woolf [*Monk's House, Rodmell, Sussex*]

Monday [14 June 1926]
Dearest M.

Very good night. *No* headache. Just off to Rottingdean with Grizzel in motor, where I shall have tea while Vita calls on Lady Jones.[1] Perhaps I shall buy you a keepsake.

Home certainly tomorrow in time for dinner. Lonely day. Longing to see all hearts

M.

Sussex

1649: To V. Sackville-West [52 *Tavistock Square, W.C.*1]

Friday [18 June 1926]

This is only a scribble to catch the post. Yes, Clive has been here, but no mischief made, though many questions asked.[2]

I'm sorry about your mother: what did the dr. say?[3] and about your despondency. But that may be circumstances, and about Sybil and the bad impression I made, and about the rats and the doves. Ever since you drove off, I've been talking—oh, and had one declaration of love; and Wells[4]—but no: I won't repeat any more great mens compliments (of course, I shall; dozens of times over)

"Among younger writers are Miss Violet Sackville West, whose Grey Wethers, strong in conception and austere in treatment, has moments of

1. Enid Bagnold, the novelist and playwright.
2. About Virginia's relationship with Vita.
3. Lady Sackville was thought to be dying, but she lived another ten years.
4. With whom Leonard had been lunching. In fact, Wells had said that Virginia was too intelligent—a bad thing (see Virginia's diary, 9 June 1926).

almost epic splendour." (Modern English Fiction by Gerald Bullet)[1] This I happen to light on, and have a thrill of jealousy.

Otherwise, I'm well disposed towards you, and if I should see a chance of coming down for a night say Thursday, should I suggest it? Anyhow write a long account of Sunday:[2] I see Clive's primed with questions: blurted out, had I read you his letter at Rodmell? So beware: dont blush: dont lead me to think you've compromised your virtue among the cedars. Yes, I do write damned well sometimes, but not these last days, when I've been slogging through a cursed article,[3] and see my novel [*To the Lighthouse*] glowing like the Island of the Blessed far far away over dismal wastes, and cant reach land.

Now Lottie is coming for this.

Never talk about my health again.

Did yours culminate in the bloody flux, or whatever its called? Are you feeling better for it?

Aint it odd that in Oct. 1922 you were still Nicolson with a aitch.

Yr
VW.

Shall you come through London on Monday?
Anyhow, dine, tea, Friday.

Berg

1650: To Vanessa Bell   52 *Tavistock Square, London, W.C.*1
Friday [18 June 1926]

Dearest,

I came back, as I am now recovered, but infinitely sensible and refusing Sybils parties.

When shall you be back? You are urgently needed: to start a Club: to get up a book of Aunt Julias [Cameron] photographs, among other things.

No one blames you for anything.[4] Everybody loves you—including

1. Gerald Bullett the novelist, anthologist, and critic. *Grey Wethers*, Vita's fourth novel, was published in 1923.
2. Vita was staying with Dorothy Wellesley at Sherfield, and Clive was among the other guests.
3. "*Impassioned Prose*" (*TLS*, 16 September 1926), on Thomas de Quincey.
4. Vanessa had denied recommending Mr Ede as an art critic to the *Nation*.

Vita, whose motives are suspect however. "So beautiful, so charming" etc.[1]
A great rush of Apostles is taking place, but I have avoided them.

I wish you had bought me linen and china in Paris: but whats the use of wishing? Clive is coming to tea—We dine with Mary tomorrow "You must see my lovely room." Did you ever get paid?

Oh how delicious for you to see me again! I'm agog with excitement at the thought. And all you think is how lovely Angelica is, how adorable, how delicious Charleston, how happy I am, what a great painter Duncan is, and I too (this is what you think) have every grace and every gift. Thank God I'm not

Virginia Woolf

Fond and frantic love to Marjorie [Strachey], whom I love passing the love of women. Also to Angelica. A letter from Quentin, who wants to attack the Keynes'.

L. went to Lydia's first night[2] with Maynard, who was so nervous he spoilt the evening.

Berg

1651: To V. Sackville-West   [52] *Tavistock Square* [*W.C.*1]
Typewritten
Tuesday [22 June 1926]

Darling Mrs Nicolson,

I think I won't come on Thursday for this reason; I must get on with writing; you would seduce me completely; I have to spend two nights (I suppose) at Garsington.

But; will you ask us (Leonard for one night, me for two) next week, if you're coming up and its convenient? which would be even nicer, or week after.

Also will you come on after your play on Thursday and see me alone? I've put off Sybil in case you can. Come early on Friday. The typewriter calls you instinctively Darling Mrs Nicolson.

1. Vanessa had written to Virginia on 16 June: "Give my humble respects to Vita, who treats me as an Arab steed looking from the corner of its eye on some long-eared mule—But then you do your best to stir up jealousy between us, so what can one expect?" (*Berg*)
2. Lydia Lopokova made occasional appearances with the Diaghilev ballet in June-July 1926. On 15 June she opened as Columbine in *Carnaval*.

I have been going through the extremes of horror, dining with the Hutchinsons to meet the [Aldous] Huxleys and feeling utterly and infinitely unhappy. I cannot control it because there is no reason for it. They say that Dorothy Warren[1] is engaged to G. Scott. They say she has had every sort of love.

Wells said . . .[2] isn't that exciting? My proposal was homosexual. I said . . .[2] isn't that exciting? You think I'm so damned vain I can be trusted to blabber everything—well, it's true.

Good by, darling Mrs Nicolson. You'll come on Thursday. Leonard says—only the usual thing, but from him unusual, about liking to see you.

Virginia Woolf
(Mrs Woolf)

Of course, if you want to meet Sibyl and you've only to say so. Will you dine with me off radishes alone in the kitchen?

Berg

1652: To Lady Ottoline Morrell

52 Tavistock Square [W.C.1]

[23? June 1926]

We will arrive at 6 at Oxford on Saturday. I'm afraid we shall have to catch the 6.17 at Wheatley on Sunday, but I hope this will leave time for Mr Bridges.[3]

Leonard is looking forward to coming—

V.W.

Texas

1653: To Vanessa Bell   [52 *Tavistock Square, W.C.*1]

[July 1926]

I forgot to ask you the one thing I wanted last night—have you any Aunt Julia letters?[4] I vividly remember reading some, to mother, I think;

1. She was a niece of Philip Morrell, and later in the '20s ran the Warren Gallery. She did not marry Scott, but Trotter, who imported Styrian jade.
2. Ellipses in the original.
3. Robert Bridges, the Poet Laureate, whom Virginia visited at his house, Boar's Hill, Oxford.
4. Virginia was writing an introduction to a selection of photographs by her great-Aunt, Julia Margaret Cameron. The book, *Victorian Photographs of Famous Men and Fair Women*, was published by the Hogarth Press in October 1926.

but can't find any here. I'm now writing about her, and it would be a great advantage to have some of her actual words, which I imagine were extremely profuse, to quote. But I daresay they've all disappeared. I dont want to have to apply to George [Duckworth] or Bee Cameron,[1] if I can help.

If you *have*, would you ring up tomorrow morning, and I will come and get them.

If not, dont bother—

I suppose you would find it too dull to dine with me, alone, on Sunday night? L. is going to Roger—

Yr B.

Berg

1654: To Helen McAfee   52 *Tavistock Square, London, W.C.*1
Typewritten
13th July 1926

Dear Miss McAfee,

I am sorry for the delay in sending you the essay I spoke of "How should one read a book?"[2] (it is, by the way, really a lecture) but I had an attack of influenza which upset all my plans.

I enclose it herewith, and hope it will be suitable for your purposes.

I should like to see a proof, if possible.

Believe me,

Yours sincerely
Virginia Woolf

Yale University

1655: To V. Sackville-West   52 *Tavistock Square, W.C.*1
[15 July 1926]

Dear Mrs Nicolson,

This is only business, not affection—I suppose you're not coming to see me; so please, as a darling, send me (oh but better far come and bring me—)

(1) Tennyson by H. N[Harold Nicolson].

(2) Venetian Glass Nephew[3] the authoress said severely "Really! Not read any of my books!" Oh what an evening! I expected a ravishing and

1. Beatrice, the daughter of Julia Cameron's son Eugene.
2. Published by the *Yale Review*, of which Miss McAfee was managing editor, in October 1926.
3. The most recent novel (1925) by Elinor Wylie (1885-1928), the American novelist and poet, who was married three times, not four.

279

diaphanous dragonfly, a woman who had spirited away 4 husbands, and wooed from buggery the most obstinate of his adherents: a siren; a green and sweetvoiced nymph—that was what I expected, and came a tiptoe in to the room to find—a solid hunk: a hatchet minded, cadaverous, acid voiced, bareboned, spavined, patriotic nasal, thick legged American. All the evening she declaimed unimpeachable truths; and discussed our sales: hers are 3 times better than mine, naturally; till thank God, she began heaving on her chair and made a move as if to go, gracefully yielded to, but not, I beg you to believe, solicited, on our parts. Figure my woe, on the stairs, when she murmured, "Its the *other* thing I want. Comes of trying to have children. May I go in there?" So she retired to the W.C., emerged refreshed; sent away her cab, and stayed another hour, hacking us to pieces. But I must read her book.

(3) Tell me if this is a real coronet, or a sham. I'm trying to prove my great Aunts descent from a Neapolitan adventurer and a French Marquis.[1] But I have no time.

Ever, dear Mrs N.

Your devoted
Virginia Woolf.

Sybil is rampant beyond belief.

Berg

1656: To V. Sackville-West   52 *Tavistock Square, W.C.*1

[19? July 1926]

You are an angel, but I didn't mean you to take so much trouble. God knows about the Marquis. Probably the whole thing is different in France—he may have been the son or the nephew of a Marquis (I think that was the legend), and anyhow I suppose I can say, vaguely, 'aristocratic', and leave it. I want to prove her base and noble—it fits in with her oddities. I might spend a lifetime over her; but can't face going to my halfbrother who knows all about the Marquis. Tennyson has not yet come; but will, I make no doubt. I quail before the Venetian nephew. Another meeting with that arid desert [Elinor Wylie] has sickened me. The only curiosity is—how does she do it—Francis Birrell, Aldous Huxley at her feet, and she no better than a stark staring naked maypole? God, again, knows.

About coming—(this letter is in the catalogue style, which reminds me,

1. Virginia sent Vita a picture of a coronet which had descended to her aunt, Julia Cameron. Vita identified it as the coronet of an English marquis and not, as Virginia had hoped, the crest of the 18th-century Chevalier Antoine de l'Etang, Julia Cameron's grandfather.

I've not yet read Wellesley, but will, and would, if Desmond hadn't turned up last night and rambled on for an hour about the character of Shakespeare —he was a smallish man, very nervous, with staring blueish grey eyes, highly excitable—did you know all this? he talked a great deal—Shakespeare: and Desmond and Virginia too.) But to return—About coming—I'm dashing off, you'll be amused to hear, on my chronic visit to Hardy.[1] I expect I shall be back on Saturday: I shall only stay one day and drink one cup of tea, and be so damned nervous I shall spill it on the floor, and what shall I say? Nothing, but arid nonsense. Yet I feel this is a great occasion. Here am I approaching the immortal fount, touching the sacred hand: he will make all of us, Leonard and me and Grizzle, seem transparent and passing, This old wrinkled dwindled man, who has, Sibyl Colefax says (who, you'll be surprised to hear knows him intimately) two very little, very bright eyes—Sibyl told him how much she liked The Dynasts. Now what did Hardy think of Sibyl? It is said he does not think. But I'll tell you all about it when we meet.

So once more, about coming. I dont think there's much good my coming with your pack of flibbertigibbets[2] (Clive has just stood me a terrific lunch and was sweet and found us an old ripe, but not quite virginal, apple, and I love him, and always shall, but not in the go-to-bed or sofa way) Clive, Mary, Evan Morgan [Lord Tredegar] etc. I should, I make no doubt, shine. Vanity compels me to admit that I should cut a very fine figure, in Todds dress (Thank God, I'm sitting in an old silk petticoat at the moment with a hole in it, and the top part of another dress with a hole in it, and the wind is blowing through me), and I'm reading de Quincey, and Richardson, and again de Quincey—again de Quincey, because I'm in the middle of writing about him ["*Impassioned Prose*"], and my God Vita, if you happen to know do wire whats the essential difference between prose and poetry— It cracks my poor brain to consider.

As I say, I don't think I'll come on Saturday, though I should cut a figure; unless you very particularly wish it: but it suddenly occurs to me, why should I not come and spend Monday night alone with you? Except that I should have to return, literally and soberly, with the lark on Tuesday morning. But that would be fun too. The fact is we all go down to Sussex in a reserved saloon, on Tuesday afternoon, and if it were feasible for you, and you had no lovers friends, mothers, poisoned dogs, or young men proposing to you (though you're a married woman as you so often and so surprisingly assert) in the house, then I should be divinely happy, and sit on a seat and chatter. Moreover, having done de Quincey by then, I should be care free of prose and poetry: I should have packed the top part

1. Her visit to Thomas Hardy on 23 July is described in *A Writer's Diary* (1953), pp. 89-94.
2. A weekend party at Long Barn.

of my dress (what is it called?) and the skirt; my books, and papers, and 3 petticoats which I bought yesterday, and now the Cook says they're not petticoats—she says they're chemises. I ask you, how is one to know? But I cannot write all that is in my head, for I should fill the entire paper supply. Answer me only with your pen: shall I come on Monday night?—or will you, perhaps, come up on Monday, and let us dine together at a new place where they have a great variety of foods and drinks; and they give you roses, and there are looking glasses which reflect the most astonishingly commonplace scenes—a fat woman gobbling—in such a way that one feels one is dangling among octopuses at the bottom of the sea, peering into caves, and plucking pearls in bunches off the rocks.

Oh Vita, I must stop writing.

Yr VW.

Leonard says he can't come because of the Press etc—but would like to.

Berg

1657: To V. Sackville-West   52 *T.[avistock] S.[quare, W.C.1]*
Sunday [25 July 1926]

I think there is a train which arrives at Sevenoaks at 6.4. I will come by this; but for God's sake stop me, if its not convenient. I feel I have rather muddled things; or you have.

Heres 7/4 for the Venetian nephew [by Elinor Wylie]. Bad, bad woman: I said LEND. You go short of twopence in punishment.

V.W.

Berg

1658: To Violet Dickinson   52 *Tavistock Square, W.C.1*
Monday [26 July 1926]

My Violet:

I ought to have written to you before, to thank you for your postal order. We have been in rather a rush, though, bringing out a book of Maynard Keynes'.[1] Unless you order otherwise, you will go on getting these horrid little books from us at intervals. They are the ones we print ourselves, and for some reason your name is down as a subscriber to them. But you've only to say if you have had enough.

---

1. Keynes's *The End of Laissez-Faire*, published in July.

I am now printing a play by a German Jewess.[1] Happily one cannot read as one prints, or I should never go on with it. And yesterday I should have been seeing Vernon Lee[2]—Do you remember taking us to see her at Florence? She is now stone deaf, and talks a great deal, very very slowly but otherwise is precisely the same—the same coat and skirt, shoes, rings, stockings. Instead of seeing her, we went to Dorchester, and saw Thomas Hardy, who talked a great deal about father, and the Lushingtons. He may well outlive us all. I never saw such a spruce lively old man, but nothing would induce him to talk about his books.

London is a frying pan in the summer, and thank the Lord, we leave tomorrow for two months at Rodmell. This is very exciting because we have just put in a bath and two waterclosets, and have not yet seen it finished. Shall you be passing? Will you look in? I should like you to see the water closet. I think I shall retire there next year, and write innumerable books. Here it is almost hopeless, what with Lady Colefax (I hear Ozzie [Violet's brother] is motoring with her) and Lady Ottoline. Leonard won't dine there, with the result that she never stops asking him.

This is not what anyone could call a letter but you must consider it better than nothing—it is written in a chaos of books and things—How I wish you had ever taught me to be tidy! Nice of course I am; but not tidy. Write some time—you have lots of little bits of paper about on which to write

Yr Sp.

Leonard sends his love. The whole family—Nessa Clive, Children; depart together tomorrow.

Berg

1. The Hogarth Press published no 'play' by a 'German Jewess' in this year. Virginia may have been referring to *The Close Chaplet*, a poem by the American author Laura Gottschalk, later Laura Riding, which they published in October.
2. The pen-name of Violet Paget (1856-1935), the novelist, critic, and cultural historian, whose essay *The Poet's Eye* was published by the Hogarth Press in July of this year.

Letters 1659-1679 (August–mid-October 1926)

August and September were spent at Monk's House, following the long-established pattern of their year. It was a summer of glorious weather, and Virginia was hard at work on To the Lighthouse, *in spite of headaches and a minor nervous breakdown in late July. Vita came to Rodmell four times during the summer, and Virginia went once to Long Barn.*

1659: To ELINOR WYLIE   *Monks House, Rodmell*
                                                    [Sussex]
July 30th [1926]

Dear Mrs Wylie,

    I have been staying away, and have only just come back to find your letter and your books waiting for me here.

    It was extremely good of you to write. I have a passion for knowing or trying to guess all that was in a writer's mind, and I shall use your letter as a commentary on your text. I am beginning the Venetian Glass Nephew tonight.

    I have put aside the weeks here to read what I want to read—London is too much of a rush; and now with your letter to help me, I shall spend my evenings shelling you out.

    With many thanks,

                                 Yours very sincerely,
                                   Virginia Woolf

Yale University

1660: To V. SACKVILLE-WEST   *Monks House, Rodmell*
                                                    [Sussex]
Sunday [8 August 1926]

Yet, it does seem hard, that we should make you spend all the fine weather with your nose to the pen [*Passenger to Teheran*]. But think of your glory; and our profit, which is becoming a necessary matter, now that your puppy[1] has destroyed, by eating holes, my skirt, ate L's proofs, and done such damage as could be done to the carpet—But she is an angel of light. Leonard

---

1. On 26 July Vita had given Virginia one of Pippin's puppies, which the Woolfs called Pinker, the model for 'Flush'.

says seriously she makes him believe in God . . . and this after she has wetted his floor 8 times in one day.

I have sat a great deal on the bank: got completely brown and bitten, feel very well, can walk any distance (what a joy after last summer) and have read, at last, Wellesley on the world.[1] I think it has great merit; but so bound up with faults—cobbled, jerked, patched—what is one to do with it? Too good to destroy: But could she re-write? Some fluency and currency and perspective—thats what it wants: but I needn't criticise, thank God. Where am I to send it? A passionate Negress has now thrown her book at my head, and wants advice.

But when are you coming our way, to stay in your little cupboard room? I am going into Lewes to buy you what is called toilet articles. Which reminds me, do tell me, what is the name and price of the Spanish wine [Allela], and how could I get it? (I ask this with grave doubt: if you so much as hint at lending me a thimblefull, never darken my door again) But tell me: Our village cider is undrinkable, and I want to buy before L's enthusiasm for strong drink has cooled.

Sibyl put us off—for the duke of Devonshire I suppose; but was not acutely missed.

Did you have Molly? Did she cry?

Thinking about copulation, I now remember a whole chapter of my past that I forgot, I think, to tell you.

Oh and my spectacles—angel, send them

Yr VW.

Berg

1661: To Helen McAfee   *Monk's House, Rodmell,*
                                     Lewes, Sussex
Typewritten
10th August 1926

Dear Miss McAfee,

I have corrected the proofs[2] and have cut out six lines on page 11, at the end of a paragraph, which will I hope meet your wishes. The proofs only reached me last night, as I am staying down in the country.

Many thanks for your kind letter. I hope I may have an opportunity of contributing again to the Yale Review.

Yours very sincerely
Virginia Woolf

[*in Virginia's handwriting:*] The above address is only temporary.

Yale University

1. Dorothy Wellesley's long poem *Genesis*, published in November of this year.
2. Of *How Should One Read a Book?*

1662: To Saxon Sydney-Turner   *Monks House, Rodmell,*
                                    Lewes [*Sussex*]
Aug 12th [1926]

My dear Saxon,
   Many thanks for the cheque. I hope you didn't inconvenience yourself
to send it.
   About the autobiography[1]—do you want it typed now, or will it do if
I wait till October? It is put away in a cabinet, but no doubt Angus could
find it if asked. I imagine it will be rather expensive, as a typist would
probably want extra for the old manuscript.
   I hope it may be possible to do something with it.
   We are just off to Charleston, hoping to escape a storm—This week
the weather has been perfect; and Clarissa[2] brightening up—seduced last
night—I should say raped—most impressive.
                                                      Yrs V.W.
Sussex

1663: To Edward Sackville West   [*Monk's House, Rodmell,*
                                    Sussex]
[mid-August 1926]

Dear Eddy,
   I have several times taken up the pen to write to you, but the weather
has always made it impossible. Its too fine (its raining now) to do anything
except sit on the downs; also, I'm de-humanised. I've sunk to the bottom
of the world, and I only see the soles of peoples feet passing above. Does
the country affect you like this? Not Knole, I imagine. I cant rise to the
top at all. It is very happy down here, I assure you. Also, I think incessantly
—so it seems. I ponder every word of your letter—about the Partridges,
about Bloomsbury, about fiction. The only thing is my thoughts blow
away—(No: Colefax did not come. She passed my door, but I averted
her. A very tactful letter—that did the trick.) Nobody has been here, except
Vita for 10 minutes. I saw the tutors[3] knees—quite enough. She was therefore shaggier and surlier than ever—broke the w.c. too before she left.
   There's not going to be a post—damnation seize my friends for not
writing to me. I'm dependent on crumbs falling down to me from life
above. (Do you still believe in life by the way? I'm reading Wells' latest
[*The World of William Clissold*, 1926]—rather thin spread—bread comes

1. Of Saxon's great-grandfather, Mr Sharon Turner. The Hogarth Press never
   published it.
2. Samuel Richardson's *Clarissa* (1748).
3. Charles Farrell, a temporary tutor to Vita's sons.

through) So, as the post wont come, I shall take my eczematic dog to the top of Asheham hill, to find mushrooms. What I do is to think—I assure you, I think about Partridge and fiction and life and—oh here is the post with a letter from Rose Macaulay. As I was saying, the thing about fiction is—its blown away, that profound thought, which settled the whole hash too. What a nuisance! Please excuse the divagatoriness of this

Yr

VW

Berg

1664: To Ethel Sands   *Monks House, Rodmell,*

                                        Lewes [Sussex]

Monday Aug 16th [1926]

Dearest Ethel,

It is very nice of you to ask us, and it is most tempting to come over.[1] The difficulty is that Leonard is so engaged here that I don't think he will manage it, and I have got to get a book finished, and if I go gallivanting off to you, I certainly shant.

I suppose the middle or end of September is impossible for you, supposing I get finished by then—dash over, if you will have me by myself for a night? (No: I see you say before Sept. 1st; so I imagine it wont do.)

Are you painting? Are you seeing a great many people? London was rather a rush—the consequence of which is that one puts everything aside to do down here. I think you are amazingly wise to put an end to it all in March.

But it will be very nice to get you to come up to tea with me and try to torment you into indiscretions in October.

Yours affect,

V.W.

Wendy Baron

1665: To V. Sackville-West   *Monks House, Rodmell*

                                        [Sussex]

[19 August 1926]

Will you come on Wednesday? to lunch at 1? Leonard will be in London for the day. Would you like me to ask Clive? If so, let me know. Sleep night. You'll be even more uncomfortable than usual.

I say, please bring 2 bottles wine (not cider) which I want to buy. Cant get any.

1. To Ethel's house at Auppegard, Normandy.

If Thursday suits you better, come Thursday.
Only let me know. Tommie [Stephen Tomlin] talking:

Yr V.W.

I thought you looked tired. I hope you're not very bothered.

Berg

1666: To V. Sackville-West   *Monks House, Rodmell*
                                          [*Sussex*]
Sunday [22 August 1926]

Yes—that will be perfect. I think I shall be alone on Wednesday—couldn't you come early and enjoy a scrambly lunch?

The title [*Passenger to Teheran*] seems very good—far the best. I'm longing, in spite of having read 3 mss, to read yours—a great testimony to you: I'm compunctious that you should have worked so hard. Seven hours a day My God

Raymonds here. You have been praised almost without stopping: "There's no one I should mind finding me out so much as Vita" says Raymond. Then its your standing gorgeous in emeralds: then knowing Persians—and so on—all making you so brilliant I shall be shy for 15 minutes and a ½ precisely at seeing you.

Poor Puppy had a tray of chicken on top of her, so is being washed. You have saved my life by explaining how to buy nightgowns: I have 2: Now, how does one make one's hair stay firm after washing? and about chemises?

VW.

Damn you for going to Normandy—I have just refused to stay with Ethel Sands, in order to write

But whats one's writing worth that one should refuse to cross the Channel?—at this moment the thing I long for: Shall we go in Sept.?

Berg

1667: To Margaret Llewelyn Davies
                                          Monks House, Rodmell
                                          [*Sussex*]
2nd Sept [1926]

Dearest Margaret,

No, we're not in Russia, but here, and its been too hot and nice to

288

answer letters—but just the right weather for reading them—(this is a hint to you—if only people would write letters and not want answers!)

We've been dining over the downs with the Keynes' in their magnificent country house, and I nearly gave him your article; but only handed on your views about the Nation questionnaire.[1] Why d'you read that paper, by the way? I'm surprised and shocked. I don't agree with you, you'll be glad to hear. I'd rather confess to Shaw than to any clergy; and the Nation, vile as it is (but Margaret can't be parted from it) is much more religious than any church. And why not out with one's beliefs? Why this timid decorous 19th century passion for reticence and dignity? So far they've had close on a thousand answers, and Leonard who rashly said he would go through them, begins every meal with a statement who's winning—God or devil. Devil is ahead today. Its amazing to see the names, but I dare not divulge.

So far, he (Leonard, not devil) has got a good deal more time for writing under the new arrangement,[2] and I hope, when the staffs' holidays are over, he will get still more. At the moment he's putting together a book of his articles,[3] under pressure from me and America. Then I think he must have read enough to make a real start, and then I daresay, working 20 hours a day as I shall insist, he will be done in no time. The Hogarth is rather pressing though. Our 'list' is becoming longer and longer—why not a pamphlet on wickedness in general by M. Ll. D? I can see your bristles flashing at this distance.

The Keynes', Lydia and Maynard, are both completely under the sway of the Webbs. Beatrice and Lydia exchange headdresses; (I know you'll like to hear this) How charming she is, says Lydia: Maynard is deeply impressed by her book [*My Apprenticeship* 1926]. I said theyd be dropped, when they were no longer useful. But Beatrice still talks of Leonards great charm. Leonard says he has long known, but concealed, her illicit passion for him. Anyhow, the great Keynes—and he gets greater and greater, and buys more and more pictures and builds more and more libraries and bathrooms—is at her feet.

Leonard sends his love, and will write.

Yrs V.W.

Sussex

---

1. On the *Nation* readers' religious beliefs and practices. The questionnaire was inserted into four consecutive issues of the journal, and 1627 replies were received. A summary of them was published without mentioning the respondents names.
2. See p. 250, note 1.
3. Leonard's *Essays on Literature, History, Politics, etc.* was published by the Hogarth Press in May 1927, and by Harcourt, Brace in the same year.

1668: To Vanessa Bell   [*Monk's House, Rodmell,*
                                          Sussex]
[14? September 1926]

I'm very sorry Quentin was so late. I didn't realise he was expected at any
time, as he suggested dining here. But he's now off—
    I see its impossible for you ever to reach us—what with one thing and
another. But I will come to tea soon—if you wish it—and consult you—on
my house—but its now too late, almost. Who is now coming here?
    Ka [Arnold-Forster]
                                                                    Yr V.
Berg

1669: To Vanessa Bell   [*Monk's House, Rodmell,*
                                          Sussex]
[15? September 1926]

I told Harrods to send you the stuff, but it strikes me that its really rather
absurd, with all your offspring and so on, to take up such a job. Frances
Marshall told me of a creature who comes and makes things very well—
Wouldn't it be better if I got her when I go back, and you supervised?
Anyhow, its a business proposition: I mean either way we must settle a
price. But I expect you will behave like Aunt Fisher
    Let me know what you think—I will send you the skirt, if you want to
do it and of course, your taste would be very superior. I doubt rather that I
shall go to Ethels.
    Yes—I heard your malicious description, over the walnuts, of the poor
Wolves and Monks—I was hovering just over the centre candle—with my
finger like a button hook
    Ever, darling Chick, (how did they end letters?)

Berg

1670: To V. Sackville-West   *Monks House, Rodmell*
                                          [*Sussex*]
Sept 15th, [1926]

They've only just sent the second batch of proofs [of *Passenger to Teheran*]
which I have swallowed at a gulp. Yes—I think its awfully good. I kept
saying 'How I should like to know this woman ' and then thinking 'But I
do', and then 'No, I dont—not altogether the woman who writes this' I
didn't know the extent of your subtleties: Here's a brave attitude—emeralds,
staircases, Raymond subjugated—thats familiar enough: but not the sly,

brooding thinking evading one. The whole book is full of nooks and corners which I enjoy exploring Sometimes one wants a candle in one's hand though —Thats my only criticism—you've left (I daresay in haste) one or two dangling dim places. Its a delicious method, and one that takes the very skin of your shape, this dallying discursive one. The danger is that one may let the discussions float off a little too high in the air. But in the main I think you've hit it off perfectly—the problem being to keep moving (which you do, for I read half the book at a sitting and was drawn on to the last words, which, emphatically are the last words) and yet somehow dally and encircle this and that and enclose them all in the one mesh. As I say, I did not altogether know Towsers resources. Indeed, it is odd that now, having read this, I have picked up a good many things I had missed in private life. What are they, I wonder, the very intimate things, one says in print? There's a whole family of them. Its the proof, to me, of being a writer, that one expresses them in print only, and you do here; more here than anywhere, I think, unless its in The Land, and Seducers. Its the very subject for you. And how did you do it, so fast and free? I daresay that was the heaven sent way of doing it, and the reason why the whole book has this fresh, unfaded-ness about it; gives this sense of your being away, travelling, not in any particular geographical country: but travelling far away. Now I see, you'll be glad to hear, what a great affair going to Persia is: By the way, how my mouth watered over the casual paragraph about a park of dromedaries and racehorses in the Ukraine before the war. Please tell me more.

Leonard is beginning tonight. I say, its very very good of you to have let us have it.

Here I am, having to face my husband this dripping evening, on his return from London with the confession, not that I've been seduced, but Grizzle has. I left the door open. Oh my God, how can I face it Then I've put my finger out, fallen on my chin and cut it, and wear a bandage.

Must one have a puppy if one copulates with a dog twice ones size and is oneself well over 60?

Puppy well.

Yr VW.

Is the Land out?

Berg

1671: To Vanessa Bell   [*Monk's House, Rodmell, Sussex*]

[16? September 1926]

My daily letter—

I rather think I shall go to Ethel (if she can have me) on 26th as I'm getting on quicker with my book.

Could you do the dress by then? if you will do it?

If not, would you send the stuff back, and I'll take it to a Grub in Lewes. But I'd better do it at once. My only skirt is now torn

Ka [Arnold-Forster] not coming, because of Mark [her son]—has grave fears that Will [her husband] is giving up painting for politics has been bathing with Nansen[1] at Geneva.

V.W.

Will you tell Quentin—I would like to come and see him, and we will certainly publish a book together.

Berg

1672: To ETHEL SANDS   *Monks House, Rodmell*
[Sussex]

[18 September 1926]

Dearest Ethel,

Is the 27th, 28th. too late for you? It seems to be the only time, what with one thing and another. Let me come next year if it is, I want to see *you*—not Normandy only as you cynically suggest.

We are broiling and baking here—the colour of bricks. It is delicious and extremely lovely—I mean the downs, not our colour. One day you must come and see. I've a room the size of a hat box for you. It is rumoured that Sibyl [Colefax] is taking a house next door to Charleston—what fun for all of us

Yours affect
V.W.

Here's a letter from Vanessa, just as I was sending this. She says you will be in Paris the 27-8th; so don't bother to answer this. I had meant to write before, but got into a muddle.

Wendy Baron

1673: To VANESSA BELL   *[Monk's House, Rodmell,*
Sussex]

Sunday [19 September 1926]

My own Lamb,
    (It is a difficult style to keep up, I agree)

1. Fridtjof Nansen, the Norwegian explorer and statesman, who was then his country's representative at the League of Nations in Geneva. The Hogarth Press published his book in 1927.

Have it your own way. If its a failure [the dress], you'll lose your time, I my money, so its equal. If a success, I'll pay you 30/- which was Grave's charge, plus bodkins and bones.

I dont suppose I shall go to Ethel then. But its possible I may cross the channel for a day or two on my own account.

Let me know when you want a fitting and I'll come. Dadie and Vita may possibly be coming, but probably not. Anyhow, I could get Vita to motor me.

As for the Paris idea, I am in your hands entirely. What I want is a cloak or coat or autumn covering of some sort. Also a hat; but you must have my head for this. I shall be only too thankful to shift the whole burden on to you—I shall pay you a modest percentage on your purchases. I had a fit in an Eastbourne hat shop with sheer horror.

I send a skirt which may indicate the length.

I think you ought to ask Molly to stay. She writes in a dismal vein, spends much of her time with the giraffes at the Zoo. As for me, I am practically non-existent with sheer heat and pleasure. You I suppose have a large week end party.

Grizzle has been seduced, so no more, darling, precious.

Berg

1674: To V. Sackville-West   *Monks House, Rodmell,*
                                     Lewes [Sussex]
Typewritten
21st Sept. [1926]

My dear Vita,
(this is typewriter writing) But when are you coming to fetch your things? Please let me know. This week? I shall be alone Thursday 23rd. Next week? Only Mrs Bartholomew to cook. Bed at your service any time. Week after we return.

Hope to bring out book in early Oct. Any names to send cards to? If so please let me have them. What is your lecture about?[1] When? Where? May

---

1. *Some Tendencies of Modern English Poetry*, a lecture delivered to the Royal Society of Literature on 27 October 1926.

I come? Will clap. Grizzle seduced again. Typewriter awfully on the spot.
No more at present from yours very

Virginia Woolf.
(Mrs Woolf)

The Hon.
Mrs Harold Nicolson
Long Barn
Weald Sevenoaks Kent.

Berg

1675: To Edward Sackville West   *Monks House, Rodmell,*
                                           Lewes [Sussex]
Typewritten
22nd Sept. [1926]

Dear Eddy,
I am ashamed not to write, and then to write on a typewriter. But there
is a paper shortage in my house—no note paper I can write on. I have hurt my
finger. So please forget and forgive.
(You have never known what it is to be without note paper.)
Yes, I like the painters, but I find their attitude a little agonising. "Poor
beetle " thats what they say; and at once I have eight legs, all squirming. It
is for this reason; their ascendancy is over all objects of daily use: tea pots,
chairs, wall paper; so that when they come, their presence is one long
criticism, from the heights. We, who deal in ideas, and are moreover,
sensitised to draw out, always more and more, other peoples feelings never
inflict this chill. How delightful if one could
I'm going over today [to Charleston] to meet Lytton. Shall I be happy—
unhappy? Anyhow, one or the other.
I like people to be unhappy because I like them to have souls. We all
have, doubtless, but I like the suffering soul which confesses itself. I distrust
this hard, this shiny, this enamelled content. We old creatures are all crusted
over with it. Now unhappiness means vapour, atmosphere, interest. I am
often unhappy. I was cursing my fate at two this morning, sitting up in bed,
wishing to be killed instantly.[1] You will never guess why.
Are you pleased with your novel [*The Ruin*, 1926]? I think the weeks
when it is first out are humiliating. People will talk about it, or they wont

1. Since the beginning of August, Virginia had endured recurrent fits of depression.
In her diary of 28 September she described herself as an "elderly dowdy fussy
ugly incompetent woman; vain, chattering and futile". See Quentin Bell,
Virginia Woolf, II, p. 123.

talk about it. Which does one want? All that is miserable; and yet a necessity
—one goes snuffing round after it.

I cannot write an elegant sentence when a flock of sparrows set on my
thoughts directly they fall to the ground and peck them out on the keyboard.

We shall be back soon. I feel entirely dehumanised by the sun now, and
wish for fog, snow, rain, humanity.

Yours
Virginia Woolf

Berg

1676: To Vanessa Bell   *Monks House, Rodmell*
                                         [Sussex]
Typewritten
[end September 1926]

I suppose you are off shortly [to France], so this is only to remind you that
what I want are:

one autumn coat, black, I should think, but leave to you.

Some simple dress to wear in the evening.

A hat—but this perhaps better wait till you can choose me one in
London.

Will you settle rate of percentage?

I dont want to give much for coat or dress I mean the sort of thing you
pay at Lafayette.

Tommie [Stephen Tomlin] very charming; incessant talk; Nick and
Barbara [Bagenal] turned up. Barbara laden with trousers and books for him,
so I left them alone, but apparently it was not necessary.

B.

I should be much obliged if you or Duncan could tell me on a card where I
could see some of the historical pictures of Benjamin Haydon?[1] in some
restaurant, I think. I have to write about him.

It is said that Condé Nast threatened to reveal Todds private sins, if she sued
them,[2] so she is taking £1,000, and does not bring an action.

Berg

1. Benjamin Robert Haydon (1786-1846). He was a painter, mainly of historical
   subjects, and is best remembered for his autobiography and journals, a new
   edition of which Virginia reviewed for the *Nation & Athenaeum* (18 December
   1926).
2. The dispute between Dorothy Todd and *Vogue* concerned her editorial policy.
   She was attempting to make the magazine more cultural than the American
   owners, Condé Nast, desired, and they dismissed her.

1677: To Gerald Brenan   [*Monk's House, Rodmell,*
                                       Sussex]
Oct 3rd [1926]

My dear Gerald,

   I was going through the Nation Questionnaire just now and came on
your name. This did not remind me of you. I hadn't forgotten you: but
perhaps if I write to you on the spur of the moment I may get an answer.
Write to 52 T.S: we go back in a day; though the sun is blazing here, like
August, only gentler and lovelier.

   Ralph said he had read enough of your novel[1] to perceive a masterpiece.
Why aren't I allowed to read it then? Am I inferior to Ralph? Certainly, in
some ways. I dont think I shall ever possess his sexual powers, for one thing,
which must be a cause of endless pleasure to him: though a little mystifying,
I daresay, to Frances Marshall. Do the sexes differ greatly here? I wish you
would explain what this vein in the thigh does to the vision of the world—
slip a purple shade over it, or what? Somebody said you live in a hotel with
a couple of Colonels, and a maiden lady. You read enormously; and sit at a
café flipping sheet after sheet, scribbled over, under a very inferior sheet of
blotting paper. When it gets too dark to see you jump up, and take a brisk
walk to the castle in the vineyards; dine; very sparely; and read till 2 or 3 in
the morning. Sometimes one of the Colonels drops in for a talk—can't make
you out quite, whereas the maiden lady finds you're sympathetic, and wishes
you weren't so lonely.

   Do you like the life of yourself? I'm very idle, sitting over the fire;
writing with difficulty in a slippery book, while the dogs (alas we have two)
snore and grumble. I finished a novel [*To the Lighthouse*] 10 days ago: and
already regard it, in which my whole life was wound and bound for 7
months, with complete indifference. I want to buy a motor car, thats all, and
wander over the Continent, poking into ruined cities, basking, drinking,
writing, like you, in cafés, and talking to Colonels and maiden ladies. Come
with me—I will drive: you shall buy grapes and bread, and discuss the state
of the wine with natives.

   People have been dropping in, but so briefly that I have discovered
nothing new about the human soul. For instance, Nick, Tommie, Barbara,
and the shadow of Saxon. Also the shadow of Lytton, Colefax, and Raymond
Mortimer. Shall you come back? What are the books to read? How is one to
live wisely? What mixture of art, literature, and society is right? Is there
anything to be said about fiction? about Wells' new novels, about Haydon's
diaries, about Eddy Sackville-Wests novel etc, etc? These questions will all

---

1. *A Holiday by the Sea.* Brenan left it unfinished but returned to it from time
   to time over the next 35 years. It was eventually published in 1961.

be debated during the coming winter at the Bloomsbury Bar, meeting in Duncan's studio alternate Fridays.[1] I hereby invite you.

It is pitch dark in the room now, except for a very coarse strong lamp, which blazes my eyes out, and illumines a pot of brilliant red and yellow dahlias. Talking of flowers, I never forget the lilies you gave me last year.

Yrs V.W.

George Lazarus

1678: To V. Sackville-West   [*Monk's House, Rodmell, Sussex*]

Sunday [10 October 1926]

Darling Mrs Nicolson,

Could you be an entire angel and tell me (for the 50th time) the name and address of the old widow who typewrites [Mrs Candy, Bournemouth]? Lost again, and needed instantly.

Well, did you like Squire?[2] I did: I think the better of him for it, though his manner is always that of a curate, a grocer, a churchwarden, someone sticky with jam and buns at a School treat, however, he admires you; and I'm jealous. Yes: that yellow moon is rising on the horizon—Everyone admiring Vita, talking of Vita. Now there remain the Times Literary Supt. for which I have an unreasoning respect: Nation: New Statesman. All of these are negligible compared with one word of mine or any other casual vivid outspoken human being: but one can't see it oneself—not the author.

I've been walking to the river and back:—But what was I going to say? Oh yes—begin your history of a Kentish village at once. Plan it out roughly on a great sheet: Let each little note branch and blossom in the night, or when you're walking (the beauty of this subject is that everything will come in—cabbages, moon, church steeple): Occasionally open some old history, or life of some unknown man, but not to read carefully—to dream over. So in a week—no, 3 or 4 days, the whole poem will be foaming and bubbling in your head: and meals seem but a temporary contrivance barring the way—(Not wine; this don't apply to Spanish wine) How I envy you, with sweet gales of praise coming from London—and this in your head, in your gaiters over your fire.[3]

---

1. This was a proposal to form a new Bloomsbury Society. The eight 'hosts' were to be Virginia, Leonard, Duncan, Roger Fry, Lytton Strachey, Clive, E. M. Forster, and Vanessa, each of whom were entitled to bring three guests.
2. J. C. Squire's adulatory review of *The Land* in the *Observer* on 10 October.
3. Vita did not write a poem about 'a Kentish village', but now began her second long poem *The Garden*, and then dropped it. It was not completed and published till 1946.

I say: did I tell you the Bloomsbury Bar was a dead secret? Eddy writes about it. I suppose I forgot, and shall be flayed alive: Can't be helped.

Are you coming up? Shall I come down for a night sometime? No: your mother.

Jack, Mary and Tom [Eliot] have just been, and Jack [Hutchinson] says we can't print Raymonds pamphlet: should be prosecuted certainly.[1]

Any more letters of praise?

The green moon is rising

Yr VW.

Eddy says he admires the Land: reminds him of Chaucer.

Berg

1679: To V. Sackville-West   [*Monk's House, Rodmell, Sussex*]

[12? October 1926]

Mr Barrington Gates (the Nation reviewer) says may he take a whole column for The Land, as in his opinion it is 'so outstanding' that it should not be lumped in with others—Sashy, Laura Gottshalk[2] to wit. So there He's going to have a column.

V.W.

Berg

1. Raymond Mortimer's pamphlet was a discussion of liberal attitudes in sexual relationships.
2. Sacheverell Sitwell's new book was *All Summer in a Day*; Laura Riding Gottschalk's *The Close Chaplet* had just been published by the Hogarth Press.

Letters 1680-1702 (mid-October–December 1926)

On 14 October the Woolfs returned to London after two-and-a-half months at Rodmell, and remained there till Christmas, apart from one visit to Cambridge and another to Long Barn. Virginia was re-typing To the Lighthouse. "My present opinion", she wrote in her diary for 23 November, "is that it is easily the best of my books." Christmas was spent with the Arnold-Forsters in Cornwall, but the visit was not a success, and they fled back to London a day earlier than intended, to find an invitation to visit the United States, by which Virginia was at first much tempted.

1680: To SAXON SYDNEY-TURNER 52 Tavistock Square, W.C.1

Typewritten
[15? October 1926]

Dear Saxon,

I think I distinguish "vapid" from "insipid" only by my ear. "Vapid" sounds to me heavy, vacant, blank; "insipid", trivial, frivolous, chattering (largely because of the three syllables I suppose) A vapid man would be silent; an insipid man would dribble along—as a matter of fact, I suspect Cobden-Sanderson did both.[1] But didnt like to say so.

I suppose the dictionaries might explain. But one writes, I suppose, by ear, not dictionary.

                                                                Yrs V.W.

Sussex

1681: To V. SACKVILLE-WEST 52 Tavistock Square, W.C.1

[mid-October 1926]
Next Tuesday (19th) seems the only day I could come down. What about the week after?

Yes, I would like to come to the Tchekov [*Three Sisters*]. Will you dine here? More reviews? More praise?

                                                                VW.

Berg

1. Virginia had reviewed *The Journals of Thomas James Cobden-Sanderson*, 1879-1922, in the *Nation & Athenaeum*, 9 October 1926. Saxon questioned her on this sentence: "The man . . . is neither vapid nor insipid nor wrapped round . . . in comfortable cotton wool."

1682: To V. Sackville-West   52 *Tavistock Square, W.C.*1

Tuesday [19 October 1926]

God knows which alternative: the telephone and Lady Gerald unnerved me completely.[1]
    Answer these questions:
1. How is your cold?
2. Are you dining here on Monday? Could you come early?
3. Are you dining with Colefax on 26th?
4. Could we leave plans till Monday? I'd like to come if you're alone, sometime.
    We cant come this weekend, as we go to Cambridge, damn it. Your Nation reviewer says you are inferior to no living poet.
    Look at this, just come [*unidentified*].

                                                            Yr VW.

I dined last night with a great admirer of yours. Oliver Strachey who begs to meet you.
    If you haven't got tickets for Tchekov on Monday, why not put it off, dine here, and I'll ask him? Or suggest another day.

Berg

1683: To V. Sackville-West   52 *Tavistock Square, [W.C.*1]

[1 November 1926]

    We hope, and expect, you to dine with us on *Friday* to meet Oliver [Strachey]. Come early and meet Virginia. Then perhaps, God willing, you'll motor us down; Leonard says he must go Sunday night. May I stay till Monday?
    Dazed and mazed with Ozzie's[2] gossip—fountains, cascades, cataracts—shining through all one steadfast star—Vita: her character, charm, greatness, goodness—Oh my God I cried at last, there's another woman whose name begins with V in this room He was like an old Badger, pouched and bristling, and we hobnobbed like old Crones over the fire, and forgot and forgave; but raked up endless embers, and burnt our fingers, gossiping—Dotty—Gerry [Wellesley]—Clive—your mother—as you can imagine.

1. Dorothy Wellesley, whom Virginia scarcely knew, had been staying for four nights with Vita at Long Barn, and they both telephoned to Virginia from there.
2. Oswald (Ozzie) Dickinson, bachelor brother of Violet, was a barrister who became Secretary to the Commissioners in Lunacy. He was a greater friend of Vita and her mother than of Virginia.

But come, dearest creature,—I will—give you one chaste kiss.

Your V.W.

Come to tea on Wednesday, do please, to meet Sibyl. I'm having such a week of conversation—mostly about you. Any letters about Persia [*Passenger to Teheran*]?

Berg

1684: To Helen McAfee   52 *Tavistock Square, W.C.*1

Typewritten
Nov 1st. 1926

Dear Miss McAfee,
    Many thanks for your kind letter and cheque for my essay on Reading. It is very good of you to ask me to send you something more, and I certainly hope to do so in the near future. Meanwhile I enclose an essay by my husband, which I think might suit the Yale Review. It was delivered as a lecture here, and caused a good deal of interest.
    Believe me, yours very sincerely,

Virginia Woolf

Yale University

1685: To V. Sackville-West   [52 *Tavistock Square, W.C.*1]

Postcard
[2 November 1926]

Then, come to tea tomorrow, Wednesday, theres an angel. At 4 Clive Sibyl Virginia all implore.
    No, I'm not asked to Ethels, Heaven consume her. Expect you dinner Friday anyhow, and to take us for week end, and Fanny—but what about Grizzle [dogs]?

VW.

1686: To V. Sackville-West   [52 *Tavistock Square, W.C.*1]

Tuesday [9 November 1926]

I think the 4th week end (Saturday 4th) would be best. L. says he would go to his brother, and in view of the other circumstances I think one would be freer, wiser, tipsier, merrier, probably more blastedly melancholy, then than now. Also, one has it to look forward to. Oh dear Desmond and Bea Howe are coming so we shall only meet at the party I suppose. And then you mustn't talk to me. You'll be whirled off by Chrissie [Aberconway], torn in pieces by Raymond. But perhaps one word in a corner will be thrown to me. Did you have a bite of food at last? I hope so, Was it nice? Yes it was. Did the insect lay an egg?

Virginia

Berg

1687: To V. Sackville-West   52 *Tavistock Sqre* [*W.C.*1]

[19 November 1926]

You are a miracle of discretion—one letter in another. I never thought of that. I'll answer when I see you—the invitation, I mean. Oh dear, Sybil has given me a headache. What a bore I cant write, except to you. I lie in a chair. It isn't bad: but I tell you, to get your sympathy: to make you protective: to implore you to devise some way by which I can cease this incessant nibbling away of life by people: Sybil, Sir Arthur [Colefax], Dadie—one on top of another. Why do I put it on *you*? Some psychological necessity I suppose: one of those intimate things in a relationship which one does by instinct. I'm rather a coward about this pain in my back: You would be heroic: But I dont want to live for ever at Rodmell with Mrs Bartholomew [daily help].

She is a woman of the world: Sybil Colefax. To me, an almost unknown type. Every value is different. Friendship, let alone intimacy, is impossible. Yet I respect, even admire. Why did she come, I kept wondering: felt so gauche, and yet utterly indifferent. This is a sign one never speaks the truth to her. She skated over everything, evaded, palliated, compromised; yet is fundamentally kind and good. Its odd for me, who have some gift for intimacy, to be nonplussed entirely.

But you dont see, donkey West, that you'll be tired of me one of these days (I'm so much older) and so I have to take my little precautions. Thats why I put the emphasis on 'recording' rather than feeling. But donkey West knows she has broken down more ramparts than anyone. And isnt there something obscure in you? There's something that doesn't vibrate in you: It may be purposely—you dont let it: but I see it with other people, as well as with me: something reserved, muted—God knows what. Still, still, compare this 19th Nov—with last, and you'll admit there's a difference. It's in your writing too, by the bye. The thing I call central transparency—sometimes fails you there too. I will lecture you on this at Long Barn. Oh why does [Robert] Bridges say my essays are poor, and Mr [Goldsworthy Lowes] Dickinson say I'm the finest critic in English literature? I cannot believe that anybody has ever been so mis-rated as I am: and it makes it much harder to go full tilt at fiction or essays: Let them damn my novels, and I'd do essays: damn essays and I'd do novels. This is one of those glib lies one's pen slips out: of course I shall go on doing precisely what I want. Only with me two inches in the top are so tremendously susceptible. Darling donkey West—will you come at 2.30—to the Press, I think: and then how nice I shall lie on the sofa and be spoilt. But my pain is going already. Was Irene[1] nicer than I am? Do you know this interesting fact. I found myself thinking with intense curiosity about death? Yet if I'm persuaded of anything, it is of mortality—Then why this sense that death is going to be a great excitement? —something positive; active?

Yr
VW.

P.S.
The flowers have come, and are adorable, dusky, tortured, passionate like you—And I've had lunch and feel ever so much better, and have read my letter, and am ashamed of its egotism, and feel tempted to tear it up, but have no time to write another. And don't I lecture you nicely Thats what comes of attacking your poor Virginia and dog Grizzle. They bite instantly.

But at the same time they adore: and if you hadn't the eyes of a newt and the blood of a toad, you'd see it, and not need telling—

Berg

1688: To Violet Dickinson   52 *Tavistock Sqre, WC.*1

Sunday [21 November 1926]

My Violet,
I hear a rumour, through Vita, that you are out of the Home and back again in your own house. I hope it's true; because half the horrors of illness cease when one has a book or a dog or a cup of one's own at hand. I've two dogs at the moment, and when I was so ambitious as to have Lady Colefax alone here, of course they disgraced me in every way. Little bits of cork from the bath mat came blowing into the drawing room. I shall never be on her level. I don't mean only fur coats and pearl necklaces: I mean I can't rattle it off like a weathercock as she does. But if one were to fall down the area[2] tomorrow (as is likely enough) who would be kinder?

Thank the Lord (if you wish to be grateful) that you're not a publisher. Instead of writing to you, I should be reading about six manuscripts; all of them not good and not bad; and at the end of each an author white with anxiety, green with envy, to whom I must concoct a letter. So you see one

1. Irene Cooper Willis, a barrister and writer. She contributed the volume on Elizabeth Barrett Browning to Francis Birrell's series *Representative Women* (1928), and was a protagonist of women's emancipation.
2. The sunken court off city pavements leading to the basement entrance.

of the reasons for taking up my pen this evening. We have been walking round Regents Park in the rain. As we go we talk rather stiltedly (for an old married couple) about the weather; the Zoo; the coal strike. But every word is in French. This is our law, so that when we meet a French man, we may have no shyness. It appears, however, that one can only say the sort of things very decrepit old people say. George [Duckworth] has sent me *a* pheasant. I'm told this is quite unknown, and should be hotly resented. Last year he threw in a bunch of radishes and a hatfull of sprouts.

It was great fun seeing Ozzie [Violet's brother] the other night—did he tell you? He seemed younger than ever, and we said many things about you which would have made you, wizened and shameless though you are, bury your face in the pillow. A gigantic charwoman bore down on me the other day at a concert; with bonnet, boot, and knobbly red knuckles in cotton gloves all complete—. Lady Cromer.[1] I like that way of dressing infinitely better than the other—pearls and powder and no skirts—all the same. Besides, if one is the Venus of Milo, one may as well pretend to be a char.

I've lots of things to say, but I'm afraid you will be disgusted and bored and chucking things out of the window in a rage—so I'll stop. But for God's sake, get well immediately—and think kindly of your devoted and humble admirer, who always cherishes a secret passion for you,

Sp.

Berg

1689: To V. Sackville-West   [52 *Tavistock Square, W.C.*1]

Wednesday [1 December 1926]

Very nice to get a letter from you, dear Creature—No, it wasn't the people yesterday—I had the shivers, due to getting wet through at Rodmell—that was all—I went to bed, took aspirin, hot bottle, quite all right today, only incredibly sleepy. Still I agree—people are the devil—What's to be done, though, if they march in unasked, like Eddy?

Moreover, you cant talk—lunch at Woking, tea Virginia, Cocktail Raymond, dine Mary, supper Kitchin—There I was warm in bed, and glad to hear it was a ghastly failure. And now you're off to Brighton heaven help you![2] I wish you hadn't that before you, but could drop in and talk—Here I am sitting or rather lying in front of the gas fire in perfect quiet.

I'm sorry about your mother—Here's Leonard. Six copies of Teheran just sold to Hachettes, so we've passed the thousand and he's sent it, with his polite duty, to her ladyship.

1. Katherine (*née* Thynne), the widow of the 1st Earl of Cromer.
2. Lady Sackville, Vita's mother, was living near Roedean, Brighton, Sussex. She was becoming increasingly eccentric and quarrelsome, and on this occasion refused to see her daughter.

Write again, do. I'm now going to read your story. Send back my essay sometime with any comments.

I'd like to stay 2 nights—but God knows. May I leave it open?

Yr Virginia

Berg

1690: To V. Sackville-West   52 *T[avistock]* *S[quare, W.C.1]*

Friday [3 December 1926]

No—I cant come. I have caught eczema from Grizzle. My hair comes out in tufts. I scratch incessantly. It wouldn't be safe for you, or, what matters more, the puppies. I shall think of you: let that console us.

That joke being done with—yes, I'll come reaching Sevenoaks at 5.22.

Its true I'm incredibly dirty; have washed my head—hair is down—skirt spotted, shoes in holes—Pity poor Virginia dragged off this afternoon by Sybil to meet Arnold Bennett who abused me for a column in last nights Standard.[1]

Oh I'm so sick of teaing dining, reading writing and everything, except seeing—well it *is* you, I admit. Yes it will be nice—yes it will: And shall you be very kind to me?

Please do.

Hows your back?

VW.

Berg

1691: To Violet Dickinson   52 *Tavistock Sqre, WC1*
[Long Barn, near Sevenoaks, Kent]

[5? December 1926]

My Violet,

I hope you won't mind my taking up a pen—Vita's pen—to write to you again, out of affection merely. I like cracking my silly joke with you. I forget where I left off. Had I been attacked by Arnold Bennett, and gone to meet him at Sibyls, and told him to his face, and he to mine, that our books are worthless trash? and then we embraced, and I am to go and see him, and his wife said she has a child called Virginia. Oh but, said Colefax, thats not his wife, only his mistress,[2] and if you go calling her Mrs Bennett you may

1. The meeting is described by Virginia in her Memoir Club paper *Am I a snob?* (see *Moments of Being*, ed. Jeanne Schulkind, pp. 189-90).
2. See p. 251, note 4.

305

find yourself in the law Court. So I came down here for the week end, and spent last night describing you to Vita, and how we went to Greece together 20 years ago, and the goats were milked under the window, and I behaved so badly and you behaved so well. There are few people I am fonder of than Violet Dickinson, I said—or have more cause to be grateful to. Ungrateful bitch as I am, I never pass her door without a smile. Then there was Ella Crum, and Beatrice Thynne.[1] So we go on talking while the eleven dogs, some in childbirth, parade the rooms, and the old Butler stumps in and out, to catch scraps of our conversation, she says, at which they laugh in the kitchen.

I wish I could send you something to amuse you or write a poem, with Rhymes to Dickinson, in your praise. A triolet for Violet. A Chicken song for Dickingsong— No. Cant be done. Prose is more my line. So please get well quick, and let us go on corresponding. Vita says may she send you her love.

Yr

Sp.

Berg

1692: To VANESSA BELL [52 *Tavistock Square, W.C.*1]

[December 1926?]

I hear from Ka (Eagles Nest, Zennor, St. Ives) that they want a flat for 4 months after Christmas in this neighbourhood. So it might be worth your writing to her. But don't stay away 4 months [at Cassis] whatever happens.

Hoping to see you

Your old friend

VW.

Berg

1693: To V. SACKVILLE-WEST

52 *T.*[avistock] *S.*[quare, W.C.1]

[8 December 1926]

Dearest Vita,

(Now why did I say that?) Yes, Monday, undern[2] 2.30. Please come, and bathe me in serenity again. Yes, I was wholly and entirely happy. If you could have uncored me—you would have seen every nerve running fire—

1. Friends of Virginia's youth. Ella Crum was Violet's neighbour at Welwyn, and Beatrice Thynne the daughter of the Marquess of Bath.
2. An obsolete word, generally unused since the late 19th century, but adopted by Virginia and Vita to identify the early afternoon.

intense, but calm. Then how hard you worked, like a navvy, and I saying to myself all the time, Anyhow this is in Vita's line.

But why, darling Mrs N., honourable Mrs N. insist upon Knole?[1] To see me ridiculous, the powder falling, the hairpins dropping, and not a word said in private between us? Is it one of your moonlight, romantic, stags barking, old man feeding them from a bucket in the snow, ideas? It shall be considered, anyhow. But Arnold Bennett[2] has sold my books twice as fast as before: 6 sell instead of one. Please be rude to him and then Teheran will leap: it is doing very well: 6 sold to Smiths, one at the door to an old woman with long teeth. Cameron [*Victorian Photographs*] moving, not fast, but with the dignity of a battleship taking the water. Logan [Pearsall Smith] to tea, very American. Raymond—I eat all my words—very charming, very gay, very simple, very what one calls nice.

But its Vita I adore.

Yr
Virginia

We want puppy back on Jan 1st. I think. Can we?

Berg

1694: To V. Sackville-West   52 *Tavistock Square, W.C.*1
Friday [17 December 1926]

Dear Vita,

Here is your mothers letter, to which I have replied in my well known 18th Century style; no, she has been most helpful and emollient. Cameron has almost paid. Yes, you are coming on Monday undern: yes, I am dining with Dotty.[3] D'you know what happened to day? I was rushing into a shop to buy a velvet coat, when a woman said Any stains to take out? Good God, I said, I have at least 12 on me at the moment—so I bought her ointment, and all my stains are vanished like snow, and I'd been cleaned unavailingly, so life has turned its rosier cheek, and everything seems possible—except indeed, I had a tooth stopped. Now my lip my cheek, my chin are all boils and blisters. When I say to the dentist, why do you do this to me? He replies, But then, Mrs W. your skin is the most sensitive in London, at which I am flattered, but Leonard paints my skin with zinc ointment which I lick and I daresay its poison and I shall be dead—here's Tom Eliot ringing up, and I've been having tea with my nieces, and sewed a frock, and was

1. Virginia spent the nights of 17 and 18 January 1927 at Knole.
2. His hostile article about Virginia in the *Evening Standard* of 2 December.
3. On Monday, 20 December, Virginia and Vita dined with Dorothy Wellesley at her house in Mount Street.

given green sweets, and lunched with Sybil and met a cousin of yours, and should be dining this moment with Lord Gerald Wellesley, but if he knew I was dining with Dotty, what a row, and Teheran is selling well, and I've been through agonies; buying shoes for my mother in law, and sending over a small boy the chocolate cigars or Turkish delight, and reading a little Tristram Shandy and Oh God I've bought a chair! My dear Vita, one sits in it and it rises round one like the clouds of summer: and . . . but, this is mere balderdash, mere chatter, stuff to make you stay sitting on my bed, and what wages d'you pay Horn [Long Barn manservant], and how much d'you give for your blotting paper; and then you get up and go, as I must, to read my book.

Monday, basement, undern.

Yr
Virginia

Have you really made it up with your mother? I hope so. Yes: my mother— I've no room.

Berg

1695: To Crosby Gaige   *Eagles Nest, Zennor,*
                                          St Ives, Cornwall
24th Dec 1926

Dear Mr Gaige,[1]
    Your letter has been sent on to me here. I am very sorry that I shall not be able to come to tea with you and your wife as you so kindly suggest, but I shall be away until the middle of January. I hope that there may be a chance of seeing you later, when I am back at Tavistock Square.
                                          Yours sincerely,
                                          Virginia Woolf
Lilly Library, Indiana University

1696: To V. Sackville-West   *Eagles Nest, Zennor,*
                                          St Ives [Cornwall]
Xmas day [1926]

Dearest Creature—
    There is an argument going on. I am writing on my knee. We look over

1. Crosby Gaige, who lived in New York City, produced a series of limited editions of English and American books. In 1928 he published such an edition of *Orlando*, before it was published commercially.

the Atlantic. You have never seen the Gurnard's Head? I should like to see you here—A tame raven taps at the window. We motor over the moors, so cold, like an 18th Century print—skeletons hanging on withered branches— Suddenly one dips into the valley, and finds rhododendrons, and palm trees, and St Michael's Mount [Marazion] riding out in a blue sea.

But the cold! the cold! I sleep in stockings, vest, a pair of wool drawers (I had to buy in Penzance) a jacket. The bed gets cold on the right if one sleeps on the left. They are kind and good and high minded and free spoken and dressed in tweeds and very public spirited—the people here. They give Christmas trees to the village children. I don't find much of that festal light, though, which stands in the door of the Sevenoaks fishmonger. I keep saying, But Vita's spoilt me—spoilt me—spoilt me! Why have you taught me this piercing cry? and then to go to Persia?[1] and leave me?

I have crept into another room, as the argument, about League of Nations breaks on my ears. Here I am with the raven and the little boy.

But what was I going to say? Fond of me? Yes, No, says Vita, a little absent minded, but then she has to give the housemaids brooches, to motor to Brighton. It will be fine, I think, and your mother will relent, and will give you 200 pounds, in a blue envelope.

We went to the Lands End yesterday. We both have colds in the head. Am reading The Constant Nymph with the painful head of a heavy woman in a bog. Have I lost all sense of fiction? Why does this flimsy trash, with one idea to a hundred pages, convince anybody? Why do we pay Miss Kennedy[2] £2000 p.a. (I think of nothing but money) for writing it? Gides memoirs[3] which I read voraciously renew the sense that I *can* read with pleasure. Otherwise I am only an eye—yes, I observe the sea incessantly very rough, blue and white, today with little tramp steamers pitching, and splashing; and at night they burn the gorse on the moor, and it is exactly like the death of Siegfried: a crimson gauze rising over crags. Oh yes, I should like to see you here—We come back on Tuesday, not Wednesday, and shall I hope, soon see you:

V.W.

Xmas post in: no letter from you. What a disappointment!

Berg

1. Vita was to return to Persia on 28 January 1927.
2. Margaret Kennedy (1896-1967), whose novel *The Constant Nymph* (1924), was a best-seller.
3. *Si le grain ne meurt* (1926).

1697: To ANGUS DAVIDSON   *Zennor, St Ives,*
                                                  Cornwall
Christmas Day, 1926

Dear Angus,

I never saw you, except through the window, to thank you for the honey, which is quite delicious and takes me back to the old days, when I climbed Mount Hymettus myself. I gave some on a crumpet, to the poet Eliot, and much sweetened him.

It is bitterly cold; we are motored over the moors to Lands End and other remote places. We look down into the heart of the Atlantic from our bedroom. All my facts about Lighthouses are wrong.[1] We come back on Tuesday. The goose is just coming into the room. I hope you have had a merry Christmas at Rochester. This is divine country—perhaps a little austere.

                                                  Yours
                                                  V.W.

Angus Davidson

1698: To V. SACKVILLE-WEST   52 *Tavistock Square* [*W.C.*1]

Wednesday [29 December 1926]

Dearest Creature,

I only got your letter this morning, so I rang up a surly butler, and heard Eddy was ill but Mrs Nicolson was better. I do hope so. Not that Eddy should be ill. Only I hate your having flu—it aint right, or honest. Why did you? How are you? *Please say.*[2]

Thank God Harold comes back [from Persia, in May], and puts an end to no lunches, motoring, your mother etcetera. I own practically everyone has it—but still its largely your reckless spendthrift life, and please curb it, and influenza's no joke: One's heart goes wrong. I say therefore (but I'm in a hurry expecting that mooncalf Philip Morrell) please don't be rash at Dottys. Let me know if you will lunch here on Monday: what time you come and how long you can stay.

We were so bitter cold at Zennor that we fled. Everyone had colds— coal gave out—endless visitors—my host [Will Arnold-Forster] testy about cigarette ends among his plants—one very lovely drive—awfully difficult to exist at all out of one's own house; and now, darling Mrs N:—there's a surprise coming, so read carefully, every word. One thing is I dont think

1. Virginia was revising *To the Lighthouse*. The book locates the lighthouse in the Hebrides, but her model for it was the Godrevy Lighthouse, off St Ives Bay.
2. Vita was in bed with flu at Knole, where she had spent Christmas.

Knole is possible; for this reason: I tore all my clothes on the gorse, and cant get any more, and I couldn't ask your butler to wait on me, nor is it for the dignity of letters that I should eat behind a screen, so I dont see how I can come to Knole, all in holes, without a pin to my hair or a stocking to my foot. You'd be ashamed; you'd say things you would regret. But read carefully whats coming. Its this

I am going to America.[1]

Now thats exciting isnt it?

But I shant be gone on Monday, so I'll tell you about it then.

But Vita darling let me hear how you are: please take care: awful awful awful haste

Yr
Virginia

Berg

1699: To Vanessa Bell   52 *Tavistock Square, W.C.*1

Wednesday [29 December 1926]

Dearest,

I found your letter last night. We fled from Zennor a day early, you'll be glad to hear, unable to stand the perishing cold and Wills slang (Ka was far better than Will) any longer. They did their best, poor people, but the coal gave out, and we all had colds, and Ka had a headache, and endless neighbours called and there was Mervyn Arnold F.[2] staying there, and in short as I say we came home. Nevertheless, Cornwall has redeemed itself for beauty: I motored from end to end; and was overcome, not so much by the moors, though they had fires burning in the cold dawn, but by the valleys. I saw a clergyman called Walke, and a picture of Rogers. Mrs Leake and Colonel Hurst were both worth many journeys to see[3]— But the cold! the cold!

I dont think I can face Julian's ridicule.[4] I am sure it is scurrilous and in the worst of taste. Never mind. I'll cook a goose for his gander, tell him. The bother is I'm now in a hideous rush putting the last touches to my

1. This is explained in the first paragraph of Virginia's next letter to Vita (30 December 1926). The journey never took place.
2. Will Arnold-Forster's brother. The Woolfs considered him for a job in the Hogarth Press, but he died in May 1927 from the delayed effects of his wounds and illnesses in the first World War.
3. These were all non-Cornish people living near Zennor. Bernard Walke was a high church vicar, who wrote radio plays. Désirée Leake was a Christian Scientist, married to a chartered accountant. Hurst an amiable retired colonel.
4. "I must warn you that an almost too painful reprisal has been prepared for you. I really don't know how either you or Leonard will take it. I will only say that its most painful points were sharpened innocently" (Vanessa to Virginia, 27 December 1926, *Berg*).

311

novel—what about the cover?[1]—and have lost so much time—it was impossible to hold a pen at Zennor—also the intellects froze—(Leonard says Will is a hypocrite, and we saw all his pictures—vague skimmings of cloud and mountain incredibly tortured and meagre) What I mean is; I dont think I can spend a night out again; but will come over, Wednesday, Thursday or Friday. Shall you be there? We come down on Tuesday. As the train left, Ka hurtled back, put her head in and said "Tell Nessa I'm really *very* fond of her". So there. It is one of the most melancholy households you can imagine. It is founded upon pretending they enjoy, what they dont: upon slang, and heartiness, and art, and humanity. Ka is to some extent genuine; Will hollow. At least so I think. I've been asked to go to America by a paper. I seriously think of doing it.

Please give Julian a hint that I'm very dangerous when roused: also, I should like to see him.

Yr B

Berg

1700: To Katherine Arnold-Forster
52 *Tavistock Square, W.C.*1

Thursday [30 December 1926]

Dearest Bruin,

Here we are safe and sound. I must say it was extraordinarily nice of you and Will to have us—Everything was at our disposal. I can't think how you manage such comfort and warmth in the howling blizzard: also the two geese; the Cornish cream; my iris and heather to go away with. Of course, the country is none of your doing (but there again, its a question of the motor car too)—that seemed to me even lovelier and stranger—more unlike anything else in the world than ever before. I like your son [Mark] too. What a crusted character he'll be one of these days! I think he will rule us for our good.

I hope we didn't break you down completely. However nice people are, to have them staying is a burden—but, then, as we agreed, as we washed our teeth, Ka is a very remarkable and a very nice woman, and we both feel very fond of her, and like to think of her tramping about the moors with the Leakes and the Griggs[2] and all the rest.

You wont read this. It will lie in the hall for days. However, it is merely

1. Vanessa designed the dust jacket for *To the Lighthouse*.
2. Maurice and Elsie Grigg, prosperous farmers at Zennor.

to thank you, dearest Bruin, for being so kind to us, and to hope you will
come to Monks House.

Love to Will
The iris is full out.
Yours V.W.

My green paper weight is the envy of beholders.

Mark Arnold-Forster

1701: To V. SACKVILLE-WEST   52 *Tavistock Square, W.C.*1

[30 December 1926]

America—
    The [New York Herald] Tribune's offered me free passages, hotel bills,
and £120 to go to New York for a month in the spring and write 4 articles.
I've said I will if I can arrange times, and not too much work—but I daresay
they wont agree—I think it would be rather fun, for a few weeks, and I
should see some odd things—dont you agree? Leonard would come.

Monday
    Alas—We go to Rodmell early on Tuesday afternoon; but I shall be
here (studio) all the morning. Let me know what you want. I'll keep Monday
free anyhow.

Pinker
    If you cant send her, couldn't you come over to Rodmell and stay? I
suppose not—with the children on you—Curse it.

Knole
    I was partly teasing. I dont mind being dowdy, dirty, shabby, red nosed
middle classed and all the rest—its only a question when and how—I do
want to see you, I do—I do.
    How did Brighton go? Write a long long letter from Sherfield.

Virginia

Just sold 20 Teheran.

Berg

1702: To G. H. GRUBB   52 *Tavistock Square, W.C.*1

30 Dec 1926

Dear Mr Grubb,[1]
    I have been asked by an American paper to write some articles in April

1. Director of Putnam & Co. Ltd. (London).

313

about American books that are appearing this spring. I should be greatly obliged if you would mention the names of any your firm is publishing which seem to you of special interest, either in biography, fiction or criticism.

I hope I am not presuming on your kindness in asking this, but it would be a great help to me if you would do so.

Yours sincerely
Virginia Woolf

Texas

Letters 1703-1740 (January–March 1927)

Virginia spent the nights of 17th and 18th January at Knole, and ten days later Vita went for the second time to Persia. Virginia's melancholy at her departure was not quite as acute as it had been a year before. To the Lighthouse was in proof, and she was pleased with it; and although she described the winter as 'my hibernating season', she was well and active, socially and at the Press, and the Woolfs even proposed to add to their labours by buying Birrell's bookshop. Virginia was winding up the Eliot fund, and helped to launch the MacCarthy fund, which was more successful. She was distressingly involved in the end of Clive's affair with Mary Hutchinson. She had her hair shingled. In March, shortly before she left for France and Italy, she felt in her mind the stirring of a new book, The Jessamy Brides, which became, in a very different form, Orlando. Her letters of this period are among her liveliest, because she had no illness, and her two favourite correspondents, Vanessa and Vita, were both abroad, hungry for news and affection.

1703: To Vanessa Bell   52 *Tavistock Square, W.C.*1

Sunday [2 January 1927]

I'll come to lunch on Thursday God willing—hope there'll be a chance of seeing Julian. I'm longing to do battle.

Here's Oliver [Strachey], so no more—I wd. have come for New Year but have to face the horror of getting proofs ready—wh. you painters escape—But my love for you remains hot and strong: yours for me thin and weak.

If another day wd. do better, let me know to Monks House.

Berg

1704: To Edward Sackville West

      52 *Tavistock Square, W.C.*1

Sunday [January? 1927]

My dear Eddy,

May we leave Wednesday open? I hope to come, but things are in rather a muddle.

I'm glad, but surprised, that you like Time Passes. I thought that

315

between The Princesse Bassiano and the translator it had got into a hopeless mess, and was too ashamed to read it.[1]

Now I must write to your Aunt Victoria [Lady Sackville] who has written about 20 pages in pencil about her miseries and loves and houses and servants and heart and daughter and secretary and Ethel Smyth and so on.

I saw Desmond. He took very kindly to the idea of Raymond at the N. S. If you see Raymond do suggest it

Your
Virginia Woolf

Berg

1705: To V. Sackville-West   [52 *Tavistock Square, W.C.*1]

[4 January 1927]

Came home to find a letter from Harold, begging me to get you to promise to be inoculated—So don't be a donkey and promise me to do it—or I won't come to Knole. Its absolutely necessary. Why risk death and typhoid and no Virginia for sake of 10 minutes bother?

Harold writes about us too—wont be jealous he says.[2] Will you send a line to me at Monks House to say you agree (*this is serious*) also tell me how I write to him—Foreign Office? Just off.

Berg

1706: To Vanessa Bell   *Monks House* [*Rodmell, Sussex*]

Wednesday [5 January 1927]

It seems perfectly hopeless to come today.
I think I'd better leave it that I'll come the first fine day for lunch.
I don't expect Leonard will leave his pruning but sends his love—We're

1. *Time Passes*, the middle section of *To the Lighthouse*, was translated by Charles Mauron, and published in advance of the book in *Commerce*, Paris, winter 1926. Princess Bassiano, the American wife of the Duke of Sermoneta, was the publisher of *Commerce*.

2. Harold had written to Virginia on 17 December from Teheran: "I am glad that Vita has come under an influence so stimulating and so sane. . . . You need never worry about my having any feelings except a longing that Vita's life should be as rich and as sincere as possible. I loathe jealousy as I loathe all forms of disease" (*Sussex*).

316

much disappointed not to see Julian. Ask him to send me his scurrilous lampoon[1] and I'll reply suitably. No coal, no anthracite, here.
We go on Sunday

V.W.

There was a very good review of Roger's book in the Manchester Guardian[2]
Oliver is in love with you—he says—not with me

Berg

1707: To Violet Dickinson   *Monks House, Rodmell,*
                                             Lewes [Sussex]
Saturday [8 January 1927?]

My Violet,
    I am so pleased that the servant who was with you when I was a baby knew my voice—how she managed it, God alone knows. But then you have always had a miraculous tribe of servants—I remember the charming Rose.
    We are riding out a tremendous gale down here. The chestnut in the churchyard has fallen on one of Leonards new fruit trees; and one cant poke one's nose out without having it blown off. I daresay you are worse off with all your trees at Welwyn. George (Sir George Duckworth)[3] says you are not in the least deaf—you are as young as ever he says—thats not true at all of George.
    Yes—Julian, Nessas eldest, is a perfect Stephen, weighs 13. 6. and writes poetry—

                                                  Yr
                                                  VW
Berg

1708: To Vanessa Bell   [52 *Tavistock Square, W.C.*1]
[25 January? 1927]

Dearest,
    I was much relieved to get your card. I hope it means that Duncan is now convalescent.[4] Any further news will be gratefully received—we all rang

1. See page 311, note 4.
2. The review by 'H. W.' on 4 January described Fry's *Transformations* as "easily the most illuminating book of art during the last ten years".
3. Virginia's half-brother was knighted in the New Year's Honours.
4. Duncan Grant had fallen ill at Cassis, with suspected typhoid. Vanessa immediately joined him there with Angelica and her nurse.

317

each other up to communicate yesterday—and let me know, theres a good Dolphin, if I can do anything here.

I'm sending the wash, except a dress shirt; as Louie [Angelica's nurse] has brought more than Angelica's things; and I daresay its better to send the lot. Leonard has written a stiff letter to Miss Beazley [*unidentified*] but has had no answer yet.

Of gossip the chief is that Herbert Stephen is engaged to Hermione Cunningham, his cousin, aged 30 I suppose—Well, well: the Stephens as you say, mature late[1]—Then Margaret Duckworth has asked us to lunch—but no: last night at Colefaxes will do me for a week or two—Sir Arthur [Colefax] was my fate: and tho' I mixed claret and champagne till my head spun, still I could not make rhyme or reason but only boredom unutterable of his doddering, chiefly about the future, past, and present of the Trades Union Movement. Afterwards, Viola [Tree] acted, and I sat hug a mugger in a Sapphists Cosy Corner. with Dotty and Mary.

Theres scarlatina at the Stephen's school, so Adrian has brought them back. Love to the old Convolvulus [Duncan]: Kiss him on his nose: I adore him.

VW.

Do get a little rest: I thought you were worn to a shred as Mary Fisher wd. say.

Berg

1709: To Lady Ottoline Morrell
52 *Tavistock Square, W.C.*1
27th Jan. [1927]

Dearest Ottoline,

If you would very kindly sign these three cheques, I think that would be the last of the [Eliot] fund.

Yr
Virginia Woolf.

Would you send Logans in the envelope I enclose to his banker, and return the other two to me.

Texas

1. Sir Herbert Stephen, 2nd baronet, was born in 1857, and married Mary Hermione, daughter of Sir Henry Stewart Cunningham, on 29 January 1927.

1710: To Ethel Sands   52 *Tavistock Sqre W.C.*

Saturday [29 January 1927]

Dearest Ethel,

But wont Thursday be a party? It would be so nice to see you without a party, so I suggest either you shall come here next Friday and find me alone, or I shall come some day when you're alone. I've heard from Nessa today that Duncan is able to go for short walks, and is getting on well. There was a muddle about a doctor, and a scare of typhoid but happily this is now all over and she sounds cheerful.

I was at Sibyl's and hoped for you—no Ethel alas.

> Yours affect
> Virginia

I'm so sorry you have been so bad—it sounded horrid. Oh what a ghastly weekend I'm just off to—the Sidney Webbs

Wendy Baron

1711: To V. Sackville-West   52 *Tavistock Sqre* [*W.C.*1]

Monday 31st Jan [1927]

My dear Honey,

It was nice to get your telegram and letters—write as many as you can.[1] It gives one a fillip. The only good thing thats happened to me is that the moment you left I became involved in a series of telephones, notes, scenes with Clive and Mary,[2] all very emotional which left me so angered, so sordidified, so exacerbated that I could only think of you as being very distant and beautiful and calm. A lighthouse in clean waters. I can't give details, which would bore you, (happy as you are, old Devil, with Harold in Persia); but I can assure you, you'll find things as usual in May: Clive giving champagne suppers to Mary. I was amused to think how angry certain charges made against me by Mary would have made you—God, if you'd been here, what fun we should have had.

But the main good was that I've been kept on the hop the whole time: so I've been restless and scattered; its like taking sleeping draughts: I try my best to put off thinking about you. Then there was the Webbs: how dreamlike things are, how skinned of flesh and blood when one's thinking of Vita going further and further My word how it blew the night you went —I was

1. Vita left for her second visit to Persia on 28 January, accompanied by Dorothy Wellesley and Leigh Ashton.
2. Clive's long love affair with Mary Hutchinson was coming to an end.

launched on a 6 mile walk on a cold common on a rainy morning with Sidney Webb. All my sentences leapt into the middle of the pond without a moment's reflection. Pausing by a beastly pool of self-conscious beauty— Surrey is detestable—Webb said one must remember what a difference Mahommedanism had made to the negroes in Sierra Leone: whereupon without a second I plunged: made some dreadful howlers, Leonard said. And there was a stunted brown woollen secretary woman at table who said "Might I trouble you for a *little* drop of water?" her only remark, except to the dog. Incredibly ugly it all was except for Lord Russell husband of Elizabeth,[1] enormous, wearing a crucifix.

Wednesday, Feb. 2nd. No letter from you today or yesterday: I suppose you're in Moscow. Here its snowy; melting though, and the rain coming through my skylight. I woke in the night, and was very dismal. My sleeping draught (Clive and Mary) is wearing off. Another long interview with Mary yesterday. We were about to fly at each others throats when in walked Eddie [Sackville West]: stayed complacently an hour or so: and only left us time for a hasty explanation. Dear, dear, its an odd story: he's [Clive] not going away. His sleeper has been cancelled. Her ferocity commands my respect: indeed we made it up: but whether she can hold him, firmly, for ever, I have my doubts.[2] He has made a fool of her all over London—Colefax that is, and Ethel Sands: Colefax came to tea. Why do people laugh at me? she asked. D'you know its a great thing being a eunuch as I am: that is not knowing what's the right side of a skirt: women confide in one. One pulls a shade over the fury of sex; and then all the veins and marbling, which, between women, are so fascinating, show out. Here in my cave I see lots of things you blazing beauties make invisible by the light of your own glory.

No: I'm not going to America. They write that they are entertaining me at dinners, but not, apparently paying my hotel bills. So the cost would swallow up all my earnings, and I think we can cry off and go to Greece.

12.30. A cable from America, asking me to come later: I suppose they may offer more money, but no, I think I won't be bribed, unless its tremendous.

Yes, honey, we are buying The Bookshop—at least negotiations are begun;[3] Francis [Birrell] is dining here tonight. He says its the chance of our lives. Leonard is like a hound with his nose to the ground. But weeks and months will pass in conversation. What fun though, dont you think—

1. The 2nd Earl Russell, who in 1916 had married, as his third wife, the widow of Count von Arnim. She wrote several best-selling books under the name 'Elizabeth'.
2. The details of the Clive and Mary affair are given in Virginia's letter to Vanessa of 2 February 1927.
3. The proposal that the Hogarth Press should acquire the Bloomsbury bookshop founded by Francis Birrell and David Garnett did not come to anything.

suppose we did it, and it was a great success, and I had a motor car, and we went bookbuying all over England

I've *not* got a cold in my head, but its like having a cold in the head, sitting here writing to you and everything at sixes and sevens. I feel dissipated and aimless for some reason. I've got to read all Morgan's novels,[1] and so far cant open a book without being interrupted. Then its you being away—I am at the mercy of people, of moods, feel lonely, like something pitiable which can't make its wants known. How you have demoralised me. I was once a stalwart upstanding woman. Then its not writing novels: this journalism is such a thin draggled straining business, and I keep opening the lid and looking into my mind to see whether some slow fish isn't rising there —some new book. No: nothing at the moment.

Yes, I like you to write good poetry. My parting lecture was not very coherent. I was trying to get at something about the thing itself before its made into anything: the emotion, the idea. The danger for you with your sense of tradition and all those words—a gift of the Gods though—is that you help this too easily into existence. I dont mean that one ought to strain, to write showily, expressively, or so on: only that one ought to stand outside with one's hands folded, until the thing has made itself visible: we born writers tend to be ready with our silver spoons too early: I mean I think there are odder, deeper, more angular thoughts in your mind than you have yet let come out. Still, you'll get the Hawthornden,[2] Oh yes, and I shall be vaguely jealous, proud, and disgusted. I'm going to read the Land through as soon as I get a chance.

Are you perishing with cold at Moscow now? It's fine again here: I have set up a little type, talked to Angus and Mrs Cartwright, must now finish this, and post it, and try to read a little, and so get control of my fidgets.

Dearest honey, are you well and happy, and did the journey go easily, and is Harold very happy, and do you ever think of the basement and—and —a kiss from Pinker: one from me to the insect.[3] I'll write weekly.

Yr V.

Berg

---

1. For her article, *The Novels of E. M. Forster* (*Atlantic Monthly*, November 1927).
2. Vita heard on 16 February that she had been awarded the Hawthornden Prize for *The Land*.
3. A pet name for Vita.

Wed. Feb. 2nd [1927]

Dearest,

I've just got your letter, asking for news. I expect you have heard by now from Clive that he isn't coming [to Cassis]. Probably he has told you about it all.

I dont quite know what I had better say, as I am constantly being warned by them both not to say anything: but of course it is all over London—so I will be indiscreet and give you my version: only don't please get me into trouble—It's only too likely I'm already embroiled.

Anyhow, the facts are (I'm in a hurry so dont expect great lucidity) that a week ago today Clive rang me up at lunch and said might he come in after dinner as he was desperate. He said he might tell me in some years why, but could say nothing now. We had Vita and W. J. Turner here; but Clive dined, and kept on hinting that he was breaking up his life, going out of England for some months, going to write a book in complete solitude, absolutely without bearings, and so on: at which we had to laugh of course, and finally he got into an aesthetic argument and everyone left. Next day he appeared in my studio with his passport, on his way to get tickets, asking me for your address. He would only say that he was going to Cassis for 3 months then to Paris and then to Charleston till October; however he asked if he might come to tea, and went off again, babbling, half excited, half bewildered as if he were talking in his sleep. Then I saw Vita, who had been at a party at Dotties the night before, and Clive had behaved there in the same way telling everyone—Sibyl, Ethel, Raymond etc—that he was absolutely wretched and was going away till the autumn. Everybody was talking, and wondering if it was Mary or what. So he came to tea, and plunged at once into a long account of his misery, again seeming very excited, yet on the whole rather happy, and high spirited. He said that for three months things had been going wrong between him and Mary, and suddenly, last Wednesday, at a play in a box with several people, he had said to her "I am wretched" whereupon she told him that the truth was she was slightly, but only slightly, in love with some one else. Thereupon he practically went mad—at any rate he said he had not slept for 3 nights, and had decided that life like this was impossible, and he was going to break with her for ever. He gave me a long account of their relationship; the upshot of which was that though passionately in love, he could not settle down with her, and also she made it impossible for him to work. He thought if he left her for 9 months he would forget about her entirely. He was sick he said of the society they lived in, and found it more and more idiotic. I should say that Mary had rung me up before he came to implore me to soothe him, and to say that he grossly exaggerated what had happened. But I could do nothing; as whenever I suggested his waiting or going for a month only he swore that he was in torture, and that his only hope was to be with you and Duncan and work. Of course I agreed about the horrors of incessant Sibyl Chrissie [Aberconway] and Leslie[1] and also thought that he must begin now if he meant to do any long book. However, I didn't have to give advice, as he had told everybody and made all arrangements. So he went off, and next day we went to the Webbs till Sunday night when I came back to find a note marked urgent, telling me that Mary had been to him in a perfect fury, especially against me, (*please don't tell this ever—be begged me not to repeat it*) She said it was a plot of mine against her, and that I wanted to break the relationship. He warned me in case she rang me up in a rage, as she well might. We went to dine with him that night, and he took me aside and said rather sheepishly that after all he was putting off going till March: Mary was suffering too much; and he could not simply thrust her feelings aside—but still he meant to go later, as he had said.

That was all we could say—except that Mary was furious with me, and he could not pacify her. Nothing more was said (aint this like a Defoe novel?) and we dined off cold pheasant and were very impersonal and cheerful. Next day he rang me up to say that Mary wanted to come and see me. She came yesterday when Eddie also arrived, so that we had a long and highly constrained conversation about books—both of us looking at each other like tigresses, for I of course was furious too and thought she had behaved like a cook; as indeed I meant to tell her—At last Eddie went, and after some palaver, she started off and asked me, ironically, if I had tried to pacify Clive as I had promised. I said that he was not pacifiable when I saw him: So then she wanted to know what he had said, finally she gave me her version, which is that she is *not* in love with anyone, had never said so, had only been rather restless and so on, was devoted to him, was absolutely horrified when she realised how he took her words at the play, was then furious when she heard that he had told people at Dotties party, was still more enraged when he said he was going for 9 months, and finally, when he rang up and said that I agreed he ought to go and called her "a little fool", her anger became such that she dashed off to see him, and abused me sky-high, and in short so stormed and raged at him that eventually he put the whole thing in her hands and said she was to decide for him what he should do. She of course told him to stay.

Then we went into the case, and she says that she detests the society they keep, longs for him to work, is often at her wits end to get out of parties, and finds him a good deal deteriorated intellectually because of his debauchery. As for its being her influence, she would have none of it. She thought I accused her of being a silly mondaine, who only wanted flirting, and had better be broken with. This was explained away I think and we parted on

1. Lesley Jowitt, wife of William (later Earl) Jowitt, the future Lord Chancellor. They were married in 1913, and she became a prominent figure in society.

323

friendly terms; but God knows what will come of it. She told me that he has plunged back at once into the old Cliveries etc—and was going out every night. But of course she said, if he goes away, as it would be best for him to do, the chances are he would leave me for ever.

So her only choice is I think to keep him here, and to try and control him. Whether she can, I don't know. I expect he will be relieved for a time at not having to work or go away and then the same thing will happen again. I've heard no more of them today; and I expect I shall be trounced by Clive next for saying things to Mary.

So dont for God's sake get me into further trouble. However, I can't think there's any harm in telling you: probably he has written already, and I daresay between us you'll get your own idea of the case—But I can't describe to you how odd he's been.

I don't think we shall go to America, as the expense seems too great—So you may see us—Love to Duncan.

Yr B.

If Roger or anyone asks you, please dont give my version which is strictly for you and Duncan only. The official version is simply that they quarrelled and have made it up—

Berg

1713: To Violet Dickinson   52 *Tavistock Sqre, WC*1

Thursday [3 February? 1927]

My Violet.

Yes. Herbert [Stephen] seems to be married. When I last saw his bride [Mary Cunningham] she wore a white pinafore and was being sung hymns to by that clodhopping woman you used to admire, his sister, Dorothea. Some 30 years must be between them. Think of the marriage bed! Like marrying a lobster which has been boiled hard as well as red. My last contact (not nuptial) with the fish was over the Dreadnought, when he fulminated against us, and said my reputation was dragged under the feet of all the blue jackets in the Navy[1]—to which there was no reply on my part.

But enough of Herbert. How are you? On your immensely long legs again? I hope so—I envy you convalescing at Brighton. I think the height and pitch of life is the Brighton pier listening to the Band—Leonard and I regularly go every summer. Now I am wondering whether to spend April in America. I've been asked to go and write articles—What do you advise?

1. The famous hoax, organised in February 1910 by Horace Cole, when Virginia, Adrian and four friends visited the H.M.S. *Dreadnought* at Weymouth in the disguise of the Emperor of Abyssinia and his suite.

I might make some money—on the other hand they say the natives are poisonous. In my articles I should have to tell so many lies I should be corrupt for ever.

Leonard sends his love—Please recover instantly and make up your mind to marry on your 70th birthday—

VW.

Berg

1714: To V. Sackville-West

52 *Tavistock Sqre, London* [*W.C.*1]

Saturday, 5th Feb 1927

Dearest Honey,

No letter since you were careering through the snow in Westphalia—that is nothing since Monday. I hope this doesn't mean you have been eaten by brigands, wrecked, torn to pieces. It makes me rather dismal. It gets worse steadily—your being away. All the sleeping draughts and the irritants have worn off, and I'm settling down to wanting you, doggedly, dismally, faithfully—I hope that pleases you. It's damned unpleasant for me, I can assure you. I had a sort of idea that I'd cheat the devil, and put my head under my wing, and think of nothing. But it wont work—not at all. I want you this Saturday more than last and so it'll go on.

You are on the Caspian? Its lovely here: an early Spring. You are being tossed up and down on a smelly ship—you and Dotty [Wellesley] and Leigh [Ashton] in his horn glasses—and I sit over the gas in my sordid room. Why cant I write except in sordid rooms? I dont think I could write a word in your room at Long Barn. Furniture that people can sit in implies people, and I want complete solitude—thats at the back of my mind, and so I get sordider and sordider. The Voyage Out was written in comparative splendour [Fitzroy Square]—a maid, carpets, fires; To the Lighthouse was written—as you know. So the next book will necessitate a shed. This fits in with my mood at the moment. I have banged my door on parties, dug myself into a dank dismal burrow, where I do nothing but read and write. This is my hybernating season. I read 5 hours yesterday, the same today. Its grim but salutary. Then May will be all festive, wont it? I'm a little nervous about Harold. I've suddenly become absorbed in a book about reading novels, and can't stop making phrases. So thats the book I see when I lift the lid and look in. Its going to be about how to read all fiction as if it were one book one had written oneself.[1] Then you're damned lustrous face, like the portrait of

1. This short book, *Phases of Fiction*, was announced as forthcoming in the Hogarth Press's Lectures on Literature Series, but it eventually appeared in the New York *Bookman* of April, May, and June 1929, and was reprinted in *Granite and Rainbow* (1958).

an ancestress by a great painter on the wall of a gallery with a light blazing on it intervenes. You hang there so fruity, so rich.

Monday 7th Feb

At last! A letter from Moscow this morning. Oh what a blessing! It has taken a whole week to come. Yes: I should have liked it if you had telegraphed: no: I should *not* have thought you foolish. Lord Bless me! Think of meeting your paramours husband![1] What did he say? And then the dinner and Lenins body! Please write everything fully when you have time. Now you are nearly at Teheran I make out, motoring across mountains; stopping at some shed I daresay for lunch, sandwiches, wine. You are very excited, all in a whirl, like a flock of birds flying across; Harold will be pacing up and down his room. I think of this journey so that I could write a book about not being a Passenger to Teheran: but its silly to tell you my version, as perhaps you have your own.

Here its pouring; rain coming through the roof; the sordidity too much for me even. I think I shall make some money and buy a carpet. Would one carpet interfere with one's solitude, d'you think? Or an ash tray? Or an arm chair?

All the harpies descend on me the moment you go: They wait for the body to be exposed defenceless—Sibyl, Ethel, now Ozzie [Dickinson]. Ozzie says "We all thought Vita very depressed at Dotties party". He tries to make out that its because your mother is jealous of anyone you speak to—thats me, I gather. And "Vita *is* so good to her mother". But I'm getting Raymond here to protect me—This is typical of Ozzie in the days when he told me how to behave, who to marry etc.

Could you and Harold go on top of a Tram up to Hampstead on a rainy Saturday afternoon? I kept trying to imagine it. Instantly all the lights went up and the whole tram became golden rosy. Aint it odd how the vision at the Sevenoaks fishmongers has worked itself into my idea of you? We went to see Keatses house, and I invented a story about two little beasts with a passion for muffins (cousins of the insect [Vita] they are) and I went into a shop and bought muffins and a woman said was I Miss Stephen whom she'd known 20 years before—then I went and sat in the room where Keats wrote his odes, and saw the engagement ring he gave Fanny [Brawne], and opened the cupboard in which he kept his books—We'll go there on a tram: but it'll be May.

America is off, temporarily at least. I'm afraid I shall have to go later though, and rather wish I'd got it over now in a month with you abroad. I think we shall go to Greece with Roger; theres also an invitation to motor in Spain with Dadie in May—this is much urged on me, but I think there are 'private reasons' against it.

1. Denys Trufusis, husband of Violet, with whom Vita had eloped to France in 1920. He was a Russophil, and Vita met him by chance in Moscow.

Clive has apparently settled down again—Vanessa writes frantic letters saying "Why is Clive utterly miserable and coming here for 3 months"— Then "Why is Clive *not* coming at all—but gives no reason?" To which I can only echo "Why?"

Tuesday 8th Feb.

Now you're just arriving I make out—driving into the gates of Teheran. Theres Harold come out to meet you. There you sit as proud as a peacock. Dotty is tactful. Well well, its all very exciting, even here in the studio with the rain coming through. My God, to be with you and the 14 cream coloured ponies, and the young mare, and the lighted window in the fishmongers shop! Still I admit that Harold has some right to this morning. I wish to God I'd asked you to wire. I wish I knew if you *had* arrived, and *were* safe, and *are* well. I trust to Dotty to tell me if you're not. Thank her for her letter. I'll write to her.

Did I lead a life of utter idleness while you were here? putting off all disagreeable jobs? I suppose so. Masses of manuscripts are now tumbling on my head; I'm to see the pillmaker of Percy Circus; I'll send you a box of vegetable pills; then theres the Eliot fund, and Desmond fund,[1] and people all at sixes and sevens. In short I'm very busy about rather dull things; not busy for you; busy for me. And now, did I tell you about Mary's bloody book? (Its confidential please) She's at last produced this thrice hardboiled egg and Leonard says its bilge, and he's going to tell her so.[2] Theres a Press crisis on too—what to do about the future of Angus[3]—another painful interview, for L. thinks he had better go. And then someone's bidding for Birrell and Garnett and will probably get it; but as Pollard[4] is a fixture and Pollard is a brute, perhaps its as well.

Wednesday

Oh and here's Clive to say he's off to France—I say But isnt that rather unexpected? Not a bit says Clive. Then what about Mary? Here he waves his hand as if he had just heard of her but thats all—Another quarrel, I suppose: but whether final or not, Heaven knows.

---

1. The MacCarthys were going through a period of financial difficulty, and their friends were collecting money to send them on holiday abroad.
2. Nevertheless the Hogarth Press did publish Mary Hutchinson's *Fugitive Pieces* in June 1927.
3. Angus Davidson resigned from the Hogarth Press in December 1927.
4. Graham Pollard, the distinguished bibliographer, who, with John Carter, exposed the Wise forgeries. He and Betty Norton (sister of H. T. J. Norton) bought the bookshop, Garnett having already sold his share to Pollard in 1924.

Sibyls latest A letter from Walter de la Mare to say he's so sorry he can't accept Lady Colefax's invitation to come to tea with me. The first I'd heard of it. And then Sibyl asks me to tell her what she does to make people laugh!

Goodbye dearest honey. Write to me please as much as you can. Yes yes yes I do like you. I am afraid to write the stronger word.

Yr
Virginia

Berg

1715: To Vanessa Bell   52 *T-[avistock] S[quare, W.C.*1]

Wednesday [9 February 1927]

Well well—in came Clive yesterday and said, casually, he was going to Cassis in a week or so. When I said I was surprised, he poohpooed it, and said he had always meant to—"But I thought Mary told me you'd given up the notion?" I said. "Mary was probably mistaken about that as about other things" he said. "Of course I didn't want to go off and leave her in a pucker; but its all settled now." "Isn't she very much upset?" I asked. He merely laughed, and turned the conversation to Desmond (who's ill in Switzerland) as if it were a matter of perfect indifference to him, and Mary an acquaintance only. So perhaps he has broken off finally. He made out that he had always meant this. I suppose after the violent scene a week ago, he cooled again, or there was another quarrel. But perhaps you know more. He's dining here tonight, but I shan't hear anything; also the subject now seems to bore him.

We've finally refused the American offer, anyhow for this Spring, as they didn't mean to pay hotel bills apparently. Theyve cabled to ask us to come later, but that wont be yet anyhow—So I think I, at least, shall manage Cassis, whether we go on to Greece or not—It would be about the end of March I suppose. Now that Clive's going, perhaps we could share the villa with him—It sounds enchanting. London is vile beyond words. I am involved with Chrissie and Sibyls over a subscription for Desmond, Vita is in Persia, I'm getting rather nervous about my novel—altogether I greatly envy you.

Do keep an eye on a French chair, a table, a chest of drawers for me in your wanderings:

I'm very happy that Duncan is better—I cant help loving him in spite of all.

Great hurry—

Yr B

Berg

328

Virginia Woolf at Rodmell in June 1926

Jacques Raverat

The Hogarth Press (a Minerva platen machine), now at Sissinghurst Castle, Kent

Vita Sackville-West in 1925

At Studland, Dorset, in
September 1923. Sitting:
Leonard and Virginia Woolf;
standing: George Rylands *(left)*
and Raymond Mortimer; in
front: Lydia Lopokova

Dorothy Wellesley

Virginia and Leonard Woolf at
Rodmell, June 1926

(Left to right) Francis Birrell,
Clive Bell and Vita Sackville-West

Virginia Woolf with Benedict and *(left)* Nigel Nicolson at Knole,
January 1927

Eclipse of the sun, Richmond, Yorkshire, at dawn on 29 June 1927.
(Left to right) Quentin Bell, Edward Sackville West, Harold Nicolson,
Virginia and Leonard Woolf

Gerald Brenan and
Dora Carrington

Virginia Woolf at Rodmell,
summer 1928

Julian, Vanessa and
Quentin Bell in 1928

(Left to right) Edward
Sackville West, Raymond
Mortimer and Clive Bell,
in Berlin, 1928

Virginia Woolf at Long
Barn, summer 1928

Vita Sackville-West
photographed for *Orlando* at
Long Barn, summer 1928

1716: To Ethel Sands   52 *Tavistock Square* [*W.C.*1]

Wednesday [9 February 1927]

Dearest Ethel,

I had a much happier letter from Vanessa this morning. She says "Duncan has taken great strides in the last few days, and really seems practically well again. He can walk and do all much as usual, and is in very good spirits". Also she thinks the Grants may be going to Rome, which would be a great relief.¹ I thought you might like to know—being a sympathetic character as you are.

By the way was I very absurd about children last night? I was rather shocked that you should think I didn't care for Nessa's. They are such an immense source of pleasure to me. But I see what it is: I'm always angry with myself for not having forced Leonard to take the risk in spite of doctors; he was afraid for me and wouldn't; but if I'd had rather more self-control no doubt it would have been all right. That's I suppose, why I don't talk of Nessa's children—it's true I never do—whom I adore. This is only a small contribution to feminine psychology, and don't I beg dream of answering. I daresay your charming character is to blame for confidences.

I wrote to Sibyl [about the MacCarthy Fund], tactfully, and she's been ringing up and driving Leonard mad. He says she sounds rather happy and will want careful management—Its always the way about money.

Yr aff
V.W.

Wendy Baron

1717: To V. Sackville-West   52 *Tavistock Sqre* [*W.C.*1]

Wednesday, Feb. 16th [1927]

Anyhow, dearest Honey, you are safe at Teheran. I saw Ozzie who let this pearl fall from his dribbling lips: also your mother has written one of her most gracious letters "Dear Mr and Mrs Woolf, bless you for being so good to my child", to which I have answered, suitably, I hope, in deep humility. Harold is a happy man and I am an envious woman. Yesterday too I got your letter from Rostov with Leigh dancing, and Miss Jebb² swinging from the rack. So now, you're there; and I like it better than when your going further and further away. Thats all I can say.

Did I say I was leading a solitary life, reading 5 hours a day? My God, what a fool to think it possible! Take yesterday: Sibyl at 4. Consultation

1. Duncan's mother and aunt had been staying with them at Cassis.
2. Marjorie, the sister of Gladwyn Jebb, third Secretary at the British Legation in Teheran. She travelled across Russia with Vita, Dottie and Leigh Ashton.

about getting money for Desmond. Sybil a little huffy with Chrissy. I try to soothe. Let her run on. Is Mollie extravagant? Are we to pay debts or subscribe for a holiday? Should there be two funds? What about the Eliot fund? Some people won't pay for Desmond's debts; others not for his holiday. Enter little Turner,[1] the one like a tipsy rook who dined with us. Sibyl goes. Turner flatters me. You have such an imaginative view of life. I get suspicious. Whats the matter? Do you live with your wife? Well thats what I want to discuss with you. Then it comes out hes in love with a daughter of Mrs Saxton Noble:[2] will I see her and persuade her to become his mistress? Here Lytton rings up. May he dine? Oh all right. Off fish? Oh certainly. Yes, Mr Turner—(but call me Walter) yes Walter I'll see Cynthia: but you'll have to marry her. Francis Birrell rings up. Bunins[3] starving in Paris. Can you help to get up a fund to pay his doctor's bill? Oh yes—certainly—I'll ask Leonard. Yes, Walter, I'll see her: but I think you'll have to marry her. But I want to keep them both. Here Pinker upset the electric lamp: the flat is completely dark. Turner goes. Lytton comes. We sit up talking about Queen Elizabeth, sodomy, love, the Antigone, Othello, when Clive rings up, will you dine to meet Elizabeth Bibesco? No I wont. Will Leonard? No. Will Lytton? No. And so to bed. Next morning Chrissie on the telephone. May I say, Mrs Woolf, I think its a great mistake to let Sibyl have anything to do with the [MacCarthy] fund? Also why subscribe for a holiday? Surely the debts are the important thing. If you will come and lunch. . . . Then Clive's brother [Cory Bell]. Look here Virginia about that motor car. If you really want one I should advise etc etc. Then supper at Clives: and so here we are.

I'm afraid I'm being very jerky and dull.

Do you realise how devoted I am to you, all the same? There's nothing I wouldn't do for you, dearest Honey. Its true, the other night, I did take a glass too much. Its your fault though—that Spanish wine. I got a little tipsy. And then Bobo Mayor[4] is a great seducer in her way. She has gipsy blood in her: she's rather violent and highly coloured, sinuous too, with a boneless body, and thin hands; all the things I like. So, being a little tipsy about twelve o'clock at night, I let her do it.

She cut my hair off. I'm shingled. That being so—and it'll look all right in a month or two, the hairdresser says—bound to be a little patchy at first— lets get on to other things. Its off; its in the kitchen bucket: my hairpins have been offered up like crutches in St Andrews, Holborn, at the high altar.

1. W. J. Turner, the poet, novelist, and music critic.
2. Cynthia Noble, who married Gladwyn Jebb in 1929.
3. I. A. Bunin, the Russian poet and novelist, some of whose books were published in translation by the Hogarth Press.
4. Beatrice Mayor (née Meinertzhagen), who married Robert Mayor in 1912. She was the author of several plays.

Darling Honey, if anything could make me say Vita's a villain it is that you didn't tell me, you'll be happier, wiser, serener, cleverer a thousand times shingled than haired. As for beauty, I looked in the glass a week ago; and I assure you, its an illusion: a mirage: I'm a plain woman; shall be plainer; so a bingling and shingling more or less dont matter: but let us get on to something interesting.

Nothing occurs to me at the moment.

There has been a good deal of talk, one way and another, about the Sackvilles. Oh said Clive, yesterday, I dreamt I was engaged to Vita. What an old nuisance Colefax is, says Roger—There I was talking to Vita Nicolson and beginning to find her so sympathetic, when in butts Colefax. Come and tell me about Alexandria, or something. Vita's at the bottom of your shingling I know, Vanessa writes in a wild fury. Vita seems to pervade the quarter curiously. I had the pillmaker of Percy Circus to tea: a red fingered woman, clumsy, woollen; obdurate and monosyllabic: but hungry for crumpets. And who should come in but George Duckworth, as fat as a louse, but beady eyed like a rat, and so condescending to us all, I first lost my temper, and then laughed; and he told us one little story to his own glory after another, till I said, they'll be making you a peer next, which he said they mean to do, at the first opportunity. Suddenly the pill maker collapsed: she must go to the water closet, she said. Was it the crumpets? or George? or if one makes vegetable pills, do they act, inconveniently, at any moment? Such is my life this week.

Please Vita dear dont forget your humble creatures—Pinker and Virginia. Here we are sitting by the gas fire alone. Every morning she jumps on to my bed and kisses me, and I say thats Vita.

But she has worms again. Leonard says, Isn't it rather remarkable you haven't had influenza this year? I say thats Vita. Oh and we are having such a to do in the Press. Wells has asked us to do a pamphlet of his: and I've got an essay out of De la Mare.[1] Our conversation with Angus was a complete misfire. He wont go. He cant see that he need go. Then Birrell's book shop is sold, I'm afraid;

I must post this, but like lingering over it, though my hand is so cold I cant write, in order to be with you. You shall ruffle my hair in May, Honey: its as short as a partridges rump.

Heres Leonard

Your
Virginia

Berg

---

1. H. G. Wells' *Democracy Under Revision* was published by the Press in March of this year. Walter de la Mare's pamphlet, *Atmosphere in Fiction*, was announced as forthcoming, but they never published it.

1718: To V. Sackville-West 52 *T.[avistock] S.[quare, W.C.1]*

Friday, 18th Feb. 1927

Sweet Honey,
    Nelly has just brought into the Studio where I'm correcting proofs of
the Lighthouse your cable "Agree about Doran".[1] Its not a very intimate
message, but it gives me a little thrill of pleasure, and I make you say instead
Good morning Virginia. Good morning Vita. Yes I want you more and more.
You'll like to think of me unhappy I know. Well, you can.
    Last time I wrote in such a tearing hurry I was ashamed to send it, so now
I'm beginning early: but there'll be endless interruptions. I want to know,
particularly, among a crowd of other things, have you talked to Harold about
giving up silk stockings and swords and gold lace and humbug and nonsense
[diplomacy] and becoming a sensible man? If so, what has he said? Now you
will have got over your torrent of talk, and might have a little serious
conversation. At a conclave here the other night it was universally agreed
that he was a loss to the world as it is: much too good for that everyone said:
but then he's ambitious, some one said. Nonsense, I said.
    You are sitting by the Kasran (I dont know what the name is) [Kasvin]
Gate, and seeing us all as little bright beads in a plate miles beneath. You see
us, and you think we dont see you. I assure you I'm conscious of you all day
long, soaring above my head. And am I a bright bead, or a dull bead, in the
plate? Or dont I exist?
    We're still talking, you'll be surprised to hear, about love and sodomy
and Bunny's last book,[2] Vita and Eddy, and Desmond's fund, shall it be for
his debts or his holiday?—with Lytton, Clive, Morgan, Raymond, Mary etc.
There we sit in Clive's smoky room, with the brandy and the tumblers, and
Mary wears a black patch on her left cheek and a golden turban. How nice
you look shingled! she says. Why dont you do it? I say. But think if I were
to look a horror for a whole six weeks! she says. I see thats a serious matter—
Then Morgan says he's worked it out and one spends 3 hours on food, 6 on
sleep, 4 on work, 2 on love. Lytton says 10 on love. I say the whole day on
love. I say its seeing things through a purple shade. But you've never been in
love they say.

Monday, Feb 21st
    It gets worse you'll be glad to hear, steadily worse. Todays the day when
I should be trotting out to buy you your loaf, and watching for your white

1. Doran, the New York publishers, were considering an American edition of
   Passenger to Teheran.
2. David Garnett's *Go She Must!* (1927).

legs—not widow Cartwrights—coming down the basement steps. Instead you're on the heights of Persia, riding an Arab mare I daresay to some deserted garden and picking yellow tulips.

My solace is what?—dining with Ethel Sands to meet Violet Bonham Carter,[1] and laboriously correcting two sets of proofs. My goodness how you'll dislike that book [*To the Lighthouse*]! Honestly you will—Oh but you shan't read it. Its a ghost between us. Whether its good or bad, I know not: I'm dazed, I'm bored, I'm sick to death: I go on crossing out commas and putting in semi-colons in a state of marmoreal despair. I suppose there may be half a paragraph somewhere worth reading: but I doubt it.

I read Cowper: The Task [1785]. Now there's a man with a dash of white fire in him. It comes so strangely, among such flummery: one line, one phrase. Theres no Cowper in Persia, you'll say: if there were, read some of the Task. The domestic scenes are lovely: and then this white fire: what I call central transparency. For a long poem of course you need a mould: and lines to fall smooth one after another: but also now and again what saves one is the wave rising solitary; a line about a hare perhaps; something said still with the formal lilt, but completely in his own voice. This seems to me the triumph of style.

Wednesday

Ethel's party wasn't bad; I liked Violet Bonham Carter, save that she gets too close, and cranes too near. Philip Ritchie told me I was the chief coquette in London. "allumeuse" Clive corrected him. Then my suspenders came down, dragging with them an old rag of chemise—why didn't you tell me one must fasten one's suspenders properly? I can dress now in 5 minutes: just think of that. But always some misery like suspenders clips my wings of glory; and Good God, I must buy a hat.

Well darling: no letter from you since Monday week. I must wait till next Monday, a whole fortnight I suppose. How are you? Any malaria? How's Dotty? Does she like Persia? My love to her. Oh I'm so solitary, except for Leonard: Clive went this morning. We had an affecting farewell. I think I cried. I feel so fond of him, and then he's in an odd state—God knows whats happening, save that I feel sure Mary is angry with me, and thinks I'm at the bottom of it. Of what, though? God knows.

I think we shall probably go to Greece the end of March and be back the end of April: and then I shall spend May motoring in Spain with Dadie— hah hah!—and June in Italy with Nancy [Cunard]; and July in Rodmell with

1. Violet Asquith, daughter of the former Prime Minister, had married Maurice Bonham Carter in 1915. In 1923-25 she was President of the Women's Liberal Federation.

Pinker; and August in Geneva with Ramsay Macdonald. But there'll be one night with you at Long Barn. Snore—Snore—Snore.

Your Virginia

P. To T. has sold 915. What about your story?

Berg

1719: To Vanessa Bell   52 *Tavistock Sqre* [*W.C.*1]
18th Feb 1927

Dearest

I cant help thinking you sound a little dismal. I hope this is only my imagination—You would tell me, wouldn't you, if anything were worrying, or if I could do anything. Are you bothered about Duncan? I suppose the Grant menage is an awful trial. I cant imagine anything I should like less. On the whole, I think you'd better marry Duncan; divorce Clive, and set up a house in a new name. But your prejudice against marriage is too great.

Your Clive news intrigues me greatly. On your word of honour, you must be indiscreet and inform me of the true situation when he arrives. All I gather from seeing them at supper at 50 [Gordon Square] the other night is that they both seem rather depressed; but there is no outward change in their manner, and the company withdrew and left them alone as usual. I doubt that she will tell me any more, and I can't ask her here unless she suggests it. I expect you and I shall rank as her enemies in future. I can't help however—foolish as I may be—rather respecting her: she is unscrupulous, but takes her fences, as they say. She don't mind what she does. I expect he will be much happier with you.

Yes, I am shingled, or rather bingled. We got slightly merry the other night on Spanish wine, with Bobo [Mayor] and Clive; and she became very insinuating and seductive after dinner and implored me to let her try the effect. So I collapsed, egged on by Clive and Leonard, who seemed both to think that my own style of hair doing couldn't be worsened—I cant describe the delight when the long coil of cold hair fell off, and my neck was exposed. I think however hideous it makes me look it is worth it. Besides, the front remains the same; it is only that one has a partridges rump behind. It was none of Vita's doing, I can assure you. She made me swear not to, and says it will utterly ruin my appearance. All the same, though it loses me the love of sister, lover, and niece, I dont regret it. For you, of course, beautiful as you are, it is a different matter. These masterpieces should be left untouched. But then I was always a second rate work, and am now much the worse for wear, so it don't matter. Its the not having hair pins, and the giving it a brush and a wollop in the morning thats such a delight—Also travelling—

think of the mercy in trains and steamers. Perhaps you'll come to it—shocking though the thought is.

All the London hostesses are engaged in a curious skirmish about Desmond. He is said to be on the verge of a breakdown. Sibyl wants to get up a fund to give him a holiday: Chrissie and I to pay his debts. Happily I have now seceded, after setting them by the ears, and only hear from Chrissie how unreasonable Sibyl is, and from Sibyl how much she fears that Chrissie etc. etc I rather expect that the MacCarthys will be set up for life, and keep a motor in the end; We are much tempted by Cory [Clive's brother] to buy a second hand Morris or Citroen: the cost is under £200 probably; and he says one need not pay insurance or tax if left at Rodmell, where the shed will be quite enough. It remains then to make £200 by the Lighthouse. At the moment it seems to me inconceivably bad—in which case, it will be a success I daresay, like Bunny's book, about which Lytton, Raymond and I agree—it is unspeakably bad.

Lytton was up last week, as Carrington has been thrown from a horse and had they thought fractured her pelvis. It turns out to be bruises only, so they have gone back—He has thrown over Philip [Ritchie], I gather, and is on with Roger Senhouse,[1] whom he wants us to be nice to. He is almost imbecile I'm told; but rather attractive perhaps. Also I'm in the thick of another love affair—that tipsy rooks, J. W. Turner. He came to tea and confided: dont spread it beyond D's area; his wife Delphine is secretary at Claridges Gallery, so you may know her. He wants to have her for friend, and Cynthia Noble, Mrs Saxton Noble's beautiful and wealthy daughter for mistress. Will I see her and persuade her to take "an imaginative view of life?" That is what he wants. But I dont suppose she'll consent—She wants a large family and a house in Bayswater. It is a sad sign of middle age being confided in.

Oh we've got to dine with the Hendersons[2] now. Tell me all you can.

VW

Give Angelica my humble and obedient love. She's shingled herself, tell her: and her beauty is famous—I wish she would write to me.

Berg

1. Senhouse was in his early twenties, a remarkably attractive man, with whom Lytton fell deeply in love. It was Lytton's last major love affair. Senhouse became a partner in Secker & Warburg, the publishers, and the translator of Colette.
2. Hubert and Faith (*née* Bagenal). Henderson was the Editor of the *Nation & Athenaeum*.

1720: To Molly MacCarthy   52 *T.[avistock] S.[quare, W.C.1]*
Sunday [20 February 1927]

Dearest Molly,
    I'm quite unaware of all the faults you find: telephone, temper, manners, deportment, cleanliness, civility, a good heart, and an open hand. All I know is, you ring up 2 minutes before I leave the house on an errand of mercy, and peremptorily insist that I'm sitting with my hands in my lap before the fender! Chelsea always thinks Bloomsbury both idle and vicious. Whereas it's Chelsea that goes gallivanting to the south, and picks the roses in January.
    What Clive may have said I neither know nor care.
    Why don't you come and see me—not this week, when I shall be at Rodmell, seeing the plumber, but the week after, say tea, 4.30, *Tuesday, 1st March.* Then we can have at each other and Desmond and Bob [Trevelyan] and all our friends with kettle and tongs.

                                    faithful
                                    sorrowing
                    Yrs.   {   traduced
                                    old, antiquated
                                    friendly, long suffering
                                    Virginia Micawber Woolf

Sussex

1721: To Dorothy Bussy   [*52 Tavistock Square, W.C.1*]
22nd Feb. [1927]

Dear Dorothy,
    You are an indefatigable and kind woman—and no doubt you shall have an ice for your tea in June. I'm much relieved to hear that the translating is good. The translators begged me not to read it in the Revue de Genève[1] as it has been altered. But their version is coming out in a book soon. I've sent on your letter, and notes. A thousand thanks. I'm glad the original keeps well; but then I think you read with greater imagination than most.
    So goodbye till the 15th. Order your tea early. China or Indian? Gunters or Buzzards?

                                    Yours
                                    V.W.

Texas

1. The *Revue de Genève* published an abridged version of *Jacob's Room* translated by Claude Dravaine and Marie Kieffer, in three consecutive issues, December 1926, and January and February 1927.

336

1722: To V. Sackville-West   *Monks House, Rodmell*
                                     [Sussex]
Sunday, Feb 28th 1927

   Are you well? Are you happy? You wont go and leave poor Virginia
again will you, even if she does have her hair cut and looks a fright?
   No letters yet for nearly a fortnight. But perhaps one is waiting for me in
the wire basket at Tavistock Sqre. We are down here for the weekend, in a
flood of wet and wind. The snowdrops are out and the w.c. has broken and
Leonard and Percy Bartholomew are stamping about the garden in waterproofs and I'm sitting in the Lodge feeling rather cold. Mrs Bartholomew is
more draggly and wispy than ever—she fetches a long breath and goes on
talking interminably. Rose wouldn't cook for us because I had forgotten to
write to her. "If you dont think me worth a penny stamp" she kept saying
standing at her cottage door. But we pacified her and she cooks far far more
than we can eat. English village life seems to me stark raving mad—their
feuds, their jealousies, their suspicions—Oh and does it strike you that one's
friendships are long conversations, perpetually broken off, but always about
the same thing with the same person? With Lytton I talk about reading;
with Clive about love; with Nessa about people; with Roger about art; with
Morgan about writing; with Vita—well, what do I talk about with Vita?
Sometimes we snore—I must go in and crouch over the fire.
   It is rather a good fire: apple tree logs on top, coal underneath: an empty
armchair opposite. Oh Vita—if it weren't for the diplomacy, you might be
sitting there now! I wasted two days on headache last week, and couldn't
write—all my own fault for sitting up late talking I suppose; so next week I
am going to sit at home and see no one.
   My 'no clothes' dodge is working admirably. I was rung up yesterday by
a woman called Lady Dilke[1] who wanted me to give the Femina Vie
Heureuse prize to a Frenchman.[2] So I said I couldnt. And she said you must.
So I said I wouldnt and she said I should. So it struck me, well I'll say I've no
clothes. At which she paled and withered, and cried off instantly: it was to be
at Claridges in May. Also, I think I've got out of lunching with her on the
same plea. Its true too. Never shall I buy another skirt. Never shall I lunch
with Lady Dilke. Never shall I give a prize to a Frenchman. (And by the
way, for your information I may add that she said something about giving

1. Ethel, the daughter of Lucy Clifford, the novelist. She married Sir Fisher
   Wentworth Dilke, 4th baronet, in 1905.
2. There were two Femina prizes awarded annually, one to an English book
   and one to a French. In 1927 the English prize was given to Radclyffe Hall
   for her *Adam's Breed*, and the French prize to Marie le Franc for *Grand Louis
   l'Innocent*, translated as *The Whisper of a Name*.

337

me the prize[1] and I blushed all over, holding the telephone, with shame and ignominy. This is true. Snobbish? No: instinctive; right.)

52 Tavistock Square, W.C.1

Last page got wet with rain: then I went for a walk: now its Wednesday, and I did find your letter, and Dotties, in the wire cage; and I cheered up considerably. But I want lots more—volumes more. Anything you write, or think.

Look here, Vita, you must wring Harolds neck, if the worst comes to the worst. You have my sanction. A dead diplomat in a dust heap. You shant spend your entire life, or even the March's and Aprils, of your life being polite in the provinces: pouring out tea: putting on emeralds. No, no, you shant. Insect [Vita] says no. Puppy (she's on the arm of the chair, sniffing the paper) says no. Virginia says no.

I'm enveloped in Desmond's affairs. I write endless letters. I engage first Chrissie then Sibyl on the telephone. They are very tactful. They cross examine poor Molly about her debts. Is she extravagant? What can she live on? Clive embroils everybody by bawling across the table. Molly says she hates everyone. Chrissie hates Sibyl. Both despise me. After all its not much different from village life and Rose Bartholomew; but it takes up the devil of a time; and I cant think what I was going to say.

We have told Angus to go: but he wants to stay. So now we are trying to combine him and Mervyn Arnold Forster[2]—a dried up little man, who makes long long jokes. And we've bought a machine for putting on stamps, only if you joggle it, it puts on 3 stamps: has triplets, I say (I've been doing it all the afternoon) and Mrs C[artwright] is shocked. The press is very busy: all the envelopes are going out. P to T sold (I think) 929. A genius has sent me the most odious copy book, written on both sides in a crabbed hand: but its very good—a tour in Bohemia, by a Welshman.[3] And we have a vast poem, and a huge novel, and a monstrous memoir.

I doubt we shall get to Greece. It takes too long. Italy? Spain? France? Now they want me to go to America 'this Fall.' What am I to say? I wish I'd got it over now. But somewhere I must go: and sit outside a cafe and drink wine and eat paté de foie gras and hear a little Latin spoken.

Yes, darling honey, I am a misery without you. So dont, I beg, be foolish walking over mountains. If you break a leg, I break my heart, remember. Puppy says I must run her in the Square.

Write again, as soon as you can.

I did like your letter. And, following your orders (P to T) I read it so as

1. Virginia won the Prize in 1928 for *To the Lighthouse*.
2. See p. 311, note 2.
3. *Welshman's Way*, by Charles Davies (October 1927).

to elicit every grain, and could write an exposition of its meanings and submeanings in 20 volumes.

Yr Virginia

P.S. Wednesday night.
Your letter just come—About Greece—All our plans are hopelessly vague at the moment. Leonard anyhow has to be back in London on the 28th: Could you be earlier? No: I suppose not. Roger probably can't manage Greece. We'd almost decided on France. Its very tempting—A sublime idea. I'll consider. I'll write in a day or two. You see, I've promised to go to Vanessa, and that uses a week and we've only 4. But a divine thought. Greece. Gangway. Vita.[1]

Yr
Virginia

(Cold fish—ho ho!)

Berg

1723: To Vanessa Bell   [*52 Tavistock Square, W.C.1*]
[end February 1927]

Here you are—standing shoulder to shoulder with the Hon John Collier.[2]
I've just been to your show:[3] great admiration: will write detailed criticism of no great importance perhaps but never mind that in a day or two.
Please write

VW.

Berg

1724: To Julian Bell   52 *Tavistock Sqre* [*W.C.1*]
[early March 1927]

Dear Julian,[4]
We shall be passing through Paris on March 30th, I think, on our way

1. Vita had proposed that Virginia should meet her and Harold in Greece on 28 April, when Vita's ship docked in Piraeus: "I leave it to your imagination to reconstruct what it would mean to me if I saw you coming up that gangway" (Vita to Virginia, 19 February 1927, *Berg*).
2. The painter and writer on art (1850-1934). He was primarily a portraitist, but also contributed many 'problem pictures' to the Royal Academy exhibitions.
3. Vanessa's one-man show at 163 New Bond Street, the show-room of the London Artists' Association.
4. Julian, who was now 19, was spending nine months studying in Paris, between leaving school and going to Cambridge.

either to Greece or to Sicily. Anyhow, will you dine with us—Clive says we have time between trains. I'll let you know the exact facts later. But keep yourself free. We shan't spend the night. But coming back in April, about 27th or so, we shall; and then I hope to see you again for a longer time. Also perhaps Luce[1] will come, and then we can get to the bottom of this business about Webster.[2] Why Webster? God knows.

Nessa says you have a Crow to spill with me about my writing. She is rather muddled and fuddled, but if you have a merry thought to split, please send it at once. I will give it full attention. What are you up to? Writing? Reading? Eating? Drinking? Quentin and I have a rod in pickle for you.

Your affate
Virginia

Quentin Bell

1725: To Vanessa Bell   52 *Tavistock Square, W.C.*1

5th March 1927

Dearest,

I dont suppose there is anything more to say about the Clive affair. My impression is that he'd like to break, but as you say, chastity is not his line. We have now, at last, settled about our travels. We shall get to Cassis on Thursday 31st, and stay till Wednesday April 6th when we take boat for Sicily. So could you angelically take us two bedrooms or one with two beds, at the Cendrillon for that time? I suppose there are other hotels—in fact I know there are—if the Cendrillon is full: but we leave it to you. I suppose a sitting room is out of the question. However, we shall no doubt plant ourselves largely upon you. In fact I'm getting very morose and disconsolate without you and Angelica; whom I depend on entirely, I find, for congenial conversation: At this moment, in this pouring rain, I could be gossiping with you: much better than sitting here, writing interminable letters to the Eliot fund subscribers, who never answer. Still, theres your blessed art to be considered, I suppose. I'm rather nervous about criticising your pictures: I made such howlers with Rogers. I said I thought he'd improved vastly, whereupon, of course, every picture I praised had been painted 10 years ago. He only sold 3 I think; Porter 4.[3] The point about you is that you are now mistress of the phrase. All your pictures are built up of flying phrases. This

1. Gordon Hannington Luce, whose *Poems* the Hogarth Press had published in 1924. For many years he taught English in the University of Rangoon.
2. This probably refers to the newly published edition of John Webster's collected plays, edited by F. L. Lucas.
3. Roger Fry had exhibited with Frederick Porter at the Lefevre Gallery in February.

is to me a very exciting and congenial stage. They have an air of complete spontaneity. The downs seem to billow; yet the hay cart is perfectly substantial. I daresay your problem will now be to buttress up this lyricism with solidity. I pronounce no opinion on that. I think we are now at the same point: both mistresses of our medium as never before: both therefore confronted with entirely new problems of structure. Of course your colour intrigues me, seduces, and satisfies me exquisitely. I do not suppose that I get to the end of the maze by any means: my susceptibilities are freakish and wayward. At the Flemish show[1] (to explain my weakness) I liked the two Breugels (Icarus: and a storm: I'm not sure of the man's name) far better than anything. But what could one see? Only troops of clergy and schoolmistresses, four thick, writing crosses and noughts in their catalogues— What d'you think they do it for? —to give their friends? But to return: I should like you to paint a large, large picture; where everything would be brought perfectly firmly together, yet all half flying off the canvas in rapture. I have now said enough—The show was only just open: there was a youth praising Vanessa Bell—"always so interesting" (the defunctive Violet Dickinson writes that "V's pictures are splendid") and a more or less idiot boy who had never sent me a card. It is rather a dismal hole, I thought.

Yes, we see the Keynes' and the Frys. We gave up Greece with Roger, partly as he wanted to go when Helen could come, partly because as L. has to be back on 28th April, we should have rushed it—which seems silly, considering the cost. Next year—God, we've had more of these interminable Press conversations with Angus, and the result is that we are asking Mervyn Arnold Forster to come and see us, with a view to his being the Manager. Angus seems to agree that he dislikes managing, and Leonard feels that he hasn't got the gift: so we are trying to arrange that he shall stay on with Mervyn in some other capacity. He seems very reluctant to go. But as it is, we could never leave the Press for any length of time. He can't think of things—and either we must give it up, or try some professional. Mervyn is a dry stick: God knows.

Did I tell you of my visit from George [Duckworth]? He and the Percy Circus Pill maker came together. George was swollen, affable, overdressed, beyond belief. He can only mumble and had just fallen flat in Berkley Sqre and strained his back. He had been to see you, but only found an old gentleman and some pictures in the hall. "Ah yes I've seen Vanessa's curtains—I should think so! And do you embroider that kind of thing too? Does poor Leonard wear them out of doors? hah hah. I see you've gone in for decoration too! Look as if they'd not taken very long to do!—But perhaps they think them out beforehand." Then he told us interminable

---

1. *Exhibition of Flemish and Belgian Art* at the Royal Academy (8 January-5 March). The Breughel paintings which Virginia mentions are *Landscape with the Fall of Icarus* (1558) and *Storm at Sea* (1568).

stories to his own glory: how he's on some commission, and has cheques made out to him for £122,000: "to me, mark you, in my own name: all the taxpayers money!" So I said, "Well George they'll be making you a K.C.B. next." "Making me? I should rather think so. Why my name's been on the list these 12 years" I never saw anyone so completely self-satisfied; so insolent; so prosperous; so condescending. He never stopped chortling and laughing. The pill maker from Percy Circus—a good stolid servant girl—was taken short and retired to the W.C. I wish I liked buggers—Lytton is giving a party at the Ivy on Monday; and I know they'll be all of that persuasion—Duncan's all right; so's Morgan: but the insipidity of the rest passes belief.

Philip [Ritchie] came the other night. Oh Molly's in a great state—says she must get Desmond abroad: Is there a place called Moursian?

Yr B

I shall be very happy to see you.

Berg

1726: To V. Sackville-West   52 *Tavistock Square, W.C.*1

6th March 1927

Dearest Honey,

It was a treat to open the wire cage and find a long sealed letter from you. Yes of course I can translate your motto:[1] what did I waste my youth on? Latin and Greek. This year you seem to me, imaginatively, more unattainable; more pearled, powdered, white legged, gay, gallant and adventurous than ever. I can't imagine you in the basement, where old Cartwright scratches her head with her pen, and the floor gets dusty with atoms of brown paper, and Angus yawns over his cigarette, and the bagmen stand dripping wet and Pinker gnaws a bit of string, and the telephone rings, and we hear the thud of Pritchards clerks galloping up and down—etc—etc—etc Why did I launch into this description? It can't convey anything to you. Still—oh yes—I'm very fond of you, all the same—I lie in bed making up stories about you. Do send me a heap of facts: you know how I love a fact: what you had for dinner: and any scrap of real talk for instance between you and Harold, upon which I can build pinnacles and pagodas, all unreal as you justly remark. No we shan't manage Greece. Roger wants to go another time: 16 days is all we should have there: and so on and so on. As at present decided, we go to Cassis on the 30th, to Sicily by boat on the 6th, home by Rome, and shall be back the 28th. This is a nice enough trip, but the other would have had one splendid moment—on a gangway. But we should have

1. *Nos patriae fines et dulcia linquimus arva.* ('We have left the borders and dear fields of our native land.')

been hurried and hustled—so I console myself: seen only coasts in the distance: a German traveller would have interrupted: they would have made us play Bridge. Next year with Harold in Whitehall,—why not six weeks, dearest?

8th March I have had a quiet dull week—no parties, except one, which Lytton gave to seduce me into liking a pink boy of his—a new pink boy— called Roger Senhouse. I got slightly tipsy and chattered (at the Ivy): came home and chattered. The pink boy said he must apologise for being so dull, was half asleep, had been up till 6: but its no use: these buggers are always dull. Now why? Do they exhaust their charm in noses and so on? Otherwise I have read a great deal, and done up 20 dozen parcels.

Two strange women have come into my life—one called Ursula Greville, a bad singer,[1] I gather who feels that I could straighten her life, and asks me to come and see her in bed—shall I?—the other, Mrs Leake of the Albany.[2] But no. I want Vita: I want Insect: I want currant bun; twilight—oh and night too if you insist, with the birds singing and the stars rising. How romantic the Sackvilles are to be sure!

You see I couldn't tell you the central fact of Clive's affair—Mary forbade. So it lacked structure. But the fragments are there—simply he couldn't work, found passion unsatisfying, parties dull, remorse gnawed him, he said he must fly, asked my advice: I gave it. Fly, I said, to your book [Civilisation] and your green lamp. But why not here in London? said Mary. If he goes he'll forget me. It's you, she said, that want to break it, she said, turning on me with an ashen face and emerald eyes—(Yes, I love passion: and she's Vénus toute entière a sa proie attachée[3] without a doubt) Damned housemaid I said, flying into one of those rare passions which its said are terrible to see, out of my house, and so on. If I want love, I have it in Persia, I said: I dont want you and your street blown roses. Clive quailed between the two of us; and at length, shuffling and shallying, made off with his tail between his legs to write a history of civilisation at Cassis. So there you are: save for one fact, which has to do with the feminine physiology, and must die with me.

I'm writing about Morgan Forster: I'm writing about Lady Augusta Stanley and Miss Emily Davies; and about street walking; and about novels

1. English operatic and concert soprano.
2. Désirée Leake, whose husband, a chartered accountant, was on the Board of Trustees of Albany, the apartment building off Piccadilly. Virginia had met her at Zennor.
3. Racine, Phèdre, I, iii.

(in a vulgar rag called The Weekly Dispatch.)[1] None of these, thank God, will you see; and then my hundred's made: I'm well ahead with the world, and need write no more till the old fish, of whom I've told you—he's Gold, but has moulted several scales—his tails quite bald by the way, and he lost one eye in a fight with a Tench—rises to the top, and I net him.[2] Yes, I've thought of an entirely new book:[3] it may be two: Each more entirely new than the other. So my fortune gilds the future for me—if my father didn't leave me pearls, this was by way of a makeshift.

Gosse still says, only two weeks ago, "Ah Mrs Woolf! doesn't respect her father"

Darling Honey, what are you writing and saying, feeling, thinking, eating, drinking, even spitting; if it comes to that. Yes, you are solidly lodged in my heart—such as it is: the cold heart of a fish: (by the way, Pinker eats a cod's head in the Square, is sick under my bed, and I say, beaming, Dearest Vita!) I'm asking Louise[4] to have Pinker for a month. Does this matter?

I'll catch every possible post. And you will too?

I'll give you addresses next week.

Yr
Virginia

I left this open, hoping for my letters in the cage. None. Only a long, scented illegible effusion from Ottoline. Curse!

Berg

1727: To Lady Ottoline Morrell

52 Tavistock Square, W.C.1

Sunday [6 March 1927]

Dearest Ottoline,

I wish I could come on Thursday, but Ethel Sands is coming here, so I'm afraid its impossible. I'm so sorry. I should have like to.

1. Virginia's articles were: *The Novels of E. M. Forster* (*Atlantic Monthly*, November 1927); Review of *Emily Davies and Girton College*, by Lady Stephen, and *Letters of Lady Augusta Stanley*, edited by the Dean of Windsor and Hector Bolitho (*Nation & Athenaeum*, 23 April 1927); *Street Haunting: a London Adventure* (*Yale Review*, October 1927); *What Is a Novel?* (*Weekly Dispatch*, 27 March 1927).
2. Cf. *Orlando*, p. 282: "Always it flies fast out to sea and always I fling after it words like nets . . . and sometimes there's an inch of silver—six words—in the bottom of the net. But never the great fish who lives in the coral groves."
3. *The Jessamy Brides*. See *A Writer's Diary* for 14 March 1927.
4. Vita's French maid Louise Genoux.

Tom Eliot [fund] again—but positively the last time.

There is an odd sum of £2.14.8. left over, which if you agree I propose to add to the cheque for Oliver's man, and so I have made out a new one.

Could you sign this?

A thousand apologies and thanks

Yr
V.W.

Texas

1728: To Lady Ottoline Morrell

[52 *Tavistock Square, W.C.*1]

[8 March 1927]

Dearest Ottoline, ·

I am so sorry I made a mistake—I enclose the right cheque.

Also I have heard from Mr Schiff,[1] so would you sign him too.

About £20 now remains without an owner. The man who gave it is said to be dead, and his daughter refuses to take it. What are we to do? But I'll have one more shot at finding him. Then there will be only one more.

Yes, I expect the stones of Bloomsbury to flower in red and gold when you come [to Gower Street].

Your affec
Virginia Woolf

Texas

1729: To Quentin Bell

52 *Tavistock Square W.C.*1

Sunday [13 March 1927]

My dear Quentin,

Would it be agreeable to you if I came down next Saturday?[2] *Let me know.* I would come in the afternoon: We would take a Bus into the furthest wilds of Berkshire: returning in time for a substantial tea. Then we would look at the Bookshops, also at the Curiosity shops. Meanwhile we would discuss our next masterpiece. The question is how can we give the utmost possible pain to everyone concerned?

Please write me a long letter, with all the scandal and gossip. I am practically the sole inhabitant of Bloomsbury as all our friends have gone abroad. Duncan has not yet found the pen, so he cannot write to me.

---

1. See p. 10, note 1.
2. Quentin Bell, now 16, was at Leighton Park School, near Reading.

What do you think of the state of China? To me it looks a bloody black business, with 6d on the income tax.

Please ANSWER.

Yrs
Virginia

Quentin Bell

1730: To V. Sackville-West   52 *Tavistock Sqre, W.C.*1

Tuesday, March 15 1927

I spent yesterday you'll be glad to hear because you are an Ogre if ever there was one, in the depths of gloom. The mousetrap filled itself and refilled itself—never a letter from you—none for a fortnight. Even Mrs Cartwright noticed my melancholy and offered me a plain bun. At last, just as hope seemed extinct, and the waters of despair were shut above my head sitting over the gas fire two arrived; full as nuts; delicious; milky, meaty, satisfying every desire of my soul, except darling, for a complete lack of endearments.[1] See how naturally my 'darling' drops out. To punish you, I shant call you honey once this letter. So there. Oh yes, Vita, I'm more subtle than you think for [me?]. Read between the lines, donkey West; put on your horn spectacles, and the arid ridges of my prose will be seen to flower like the desert in spring: cyclamens, violets, all a growing, all a blowing.

I shall attend the Hawthornden Prize giving if possible—Should be soon.

This very moment a young man—39 I suppose though—has just left the room with these identical words on his lips. "I say, is V. Sackville West the same person as Mrs Nicolson? I've just read "The Land," Its a master-piece—a classic—the best poem of our age. I dont know when I enjoyed a book so much. And whats so exciting is that I'm going to teach her little boys at Summerfields."[2] My face fell—I was furiously jealous. This was Mervyn Arnold-Forster, who may become our partner (you'll agree he ought to be a publisher—and by God, we'll get your next poem out of you—see if we dont) He's doing schoolmaster for a term. Ben and Nigel will catch some of your glory I hope. Really he's a sensible little creature, dry as

1. Vita had omitted any opening endearment in her letter to Virginia of 23 February. On receiving this reply from Virginia, she immediately answered: "I always get devastated when I hear from you. God, I do love you. You say I use no endearments. That strikes me as funny, when I wake in the Persian dawn, and say to myself, 'Virginia—Virginia'" (Vita to Virginia, 30 March 1927, *Berg*).

2. Summer Fields, a preparatory school on the outskirts of Oxford. Arnold-Forster died before he took up this post.

a biscuit, with a passion for fields and hedges. I think he's going to come to us. But say nothing to nobody—dont go blurting Hogarth Press secrets to the Bachtiaris.[1] I shouldn't take your sterility much to heart, if I were you. One's mind wants to lie under the leaves and let them rot on top. Solitude is the one thing I want to write about. Lets see how differently we do it. Dotty also wrote. I rather flinch at 15 miles a day for 14 days; but I daresay its all in your stride. I must warn you that if you come back lean as a flail and brown as a berry, with any damage to body or brain, I shall no longer respect you; I shall come back plump as a partridge and red as a rose—a very different matter. I'm going to do nothing but sit in the sun, eat hugely, and watch landscapes. Thats the way I travel. Looking, looking, looking and making up phrases to match clouds. It is the passion of my life. You cant think how dry and gravelly my mind gets when I dont take it to the South where things have a dash of red and blue to them, and dont wobble in pale grease as they do here.

Do *not* buy me a coat. As you know I utterly refuse and abominate presents; and I dont want to spend a penny on clothes this summer. Last summer I spent £12.10: this summer 6½d. I want to buy carpets and beds for Rodmell. I'm that sick of making money I'd rather walk into Argyll House [Sibyl Colefax's house] naked, than earn another guinea. But if you have bought it, of course I'll joyfully flaunt in it, in the Haymarket, d'you remember, in the dusk. Sibyls dropped me. Everybody's gone—no, there's Eddy coming to tea—We linger like ghosts in a world of incredible beauty— I take back my insult to England. I've just been buying cigarettes in the Tottenham Court road—rivers of silver, breasted by plumes of gold: omnibus and shops equally beautiful—Why go to Persia when the T. Ct. Rd. is like that? Now Roger wants to go to Greece—too late. We've plunged for a week at Cassis, then Sicily, then Rome. About addresses—We shall be at the Hotel CENDRILLON CASSIS FRANCE, from March 30th to April 6th.* Then by boat to Palmero. But I'm not sure of dates or hotels so you'd better write to Tavistock Sqre. after that and they'll forward. Do write, any scrap. I shall count on it. I know there'll be a fortnights break. Damn you Vita, why do you insist upon taking the world by the scruff of its neck and shaking it? Why these great and gallant ways? being so adventurous and athletic and spartan? So we lose a fortnights friendship.

Talking of my subtlety and the disguises it puts on my respect for you,† I tell you this story—a true one—We were asked to a party by Todd. We

* No: you cant get this in time to write to Cassis, I suppose
† (hah hah! who said 'respect' once?)

1. The Bakhtiari tribe migrated annually through the mountains of southern Persia. Vita, with Harold and Gladwyn Jebb, walked for twelve days through these mountains to the Persian Gulf, and described the journey in her book *Twelve Days* (Hogarth Press, 1928).

were dining near by: when we stood at her door, what decided me not to go in? Not Leonards exhortations to come back to bed; but my certainty that Raymond would come up to me, kind and grave, and say, kindly and gravely. You've heard of Vita's accident? To avoid this, I came home.

Wednesday March 16

Heaven's be praised! Another letter from you just found in the cage! A very very nice one: all about splinters of my mind. Dearest honey (damn, there its out) dont be glooming about not writing poetry. I like your prose. Eddy's coming in a moment. Shall I lecture him about his party? I'll be highly discreet.

All news seems too unreal to send. You can't be interested in my dinners and teas, nor am I much; nor in Clive's heart; nor in anything but the depths of the soul, which I've no time to fish up. It must all seem incredibly silly and thin. Not my respect though: thats all right, I can assure you. Crush this in your fingers as you walk over the hills, and float on a swollen goat skin. I'm glad Dotty dont pan out well in the East. Bloomsbury's the right training for Persia. Yes I'm perfectly well: was rather headachy and had a sore throat; and recovered completely; and Lydia Keynes said she'd never seen me look better last night. But then she admires my shingled head. I dont. Its like the hind view of a frightened hen partridge.

My dear, I must stop.

Please Vita as you love me take care of yourself on the Expedition (curse it) Tell Harold he must be careful of you, and not let you go on if you're tired. What about the Bloody Flux and all the rest of it?

Now darling honey (its out) goodbye

Yr
Virginia

1731: To Vanessa Bell   [52 *Tavistock Square, W.C.1*]

Wednesday [16 March 1927]

We thought you knew what to do[1]—The same as Mrs Dalloway, I suppose. You have to put Harcourts name and the price—both the same. But perhaps you cd. alter the jacket I sent. I sent their address at once.

383 Madison Avenue
New York.

That is it.

Will you deal with them direct?

A thousand thanks to Duncan for his enchanting effusion. Eddy and I

1. Vanessa was designing the jacket for the American edition of *To the Lighthouse*.

get together and mouth his phrases. As for the chorus of praise wh. is sung in your and D's honour—I cant abear it. Never could

Will write in a day or two.

Hope to see Q. on Saturday.

V.W.

Berg

1732: TO VANESSA BELL   52 *Tavistock Square, W.C.*1

Sunday 20th March 1927

Dearest,

I dont know how your sense of justice reconciles itself to asking me for 20 pages when you send me one, written on a kind of Bromo too, However; let me see, I have several things to tell you—First, I went down to see Quentin yesterday, he having been impounded the week before for roof climbing I think. We had a walk by the river and a good deal of gossip. He said I was to tell you that he was following in his elder brother's footsteps—ragging, I gather. He seemed very well, very tall, cropped like a convict, rather bored with school I thought, and wanting to talk about pictures. We had tea and he met several cronies but said he did not want to talk to them. He was going to a Debating Society dinner so ate a comparatively small tea. We went to the movies, and he was very scornful of a great seduction scene in China. We also talked a great deal about our next satire: He was very charming as usual, and if anything older and better informed than I am. We cracked the usual jokes about the Keynes'. We dined there [at 46 Gordon Square] the other night, by the way. Lydia and Harland [servant] between them have consummated the decoration of the drawing room by picking up at a sale some primrose coloured satin curtains, sprinkled with violet wreaths, which hang tight and shiny across the windows and are met by a sky blue carpet of the thickest pile. Your ceiling decorations have been whitewashed; several 18th century candelabras from Maples' imported and the whole effect is bright and tight and shiny as you could wish. But Maynard is apparently conscience stricken about luxury, and gave us no wine, a poor dinner, and only old broken springed lodging house chairs to sit in. They are off to Tilton; how you must be looking forward to your tennis parties in the summer!

Then a voice on the telephone recalled me 30 years at a leap the other day. Something mincing, powdered, affected, vulgar, effusive, fawning,—who do you think? Ethel Dilke! She wanted me to lunch with her and give a prize to a Frenchman. But I promptly invited her here for a date unknown, and so shall escape—unless you insist upon a rapprochement. Then we dined

349

with the Sangers, and who should be there but an incredibly touzled, long coated woman—blurred—bleared—smudged—muted—like a wingless bluebottle—old Dobbin and her husband.[1] I took strongly against her, though no doubt she is harmless enough. She has taken up furniture decoration, and her finger nails have permanently suffered.

Roger of course changed his mind, as soon as we had taken rooms at Cassis, and would have gone to Greece. This is remitted till next year, when a large party is going for several weeks, you'll be glad to hear. Duncan has refused, if I am of the party. I bear him no grudge. I submit to all his spites. People say that he is a great genius. Who am I that I should complain?

Then Dick Strachey[2] has got his girl with child and has had to marry her. As for the Hogarth Press, some strange compromise too difficult to explain, has been arrived at. I rather think Mervyn A. F. [Arnold-Forster] will become Manager in the autumn. Mrs Cartwright is decidedly queer, and I hope in time to supplant her by Rachel MacCarthy[3] who is exquisite merry and like a lustre tea pot to look at. The MacCarthys of course being on their beam ends gave us a magnificent dinner of 7 courses the other night. Desmond was in great spirits; is going to Contrexéville to do a cure, and then to Italy in May; The fund is already about £350 I think but he says he intends to regard it merely as a loan. He has prospects of great wealth in the near future.

Do you want me to do anything or bring anything? If so, write. I want to bring a little cadeau to ingratiate myself with Angelica—Is there anything she wants? I count the days till we leave. Society here has become intolerable —save for Edith Sitwell who was fascinating the other day—very beautiful —and full of astonishing stories about her mothers frauds: how she was made to catch bluebottles as a child and so on: otherwise I pine for the society of Cassis, which seems to me perfect: I rather wish we were spending all our time there—Can we go to Toulon? Can we buy some furniture? some china? Now I must do my Italian lesson on the gramophone—

Yr B.

I am asking Julian to dine with us on our way through Paris. He wrote me a very nice letter about Luce and Webster (the poet—there was a poet called Webster once.)

Berg

1. Mary Creighton, daughter of Mandell Creighton, Bishop of London.
2. Richard P. F. Strachey, Lytton's nephew, aged 24. He married Frances Esmé Rudd.
3. Daughter of Desmond and Molly MacCarthy. She later married David Cecil.

1733: To Lytton Strachey   [52 *Tavistock Square, W.C.*1]
[21 March 1927]

Could you be so angelic as to tell us the name of the hotel in Rome? any other information gratefully received.

I'm afraid I seemed rather brusque—not sympathetic last night—owing to circumstances. I do feel that love is such a horror I would advise anyone to break off. But I see the difficulties. I hope to make the young man's [Roger Senhouse] acquaintance when we come back.

We have collapsed under typhoid—I verge on 102—is it worth it? I wonder. So goodbye—

V.W.

Strachey Trust

1734: To Julian Bell   52 *Tavistock Sqre W.C.*1
[23? March 1927]

My dear Julian,

Will you meet us next Wednesday at 7.15 outside the door of the Restaurant at the P.L.M. station—Perhaps you know a good place to dine or we could dine there.

I have been entirely miserable with typhoid germs too or I would have written. It seems to me an evil superstition—probably useless.

I dont follow Professor Luce on Webster—but hope to see him some time and get to the bottom of it.

Please offer him my love if he does not think it presumptuous.

I saw Quentin last week. He had been roof climbing, bed wrecking and otherwise enjoying himself. He said he was following his elder brother's steps.

Have you got your lampoon? Ours is withering in the highest degree, I must warn you.

Your
Virginia

Quentin Bell

1735: To V. Sackville-West   52 *Tavistock Sqre* [*W.C.*1]
March 23rd 1927

Dearest Honey,

Are you well? Did you enjoy the [Bakhtiari] walk? Were you drowned, shot, raped, tired? Lord! I'd give a good deal to know. But the silly thing is that I'm writing before you've even left Teheran, I suppose. What I pretend to be past is all in the future. Yet to you, reading this, its over. All very confusing, and pray God I may never have to write to you in Persia again.

How you'd laugh to see me stretched out comatose recovering from two

351

days high temperature—all owing to inoculations, and my principles—I know I deserve it. I urged you so lightly into it—how little I pitied you—and now you shall laugh at me. How I wish you'd walk into the room this moment, and laugh as much as you like.

Why do I think of you so incessantly, see you so clearly the moment I'm in the least discomfort? An odd element in our friendship. Like a child, I think if you were here, I should be happy. Talking to Lytton the other night he suddenly asked me to advise him in love—whether to go on, over the precipice, or stop short at the top. Stop, stop! I cried, thinking instantly of you. Now what would happen if I let myself go over? Answer me that. Over what? you'll say. A precipice marked V.

I had a visit from Edith Sitwell whom I like. I like her appearance—in red cotton, many flounced, though it was blowing a gale. She has hands that shut up in one's own hands like fans—far more beautiful than mine. She is like a clean hare's bone that one finds on a moor with emeralds stuck about it. She is infinitely tapering, and distinguished and old maidish and hysterical and sensitive. She told me awful Brontë stories about being cursed by her mother as a child and made to kill blue bottles in a hot room. I like talking to her about her poetry—she flutters about like a sea bird, crying so dismally. But honey, can one make a new friend? Can one begin new intimate relations? Dont mistake me. No precipice in this case—Only I was discussing friendship with Morgan Forster. One cannot follow up human relations any more he said. Theres Dante to read. Solitude—ones soul. He is half a monk. An elderly bugger is always something of a priest. Leonard went down to Sevenoaks with puppy. Louise [Genoux] met him and Leonard was very downcast Puppy didn't seem to mind going he said. Half laughing I said I'd ring up and ask after her. He took it quite seriously. This shows where you've led us in dog worshipping. He thinks she's hermaphrodite: Lizzy has the flux: puppy still hermetically sealed.

Sunday 27th

The germs are clearing off: so you shan't laugh any longer. But I'm being as careful as a cat on eggs in terror lest I shouldn't be able to start on Wednesday—you know what Leonard is. A visit from Eddy, and a talk about promiscuity. He deplores the taste as much as you do. He swears by love himself. I gather he is becoming the other way inclined, or balances between the two. He is wildly romantic, dreams I'm sure, of princesses with violet hair, leaning out of mullioned windows, scribbles endlessly, has boundless belief in himself, and in 20 dozen other people too.

Look here—will you come to Oxford on May 18th, and lecture some undergraduates?, on poetry and fiction, I think.[1] I agreed, at Eddy's per-

1. Virginia spoke at St Hugh's College, Oxford. Her lecture was subsequently published as *Poetry, Fiction and the Future* (*New York Herald Tribune*, 14 August 1927).

suasion—the charm of his absurdly serious literary views. As if I—or anyone—did any good by being set up to chatter for an hour about impassioned prose—I'm banging about this way and that like a ship at anchor in a rough sea. Millions of things have to be done before we start. The question of the book shop has started again—we may get it very likely. I've had to buy skirts, hats, shoes, boxes, mackintoshes. I find myself in the wrong department. I dream. I saunter. People trample on me—they inflict the most dreadful insults at Marshall and Snelgroves. Its humiliating to be in the Babies Sock Dept. when one wants Ladies handbags. The Dr's been, and refuses firmly, to give me another dose. So I shall go half oculated: but I stuck up for my principles all the same. I'm in robust health. I get so excited, dreaming of Paestum, Segesta, the Campagna, Palermo, first sight of Sicily and so on. Oh and about the Hawthornden—take it for granted that they are putting off the presentation till you come back. It must be so: or they would have given it already. Your mother writes me long letters on slips of paper with holes through the corners about love and death and you and Ebury Street[1] and money. I answer suitably—rather more 19th than 18th Century now: profuse, romantic. Imagine us prancing and caracolling together; but like a pair of courting butterflies, never coming very close together.

Tuesday [29 *March*]

Oh damn, Vita—no letter at all. This is the first bag you've missed since you've been away. And for me the worst, because now I shan't hear till goodness knows when—what can have happened? Illness? But then you'd have written and said nothing: or I'd have heard. I don't suppose you're angry. Then you must have gone on an Expedition, or the bag is late. And I'm off early tomorrow without a word. I assure you, this does sadden me rather. You seem utterly disappeared, at the moment. I'll write to Cyprus. You seem gone, gone, for ever. But dear honey write to Tavistock Sqre all the same, and forgive this execrably scrawled letter. They will forward.

Are you well? Are you happy?

(No, I don't for a moment suppose your angry—its the malice of fate, thats all: and I daresay I'll hear by the ordinary post on Wednesday)

Yr
Virginia

We leave Cassis for Sicily on the 6th by Boat from Marseilles: wander about Sicily for a fortnight: then a week in Rome—Back April 28th.

Berg

1. Lady Sackville's house in London.

24th March [1927]

Dearest Molly,

I have been asked to send you the enclosed cheque for £300 which your and Desmond's friends hope you will both spend on taking a complete holiday abroad for three months.

Nobody wants to be thanked or named or to have any notice taken of this whatsoever, but only that Desmond and you shall get away and have a good rest. As for Desmond's thought of repaying, that will be thought nothing short of an insult.

I'm afraid I shan't see you before we go, but I implore you to remember the existence of the inkpot and pen, and let me know what happens to you, whether you fall into a crater, or kiss the Pope's nose, or whatever it may be.

I am finding great consolation for innumerable typhoid germs in the poetry of Cowper.

I can't tell you how much affection I haven't heard expressed for you and Desmond during the last few weeks—to which I've added a few lugubrious stanzas of my own.

Your attached
V.W.

Sussex

Sunday [27 March 1927]

Dont bother about a taxi—we will come by the Bus, as we shan't bring more than we can carry. I hope not having an evening dress wont cut me off from Cassis society to which I look forward with passion.

Your caryatids have come—and greatly improve my room—The old char is a little surprised. They only just get in.

Roger lectured for 2 hours at the Queens Hall to 2,000 people and was a great success, but I had the typhoid germs strongly and couldnt go. I'll keep the news of the quarter though, so that you may have some motive for wishing to see me.

No tea, no paints come yet, but I'll take steps if they dont.

Adrian, Helen and Roger are about to drop in:

I'm very excited already and have just been putting all my clothes on the floor—that is the beginning of packing, I suppose.

354

Julian is dining with us on Wednesday.
We'll come up on Thursday I daresay—

Yr B.

We are of course travelling on the same boat as Ethel [Sands], Nan [Hudson], and Raymond [Mortimer].

Berg

1738: To Violet Dickinson   52 *Tavistock Square, WC*1

Typewritten
Sunday 27th March [1927]

My Violet,
     I am ashamed never to have answered you before, but I am so sick of writing. I shall give it up. It bores me beyond belief. You see I can no longer use a pen. However I should very much like to know how you are. Nelly [Cecil] says she has seen you, and you walk about spit, swear, pick up your skirts and run after donkeys along the sands of Brighton. Lady Sackville watches you through a pair of highly ornamented glasses from her terrace. It sounds to me so unreal that I should be perfectly in my element. Lady S. writes me pages and pages—about secretaries, Ebury Street, Vita, death, life, food, money—in pencil on narrow pages with a hole through them, such as middle class women I think use (I am middle class but I never buy my own beef) to write down how many pounds of beef they must buy. Being ill is rather nice in some ways: it brings one in to touch with oddities. I have been having, not an illness, but an experiment with typhoid germs before going to Italy which has reduced me from spry middle age to senile decay in three hours and a half. They squirt a little sticky juice into one's arm; next moment one has a temperature of 102 and can't move, think, read, or laugh. I am only just emerging.
     But I thought of many odd people, you and Lady S. and Katie [Cromer] whom I sat next to at a Mozart opera the other night. She has bought a complete charwoman's outfit, bonnet, boots, shawl and all; but forgotten that nature provided a Greek Goddess for the head piece; there she sat more incongruous than you can think, in the middle of the stalls, and never noticed me. It is a most effective style of course; had there been Lady Diana [Cooper] present in all her pearls she would infallibly have looked like a—the word is improper, I will not use it. Are you back in Manchester Street? We are off on Wednesday to Nessa at Cassis; to Naples, to Sicily to Paestum, to Rome and so home—ruined, but happy. I will try to learn how one writes. I hope you will by then be better than you have ever been in your life.
     Leonard's love   Yr VW.

Berg

355

Sunday March 27th [1927]

My dear Edith,

I'm not going to write to you about your poems[1]—I'm going to talk to you about them. They interest me greatly: I dip in and pick up something that makes me spend 20 minutes staring at the fire, inventing theories about you. Are you changing? Then where are you going? And what sort of loveliness are you reaching down from your strange and very high trees? I ask myself question after question; but I warn you, there are many more to come, more intelligent than these, I hope to Heaven, for I am only dipping into you as yet: I've been rather wretched ever since I saw you with a temperature caused by typhoid inoculation. This leaves one no vigour of mind, so I dont pretend to read you. I shall, though. Then you will come and talk to me I hope. I will talk to you for hours about your poetry. Did that little grocer Gosse write about you? In a rage, I cancelled his paper:[2] but I wish I had seen what he said—

I did enjoy your visit the other day. I hope you will come often again. It would be a great pleasure. Of course you are a good poet: but I cant think why. The reason may strike me in Sicily.

Yr
V W.

By the way, the Hogarth Press wants you to write another pamphlet.[3] Will you?

Berg

Typewritten
29th March 1927

Dear Miss McAfee

You were so kind as to ask me to send you an occasional article. I have written the enclosed [*Street Haunting*] which you may perhaps like to have

---

1. *Rustic Elegies*, 1927.
2. In 1918 Edmund Gosse began to write weekly literary articles for the *Sunday Times*, and continued them until his death in 1928.
3. The Press had published Edith Sitwell's *Poetry and Criticism* in 1925.

for the Yale Review. If so, I should be much obliged if you would tell me when you propose to publish it so that I may arrange for simultaneous publication over here.

With kind regards,
yours sincerely
Virginia Woolf

Yale University

Letters 1741-1748 (April 1927)

Virginia and Leonard left London on 30 March for a month's holiday in France and Italy. They went by train, through Paris to Cassis on the Mediterranean, where they spent a week with Vanessa, Duncan and Clive. Then on to Rome for a day, and so to Sicily, basing themselves on Palermo and Syracuse. On the return leg, they stopped in Rome again, this time for a week. They were back in London on 28 April. Virginia had enjoyed the holiday immensely. When in France, she thought of throwing up their London life to live at Cassis for half the year; when in Rome it was to be the Campagna. But unlike Vanessa and Duncan, who bought and converted a house at Cassis the next year, the Woolfs never owned a place abroad.

1741: To V. Sackville-West   *Villa Corsica, Cassis*
                                     [France]
Tuesday, 5th April [1927]

I was in a towering passion—Clive had a long letter from Harold, I none from you. For some inscrutable reason after 4 days two arrived from you and one from Dotty. This has assuaged my rage, which threatened to make our journey one black and bitter pilgrimage of despair. I was very unhappy.

I am writing, with difficulty, on a balcony in the shade. Everything is divided into brilliant yellow and ink black. Clive is seated at a rickety table writing on huge sheets of foolscap, which he picks out from time to time in red ink. This is The history of Civilisation. He has by him Chamber's Dictionary of the English Language. We all sit in complete silence. Underneath, on the next balcony, Vanessa and Duncan are painting the loveliest pictures of rolls of bread, oranges, wine bottles. In the garden, which is sprinkled with saucers of daisies, red and white, and pansies, the gardener is hoeing the completely dry earth. There is also the Mediterranean—and some bare bald grey mountains, which I look at, roasting in the sun, and think Vita is climbing over hills like that at this moment. I hope your rubber shoes are doing well. Talk of solitude—I think your analysis highly subtle (oh yes and you're a clever donkey West: an original donkey: for all your golden voice, which has the world by the ears) It is the last resort of the civilised: our souls are so creased and soured in meaning we can only unfold them when we are alone. So Leonard thinks; and is determined to buy a farm house here and live alone, with me, half the year. It may be our form of religion. But then what becomes of friendship, love, intimacy? Nessa says, suddenly, she has been wondering why one is supposed to attend to people.

Other relations seem to her far more important. I say, thats what Vita says in her letter this morning. Heard from Vita? says Clive, pricking up his ears, like a war horse, out at grass—(for he has renounced the world, and puts water in his wine, and looks incredibly pink and fresh) Yes, I say. And off we go, discussing you and Harold and Dottie, whom we gather, (Clive and I that is) is not altogether cut out for the life of a diplomatists friend in Teheran. This may be over subtle, and malicious, on our part. But you know what Clive is, and Virginia too, when they get together.

Then Colonel Teed and Miss Campbell come to lunch—he a retired cavalry officer, she his mistress: both together vine growers, living in a divine 17th Century manor house, set with cypresses, painted, tiled, with tanks of frogs and Roman aqueducts. Miss Campbell was sitting in the dusk listening to the frogs last night when we went there. So there we all sat quite silent; and then the frogs began again; and the Colonel made us come in and drink several different kinds of wine in his great empty room, and we were given bunches of wild tulips, Vita, and why don't we all live like that, Vita? —and never go back to Bloomsbury any more? You meet a Miss Brown here, and she says her eldest son is 17. Yes. She has three children by the Italian singing master in Genoa. Madame Labrotte was afflicted with a gigantic tumour—had all the doctors of London and Paris to consult—came to Cassis to recuperate and was delivered, at the age of 50, in one quarter of an hour, of a child. That is our atmosphere—slightly detached, from reality—or Argyll House: mute: they are all painters: every street corner has an elderly gentleman on a camp stool; austere; The sink of the bath has to be filled with flannel: Clive does it for me: I stand in a chemise with jugs of cold water, since the pipe is blocked. Our grand extravagance is wine, which the peasants sell, and Clive and Duncan fetch in great baskets, dressed in cotton clothes, with rope slippers: Duncan smuggles brandy in, and so we sit, talking, for hours—now we are off to Sicily, not alas by the Pierre Loti which has sunk or disappeared, but by train, early tomorrow.

I am all the time thinking about poetry and fiction and also of Vita: and the Insect. The best piece of news I have had is that Harold is in travail.[1] Say nothing: his own good sense will deliver him. But then you must persuade Leonard not to embrace the religion of solitude in Provence. In her latest letter your mother says you are thinking of living near me in Bloomsbury. I assume that this is merely your mothers exquisite good manners—Live near me in Provence: we will sit under the cypresses and drink wine, and you shall write poetry—which by the by I'm going to tell the Oxford Undergraduates is a hobbled, shackled tongue tied vehicle now for the voice of the soul, which—did you know it?—now speaks in prose.

1. Vita told Virginia that she observed "a struggle going on in Harold". In fact, he had decided to resign from diplomacy, and applied for a job with the Anglo Persian Oil Company. When he did not get it, he remained in the Foreign Service.

Now I'm going to stop; rather tipsy in the head after lunching in the hotel. And oh damn! a familiar sound floats up from the courtyard—I look out and see, at a little table, Julia Strachey, Tommie,[1] and Douglas Davidson! The shades of the prison house descend. I trust we don't meet Raymond and Ethel in Palermo.

Please darling honey come back safe. We will have a merry summer: one night perhaps at Long Barn: another at Rodmell: We will write some nice pieces of prose and poetry: we will saunter down the Haymarket. We will *not* dine at Argyll House. We will snore.

1. Virginia is completely spoilt by her shingle.
2. Virginia is completely made by her shingle.
3. Virginia's shingle is quite unnoticeable.

These are the three schools of thought on this important subject. I have bought a coil of hair, which I attach by a hook. It falls into the soup, and is fished out on a fork.

Are you well?

Virginia

My last letter, thank God.

Berg

1742: To Vanessa Bell   *Hotel de France, Palermo*
                                          [Sicily]
9th April 1927

Dearest,

Will there be a special allowance for letters written under circumstances of great difficulty? If so, this one must be paid at a rate of 17 inches by $8\frac{3}{4}$: oil: canvas: still life.[2] We are sitting in our bedroom after dinner. The light is suspended in thick glass some feet above my head. Leonard is dusting the table with his bandanna. I have made an awful mess with various odds and ends accumulated during my travels: several packets of cigarettes for instance have been ground to powder. There are explosions going on in the street and a general buzz and hum which rather entice me to step out into the Square and go to the movies; but we are off to Segesta[3] early tomorrow so we are having a quiet night. However, they are at this moment marching through the Square, playing a band, with lanterns, and some sacred object under a panoply—It is Easter, I suppose—I like the Roman Catholic religion. I say it is an attempt at art; Leonard is outraged—We burst into a service of little

1. Stephen Tomlin. He married Julia Strachey, a daughter of Lytton's brother Oliver, in July of this year.
2. In return for Virginia's letters, Vanessa had promised her a painting.
3. The Doric temple, late 5th century B.C., a few miles from Palermo.

girls in white veils this morning which touched me greatly. It seems to me simply the desire to create gone slightly crooked, and no God in it at all. Then there are little boys brandishing palms tied in red ribbon and sugar lambs everywhere—surely rather sympathetic, and to me more attuned than those olive trees which the old gentlemen are for ever painting at street corners in Cassis.

Looking out of the carriage window at Civita Vecchia, whom should we see, sitting side by side on a bench, but D. H. Lawrence and Norman Douglas[1]—unmistakable: Lawrence pierced and penetrated; Douglas hog-like and brindled—They were swept off by train one way and we went on to Rome. I am sure Rome is the city where I shall come to die—a few months before death however, for obviously the country round it is far the loveliest in the world. I dont myself care so much for the melodramatic mountains here, which go the colour of picture postcards at sunset; but outside Rome it is perfection—smooth, suave, flowing, classical, with the sea on one side, hills on the other, a flock of sheep here, and an olive grove. There I shall come to die; and I suggest, as an idea you may consider, the foundation of a colony of the aged—Roger, you, Lytton, I: all sunken cheeked, tottering and urbane, supporting each others steps along Roman roads; I dont mind if one does die at the street corner: you with a beautiful handkerchief over your head (how ashamed you made me feel of my poor partridges rump!) and the rest of us with large sticks in our hands. A death colony will certainly become desirable. However we only had time to see the Coliseum and to eat a vast dish of maccaroni. Then we crossed over to Palermo by night and I shared a cabin with an unknown but by no means romantic Swedish lady who complained that there was no lock on the door, whereupon I poked my head out from the curtains and said in my best French "Madame, we have neither of us any cause for fear" which happily she took in good part. Its odd how much the Scandinavians scrape, scent, gurgle and clean at night considering the results next morning: as hard as a board, and as gray as a scullery pail. She suggested nothing but paring potatoes. Much though I love my own sex, my gorge heaves at the travelling female. We had two with us from Toulon to Mentone, arch and elderly, with handbags packed with face powder and complexions that not all the thyme and mint in England could sweeten—elderly virgins from Cheltenham, playing golf in France; but one feels sure they cant hit the ball—they cant do anything—they spend enough to keep you and me a year on their clothes—they have no reason to exist in this world or the next.

We have run into Cecil Taylor[2] and a young man called Cox (not Fox)

---

1. This is the only recorded instance when Virginia saw D. H. Lawrence and Norman Douglas. Lawrence was then 42, and within three years of his death. Douglas (1868-1952), the author of *South Wind* (1917), had settled in Florence.
2. Master at Clifton College until 1948.

361

here; but happily they are devoted and inseparable. Otherwise I find the clergy and the old ladies very fascinating; I find the architecture divine. Pillars of pale green and pink marble like avenues of birch trees disappearing one behind another: immense distances; vast spaces; people like ants; everything very light, gay and spacious—Why, I ask you, cant we build like that? You cant think how beautiful the human figure looks properly displayed on these staircases. I have seen the mosaics [at Monreale]: there is one of hunting which I liked; but the gilt tends to be tinselly. My taste is naturally so bad that I dont in the least mind exposing it.

Would you write to me at
Hotel Hassler-New York
8 Piazza Trinita dei Monti
Rome. (we shall be there from 22nd to 26th)
Please say
1: What did the oculist say about your eyes? Where could I buy old stuff? rings? china?

2: Which are good places to dine at in Rome? Leonard would like to have kissed you; but was too shy. We get on with my dog Italian and Leonards pure Latin. The people are charming to us.

My love to my nephews, if they are there—I long to be at Julian about his dancing mice—

Yr B

Berg

1743: To Vanessa Bell   *Hotel de Rome, Syracuse*
                                         [Sicily]
14th April [1927]

Dearest,
This is again written in great difficulties sitting beside the fountain of Arethusa (she was pursued by Alpheus as you know and they now spout together eternally) in a glare of sun and dust with Italians asleep, one singing, a man playing a mandoline; a beggar. But the worse I write, the better you must paint: were it not for a picture, I should not bring myself to write at all. We got here last night, and who should we meet driving from the station, but Osbert Sitwell, who stopped the cab and was very friendly, but he is lodged in a grand hotel outside the town, whereas we lodge in a cheap Italian inn, where no one speaks English, and we get delicious food, and there are only Italian officers and widows, and thank God, no Germans —so I dont suppose we shall see Osbert. There is a courtyard, with two cats in a basket, a waiter varnishing a table and an old woman picking over mattresses: I am rapidly falling in love with Italy. I think it is much more congenial than France—All the men must be womanisers. The old innkeeper cooks an omelette specially for me. I dreamt all night of Duncan and

Carrington. She asked him to get her with child, which he did. This was so vivid I woke and asked Leonard if he would think it a compliment should Bea [Howe] ask the same of him. But alas—my dream is gone like smoke; Carrington bears none of Duncan's children within her, I'm sure. Aint it odd how all the flowers of female youth will die with their buds unopened— Carrington, Alix, Frances,[1]—This is the sort of thing Leonard and I maunder on about as we sit in the ruins.

Last night we explored Syracuse by moonlight. But how am I to describe without boring you, particularly as you won't have drunk a bottle of wine, and be half tipsy as I was—the bay, the schooners, the blue sky, with the white pillars, like paper, and clouds crossing, and people sauntering, and a man on stilts—no it cant be done. One's mind is such a hotch potch of different things, always on the bubble—I daresay painters are more concentrated, but less amiable and lovable in their marmoreal chastity than we are—you and Duncan always seem to me, though some appearances are against it, marmoreally chaste—You have cast out so many of the devils that afflict poor creatures like me—Ever since I left Cassis I have thought of you as a bowl of golden water which brims but never overflows. A back hander? Eh? Well, I am being brushed off my seat by an old man who is sweeping the ground.

We have just lunched, and had another bottle of wine. No letters ever get forwarded when one is abroad, except bills and letters about beating carpets —only one from that old lady at Cheltenham, whom Snow[2] has now been to see "such a particularly nice person" Mrs Smith says; and as Mrs Smith also paints, they have much in common. I dont bear my friends ill will, but I think of them all as dead, or far removed behind a painted curtain, which I have no wish to draw aside—I should like to go on travelling from town to town all my life. rambling about ruins and watching schooners come in, and falling in love with Italian girls, who all look like Millais drawings in the Cornhill. I should rather like to write; which one cant do; but perhaps it is nicer to imagine books, which I do all day long, until I have to tell them to poor old Leonard—We spend a lot of time on the balcony looking at people in the street. All the horses wear ostrich feathers. Tell Angelica I woke up in the night travelling to Rome and found her matchbox. It came in very handy—I have several secrets to tell her, in great private—I have seen three new witcherinas. They sent her their love. I said she had a beautiful tribe of Elves, and also a crested newt but this is *very private*.

Did Tommie and Julia confide in you? How anyone can think him attractive, physically, passes me—But I am not a judge of the manly form, I suppose—He reminds me of Georges opera hat—the thing he carried under

1. Carrington died childless in 1932; Alix (Mrs James) Strachey died in 1973, also childless; Frances Marshall (later Mrs Ralph Partridge) had one son.
2. Margery Snowden, Vanessa's closest friend before her marriage. They had met as art students.

his arm to make him look diplomatic—and God knows why, here is a letter from George about some book of his, which he wants Leonard to praise. I dont think I shall ever come home. But please, good Dolphin, write to Rome. You have kept your hair. You are beautiful, beloved, chaste: and I am none of these things

V.W.

Berg

1744: To Angus Davidson   *Hotel de Rome, Syracuse*
                                                  [Sicily]
14th April, 1927

My dear Angus,

We are both burnt bright brick red; we are both slightly tipsy; we are almost decided never to come back to England again. It is perfect here. If only God had forgotten to create male Germans and female Germans, I should have no complaint to make. Happily we have pitched on a purely Italian inn—rather humble; W.C.'s fair; no English spoken, and we sit drinking coffee with Italian sailors and officers after dinner. We have been all day (I add, lest you should draw wrong conclusions) among the ruins of the Greek theatre, where they are getting up a play to act next week before the King and Queen; so we saw Medea in a sulphur-coloured wig, and Alcestis, in a bowler and overcoat, shouting their parts. It was rather beautiful. In fact everything is charming; and though we ran straight into Osbert Sitwell on arriving, it seems unlikely that we shall see anyone else. I am getting as unsocial as Nessa. They were all very well at Cassis, extremely happy, and hoping not to see a soul for 6 months. Naturally, Douglas [Angus' brother], Tommie, Julia and I think Roger, instantly arrived.

I hope the Press is not too gloomy. The widow [Mrs Cartwright] is in Wales I imagine: and I suppose you'll get a few days off now. Why anyone lives in England I can't imagine at the moment; but I suppose we will soon recover our sanity, and not take the widow by the neck or create any other disturbance. Leonard sends his love.

Yours
V.W.

I see we're in for a hot time with Mary [Hutchinson]; but if she treats us as she does, what does she expect? That book [*Fugitive Pieces*] has been half in and half out of the womb these 9 months.

Angus Davidson

1745: To Vanessa Bell   *Hotel Hassler-New York*
                                Piazza Trinita dei Monti, Rome
21st April 1927

Dearest.

We got here last night, and found your letter, which I read twice, at dinner, once in the Pincio this morning, so let your modesty, which is only sham after all, hide its head. I am always on the look out for some huge revelation lurking in the boscage about life in your letters. Undoubtedly I shall settle here—it surpasses all my expectations: It is a holiday today and all sights are shut so we have done nothing but sit in the gardens and stroll over to St Peters. I dont know why one feels it to be so much superior to other cities—partly the colour I suppose. It is a perfect day; all the flowers are just out, there are great bushes of azalea set in the paths; Judas trees, cypresses, lawns, statues, among which go wandering the Italian nurses in their primrose and pink silks with their veils and laces and instead of being able to read Proust, as I had meant (by the way he is far the greatest modern novelist, and I think it would repay you one of these days if you should take to book reading to look at him) I find myself undulating like a fish in and out of leaves and flowers and swimming round a vast earthenware jar which changes from orange red to leaf green—It is incredibly beautiful—oh and there's St Peters in the distance; and people sitting on the parapet, all very distinguished, the loveliest women in Europe, with little proud heads;—but you will not attach any sense to all this.

By the way, I ran into two pictures by Breugel at Naples; The blind leading the blind, one was; but I didn't care for them so much as the London one[1]—Too melodramatic—Then there was a Titian, and some Italians, which we said, loud and bold, as we do when we're alone, were very good pictures. But then the Roman works of art at Pompeii are profoundly depressing—At first I thought the ruins were merely a deserted mining town, but later I became very much impressed; mostly by the hills outside, but also by the colour of the bricks; one or two skeletons, people dead on the top of their treasure chests; and the general atmosphere of [the] place, which is very strange. In August 76 A.D. the lava came down and covered the whole town—this you may not know, but really it is necessary to remember it, should you talk about Pompeii. At Syracuse we were exploring the quarries when Osbert Sitwell and Adrian Stokes[2] came after us. Otherwise, we have met no one. And we escaped Osbert, who was much excited by a telegram to say that Sashy [Sitwell] has a son.

I'm sure, to return to your letter, that I should make a vile mother.[3] For

1. See p. 341, note 1.
2. The writer and art-critic.
3. Vanessa had written to Virginia on 16 April: "I wonder how you'd really like the problem of children added to your existence. I don't feel at all equal to dealing with it myself" (*Berg*).

365

one thing (though this I try to hide from you) I slightly distrust or suspect the maternal passion. It is obviously immeasurable and unscrupulous. You would fry us all to cinders to give Angelica a days pleasure, without knowing it. You are a mere tool in the hands of passion. Other mothers are much worse, and I've no doubt I should be worst of all—Helen Anrep and Faith [Henderson] appal me when they talk of their children: In fact what you feel about marriage I feel about motherhood, except that of the two relations motherhood seems to me the more destructive and limiting. But no doubt I'm merely trying to make out a case for myself: there's some truth in [it] though; I dont like profound instincts—not in human relationships.

Friday [22 April]

Now we are just off to our days work—St Peters, the Vatican etc. It is again perfect—hot and still. I dont want to go back to the telephone and the omnibus at all. Why not settle here, rather than Cassis? I believe one could be more aloof—At Cassis people would come and stay—Here they could only drop in for half an hour. Unhappily, Wednesday is the Rag market day, and of course we shall be gone. What a bore! I shall go to the antiques instead.

But if we come to live here—and really I think we may, should Mervyn [Arnold-Forster] take on the Press—then I shall go to the Rag market every Wednesday.

I'm afraid this is a dull damp letter, but then traveller's letters always are. But I have tried to be as annoying as possible—to drop a little salt on Dolphins snout so that she may spout columns of fury into the air: You must write to Tavistock now. First defend your position as mother; next as artist. Why do you say that the chief end of life is one's work?

B.

Berg

1746: To Lady Cecil   *Rome*

Postcard
24th April [1927]

This is where we are at the moment. I hope some day we may meet, *not* at Geneva.[1] We are just coming back, but if I had my way I should live here for ever.

Love from
V.W.

Hatfield

1. In 1927 Viscount Cecil was a British delegate to the Coolidge conference on naval disarmament, in Geneva.

366

1747: To Vanessa Bell   *Hotel Hassler, Rome*

26 April 1927

Dearest.

You see how hard I work for my picture[1]—or have I the right to exchange for a decoration, or what is my position exactly? It had better be drawn up accurately to avoid those fierce broils which may well break our sisterhood before its over. For example, the gramophone: a yellow brown object, like Bromo: would you paint that?

I am again writing under difficulties with Leonard catching his 4th flea, on our last morning. We are off early tomorrow, and shall travel straight through and get to London late on Thursday night. Damn it all. The telephone will ring: Raymond will ask if he may come to tea. The only thing that reconciles me to going is that it has set in to rain, and Germans pullulate. Otherwise I only wish to be allowed to stay here—for ever and ever—never to see a soul; to buy a little paper and write a book, as Shelley did, in the Baths of Caractacus [Caracalla]. We went to Nemi yesterday—We rambled over the Campagna on Sunday. I suppose France is all right, and England is all right, but I have never seen anything so beautiful as this is. Figure us sitting in hot sunshine on the doorstep of a Roman ruin in a field with hawk coloured archways against a clear green grape coloured sky, silvery with mountains in the back ground. Then on the other side nothing but the Campagna, blue and green, with an almond coloured farm, with oxen and sheep, and more ruined arches, and blocks of marble fallen on the grass, and immense sword like aloes, and lovers curled up among the broken pots. Nemi perhaps you have seen. We lunched at a restaurant hung above the lake, which is almost round, very deep, with Roman ships sunk in it, and of the colour first of olive trees and then of emeralds. It was rather cloudy so the colour was always changing very slowly, and round the lake was a little path with horses and goats. We went down after lunch and found wild cyclamen and marble lapped by the water. Dear, dear, and then one goes and sits in a basement in Bloomsbury!

As for the works of art, all I can say is that Raphael comes out very much better than I expected. But we had only one morning. Moreover, your tooth and Duncans venom sweetly though it is exuded through a stalk of silver, slightly inhibit my art criticism. (I enclose an article from the Times on Duncan.) Still I get a good deal of pleasure even from the pictures. How did Michael Angelo paint the ceiling? Slung on a board? What do you think of Raphael? and of Michael Angelo? Please tell me.

As I have not seen a human face, and scarcely an English tourist, for they are all German and American, I have no gossip. Tom's father in law has died at Bexhill and Tom [Eliot] is very busy winding up affairs. Dotty has reached

1. See p. 360, note 2.

367

England safely, though she flew over the Persian alps. Mary is said to be in a rage because we dont bring her book out at once. As she wont correct the proofs, and perpetually adds and scratches out, we put the blame on her.

I must stop now—L. has caught his flea—Our only failure is the antique shops: we have beat up and down all the streets in the neighbourhood of Castel Angelo and St Peters without success. I had hoped to bring home all sorts of china; but it cant be helped. The moral is we must come next year. I will try to be more amusing, but I have no wish whatever to see my friends, or to gossip, or to dine with Colefax—

Your B.

Berg

1748: To Vanessa Bell   52 *Tavistock Sqre, WC*1

Sunday. 1st May [1927]

Dearest,

Damn it all—I'm afraid I shall have to make an end of our agreement and lose my picture. Directly I get back I'm told that Clive is making Raymond etc in Paris roar with accounts of my rhapsodies about Italy—how they were obviously all humbug—how horribly bored we both were etc. etc. God knows what I did say. Of course nothing was said about your reading my letters aloud or showing them, so I suppose I've no right to complain. But it makes one so self conscious if one thinks what one writes to you is going to be shown round and made up into stories that I am reduced to silence or mere facts and gossip, which bore me rather. So what am I to do? If its not Clive, it'll be Roger or Tommie or some one, and these things always get round in about three days and are far more irritating, as you'll agree, than they're worth.

We came back to the usual disaster—Nelly [Boxall] has been having an abcess on her kidneys, and was ill in bed. She's now gone home for a fortnight anyhow, and we are reduced to an old char and in rather a turmoil. People pullulate at every corner: I've just had the strength of mind to say not at home to Francis Birrell; but what with the books coming out and the everybody coming back to London I rather envy you at Cassis.

I shall try to get hold of Quentin. We dine out every night—at a restaurant I mean—so he might come with us.

Let me know what you think about the letters. Its a sad business. How it takes me back to the old days! However, I'm more philosophic now.

Yr B.

Berg

368

Letters 1749-1792 (May–July 1927)

A few days after Virginia's return from holiday, Vita arrived back from Persia, this time with Harold Nicolson, who was still seriously considering resignation from diplomacy. Vita attended Virginia's lecture at Oxford in May, and Virginia Vita's award of the Hawthornden Prize for The Land *on 16 June, and with a party of friends they travelled by train to Yorkshire to watch the eclipse of the sun at dawn on June 29. But the great event of these months was the publication of* To the Lighthouse *on 5 May. It was acclaimed as Virginia's most accomplished novel, and the good opinions which meant most to her were Vanessa's and Roger Fry's. A spate of headaches in June was her only illness of the year, and it was while she was convalescing at Rodmell that the idea of* The Waves *flashed into her mind. After her recovery, the Woolfs bought their first car with the profits of* Lighthouse, *and Virginia took driving-lessons, but never became proficient enough to pass her test.*

1749: To HELEN McAFEE   *52 Tavistock Square, W.C.1*

Typewritten
1st May 1927

Dear Miss McAfee,

I am glad that you like my essay Street Haunting [for the *Yale Review*]. I will arrange that it is not published in England before the 20th of September.

Would you be so very kind as to let me have two sets of proofs, in good time? There are some passages which I should like to alter.

With many thanks,

yours sincerely
Virginia Woolf

Yale University

1750: To VANESSA BELL   *52 Tavistock Square [W.C.1]*
Sunday 8th May 1927

Dearest,

Well, well. Clive must have a genius for invention. He not only kept them all—Dadie, Raymond, Nancy [Cunard] and some American—on the roar with his account of what Leonard said and what I said, but he made Dadie, who was my informant, so convinced of the truth of it that I had great difficulty in assuring him that the whole tour hadn't been a complete

369

failure. I should be much interested to know why he does this. There must be some obscure jealousy at work I think. He grudges, not your affection for me, which doesn't exist, but mine for you—Or he wants to parade his knowledge of our affairs. You are kind but foolish to hand me on his praises, by way of solace.[1] Dont you know that Singe[2] knows flattery now a mile off, and it has no effect on him? But I'm so badly in want of your pictures that I shall risk more indiscretions. Clive, I believe, is the only real danger, and he, I hear, is expected at 50 [Gordon Square] tonight. But warn me next time anyone malicious is in the house, and I'll change my tone.

I haven't as much gossip as I might have, as Nelly is still away, so I cant ask people to dinner, and I am in an unsociable mood. A ring came at the bell last night and we refused to budge; at last we peered out of the bathroom window and saw Julia Strachey standing looking up at us: we ducked, and she went away. But Ottoline is at Gower Street; Vita is back; Raymond is back. Vita I have just seen, but only flying through London, rather distracted. Here's a profound secret (which I expect the whole of London knows) Harold is leaving the Foreign Office. You must admit this is to his credit. He is over 40: has no money of his own; and is throwing up his career just as he's getting to the top—Apparently diplomatic society is so boring that he cant face even becoming an ambassador. Really, I think its a feather in Bloomsbury's cap: a goose feather if you like. No doubt he'll step into something much better; they always do: still, all his relations, Vita says, will be heart broken. She was appreciative, I admit; had passed Cassis on Tuesday in her ship, and thought of you. I could not hold out hopes that you had thought of her.

I sent you two copies of the Lighthouse, one from the Press, and one from me (but I think I forgot to write your name in it.) I hope you'll write and criticise it. I would like your good opinion, which is more than one can say of most people. Probably the subject was a little unwise: But then one falls in to these things all in a second—I made it up one afternoon in the Square—without any premeditation, that I can see—How do you make up pictures? Suddenly all in a second? The bore with a book is that everyone thinks they have to talk to one about it. This will begin next week, I suppose: and they will all say different things, and I shall be very angry and very pleased and all the same, rather bored; because I have 2 other books I want to write; but still I should like your opinion, good or bad, Duncans, Morgan's, Lyttons: that's all, I think. Leonard says its my best book; but then I think he has to.

There seems a curse on the Press—We were about to see Mervyn

---

1. "Clive simply raved about your brilliance and we discussed your gifts as a letter writer compared to Mrs Carlyle" (Vanessa to Virginia, 4 May 1927, *Berg*).
2. 'Singe' ('Apes') was one of Virginia's names for herself when writing to Vanessa.

Arnold-Forster and settle the future; and now Ka writes to say he is probably dying. He suddenly became paralysed, and has pneumonia. So what are we to do now? Angus, Leonard says, was cheered by the news, but can we do with Angus? Then our lives have been made a burden by Mary [Hutchinson]. I told you, I think, how furious she was that we were not bringing her book out now. She so rattled poor old Angus that he promised to do it by the end of May. Now begins a series of letters and telegrams. One comes to say "Please wire printer to change BOULE on page 79 to BUHL." So we wire printer. Next day another wire, "very sorry, please wire printer to change BUHL to BOULE unless you ascertain from authorities that BUHL is correct." I fly upstairs, search through dictionaries; discover that BUHL is the German form of BOULE and is now in use. So we leave it. Next morning comes a long letter marked urgent. She has been to an antiquary in Sussex and he tells her that the most correct form is certainly BOULE, as that is the original name of the maker, who was French. Still she has her doubts, and will we consult Roger Fry, by whose opinion she will abide? Meanwhile the book is to be held up: Roger is in France; and so on and so on. But I'm not going to renew friendship without an explanation. Doubtless she won't want to renew friendship: But I'm not going to decorate her table (I dont mean aesthetically —its my mind thats my jewel) when all the time she's accusing my heart of corruption and my liver of rottenness. Besides, I should like a good scene. Colefax is testy about the Desmond fund, I hear, and so I'm not invited; but the MacCarthys have netted £700 and are, now, it is said, in the depths of gloom, scraping and paring to pay it off. At least this is Molly's view of it— "What are we to do with all this money? It only means more debts" but Desmond has vanished to the continent, in the highest health and spirits.

What else? Quentin came to lunch. That boy is really a marvel. He drank two full tumblers of strong Spanish wine, where I can only take a wine-glass; and it was a hot day; and then he went off to shop, and seemed quite as steady as usual, and came back to tea, and had a long argument with me about poetry and painting. Probably I am almost as spotted with the maternal taint as you are. My pride rises at the sight of him, and I find myself boasting to the char about his height and his age as if I were Aunt Mary. I only wish they didn't both (Quentin and Julian, I mean) think Bernard Shaw greater than Shakespeare. Quentin sees nothing in poetry. For God's sake dont tell me you put in by mistake a drop too much of the old Bell in them—I always thought you were playing with gunpowder in that marriage, and you scarcely deserved to come off as well as you did.

I have written to Mr King [doctor] to say that you will take Angelica to see him as soon as you come back. He lives somewhere at the other side of Maida Vale. Burn Wilson's[1] letter—

London is pretty horrid, for some reason: so flat, so obvious, after Rome.

1. Vanessa replied that 'Wilson' was really a Mrs White (*unidentified*).

But no more of that. Only to make up for your indiscretion you might tell me what you think of Raphael and Michael Angelo: but not until you've told me about the Lighthouse.

Our motor car depends on the sales: so far much better than Dalloway but it may stop all in a second.[1]

What a terrific letter!

By the way, your story of the Moth so fascinates me that I am going to write a story about it. I could think of nothing else but you and the moths for hour's after reading your letter.[2]

Isn't it odd?—perhaps you stimulate the literary sense in me as you say I do your painting sense.

God! How you'll laugh at the painting bits in the Lighthouse!

Yr B.

Berg

1751: To VANESSA BELL   [52 *Tavistock Square, W.C.*1]

Monday [9 May 1927]
Post Script.

For God's sake—say nothing to anybody about Harold Nicolson and the Foreign Office—I find it is a dead secret. Dont, above all, breathe a whisper to Clive—whom I've just seen.

VW.

Berg

1752: To V. SACKVILLE-WEST   [52 *Tavistock Square, W.C.*1]

Monday [9 May 1927]

Dearest donkey West,

Did you understand that when I wrote it was my best book I merely meant because all the pages were empty?[3] A joke, a feeble joke: but then it might get round through Jack Squire, through Hugh Walpole to Gosse: seriously such are your friends.

1. On 5 May, the day of publication, Virginia recorded in her diary that *To the Lighthouse* had an advance sale of 1690, twice the number for *Mrs Dalloway*.
2. Vanessa's letter is quoted by Quentin Bell, *Virginia Woolf*, II, p. 126. This story was one of the inspirations for *The Moths*, which became *The Waves* (1931).
3. On her return to Long Barn, Vita found a copy of *To the Lighthouse* which Virginia had inscribed "In my opinion the best novel I have ever written". When Vita opened it, she discovered that it was a dummy, and all the pages blank.

These things made me shiver like a fish on a hook about 2 a.m. so I am writing.

Then, second: Oxford is *May* 18*th*. and I've written to take rooms at the Mitre.

And shall I see you before? And where does one buy a black coat? I have to broadcast, and think it should be done in broad cloth.

Yr
VW.
Virginia
(I forgot)

Berg

1753: To Clive Bell   [52 *Tavistock Square, W.C.*1]

Monday night [9 May 1927]

It suddenly comes over me—you know how these dragons afflict one—that you thought I meant the inscription in Vita's copy of my book seriously. It was a feeble joke—"my best book" referred to the blank pages of her dummy copy.

Then, secondly; another dragon: affection for Clive: Glad he's back. Can one say so without being sentimental? Well, perhaps hardly.

V.W.

No answer

Quentin Bell

1754: To V. Sackville-West   52 *Tavistock Square* [*W.C.*1]

Friday [13 May 1927]

Darling Vita,

What a generous woman you are! Your letter has just come,[1] and I must answer it, though in a chaos. (Nelly returning: her doctor; her friends; her diet etc) I was honest though in thinking you wouldn't care for The Light-house: too psychological; too many personal relationships, I think. (This is said not of the dummy copy) The dinner party the best thing I ever wrote: the one thing that I think justifies my faults as a writer: This damned 'method'. Because I dont think one could have reached those particular

---

1. Vita had written: "Everything is blurred to a haze by your book . . . I can only say that I am dazzled and bewitched" (11 May 1927, *Berg*).

emotions in any other way. I was doubtful about Time Passes. It was written in the gloom of the Strike: then I re-wrote it: then I thought it impossible as prose—I thought you could have written it as poetry. I don't know if I'm like Mrs Ramsay: as my mother died when I was 13 probably it is a child's view of her: but I have some sentimental delight in thinking that you like her. She has haunted me: but then so did that old wretch my father: Do you think it sentimental? Do you think it irreverent about him? I should like to know. I was more like him than her, I think; and therefore more critical: but he was an adorable man, and somehow, tremendous.

Look here, dearest creature, the young men [at Oxford] have taken us rooms together at the Clarendon before getting my letter: also they want us to dine with them first at 7: so we must get there about 6. I daresay train is simplest. Let me know what suits you. I'm rather bothered about my paper; it mayn't suit; it may be dull. Ask Harold whether one can say that God does not exist to Oxford undergraduates? As one could to Cambridge. Also would you please, please please send us that story you said you had almost ready? This is most important, as Lord Olivier is not alive enough to support the story series.[1] Couldn't you bring it with you on Wednesday?

But why do you think me "lonely". Lovely I understand: not altogether, lonely.

Yes, its an immense relief that you like it; I had been sure you wouldn't. I have so many more books in my head that I should be unhappy to think the whole progeny was doomed to drive us further asunder. The next will be better than this I think. An old creature writes to say that all my fauna and flora of the Hebrides is totally inaccurate. Dear me! whats to be done about it?

So dearest, train, Wednesday, to arrive for dinner. I rushed into a whore's shop in Leicester Sqre and bought a coat

Come here any time you like. Tell Harold we want him to come and dine with us, and I see some hope now of getting dinner soon. Will he?

The Story! The story!

VW.
(oh I forgot—
Virginia Woolf)

One needn't dress for the young men, need one? No.

Berg

1. The 'story series' did not progress beyond the publication of a single title, Lord Olivier's *The Empire Builder* (May 1927). Sydney Olivier was formerly Governor of Jamaica and a prominent Fabian. The story which Vita was to contribute to the series cannot now be traced.

[52 *Tavistock Square, London, W.C.*1]

Sunday [15 May 1927]

All right, dearest donkey. I will be outside the place where one buys tickets at Paddington at 4.35 on Wednesday, carrying a neat bag, otherwise slightly shabby, but distinguished. Suddenly it strikes me that its all great nonsense your coming—except that I shall enjoy it. The dinner, the paper— what a bore for you! However in the relics of time left us, the scrapings and parings, we may make hay. Herbert Fisher[1] has asked me to stay: Mr. Driberg[2] wants us to lunch. No, I say—How did the Colefaxes go? a little damp, I should guess. D'you know the first time I met her she struck me so hard and bright I compared her to artificial cherries in a servants hat—nor can I ever quite obliterate it.

> Yr
> Virginia
> in haste.

Yes, bring the story: but if you dont want to come say so like a man. Ring up.

Berg

1756: To Vanessa Bell   52 *Tavistock Sqre, WC*1

Sunday 15th May 1927

Dearest,

No letter from you—But I see how it is—

Scene: after dinner: Nessa sewing: Duncan doing absolutely nothing.

Nessa: (throwing down her work) Christ! There's the Lighthouse! I've only got to page 86 and I see there are 320. Now I cant write to Virginia because she'll expect me to tell her what I think of it.

Duncan   Well, I should just tell her that you think it a masterpiece.

Nessa   But she's sure to find out—They always do. She'll want to know why I think its a masterpiece

Duncan   Well Nessa, I'm afraid I cant help you, because I've only read 5 pages so far, and really I dont see much prospect of doing much reading this month, or next month, or indeed before Christmas.

Nessa   Oh its all very well for you. But I shall have to say something: And I dont know who in the name of Jupiter all these people are

---

1. Virginia's cousin, Warden of New College, Oxford. For Virginia's lecture, see p. 352, note 1.
2. Tom Driberg was then an undergraduate at Christ Church. Later he had a distinguished career in journalism and politics, and died in 1976.

	(turns over some pages desperately) I think I shall make a time-table: its the only way: ten pages a day for 20 days is—

Duncan	But you'll never be able to keep up ten pages a day.
Nessa	(rather dashed) No—I suppose I shant. Well then, one may as well be hung for a sheep as for a goat—though whats the sense of saying that I never could see: a sheep is almost identical with a goat in some countries; except that one can milk a goat of course. Lord! I shall never forget Violet Dickinson at Athens and the goats milk! But what was I saying when you interrupted me? Oh yes: I shall take the bull by the horns. I shall write to Virginia and say "I think its a masterpiece—" (she takes the inkpot and prepares to write, but finds it full of dead and dying insects). 'Oh Duncan, what have you done with the inkpot? used it to catch flies in? But thats a beetle! Yes it is. Beetles have 12 legs: flies only 8. D'you mean to say you didn't know that? Well, I suppose you're one of those people who think a spider's an insect: Now if you'd been brought up in Cornwall you'd know that a spiders not an insect; its—no I dont think its a reptile: its something queer. I know. Anyhow, I cant write to Virginia, because the ink is nothing but a mass of beetles or spiders legs—I really dont know what they are: but one man's meat is another man's poison; and if you will use the ink pot to catch flies in, then I dont see how even Virginia herself could possibly expect, or even wish me to write to her—(they settle down again to discuss spiders etc etc etc)

Now isn't this word for word the truth?

Well; I must leave a little room for mere fabrications. Clive has been here: in my opinion utterly distraught. I think, seriously, he's verging on collapse of some sort. He said his stay at Cassis had been a failure, so far as his book is concerned. He gave me the impression of having lost all his illusions, like a bat in the day time—Yet he sees Mary. Only he calls her Mary Hutchinson rather stiffly. He rambles just as he did before he went away; half apologised for laughing at my letters (you must have told him) and then said he couldn't sleep at all—and Mia had come in drunk, and he had been put in his place by Robin Mayor; he was off to Seend but I've never seen him so disjointed, and twitchy and queer.

We dined with the Keynes': he almost brought the tears to my eyes (though he gave us not a drop to drink) by his doglike affection for you; it is conveyed I scarcely know how; but I'm convinced he feels at his heart your malicious ways, and yet cant overcome his superstition that you and Duncan are the soul and salt of the world. Vanessa says this—and Vanessa used to do that—All his talk was of you; but in the past. Lydia ripens visibly. She has her little stories and jokes; but is settling into house keeping, and talks, religiously, of the fresh fish she gets at Selfridges, and how, by making eyes at a certain shop man, he pulls the kidneys fresh and bleeding from the sheep (or is it cow?) in her presence. I see in this all the tragedy of the childless, which, no doubt, will corrode her entirely—She's off to catch butterflies with old Dr Keynes[1] in the Tyrol—Thank God, I'm not.

Otherwise, I'm engulfed in writing a paper on poetry to read to some Oxford undergraduates on Wednesday—Vita comes with me—We stay at an hotel. Let us hope for nightingales, moons, and love—At present its damnably cold, and I cant get over my impression that London is built on a graveyard. Its flat; its grey; its drab. Its walked, too, by the Alixe's and the Bunnys: who all seem to me phantom and futile. Poor Mervyn Arnold-Forster—yes, he's dead; almost the most disappointed pinched starved man I've ever known; and we're in a fix what to do now.

Adrian and Karin [Stephen] have patched, she tells me, a working marriage; which means she will visit American asylums 6 months of the year; and the other 6 live here. But her sterling qualities are now uppermost, and I was deeply touched—I dont quite know by what—It came over me sitting with her, dumb, and deaf, and resolute, in front of the open window, watching Alix and [Arthur] Waley march round and round the square together. These things do come over me—Its what makes me so undependable as a friend—Tomorrow I am lunching at Simpsons with Saxon [Sydney-Turner] to meet some Swedes—"not exciting people exactly" he said; so I expect an uproarious time. We are, by the way, taking a first class carriage to see the Eclipse in June.[2] Will you share? It stops in Yorkshire as the sun disappears, for 5 seconds; we all get out and look up; hot coffee is then served and we return to London—Saxon is coming; also the Swedes.

When are you coming back?

Damn Duncan's show:[3] it was shut; they cant afford, Maynard says, even a cretin to sit there with her knitting; so one finds it shut.

Yr B.

Berg

1757: To Lady Ottoline Morrell   *Monks House, Rodmell*
                                   [Sussex]
Sunday [15 May 1927]

Dearest Ottoline

I am so glad you like parts of the Lighthouse—I accept it all gratefully and humbly. I daresay its flattery, but I like it so much that I swallow it all the same. I'm specially pleased that you like Time Passes—It gave me more

1. John Neville Keynes, Maynard's father, who was a philosopher and economist, died at the age of 97 in 1949, surviving his son by three years.
2. See p. 382, note 2.
3. At the London Artists' Association, New Bond Street.

trouble than all the rest of the book put together, and I was afraid it hadn't succeeded.

Shall you really be in Gower Street? I can hardly believe it. I look forward to your creation there—people, colour, furniture, china, lights and all the things you create with so singularly and remarkably—more than you can do to anything I write—And that isn't flattery.

Your aff^{ec}
Virginia Woolf

Texas

1758: To Duncan Grant   52 T[avistock]. S[quare, W.C.1].
Monday [16? May 1927]

Dearest Duncan,

Would you be so very kind as to buy Nessa a birthday present with the enclosed?[1] something frivolous and foolish. I couldn't find anything abroad; and then if I send it to her, she pays for Julians toothbrushes, or the drains; and then your taste is so good. So excuse.

Yrs Virginia

Duncan Grant

1759: To Charles Sanger   52 Tavistock Sqre W.C.
17th May 1927

My dear Charlie,

You are amazing in the way you read your friends books. It is the greatest encouragement. I can't say how glad I am that you like the Lighthouse. You said Mrs Dalloway lacked humanity; and if this is better in that way, it is a proof that I took your strictures to heart. I confess I sometimes want to cut the whole psychology business altogether; it is so endless, but I get drawn in against my will. Those jumps and jolts you complain of are not at all to my liking. Unfortunately one is doing a very difficult thing with imperfect means: I can never scrape through a book without disaster. But I wont bore you with all this.

Wont you dine with us on Wednesday 25th 7.45? That would be very nice.

Yours ever
Virginia Woolf

Daphne Sanger

1. Vanessa was 48 on 30 May.

1760: TO VANESSA BELL

Monks House, Rodmell
[Sussex]

Sunday—22nd May 1927

Dearest,

I was so pleased and excited by your letter[1] that I trotted about all day like a puppy with a bone. In fact you entirely destroyed my powers of work: I was always taking it out and reading it again, until I thought perhaps I exaggerated, and ran off to Leonard with it to ask him if he thought you really meant it. Taking into account your well known character, he decided, finally, that you probably did. So then I settled down to complete satisfaction, which no one else's letters have given me—(here's one that may recall the character of Dora Sanger to you—I dont want it back)

But what do you think I did know about mother? It can't have been much—What would Quentin have known of you if you had died when he was 13? I suppose one broods over some germ; but I specially refrained either from reading her letters, or father's life. He was easier to do, but I was very much afraid you would think me sentimental. I seem to make people think that the Stephen family was one of insane gloom. I thought it was a cheerful enough book. I don't defend my accuracy, though I think Watts used to buy lapis lazuli, break it up with a small hammer, and keep it under damp cloths. I think, too, the pre-raphaelites thought it more like nature to use garden clay, whenever possible; to serve for colours. Lord Olivier writes that my horticulture and natural history is in every instance wrong: there are no rooks, elms, or dahlias in the Hebrides; my sparrows are wrong; so are my carnations: and it is impossible for women to die of childbirth in the 3rd month—He infers that Prue had had a slip (which is common in the Hebrides) and was 9 months gone. This is the sort of thing that painters know nothing of.

If we weren't down here for Sunday, I should be seeing Clive: and so might throw light upon the mystery. The position seems odd: he has Mary there; seems in good spirits with her; and then goes about (this is from Eddy) saying that he is wretched; twitching; complaining; maundering on about life being over, and his bolt being shot, as he did before he went away. I think the truth must be that he's back again where he was, with Mary; she exacerbating and exasperating him; and he now without any prospect of escape. I'm lunching with him on Tuesday, but shan't see him alone. I think he wants, not exactly to confide, but to talk round and about himself. You'll be back though. Now, Dolphin, you've got to face it and do it. People feel very strongly about you and Duncan—Whats life without those prime jewels of our coronet, people say—the most unlikely people are moved to a bastard kind of poetry on this occasion; people who have never spoken save

1. See Appendix for Vanessa's letter on first reading *To the Lighthouse*.

379

plain prose before; people like Arthur Walcy, Ray Strachey,[1] and Lisa Stillman[2]—A voice on the telephone plunged me into the wildest memories —of St Ives—Gerald[3]—the trapeze on the landing—yesterday. "I am trying to find Cameron photographs of Mama—Can you lend me any negatives?. . . . I should so much like to see you and Nessa again . . . Oh in France is she? Vanessa's always in France! I shall try again in a few weeks time." Then the whole apparition, which was of the utmost vividness, vanished. But as I was saying, you must face life again. Whats the use of flowering in a nettle bed t'other side of Europe? Ottoline impends; but she never fades—She's still at Garsington; Philip sits in the Nation chucking Mrs Jones on the chin, and Leonard comes in to find "P.M" [Philip Morrell] marked on all the best books. "Uncle Philip would like these, please, Mr Woolf" says Mrs Jones archly. Leonard says nothing. He says, going out, casually, "Mr Morrell may do a briefer notice of the Aztecs if he likes: but if he writes more than 50 words, I shall cut it." With the Morrells in London, this snuggling and chucking, to put it euphemistically, may increase; and not wanting a whole clutch of bastards, Ottoline may stay away.

Then I went to Oxford to speak to the youth of both sexes on poetry and fiction. They are young; they are callow; they know nothing about either— They sit on the floor and ask innocent questions about Joyce—They are years behind the Cambridge young, it seemed to me; Quentin and Julian could knock them into mud pies. But they have their charm—There was a man called Martin (I think) an adorer and disciple of Roger's, who was the most intelligent. We went on to somebodies rooms, and there they sat on the floor, and said what a master they thought Roger Fry; and were Bell and Grant able to make a living by decorations; and was Tom Eliot happy with his wife. They're oddly under our thumb, at the moment—at least this particular group. Roger, the old wizard, has them all entranced—I pretended to a degree of intimacy which, alas, is not mine, to colour my cheeks for them. Clive, they said, was very good fun; but we always feel Roger Fry's the real mind. Then there was Vita, very striking; like a willow tree; so dashing, on her long white legs with a crimson bow; but rather awkward, forced indeed to take her stockings down and rub her legs with ointment at dinner, owing to midges—I like this in the aristocracy. I like the legs; I like the bites; I like the complete arrogance and unreality of their minds—for instance buying silk dressing gowns casually for £5 and then lunching off curd cream (a yellow mess) which she picked out of tartlet with a fork, dropping the pastry back into the dish; and then tipping porters a shilling for

1. Rachel Strachey (née Costelloe), Oliver Strachey's second wife and Karin Stephen's sister. She was prominent in the Women's Suffrage Movement and other political causes.
2. The daughter of W. J. Stillman, the American painter and writer, and herself an artist.
3. Gerald Duckworth, Virginia's half-brother, and her first publisher.

doing nothing; and then—the whole thing (I cant go into details) is very splendid and voluptuous and absurd. Also she has a heart of gold, and a mind which, if slow, works doggedly; and has its moments of lucidity—But enough—You will never succumb to the charms of any of your sex—What an arid garden the world must be for you! What avenues of stone pavements and iron railings! Greatly though I respect the male mind, and adore Duncan (but, thank God, he's hermaphrodite, androgynous, like all great artists) I cannot see that they have a glowworm's worth of charm about them—The scenery of the world takes no lustre from their presence. They add of course immensely to its dignity and safety: but when it comes to a little excitement —! (I see that you will attribute all this to your own charms in which I daresay you're not far wrong).

How many paintings shall I have? Monks House is in need of some. I think you'll have to come here for a week end—Well, I daresay you could get off with one night—before July. There are several problems waiting you: I have my own ideas, and my own taste, but its all ineradicably bad. The garden is this year a miracle of order. But that damned Allinson,[1] in concert with Durrant, has changed a farmbuilding into a florid surrey villa in 6 weeks. Marjories book[2] twits us all, practically by name; and compares us with Jos [Wedgwood] and herself, much to our disadvantage. It has rather more merit than the others, but that is chiefly that she has taken over some modern tricks, and the interest of finding the Barley Mow, Fitzroy Street, and the Beanstalk in print keeps one going.

Both Dick and John Strachey[3] have been drowned—according to Lottie. That is to say they stole the Stephen's boat which had a hole in it and sailed away and have never been heard of since. Lottie says they were washed out to sea. Nellie says they have gone to visit Johns, or Dicks, wife at Harwich. Adrian says nobodies heard anything for ten days but he doesn't see any particular reason for anxiety. I creep up and peer into the Stephen's dining room where any afternoon, in full daylight, is to be seen a woman in the last agony of despair, lying on a sofa, burying her face in the pillow, while Adrian broods over her like a vulture, analysing her soul[4]— It is exactly like a picture by John Collier. This is a very very long letter, I would have you observe.

Yr B.

If you could bring me back a few penny cigars such as one buys in Cassis I

1. J. M. Allinson (1877-1929), formerly advertising manager of *The Times*. He owned a large house and land in Rodmell.
2. Marjorie Strachey's *The Counterfeits* (1927), a novel about Bloomsbury. Virginia appears in it as Volumnia Fox. The 'Beanstalk' was a house, and 'Barley Mow' a pub, near Charleston.
3. Ralph Strachey's children.
4. Adrian Stephen was in his last year of training as a psycho-analyst.

should be eternally grateful and, what is more, pay you: I got the habit of cigar smoking in Italy and can't break myself of it.

Berg

1761: To V. Sackville-West   *Monks House* [*Rodmell, Sussex*]

Sunday [22 May 1927]

Yes, honey, do come on Tuesday. Only stay longer than they do, whatever happens. I don't like seeing you between the legs and over the heads of Logans and Hendersons. I think it would be a tactful thing on your part if you asked L. to come to Long Barn in person. He probably thinks you dont want him etc: being a modest man. A very stormy week end, but infinitely lovely on the marshes. D'you remember the birds that ventrilocute? —They're swarming—redshanks, I think. And you entertaining Hugh, and Eleanor![1] Eleanor will say "Might I . . . Mrs Nicolson?" You'll take her. "Its my miscarriages" she'll say coming out. "I've had six". And then, having thought yourself rid of her, she'll settle in for another two or three hours, and tell you the whole story.

I think the Eclipse affair is all right.[2] But I'll know for certain on Tuesday.

Many thanks for Leigh's [Ashton] hat. I feel like a nice puppy; wandering about under a dinner table, and now and then you give it a titbit off your own plate.

Just off to London.

Berg

1762: To Vanessa Bell   52 *Tavistock Sqre* [*W.C.*1]

25th May 1927

Dearest,

I am horrified to find that my letter will probably have missed you at Cassis. Not that it was anything particular in the way of a letter; but I was so much touched, and excited and overcome by yours (I can never believe that you approve of me in any way, strange though it may seem) that I particularly wanted you to get it. I tried to express my thanks. But it was

1. Hugh Walpole was staying the weekend at Long Barn, and Vita and Harold took him to Knole on Sunday, where they met Elinor Wylie.
2. On 28 June Virginia, Leonard, Vita, Harold, Eddy Sackville West, Quentin and Saxon Sydney-Turner left London by train for Richmond, Yorkshire, where early next morning they watched the total eclipse of the sun from Bardon Fell. It is described in *A Writer's Diary*, pp. 109-13.

such a rush here, what with going to Oxford and so on, that I put off writing till I got to Rodmell, and then found we had no stamps, and so brought the letter back to London, and now I see that you are leaving Cassis today. I'm afraid I shall have missed you. However, no letter pleased me one tenth as much as yours did. I was, truthfully, unable to write at all that day. Finally, incredulity that you could like the Lighthouse led me to consult Leonard, and when he said he thought you meant what you said, I was in such a happy state, no tea kettle, no cat, not all the contented and happy creatures in the whole world, were a match for me. I'm in a terrible state of pleasure that you should think Mrs Ramsay so like mother. At the same time, it is a psychological mystery why she should be: how a child could know about her; except that she has always haunted me, partly, I suppose, her beauty; and then dying at that moment, I suppose she cut a great figure on one's mind when it was just awake, and had not any experience of life—Only then one would have suspected that one had made up a sham— an ideal. Probably there is a great deal of you in Mrs Ramsay; though, in fact, I think you and mother are very different in my mind.

Why do I attach so much importance to what you and Duncan think? illiterate, simpletons, as you are? I daresay you are qualified however, much more than many of my literary friends to judge of things as a whole, as works of art—Anyhow, next to your letter, Duncan's gave me most pleasure; and I'm going to write to him. But then you say that you cant judge of it as a work of art yet. Please think it over and tell me if anything emerges. Duncan's hit upon the thing I thought best—the dinner party. But you will have had enough of this egotism, poor Dolphin. The talk about it here is practically over. One very soon gets through it, and if it would only sell well, and I could buy a motor car, I should now be content (you'll be glad to hear) to dismiss it from my mind. In fact; it is rather a distraction from the thing one wants to write now:

I saw Lytton yesterday and asked him about Clive. He was, of course, highly discreet, and would only say that he could see no reason why things should not now settle down again. He said that he thought Clive would find that the habit, after 13 years—of seeing Mary, was too strong to be broken. I lunched with Clive, and he seemed again in the highest spirits, and gave me obscurely to understand that it is at the moment all right between them. He was beset by ladies. Bea [Howe] was coming to tea; Bertha [Penrose] to dinner, but he called her "a little bitch" and said he must find some way of not going to bed with her. Then he gave us (Dadie and me—Lady Violet Bonham Carter had to go—rather a dull lunch, on the whole) a great discourse upon the pains of love, which, he said, were amply made up for by its delights which, he said, I had never known, and never could know. So I denied it, and then Dadie said that Clive was undoubtedly a great lover, and Clive was highly pleased, and seemed to think that he had been very gallant and adventurous and romantic during the last few months, and deserved a medal: so thats all as it should be—He dresses in sky blue flannel, with blue tie and pocket handkerchief and says he has lost a stone and a half.

Yesterday was such an awful day of incessant conversation that my head is still bemused. Clives lunch party; then Faith, Logan, Eddy and Vita to tea; then Lytton in the Square; then dinner at 37 [Gordon Square] with Douglas and Dadie and Cynthia Noble—a dull girl; then they went to [C.H.B.] Kitchins party, but I had the strength to refuse: I am going to entreat your help in leading a nice quiet life, with little excursions to Reading and Hampton Court. This gabble is senseless. Lytton however was affable and urbane and charming though apparently he has gone through tortures at the hands of [Roger] Senhouse. The whole affair is over. He has been in the depths of despair, and is now trying to get on with his book. Dadie and Clive take it very seriously; and say that a week ago he was desperate, and that nothing has hurt him so much for years. Roger refused to bed in the end—I think that was it. But there'll be another for certain—I don't see how one can take it as a death blow considering how he revives.

Nobody seems to know when you will be back. We hope for the best, as they say: and if anything could touch your hearts of glass and emerald— for I dont deny they are beautiful hearts in their way—it would be this chatter we all keep up about Nessa and Duncan, whether they're coming and when they're coming and what we can do to make them stay with us, and not go for ever to live among the frogs of Cassis.

No, I shirked Helen [Anrep]. She rather smears my mind—she has a trailing foot. We talk too much about people's characters and I'm afraid her milieu is rather underworld. But this is only a murmur—not a groan. I like people to have a little bone in their heads—something one can argue about. Not politics, but art or something. Faith [Henderson] afflicts me rather in the same way. One cant talk about Saxon and Barbara for ever.

Now with Dolphin I can always put up a hare or two, but this is drivelling, and I ought to be writing an article on Morgan's novels, which I cannot finish.

But dearest Dolphin, you were a good kind creature to write me such a nice letter

Yr B.

Berg

1763: To Vanessa Bell   52 *Tavistock Square* [*W.C.*1]
Thursday [26 May 1927]

We hope you and Duncan will dine with us—both or singly—whatever

384

night you come back—Thursday next week is our only engagement—
Would you let me know if possible.

V.W.

We've had an offer for Hyde Pk Gate[1]—they will take it on at £300 or buy
for £4,500. What do you think?

Berg

1764: To Roger Fry   52 *Tavistock Sqre* [*W.C.*1]

May 27th 1927

My dear Roger,
        Thank you very much for your letter. I am immensely glad that you like
the Lighthouse.[2] Now I wish I had dedicated it to you. But when I read it
over it seemed to me so bad that I couldn't face asking you. And then, as it
happened, that very day, I met you somewhere,—was so overcome (did you
guess it?) by your magnificence, splendour and purity (of intellect, not body)
that I went home and was positive it was out of the question—dedicating
such a book to such a man. Really therefore the not-dedication is a greater
compliment than the dedication would have been—But you shall have a
private copy, if you'll accept it. What I meant was (but would not have said
in print) that besides all your surpassing private virtues, you have I think
kept me on the right path, so far as writing goes, more than anyone—if the
right path it is.
        I meant *nothing* by The Lighthouse. One has to have a central line down
the middle of the book to hold the design together. I saw that all sorts of
feelings would accrue to this, but I refused to think them out, and trusted
that people would make it the deposit for their own emotions—which they
have done, one thinking it means one thing another another. I can't manage
Symbolism except in this vague, generalised way. Whether its right or wrong
I don't know, but directly I'm told what a thing means, it becomes hateful to
me.

1. 22 Hyde Park Gate, Kensington, was the childhood home of the Stephen
    family, but none of them had lived there since 1904. They sold it in May 1928
    for £4,925.
2. Roger Fry had written to Virginia that he thought it "the best thing you've
    done, actually better than Mrs Dalloway. You're no longer bothered by the
    simultaneity of things and go backwards and forwards in time with an extra-
    ordinary enrichment of each moment of consciousness. I'm sure that there's
    lots I haven't understood . . . for instance, that arriving at the Lighthouse has
    a symbolic meaning which escapes me" (*Sussex*, quoted by Quentin Bell, II,
    pp. 128-9).

I did not consciously think of Nessa when I was doing Mrs Ramsay. In fact she and my mother seemed to me very different people. But no doubt something of Nessa leaked in. After all, my mother died when I was 13, so that the idea must have been developed somehow. But the whole process of writing remains to me a complete mystery; the only thing I realise is that at last, for some reason, I am beginning to write easily, which may be a sign of decay, of course. I turn to your essays to find out; of course, some one has stolen them, some black-hearted devil. I was just saying to myself now I will read Roger through properly, and you're nowhere to be found. A starved young man—but I forget who—begged it of me one day—thats all I remember. So you must come back, and let us have an argument in person.

London is rather a grind—nice people and nasty people stuck together in bunches, so that one cant get at them separately but has to bolt them whole. I get a little bothered by the idiocy of most human intercourse,— think I shall retire to Rome. But then there too one would be hooked in to the quarrels and loves of the detestable English. Clive is specially rampant at the moment, rolling in the pigsty after his three months abstinence, and rather a repulsive sight. Its an amazing recantation of all he said 3 months ago, but he's so outspoken and innocent in his queer way one can't object. Love is the only God, he says, and art and fame an illusion, which means, I suppose, that he intends to dine out at the Ivy with Mary every night of his life and never write a word. One sees the top of his bald head disappearing into the waves. I don't think Nessa will be able to fish him out this time.

I've been lecturing at Oxford, and ran into a wave of Fry worship that was positively oppressive. The only intelligent young man came up and introduced himself as your friend—had met you in France—his name, I think, was Martin. Anyhow he sang a rhapsody about you, which I could not stop. Really Roger, if you go on like this they'll be making a Christ of you within a century. You're becoming a legend to the young. Of course its the only sort of fame worth having—I see that: but I'm a little alarmed at the size and luminosity of your halo. Then the girls rhapsodised about Margery[1]— said Somerville was a different place: plants grow, love grows, learning grows—all due to Margery. Its time I set about the Fry memoir which I have it in my mind (as you Quakers say) to do before I die. Theres not much gossip: Lytton is out of love: Tom Eliot has buried a father in law at Bexhill: Dick and John Strachey are not drowned, but should have been. Marjorie's book is a pretty dismal affair:[2] Bloomsbury shown up against the radiance of Jos's [Wedgwood] private parts—thats the plan of it—and how anyone can be such a fool as to think the mind dull compared with the body, Lord knows. I'm sure I live more gallons to the minute walking once round the square than all the stockbrokers in London caught in the act of copula-

1. Margery Fry, Roger's sister, was Principal of Somerville College, Oxford, 1926-31.
2. See p. 381, note 2.

tion. As for you—but I've flattered you enough—and it isn't flattery: its sober truth, which makes it worse. Love to Helen.

Yr
V.W.

Please tell Helen I had to stay at home and polish off the poem of a poet whose mother wished to see his work printed before she died. But not by us.

Sussex

1765: To V. Sackville-West   52 *Tavistock Sqre* [*W.C.*1]

Sunday [29 May? 1927]

Yes, it did amuse me, the picture of you on your donkey, or was it a mule perhaps?[1]

That damned chill has landed me in a damned headache, so I am staying in bed.

I wish you would come in—I suppose you're entertaining Eddy instead.

I'm much better today and hope to be all right tomorrow. What a curse it is, to be sure!

I think probably it would be more tactful only to stay one night this time. Perhaps you'll ask me for 2 later.

The end of this young man's letter may amuse you—What do you think he means?

You're the only person I want to see when I have a headache—thats a compliment—But its going off fast.

Write, dear honey, a nice letter to me.

Yr Virginia

Berg

1766: To V. Sackville-West   52 *Tavistock Square, W.C.*1

Wednesday [1 June 1927?]

I'm hoping to get Leonard to ask you to come and see me tomorrow. Nessa I think comes Friday. Its frightfully selfish, as I'm too stupid to talk. But I should so like it, if it isn't difficult for you. I'm much better. I had rather sharp pain for two days, and so feel rather done up, but I've slept almost all day. for 3 days, not thought or read: and there's nothing to worry about. I'm very comfortable.

1. In southern Persia. It was published as an illustration to Vita's *Twelve Days*, her account of this journey.

The flowers are quite divine How good you are to me! dearest creature. *Dont come if its the least bother*

Berg

1767: To V. SACKVILLE-WEST   52 *Tavistock Square, W.C.*1

Sunday [5 June 1927]

Oh I envied Raymond driving off with you through the hop gardens to hear the nightingales—It was a great joy seeing you; and if you would send me one line daily I could go on building you up. I am a great adept at this game. I am lying under a blue and purple forest, the lupins you brought. Enormous trees they look like, and I am a little rabbit running about among the roots. Its odd how being ill even like this splits one up into several different people. Here's my brain now quite bright, but purely critical. It can read; it can understand; but if I ask it to write a book it merely gasps. How does one write a book? I cant conceive. It's infinitely modest therefore,—my brain at this moment. Theres Vita, it says, able to write books: Then my body—thats another person. So, my body is a grey mare, trotting along a white road. We go along quite evenly for a time like this . . . . suddenly she jumps a gate . . . ∧ . . . This is my heart missing a beat and making a jump at the next one. I rather like the gray mare jumping, provided she doesn't do it too often. I have walked round the Square, but I much prefer lying on my chair under the blue and purple forest.

I've seen noone, except Nessa, who met Ottoline in Wigmore Street the first day she came back, and had an indecent proposal made her on the telephone by an unknown man—thats London, she said. She is going to wear earrings. I say, Vita, it was good of you to come. And you'll come on Friday, and you'll write wont you? You make such a figure in this forest: coming out of a glade; yellow; golden.

The Seafarers Educational Society has bought 2 copies of The Lighthouse. Its an awful thought that the merchant service will be taught navigation by me: or the proper use of foghorns and cylinders. Its a compliment never paid to you poets. I think I deserve it. The Trouble I took with that Lighthouse! Its going to be reprinted so send me any corrections: I'm rather pleased. Not very. But then the only thing I did much want, to tell you a secret, was to be given a medal by Drinkwater.[1] Thats what cuts me to the quick. Whats a Lighthouse if Drinkwater dont approve? Eh?

Virginia

We go on Tuesday

Berg

1. John Drinkwater was to present the Hawthornden Prize to Vita on 16 June.

1768: To Violet Dickinson   52 *Tavistock Sqre.* [*W.C.*1]

Sunday [5 June 1927]

My Violet,

I'm so glad that you like some of The Lighthouse. People in The Hebrides are very angry. Is it Cornwall? I'm not as sure as you are.

I've been nursing a headache in bed all this week, and now we go to Rodmell, to lie in the sun—so please excuse my illiteracy. I think I should prefer an operation to a headache—

Are you really all right again? At Welwyn? Digging? with Dogs? Leonard sends his love.

Yr
VW

Berg

1769: To Gerald Brenan   [52 *Tavistock Square, W.C.*1]

Whitmonday [6 June 1927]

My dear Gerald,

I think I appreciate lilies more than the altars do—nevertheless, I dont approve of this lavish generosity of yours. Do I send you venison if you have a cold? At the same time, your lilies are triumphant and resplendent in my big jar. Thank you very much.

I have been very wretched with a pain at the back of my neck all this week—can't read or think; but we're going to Rodmell tomorrow where I shall do nothing for a week and recover.

Please come and see me quietly alone when I get back.

Yours ever
Virginia Woolf

George Lazarus

1770: To Clive Bell   52 *Tavistock Square W.C.*1

[6? June 1927]

Dearest Clive,

I am afraid I can't come tomorrow. This bloody headache after the flu seems to have settled in again; I'm really desolated, and feel too I have gone as usual and been a killjoy. But I shall now retire to Rodmell for a bit and come back recovered.

Please forgive, and if you can, still cherish some affection for your most vexatious sister in law.

V.

Quentin Bell

1771: To V. Sackville-West

52 *Tavistock Sqre* [*London, W.C.*1]

[7 June 1927]

Health.

Better but not quite right yet—I mean I get the jumping pulse and pain if I do anything: Cant write sense. Will you please be rather strict for a time? Its so easy, with this damned disease, to start a succession of little illnesses, and finally be sent to bed for 6 weeks, as happened last time. I expect to be perfectly well by Sunday, after a few days at Rodmell. All I pray is that you will not encourage me to excitement, even so: and you wont say I'm a molly coddle will you? Life in London is difficult: Ottoline, Clive, and so on. Now this is enough about health. We need not mention it again I hope.

Sofa: Yes.[1] But the difficulty is that few decent sofas can get up our stairs. I sacrificed my old one for that reason.

Hawthornden

Yes: the 16th: Damn Raymond. I'd been planning a party here—all the lights of London to meet you—and only waited to be steadier on my feet to ask you. I'm dining with Clive on the 17th. "to celebrate the success of Fugitive pieces" [Mary Hutchinson's book].

Long Barn.

I'd like 3 days doing nothing but eat and sleep at Long Barn more than anything. An occasional kiss on waking and between meals.

Rodmell. You'll come Friday, honey, wont you?

Virginia

Berg

1772: To Molly MacCarthy

52 *Tavistock Square, W.C.*1

Wednesday [8 June 1927?]

Dearest Molly,

It is said that you've asked us to dine on Sunday. Alas! I'm afraid we shall be off to Rodmell, to get rid of this damned flu, with which I'm still infected.

---

1. Vita had offered to buy Virginia a sofa.

But why don't you ever come and see us?
Stiff, and set up with your own importance I suppose.

yr
V.W.

Mrs Michael MacCarthy

1773: To Vanessa Bell   *Monk's House* [*Rodmell,*
                                         Sussex]
Wednesday [8 June? 1927]

Dearest,
    I see there's a bus which would get us to you about 1.45, so if it is fine on
Friday we will come to lunch, and perhaps go rather earlier (but we must
have time for a good gossip)
    I wish you'd signed your cover[1]—Privately I thought it lovely—so did
Lytton—but I was too much dashed by your letter to say so. The lines on
the back were a great improvement. Your style is unique; because so truthful;
and therefore it upsets one completely. Still I see what you mean.

B.

Berg

1774: To V. Sackville-West   [52 *Tavistock Square, W.C.*1]

[14 June 1927]

    You see I was reading Challenge and I thought your letter was a
challenge "if only you weren't so elderly and valetudinarian" was what you
said in effect "we would be spending the day together" whereupon I wired
"come then" to which naturally there was no answer and a good thing too I
daresay as I am elderly and valetudinarian,—it's no good disguising the
fact. Not even reading Challenge will alter that. She is very desirable I agree:
very. (Eve).[2] Here's Clive. So London begins. Thursday then.

1. The jacket of the American edition of *To the Lighthouse*.
2. Eve, the heroine of Vita's novel *Challenge* (1924), was based upon the character
   of Violet Trefusis. Vita was staying with Dorothy Wellesley at Sherfield in
   Hampshire, and wrote to Virginia on 11 June: "Do you know what I should
   do, if you were not a person to be rather strict with? I should steal my own
   motor out of the garage at 10 pm. tomorrow night, be at Rodmell by 11.5,
   throw gravel at your window, then you'd come down and let me in; I'd stay
   with you till 5, and be home by half-past six. But, you being you, I can't;
   more's the pity. Have you read my book? Challenge, I mean. Perhaps I sowed
   all my wild oats then. Yet I dont feel that the impulse has left me; no, by God;
   and for a different Virginia I'd fly to Sussex in the night. Only with age,
   soberness, and the increase of consideration, I refrain. But the temptation is
   great" (*Berg*).

You won't think from this that I mean I seriously expected you: it was all a kind of tipsy vision of driving along the downs with you in the dawn. I was very excited all day.

Berg

1775: To Harold Nicolson   52 *Tavistock Square, W.C.1*
Wednesday [15 June 1927]

My dear Harold,
    It was more than angelic of you to send me an early copy of your book.[1] It is now half past ten: Leonard is saying we must go to bed; but I must scribble a line in haste to say how absolutely delightful I think it—how I laughed out loud to myself again and again. Yet at the same time it is rather serious—I can't make out how you combine the advantages of fact and fiction as you do. I am also jealous—I cant help it—that all these things should have happened to you, not to me. And also, for some reason I feel profoundly and mysteriously shy. What this arises from I have not yet discovered: some horror of the past no doubt: but I think it is a great tribute to a book when it makes one fumble in ones own inside. I was so glad to find poor dear Bloomsbury playing its games in its corner—and Sibyl Colefax popping in for one moment. You must write another and another, and for goodness sake, send them to the Wolves.
    I hope we shall meet tomorrow. Tell Vita I tried to buy a pair of shoes to dignify the occasion [Vita's Hawthornden Prize], but my heart failed me.

Yours Ever
Virginia Woolf
(in great haste, but also in great delight)

Berg

1776: To Lady Ottoline Morrell
                                52 *Tavistock Square, W.C.1*
[June 1927]

Dearest Ottoline,
    Welcome!!!??? (this is in imitation of Lady Colefax)
    It is a great pleasure to think of you again in London, exercising your natural genius, and I at once flock to your standard—but not this Wednesday, as we have people dining here—We shall come next week I hope—if you mean Wednesday will always find you.

1. *Some People,* which was published on 23 June.

I don't think I can manage this Tuesday, owing to the rush here in the press in the afternoon.

However, its a great excitement and illumination of the perfect dulness which broods over Chelsea swamps in my mind to think of you there.

Excuse this scrawl—I am having to talk as well as write.

Ever yours
V.W.

Texas

1777: To V. Sackville-West   [52 *Tavistock Square, W.C.*1]

[1927?]

Look here Vita—throw over your man, and we'll go to Hampton Court and dine on the river together and walk in the garden in the moonlight and come home late and have a bottle of wine and get tipsy, and I'll tell you all the things I have in my head, millions, myriads—They won't stir by day, only by dark on the river. Think of that. Throw over your man, I say, and come.

Berg

1778: To Ethel Sands   52 *Tavistock Square, W.C.*1

June 23rd [1927]

Dearest Ethel

I have been a wretch not to answer you before, but I have been awfully bothered with headaches and detested the sight of a pen.

What a bad psychologist you are! You know I don't care a damn for your praise, and think you know nothing about it—that's your mistake. If you were here this evening (and I'm alone in my drawing room, and wish you were sitting in your arm chair opposite) I should examine you closely into the meaning of all you say, and perhaps dont say about the Lighthouse. It would interest me enormously to know what you mean by 'a more intense vision of the outer world'. The Lighthouse seemed to me almost too much the inner world. But thats only the beginning. You'll have to rub up your memories, and stand a lot of questioning. Why, if you object to this, do you know authors?

Yes, Eleanor Brougham[1] has sent her ms. and it lies, with a gigantic coronet and plenty of scent on my table. I will read it, but I feel slight

1. Eleanor Mabel Brougham was the daughter of Lord Brougham and Vaux. She had already published two anthologies of English verse, and had submitted the short anthology *Epitaphs* to the Woolfs, who rejected it.

shivers. She has dogged my life at a distance for many years. And I've always heard or understood, that she's a bore. I see you say she's an old friend of yours. But then you're so exquisitely composed that no one bores you—thats my belief, not even. . . . .[1]

I can't settle down completely to London after Rome. It was a revelation to me—flowers coming out every moment, ruins, Roman roads, nightingales, the Campagna. I'm going back—certainly I shall never go anywhere else.

I should like extremely to come to you some time. (I think it is extraordinarily nice of you to ask me). Could it be for two nights about the 25th of July? I can't be quite sure, as one or two things have to be fitted in: but it would be great fun; and I dont suppose, if you dont mind, that Nessa and Duncan would. May I let you know?

I've not seen Ottoline or Sibyl, in fact I've no news whatever. But Lytton tells me that Ottoline has crammed two Garsingtons into one small house [10 Gower Street], wears pink plush, and is so much of a ruin (without a sunset or nightingale or anything) that one can only drop a wreath and heave a sigh so I suppose I must go round and see.

Yours affect
V.W.

Wendy Baron

1779: To V. Sackville-West   52 *Tavistock Square*, *W.C.*

Friday [24 June 1927]

Yes, my dear Honey, it was a great pity you didn't come yesterday. You'd have found me alone. So am I today—and there's your empty chair. The only solution of the problem is that you should take a flat in London— please consider this: Yes, the Wolves would like to come next week end—I mean Saturday 2nd. Leonard says he must go on Sunday night. Could I stay till Monday? Shall you be alone? If so, I might catch a few minutes talk with you.

Our traveller went to Bumpus, who said they'd brought up 4 copies of Teheran from the cellar, put them in the window, and sold them at once. On this showing, the Land must be selling like melting snow. I think I'm going to see Edith soon—I like her: she's a character. I dont think you probably realise how hard it is for the natural innovator as she is, to be fair to the natural traditionalist as you are. Its much easier for you to see her good points than for her to see yours. Also, she hates Squire (with some reason— he's the spit and image of mediocrity) and the Hawthornden tars you, you must admit, with that brush; and then you sell, and she dont—all good reasons why being a Sitwell she should vomit in public: I wish, by the way,

1. Dots in the original.

you, on your side, would find out what's up between me and Sibyl. Save for a scold on the telephone I've not had a word from her since February. I'm afraid some one's gossiped. But don't let her suspect that I've noticed—it may be Desmond, of course.

I'm rather in the dumps. I have to put off everything and see nobody and go nowhere or I get a pain in my back or I sneeze or my heart jumps or something; and so I footle my time away when I want to see 150 people and write 26 books. I do write a little, but thats about all. However, I think its better, and I'm saving up for Tuesday.

You'll come early Tuesday afternoon, wont you and stay late? I wanted to ask you to dine, but Leonard thinks I shall then get excited, and start the Eclipse with a headache—Damn, oh damn!

I should now be at Carmen with Raymond.

Arnold Bennett wrote quite a friendly article about the Lighthouse last night.[1] Why, I wonder? I've rejected Miss Brougham. I liked your husband.

Yes. I've lots of things to say.

Yr Virginia

Berg

1780: To V. Sackville-West   [52 *Tavistock Square, W.C.*1]

Monday [4 July 1927]

Yes you are an agile animal—no doubt about it, but as to your gambols being diverting, always, at Ebury Street for example, at 4 o'clock in the morning, I'm not so sure. Bad, wicked beast! To think of sporting with oysters—lethargic glucous lipped oysters, lewd lascivious oysters, stationary cold oysters,—to think of it, I say. Your oyster has been in tears on the telephone . . . [7 *words omitted*]—thats all the faith there is in oysters. But what did I come back to? A message from Dadie, and he's coming in next minute, and I'm alone, and Leonards motoring, and we shall have 2 or 3 hours tête à tête—I and Dadie. Hah Hah! Bad Wicked Beast.

At the same time, there were the mushrooms: the crab: the bed; the log fire: All shall be credited to you. I'm a fair minded woman. You only be a careful dolphin in your gambolling, or you'll find Virginia's soft crevices lined with hooks. You'll admit I'm mysterious—you don't fathom me yet— Who knows what—but here's Dadie:

Honey, could you remember to bring my waterproof (rose pink) and my gloves (scarlet) I flung them down in the hall I think. I'll keep Tuesday, miraculously free, for any purpose you like.

1. Bennett wrote in the *Evening Standard* of 23 June: "I have read a bunch of novels. I must say, despite my notorious grave reservations concerning Virginia Woolf, that the most original of the bunch is *To the Lighthouse*. . . . Her character drawing has improved. Mrs Ramsay almost amounts to a complete person."

Tray[1] and I fairly hymned and carolled and chanted the praises of Vita and Harold. The Weald of Kent was a mere back cloth for your splendours ... This is something very interesting.[2]

Only one reservation I made—about beds in Ebury Street: and lost ear rings.

Yr Virginia

Pale: pastyfaced, muffin minded Shanks, your brother in the Hawthornden, calls me 'a dishonest writer'—so you see, if you have Edith, I have Shanks.[3]

Berg

1781: To V. Sackville-West   52 *T.[avistock] S.[quare, W.C.1]*
[8? July 1927]

Yes, do come as early as ever you can on Tuesday. I'm now told that I engaged myself to go with Nessa, Duncan and Clive to Hampton Court on Tuesday. If so, you'll have to come—We'll dine; we'll haunt the terrace. For my part, I should prefer solitude. For yours, you'd prefer oysters. Bad Vita, bad wicked Vita. Whats become of your fine gesture about promiscuity? Dadie looked divine last night in a new plum coloured suit. I'm outraged by your mother's habits[4]—

Still I've had 3 hours today of Susie Buchan,[5] thanks to you. She says she knows you—I said why chaperone your daughter? All girls go to bed with young men as soon as look at them. Not a successful remark: she says—oh she says thousands of things.

What a good review [of *Some People*] Harold had in the Lit Sup: What a bad one your oyster had. But have you committed incest with Eddie? I can well believe it. I can believe anything—the creeping newts, the toads that spawn in the ditch. What would Susie say, or John either, for the matter of that?

1. Raymond Mortimer, who had also been staying at Long Barn that weekend.
2. Virginia heavily scored out a short preceding sentence.
3. Edward Shanks, the poet who had won the first Hawthornden Prize in 1919. In a series of articles, Edith Sitwell had abused *The Land*.
4. On 5 July Lady Sackville had kept Vita up until 6 a.m. abusing everybody and pretending to be desperately ill.
5. Susan Grosvenor, the novelist and biographer, had known Virginia since their youth. She married John Buchan, later Lord Tweedsmuir, in 1907.

A thousand million thanks for the pink coat. I've no stamps, so be content.

VW.

I've just written, or re-written, a nice little story about Sapphism, for the Americans.[1]

Berg

1782: To V. SACKVILLE-WEST   52 *T*[*avistock*] *S.*[*quare, W.C.*1]

Friday [15 July 1927]

Dearest Creature,
    We have now got our own motor[2] and so will come down in it for lunch on Sunday, if thats all right. But heaven knows what excuse I can make for staying the night. Can you invent one? I'm afraid I shall have to go back with our Mr Harris[3] after tea or dinner. Perhaps I could have a fit on the lawn.
    Just off to broadcast;[4] not a bit nervous; more likely to be deadly bored. I know what'll happen—I shall yawn and say, . . . [*eleven words omitted*]. This will be broadcast and ruin the chastity of 12 million homes. Thats what you've brought me to.
    Goodnight dearest honey, my voice will soon be mingling with the nightingales at Long Barn.

Yr Virginia

Berg

1783: To V. SACKVILLE-WEST   52 *Tavistock Sqre, W.C.*1

18th July 1927

My dear Mrs Nicolson,
    I cant tell you how I enjoyed myself on Sunday. It was so good of you and your husband to let me come. And what a lovely garden! I cant think how you can ever bear to leave it. But then *everything* was so delightful. London seemed more commonplace than ever after your delightful Long Barn. And I still have some of your lovely flowers to remind me of the happy time I had with you, and your husband, to whom please give my best thanks and remembrances, and with much love to you both, I am. There,

1. *"Slater's Pins Have No Points"* (*Forum*, January 1928).
2. The Woolfs had just bought their first car, a second-hand Singer.
3. Fred Harris, Virginia's driving instructor.
4. Virginia and Leonard broadcast for the B.B.C. for the first time.

you ramshackle old Corkscrew, is that the kind of thing you like? I suppose so.

What I think will be so nice next time is the porpoise in my bath—steel blue, ice cold, and loving hearted. Some prefer dolphins—I dont. I've known one dolphin, the Mediterranean kind, ravage a whole bedfull of oysters. A lewd sort of brute that.

I've been motoring all the evening. Rather good at gears now. What else? A sordid scallywag dinner last night; room smelling of cheese, but very bright in the head. I've engaged myself to write a book on architecture with a man.[1]

Honey dearest, don't go to Egypt please. Stay in England. Love Virginia. Take her in your arms.

Three o'clock Thursday.

I may motor down—so there.

Yr Virginia

Berg

1784: TO CHARLES SANGER   52 *Tavistock Sqre W.C.*

July 18th [1927]

My dear Charlie,

Yes it is very annoying never to see you. But I dont believe its possible in the summer. Let us hope for the autumn. We've just bought a motor car, and I hope this will take us to Chelsea.

Daphne has written me a very just and rather severe letter about the inaccuracy of the Lighthouse. But she also flatters me by liking it which pleases me greatly.

My love to Dora.

Your affte
Virginia Woolf

Daphne Sanger

1785: TO DAPHNE SANGER   52 *Tavistock Sqre W.C.*

[18 July 1927]

Dear Daphne,

It was very nice of you to write to me about To the Lighthouse. I am very glad that you enjoyed it, as I did not much expect you would. I also like your reason for liking it—that it is 'an organic whole'. That is what I wanted it to be. I don't myself much mind about peoples' ages and topo-

---

1. George Kennedy, the architect. The book was never written.

graphy—not, that is to say, in a book like mine where the writer is trying to do something else. I should mind in Jane Austen, because I think she leads you to expect that kind of accuracy. Still I will try next time to be either quite inaccurate or quite accurate.

I am very sorry we didn't see you this summer. I hate the summer in London as one sees all the people one doesn't want to see. But I suppose you are happy down in Somerset, except that I remember you much prefer towns.

Thank you again for your letter.

Yours sincerely
Virginia Woolf

Daphne Sanger

1786: To Susan Buchan   52 *Tavistock Square, W.C.*1

July 19th [1927]

My dear Susie,

It was very good of you to send me Huntingtower,[1] but I was so in-discreet as to leave it on the table and it was at once seized by someone who was going on a journey and has not been returned. This seems to me a great compliment to the author, but not at all pleasing to me. I hope to get it back next week, and then I shall at once read it, but I dont like not to thank you for so long.

Please dont become entirely political[2] and thus have to drop me once and for all. I hope next autumn you will come again, or let me come and see you.

I am sure you will be glad to hear that Sibyl Colefax is coming to tea on Tuesday. This is a great relief to me.

It was so nice of you to send me the book.

Yours very sincerely
Virginia Woolf

Lady Tweedsmuir

1787: To Helen McAfee   52 *Tavistock Square, WC*1

Typewritten
19th July 1927

Dear Miss McAfee

I am so sorry that you had the trouble of cabling to me. I have been

1. John Buchan's novel *Huntingtower* was published in 1922.
2. Buchan was elected M.P. for the Scottish Universities at a by-election in May 1927.

delayed by illness, but I hope I have been able to improve the essay [*Street Haunting*] a little. I shall be very grateful for the double set of proofs which you are good enough to promise.

I am very much pleased that you should like To the Lighthouse. It is very difficult to judge ones own work; but I certainly enjoyed writing it more than any other of my novels.

Please accept my apologies for the delay, and believe me

yours sincerely
Virginia Woolf

Yale University

1788: To Ethel Sands   52 *Tavistock Sqre, W.C.*

Friday 22 July [1927]

Dearest Ethel,

I'm sorry I've been so long about writing, but I couldn't be sure about days. I will come[1] on Wednesday 27th if that suits you. The boat arrives some time in the afternoon I think. May I stay till Saturday? I am very much excited at the thought of coming. You won't mind talking for 24 hours on end, I hope? It will be mostly about motor cars, I can think of nothing else. I have driven from the Embankment to the Marble Arch and only knocked one boy very gently off his bicycle. But I would rather have a gift for motoring than anything.

Nessa and Duncan sound very happy. It will be alarming to be alone among so many painters. They are so mute and highminded compared with us poor creatures. I am leading a very impure life at the moment—what with motoring and Sibyl who is having a reconciliation with me, and so on. But it will be great fun seeing you, and I must say I think it is very nice of you to ask me.

Yours aff
Virginia

Wendy Baron

1789: To Vanessa Bell   [52 *Tavistock Square, W.C.*1]

Saturday, July 23rd [1927]

Dearest,

I have written to Ethel, which I suppose I should have done before—I'm coming on Wednesday—a little alarmed, as I foresee you and Duncan

1. To Ethel's house, Château d'Auppegard, near Dieppe.

will be occupied all day, and I shall have to do my tricks with Ethel (now don't leave this lying about). I shall be rather glad however, to see you—partly as a relief from Ottoline, Colefax and such like. But my whole life is spent motoring with Harris. Not that I've had as many lessons as I should like. I'm now competent to drive alone in the country, he says. I think it is a very exciting employment. and he says (but this may be flattery) that I'm well above the average. We both have the same fault—you and I—we keep too much to the left. But my gear changing is very good.

We went to Tommies wedding [to Julia Strachey] at St Pancras Church yesterday, a prosaic affair, though the service always fills my eyes with tears. Also the grotesqueness is so great. The Strachey women were of inconceivable drabness on one side, Aunt Loo[1] having also an aroma of hypocrisy about her which makes me vomit; on the other side sat the Judge[2] in frock coat and top hat, like a shop walker. He got locked into his pew, and could not get out, except at the last moment, to sign the register. He mistook the hinge for the door handle. Julia was highly self possessed, and then Angus was glowering behind us. I daresay he takes it to heart, though I repeat for the 1000th time; I cannot see the physical charm of that little woodpecker man. They dined with us afterwards. I handed on your curse, just before the ceremony—Nessa's curse on marriage, it is called; and has been known to strike a Bride dead on the altar steps.

Vita has had a letter from Clive telling her the good news that he is now completely happy: life is treating him well; he has nothing left to wish for. I think that Parrokeet is one of the vainest and silliest of fowls: if he can make us think that he goes to bed with Valerie,[3] thats all he wants—I believe half his misery has been outraged vanity. Now he's Don Juan again, nothing matters. But I very much doubt that he is Don Juan. I hear he's gone to Charleston. I also hear that Fred [Harris] can't get off till 4 on Saturday, so Leonard won't be able to meet us. Fred will stay the night, and motor us to Charleston next day. Then you will see me take the wheel and return—It is an awesome sight.

But all this will be told you when we go to our rooms to write letters. How fascinating the whole thing will be! Duncan reading—"the kettled lips of graves"—the ladies sewing; but poor Billy [Virginia] isn't one thing or the other, not a man nor a woman, so whats he to do? run up the ladies skirts. Nan[4] terrifies me. Ethel makes me silly. But the food will be nice, and Nessa will kiss me.

B.

Helen [Anrep] is going to Romney for the summer—We dined there with the

1. Alys Pearsall Smith (Mrs Bertrand Russell), the aunt of Julia's step-mother.
2. Thomas Tomlin, a judge of the High Court, and Stephen Tomlin's father.
3. Valerie Taylor, the actress.
4. Nan Hudson, the American painter and life-long friend of Ethel Sands.

[George] Kennedys—too many handkerchiefs in the pot for my taste, which may be hypercritical, of course—One has a sense of ashes in the soup. One of her legs—supposing she were a fly and had 6—has come off. But it was all very nice. Then we had Bob [Trevelyan].—but I've no room.

Berg

1790: To Edward Sackville West   52 *Tavistock Sqre, WC*

Saturday [23 July 1927]

Dear Eddy,

I'm afraid Wednesday won't do, as I'm going to Dieppe that day.

Could you come to tea on Tuesday? Thats the last chance of seeing you. Sibyl will be here, but you would alleviate the situation for both of us, and then she'd go, to some Duke in a hurry, and we could gossip on.

We had Tommie and Julia to celebrate their wedding last night: it was at St Pancras at 2.—the most dismal ceremony.

Your
Virginia Woolf

Berg

1791: To V. Sackville-West 52 *T.[avistock] S.[quare, W.C.*1]

Sunday [24 July 1927]

Dearest Creature,

(by the way, why is it that you always come into my presence in letters simply and solely—not even My dear Virginia, whereas I always invent some lovely lovely phrase?) how nice it is of me to be writing to you, when you're not writing to me. No, you're not. You're talking to Dottie. By God, at 3 this morning I'll ring you up. Noodles [butler], or whatever his name is, will catch you in the act. You will summon all the blood of all the Sackvilles:—

But listen. I bought the stockings with lisle thread heels—you're quite right. They have existed it seems these 30 years. Queen Victoria wore them. And I bought a mixture which is applied with a sponge to shoes. They have ripened in the night to a patchy nut-brown. But tell me—when a shoes inwardly sound, yet outwardly corrupt, what can one do? It goes against my conscience to throw them after a bride or otherwise destroy. (We went to Tommie's wedding at St Pancras Church: hence the metaphor, or whatever it may be.) But listen: now what am I to do about powder? Ethel will take it ill if I don't powder my nose. Once you gave me some which didn't smell;

402

but I dont know what it was: I bought some which permeates every pore, and I daren't stink like that: I loathe scents. (except on you, when they are merely the ripeness of the apricot) Tell me quickly what to get and where. I will rise to powder, but not to rouge. So thats finished.

I forget what has happened since I let you out in the moonlight, to go whoring in Mayfair. I was very happy at Kew.[1] Very, very.

Leonard says he will spend Thursday nights in London. Wouldn't Thursday be the day you come back from Brighton? and sleep at Rodmell? But this wont be till the 12th, so you must come before.

You'll be glad to hear I've sold 4000 of the L[ighthouse]: in America in a month: so they think I shall sell 8000 before the end of the year. And I shall make £800: (that is with luck.)

I've got to go and see Ottoline now, which is the most incredible effort. To step from Pinker asleep in the big chair to all those satins and jade greens and little yellow books with tassels hanging out of them!

I say, you won't be in London on Tuesday I suppose?

My love to Dottie

Virginia

Berg

1792: To Janet Case   52 *Tavistock Sqre* [*W.C.*1]

July 24th [1927]

My dear Janet,

It was very nice of you to listen in and to hear us so clearly.[2] One is shut up in a soundproof room, with a red light over the door, and a notice to say that if one rustles one's manuscript thousands will be deafened. All this makes one rather bored and dismal, but I'm glad it got through to the New Forest all right.

We are just moving, I to France for a few days and Leonard to Rodmell. We have bought a motor car (this is the cut of the Lighthouse) and I have been wobbling round and round Windmill Hill, every day, trying to avoid dogs and children.

But when we're expert perhaps we shall call on you one day. Everything seems to be within ones reach of a sudden.

Leonard's love.

Yours
V.W.

Sussex

1. Virginia and Vita had been to Kew Gardens on 21 July after Vita had given her driving lessons in Richmond Park.
2. Virginia's and Leonard's broadcast of 15 July.

403

Letters 1793-1818 (August–early October 1927)

Before going to Monk's House for the usual summer recess, Virginia spent four days with her American painter-friends, Ethel Sands and Nan Hudson, at their house in Normandy. During August and September the Woolfs made constant local expeditions in their car, and Virginia went three times to Long Barn, where Vita was becoming deeply involved with Mary Campbell, the wife of the South African poet Roy Campbell, who had rented a cottage in the village. Virginia herself had a declaration of love from Philip Morrell, but responded less ardently. She was writing, without much pleasure, a short book on the novel (Phases of Fiction) *and several articles for American papers, but she was longing to make a start on* The Waves.

1793: To ETHEL SANDS

Monk's House, Rodmell,
Lewes [Sussex]

Aug 1st 1927

Dearest Ethel,

I was covered with shame and remorse when I found that you had sent Loomes [butler] all the way into Dieppe with my bag. It was angelic of you and very skilful of him and idiotic of me. Will you please express my gratitude and thanks! And then, in mid-channel, I found myself grasping your copy of Maurois' Disraeli, which I will send back. I don't know how I purloined it without knowing.

But I feel that I came away so laden with all sorts of things that one more or less don't much matter. There's the Seine that day, and Jumiège, and the house, and the sea, and Dieppe and the furniture shop, and then the food, and the clothes, and the flowers and the furniture, and in the middle, so exquisite, such a type to my mind of civilisation and rightness, Nan and Ethel—Ethel and Nan—which way ought it to be? Here I stop short, seeing the prospect of disaster before me. I shall be comparing you to birds of paradise or sea-horses or something and you will each write me a separate letter of acute disgust (I found a declaration from Philip[1]—how exciting!—how nice, at my age to have a little love—but what am I to do?) You see, at

1. Just before she left for France, Philip Morrell had called twice on Virginia, and told her that he loved her. She treated his advances with light amusement.

least 300 pages could be written about my three days. But in one word, I was astonishingly happy, and I can't get over your being so good to me.

The transition from you to us was highly abrupt. I had forgotton to order beer for the Chauffeur. I scraped together some cold lemon coloured cheese. They did not get here till after nine, and what dinner we had was eaten in such chaos as you can't conceive. Next day we went to Charleston and Clive was so damp and dismal and shrunken that I hadn't the heart to plant any darts in his flanks, nor he in mine. The sacred subject was not mentioned. But it will be—he is coming to tea. Then we played dressmakers with Angelica, then we compared our cars, then we drove home, then we knocked a bit off the car getting it into the shed, then Nessa came round in her car, then we hoped sudden death would befall the Keynes, then we said some very nice things about you, and now it is pouring wet, and I must go and see what that poor gaping imbecile my charwoman is doing about dinner.

A thousand thanks again. I was so happy.

Your affect
Virginia

Wendy Baron

1794: TO NAN HUDSON   *Monk's House, Rodmell,*
                                        Lewes [Sussex]

1st August 1927

My dear Nan,

It is rather an awful undertaking writing to a woman who fills me with such awe and envy (no, I'm not really afraid of you at the moment) and also makes me talk about Greek heads and Chalcedony. But gratitude and I suppose greed drive me to it. You can't imagine how delightful it was being with you and Ethel; the only drawback is that I should soon be spoilt for the extreme simplicity of home life. As it is, even after 3 days with you, I find the tapioca pudding almost incredible. It comes up in a slab like glue, not hot, not cold, very sticky, yellowish, sweet. Then there's the suet pudding and the pastry. What do they do with things over here? Poor woman [Rose Bartholomew], she is very plaintive, has several children, no larder, poisoned gums, so I suppose one must face it But Leonard thinks me grown rather pernickety in my absence. We talk a great deal about you and the dog and the garden. Our only piece of luck is that two swarms of bees settled in the orchard and we caught one of them and hope to have some honey next summer. Now would you come to Tavistock Sqre and eat my own honey off plain bread? I shall ask you. One can but try these things. You can be as haughty as you like. I shall continue to be humble. Why are writers so much less well equipped for life than painters? Why is my writing table all of a mess (do buy me the next writing table the furniture man has, and a chest of drawers, and I will bless you for ever and I am rather rich at the moment) and why does my spaniel jump onto the chairs when she is dripping from a swim in the river? The answer is that instead of controlling life as you and Ethel do, we writers merely contemplate it. I make up little pictures of Auppegard. I think of the Seine that day at lunch; of the windows of your house. And now I must answer M. Blanche[1] and pretend that I have already read his six volumes. What I have done is to begin a new book on fiction,[2] all in a rush, thanks to feeling so spry and fresh. But I mustn't go on chattering or you will say to Ethel "What a bore the woman is!" when the poor creature is only trying to thank you for being so good to her, for it was astonishingly nice of you to let me come.

Yours affect
Virginia Woolf

Wendy Baron

1795: To V. Sackville-West   *Monks House [Rodmell, Sussex]*

Wednesday [3 August 1927]

Yes, darling creature, your letter was handed me just as we left Auppegard, and caused me, I suppose, to forget my box, so that the exquisite butler had to motor into Dieppe after us. Yes, darling, it was a nice letter. Sauqueville[3] aint a very grand place, all the same. I looked for traces of you. Did your ancestors own a saw mill? Thats what they do now, and not a specially fine leg among them. But I'll tell you all about it when you come. When? Choose your day and night—your 2 days and nights even better—whenever suits you. All I impress upon you is that until next Wednesday, when Nelly returns, we are living on potted meat and sardines: only Mrs Bartholomew to do, and she in the last stages of decrepitude. I really advise you to wait. Then Leonard goes up on Thursday 11th and comes back on Friday. I shall be alone Thursday night. Could you stay two nights? I dont want to seem as if I had you in secret, though its infinitely more to my taste, exploring about in the recesses secretly. Write me a tactful letter, making out a good case for whatever it is: and let it be as long as you can. (Your stay and your letter) No one else is coming.

Ethel's was great fun—eating and drinking, motoring, and chattering.

---

1. Virginia met Jacques-Emile Blanche, the portrait painter, at Auppegard. The 'six volumes' were his memoirs, *Les Cahiers d'un artiste*, 1914-19.
2. See p. 325, note 1.
3. The village near Auppegard, Normandy, from which the Sackville family came to England in the 11th century.

Oh the heavenly food! I said to myself I shall grow so fat Vita won't like me. Still I ate and ate. Nan is the discovery of the two. Nan is a sterling dignified upright character, with more sound and fury in her than Ethel. Yes, I like Ethel (I read that aloud, the praise that is, at lunch and it had a great success: Ethel blushed, so did Nan, who likes Ethel praised better than anything) but Ethel's a little fine ladyish, pernickety, acid, occasionally. She longs for society. Nan for solitude.

Tell me about your poem.[1]

My God, how you would have laughed yesterday! Off for our first drive in the Singer: the bloody thing wouldn't start. The accelerator died like a duck—starter jammed. All the village came to watch—Leonard almost sobbed with rage. At last we had to bicycle in and fetch a man from Lewes. He said it was the magnetos—would you have known that? Should we have known? Another attempt today, we are bitter and sullen and determined. We think of nothing else. Leonard will shoot himself if it dont start again.

Come down, dearest Creature

Yr Virginia

Berg

1796: To V. Sackville-West

Monk's House, Rodmell
[Sussex]

Friday [5 August 1927]

Yes its odd, as you say, how the crowded night is succeeded by the empty day. The only consolation at the moment is that Leonard has gone up for the day this week not night so our intercourse would have been limited. All the same, here I am alone, shivering, crouching over the fire; and we might have talked about English prose.

I've seen too many people, and talked too much. and I've no time now to write this out 6 times over, as I had meant. Yes; that sticks in my throat; that I bubble. I'm going to polish and preen in future.

Dont, dearest, think you must pay me compliments. I've a very low opinion of my writing at the moment. This comes of correcting proofs [of *Street Haunting*]: its all bounce and jerk; I want to spin a thread like a spider.

Where did you meet Lord Gage?[2] Shall you marry him? Clive hinted that he knew, and I knew, about a night in the oyster bed yesterday; but we were both very discreet.

Oh Lord! Stock brokers [Herbert Woolf] tomorrow. I wish I could see no one till October—excepting someone whose name has a V. in it—which may mean Vanessa, mayn't it.

1. Vita was contemplating a poem about solitude, but did not finish it until 1938.
2. The 6th Viscount Gage, who succeeded his father in 1912. He was the owner of Firle Place and Charleston.

Be sure to come Thursday, as early as you can. You must come, even if Leonard dont spend the night away.

And write again before that, honey, do. When's your book out?[1] Not in September so that I could review it for America?

Any news from Foreign Office?[2]

I've been reading Katherine Mansfield[3] with a mixture of sentiment and horror. What odd friends I've had—you and she—

Your
Virginia

Berg

1797: To V. Sackville-West   *Monks House* [*Rodmell, Sussex*]

Sunday [7 August 1927]

Musha—i—djabah—dal—imam—[4]

Which being interpreted means, Darling—West—what—a—donkey—you—are—all my letters in future are going to be addressed to Pippin [dog], since it is clear you cant read them. "Something wrong I feel by your letter." —What do you mean? It was the nicest, lovingest, tenderest letter in the world: a little rasped at not seeing you perhaps, but after all thats to your taste isnt it? Or did you, with the marvellous intuition of the poet, discover what I have tried to keep concealed from you? that I am loved, by a man [Philip Morrell]; a man with an aquiline nose, a nice property, a wife of title, and furniture to suit. The proposal was made the day before I left, and I have a letter now confirming it. What do you wish me to do? I was so overcome I blushed like a girl of 15. It was seeing me in my black hat and cloak that did it, he said; and then Colefax came in, and we were caught.

So, you see, nights and days must be devoted wholeheartedly, not just as you might tickle a trout with the tip of your finger, to keeping me servile. You must lay yourself out to enchant me every second.

Yes, Thursday, dearest: but earlier than 5 please. make it 4. Then Leonard will see you (and he wants to) and we'll motor him to Lewes.

Do you want to lunch at Charleston on Friday? Say yes or no. I've made no promises.

One thing—no two things—more—First, unutterable villain about powder: did I ask you to *give* me a box? No. And its not the first time I have had to complain either. True, I spilt most of it on Ethels floor—but never

1. Vita's *Aphra Behn* was published on 27 October.
2. About Harold's next appointment.
3. Her *Journal* (1927).
4. This phrase, and its equivalent before Virginia's signature to this letter, were mock-Persian, and have no meaning in either case.

do I ask you anything again, except this very instant, when I ask, could you bring your camera and do 3 or 4 snapshots (me paying 2/6 each) which could be printed (me paying 6d each) and sent to M. Blanche, who is writing an article called An Hour with Virginia Woolf,[1] and wants to substantiate his statements by a large untouched portrait. If so I should be infinitely grateful; and for the last time.

I think its a very good plan to have some straightforward work like Aphra to keep one's machinery engaged: because then the other part of one's brain can take a rest and form little nuggets of gold, drops of pearl: your solitude. Will it be dedicated to me? Or to Dotty? Or to a certain lecherous oyster?

By the way, Miss Valerie Taylor has taken up her lodging in Clive's flat, so thats that, to put it poetically: all the same Clive still looks a little moped, and eats baked bread called Vita bread to keep his figure at its present level.

So 4 on Thursday, dearest—Mishka—na—y—ralt—ta—vera. You wont miss the significance of *that* will you?

Virginia

Stay Friday if you can—I shall be alone till 7.
Why has your friend Hugh Walpole set Ellen Glasgow upon me, and who is Ellen Glasgow?[2]
Bring Pippin.

Berg

1798: To V. Sackville-West   [*Monk's House, Rodmell, Sussex*]

[10 August 1927?]

all right. Come then: be enchanting: This is only to say your d—d wine merchant hasn't sent our wine, so would you let me BUY off you a bottle of Alletta? [Alella]
     BUY I say. *BUY*

Your
Virginia

Dont be later than 4 please, or I'll have to go into Lewes without you.

Berg

<hr>

1. *An Interview with Virginia Woolf* (*Les Nouvelle Littéraires*, 13 August 1927).
2. The American novelist (1874-1945).

1799: To HELEN McAFEE   *Monks House, Rodmell,*
                              Lewes, Sussex
Typewritten
17th August 1927

Dear Miss McAfee

Many thanks for sending me the double set of proofs. I have returned one, with a few very slight corrections which will not affect the length. I have let the title stand as you altered it. I agree with you in thinking it an improvement.

With many thanks,

yours sincerely
Virginia Woolf

Yale University

1800: To SAXON SYDNEY-TURNER   *Monk's House, Rodmell*
                                      [Sussex]
Sunday Aug 21st [1927]

My dear Saxon,

I am sorry to hear that you are back again, as I should like to have gone on getting particulars about your Finnish journeys. You left off at a highly romantic moment, just as you entered a very old church in company with a Princess. The Sacristan was about to show you a holy chalice—This reminds me—as you will see why—to ask you if you have and would lend me the Mysteries of Udolpho [1794] by Mrs Radcliffe. I am in urgent need of it. Naturally the London Library thinks it may have it in a month or so. I am writing about Romance—a silly thing to do; but then Leonard and Dadie have started a series, and my summer is being ruined by the need of writing a book for it on fiction;[1] which I hate more and more, and become more and more incapable of reading, let alone criticising: But what am I to do? Leonard will take no excuse; and then there's Dadie, as pink as a daisy and as proud as a wood-lion. Where does one read of wood lions?

I am keeping a copy of a book called Jakobs RUM [Swedish edition] to give you; and here are some comments on it, which leave me cold.

A good way of writing a letter would be always to begin the next sentence with the last word of the one before. Thus, cold—It is very cold; it is devilish cold; it is also blowing a hurricane and yesterday rained an atlantic ocean. (I cant remember what the word that goes with rain on a large scale is.) Our motor car which is the joy of our lives, has to turn back,

---

1. *Phases of Fiction.*

on the road to Bodiam,[1] just as we are passing through Mr Bottomleys[2] village, the Dickers. We can stand it no longer. So you see, though I meant to write you a description of Bodiam, in your own style which is the envy of my heart, I can't. There's no news in the whole of Sussex. We drive over to Charleston and find Nessa has driven somewhere else. Clive to protect himself is going to learn to drive; because we talk of nothing but gears and cylinders.

I am reading a new classic every night. But what is happening to you? and to Barbara [Bagenal] and to Barbara's child and to Mrs Stagg[3] and to your uncle the ichthyologist? This is the group, you see, in which I compose you. Then there's your great grandfather's life. Do you agree that one never thinks of Saxon or Barbara singly, but always as the centre of a nest of other objects? This fact has never been observed by the novelists—but my word, what a set of dunderheads and duffers they are! Even Scott has passages of an incredible imbecility. Trollope has gone up in my estimation however. But then, as its all a question of mood, and of what one's just read, or whom one's just seen, whats the good of criticism? And, anyhow, vile as they are, the novelists outdo the critics. You probably have no notion what the criticism of fiction amounts to—you, who have passed your entire life on the highest peaks of Parnassus where only a few asphodels grow in the snow. Grow and Snow ought not to be there; but there they are.

Please forgive the incoherency of this letter, which does injustice to my affection, and send me Udolpho if you have it.

Yrs
V.W.

Sussex

1801: To V. Sackville-West   *Monks House, Rodmell*
                                           [Sussex]

Monday, 22nd Aug. [1927]

Yes, dear Creature—but what was I saying 'Yes' for?[4] I forget. Pinker has been sick, and an apple tree blown down. But none of this was what I had in mind, as I came across the lawn in a hurricane to my lodge. (Its used for storing potatoes now.) I was going to say you needn't have bothered about the photographs—which I return; and I dont much like the looks of

1. The 14th-century moated castle in East Sussex, which Lord Curzon had restored and bequeathed to the nation.
2. Horatio Bottomley (1860-1933), the journalist and financier, who in 1922 was found guilty of fraud, and sentenced to seven years' penal servitude.
3. The landlady of Saxon's London lodgings in Great Ormond Street.
4. Virginia had agreed to review Vita's *Aphra Behn* for an American journal. No such review has yet been discovered.

Virginia Woolf myself: for Blanche has written his article and used an old photograph of me at 19—which is just as well. Dear, dear, I suppose you wouldn't accept a p.o. for 3/7 if I sent it? It would only be handed me 6 months later in a 3rd Class railway carriage between Orpington and Sevenoaks. No: though I dont think snaps are gratifying, they are salutary: so I wish you'd give me one of you. I've only the incredibly noble and highminded Hawthornden prize winner, the loved of Gosse (who's dying it seems) and praised of Squire. Mightn't I have a blowsy scallywag once in a way? or are you too vain? Yes, you are. Another scene comes to mind—at Knole this time, and Vita tearing up a snap (Nelly's word) which made her look like Bill Sykes she said. But then you are like Bill Sykes I said. I'm not, Vita said, flushing crimson and stamping her foot.

Now, shameless that I am, having said I would never ask again, I ask again. Only a loan this time. *The Mysteries of Udolpho* by Mrs Radcliffe. I think you may have them. After all Long Barn combines the luxury of etc. with the refinement of etc. Then, 2nd, would you lend me whichever is in your opinion the most romantic novel of Mrs Behn's. The truth is I'm stuck in Romance; am battered back by the hellish storms outside and do nothing but fabricate theories for my dull, dreary, long winded asinine book on fiction; and I cant get a single thing I want from the London Library.

Now, honey, if you've time on your hands why not turn it to the advantage of the Hogarth Press? You have to write a paper for the Oxford young men: make it a pamphlet for us.[1] *Please do.*

I like your energy. I love your legs. I long to see you. Leonard says "Will Vita motor me in, and fetch me back on Friday?" "The way we treat Vita!" I say. "Yes, but I can't help it" says L: I say, it is going rather far. But if you could be here by 4 on Thursday, with Udolpho and Behn, we should be very grateful

Yr
Virginia

I hope Nigel [Vita's younger son] is all right. Give him my love.

Berg

1802: To T. S. Eliot   *Monk's House, Rodmell,*
                                        Lewes, Sussex
Typewritten
24th August 1927

My dear Tom,
    I'm glad to think that we now have another subject in common—motor

1. On 14 November Vita spoke at St Hugh's College, Oxford, on modern poets. The paper was not published as a Hogarth pamphlet.

cars. Did Leonard tell you how our entire life is spent driving, cleaning, dodging in and out of a shed, measuring miles on maps, planning expeditions, going expeditions, being beaten back by the rain, eating sandwiches on high roads, cursing cows, sheep, bicyclists, and when we are at rest talking of nothing but cars and petrol? Ours is a Singer.

But the business of this letter must be put through. Will you come and stay for the week end of the 24th September? It is some way off; it is the last before we leave; we shall be alone; for all these reasons we think you must come. Needless to say, a car will meet you and take you.

What on earth makes you think I was at Pontigny?[1] I've never even been asked, and I understand that an invitation is necessary. No; I was far better employed—living in luxury and purity of spirit with your compatriots Miss Sands and Miss Hudson near Dieppe. For the cooking alone I would sell my soul twice over. Then there was M. Jacques Blanche. On the table lay the Adelphi and the New Criterion.[2]

Keynes is at Firle. We will take you over there. They have the highest opinion of you—Heaven knows why. I thought your poem rather a nice one, myself.[3] But I dont like these authors' civilities.

Ottoline was devoted to me; I made a very good impression that Sunday you rang up and were so short with her; but I undid it that same night by writing a letter in which I compared her to a Dolphin shedding its scales. Philip came round and told me she said I didnt understand her mystic side. [Richard] Aldington I know nothing about, so must let that thrust of yours remain unmet; but I think he belongs to the Murry world, where dog eats dog.

But we will go at length into all these matters when we meet.

No policeman has yet called. Why should he? Are you taking a house?

Yours affly
Virginia

Houghton Library, Harvard University

1803: To Saxon Sydney-Turner   *Monk's House, Rodmell*
                                      [Sussex]

29th Aug. 1927

My dear Saxon,

I am much chastened and humiliated by finding the 4 volumes of Mrs Radcliffe on my plate,—a lovely edition—when I only asked you for a loan.

1. The annual literary conference, which met at the home of its founder, the writer and philosopher Paul Desjardins.
2. The *New Criterion* was edited by Eliot, and the *Adelphi* by John Middleton Murry.
3. *Fragments of an Agon* (1927), also published in Eliot's *Sweeney Agonistes* (1932).

However, it is most opportune, and I am most grateful. But you should not be so extravagant. You will have a pauper's burial, I make no doubt. But if I survive I shall be among the grateful at your graveside. I think, as far as I have got, that Mrs Radcliffe is a remarkably good writer. I can't see why she is a mere laughing stock at all. She writes like a lady (and the ladies of England knew how to write, anyhow until 1850, when a rot set in) and she has a beautiful sense of landscape. So far, which is the end of vol. one, I have met nothing to raise a laugh, except a hole in the drawing-room floor where the family papers seem to be kept. But why not? I expect Jane Austen went too far the other way; and I'm not sure I shan't lead a Radcliffe relief party: but it remains to finish Udolpho, of which I see little chance so long as I am interrupted by the visits of friends in motor cars.

I have to scratch out every other word, my hand trembles so, partly with heat, partly with rage. I have just been over to Asheham to look for mushrooms, and find a railway with little trucks being built in the field, and a great chalk pit dug out in the hollow behind. There is an engine at work, and I can only suppose that they are starting some damnable lime works, and killing all my ghosts. I doubt whether this country will be possible much longer.

I hope Barbara [Bagenal] and Judith [her daughter] are now recovered. Give her, Barbara I mean, my love.

It is the first hot day we have had, and I shall spend the evening reading Udolpho. Many thanks: but remember the pauper's grave, and Stagg and me weeping in rusty crape.

Yours
V.W.

Sussex

1804: To Vanessa Bell   [*Monk's House*] *Rodmell*
                                [*Sussex*]
[end August 1927]

Dearest,

We have already accepted the Keynes' for dinner on Friday. What we suggest is that we should come to tea with you, go on to them, and then, if possible, induce them to come round after dinner for the fire works—if that suits you—I don't suppose they want much inducement. Has Lydia got full use of her legs?—after not being thought about so long. My great toe is quite numb. However these frivolities are ill timed, as I have an awful confession to make—really something ghastly: Either Nelly has thrown away the [embroidery] design you lent me, or the puppy has eaten it. It disappeared completely yesterday, after I had been working at it the night before. What am I to do to express my apologies? I had traced it exactly onto

414

the canvas. Could you re-paint it if I brought this? [Raymond] Mortimer admired it so much that I half suspect him. I will write you a story in return, but then you dont think much of stories.

I wrote the Tiltoniad[1] in such a hurry that I think a good many indiscretions, not to say indecencies, may have crept in. Also it is very vulgar. I think it would be better to keep it for the Bells alone; unless you go through it and blue pencil it, for which you have my permission.

I am stained with blue all over. For Gods sake take up the making of wall papers. I'm sick of the long monotony of distemper, besides which, when dry it is totally different from what one expects.

No: Ka [Arnold-Forster] is still to come—She asked herself, having been dreaming of Rupert [Brooke]. Why can't she ever wake up from the year 1911? There she sticks with Rupert copulating in Berlin and Dudley Ward and Gwen and Jacques [Raverat]. Pah!

Mortie [Raymond Mortimer] was as fresh as a lark, and as chirpy as a sparrow, as lively as a trout, and as—in short highly agreeable company: but then tastes differ, and when you tell me you're having Saxon and Barbara for a week or two, also Hope Bagenal, I turn up my nose.

Are you going to stay with Ethel at Dieppe?

Yr B

Dont let Quentin come this week: as we're having Vita and going out; but next I hope.

Berg

1805: To V. Sackville-West   *Monks House, Rodmell*
                                     [Sussex]
Friday, Sept 2nd [1927]

Dearest Mrs N:
    Well its all settled. Lady G. Wellesley has bought me.[2] She paid £25 thousand down and the rest on mortgage, so I'm her's for life. I have the use of the Rolls Royce and wine to taste.
    Speaking sober prose, however, I wont belong to the two of you, or to the one of you, if the two of us belong to the one. In short, if Dotty's yours, I'm not. A profound truth is involved which I leave you to discover. It is too hot to argue: and I'm too depressed.

1. A skit on the Keynes's written by Virginia and illustrated by Quentin.
2. Dorothy Wellesley had agreed to sponsor and edit the Hogarth Living Poets series, which started publication in 1928. There were 29 volumes, all original poems.

It aint so much that I'm a bad writer though that I am, as that I'm a sold soul. The body to Lady G. W: the soul to Mrs Van Doren. Here am I bound hand and foot to write an article on the works of a man called Hemingway. There are 3 more to follow.[1] For this I shall be paid £120. Not a penny more do I earn as long as I live; so help me God. Rather would I go without shoes, stockings, facepowder, love; be ashamed of me if you like; tell me to my face you cant be seen in the street with me; may my stairs rot, and my pictures fall to the ground, and rats devour my carpet and linen; may the thistle sow itself in my drawing room, and the barley grow where my pillow used to be—write for the Americans again, write for money again, I will not.

I'm in a temper. How I longed to write the first page of The Moths [*The Waves*] this morning! And after this I'm tied to Romance and Psychology— as if I knew anything about *that*: now I do know one or two facts about moths: and they must keep.

Then I'm quite alone. Leonard went up after all; but I don't suppose you could have come. And next Thursday—will you come then? I'll promise to be sweet as honey, soft as silk. Let me know.

If anything comes of the Wellesley-Monro marriage,[2] the fruits belong to me, not to you. After all, *the idea* was mine: you only did the *menial work*. Anyhow, it was a triumph, if not for the art of poetry, at least for the life of Dotty. Monro will cease chewing the relics of his dinner: he will fall in love with her; and so she is happily launched on a career of exaltations, renunciations, explanations, tergiversations: This is what some people call life. I dont. How cross I am! The only cheerful event was walking with Pinker through a field of clouded yellows this afternoon. The Clouded Yellow [butterfly] has played more part in my life than almost any other body or thing. Then Pinker swam in a dew pond. And now, dearest, I must wash, and catch the 3 penny bus into Lewes, and meet Leonard, and drive out to dine with the Keynes. Lydia will sing "My ear rings, my ear rings:" old Mr. Sheppard[3] of King's will act the part of a Regency Buck; we shall sit out under the downs. Nessa will come across with holes in her stockings— Quentin will come across with a hole in his trousers. I shall think, "How Shakespeare would have loved us!" for this sort of thing, the gramophone playing Mozart, the stars, the heat, the combination of shabbiness and

1. In September and October Virginia published five reviews in the *New York Herald Tribune*, including a review of Ernest Hemingway's *Men Without Women* on 9 October. The editor of the *Weekly Book Supplement* of the *Herald Tribune* was Irita Van Doren, who was married to the critic and biographer Carl Van Doren.
2. Harold Monro (1879-1932), the poet and editor. He founded *Poetry Review* and owned the Poetry Bookshop. Vita had introduced him to Dorothy Wellesley.
3. J. T. Sheppard, the classical scholar.

splendour (we are a very good looking family) always starts my tears. How many phrases I shall make,—which will die like falling stars, all that my article on Mr Hemingway may be written and earn me £120 pounds. So good night

Virginia Woolf

Berg

1806: To Ethel Sands

Monk's House, Rodmell, Lewes [Sussex]

2nd Sept [1927]

Dearest Ethel,

Here (or will be) is your Disraeli [by André Maurois] which I have enjoyed very much, though I think you say you didn't. But then I envy Frenchmen their French so much that it casts a glamour, I suppose.

I heard from Leigh Ashton the other day that both he and you are looking for a working desk for me. It is most angelic of you. But I'm afraid—unless you should have already found one—that I must put it off till next summer. My room is so damp—dark sweats break out on the walls and ooze up underneath one's feet—that I think I must have what they call a damp course put in before I buy anything nice. But next summer when I am dry and have two water closets and a bathroom I shall consider that I've done my duty by the decencies, and rush to M. Benoni. It was very good of you to remember it, and to inspire Leigh Ashton.

We still do nothing but talk about motors. Most afternoons you would see Leonard and me hauling the Singer in and out of the cowshed, or greasing, or cleaning, or running it backwards up a bank, because the engine's jammed. But its a heavenly invention—We motor all over Sussex—to Bodiam, Herstmonceux and so on, and have motor picnics, and compare our engines, and deride the Keynes'—who have a Morris Cowley, secondhand. You can imagine Nessa's derision. But my engine runs sweeter than hers—tell her so, please, with my love, next time you see her. I hope you are enjoying yourselves. You must be. Merely to eat at Auppegard is enough. I hope your chauffeur caught lots of trout and that the white pinkish eyed dog is well, and that Nan isn't lumping us all together with the Colefaxes and the Morrells. Please assure her I'm different. Vita came over the other day, very garish, in bright autumn tints: oranges; violets; not—the tints—very nice, but I forebore to say "Ethel thinks you dress disgracefully". So tactful am I.

Then Clive is still talking about love: and he still says Virginia knows nothing about love, and then I say what about Philip Morrell?—and so on. Love to Nan.

Yrs
V.W.

Wendy Baron

417

Monk's House, Rodmell
                                        [Sussex]
3rd Sept. 1927

Dearest Lytton,

A rumour has reached me via Nessa and Raymond that you aren't well. I hope this may be untrue; but if true, please bestir yourself and get well instantly. If you can't sleep, try Audit ale; very effective, with no evil consequences, and any fellow of any college, of whom you must know millions, can get it for you. I was going to recommend the Mysteries of Udolpho; they send one into a mooney trance which is very refreshing; but also Mrs Radcliffe has her moments of inspiration. Her landscapes are sublime. I adore soft music at evening, and indeed I think Jane Austen might have done worse than take a leaf from Radcliffe's book. This you may put down, with other notorious faults, to my unfortunate romanticism—I can't help it. What's more, I don't want to help it. I have come to a time of life when I can help nothing.

This was, in fact, what I was saying to Sheppard last night, at Tilton, when we picked the bones of Maynard's grouse of which there were three to eleven people. This stinginess is a constant source of delight to Nessa—her eyes gleamed as the bones went round. We had a brilliant entertainment afterwards in the new Loggia, with a rustic audience. Sheppard half naked, tightly swathed in red silk, shingled as to his head, with coloured garters, was Miss T. [Todd?] to perfection: Maynard was crapulous and obscene beyond words, lifting his left leg and singing a song about Women. Lydia was Queen Victoria dancing to a bust of Albert. What did the yokels make of it? I wish you had been there—which reminds me, there was a good deal of talk about you at dinner, some for you, I, of course, against; some saying you had a good influence, Sheppard and I sticking it out it was wholly vile. I said, if you drop a little salt on a snail it foams. Lytton was the salt: Sheppard the foam. He said this summed up, admirably and completely, his entire life, which has been a failure. That round faced innocent [Cecil] Taylor was there, and seemed to take it all very seriously.

All the rest of the news is motor car gossip. We flash through Sussex almost daily; drop in after dinner; visit ruins; muse by retired moats, of which Sussex is full; surprise Colonels—it is a perfect invention. What we did without it passes comprehension. Most of the Victorian horror seems explicable by the fact that they walked, or sat behind stout sweating horses.

Do you know the story of L.E.L.?—the poetess, who committed suicide, as some say; but others feel sure was murdered? Your blue stocking Hampstead friend, Enfield, has written a life of her which we are to publish.[1]

1. *L.E.L., A Mystery of the Thirties*, by D. E. Enfield, was published by the Hogarth Press in March 1928. L.E.L. was Letitia Elizabeth Landon (1802-1838), the popular poet and novelist. She was found dead in the Gold Coast from a dose of prussic acid.

If only every good spectacled Don and schoolgirl did not think themselves Lytton Strachey and proceed to put it into practice! But I have made this complaint not for the first, nor the second, nor the last time. For God's sake, come out with Betsy [*Elizabeth and Essex*, 1928] and make them all skip. It's better in French: I have just read Disraeli by Maurois.

They are starting a cement works at Asheham. A railway line runs round the field, and the down behind is nothing but chalk. Isn't it damnable? What is to become of us? Are we to migrate to the South of France? or Rome? or where?

Raymond was here last week end, very polished and agreeable; and I daresay it's supercilious to refer to the end of his nose, or his clothes, or his modernity which seems to me miraculous, as if he had already been to a lunch party which has not yet been given. Still,—Still, he's very intelligent, which as the old Serpent [Lytton] used to say—in his fiery days when he branded so many of us for ever—is the only thing that matters. And Roger was here with a new theory about Lord Salisbury's foreign policy which drove Leonard almost frantic. He has taken up meteorology, and is off to Vichy with Ha!!¹ (if that's how you spell her)

Morgan is coming here next week, and Dadie some time; but I hope I shall see you if you are at Charleston. I should like you to see me driving along the Eastbourne road at 50 miles an hour.

Leonard sends his love.

Yr V.W.

Frances Hooper

1808: To Vanessa Bell   [*Monk's House, Rodmell, Sussex*]

Postcard
Tuesday [6 September 1927]

We shall be ready to go on picnic tomorrow if fine between 2 and 3, if you like to come: but can't go Thursday or Friday.

V.W.

We shd. be much pleased if you and family would come to tea anyhow

Berg

1809: To Vanessa Bell   [*Monk's House, Rodmell, Sussex*]

Friday [9 September 1927]

Leonard is away, so I can't answer for our coming for *certain* on Sunday;

1. Roger Fry called his sister Margery 'Ha'.

humanly speaking we will—and bring as you so kindly suggest, Saxon, Barbara, Sibyl Colefax, who's taking Firle Place for 6 years: also, perhaps, one of the Oliviers, and Morgan.[1]

But I dont see whats the use of my wasting vocables on you, since the only upshot is confusion irreparable.

Think of my post card, with its explicit directions *not* to come after 3 if it was fine, but to come *before* 5 if it was wet—and what a mess you made of it.

Hoping to see you Sunday

Your old familia
Wolf

Berg

1810: To V. Sackville-West   [*Monk's House, Rodmell,*
                                     Sussex]
Sunday [11 September 1927]

Here, enclosed, you will find a type written document—not intimate, but precise. It would be quite a good idea, I think; but for God's sake don't let Dottie think of it, except from the point of view of her own amusement.[2]

I think of nothing but Laughton Place.[3] Leonard is enthusiastic. We have written to ask if we can buy—and are ready to pawn our shoe laces to raise funds. Of course they'll say they won't, or will ask too much. But suppose they did! My word!—there would be an entire barn given up to Vita: and the garden: and the moat: and scraping off wall papers and so on—one's life would vanish into Laughton like smoke. But we shant hear till Tuesday, I suppose.

Morgan is here; we're going to Charleston for a birthday party. So I am hurried.

I say, I was ashamed and furious to have put you to all that trouble. I had a vision you would rush to meet Harold, skid, be killed—all my fault. Never a hitch with the motor except when you're here.

1. Virginia was joking about the arrival of all these people, except for Morgan Forster.
2. See p. 415, note 2.
3. Vita and Virginia had visited Laughton Place, near Glynde, on 9 September. It was a 16th-century moated house, the property of the Pelham family for many centuries, of which the main surviving building was a brick tower, converted in the 18th century into a Gothic farmhouse. After closer investigation of the interior, Virginia and Leonard decided not to buy it.

I dreamt all night that you were going back to Teheran by air. How I raged, and woke to hear the rain.

Yr V.W.
Virginia
Woolf

Berg

1811: To Harold Nicolson   *Monks House, Rodmell*
                                             [Sussex]
Tuesday [13 September 1927]

Dear Harold,

Yes, the flattery was delicious, exquisite, charming and certainly would have been effective, had I not already written to the Tribune and said I would do your book:[1] But I'm rather nervous. You say its out on *Sept* 16th: you dont mean October, I suppose? If it is Sept: I am afraid they may have done it already. However they are proving so incompetent, that I'm taking the law into my own hands, and will do it unless they positively forbid. I'm afraid though that I shall have to mush you up with Harriet Martineau and some general reflections, as it is to be a general review, a commentary or whatever they call it. I am so bothered with these articles that I dont think its worth it, even for the money. One polishes off Hemingway and without a second's pause plunges into Shelley:[2] and I find it difficult to get up indignation about Harriet, or even to care whether she spells her name with two ts.

Anyhow,—this is genuine, because I'm not, at the moment, asking you for anything, though no doubt I soon shall—I shall be very happy to write about a real book, (I mean Some People) instead of these Stuffed Americans.

Love to Vita: whom I shall soon cease to love, tell her. Clive's rhapsodies about her go too far. I am dragged round and round the garden at Charleston listening to her praises. Not a quality, he says, is lacking:

Yours Ever
Virginia

Leonard says if Vita would send him an itinerary he would motor us over to you, if we were asked.

Berg

1. *Some People*, reviewed by Virginia in the *New York Herald Tribune* of 30 October, under the title of *The New Biography*.
2. Review of *Shelley: His Life and Work*, by Walter Edwin Peck (*New York Herald Tribune*, 23 October 1927).

421

Monks House [*Rodmell,*
                                                   Sussex]
Thursday [15 September 1927]

Thanks for Dottie's letter. It sounds as if Heaven had brought us together. But I daresay some fatal flaw will develop. We would like to come over for an hour or two either Sunday or Monday about 2.30, I suppose—But this is doubtful, so dont alter your long country walk, or whatever it is.

Laughton [Place] has become a possibility—its frightfully exciting—but I wish poor Philip Ritchie wouldn't die.[1] I wasn't very nice to him: anyhow its a pity—dear, dear. So be very careful, and dont get ill, or be smashed somehow—Please, dearest.

Also, could you lend me Mrs [Olwen Ward] Campbells Shelley? Could you send it? I'll be sure to return it. But perhaps you haven't got it.

Shall you come next Thursday? I shall be alone.

                                                   Yr Virginia

Any Foreign Office news yet? No: I suppose not. Many thanks for itinerary If we don't come, we'll write to Dotty

Berg

1813: To V. Sackville-West   *Monks House, Rodmell*
                                [Sussex]
Wednesday [21 September 1927]

The M.S. has just come. So sorry I forgot it.

I shall be in London on Friday till 4—no chance of seeing you, I suppose —If so, write to 52 Tavistock Sqre.

Very hurried, so I cant write. And rather melancholy. This I'll explain when we meet, if you are kind.

                                                   Yr Virginia

Do let me know any news from the F.O.[2] Is your cold gone?

Berg

1. Ritchie, then aged 28, had died on 13 September from septic pneumonia, following a tonsillectomy.
2. Harold had already turned down an appointment to the British Embassy in Budapest, and now heard that he might be sent to Rome.

Monks House [*Rodmell, Sussex*]

Sunday [25 September 1927]

Look here, I want to be told,
(1) *how you are*, truthfully.
(2) any news from Foreign Office?

Hows Ben? Anybody else got it [flu]? My God, I do think you deserve death and disaster for coming to London in that flood after a temperature of 104! But tell me truly how you are.

Then (this is all dull business, written in a rush going off with Dadie to Charleston, and still rather melancholy and cross, and unable to get anything finished) then, about Thursday. Can you come? Let me know as soon as you can. Leonard I think wants me to go up to London with him, but if you can come, I'd much rather—yes much rather—see you. Only, again, there'll be no cook: no food, except of Bartholomew's cooking. If you're feeling ill, dont take risks.

But I own I'd like to see you. Then I'd tell you about my melancholy and a thousand other things Its the last chance of a night before London's chastity begins.

Let me hear on all these points, especially your health and coming here, at once.

Yr Virginia

Berg

Monks House, Rodmell [*Sussex*]

Thursday, Sept. 29th [1927]

Dearest,

How good, how faithful, how tender, how devoted I am, to sit down to write to you. And I've given up hope of reward. And Heaven knows if you're alive. You were last heard of at Crawley. All the children were popping their heads (Angelica's is lovelier than Judith's [Bagenal]) out of the window to look for you. You may still be marooned at Crawley, or dead, or at Gordon Square: mystery shrouds you, (and by the way, it occurs to me that you are, fundamentally, mysterious) Still I write.

I have a little favour to ask of you, it is true. Could I, if necessity obliges, lodge at 37 [Gordon Square] from Monday or Tuesday to Thursday next week? I should only want a bed, and cook my own breakfast: I've had to let Nelly go home to a wedding, and we can't get in to 52 [Tavistock Square] till Thursday. Should the conditions have become intolerable, as they threaten, I think I shall depart, leaving Leonard, who means to stay in spite of everything.

But this is only a bolt hole in case of emergency. And I daresay you are occupied at 37. So dont bother to upset anything.

I had an odd interview, entirely unexpected, with Clive, when we came to get Leonards hat and you were at Crawley. He suddenly became moved, indeed emotional—as I expect he did to you—and told me, as I've no doubt he told you—how he has found a new love. In case mine may be a different version, I will repeat. Before leaving London he said, he met an entrancing girl, less than half his age, witty, beautiful, sought after—He had an instant success; but could not believe that she was serious. Many obstacles prevented their meeting, and extreme secrecy was essential, as she is closely supervised. However, beyond belief, they had four days together last month of entrancing happiness. Incredible though it sounds she has declared herself passionately in love with him. Their jaunt succeeded completely. Though he dare not trust himself, and does his best to control himself, he now believes that the feeling may be permanent on her part. If so, his happiness will be incredible. He is living in the wildest state of excitement—He has letters and telegrams from her incessantly. He was going to lunch with her yesterday, and on Monday when he comes back, the drama will begin. He swore that he could not on any account give her name, for reasons which affect her, not him. He says that they can only meet at long intervals, as she is much occupied, and often, I gathered, away. But he hopes that it will mean that he sees more of his old friends than for some time past. Not a word about Mary. Leonard came in or I think—we were both by this time in such a state of emotion—he would have told me who she is.

I guess Valerie Taylor, though he talked of her with the appearance of indifference. She is young etc: also her acting makes her often away: also she has some liaison with some man which might make secrecy necessary. However, you may know all, in which case, please tell me:

There is a sense here of complete disruption, finality and misery—It is pouring hard and blowing a gale. I have had a visit of two hours from old Mr Hawkesford [Rector of Rodmell] which pleased me, and he said we could now get £2,000 for Monks House: in which case I think I shall sell, and buy a villa on the Coast of Italy.

Love to Ethel and Nan, provided you are not settled down more or less permanently at Crawley. We were amused, indeed pleased, at least Leonard was, to hear you had both failed at your [driving] exam.

Let me know about 37.

and write
and kiss Duncan
Yr B.

Berg

424

1816: TO JULIAN BELL   [*Monk's House, Rodmell,*
                                         Sussex?]
Typewritten
[September 1927]

My dear Julian
    Could you possibly show your good heart by bringing me back fifty
voltigeur cigars? in a box.[1]
One declares them, and they make no fuss. But dont bother if in hurry and
torment unutterable.
I will repay.
    But I expect this is too late.
    I am as you see inventing an entirely new style, but what about yours?
Come and dine on your way through.
                                                Aunt Virginia Woolf
Berg

1817: TO VANESSA BELL   *Monks House* [*Rodmell,*
                                         Sussex]
Wednesday [5 October 1927]

Dearest
    It was angelic of you to wire, and I'm most grateful. I should certainly
have gone to 37 had it continued to pour, as what with a broken pump and
Mrs Bartholomew life was hardly worth living. But it suddenly became warm
and sunny, and so has remained. In fact since Sunday we have had the best
weather this year—quite astonishing—I hope you have too.
    Your letter has just come. No. I never said a word to Nelly [Boxall]
about Fred, nor did Leonard. But Leonard thought she suspected something,
and supposed Fred had given her a hint. If you like, I'll tell her not to say
anything: but I'll wait till I see you.[2]
    I saw Vita who is positive it isn't Valerie Taylor [whom Clive loved].
Valerie had been staying with her, and had talked of Clive with apparent
indifference: and discussed a washing bill and so on. The mystery will be
solved soon I suppose: except that the lady seems to be out of London a good
deal. We went for a drive yesterday, came back through Brighton, and
getting out to eat a bun ran straight into Mary and Barbara! Mary was
friendly in the extreme, and said they had been on the point of coming over
to see us with Leslie Jowitt. We had tea together and were all as amiable as

---

1. Julian was returning from Paris before going to Cambridge for his first term.
   Virginia had started smoking cigars during her journey to Italy.
2. The details of this domestic drama are not recoverable, but it had something
   to do with Clive's attempt to hire Fred Harris as a chauffeur.

possible. She [Mary] looks, I think, a little wrinkled and arid, and seemed anxious for news. She asked if we had had a very exciting summer, upon which I said "Nothing to what the autumn's going to be!" and could only get out of it rather lamely, on being cross examined, by supposing that there might be an eruption, or the animals might break from the Zoo. However, all passed off; and she kissed her hand to me on parting, which, remembering I hadn't seen her since our set to was a little queer.

As for Clive, I give him up. Among other things that day he said, as I thought, that of course you were sharing the money,[1] which meant that he was not really much richer: in fact I understood that you had already got your share. I think if nothing happens this time Bloomsbury must present a round robin. Its outrageous if it all goes on some new parrokeet. I dont suppose you'll get this letter, by the way. Ring up and suggest your coming or our coming, theres a good Dolph. Leonard will discuss the proofs[2]—he is going into it.

Yr VW.

I'm so sorry about Duncan—I hope he is all right again.

Berg

1818: To Julian Bell   [*Monk's House*] *Rodmell*
             [*Sussex*]

[October 1927?]

My dear Julian,

I submit the enclosed card with its reference to Fred [Harris?] for your arbitration. As I read it, I understood that both Fred and I were implicated in the same astonishing conduct. I think you will agree that the construction is such that it will bear almost any interpretation.

I also enclose a letter which you may give your mother, but I *should like it back*—It asks certain questions about you and Quentin which I have had, alas, to answer in the negative.

Yr
Virginia

Berg

1. The legacy of Clive's father, who had recently died.
2. For the third English (limited) edition of *Kew Gardens*, which Vanessa had decorated on each page.

426

Letters 1819-1843 (October–December 1927)

It was on 5 October, the day before she left Rodmell for London, that the idea of Orlando *suddenly crystallised in Virginia's mind, and she began it three days later. It thrust everything else aside, and she spent 'a singularly happy autumn' writing it. Already by late October she was visiting Knole to choose illustrations with Vita, and dragged her to London to have her photographed for the book. At first she planned it as 'a little book', to be finished before Christmas, but it grew as she progressed. Vita was delighted and tantalised by Virginia's probing questionnaires about her past, and they met frequently.*

1819: TO V. SACKVILLE-WEST   *Tavistock Square* [*W.C.*1]

Thursday [6 October 1927]

It strikes me—but I may be wrong—that you may be up tomorrow, dining with Sibyl, dining with Clive, God knows.

But if you would like to see me—I say IF—I can be in, alone, tomorrow (which is Friday I think) undern, or tea, or after tea. Only in that case ring me up before 10, or I shall be in the basement.

It would be heavenly delicious to see you: but I hardly expect it.

I'm frightfully excited: I will tell you why.[1] Just back: Pinker has messed copiously in the hall.

I hope lunch was good at the Metropole [Hotel, Brighton] on Tuesday.

I had such a brilliant and agitating tea party in Brighton on Tuesday [with Mary Hutchinson].

Berg

1820: TO V. SACKVILLE-WEST   *52 Tavistock Sqre.* [*W.C.*1]

9th Oct. [1927]

Look, dearest what a lovely page this is, and think how, were it not for the screen and the [Mary] Campbell, it might all be filled to the brim with lovemaking unbelievable: indiscretions incredible: instead of which, nothing shall be said but what a Campbell behind the screen might hear.

1. On 5 October Virginia wrote in her diary: "And instantly the usual exciting devices enter my mind: a biography beginning in the year 1500 and continuing to the present day, called Orlando: Vita; only with a change about from one sex to another."

Really, its worse than being bound in morocco by Lytton, and read by all the tarts of the moment. Which reminds me, do you know a man of that persuasion called Cecil Beaton[1]—who wants to photograph me, and Osbert will comment upon the portrait in a catalogue; and shall I go and be done? I say no: I say I am living perpetually in Sussex. I say, judging from your style and manner (this is what I say to Cecil Beaton) you are a Mere Catamite. Clive who came in yesterday, dropping with sleep after what I understood was an orgy, confirmed this. Why was he dropping with sleep? Oh, he said, after they'd all gone, he got into bed, but couldn't shut his eyes. Being in a close costive contrary mood I did not egg him on. So he went to Paris, and will be back next week, and then I'm to dine with him. Aint it romantic —this visionary and aetherial presence brooding diaphanous over Gordon Square, like a silver spangled cloud? What are we to call her? Clive bursts into Nessa who's solidly carving mutton for the children and rambles about, romanticising about Life, London, Autumn fires being but a man of 46 at his prime. Only in August I was thinking he would string himself from a lamppost. But Vita, my dear, please not a word to anyone about Clive's money and Nessa: that would be fatal, and no doubt he has honourable intentions and will make a rich woman of her next quarter day. She seems perfectly serene.

Here occurs a terrific gulf. Millions of things I want to say can't be said. You know why. You know for what a price—walking the lanes with Campbell, you sold my love letters. Very well. So we will skip all that and move on to Mrs Wells,[2] and death, and the funeral at Golder's Green, to which I'm going tomorrow, if I can scrape together a sufficiency of clothes. Wells wrote Leonard the oddest post card. I wont say that it was a picture post card, with a view of Easton Church, but practically that; and just a line to say "my wife died last night; or we had hoped to ask you and Mrs Woolf down for a week end." I'm going to the funeral to see whats done with the bodies of unbelievers. What fun! How I love ceremonies, and odd collocations (is that allowable?) of the human kind!

Yesterday morning I was in despair: You know that bloody book which Dadie and Leonard extort, drop by drop, from my breast? Fiction, or some title to that effect [*Phases of Fiction*]. I couldn't screw a word from me; and at last dropped my head in my hands: dipped my pen in the ink, and wrote these words, as if automatically, on a clean sheet: Orlando: A Biography. No sooner had I done this than my body was flooded with rapture and my brain with ideas. I wrote rapidly till 12. Then I did an hour to Romance. So every morning I am going to write fiction (my own fiction) till 12; and Romance till 1. But listen; suppose Orlando turns out to be

1. Cecil Beaton, who was only 23, was already making a reputation as a photographer.
2. Amy Catherine Wells, the novelist's second wife.

428

Vita; and its all about you and the lusts of your flesh and the lure of your mind (heart you have none, who go gallivanting down the lanes with Campbell)—suppose there's the kind of shimmer of reality which sometimes attaches to my people, as the lustre on an oyster shell (and that recalls another Mary) suppose, I say, that Sibyl next October says "Theres Virginia gone and written a book about Vita" and Ozzie [Dickinson] chaws with his great chaps and Byard [of Heinemann] guffaws, Shall you mind? Say yes, or No: Your excellence as a subject arises largely from your noble birth. (But whats 400 years of nobility, all the same?) and the opportunity thus given for florid descriptive passages in great abundance. Also, I admit, I should like to untwine and twist again some very odd, incongruous strands in you: going at length into the question of Campbell; and also, as I told you, it sprung upon me how I could revolutionise biography in a night: and so if agreeable to you I would like to toss this up in the air and see what happens. Yet, of course, I may not write another line.

You will come on Wednesday undern? You will write, now, this instant, a nice humble letter of duty and devotion to me.

I am reading Knole and The Sackvilles. Dear me; you know a lot: you have a rich dusky attic of a mind. O yes, I want very much to see you.[1]

Yr V.W. (thats because of Campbell)

Berg

1821: To V. Sackville-West   52 *T.[avistock] S.[quare, W.C.1]*

Friday, Oct. 13th [14th 1927]

"Well thank God Vita aint coming" I said, putting the telegram down with a snort.

"And why do you say that?" asked Leonard, looking up from his pocket handkerchief. To which I had no answer ready: but the true one was: Because my nose is red.

The poor Wolves have been having colds in the head. Mine I caught in a dentists waiting room: but thats neither here nor there. The point is the incident symbolises our friendship. Now think carefully what I mean by that. There's a dying hue over it: it shows the hectic dolphin colours of decay. Never do I leave you without thinking, its for the last time. And the

1. To this letter Vita replied on 11 October: "My God, Virginia, if ever I was thrilled and terrified it is at the prospect of being projected into the shape of Orlando. What fun for you; what fun for me. . . . You have my full permission. Only I think that having drawn and quartered me, unwound and retwisted me, or whatever it is that you intend to do, you ought to dedicate it to your victim" (*Berg*). Virginia did.

truth is, we gain as much as we lose by this. Since I am always certain you'll be off and on with another next Thursday week (you say so yourself, bad creature, at the end of your last letter, which is where the viper carries its sting)[1] since all our intercourse is tinged with this melancholy on my part and desire to be white nosed and so keep you half an instant longer, perhaps, as I say we gain in intensity what we lack in the sober comfortable virtues of a prolonged and safe and respectable and chaste and cold blooded friendship.

I am writing at great speed. For the third time I begin a sentence, The truth is I'm so engulfed in Orlando I can think of nothing else. It has ousted romance, psychology and the rest of that odious book completely. Tomorrow I begin the chapter which describes Violet [Trefusis] and you meeting on the ice. The whole thing has to be gone into thoroughly. I am swarming with ideas. Do give me some inkling what sort of quarrels you had. Also, for what particular quality did she first choose you? Look here: I must come down and see you, if only to choose some pictures. I want one of a young Sackville (male) temp. James 1st: another of a young Sackville (female) temp. George 3rd. Please lend yourself to my schemes— It will be a little book, about 30,000 words at most, and at my present rate which is feverish (I think of nothing but you all day long, in different guises, and Violet and the ice and Elizabeth and George the 3rd) I shall have done it by Christmas. That's to say, if we dont go to Russia. Do you want me to go to Russia? We've been asked to go there, free, by the Government, to celebrate the anniversary of Revolution for one month. Dont you think one should take the chance, buy furs, and risk the cold? Tell me what you think. I must settle by Tuesday.

Orlando will be a little book, with pictures and a map or two. I make it up in bed at night, as I walk the streets, everywhere. I want to see you in the lamplight, in your emeralds. In fact, I have never more wanted to see you than I do now—just to sit and look at you, and get you to talk, and then rapidly and secretly, correct certain doubtful points. About your teeth now and your temper. Is it true you grind your teeth at night? Is it, true you love giving pain? What and when was your moment of greatest disillusionment? And then you say there's a squalid reason, the flux I suppose, and you cant come! Still my nose was red, so I forgive you.

This is written 500 words to the minute with Leonard looking suspicious in the arm chair, Pinker snoring and Nelly [Boxall] playing fox trots on the gramophone upstairs.

I'm to see Dotty alone, at night, next week. But then she bought me —paid £20,000 down. About Laughton [Place]. How you upset me! But

1. "I am good, industrious and loving; how long will it be, though, before I break out? I would never break out if I had you here, but you leave me un-guarded" (Vita to Virginia, 11 October. *Berg*).

the place is bewitched. Seen with you adorable: with Leonard utterly detestable, so that the very thought depresses me.

Sixty pounds just received from America for my little Sapphist story[1] of which the Editor has not seen the point, though he's been looking for it in the Adirondacks.

Please tell me beforehand when you will come, and for how long: unless the dolphin has died meanwhile and its colours are those of death and decomposition. If you've given yourself to Campbell, I'll have no more to do with you, and so it shall be written, plainly, for all the world to read in Orlando. Tell me if you will come and when: because I'm already rather harassed by decayed actresses, Treasury Officials and so on.

Dearest Mrs Nicolson, Goodnight

V. (for Vita)
W. (for Campbell)

Berg

1822: To V. Sackville-West   [52 *Tavistock Square, W.C.*1]

[15 October 1927]

Oh how damned! I'd been hoping for London, unreasonably.[2]

Yes, I shall be free all Tuesday; come as early as you can.

I am so unhappy.

Will the people there be an awful bore? Shall you hate it? Does Harold? You won't go for long will you?

Yr
Virginia

Berg

1823: To Julian Bell   52 *Tavistock Square, W.C.*1

Typewritten
16th Oct. 1927

Dear Julian,

I was very glad to get your poems. As I have often told you, I consider that any wits you may find in your head (for writing I mean) come solely from me; so I think I have a right to see your works. I may be partial of course; but I like these poems very much. I will try to tell you what I

---

1. *Slater's Pins Have No Points.*
2. Harold had just heard of his appointment as First Secretary to the Embassy in Berlin.

431

think good and bad in them. In the first place I think you have sometimes some very nice and original lines which express what you have seen yourself; for instance; "in rain bright air"; "The lantern closes, leaves an instants dark, Then lights the brown beads on the pear trees bark." "Or the draught moved curtain scrapes the edge of the windowsill"

I like the freedom from any hackneyed or conventional phrasing. It makes one feel that you have looked at the thing until you have, by looking at it, found the words which express it yourself, without thinking what other people would expect you to say. I think this is probably the right way to begin. But of course you will have to learn to express yourself more fluently. I do not mean by that only that you will have to get greater command of words and use more of them. I think you will have to learn to leave out details, even though they are good in themselves, so as to give a more generalised view. Some of the poems are very difficult to read because they pile up so many separate facts that one cannot put them together. *The Moths*[1] avoids this fault, and gives one a much more complete idea therefore of your emotion. I think I like it best, but that is partly because I like the subject so much. Of course I understand that you are not trying to write about moods so much as about your feelings as a naturalist. But I think both Jefferies and Hudson[2] succeed because they are very careful what they observe; I mean they do not make a catalogue of things, but choose this that and the other. I admit that in poetry you get greater intensity than in prose, and have the right to be more jerky and disconnected. But I think you carry this right a little far. These are the chief criticisms I have to make; too much detail; too jerky; not sufficiently seen as a whole. On the other side; vividness; truthfulness, and often some striking observation. Wouldn't it be a good thing to write more prose so as to get more freedom of expression? But as I began by saying, I like these poems very much, and think you should certainly continue to write them. I will always give you good advice. I will keep them till I see you, (which I hope will be soon); and not show them. Leonard opened the envelope by mistake, but did not read them.

I should be very much excited to hear about Cambridge[3] any time you would write and tell me a little gossip. Kiss [J. T.] Sheppard on the top of his head from me.

Your affectionate AUNT VIRGINIA

Quentin Bell

---

1. Published in *Winter Movement*, 1930. The second quotation in the first paragraph is from that poem.
2. Richard Jefferies (1848-87) and W. H. Hudson (1841-1922), the nature writers.
3. Julian had gone to King's College this autumn.

Friday [21 October? 1927]

I had a slight suspicion/contrition after telephoning to you that it was awkward for you to have us on Sunday—anyhow for me to stay the night —servants, plans, family, anything (I only mean I'm not afraid of your not wanting me; only of what one calls circumstances.) So please say honestly. There's no reason on earth for walking this Sunday. My questions about your past can wait till you're in London. I should hate forever to be for an instant a burden to you. And you would never offend your devoted poor mole whatever you said or did. except by letting her bore you.

So if there's any reason against, Ring up. If we dont hear we shall come between *4 and* 5.

Berg

1825: To V. Sackville-West 52 *T.[avistock] S.[quare, W.C.*1]
Sunday [23 October 1927]

Dearest Creature,
I'm afraid you are feeling lonely tonight.[1] I wish I were with you. Harold is a very nice man, and I'm glad I know him.
Would Wednesday, Thursday suit you for me to come, suppose Friday was difficult? But I'm not sure. What used you and Lord Lascelles[2] to talk about?
Am I to buy a moleskin coat?
Are you well?

Yr
Virginia

I've sold Orlando in America.

Berg

1. Harold had left that day for Berlin.
2. Lord Lascelles appears in *Orlando* as the Archduchess Harriet. He had been in love with Vita in 1912-13, but in 1922 he married Princess Mary, only daughter of King George V.

1826: To V. Sackville-West 52 *T.[avistock] S.[quare, W.C.1]*

[30 October 1927]

1. Should I hire a wig for you? or can you make up?[1]
2. D'you think Valerie Taylor would do for the Russian Princess, if disguised?[2]
3. Many thanks for pleasant week end.
4. Let me know what time Wednesday.
5. Have you been eating mushrooms?
6.7.8.9.10. What a nice creature I am.
11. and 12. Will this letter go into the cupboard?
13. *Bring photograph of Orlando.*[3]
14. dined with 14 stockbrokers last night[4]

Berg

1827: To V. Sackville-West   52 *Tavistock Square, W.C.1*

Friday [4 November? 1927]

Shall I see Orlando next week?
Say yes.
But when?
Let me know in good time.
Was Orlando presented at Court?

                                          Poor Virginia
                                               in a
                                              d—d
Berg   hurry

1828: To V. Sackville-West

                                    52 *T.[avistock] S.[quare, W.C.1]*
Sunday [6 November 1927]

   If you haven't already got the man to do the photographs [at Knole],

1. Virginia was already beginning to assemble illustrations for *Orlando*. She and Vita had been to Knole on 28 October to choose portraits of the Sackville family, of which three were used in the book. She needed more of Vita herself for the second part of the book, and was arranging to have her photographed in various guises.
2. In fact, Angelica Bell posed for the portrait of 'Sasha'.
3. Photographs taken of Vita by Lenare at the time of the Hawthornden Prize presentation.
4. It was a family birthday party for Leonard's mother. Two of her sons, Herbert and Edgar, were brokers, and a third, Harold, 'interested' in the market.

would you wait a little—The characters are sprouting up rather differently than I expected: and the pictures maynt fit (but the 2 Orlando's[1] certainly will) Also, Nessa and Duncan suggest that they would take photographs of group and dress them up, which would be rather exciting, and lends itself to many new ideas. But if taken, all right.

I shall be alone here to dinner on Thursday. Why not come then—if you're coming—and let us have a lark? Come in the afternoon or any time

Thanks a million times for Book [*Aphra Behn*] which I see is Booming. Goodnight.

Berg

1829: To V. Sackville-West   [52 *Tavistock Square, W.C.*1]

Friday night [11 November 1927]

Dearest Creature,

You make me feel such a brute—and I didn't mean to be.[2] One can't regulate the tone of one's voice, I suppose; for nothing I said could in substance make you wretched for even half a second—only that you cant help attracting the flounderers—Nor you can; and its not your fault, or only partly. And I'm half, or 10th, part, jealous, when I see you with the Valeries and the Marys: so you can discount that.

And thats all there is to it as far as I'm concerned. I'm happy to think you *do* care: for often I seem old, fretful, querulous, difficult (tho' charming) and begin to doubt.

But enough of these megrims.

You'll lunch here at *one sharp* on Monday wont you: bringing your curls and clothes. Nessa wants to photograph you at 2, that is if she thinks the Lenare too bad.[3] I'm not sure.

Then, we might have some fun.

Clive's just been in. No, its only old friendship—nothing more.

1. The illustrations captioned in *Orlando* as 'Orlando as Ambassador' (male) and 'Orlando on Her Return to England' (female).
2. Roy Campbell had found out about Vita's affair with his wife, and threatened first to kill Mary and then to divorce her. Vita, dreadfully distressed, told Virginia the whole story on 10 November. Virginia reproached her for 'muddling her life', and Vita burst into tears.
3. The photograph which Vanessa and Duncan took of Vita appears in *Orlando* as 'Orlando about the year 1840'.

I'm just going to sleep in my Heal Bed; and you're listening to Genesis in Sheffield[1]—Good God.

Love, my dear honey

Yr Virginia

Berg

1830: To HELEN McAFEE   52 *Tavistock Square WC* 1

Typewritten
14th Nov. 1927

Dear Miss McAfee

I ought to have thanked you long ago for your cheque for my article Street Haunting, and for the copies of the Yale Magazine which reached me safely.

I shall be delighted to send you something more later.

I am afraid I put rather a higher price on my stories than on my articles —that is to say I would ask £30 instead of £20; and I daresay this is more than the Yale Review would be able to give.

But if I do another article I shall be very glad to let you know about it in good time as you suggest.

With many thanks,

yours sincerely
Virginia Woolf
(Mrs Woolf)

Yale University

1831: To V. SACKVILLE-WEST   [52 *Tavistock Square, W.C.*1]

Wednesday night [16 November 1927]

Why no letter? I want to write one, but have no time—you have. This is to say, come to *dinner* on Monday with me *alone*. Please do. Lunch is a bore; and I dont think I can cheat the Press of an afternoon—the Xmas cards and things are beginning—And dinner means longer—for you can come early. And I ought to be dining with Sibyl.

So say you'll come—I've a heap of things to ask you about: your first

---

1. On 11 November Vita and Dorothy Wellesley went to Sheffield, where Dorothy read from her own poem *Genesis* and Vita's *The Land* to the Sheffield League of Arts.

party etc—But Orlando's bad and wont be out, if at all, till the Autumn.
Come Monday then—and write a long long loving loving letter

                                                                V.

Tell me about Oxford [Vita's lecture on Modern Poets].

Berg

1832: To E. M. Forster   52 *Tavistock Square* [*W.C.*1]

Typewritten
16th Nov. [1927]

Dear Morgan,

I'm not particularly inspired to repartee by your letter.[1] But I reply:—
You say "Each sentence leads to . . . a casket of which the key has unfortunately been mislaid, and until you can find your bunch I shall cease to
hunt very anxiously for my own"

Very well—but then I'm not writing a book about fiction. If I were,
I think I *should* hunt a little. As a reviewer, which is all I am, it seems to
me within my province to point out that both bunches are lost.

I agree that Tolstoi "vitalises the guillotine" etc. But by means of art
I think; admitting that I cant define the word.

No; Percy Lubbock [*The Craft of Fiction*, 1921] doesn't "altogether
satisfy" me. But then I dont agree with you that he's a critic of genius.
An able and painstaking pedant I should call him; who doesnt know what
art is; so, though his method of judging novels as works of art interests
me, his judgments dont.

                                                                V.

[*in Virginia's handwriting:*]

The above is official and impersonal. Unofficially and personally I'm
fraid I've hurt or annoyed you (perhaps I imagine it) I didn't mean to.
The article was cut down to fit The Nation, and the weight all fell in the
same place. But I'm awfully sorry if I was annoying.

Berg

1. Forster had written to Virginia about her article on his book *Aspects of the
Novel* (1927). The article first appeared in the *New York Herald Tribune* (16
October 1927), and was then republished, slightly shortened, in the *Nation*
of 12 November. Their argument was about the importance of 'life' in fiction
(Forster) and 'art' (Virginia). Quentin Bell (II, pp. 134-5) discusses their
correspondence on this subject.

1833: To V. Sackville-West   52 *Tavistock Square, W.C.*1

[18 November 1927]

But I let you know about being alone on Monday the very moment I could—What a d—d bore.

Lunch is unromantic: still, better than nothing; so I shall expect you to turn up here at ¼ to 1 on Monday and we'll lunch out or here and sacrifice the afternoon—to love, not the Press, if Vita stands for love which I doubt. Then I'll settle with you about everything and coming and French[1]— Raymond and Kitty West[2] are on me—

Virginia

Berg

1834: To Clive Bell   52 *T.*[*avistock*] *S.*[*quare, W.C.*1]

Saturday night [19 November? 1927]

Dearest Clive

I've just finished your manuscript[3] which indeed I couldn't stop reading. I think it most brilliant, witty and suggestive—I'm sure its the best thing you've done—not a doubt of it. One or two suggestions perhaps I could make; but nothing of the least importance. You must go on with it. I want to have another look at it, as I've galloped through it, and then we must meet and talk about it. It seems to me, at first go off, full of really new and original things, and what a mercy to read anything so reasoned and written throughout.

But you must leave out your compliment to me. Yes: I've no doubt of its goodness—none whatever.

This is written hastily to thrust into Lottie's hand as she goes out.

Yrs
V.W.

I thought I'd just tell you how good I think it.

Quentin Bell

1835: E. M. Forster   52 *Tavistock Square, W.C.*1

Typewritten
21st Nov. [1927]

Dear Morgan,

I'm so glad I was not annoying—only wrong. (I dont think I'm as

1. Virginia was planning to take French lessons.
2. The daughter of Walter and Charlotte Leaf, Madge Vaughan's sister. She had recently married a young journalist, Raymond West.
3. *Civilisation*, which was published in 1928.

wrong as Arnold Bennett in the Standard, all the same.) But where we differ is I think plain from your letter. Both bunches have been lost, you say, "and yet we persist in reading fiction." But I don't. Nothing induces me to read a novel except when I have to make money by writing about it. I detest them. They seem to me wrong from start to finish—my own included. And I suppose I wanted you to say something to explain to me why I feel this. Naturally you didn't, because you dont feel it. Youve lost your bunch; but still you go on. And I dont want to go on, either writing them or reading them. This only proves I think that I am not a novelist and should not criticise them either. As for your book [*Aspects of the Novel*] —its perfect I think, better than anything I could ever write; (I mean this) only it doesnt light up my own particular boggle. Never mind. It is delightful and brilliant beyond words.

I hope we shall come up for a night, and shall ask Julian to arrange about seeing you.

No; I dont care for his play[1] either.

Yr
Virginia

Berg

1836: To Julian Bell   52 *Tavistock Square, W.C.*1

Tuesday [22 November 1927]

My dear Julian,
I was very glad to get your play. I dont think I like it as much as the other things you've shown me. I dont think its exactly dull; but I think its awkward and there's not as much observation of character in it as there was in your devilish brilliant attack on me.[2] This means that the jokes are rather obvious. You don't make your people real enough to rouse interest: Still I did laugh. I have never written a play so I don't know much about it. But I think you have to be frightfully careful not to sprawl about; but to hit every bird through the head. (This sporting metaphor may be wrong). Here you whack about rather at random, and so the birds fly away. I hope you will go on, and write and write and write—every sort of thing. I rather hope it wont be a novel. Anything is better than a novel. Try an auto-biography. Try sporting sketches. Try 'a day of my life'. Write long letters and send them to me.

I rather think we may come down for a night [to Cambridge] some time before the 7th. Could you get us a bedroom? I want to see you and Morgan also, who says he likes you very much. That is a tremendous compliment from Morgan. I would rather have it than a Gold Medal at a dog show as Nessa would say.

1. See next letter.
2. See p. 311, note 4.

I'm going with her to see Quentin [at school] tomorrow. He is very hungry, so I'm taking him some scraps of bread, bones etc. I dont see why you envy him. Think of being a painter, my God!, when you might be a writer! Its a pleasant lazy life, I daresay, humming and hawing over one's paper; but then so's a cows.

I'll bring your manuscripts if I come; or keep them if I dont.

I admit you made me laugh; and I liked some of your diaiogue. If I criticise your writings, I shall tell you exactly what I think: on condition you don't mind when I blame, and don't think me being kind if I praise.

Your old Aunt

V.

Quentin Bell

1837: To V. Sackville-West   52 *Tavistock Square, W.C.*1

Tuesday [22 November 1927]

I'm awfully anxious to hear that everything has gone well.[1] What an odious beginning to your day, I thought, at 9 this morning; and poor Ben waiting for the doctor. It was brown fog here. Write, if you aren't tired out.

The poor little Mole [Virginia] died half an hour after you left: came up to snuggle: found no warmth; and so heaved once, and sighed, and was dead. Would you like the pelt kept for you? It was all very warm and cosy so long as you were here—odd that, driven and hunted as you are, you should yet be to me like a sunny patch on a hot bank. God—I'm angry that your time should be frittered and tittered like this. Nothing is more fidgetting and exasperating; and why should it be *you*, of all people? Because if I were to have the training of you, you might sit down and write a nice poem. However, you will: throw Harold to the sharks this summer—drown Lady Sackville; immure the boys: all crimes against relatives will be forgiven after this flagellation: Here am I cursing God because I have to go to Reading tomorrow and so cut short my morning's work. You see, when, as with us, the mind's bent one way, its physical and moral torture to unbend. The mere reeds in the river bed can take this turn or that—the Mary's the Valerys the Dotties: what hurts them is concentraiion: But then they dont write poems; I'd forgotten Genesis. They dont even write novels (as bad as mine are.) At this point, Dottie rang up to ask us to an oyster supper after the Sitwells: had to confess I was already engaged to Clive, at which she sniffed rather.

I find Leonard's going to a brother on Sunday; so perhaps I could come

1. Benedict ('Ben') Nicolson, Vita's elder son, had had an emergency operation for tonsilitis at Oxford.

down on Saturday night as you suggest. But it might be nicer to put it off till you come back. I dont suppose I could do both—And you might (and I shouldn't blame you) like an evening alone. Let me know any time before Saturday. Anyhow you'll come as early as you can on Sunday. Would you bring Gorboduc,[1] or whatever its called. Did you hear Hugh Walpole? And what are you doing at this moment? Leonard is lecturing, and I'm— you'll be surprised to hear—reading 3 manuscripts and a book to review —Clever, aint I, to be able to write to you at the same moment.

Yes, it was very nice when you came in unexpected yesterday. Clive sent me a huge box of chocolates—Am I six years old? But they're rather good. And I think I shall want a photograph of Orlando in the East: Settle which ever way you like best about Saturday. I could certainly come later.

I say I do hope everything is all right, and you're not anxious—He's a very nice boy, Ben, jealous though I am of your nice boys.

Yr Virginia

Let me tell you, Philip Morrell is again to the fore.

Berg

1838: To Clive Bell   52 *Tavistock Square W.C.*1

[November 1927]

Dearest Clive,

I am very sorry for my outburst which as I realised at the time was foolish and excessive. My excuse is that I was rather hurt at the moment that you should accuse me of insincerity when I had been really moved and stirred by your book [*Civilisation*] and had tried to say so. Also I am enough of a prig and conceited enough to attach some value to my judgments of books and dont like it to be assumed that though I may lie about everything else, I lie about them (except indeed when they're by Topsy.[2])

As I daresay you saw, fate has been belabouring me almost incessantly on that very spot these past ten days. This morning on my breakfast table I found a novel from a friend of Goldies [Dickinson]: on my tea table, a manuscript from the sister of an officer in the Flying Corps.[3] I shall have to read both: to write to both. But if you crown these occasions with boxes of chocolates, Heaven knows I shall indulge again.

1. A tragedy (1561) by Thomas Norton and Thomas Sackville, Vita's ancestor.
2. Emily Lucas, wife of F. L. Lucas, the critic and poet and Fellow of King's College, Cambridge.
3. Probably *The Peacemakers* by Alice Ritchie, which the Hogarth Press published in 1928.

But seriously; forgive your irascible sister once more: I hate to think that I annoyed you when I would much rather please you (but not by insincerity —no). And show your forgiveness by sending me the second part, as I show mine by eating your chocolates—which are delicious.

Virginia

Quentin Bell

1839: To S. S. KOTELIANSKY   52 *Tavistock Square W.C.* 1

27th Nov. [1927]

Dear Kot,

I have always meant to say that I am not at all cross with you—Why should I be?—and that I am very pleased to hear that you liked The Lighthouse.

This needs no answer of course.

Yours ever
Virginia Woolf

Leonard says could you look in at the Nation office on Tuesday afternoon, as he wants to ask you about something?

British Library

1840: To V. SACKVILLE-WEST   [52 *Tavistock Square, W.C.*1]

Monday [5 December 1927]

The photographs are perfect, and the two Orlando's fit like a glove.[1] I think we must get Lord Lascelles done next, and then—?

Oh what a tantaliser Friday night was[2]—always a shoulder between us; damn Raymond, damn everybody. And I feel rather loving at this moment. Two poor moles born—died instantly.

Shall I come Saturday for the night?—seems the only chance. Let me know.

A thousand very interesting and instructive things to say. I went into the country and got a stiff neck yesterday with the stockbrokers [Herbert Woolf]—We had 5 hours such talk you can't imagine: in damp drizzly woods for the most part—My passion for stockbrokers is dead.

Remember Gorboduc.
Remember Virginia.
Forget everybody else.

1. See p. 435, note 1.
2. A party on 2 December at Ethel Sands's house. The guests included Raymond Mortimer and Arnold Bennett.

Should you say, if I rang you up to ask, that you were fond of me?
If I saw you would you kiss me? If I were in bed would you—
I'm rather excited about Orlando tonight: have been lying by the fire
and making up the last chapter.

Yr
Virginia

Berg

1841: To Philippa Strachey   52 *Tavistock Square, W.C.*1

Tuesday [13 December 1927]

Dear Pippa,
  What am I to tell this good woman about your Uncles, or Cousins',
poems?[1] Would you object to my sending her a copy of the one I quote?
If so could you send me the right version? at your leisure, if you ever
have any.
  Also can you inform me about Miss Goddard, and her missionary
colleges? Ought one to support her? Also, can't we come and see you
some time and your mother? Or is she not well enough? Please give her
my love; and answer all this only at your convenience.

Yours ever
V.W.

Would you return the letter some time.

Strachey Trust

1842: To V. Sackville-West   52 *Tavistock Square, W.C.*1

[21 December 1927]

  Directly you had gone, a faint smell, Orlando's, led me to look under
a book and there they were: but not Vita. No. And where was Vita last
night, and what did she do there? And is tickling a game for ladies or for
housemaids? (This might be a passage from Orlando—so now you need
have no doubt that it is the wittiest and most profound book in the world:
the very spit and image of you into the Bargain.) I write Bargain with a big
B because I have been buying presents, and feel degraded in consequence
—but I bought 2 yards of pearls at Whitworths, or is it Woolworths, for
6d to wear tonight. Shan't I look nice? Heres 12/6. I like writing cheques,

  1. The poem *Luriana, Lurilee*, which Virginia quotes in *To the Lighthouse*. The
  lines are from a poem by Charles Elton (1839-1900), who married, in 1863,
  Mary, daughter of Richard Strachey. It was first published in full in Vita's
  and Harold's anthology *Another World than this* (1943).

it makes me feel more like other women. I bought a spring of mistletoe, too, as Dadie is dining here.

Oh and I must go and dress now, and have the most important conversation in the whole history of the Hogarth Press.[1] Don't give away my newspaper plan.

And let me know when we're to meet.

Yr poor dear

V.

Berg

1843: To Lady Cecil   *Monks House, Rodmell,*
                                       Lewes [Sussex]

28 Dec [1927]

My dear Nelly,

I was sitting next a charming nephew[2] of yours the other night, which has emboldened me to write to you. Vanessa had also sat next to him at dinner, and also thought him very charming, and they had talked about you. So then Nessa and I began to talk about you, and said many things which should have made you blush, being a modest woman. We talked about your nice room at St Johns Wood, and how we used to dine with you—how lovely we thought you. It is said by Lord David that you are lovelier than ever and even more charming. How clever of you to make the younger generation take this view of you! Indeed, I have always thought you a very clever woman. So you see I am writing to you to offer you our compliments and thanks—rather late in the day, I admit. Still I think you must have been a very charming woman to ask us to dinner when all my clothes always fall off, if they were ever properly speaking on, and Nessa says she never opened her lips.

I want to come over one day in my motor car to see you. Perhaps one day next summer we might exchange visits. Did you know I have a motor car? It breaks down on the coldest part of the road, and Leonard gets out and we think we shall have to walk 5 miles home; happily it recovers miraculously and here we are, sitting over the fire.

I am trying to write about Lord Chesterfield and de Quincey.[3] But the moment I start writing, I think I should like to write a story. Then I begin

1. The Woolfs were considering Francis Birrell as a partner in the Press, and the publication of a journal to be called the *Hogarth Miscellany*. They did not proceed with either plan.
2. Lord David Cecil, the critic and literary historian.
3. Review of *The Characters of Lord Chesterfield*, edited by Charles Whibley (*TLS*, 8 March 1928).

a story: then I think about de Quincey. Then I ought to read some horrid manuscripts for the Press. I have a nephew, Nessa's son, who does nothing but write plays, though he is said to be an undergraduate at Kings. So I must read his plays.

I dined with Arnold Bennett the other night. Do you know him? He is a kind old walrus, who suddenly shuts his eyes like a dead fish and waits three minutes before he can finish his sentence. He makes enormous sums of money; but has horrible dinners; slabs of fish: huge potatoes; everything half cold; and then he took me to look at his bed. I should say that I had led to this by talking about comfort. All his furniture is very solid, but not comfortable; and uglier than you can even begin to imagine. So was his bed. He says that great artists need all the comfort they can get. But is he a great artist? I detest all novels, so I cant say.

What do you read? Thats the sort of question Mrs Sidney Webb asks me. But it is all Lord David's fault—

Leonard wants me to send you his respects.

Your aff: Virginia Woolf

Hatfield

Letters 1844-1874 (January-March 1928)

All through January Vita's father lay at Knole, dying painfully, while Virginia pressed on with Orlando, *less exuberantly than before, and when she finished the first draft on 17 March, thought it bad. Her work was interrupted by two bouts of illness, headaches in January, flu in February, and by many visitors. T. S. Eliot came to talk about his Anglo-Catholicism, Roger Fry about his career, Clive about his love-life, Noel Coward about Society, and Desmond MacCarthy and Dorothy Todd about their new magazines. Virginia's letters (mainly to Vanessa at Cassis, and to Vita in Berlin) reflect little of the melancholy which she recorded in her contemporary diary.*

1844: To V. Sackville-West   *52 Tavistock Square, W.C.1*

[7? January 1928]

Dearest Creature,

I'm frightfully sorry about your father.[1] Lord! What a time you have of it: I do hope he is better: and for God's sake dont catch it yourself. Please, darling creature, be careful.

I'd like to come for a night, if I could. The horror is I'm let in for a rush of work this week,—all my own fault. But I'll write later if I may. This is only a scrawl.

Damn Rebecca[2]—who doesn't know a turnip from an umbrella, nor a poem from a potato if it comes to that—what right has she to pontificate about the Land? Let me see it.

No—the prize [*Femina Vie Heureuse*] is still to give—that was last years: so you may laugh: but I think not.

A marvellous letter and present from your mother.

Please send me a line to say how you are and your father, and about seeing me and about life, love, literature.

Love Virginia (imperative)

Love Virginia (absolute)

Love? Virginia? (interrogative)

Mine was the 1st.

V Woolf

Berg

1. On 2 January Lord Sackville fell ill at Knole with suspected pneumonia.
2. In *T.P.'s Weekly* for 7 January, Rebecca West had reviewed the poetry of 1927. She described *The Land* as "a very fine achievement, but a poem unlikely to survive".

1845: To V. SACKVILLE-WEST   [52 *Tavistock Square, W.C.*1]

Tuesday [10 January 1928?]

I hear they never told you about the dog [Pinker]—imbeciles.
I'll bring it to Long Barn on Saturday—dear me how nice! But don't
please spoil it all by getting the flu. That I couldn't bear. So all depends
on your being well: if not, we don't meet till May. And I've a million
million things to say, and one or two to do.
Dearest be careful. I'll look out a train—afternoon: and stay till Sunday
afternoon. Oh what a pleasure ahead.

Virginia

Berg

1846: To CLIVE BELL   *Monks House, Rodmell*
                                       [*Sussex*]
Saturday 21st Jan [1928]

Dearest Clive,
Here we are at Rodmell. It is decidedly damp.
The clergyman [Hawkesford, Rector of Rodmell] as you know is dead,
and his widow has commanded a seven foot grave in order that she may
lie beside him when her time comes.
The only substantial advantage of a week end, or the tail end of a week
end, in the country is that by no human means can the voice of Ka call
me across to the telephone; to hear her uneasily playing with the eternal
theme of Lady Colefax and Veda (as she calls her) "I suppose you're
entirely taken up with great people now" etc etc.
No, thank God, 50 miles of Sussex and Surrey, under water too to
make them more impermeable, lie between us.
But the voice of my brother in law penetrates the Moravian forests (my
Geography is rusty, but romantic) amazingly clear.[1]
"Now tell us the news, Virginia". The news is I've seen Snow[2]: seen
Lytton; seen Hope; Oliver; Ottoline:—of which would you like an account?
To me the most fascinating is of course the pale and withered but still
tremulous harebell Snow: so caustic still, so facetious. D'you remember
the way she rolls ones' sayings into little pats of butter, so that nothing,
nothing can be stated and left? But now an unalterable pathos pervades
even the pats of butter. She tells me of tea parties at Cheltenham when the
Miss Hattersley Smiths, who were almost, but not quite, up to Wimbledon
standard, condescend, since they are past 50; and their game is over; but
their huge muscular arms remain and their prodigious but fallen pride. Well,

1. Clive was travelling in Germany, not Czechoslovakia.
2. Margery Snowden, Vanessa's painter-friend when they were young.

447

all this Snow tells sadly, for her pride is over too; she comes into the Thackeray hotel, and people think "There's an elderly woman!" And what has she made of her life? she asks me. But I beg and implore her to tell me more, infinitely more, about the Hattersley Smiths: and their fallen pride.

Lytton now—dear old Lytton—well, he was in very melodious humour returned to his [Roger] Senhouse, his Partridge, his book, at peace with the world. Moreover, he is buoyed up by the gigantic vanity of authors. And there they sit, the Stracheys, at their peep show: a peep show I may tell you is a frog or insect or a piece of grass pressed between glass: I had one once: and you put it in a cardboard box; and there it is, quite complete. I mean by this, he detests Hardy:[1] and also, doesn't talk quite as much about *my* books as about his own. Noll [Oliver Strachey] is chubby, flirtatious; Hope [Mirrlees], too well up in the Romantics for my taste; but a woman of wit none the less, and passable, even now, in a darkish room; whereas Ottoline, in her taffeta dress, with a pink plush rosette at the breast always slipping down, was a trifle garish. Pipsy [Philip Morrell] plays Bridge every night at the club, or he goes to sleep. Middle life!—my God! So she's out hawking the streets of Bloomsbury by night, and has, as you can guess, already befouled a good many twigs here.

I suppose you've heard that Harold has had to come back as Lord Sackville is worse. Vita sounds very miserable, but Dottie, last night (Sunday) said he was better.

We are back again. And here's your letter about Wagenseil.[2] I will send a copy of Monday or Tuesday, but Wagenseil has been pestering us for some time—asking for my books and offering his own and never paying—so I haven't much hopes. Mrs Dalloway is coming out in Germany soon—so is the Lighthouse I think.

Now begins my life of labour again: Dottie, Ethel, Ka, Roger, Jane Harrison, M. Jean Aubry,[3] Mr and Mrs Southorn[4]—but no Clive—And so in my world the lights are dim.

Tom [Eliot] has become an Anglo-Catholic.

Yrs V.W.

Quentin Bell

1. Thomas Hardy died on 11 January 1928, and Virginia attended his funeral at Westminster Abbey.
2. Hans B. Wagenseil, the translator into German of many current English books, including several of Virginia's stories and essays. In 1929 he published in *Die Neue Rundshau* his translation of Virginia's *An Unwritten Novel*, a story in *Monday or Tuesday*.
3. Jean Aubry (1882-1950), the professor of literature, poet, biographer, and French translator of Conrad.
4. Thomas Southorn was Bella Woolf's second husband, and a member of the Colonial Civil Service.

1847: To V. Sackville-West   52 *T[avistock] S.[quare, W.C.1]*
Sunday night [22 January 1928]

I've been thinking of you all the time, dear Honey. Now Dottie rings up to say your father's better. I am so happy to think you may be less wretched tonight. You can't think how I mind your being unhappy—it spoils everything. You must be a heavenly comfort to him.

I could come any afternoon—for an hour; but I dont suppose you'll be able to see anyone for some time. This is only by way of goodnight, and to say that should you ever want to see me, I am your entirely devoted but helpless and useless creature.

                                                                    V.

Berg

1848: To V. Sackville-West   [*52 Tavistock Square, W.C.1*]
Thursday [26 January 1928]

What a disappointment not to see you yesterday—I was in bed alone. But I do hope your father's not worse—I suppose there's no chance of seeing you? Let me know if there is. Would you thank Harold for his letter which I will answer, and am ashamed not to have answered.

I'm going to keep quiet so as to get back to Orlando as soon as I can.
                                                                Love.
                                                            Yr Virginia

A letter would be nice. I've been reading the Land—so good, I think, some lines.

Berg

1849: To V. Sackville-West   *Tavistock Square* [*W.C.1*]
Friday [27 January 1928]

Dearest Honey,
This is only to send my love, which you have always by you, and to say I'm keeping Wednesday free, should there be the remotest chance of your coming. But I'm afraid not.

I get news through Dotty. I wish, I wish I could do anything, but the only thing I can do is to be your loving creature Virginia, which I am.

Berg

449

1850: To V. Sackville-West   [52 *Tavistock Square, W.C.1*]

Sunday [29 January 1928]

Darling honey,

This is only to send you my love.—You dont know how much I care for you.[1]

> Yrs
> Virginia

Dont dream of writing—I hear from Dottie.

Joanne Trautmann

1851: To Harold Nicolson   52 *Tavistock Square, W.C.1*

Sunday [29 January 1928]

My dear Harold,

Would you let me know if there were anything you think I could do for Vita? I'm afraid there isn't, but if there were, nothing would give me greater happiness, as you know, and I am perfectly free.

I'm so glad I knew Lord Sackville enough to feel his great charm and sweetness. I loved seeing him and Vita together.

With deep affection

> Yours
> Virginia

This of course is not to be answered unless I could be of use.

Berg

1852: To Vanessa Bell   [52 *Tavistock Square, W.C.1*]

Saturday [Sunday], 29th Jan. [1928]

Dearest,

Your letter was extremely welcome, and devoured at once by poor dear Singe, who is, or was rather, in bed with a headache; so his services to you are not worth much. I'm much better and hope to begin my usual life again on Monday. Meanwhile, only Echoes of the great world have reached me—no—I remember—I've seen Snow [Margery Snowden] since you left, and Ottoline and Lytton. But dont expect any very brilliant

1. Lord Sackville died at Knole of pericarditis, a few minutes after midnight on 28 January.

450

reports, though Snow impressed me profoundly. A withered harebell, lightly dancing on its stem—such she is. So shrunk and worn and secluded. Her age seems to weigh on her; she is about to be 50. I doubt that she is very happy. What d'you think? Ought she to have married a drawing master? I can't remember. But she has her remarkable quality still—everything is slightly tart. And I utterly distrust my own insight into character. It is infantile.

Lytton by the way said you were the one person who had completely understood his case[1] and sympathised with him last summer. "It was terrific." So I said yes—those glacier torrents, sea green and immobile on the mountain top for so many years, are now the fountains of spring—In other words we puzzled our heads to account for your astonishing powers of sympathy. She has every gift, damn her, I said at last—Lytton agreed. He is once more a-simmer. Senhouse is kind, sweet, good, divine—I am to ask him to dinner. Lytton says he likes his old friends to like his new ones, but is afraid we are cruel about Roger. Can one know one's friends friends, d'you think? My poor dear Vita is now very miserable: Lord Sackville has just died. The passion of her life is Knole, I think, and now this will belong to an uncle[2] with a detestable American wife, and I suppose Vita will feel outcast—Also she was very fond of her father, who was a disappointed man, never able to marry Mrs Rubens:[3] who is now also desolate: Old Lady Sackville sits at Brighton being intolerable, and likely to live 100 years.

Lord, Lord—I have heard from Clive, chiefly about the legs of the German ladies, which are thinner than he expected. I quite agree that his head is turned; and I rather dread the weeks with him here, and you away. Lytton says he [Clive] has mismanaged the Mary affair and had he been wise would have told Mary he had no wish to go to bed with her, in which case Mary would have reverted to him. He thinks her very lonely and anxious to come back—She rang up and asked us to tea, but I was in bed and Leonard couldnt: since then I hear she's lunching with Ethel, and completely silent. I daresay I shall see her; but that only means putting my fingers in the fire—However, it amuses you.

We have been in great ups and downs at the Press. A brilliant American lady appeared from the blue: also a rich young or youngish man. She wanted to be manager and he partner. So we engaged her, and then she said a better job had turned up; so we gave the post to old Cartwright; and now the American wants to come to us; but alas, old Cartwright is engaged,

1. His love for Roger Senhouse.
2. Charles Sackville-West, who succeeded his brother as 4th Lord Sackville. He married Anne Bigelow of New York, an actress.
3. Mrs Walter (Olive) Rubens, the singer, whom Lionel Sackville had loved for many years, but could not marry because Victoria Sackville refused him a divorce.

though nobly self effacing; and we can't let her efface herself, so she stays and the American goes, and we don't know whether to take the rich youngish man or not. Where on earth does dear old Angus get his versions of Cartwright from? If only she would give us notice!—but no. She wallops round the basement, more energetic than ever; but I doubt her competence; and expect her at any moment to foam at the mouth or fire at the head.

You will be sorry, but not surprised, to hear that Leonard passed his [driving] test at Brighton without any difficulty first shot. I never thought he would. We almost collided with a bus, and then ran into a culdesac unexpectedly.

I see you and Duncan are now completely, absolutely, and eternally happy.[1] This gives me a certain amount of pain, I admit. It must be a divine joy to sit in one's own vineyard in the sun. I think I shall run out for a week or two—Life is too dismal here. There's Ka coming to tea today with Mark. Theres poor Vita wretched. There's a general murk and damp everywhere. (But dont be alarmed—I shan't come really; and I'm really quite happy; sitting over the fire; and I shall even enjoy being bored by Ka, I daresay.) Yes: trouble has already begun with Helen [Anrep]. We asked Roger to dinner to play chess: he rang up and said did we mean Helen to come too? I had already asked Elizabeth Bibesco, so had to say no. The party fell through, as I got a headache; but L. went to Rogers, and said relations between him and Helen were strained. I shall now ask her to tea. That will make things worse.

Have you got your clothes? God, God, how I miss you! There's nobody to chatter with—And I miss Angelica; whom I find essential to my pleasure. And I miss Duncan, whom I adore; and I miss dropping into tea; and I miss the whole atmosphere of ragamuffin delight—But it is useless to complain: Dog and Dolphin [Duncan and Vanessa] are lost to me lost to me. So write, and long long letters.

Yr B—

Berg

1853: To V. Sackville-West   52 T.[avistock] S.[quare, W.C.1]

Tuesday [31 January 1928]

My darling

Any time you come you know it will be more than happiness to see you. I've no engagements, and if I had any would put them off. But consider, honey—wouldn't you let me come down to you instead, and you stay

---

1. They had gone to Cassis to occupy for the first time the villa, 'La Bergère', which they had built on Colonel Teed's land.

quiet in bed and let me chatter to you about life in the tropics or any such subject, and you should cut my hair and lots of little moles would be born. You must be so tired now—so terribly tired after this strain. And I'm at your beck and call as you know.

Or perhaps, with your invincible modesty, you dont know.

But I do adore you—every part of you from heel to hair. Never will you shake me off, try as you may. Lord—how I wish we were so constituted that we could help each other. But there you are, quite alone, and I cant do anything.

But if being loved by Virginia is any good, she does do that; and always will, and please believe it—And rest, and be careful and dont write letters.

Yr
Virginia

Berg

1854: To Clive Bell   52 *Tavistock Square* [*W.C.*1]

31st Jan 1928

Dearest Clive,

A London letter in these circumstances, is rather difficult. There's poor dear Vita very miserable about Lord Sackville—in fact it seems a bad business altogether. Added to this—your poor sister-in-law has been a-bed all last week with the headache. Only rumours of the great world have reached me, many, by the way, from Dottie on the telephone. Is she to drive down to Knole and take away Olive [Rubens] by force? What can we do to prevent Lady Sackville from making a scene at the funeral? How can we prevent Vita from going there? Aren't funerals awful? Dont people dream of them for years afterwards? Will I read her poem[1] and tell her what I think of it?—As you see, nothing very much to the point. I heard from Vita this morning that she is going back to Long Barn today, and then I suppose Harold will return [to Berlin]. Whether this makes any difference to your plans, I dont know.

Your letter was very cheering. A little sanity, a little pleasure is what I want. Sibyl came to tea yesterday, now I come to think of it. And she stayed till past seven, and we advanced some inches in that perilous undertaking which is called human intercourse: a nice, good, discerning woman, I think her. And she is adopting Roger's lectures, I gather. Christa [Aberconway] (so she says) has the meanness to say that she can't afford to have lectures in her house because of the housemaids time dusting up afterwards.

1. Probably Dorothy Wellesley's *Matrix*, published by the Hogarth Press in May 1928.

"Now two charwomen clear up after my parties the very same night" says Sibyl. She and Christa aren't exactly sympathetic I gather. Ka? d'you want to hear about Ka? Well, she and Will are dining with Mr Alfred Lyttleton next week. Thats nice, aint it? Oh and the Princess Libby-Bebby [Elizabeth Bibesco] is very vocal on the telephone and had a wet dream about us the other night—which was so delightful, she says. A cloud, no bigger than a man's hand is on the horizon with the Frys. We ask Roger to dinner "Do you mean Helen to come too?" he asks, "No, I dont" I reply. But I am taking the nettle by the root; I am having Helen to see me alone; only then Roger says "Do you mean me to come too?" and I again say "No I dont" so that the maze seems to lead to nowhere.

Will you take me to the Maze [Hampton Court] this summer? We were once lost there, years ago, I daresay with Dobbin [Mary] Creighton.

I was asked to go and see Mary [Hutchinson], but being bedded, had to refuse. She was lunching with Ethel the other day though, and so is recovered I suppose.

All these little snippets are hardly worth sending; Happily, for we are all profoundly egotistic both at bottom and at top, my head is now recovered enough to let me begin writing a few feeble fancies in the morning; and as you know, this habit has much of the irrational intoxication for me that certain other habits not connected with the pen, have for you. Otherwise I should die of envy to think of your life.

By God—I mean never to spend February, March, April in London again. Rome, Munich, Moscow—anywhere anywhere out of this damp, dull, dripping dustpan. With Clive away its like a cage where they've forgotten to give the poor bird its groundsel. She has corns on her toes: she hops: she moults. But I am re-entering the arena. I lunch with Sibyl to meet Noel Coward.[1] I am reading Michelet.[2] Does it strike you that history is one of the most fantastic concoctions of the human brain? That it bears the remotest likeness to the truth seems to me unthinkable. Consider the character of Louis 14th. Incredible! And those wars—unthinkable. Ought it not all to be re-written instantly? Yet he fascinates me. And what about Lytton's articles?[3] I can't get into the skip of them. But they enchant the fashionables; and I have every reason to suppose that his Elizabeth [and Essex] is a masterpiece. I have every reason to suppose that my own judgement is vitiated. I have been writing to Max Beerbohm—now that's a good sentence to leave off with.

1. Noel Coward was then 28, and was already well known as a playwright.
2. Jules Michelet, *L'Histoire de France* (1833-43).
3. The articles appeared in the *Nation*, 7-28 January. They were about the four historians, Macaulay, Hume, Gibbon and Carlyle, and were collected in a book with the title *Portraits in Miniature and other Essays*, 1931.

Love to Raymond, and please, please, write.

Yr V.

You will write a very very nice letter to Vita, wont you? I hear from Harold that she is very wretched. It was a ghastly affair, his getting better and then worse, and she feels she has lost Knole too. So tell her you love her, as you do.

Quentin Bell

1855: To V. Sackville-West   [52 *Tavistock Square, W.C.*1]
Friday [3 February 1928]

Yes, darling honey, I shall be in all Monday evening, and shall expect you any time after five. And will you stay and dine with me alone? Please do if you can. That would be nice.

Don't mind being as miserable as you like with me—I have a great turn that way myself—

A thousand useless but quite genuine loves descend upon you at this moment—which is I know very very horrid, my poor dear honey.

Berg

1856: To Clive Bell   52 *T.[avistock] S.[quare, W.C.*1]
Tuesday. Feb 7th [1928]
(your wedding day)

Dearest Clive,
    Yes, we shall be delighted to dine on Sunday.
    Yes, I am recovered.
    Yes—oh yes—you'll be seeing Desmond, and Michael [MacCarthy] and Bob: and Desmond is starting a new paper,[1] and Bob has £10,000 a year and is called Phillips.[2]
    And I've been talking for two hours to Tom Eliot about God: and so no more, till we meet, except thank you for your exhilarating and enchanting letters.

and so
farewell
V.

Quentin Bell

1. See p. 457, note 2.
2. Robert Trevelyan's mother died on 26 January. She was Caroline, the daughter of R. N. Philips, M.P.

1857: To V. Sackville-West   [52 *Tavistock Square, W.C.*1]
Thursday [9 February 1928]

I shall arrive at Sevenoaks at 1.12 tomorrow—that seems the only train
—and stay till 6.30 so I'm afraid you'll have to give me not only a bun
for my tea but a bone for my lunch. Ring up if for any reason this don't
suit. But I'm longing to see you, and we could sit out in the sun; anyhow
talk, talk, talk, and by the way I'm now called Bosman's Potto,[1] *not* V.W.
by arrangement—A finer name, don't you think? more resonant.
    Have you slept? Have you dreamt?
    How are you?

                                                            Yr
                                                            B.P.

Berg

1858: To Vanessa Bell   52 *Tavistock Sqre* [*W.C.*1]
Saturday, 11th Feb. [1928]

Dearest
    Your letters rather depress me—my vanity I mean. They are so expres-
sive.—yet you only dip your paw in the ink, and scarcely know one word
from another. How is it? We literary gents, Clive and I, never get your
effects at all. Clive has just rung up, and we are to dine with him tomorrow
and lunch on Tuesday to meet Bobo [Beatrice Mayor], so you see my deluge
has begun. I haven't seen Mary; but I daresay she will try something now
he [Clive] is back again.
    I am quite recovered, which shows how sensible I am, and I rather
wish I had an excuse to leave this ghastly dreary place, where a blizzard
rages so that Nelly thinks there are burglars on the roof at night. A man
was standing by a van this morning when the wind blew the doors open
with such violence that he was struck on the head by an iron bar and
carried off insensible. Bits of hoarding go whirling about perpetually; and
Pinker has the lice, which means that she is soaked in methylated spirits
and must not go near the fire—I have to beat her off all the time I write
—so excuse slight irrelevancies and otherwise; I can think of only some
few pieces of gossip. Helen [Anrep] came to tea, and we agreed that it is
always better to ask husbands and wives separately. Also she says she isn't
silent from fear; but from awe of you and me, and she enjoys her Bloomsbury Evenings thoroughly. I think there is a good deal of truth in what
you say about her—She is intelligent and tart and rather a sharp tongued
harlot. Wasn't it clever of me to come to terms? Of course she flatters; but

    1. Another of Virginia's fantasy names for herself. A potto is a lemur.

                                    456

then, one can forgive that, though her flattery of you runs to the outrageous. Roger says she is even more in love with you than he is—what a complicated and indecent association the three of you make together! Do you have Helen one way and Roger t'other? Well well, I never suspected you of that. This reminds me, for reasons unknown to you, of Vita, whom I saw yesterday. Complete chaos has reigned ever since the funeral. Often I was rung up twice at night by Dottie with some absurd question about Lady Sackville. That old wretch has done her best to upset everything, has insulted Vita, made off with Marie Antoinette's diamond necklace, won't answer lawyers letters, and holds up the whole will—But Vita has twenty dogs, some with lice, others pregnant, and seems more or less composed. She chose the drawing with the hair;[1] the others, though beautiful and very young, dont, I'm sorry to say, seem to her like. You've let me in to sit to Roger by the way. He says he can make a perfect likeness and yours are poets dreams. Now I should have thought you took a sufficiently prosaic view of me: Caustic, severe.

Bob Trevelyan has come in for £10,000 a year on his mothers death, and is almost frantic with worry. His miserliness, great as it was when he had £800, has to be vast to cope with £10,000. And Julian [Bob's son] gets £100 down, as a legacy: this, Charlie Sanger says, is more than Bob can stand—So he's off to Italy, and good Bessy [Bob's wife] is staying to settle the affair—which won't bring any good to anyone I suppose.

Desmond has been given £6,000 by Oliver Brett to start a monthly magazine with.[2] How bored you would be to hear all us authors chattering about it!—not that it will ever come out; but if it did come out it would be the most brilliant, the most advanced the best paid paper in the world —Also it would make Desmonds fortune, so he says. But I say it won't come out: now Raymond is back too, so we shall hear about the Quarterly, I daresay. We are dining with Ka next week, and should have seen a good deal more of her and Mark, she says, if Vanessa had not forgotten to pay the telephone bill: so that they have been cut off.[3] They are now on again: Will is having a show; so is Roger; and I must go to both, which is hard on a quiet sedentary creature—buffeting about Bond Street looking at pictures by daylight is hardly in my line.

Then I have had a most shameful and distressing interview with poor dear Tom Eliot, who may be called dead to us all from this day forward. He has become an Anglo-Catholic, believes in God and immortality, and goes to church. I was really shocked. A corpse would seem to me more

1. A drawing of Virginia by Vanessa. Its present whereabouts is unknown.
2. Oliver Brett, later 3rd Viscount Esher, was to become chairman of the National Trust and many other cultural bodies. The magazine was *Life and Letters*, which Desmond MacCarthy edited for the next five years.
3. Ka and Will Arnold-Forster, together with their son Mark, had temporarily rented Vanessa's rooms at 37 Gordon Square.

credible than he is. I mean, there's something obscene in a living person sitting by the fire and believing in God. But will Angelica be one too?

Talk of the Devil! The telephone rang at this point—There's Mary asking us to lunch tomorrow! If not lunch then tea! Anyhow do let us meet soon! So there!

One thing I'm determined—no more Februarys and March's in London for me. It is detestable beyond words this year; and one might be sitting among tulips [in Cassis] in the sun with lizards licking ones boots and Miss Campbell talking to the frogs. As arranged now, we leave London on March 28th. get to Cassis in 5 or 6 days: stay there a week; and then amble back again: This will be too early for you to come, I'm afraid: but you might try. We went in floods and gales to Staines the other day: but it was more discipline than pleasure.

Tell Angelica I saw Clinker[1] yesterday—She is most charming: very gay; skittish, elegant, and provocative—She sent Angelica her best love, and looks forward to being hers in the summer. So do I, tell her—I miss her inconceivably; and have six witcherinas sitting on my shoulder at this moment a-whispering love songs about Angelica. May I ride the donkey? Is it called Topsy or Duncan?

Love to all the Creatures

Yr B.

We are lunching with Mary!
We think your cover[2] a great success—one of the best—Dottie has still to see it—

Berg

1859: To Edward Sackville-West

52 *Tavistock Sqre.* [*W.C.*1]
Sunday, Feb. 12th [1928]

My dear Eddy,

It is shameful of me not to have answered your letter, when I was so much pleased to get it. But a series of impediments—going to bed for a week, expecting to see you perhaps and Sloth and age—have prevented me from writing.

I have just been down to Long Barn. Vita seems better, and has answered about three hundred letters [about her father], but I'm afraid it is a dismal affair for her; and your aunts [Lady Sackville] behaviour could only be tolerated in an Elizabethan play. That she may take a dagger to her own throat or drink broken glass is rather my hope, I admit. What an odd race you are!

1. A spaniel puppy, which Vita gave to Angelica.
2. For the Hogarth *Living Poets*, edited by Dorothy Wellesley.

458

I am greatly charmed by your old German ladies.[1] But how do you account for the size of their posts? In trying to construct their lives, I cant get this right, unless we suppose that the post is a fabrication: in which case they become pathetic and slightly crazy. Do you remember whom I'm talking about?—the two old ladies you talk to in The Pension.

Does this indicate that your novel[2] is to be packed with observations? I am at the moment disinclined for fiction of all kinds. But then I was forced to read all Meredith in a week. I did get through three of them; and feel like an old sheep which has torn off half its fleece in a hedge. But it may have grown again by the time your novel is out, and then the old sheep will read it with her horn spectacles on.

Bloomsbury has been so quiet on the whole with Clive away; Nessa and Duncan are so quiet always that when they go, it isn't the noise that is less, but the substance. We become more flashy and meretricious. We have all been laughing maliciously at Bob Trevelyan whose mother has died and left him £10,000 a year and a vast house at Stratford on Avon.

He has had £800 so far, and been the most miserly of men. Often his wife wont let him have a second help. They never burn coal, but only some compound of vegetable produce which is home made and so on. I think they have one of Charlie Sangers second hand bees to make ginger beer with into the bargain. And now he has £10,000 a year. What is he to do? Kill the bee, buy coal, and eat six helpings? But he will die. Besides it goes against the grain. He is almost frantic with the effort

And Desmond has been given £6000 (what a rich letter this is!) to start a monthly magazine with. It is to be incredibly brilliant and to come out punctually the 1st of every month. He says his fortune is made: but I shan't subscribe till it is in my hands. There was once a paper called the New Quarterly. This died so thin, at the wrong time of year too, it made one cry to see it: and this was to make Desmond's fortune—before you were born.

I've been lunching with Mary Hutch: and am dining with Clive.

Dont draw any inferences: there are none, I'm told, to draw.

But do write again in your verdant ink.

Raymond I'm told is back at dawn.

And so the snake its skin renews (Shelley)

Your
Virginia

Berg

1860: To Harold Nicolson   52 *Tavistock Sqre, WC.*1

Feb 19th 1928

My dear Harold,

You have probably long ago forgotten a delightful letter you wrote me.

1. Eddy was in Dresden, and later went to Berlin.
2. *Mandrake Over the Water-Carrier*, 1928.

But I have not, and have at last found a copy of the Lighthouse and sent it to the Embassy in case your Editor still wants it. The Germans are apt to be very effusive and very ineffective about translating and writing, but I think Mrs Dalloway will soon appear in German, and any notice is likely to be to my good.

I'm delighted—this is the kind of way literary people talk—that Some People is triumphing in America, and Vita tells me your offers are of so fabulous a kind that you blush to think of them. You will soon be asked to write for Desmonds new paper, which comes out in May, and then for Miss Todd's new paper, which also comes out in May.[1] A great deal of caballing is going on with Todd, Raymond and Francis. Do you know that rather alarming woman?—she reminds me of an extinct monster pushing through the mud: in my direction. We are all also a good deal amused, if that is not impertinent, by the Foreign Office affair, and asking if Tyrrell goes to France, will you come back here?[2] I hope so.

There are masses of books for you to write, and directly I am allowed a copy, I'm going to read Nicolson's Biography.[3]

I saw Vita a day or two ago. She seemed to me ever so much better, and working hard, which I'm delighted by. I am sure it is the mainstay of life—an old fashioned view. but none the less true. Then of course we are also discussing Raymond [Mortimer] and Valerie [Taylor]; and Clive is making the whole quarter ring with his descriptions of the Legs of German women. But you'll have heard all this.

Leonards love

Yours
Virginia

Berg

1861: To Philip Morrell   52 *Tavistock Square, W.C.*1

Sunday [19 February? 1928]

Dear Philip,

You've put me in a quandary[4]—that is I shall probably lose all such respect as you may have felt for me, if I confess: that for some reason

1. After Dorothy Todd's resignation from *Vogue*, she planned to start a new quarterly which would combine fashion with cultural interests. The project collapsed for lack of financial support.
2. J. D. Gregory had been dismissed from the Foreign Office for allegedly giving away financial secrets to a woman with whom he was involved. Sir William Tyrrell was Permanent Under-Secretary of State at the Foreign Office from 1925 to 1928, when he was made Ambassador in Paris.
3. Harold Nicolson's *The Development of English Biography* was published by the Hogarth Press this month.
4. See p. 441.

460

probably discreditable to my adult intelligence; I had much rather you came here, and much rather write to Gower Street, than have tea in a shop and address letters to your Club.

Now you'll have no respect left over. Never mind: I cant be bothered to go into reasons: but only blurt out impulses. After all, Leonard is not a frightening man, and if Ottoline has her severities, I dont pay any attention to them—Nor should you. So having made a clean breast, I break off, before further damning myself: and leave you either to curse me in silence or say whatever you choose.

The influenza still clouds my faculties, so excuse illiteracy; and brevity.

Your
Virginia Woolf

Texas

1862: To V. Sackville-West   [52 *Tavistock Square, W.C.*1]

Monday [20 February 1928]

Would Friday be too late for you?[1]—if I came then and spent the night? I've had to go to bed with a sore throat and a little temperature, but shall be cured tomorrow and in robust health (*in every sense of the word*) on Friday: so do try to manage it—

And couldn't you send me one of your new poems? Please do. And how are you?

And do you love me?

Yr

So cross: I was just finishing Orlando.

Berg

1. Vita was leaving for Berlin on Saturday, 25 February, so this visit to Long Barn was changed to Thursday.

461

1863: To V. Sackville-West   [52 *Tavistock Square*, *W.C.*1]
Tuesday [21 February 1928]

Dearest Honey;
    Here is Bosman's Potto and the Pinche Marmoset, and some other of
Virginias animals—which will you keep for her till Friday.
    Lord! how I look forward already to seeing you again!
    Wednesday's Bob Trevelyan: a dull green.
    Thursdays Miss Dudley's pill factory [in Percy Circus]: a worthy but
            unattractive duffle grey.
    Fridays Vita: orange and rose, tipped with amethyst—
    Please see to it that its a fine day, that there's a bun for tea, a porpoise
in the fishmongers: and darling, write me something—a little poem: prose
if nothing else, and we'll sit and talk and talk: or walk. Only be well and
glad to see me: or Noodles [butler] will have to wipe me up.
    Love a thousand times.

                                                                                V

Berg

1864: To Vanessa Bell   52 *T*.[avistock] *S*.[quare, *W.C.*1]
Tuesday 21st Feb. [1928]

Dearest,
    I take your snub very unkindly. I wrote to you a long loving letter,
and then you answer my husband. You don't deserve another word, but
as I am temporarily unable to write my book, owing to a slight attack of
the flu, I will give you the relics of my mind. It is a very slight attack, only
a bad throat and a little temperature and I am up today, in fact have only
been one day in bed, and hope to be recovered tomorrow—when I ought
to be lunching with Colefax—but I shant. By the way, we dined with Ka
the other night, and there I saw a letter to you from Colefax. Are you
intriguing with her? Oh God! Ka was beyond belief worthy, scraped,
dismal, patronising oppressive. Not so much Ka herself; but her surroundings. Scores of tired damp muddy people called Campbell or Dent or
something came in afterwards. And in some miraculous way she has completely altered your rooms—partly the lights, which are very bright; partly
the spirit; and then the talk is all of respectable peers and politics; something
like the Sangers with a dash of art. Will's pictures were praised skyhigh.
"What wonderful blues you give us! Mr Arnold-Forster. It makes one
feel oneself in the Alps." Then Will is very offhand and manly: but as
vain as a peacock, and somehow lets fall that they are all sold, some to
the Cecils. "Spiffing that" Meanwhile, the wretched Mark is heard sobbing
upstairs.

Then we lunched with Mary—For an hour it is very nice, as the food is delicious, and I like Jack's stories for precisely 60 minutes. But when the clock strikes two, the Princess turns into a rat—is that the story of Cinderella?—perhaps not—and one can't think of another word to say. Leonard yawns. But I admired the adroitness with which Mary discovered that Clive was back, and found out about his doings in Berlin. She was rather depressed perhaps, and very affectionate. We had some banter about her quarrel with me. And I said she had bitten me over the left breast and left a blue stain like an Asp (see Antony and Cleopatra, by Shakespeare) and she said she had only bitten me once, and then not really hard. I don't think Clive shows any disposition to go back to her. I see him constantly, but not so far alone, except at the play the other night, but then he was so excited by the presence of the Beau Monde that he was incapable of intimacy. He took me to a play about a school boy who falls in love with the masters wife.[1] It is strange how sentimental one becomes about the young—Clive and I both cried—not at the same places, but both at the thought of love and youth. Why is Julian depressed? Do you think he is in love? I should like to go and see him, but I dont suppose he would confide in me. I have just found his plays, so I shall write to him; and I think we may go up for a night to see Dadie act, but the thought of Cambridge is slightly abhorrent. Its amazing weather here at the moment; everything coming out.

Have you heard all the Todd cabals? She came to tea here to discuss her new quarterly with Clive and us. It is to be Vogue, only quarterly— She is very anxious that you should do caricatures for her, and is writing to you. There is no sign that she means to give any power to Raymond[2] or Francis [Birrell], or to take their advice. I gather that she is putting up most of the money herself, and intends to be in complete control with [Madge] Garland under her—This will be rather a blow to them; but she is a truculent determined old Brute, fatter and more snouted than ever— very disillusioned and commercial and without ideals: so I think she will take her own way.

It seems to me that everybody is going to Cassis at the same moment. Won't it be rather a bore? I can't believe your amazing stories of the Male and Female parts of the Renault. Do the French sexualise their engines? The Singer I know for a fact to be hermaphrodite, like the poet Cowper.

I'm afraid this letter is tedious in the extreme. I am rather muddle-headed. But I assure you there is nothing beyond a very slight 'flu the matter with me. (I put this in remembering how even the cold hearted like

1. *Young Woodley* by John van Druten. It had first been banned by the Lord Chamberlain, but he withdrew the ban on 17 February.
2. Raymond Mortimer had succeeded Aldous Huxley as literary and dramatic critic on *Vogue*, and was now suggested for the same job on the new quarterly.

you exaggerate peoples ills when they are abroad.) I am rather depressed, however, that I can't write, because my head is easily affected as you know, and I have only just time to finish Orlando before we go abroad. So please write me a long and loving letter: if Duncan would too, all the better; since I cherish for him a withered, unspoken adoration, such as I imagine Aunt Daisy[1] has for a Cavalry officer in Calcutta—As for Angelica, my sentimentality overcomes me beyond belief, and when I saw a little girl in the street just now I almost burst into tears. Not that she was a patch on Angelica. Angelica has spoilt me for other children. Mark [Arnold-Forster] says I am one of the nicest people he knows—the others being Mr Nevinson and Mrs Swanwick[2]—but even so what a dried up little twig he is compared with her! I think she must have an extremely queer imagination: her sensibility is rather like mine—What higher praise can I give her? But in beauty she transcends my highest moments. Is she learning anything? What about God?[3]

Yr B

Berg

1865: To Julian Bell   52 *Tavistock Square, W.C.*1

Sunday [26 February 1928]

My dear Julian,

I have been meaning to write and confess to you that I have found your plays. I apologise most profoundly for wrongly accusing you. They had laid themselves beneath a vast and hideous deposit which one could only touch with a broomstick. It fell at last. Shall I send them, or wait for you to fetch them?

Why have you sent me no more writings? Dont tell me you have given up writing. What else is there worth doing? Politics? Pooh! Beagling? Pish! Conversation? Tosh! Write some poetry and send it me at once.

I dont know, and cant imagine, what you're up to at Cambridge. Here we are printing a great many books, and taking on a new staff, buying a typewriter, and talking as usual masses of nonsense.

We are motoring to Cassis through France at the end of March.

The old umbrella [the Singer] is absolutely sublime, and lives at Richmond, and we take her for a 60 mile spin on Sundays.

Nessa sends me astonishingly indecent details about the Renault. It cant go, she says, because its hermaphrodite. So it is being mated with a Citroen,

1. Daisy McNeil, sister of Duncan Grant's mother.
2. H. W. Nevinson, the journalist; and Helena Swanwick, who was prominent in the Women's Movement.
3. Angelica was going through a religious phase.

and they hope for the best. Meanwhile, Duncan turns the screws the wrong ways and mechanics have to be wired for from Marseilles to turn them the right way.

I am reading Michelets History of France—God knows why. I find it fascinating, but wholly fictitious. Do you think any history is even faintly true?

Now I must read the History [*After the Deluge*] which Leonard is writing.

Please come and see us directly you set foot in London—There are lots of things I want to talk about.

Your affectionate
AUNT
Virginia

Quentin Bell

1866: To Vanessa Bell   52 *Tavistock Sqre* [*W.C.*1]

Sunday, 26th Feb. [1928]

Dearest,

This is a brief Business letter. Will you please take us rooms at the Teeds from April 2nd to April 9th as you suggest as many rooms as possible, and any meals they can supply. This seems now settled—We shall start on the 26th I think. I suppose if by any chance we could stay on a few days, something could be arranged. But I'm afraid its not likely.

I saw Nan [Hudson], and I think she may stay longer—and I believe the Roy Campbells are going to settle at Cassis—in fact I see you're already a Colony. I had an interesting talk with Clive, but haven't time to report it—except that he told me he could never go back to Mary as she had treated him so badly, and he has now discovered that all her views on art and literature were taken from him: He can now see no advantage in her, and her friends and ways are not nearly so congenial to him as ours are.

But we've got Roger coming in; and we are dining with Clive, so I must stop.

Moreover you owe me a letter, I think—but I wont be a grudging curmugeon and will write soon.

Yr B.

Do keep a look out for any nice objects—chairs or pots—or chests of drawers—that I could buy if you don't want them. I hope to do some chaffering

Berg

465

March 5th 1928

Dearest,

I don't know whose turn it is to write—I expect yours; but your picture gets so much praise from the Cognoscenti that I am feeling mercenary towards you. Also affectionate—Also desperate—and a thousand other things. About our rooms—Clive changes his plans daily—now he's going to Madrid, now to Cassis at once, now not at all. Perhaps he is more stable in his letters to you. So I dont see how to combine with him, and shall throw myself on your hands. Do the best for us you can—it'll only be a week alas, unless I can wangle something.

I'm rather void of interesting gossip, I'm afraid, as I'm being as careful as a cat walking on eggs, and have refused Colefax and now Clive (to meet Lord Berners), my head not being quite established. We are going to Rodmell for three or four days, and there I shall finish Orlando, I hope.

I think I told you something of my last talk with Clive. He seems now completely disillusioned, and says that his feeling for Mary was founded on a misunderstanding of her real nature—or rather intellect, which he had thought subtle, exquisite, witty and original, and now finds merely a slavish copy of himself. Dont you think it odd that he never guessed in 13 years what we could see in ten seconds? She is now returning to her attack on Bloomsbury—that is, she asked Leonard to dinner, and wants to come to tea. But, seriously, something must be done to control Clive. We see him every other day almost—not that we mind that—and every kind of supper and drink is lavished upon us: but when he meets a virgin, as he did the other night here (her name was Jenkins and she comes from Newnham) his behaviour is such that one wonders whether he's crazed or about to be so. He sat beside her on the sofa talking about her youth and his age (this is now his mania—that he's middleaged, and he goes to a beauty specialist about his hair, which is not growing however) and paying her compliments and talking about Princesses and Prime Ministers and finally asked her to dinner—whether seriously or not I dont know. When you come back I think you must quieten him. Also he never keeps off his own happiness or unhappiness, as the case may be. Raymond caterwauled like the most lamentable housetop cat. I suppose his affair [with Valerie Taylor] is on the rocks. He has never been so unhappy he says—the pair of them answered each other across the room like a couple of nightingales— moulting nightingales. Then they say how happy I am; and how happy you are. I daresay you can imagine it at Cassis, and thank your stars the seas are between us.

Still, talking of the seas, whats the use of them if Barbara can swim? A week of Barbara [Bagenal] seems to me to outweigh 6 weeks of Ka, Colefax, and the rest—I can hardly picture it. One evening broke my spirit for 8 weeks, 7 days and .. And who should ring up this very moment but Nick [Bagenal]? In the extravagant hospitality of our hearts we agreed to let him come in for one hour after dinner—upon which he discloses the horrid fact that Saxon is attached to him—Still one hour after dinner isn't a whole week—Then you've Nan: so solitude seems to me to have its drawbacks. I suppose though, the car is now in perfect order—So is ours—You'll be amused to hear that I'm at last having French lessons. What will surprise you is that my volubility is extreme, and my teachers say I talk so well that I dont really need lessons. I suppose this is flattery—I'm afraid so— Still its wonderful how much easier it is to talk to some one professional. Occasionally I use phrases which have been out of use for a century or so. But once the blood is up one flurries along somehow: genders, or no genders.

Angus seems gloomy and determined, and so far has not got a place. He hangs on to the hope of Agnews, but Roger doesn't seem sanguine; and I must say (this is not through my husband) his lethargy takes the life out of one, absolutely. I had a small job which might have been worth £20—to write a description of some pictures of Hardy's county— but he was so pessimistic and so languid, I gave it up. We have Miss Belcher now—a brisk girl, who says very tart things, but is already Mrs C's right hand.

Roger is a good deal run after I gather by Astors, Stoops,[1] and so on. I haven't seen him, but Leonard dined there, and was given rhubarb fool made with Mary's hair oil (by mistake.) But this was a mere bagatelle— The couple seem invincible and triumphant. Molly [MacCarthy] came to tea yesterday—a fair grind, I must say. I got on by saying she must ask me 3 questions, and then I ask her another 3. So I elicited an account of copulating with Clive on a hard bed on a cold night at Asheham; and how she flared up next morning and went home. Desmond never much enjoyed copulation. As for Philip M[orrell], he never got that far—(I saw Ott. by the way, and find her fascinating: old, erratic, random, ribald; very shabby and dressed up in relics of plush at least 10 years old.) An odd thing about the MacCarthy ménage is that Michael is so violently jealous of Rachel that they cant be in the house together. He flies into rages, for no reason, as Rachel is perfectly good humoured, and it is thought to be sexual, as he threw an iron bar at [her] when he was two.

I saw Peter [F. L.] Lucas the other day, who says that Julian is charming and intelligent, but frightfully lazy—Peters standards are impossible though, and so long as Julian dont start telling the truth, I shouldn't worry. LOVE TO ANGELICA. None to Duncan, because he's vile, heartless, and not worth having as a brother-in-love. So tell him. I saw his mother too; all her beauty recovered, and Pippa and Gumbo [Strachey], who excel in the

1. Bertha and Frank Stoop, art collectors and patrons of music.

467

sterling qualities of the English woman rather than that. Heres Nick. So goodbye, and write Dolphin, do

B

Would you like me to print you some [writing] paper like this?

Berg

1868: To V. Sackville-West   52 *Tavistock Square, W.C.*1
Tuesday [6 March 1928]

Dearest Honey,
      Why do you write a letter on Wednesday and I only get it on Monday? Might be Persia over again: I'm afraid you're not very happy—you sound unhappy. Whats to be done about Berlin and the Ambassadors Coach with the purple footman on the box?[1] Dottie will no doubt speak her mind to Harold. My mind is at your service if you can use it. And Potto has a large warm heart, but then he can't write and its Virginia who writes.
      And I ought to be dining with Clive to meet Lord Berners, and all owing to you I'm sitting over the gas fire instead. Its this damned Orlando —I want to finish it, and I cant finish it; and then I wake in the night so excited and have to take a sleeping draught and so spend my day moping. But we are going to Rodmell for three or four days and there—please God—you'll be finished off; and I shall come back refreshed. I rather think, too, its an addled egg: too hasty, too splash-dashery, and all over the place. But I shall put it in a drawer till May. Why lecture the Danes on poetry[2] when you might give Virginia (who is worth all Copenhagen) a practical demonstration in the art of love? No: we start on the 25th: and so shall miss you completely.
      I do miss you. There's no fishmonger and porpoise in my life without you. All's a grind over cobbles. Sibyl, Clive, Stockbrokers, Ottoline, Molly, The Press—such is my round, with Dotty hovering on the outskirts and Lady Margaret [Duckworth]. Shall I lunch with her, and be condescended to by George? I think not. So what is there left? The art of literature. But I don't think I have anything of profound importance to say about that. Lucas was so smug on the telephone that I refused to give him my article: and I've refused to write for the Evening Standard on the 9th year of marriage: and I've refused to write for the Encyclopaedia and on the other

1. Harold had told Vita that he now wanted to become an Ambassador.
2. On 26-27 March Vita lectured on poetry, and Harold on Byron, in Copenhagen.

468

hand, I think I shall write a little article on Queen Elizabeth's nose for Eve.[1]

At Ottoline's I met James Stephens;[2] a little barrel organ monkey man, loquacious as a — oh I cant think at the moment what is loquacious except my gas fire. He said Yeats spent 20 years writing Leda [and the Swan]; and used to say it over and over, till the weight of every word was right: sometimes he would take one out, and then next year put it in again.

For Gods sake, translate Rilke:[3] only be sure of your rights; and that there's no other in English—I read some (prose) in French; and thought it good *up to a point*; subtle, melodious; but not quite getting over the obstacle. His poetry may be better; probably, from what they say, it is. Yes, certainly do it. Did you know that I talk French very well? That is with great fluency, some inaccuracy, and a good many words not in use since Saint-Simon? This is the report of my French teacher. I have lessons. It is the greatest fun. Now a youngish woman; then an old man; then again a very seductive elderly Bohemian; who tells me she 'loves Englishwomen'. From each I get a different story. I am thinking of learning Italian, Spanish, and Russian, not for the languages, but for the life histories of the professors. I only want you to know this fact: that I do talk French: because you will never hear me; and then I get a little more even with you in real-womanliness— All real women talk French, and powder their noses.

By the way, do you think I know you? Intimately? A question that I shall ask myself tomorrow morning—You are driving down to Knole [in *Orlando*], and as you go, you exhibit the most profound and secret side of your character.

Eddy writes a very very testy letter about Herr Wagenseil. Never have I met anyone so frankly peevish. It can't be the aristocracy—I mean some obscure self-assertiveness bred (very mistakenly) by thinking oneself superior—because Orlando hasn't a touch of it. He should marry Miss Spender Clay.[4] I met her and she seemed intelligent, and amiable, and very pretty, but to marry Eddy seems to me wearing a hair shirt for life. Raymond is 'the most unhappy man in the world"—or so he said the other night: but I asked for no details.

Goodnight now. I am so sleepy with chloral simmering in my spine that I can't write, nor yet stop writing—I feel like a moth, with heavy scarlet eyes and a soft cape of down—a moth about to settle in a sweet, bush—Would it were—ah but thats improper.

1. *The Waxworks at the Abbey* (*Eve*, 23 May 1928).
2. The Irish poet and story writer (1882-1950).
3. In 1931 the Hogarth Press published Vita and Eddy Sackville West's translation of Rainer Maria Rilke's *Duino Elegies*.
4. Phyllis, daughter of H. H. Spender Clay and Pauline Astor. She was 23 years old.

Please darling, creature, be happier—Or at any rate tell me the truth about yourself

My love to Harold. His book [*Biography*] is doing very well, and we're very pleased altogether. Would he like reviews sent him?

Yr Virginia

Potto

Berg

1869: TO PERNEL STRACHEY   52 *Tavistock Square, W.C.*1

8th March 1928

My dear Pernel,

I am a wretch, never answering, never doing anything. But the influenza has unmanned me; and what is worse—for I don't much mind that—got me so behindhand with a wretched silly thing [*Orlando*] I have to finish this summer—or I shant be paid if I dont—that I have had to put off coming in May. I am coming in October instead. So may I transfer your invitation till then?

But that doesn't mean that I want to transfer seeing you. But how is it to be managed? We are going to France on the 25th, motoring. And you're going to Egypt and Syria and Meccah, I make no doubt—somewhere romantic in a select distinguished way. For—but I must not take up your time which is so valuable and your attention which is so magisterial—by writing an entire and truthful life of you, as I should like to do. Did you know that has been my ambition always? Ever since I discovered about your dusty ears and pearl buttons. Dusty Ears it will be called—a pendant to Dusty Answer.[1] Perhaps it will be the most popular book of its time, like that. I think I should like it better; but then this is professional jealousy.

I saw Pippa and Marjorie the other night, and both gave me the liveliest joy; such integrity, such humanity—but there! You must go back to your labours, while I, thank God, can sit over my gas fire and imagine the first chapter of Dusty Ears: a Biography.

But for God's sake, come and see me—I'm on the telephone.

Yrs
V.W.

Strachey Trust

1. The novel by Rosamond Lehmann (1927).

1870: To V. Sackville-West   52 *Tavistock Square, W.C.*1

12th March 1928

Dearest Honey,

But why haven't you got my letter—sheets and sheets?—written directly
I had yours. I had one from you this morning, written on the 8th. True,
it was sent to Rodmell; but why 4 days from Berlin? Another tribute to
the efficiency of the British Embassy, I imagine.

We went down for 3 days hot sunshine at Rodmell, and were beat upon
and caged up by the worst frost and gale and snowstorm since Christmas
—after a week of June weather. So parched and frozen was I, I couldn't
write a word of Orlando, and have brought him back, like an old man of
the sea, to finish here. And the Americans must have the first chapter by
May 1st! All your fault. I could write another 3 volumes—easily, easily.
Appendixes blossom in my head. Then there's the Index, and the bibliography. Oh Vita Vita, how you have brought my life to ruin, and wasted
the fair taper in a sea of grease!

I lunched with—yes, you know who [Sibyl Colefax]: and she wants
me by the way to call her Bloody Poll in future—at least so the last orange
hieroglyph reads—and there I met a little gnome called Knoblock[1] and we
stood in Sibyls window half an hour saying this sort of thing:

V. "Oh she's enchanting:

K. "Enchanting? Thats not strong enough, Mrs Woolf. Great. Vitas a
   great woman.

V: Yes. Great. But so adorable; not merely great.

K. Adorable, I admit. But her character—thats whats so unsurpassable.
   I've known her since she was a lovely girl, very shy, her hands and
   feet running away from her, in yellow, at her first party. And the
   more I know the more I find to admire.

V. Admire? No Mr, Knoblock, thats not strong enough. Love.

K. Yes. Love it is.

and so on and so on.

Meanwhile, in between this fulsome rhapsody, I fell in love with Noel
Coward, and he's coming to tea. You cant have all the love in Chelsea—
Potto must have some: Noel Coward must have some. I played a funny
trick. I had no hat. Bought one for 7/11¾ at a shop in Oxford Street: green
felt: the wrong coloured ribbon: all a flop like a pancake in midair. Even
I thought I looked odd. But I wanted to see what happens among real
women if one of them looks like a pancake in mid air. In came the dashing

---

1. Edward Knoblock (1874-1945), the American-born playwright. He was a
   great friend of Vita and her mother, and in 1934 dramatised Vita's novel *The
   Edwardians.*

vermeil-tinctured red-stopper-bottle-looking Mrs Edwin Montagu.[1] She started. She positively deplored me. Then hid a smile. Looked again. Thought Ah what a tragedy! Liked me even as she pitied. Overheard my flirting. Was puzzled. Finally conquered. You see, women cant hold out against this kind of flagrant disavowal of all womanliness. They open their arms as to a flayed bird in a blast: whereas, the Mary's of this world, with every feather in place, are pecked, stoned, often die, every feather stained with blood—at the bottom of the cage.

Couldn't you make it the 21st instead of the 28th, honey? Do. I hear from Vanessa that motoring in France is no joke: She's just gone bang into a bus and smashed her Renault; so think of me in my Singer, and you not back to see the last of me. Did I tell you how well I speak French? Madame, you must have French blood in you! "Yes Sir, my Great Grandmother was a French Marquise"—ah, but I think I told you of the exquisite joy this gives me before. And you'll never hear me—thats whats so tantalising for you: the great grand daughter of the French Marquise.

I told them to send your books. I will write to Harold, whose letter enchants me, but shows a guilty conscience. He is ashamed of being an Ambassador. I am ashamed that any friend of mine should be married to a man who may be an Ambassador. Better be a footman—no, no, this must be written to Harold himself. Leonard is indignant that Harold should think he wrote the article about the F.O. in the Nation. It was [Hubert] Henderson probably. Leonard has written nothing; has been meeting Bernstorf[2] at Clives: Clive being ubiquitous and really I think, March-hare-mad: one hears his drumming through the Squares at night.

Darling, are you happy or unhappy? Writing? Loving? Please send me a long letter, on big paper, because Potto likes that best. Look [*squiggly design*] thats Potto: this is

Virginia

I have been flying:[3] but no room to tell you how I just missed death. I will kiss Bottome[4] if I may see her story.

Berg

1. Venetia Montagu was the widow of Edwin Montagu, formerly Secretary of State for India.
2. Albrecht Graf von Bernstorff, Counsellor of the German Embassy in London 1923-33. At the end of the Second War he was murdered by the Nazis.
3. On the last page of the book, Orlando hears an aeroplane bringing Shelmerdine (her husband) back to her.
4. Phyllis Bottome (1882-1963), the novelist and short-story writer. Vita had met her in Berlin, and told Virginia that Bottome was anxious to make her acquaintance: "As she thinks this beyond her reach, she has consoled herself by writing a story in which she describes the meeting between you and herself" (*Berg*).

1871: To Vanessa Bell   52 *Tavistock Square, W.C.*1

Tuesday [13 March] 1928

This is not a letter only an urgent request: could you lend us your Michelin guide and send it off at once? It is out of print, and we cant get a copy, which is said to be essential. We will bring it—of course, with us. Horrified at your accident.

Clive says we can have the other 2 rooms at Fontcreuse[1] as he will be alone.

Berg

1872: To V. Sackville-West   [52 *Tavistock Square, W.C.*1]

Postcard
[14 March 1928]

See whether you can read this—it will remind you of Kent.[2] An orange fog here, the King of the Afghans very miserable[3] and Dottie coming to tea.

Love,
V.

Berg

1873: To V. Sackville-West   52 *Tavistock Square, W.C.*1

Typewritten
[20? March 1928]

Dearest, Mrs Nicolson,

O what a curse these translators are! Tell your Bosom friend Mrs Voigt[4] Something or other that all I can say is that I have received a cheque from, and signed a contract with, the Insel Verlag which is I understand the Fischer Verlag by which they are to produce Mrs Dalloway this autumn and The Lighthouse later. But all communications must be through Curtis Brown.

1. Colonel Teed's house, a mile or two from Cassis.
2. On the reverse was a reproduction of a charter in the British Museum, by which King Canute granted land in Kent to the Archbishop of Canterbury.
3. The King and Queen of the Afghans were on a state visit 13-15 March.
4. Margaret Voigt, *née* Goldsmith, had met Vita in Berlin, where her husband Frederick Voigt was Correspondent for the *Manchester Guardian*. She was herself a writer, and acted as literary agent for British writers in Germany. She hoped to arrange the publication of Virginia's books in German.

473

Our address will be from the 2nd and till the 9th
La Bruyère [error for La Bergère], Cassis, Bouche du Rhone, France.

[in Virginia's handwriting:]
There! Thats business like aint it? The worst of business is it dries the
finer faculties, and I now find it very hard to continue. Potto has gone out
for a walk with Pinker so I cant get him to help.

[typewritten]
ORLANDO IS FINISHED!!!

[in Virginia's handwriting:]
Did you feel a sort of tug, as if your neck was being broken on Saturday
last [17 March] at 5 minutes to one? That was when he died—or rather
stopped talking, with three little dots . . . Now every word will have to
be re-written, and I see no chance of finishing it by September—It is all
over the place, incoherent, intolerable, impossible—And I am sick of it.
The question now is, will my feelings for you be changed? I've lived in
you all these months—coming out, what are you really like? Do you exist?
Have I made you up?
But I dont want to write another word for months—not a letter even—
Do you ever feel words have gone dry and dull in your mind? Your mind
like a sponge in the dust? You squeeze it and nothing comes? In October
my mind was dripping: That is the only life.
Last night at 12 Clive rang me up. He was quarrelsome drunk. Dotty
rang me up. She was merry drunk—They were in the same room. Also
there were Christa, Raymond and an unknown man. Here in my room at
12 o'clock were Roger and his mistress: the Arnold Forsters.
But we were sober.
That sort of instant communication of two rooms fascinates me—you
put down the telephone, and the whole Atlantic; very dark is between
you: having been so near you could see into the lights of the billiard room.
I have been reading Hazlitt. For 5 minutes my mind runs on the same
rails that the book runs on. I can only think in the same curves. Could you
tell me where I began to read Hazlitt and where I left off? Are you a critic?
Now Vita, sit down and think about yourself.
Sibyl says,
"Yes, I just saw Vita for a moment before she left"
She didnt. did she?
Is it because she tells these lies that one is never intimate with her?
I have just listened in—in Nelly's bedroom—to the Prince of Wales
speaking about merchant seamen. In the middle Leonard came in, with
Pinker. Again, this was very odd: the dinner, the cheering, the Prince

stumbling along like an old stiff cart horse: and Pinker scratching my legs at the same time.

Bottome! Bottome! If she don't come quick I shall miss her.

My French teacher is of your persuasion. She is now irritated with me, for some obscure reason—Still, my accent is admirable—(this I shall repeat and repeat, because it is one of my secret shames—like not being able to do my hair, or powder—

God Vita what a dull letter! The truth is, I'm talking to Leonard about Sir Thomas Browne; and about buying a rug; and am incredibly sick of my own words.

Darling Creature, send me a long lovely letter to Cassis.

I am rather depressed.

Orlando so bad.

Cant write.

Can Love but then Vita's away.

Shant see her for ever so long.

But continue please to think me charming and write to me.

Virginia

Berg

1874: TO VANESSA BELL   52 *Tavistock Square, W.C.*1

20th March [1928]

Dearest,

Many thanks for all your good kind acts. I will do anything here you want done—as I meant to say before, and now there is no time for you to ask me: except for sanitary towels, which I will bring in masses. Oughtn't we some day to be coming to the time of life? Gumbo [Strachey] has already they say. But you and I hang on; so does Molly: a sign doubtless of a rich temper. Ask Nan what her state is. Doubtless never had a time at all.

I am on tip toe to see you and the house. I shall be very envious I suppose: you will have lovely pots and dishes and chairs. One day I must spend rummaging for things, as we might easily take a few tables and beds home on top of the Singer.

Already everything is rather chaotic, and people pullulate: Ka and Roger dining here tonight, which he says is my devilry; but I owned up to Ka in asking him—And then Will comes in, which is, Roger says, so cruel an infliction that if it weren't for love of me he couldn't come. And Helen is coming in, and Morgan, and after that thank God, I shall have no more people. I rather wish Cassis were only to be you and Duncan. Not that I have a word against Clive or Nan [Hudson]: but you know what one gets with talk talk—and never has Clive been in such a state of

475

loquacity. I haven't seen so much of him since the year 10. Bobo [Mayor] seems mildly to rule him, but he is, as you will see, very wild and queer, and has run amok in the Beau Monde again, and carries drunk guardsmen to bed from great houses in Grosvenor Square—You'll hear the story, so I say no more. But not a word of Mary.

Angus has some hopes of Agnew who has offered to see him: Also your old friend the man I call Benwick—but thats not his name—is leaving Lefevre; so he may try there. I shall be glad to be quit of it all. It is not agreeable, his going, and Mrs Cartwright putting her best foot forward so vigorously one has one's nose cut off every time one speaks.

We had a Bloomsbury meeting on Sunday at Clives, and did our best, but agreed that it was useless without you—We tried to make you speak, and invented your opinion of Queen Victoria's letters: but no. Dolphin is inimitable, and life is dust and ashes without her. Then everyone longs for Duncan's society. But it is thought that you don't particularly long for us. I hope you will have your settlement with Clive. I can't see how he can have his daimler and his supper parties and not increase your money. I see that London is very complicated. But wouldn't Cassis for ever be rather monotonous? I should die—if you left for ever—But thats a mere bagatelle I agree. I cant help thinking that Lord Gage is only a threat.[1] Still its all very gloomy and unsettling. But I can't understand the money difficulty— judging from Clives own state.

Ka says she is doing her best to let 37. I think she is well placed for that sort of thing: she moves among the dull and the rich who talk of houses perpetually. George and Margaret [Duckworth] asked us to lunch—but we did not face it. Mrs Dominic Spring Rice has run away with Mr Micheson, and Mr and Mrs Francis Meynell[2] have parted: all this means nothing to me, or to you, I daresay: but I am scribbling in haste, and so am very dull. I must dress, or wash, thats the truth; and Roger will be crusty, and Ka suburban, and Will intolerable. What an evening, and why did I contrive it?

The Michelin map has come; I meant the Guide: but we have now borrowed one.

This will be my last letter. We think of coming *home* through Tarascon, Leonard says: couldn't you go back with us and meet us somewhere else?

But I will get him to send you a line about our route before we start. It is still rather unsettled.

Do try and meet us somewhere.

Yr B.

Berg

---

1. Lord Gage, the owner of Charleston, whose agent had given Vanessa notice that she had to leave the house, but the notice was withdrawn.
2. The typographer and designer, founder of the Nonesuch Press.

Letters 1875-1910 (end of March–mid-July 1928)

Virginia and Leonard went to Cassis on 26 March, driving themselves for the first time abroad, to see Vanessa in her new villa. They left the Hogarth Press in charge of Mrs Cartwright, Angus Davidson having now departed, to be replaced by the young Richard Kennedy in April. Their holiday was briefly marred by a sharp row between Virginia and Clive, and later she suspected that he had read the letters she wrote to Vanessa. The journey home by car was perilous, but they arrived safe in London on 16 April, and Virginia immediately began the revision of Orlando. *Leonard read it at the end of May, and took it rather "more seriously than I had expected. Thinks it in some ways better than the Lighthouse. The truth is I expect I began it as a joke, and went on with it seriously" (Virginia's diary).* Orlando *was not published until October, but there were still reverberations from* To the Lighthouse, *for which Virginia was awarded the Femina Vie Heureuse Prize, presented to her on 2 May by Hugh Walpole, who became an affectionate and patient friend. Virginia did not immediately embark on* The Waves, *but wrote journalism for the* Nation *and* America. *Her letters to Vanessa give the false impression that she no longer cared for her friends: only Rebecca West emerges from them with credit. But she was worried, by the superficiality of* Orlando *which she thought might do her reputation harm, by the threatened devastation of the countryside around Rodmell, by the continued absence of Vanessa, and the feeling, as she expressed it in her diary, that "I detest my own volubility".*

1875: TO VANESSA BELL

Monks House [Rodmell, Sussex]

Sunday. 25th March [1928]

Dearest,

We are perching here before starting tomorrow. We are just off to test the car by driving to Rye; everybody is full of gloomy prognostications, and says we shall break down. If we are both killed simultaneously, please remember that I leave you all my possessions, in land, house, gold silver, stocks, jewels, books, carpets: Pinker is to go to Clive; who will I know, cherish her for my sake.

Really I am waiting for Leonard to come in from the garden with Percy and tell me our route, which is now finally settled. But they have got talking about the cesspool which is full up, and must be emptied on to the

477

vegetable beds with a bucket. Perhaps you might meet us somewhere, if the old char's bonnet [Vanessa's Renault] is once more on its legs.

Did I tell you about Noel Coward? He is in search of culture, and thinks Bloomsbury a kind of place of pilgrimage. Will you come and meet him? He is a miracle, a prodigy. He can sing, dance, write plays, act, compose, and I daresay paint—He rescued his whole family who kept boarding houses in Surbiton, and they are now affluent, but on the verge of bank-ruptcy, because he spends so much on cocktails. If he could only become like Bloomsbury he thinks he might be saved. But I wont ask you to meet him, unless you swear to come back by the *14th May* at latest. You can't neglect Angelica's education: like this—my most promising niece:

Here's Leonard: here's the list.

On Friday 30th sleep at Lyon.
   Sat—31st sleep at Montelimar
   Sun. 1st. sleep at Aix

Our route will be,

                Tournus
                Lyon.
                Vienne.
                Valence
                Montelimar
                Orange.
                Carpentras.
                Cavaillon.
                Orgon.
                Aix
                Cassis.

But this is at the mercy of the Gods of course.

I am very excited, partly at the thought of seeing you again. I am like a sea anemone which has had to keep all its tentacles curled up, and when its put in water (i.e. Dolphin) they come out and wave and tumble and are of an exquisite and incredible beauty: but Lord! Dolphin bites: or she squirts acid: Dolphin cant be depended on for more than 2 seconds—Dolphins a heartless brute, but nothing to Duncan, whose heart is made of purest emerald—hard, precious, beautiful, unmelting—We had, I thought, a slightly painful parting with Angus, (who seems to think he's coming to Cassis) They have been doing the accounts; and sometimes they discover debts and sometimes windfalls. All is complicated by the exact date; that is, whether Angus shares or not. He is hopeful, however, about Agnew [art-gallery], which is a mercy. Never never will I have another young man as partner.

Are you drawing for Todd? She is like a slug with a bleeding gash for a mouth—She paints badly. The whole of London does nothing but talk about bringing out magazines:

Have you done some pictures?

Do you love me?

Does Angelica?

Here's the Singer.

I could only get 1/8 towels: but I find them absorbent sufficiently

V.W.

Berg

1876: To V. Sackville-West   *Orange [France]*

31st March 1928

Dearest Honey,

Are you back? At Long Barn? Happy? With the dogs? Comfortable? Well?

I can't remember how one writes. Nothing but a heart of gold would make me try to write now—perched on a hard chair in a bare bedroom in a bad inn—Perhaps there will be bugs in the bed. But all the other inns have been divine. Even here, I have drunk a bottle of wine for dinner, and the world goes gently up and down in my head. Suppose one had wine every day, at every meal—what an enchanted world! I forget the bugs and the rain as it is: I think of Vita at Long Barn: all fire and legs and beautiful plunging ways like a young horse.

No accidents so far; and every day we drive quicker, and shall be at Cassis tomorrow. This is the way to live, I can assure you. Driving all day; an hour or two for lunch: a few churches perhaps to be seen; one's inn at night: wine, dinner; bed; off again—gradually it gets Southern, and we take off our jerseys and I have had to buy a silk one. One drops in upon people playing dominoes in cafés: or one stops on a mountain, and I sit on a stone, and L. tries to discover why the umbrella leaks at the nose.

But these travellers letters are too dull; and I've lost all touch with language; am a revolving brute, merely; a creature who sits 8 hours a day looking out of the window.

But we must do this together one day, Vita, my dear: unless you are, as I think all my friends are, a myth, something I dreamt.

I buy a new book at each town, and read it in bed—I'm extremely well. I've not seen a paper or had a letter for a week. So it is a nice proof of my affection that I find my mind settling on you, like a butterfly on a hot stone.

The day before I left I read in the Times that I had won the most insignificant and ridiculous of prizes[1]—but I have heard nothing more; so it may be untrue. I dont mind—you will laugh either way.

1. Virginia won the *Femina Vie Heureuse* prize for *To the Lighthouse.*

We shall be back on the 17th.

I will write from Cassis: This is merely the bubble of affection, which is stupid and inarticulate, but risen from Potto's heart. Tell me if you are fond of me; and about your mother—pray God she don't come to Knole[1] —and have you written anything? Tell me everything. My mind is like a deep irreflecting river in which facts are slowly turned. I'm not allowed to drive. All the fruit trees are out. Pink, red, white. But it is pouring here.

> Yr
> Virginia

Berg

1877: To Quentin Bell
Fontcreuse, Cassis,
B du R. [France]

5th April 1928

My dear Quentin,

I think you are rather a mangy beast to put me off with a postcard after all these months. Still, if you now write me a letter, very indiscreet, affectionate, interesting and full of reflections upon life—but also describe your German family in detail[2]—then I will forgive you.

We arrived here before our time, owing to the impetuous and fiery nature of the Singer, which went quicker and quicker, so that we were almost run away with through France. Everybody here was, and is, doing something odd. Clive has just given away a pair of sky blue pyjamas to a young lady: Duncan dances to the gramophone; the little girls collect frogs; Leonard collects spiders for the frogs; Nessa lets the frogs loose. Miss Campbell breeds innumerable chickens. Colonel Teed gives me sips of wine. We are thinking of buying a house here: I could go on in this style for ever, but it is not very interesting, I daresay. The frogs—the garden is full of them, all amorous, all vociferous, and none satisfied—make consecutive thought, such as you and I like, impossible, otherwise I would tell you about the state of England.

Roger is fast crumbling, like a lump of sugar in hot milk; that is to say, he remembers nothing and invents everything. Sometimes his pocket handkerchief has eleven knots in it by nightfall; and he and Helen sit on the edge of the bed till the small hours untying them and trying to remember which is which. But his decline is beautiful as the sunset, and it is certain that he will be alive when you and Julian are old, old men, prodding each other in the back with umbrellas. Julian is the very spit and image of a

---

1. Lady Sackville had written to her brother-in-law, the new Lord Sackville, asking if she could take a two-year lease of Knole.
2. Quentin was staying in Munich.

German Professor: with a bag on his back, spectacles, straw hat; very huge; amiable and apparently innocent, but if you observe his teeth, of which he has a great many, you will see that they are pointed and turn inwards—a sure sign of a sarcastic and biting disposition.

Every night we sit round the lamp in Nessa's studio, while the moths batter at the window, and Nessa tries to cut their heads off with a pair of very large scissors. She says Moths dont mind this, but soon grow new heads, or tails, as the case may be. Whenever Clive becomes inspired, about Proust or the French Revolution, and is about to say something which has never been said before, an old male frog, who has been bitterly disappointed, and would kill himself if he knew the way, barks. Thus Clive's words are never heard, and the truth is lost—which is a great pity, but after all, why should not frogs have their will now and then? Answer me that. I am so set upon, chiefly by Julian, for asking questions which have no answer, at least in this hemisphere, that I scarcely dare say How are you? or How do you think that Colonel Teed proposed to Miss Campbell, because showers of things are instantly thrown at me. We discuss everything in the world. Cassis is becoming as notorious as Bloomsbury. Characters of the strangest sort abound. We motor back again to Dieppe on Monday.

I haven't yet asked you a single question; but I have told you the reason. I entirely depend on you for protection in the Bell family which is ferocious beyond words. Judith [Barbara Bagenal's daughter] is here, and has a bottom of common sense, as Dr Johnson said: but you dont know why he said it, or what happened, being only a painter, poor boy: we were discussing this at lunch today, and saying you would be ignorant always. Probably you are extremely happy: and I shall hope to see vast allegorical works, upsetting all theories and establishing a new form, when you come home. I will take you to the United Service Museum in Whitehall to see the Duke of Wellington's top hat. So please write me a long long letter. As there are no frogs in Germany you wont be able to have that excuse for being as dull and prosy and disconnected as your afflicted Aunt.

Please consider our summer libel.[1]

Yr V.W.

Quentin Bell

1878: To ANGUS DAVIDSON

Fontcreuse, Cassis
[France]

Saturday [7 April 1928]

My dear Angus,

I am very sorry to hear that you have been ill. I believe it is a most painful disease, and fills one with melancholy. Morgan Forster has just been

---

1. Virginia and Quentin sometimes collaborated on satirical pieces about their friends.

having it. Poor Cartwright must feel hereby doubly widowed, now you are gone. I shall go through the stages of your departure every year with her, just as I've finished the typhoid. But that is only one of the reasons which makes me very sorry you are going. I doubt that I shall ever do up a parcel again, and as my gift in that line is astounding, it seems a thousand pities.

Everyone here is as odd as usual—Julian has actually made himself sick laughing at Duncan and me. Our eccentricities seem to flower in the South, and the frogs keep talking incessantly. We went to Toulon with Nan Hudson, and should have gone to Marseilles today, but it is pouring. The Singer runs so fast on French roads that we got here early. It is undoubtedly what one will do in Heaven—motoring all day, and eating vast meals, and drinking red wine and liqueurs. But don't tell your mother this. I suppose you are at Bath today. Clive has just given away his best silk sky blue pyjamas to a young lady who is of fascinating beauty, and he dines out most nights with the aristocracy of Cassis.

Leonard has almost done the accounts and thinks we should each get £70 profit—which is more than I expected after Mary.

I hope you are really recovered. What about Agnew? Have you heard anything?

Yours ever,
Virginia Woolf

Angus Davidson

1879: To Violet Dickinson   *Fontcreuse, Cassis,*
                                   B du R., France

[7? April 1928]

My Violet,

Here we are sitting in the sun in a vineyard miles from prizes and novels thank God.

But it was very nice of you to make your tail wag in my direction; and Leonard and I send our love.

Nessa is down the road in her new villa, painting hard, and I shall take the liberty of sending her love. Angelica's, Clive's, Duncan's and Julian's too.

Julian is 6ft two and very charming.

Yrs
V.W.

Marquess of Bath

1880: To Gwen Raverat   *Fontcreuse, Cassis,*
                                          B. du R., France
7th April [1928]

My dear Gwen,
    I wish I could have gone to see your pictures,[1] but we left England
the day after the show began, and I suppose it will be over when we come
back—about the 20th. I should have liked to see them, not from artistic
reasons, but to make up my idea of your character. I have no illusions
about my artistic criticism. It is all literary. Were you pleased with the
show? I have a kind of idea that we may meet one day this summer. It is
an almost impossible achievement. Human beings are so terrified of each
other. If I rang your bell I should feel certain you did not want to see me,
as I walked up stairs—I should feel I am committing an intrusion. All the
same, I think I shall.
    We motored from Dieppe to Cassis—absolute heaven, I think it.
Everything looks odd and new, coming along the road to it gradually. I'm
half inclined to buy a barn here in a vineyard. The sun and the hills put
my dear London rather in the shade—and then one does exactly what one
likes here.
    What are you up to?

                                                    Yours,
                                                    V.W.

Sussex

1881: To V. Sackville-West   *Aurillac [France]*
Wednesday, April 11th 1928

    We are on our way back, and have been up in the mountains, snowed
upon, punctured 3 times, changing wheels in snowstorms in pitch darkness
on the edge of precipices and have come 130 miles today so I'm very
sleepy—but extremely well—and rather tipsy. This is to say will you
come as soon as you can and *bring Pinker*—let me know to Tavistock
Sqre. We expect to get there on Monday night. No engagements so far—
all days, all meals at your service. Yes—you have survived the death of
Orlando: but as I must re-write him entirely, he's only suspended, not
dead.

---

1. Gwen Raverat's exhibition at the St George's Gallery, 23 March to 12 April.

Yes I do want to see you—Yes I'm very fond of you—Yes-yes yes. Potto is here

Goodnight—

Potto [*squiggly design*] there!   Virginia

Its all great fun—We must, must, do this together.

Berg

1882: To Hope Mirrlees [*from Leonard and Virginia*]
                                         52 *Tavistock Square, W.C.*1
[17 April 1928]

Dear Hope,

We are both so distressed to see the news of Jane's death.[1] We only got back from France last night and had looked forward to coming to see her again. We know what it must be to you.

If there's anything at all which I could do for you these next few days, will you let me know?

Yours
Leonard Woolf

Anyhow, what a comfort for you to have been all you were to her.

Love V.

Mrs T. S. Eliot

1883: To V. Sackville-West   52 *Tavistock Square, W.C.*1
Tuesday [17 April 1928]

Would you bring a bookplate or something with your Arms on it— very important—also the photograph of the man at Worthing: Did you get Shelmerdine photographed?[2] I'm being pestered to send all these things to America at once, and see that every word will have to be re-written.

Come punctually at 4 with Pinker, or Leonard will be gone. May I come to the broadcasting with you? And aint it wretched you care for me no longer: I always said you were a promiscuous brute—Is it a Mary again; or a Jenny this time or a Polly? Eh?

1. Jane Harrison, the classical scholar, died on 15 April at the age of 77.
2. A portrait painted by an unknown artist in about 1820 of an unidentified young man. Vita had bought it from a London dealer, and it was used in *Orlando* as a portrait of Marmaduke Bonthrop Shelmerdine. The picture is now at Sissinghurst.

The truth shall be dug out of you at all costs.

Am I to be wearing my heart out for a woman who goes with any girl from an Inn!

Yr Virginia
Woolf

Potto

Berg

1884: To Vanessa Bell   [52 *Tavistock Square, W.C.*1]

19th April. 1928

Dearest

Here we are back again after the most adventurous cold journey you can imagine. Once we were marooned on the top of a mountain pass in the snow. Once a runaway horse missed us by two inches. Innumerable nails stuck in our tyres. —But to business. Would you let your rooms, or 3 of them, to some friends of Vita's [Frederick and Margaret Voigt], poor but respectable, for £2.10. a week for a month from next week or the 1st of May? Details are a little vague as they are in Germany, but if you would state your terms and leave me a little latitude I expect I could arrange something. I said I thought you would want £3.3. I think they only want a bedroom, sitting room and kitchen.

Now I will just run over my first day here, not to excite your envy, for really I wonder why one lives the way one does when one might the way one doesn't—in the tower at Fontcreuse, for example, seeing the tip of Dolphin's tail once a week (For I should be strictly independent) But to return: the telephone rings as I have my bath: Leonards mother: will we go there: an hour or two at Orlando, which is wretched, and must be entirely re-written in one month; then out across a churchyard to look for a garage; and accosted by two drab wandering women, distraught, sobbing, one Hope, who cried that Jane was just dead and would we come to the funeral: never have I seen anyone so mad, wild, frantic: and we kissed among the tombs: (Cromwell's daughter is buried there, as perhaps you know— anyhow Duncan would) so to the office; and there's Raymond: just been flying; may he come to tea; theres a Jew called Namier;[1] so home; Lydia and Maynard: will we come to dinner; telephone; Vita; may she come to tea next day; and so to bed. The net result is that we're just off to Jane's funeral at Finchley and dine with the Keynes's tonight. I think Duncan might fitly and gracefully write to Hope.

1. Lewis Namier, the son of Polish Jews who emigrated to England, was the historian of the 18th century and a strong advocate of the Zionist movement.

I found an odd letter from Clive waiting me here. He apologises for having been angry with me, but says that he found I had been making merry at his expense, and that he couldn't help bursting out,[1] though he should have been angry not with me but with the person who repeated my sayings. What can he mean? Did you repeat anything? I shouldn't blame you; but on the whole I suspect he read some of my letters to you, the day we went to Toulon. Lord, Lord! He says I ought to remember how unhappy he has been. But when will the days of his widowhood be over? Oughtn't he to remember how mad I have been? And hasn't he forgotten the blue parrokeet [Mary Hutchinson] entirely? And is this love? And would you or I forget Duncan or Leonard in six months? And whats the truth of life?—for I am convinced it is lodged with you.

I came to a million conclusions about you and Duncan during my stay: Happily for you I left with about 20 thousand questions unasked. The few I managed to get spoken were mere midge bites—I should like to write a book about Duncan. Are you the only person who is really acquainted with him? intimately profoundly? I daresay.

But now I must rake out my black clothes and be off, in this bitter cold. Write please instantly; and I will answer. I have a thousand very interesting things to say. No news of Angus—Adrian away. His dog has torn Alices lip open and she had to go to the hospital and threatens to have the law on Adrian. And there's Will Arnold Forster inviting himself to dinner.

Yr B.

Please tell me if you can throw light on Clive.

Berg

1885: To Clive Bell   52 *Tavistock Sqre* [*W.C.*1]

21st April [1928]

Dearest Clive,

I own I don't like being smacked in public—it makes us both slightly ridiculous; and I cant for the life of me think what I did this time to deserve it. I shouldn't mind owning [up] if I'd made merry at your expense—its a way you have too, you'll allow—but the occasion escapes me. I sometimes wonder what itch this smacking gratifies—why I'm so often the victim. Psychologically, I'd like to understand it. And if I ought to remember that you've been unhappy, so ought you to remember that I've been mad.

1. In her diary for 17 April, Virginia alleges that Clive "smacked me in public—curse him for an uneasy little upstart", but it is doubtful whether she meant it literally.

These slaps and snubs—unexpected as they are—annoy me more than they should. But enough—

Life, if life its to be called, has been breaking in. That is to say I've dined with the Keynes', been to Jane Harrison's funeral; had Vita to dinner; Raymond to tea; Elly [Dr Elinor Rendel] to pull wax out of my ears, written some pages, and have to see the Crolys,[1] Dadie, Angus, Stella Benson,[2] God knows who else, in the near future. Meanwhile its as bitter as sin and as dark as a coalhole. Julian turned up to eat the remains of our dinner the other night, and caught the last train to Cambridge.

Of gossip the chief is that Vita has had a terrific culminating and final scene with Lady Sackville in a solicitor's office, with witnesses to take down all insults—The woman seems utterly mad, called her liar thief and harlot, cut her pearl necklace in half, and pocketed the twelve best stones, and then announced that she would consider her dead henceforward and stop every penny of her allowance. Vita swears she is going to earn her own living by her pen. Dottie is selling Sherfield and buying a place at Groom-bridge,[3] chiefly remarkable for the gigantic rocks in the garden, which have taken Vita's romantic fancy. But you'll hear all this in detail—and a thousand other titbits—from Raymond, who is flowing, scintillating, brilliant.

Oh and Fredegond[4] has been taken for a Roman Catholic—and Lydia [Keynes] is a woman of parts.

Yr V.W.

Quentin Bell

1886: To V. Sackville-West   *From Monk's House [Rodmell, Sussex]*

Friday [27 April 1928]

I rang you up just now, to find you were gone nutting in the woods with Mary Campbell, or Mary Carmichael, or Mary Seton,[5] but not me— damn you—to say:

I've forgotten the right name and address of Mrs Goldsmith [Margaret Voigt]. She rang up and said she was staying possibly with you. Would

1. Croly was an American who invited Virginia and Leonard to lecture in the United States in the autumn. They refused the invitation.
2. The novelist (1892-1933). After her marriage in 1921, she lived mostly in China, where her husband was a customs officer.
3. Penns-in-the-Rocks, Sussex.
4. Fredegond Shove (*née* Maitland), Virginia's cousin.
5.   "There was Marie Seaton, and Marie Beaton,
                  And Marie Carmichael, and me."
   (*The Ballad of the Queen's Maries*). Virginia used these names for imaginary novelists in *A Room of One's Own* (1929).

you tell her that the rooms [37 Gordon Square] will be ready on Monday, and the keys will be here any time on Monday morning. Tell her this, but dont tell her how violently I disliked her for talking of 'Vita' on the telephone: how vulgar, pushing, crude, coarse, American, I thought her voice —This is one of the effects of jealousy. I can't say how I detest hearing some one call you 'Vita' in American on the telephone at 8 in the morning

Second

I wanted to ask if it would be convenient should we call in on Sunday on our way back; at Long Barn. It has now become essential to have a photograph of Orlando in country clothes in a wood, to end with.[1] If you have films and a camera I thought Leonard might take you. We should come about 2 or 3 or earlier: not later, so dont stay in. Would you wire if this won't do: like an angel. And we won't come if your house is flooded with people. And I dont want to meet that voice inside a woman. Not hearing, we shall understand it suits.

                                                                         V.W.

A thousand thanks for translations [Rilke]: life exciting: hectic: old friends, turning up: Dadie—dadie—dadie Hah!

Berg

1887: To Vanessa Bell   *Monk's House* [*Rodmell, Sussex*]

Sunday April 29th [1928]

Dearest,

The letting of the rooms seems to be accomplished. Old Uppington[2] arrived in the Press with your letter and will have the rooms ready on Monday. A hard American voice [Voigt] roused me at 8 in the morning with a torrent of enquiries. (I put this in to show how much I have done for you; and thus what a claim I have to your kindness)

We are down here for the weekend. It is suddenly full summer; everything is out; the garden blazing with lilac, apple, pear blossom and every flower you can imagine; and the country is far far far away better than Cassis. Really, the downs are astonishing at this moment. (Here I cut out a long rhapsody, just as I suppressed a very brilliant and profound account of Chartres, because of Duncan's viper tongue) But in 5 years we shall be driven out—theres no doubt of it. I went for a walk to the river this

---

1. A photograph of Vita at Long Barn is the final illustration in *Orlando*. It is reproduced in this volume as Plate 8b.
2. Mrs Uppington was regularly employed at Charleston as a 'daily help'.

evening and found a race course on the flats by the halt, with stables and a stand run up in cheap wood. It seems inconceivable, but the man who has bought Southease farm is starting a pony race course, and they're said to [be] going to make a side line from the halt to Southease. And they say they're going to build 30 cottages at Asheham. Undoubtedly, this country is doomed; but where to go next, I dont know. I wish Cassis hadn't an English colony attached, and weren't so hilly. Wont you migrate to a little terrain somewhere between Tarascon and Uzés, which seemed infinitely lovely, and entirely French, and one had asparagus and truffles, which is my favourite food, for about sixpence? Thats my notion of bliss.

I've written to ask Clive for an explanation, but I dont suppose he'll give one. I feel pretty sure, from the definite way in which he said he had been told I had laughed at him; that he had really read it. So I think it would be safer to lock up letters. His anger began, (and he could have seen no one, and had no letters himself) directly after we went to Toulon. I've no doubt I did write something about him—but I cant remember what.

Please send the photograph of Angelica [as Sasha in *Orlando*] *as soon as you can.* Harcourt Brace is badgering my life out to get the whole book and pictures during May.

London has become, largely owing to the heat, rather attractive. I have had one or two odd encounters—one as we were crossing Piccadilly at night to go to the play. Someone plucked at my shoulder and I saw to my amazement Katherine Furse![1] "I was just thinking of Madge" I said, which happened to be true. "I wasn't" she said. "I was thinking of a woman policeman with whom I'm to spend the night." She is going to come and see us—She is much the same—strapping, tailor made, a little pinched and weather-beaten; and it must be 20 years since I saw her. She is a masterly woman, I gather, an official, and spending the night with a policewoman only meant supervising morality, I am sure. Then I was rung up by Marjorie S[trachey]. in a great state of emotion. "May Boris and I come and see you at once?" she asked. I, understanding by this that she had eloped with Anrep and wished for my blessing agreed enthusiastically. But she turned up with Doris—Enfield it was: a worthy and highly intelligent woman; but not what I wanted. Then we had a most curious wizened monkey-like woman, Stella Benson, to dine. As you are now a library subscriber, perhaps you can tell me about her books. She was second for my prize; and she took it very seriously; but I had to admit that I had never been so sneered at in my life as for getting it. Why does almost every bodies intelligence stop short beneath the chin? One finds somebody intelligent, amusing, educated, and then Hey Presto (as you would say) they take the Femina prize for the voice of God, and become no better than a suburban lodging house keepers scullery maid. But she has seen rivers in Manchuria

1. The daughter of John Addington Symonds and sister of Madge Vaughan.

freeze from side to side in ten minutes, and is of two minds whether to leave her husband or not.

I think I have secured an interesting piece of gossip for you—which I will tell you when you come back. You must be back on the 30th. I am rapidly drying—Angelica has become essential to me. An awful kind of spurious maternal feeling has taken possession of me—which reminds me, don't let Julian become too like his father in twitching persisting uneasiness—he takes his poems a little too much to heart; as Clive does his derision at the hands of the great Stephen family. What a mass of vanity that man is! (now dont leave this lying about) I'm seriously rather concerned about his future; when you're not there especially. He is so exacting and pertinacious, and yet to have him with young women, as he insists, is almost intolerable; to Leonard indeed quite so. I rather hope he and Raymond will knock about Europe for a time. Could one tell him not to talk so much about himself? Thats what gets him laughed at—this perpetual description of his own ecstasies and agonies: after all this bedding or not bedding becomes a little dull; when one's out of it: as I am; and Vita is; and Dottie is; and various other people.

I dont advise you to motor back the way we came, unless it is hot. Leonard caught a violent cold and I went completely deaf in one ear. The ground is strewn with nails. When I was deaf I thought only Angelica will be kind to me. I shall retire and trouble my friends no more—Happily Elly came and by blowing trumpet like through a tube shook out a piece of wax and suddenly I heard the gas fire roaring and was cured. Apparently I did it with my ear stoppers.

Angus is seeing Agnews today, and I think they must mean to offer him something. The Press has revived astonishingly with Cartwright only; Leonard gains a good half hour every morning. On Monday Kennedy[1] comes; Belcher has not been pert, but is apt to be flustered and to need looking after at her accounts. I know you like these details of the basement world.

Are you going to Germany? I hope not. I'm jealous of Roger being with you. I must go to the London show; but wild donkeys and tigers shall not make me commit my views to writing—with Duncans flickering adders tongue a-playing round my verbiage. Nevertheless, kiss that adorable man from me. I often wonder how we should have done married.

B

Berg

---

1. Richard Kennedy, nephew of George Kennedy, the architect. He joined the Hogarth Press when he was 16, having just been superannuated from Marlborough for idleness. He described his experiences in *A Boy at the Hogarth Press* (1972).

Typewritten
May 2nd [1928]

My dear Julian,

I have been in the devil of a hurry, and am still, owing to my dog show prize [the *Femina*], and to having to finish an extremely foolish book [*Orlando*] all of a sudden. So I have not written. However here are my remarks for what they are worth. I still think much as I did about the poems you showed me last summer. I like them. I think they show great promise—I mean power of observation, and of putting your facts down accurately. But I still think you need to get a broader view of nature as a whole before you can make your observations into poetry. They dont make poems yet; only lists of things one after another. This applies most to the natural history poems. I think you want some mood to give them unity and driving force.

But this doesnt apply to the later ones—more especially to the Ode to Jefferies. I think this is much more coherent and pulled through. There you have given one emotion which subdues the details instead of leaving them separate and unjoined. I like this very much. I hope you will try to give more emotion and less observation; or rather to combine them more. I think you want to write a great deal still so as to get things to run quickly in words. But I quite agree that one must begin by being a pettifogging character, with a note book, trying to get the colour of the sunset right, at the beginning. Please send some more. I think you are beginning to creep out of your shell; and it is a very grave question whether you are a duck, or a swan, or it may be some odious reptile. I hear you have done a good review for Leonard. I shall be greatly amused to read it in print.

Now I must go to the Institut Français to be given forty pounds by Hugh Walpole and make a speech of thanks. My god! Is it worth it? Echo answers no.

I think we shall come up [to Cambridge] soon, and descend on you for lunch.

Yours affectionate and loving (but what on earth is the distinction?)
Aunt Virginia

Quentin Bell

4th May [1928]

Dear Mr Walpole,

It is extremely nice of you to write when you have already been put to so much trouble on my account.[1] I wanted to thank you at the time, and should have liked to start an argument had it been feasible but when I turned and saw the audience I was overcome with horror, could think of nothing to say, and so fled. But I do thank you very sincerely. Apart from the very generous things you said, and seem always to be saying in print, about me, I was immensely interested by your theories.

I suppose you would not be able to dine with us next Friday, 11th, at 7.45 without dressing. I hope it would be less gloomy than South Kensington and we should enjoy it very much if you could come.

Yours sincerely
Virginia Woolf

Texas

1890: To V. Sackville-West   52 *Tavistock Square, W.C.*1

Friday [4 May 1928]

Orlando,
I think I must tell Eddy about you [and *Orlando*]. What do you say? He is so passionate about Knole and Sackvilles. I feel it awkward to spring the whole thing without warning—Would he keep it secret? Let me know what you think—I am seeing him on Tuesday. I'll tell him myself, if at all.

I hear Mrs Nicolson and Mrs Woolf gave some offence on Wednesday by coming to the prize dressed as if for a funeral. Still it *was* my funeral. Hugh has now written me an eloquent letter of affection and regret—says he was stunned. He must be a man of the tenderest heart, and so I've told him.

Life flows on—Oh Lord what a lot of people I've seen.

And you're alone listening to the Nightingales damn you—with Mary [Campbell]—

Yr
Virginia

Berg

1891: To Quentin Bell   52 *Tavistock Sqre, WC*1

May 6th [1928]

My dear Quentin,
Your letter has been rather a surprise to me; because, if you can write

1. Walpole had presented the *Femina* Prize to Virginia on 2 May. He wrote in his diary: "A *frightful* occasion. Rows of old female novelists glaring at me. I made a rotten speech. Everyone desperately nervous" (Rupert Hart-Davis, *Hugh Walpole*, 1952, p. 289).

as well as all that, with such abandonment to devilry and ribaldry,—for I dont believe a word of what you say—how in Gods name can you be content to remain a painter? Surely you must see the infinite superiority of the language to the paint? Think how many things are impossible in paint; giving pain to the Keynes', making fun of one's aunts, telling libidinous stories, making mischief—these are only a few of the advantages; against which a painter has nothing to show: for all his merits are also a writers. Throw up your career, for God's sake.

Here we are back again, after a most exciting journey in the Singer, which is now pronounced as the French pronounce monkeys, across France. Often we were suspended on a precipice with the crows ogling us. Often only a hairs breadth was between the left wide wheel and a drop of some 80,000 feet. But we came through, and are, as I say, here; which is London: very hot; all ablooming; have just been to St Albans for a drive; come back; Roger rings up; he and Helen will come in after dinner, which will consist of a cold chicken, but no wine.

Here you have the very latest information from the metropolis of the world.

I was fascinated and appalled by the story of your adventures—That a nephew of mine! I cried, between tears and laughter—Should one be proud of you or the very opposite—climbing the Monument naked, and sleeping with a professor of divinity, who is, unfortunately, but its the way in Germany, of the female sex—such is your way of life, and I tell it at many a merry party, half crying, half laughing.

I wish though you would come home. I want to visit the Museums with you and to consult you on many points. I dreamt of you all last night, but I shant tell you what we were doing, for fear it should shock you.

Julian is a very odd sort of phenomenon—about the size of a moderate Indian rhinoceros; said to be good tempered—I doubt it. He's a clever reptile, and is writing—there, that's what you should do.

I have had no news from your blessed mother for a fortnight, except about letting her rooms to an American. Of course Duncan went and let them to another American; of course Mrs Uppington went off with the keys; of course I was blamed for everything—of course—of course.

I am scribbling away to finish my nonsense book. Have I your permission to mention you in the Preface?[1] Because I've done it.

Now sit down and write to me, dearest Quentin, a long long letter. I assure you, without flattery, and we know each other too well for that, you write the best letters of anyone I know.

And do come back because of our Libel.

Yr loving V.W.

Quentin Bell

1. In the Preface to *Orlando* Virginia acknowledges "my nephew Mr Quentin Bell (an old and valued collaborator in fiction)".

1892: To V. Sackville-West   [52 *Tavistock Square, W.C.*1]
Sunday [6 May 1928]

Hugh Walpole is dining here on Friday.
Will you come?
Please do.
And let me know AT ONCE (as I must get someone)—or as soon as you
can.

VW
Virginia
in haste

And when shall I see you? If you like to telephone, I shall be here before 10?

P.S.
IF—you are driving Clive back on Monday—but dont—come both of
you and lunch here.
Let me know
    And Harold
    Why do I like Harold so much?
    Does Harold like me?
    These remarks are all strictly *Private*

Berg

1893: To Vanessa Bell   52 *Tavistock Square* [*W.C.*1]
May 9th [1928]

Dearest,
    It is a proof of affection how quick I answer your letters. Indeed I am
getting very wizend [*sic*] and dry without you. We are overcome with
your horrors—Gordon Sqre I mean[1]—My practical suggestion is that you
should take Gwen's [Raverat] house which is nice, cheap, and can be let
without difficulty. She seems settled to go and live in Grantchester. Has
nothing yet been done about your money?—with considerable skill I
contrived to get Mrs Goldsmith, Dick Wood and Mrs Uppington, together,
and Dick Wood is now in residence. I've just rung up to ask how many
rooms they're using, but no answer; so I will write to her—she's American
too and always out—and let you know.

1. The landlord was threatening legal action against Vanessa to force her to repair
the house before subletting it.

London of course teems with gossip—Ottoline (no doubt you've heard) has almost died. She has necrosis of the jaw, had two operations; agonies of pain, 7 teeth out without gas; and is still very ill—also much disfigured —I saw Philip who was distracted and pessimistic—in fact hinted at cancer. But they say she will recover. Then there's Eddie back and as prickly as a hedgehog. Old Lady Sackville is bringing a case against his father, which will mean that all their characters will be blackened in the Law Courts— Already she has scattered it broadcast that Harold's a bugger, and Vita a sapphist. This upsets Eddy considerably; but he was rather nice, queer, acid, prickly; and immensely sorry for himself. Rogers back—We had a sham Bloomsbury evening with Molly and Desmond at Rogers; with Molly entirely sunk into a lump of white jelly—I have never seen her so gloomy. After an argument lasting 2 hours, she said she hadn't heard a word the whole evening—Lord, Lord! And I was given my prize by Hugh Walpole in a South Kensington drawing room full of elderly fur bearing women, among whom the loveliest and sprightliest was Ethel Dilke.[1] I was made to speak; which I did with dead and melancholy composure. I told them my great grandmother was a Frenchwoman—then I was given a very strong smelling purse with a cheque for £40—but I think it aint worth it. I still scratch a good deal at nights to get rid of the feel. Of course George [Duckworth] writes to congratulate me; and says he met Sir Somebody at dinner, who had heard of me—or the prize; but he has had all his teeth out—so has Gerald—and he and Margaret are feeling very stiff in the back. Florence B. may amuse you.[2] I maintain that I live wholly at Rodmell.

I suppose you've heard that Angus has not got Agnew's job. and I gather that he's not going to Cassis—He seems very cheerful, and smart; and the Press is 50 years younger without him. Kennedy says he is going to put up a shelf, as he knows a man who sells wood wholesale, and he is very fond of putting up shelves. He is a nice, simple-minded boy, delighted to escape home life, I gather. But as Leonard and I were saying, Julian seems a different order of creature altogether. These young people—I've just been to tea with Miss Jenkins[3]—might have come off chocolate boxes —What happens when they take to life, I cant conceive. Or are Julian and Quentin prodigies of brain and character? Julian has written a very good review of a French history for Leonard, in about 2 days. And I had a really brilliant letter from Quentin, in which he says, "I am I believe one

1. See p. 337, note 1.
2. Virginia enclosed a letter from Florence Burke (née Bishop), the wife of a naval doctor, and an old friend of Leslie and Julia Stephen.
3. Elizabeth Jenkins, the author. Her first novel *Virginia Water*, 1929, dealt with a girl's love in a Bloomsbury setting.

of nature's puritans, which is surprising considering my beloved parents isn't it?" Fancy our writing like that about father to the Quaker![1]

As for Clive; I feel rather embarrassed. He'll be back on Sunday, and there will, I am sure, be some sort of explanation—Shall I accuse him of reading my letters? He wrote to me again, saying that he has an inferiority complex which leads him to fly into passions with me: but he is now radiantly happy, thanks to you and Duncan and Angelica, and wishes never to leave Cassis. What do you advise me to do? Mary seemed very wistful, yet frigid, on the telephone, scouting for news of Cassis; yet refusing to dine with us. I saw Lytton, by the way, who thinks she misses Bloomsbury considerably, but is settling down—how he knows not. He has sold Elizabeth[2] it is said for £6,000 to an American newspaper, and was just off, mysteriously, to Provence. No doubt he will settle on you like the rest of us. I entirely sympathise with your brilliant and caustic remarks about Raymond—to have a week of him would make me take to sack cloth and ashes, wear wool next the skin, put peas in my boots—anything anything to be out of fashion, out of date obsolete. I had an amusing account from Eddy of the final rupture with Valery [Taylor] which took place at Long Barn, just before he started. They reached a point where they couldn't speak to each other, so Vita was sent from room to room with notes, each sobbing loudly the whole time. It is now completely over, Eddy says: and both are much relieved.

But the real weakness of Cassis as a place of residence is not the landscape nor the Crowthers:[3] it is the liability to Raymond—and the Wolves I would say, if I were modest—To be exposed without any protection to Barbara and Raymond seems to me an infliction only to be visited on the damned. But I think you are damned. Theres Barbara, condemned by you to have three children and decorate her house; and now—all thanks to you and Duncan—the poor woman has moved into a caravan, where she sits all day on the ladder, shelling peas. Somehow she thinks this is in the Bloomsbury manner. She has just sent me a message through Saxon that she thinks me a pig: perhaps she has heard what I think of her. And a pig's nothing to that.

Now this is a fine collection of gossip—and deserves a return. Then I'll tell you, perhaps, what I think of your pictures. We had a private view of Roger's latest—but is it true he has fallen into despair and is giving up painting altogether? Clive says so. Karin's back; all askew; and thinks she will live half in America in future. They have given Alice £5 and hope to have settled the bite. The dog is at this moment on our stairs—very dirty, but kind hearted.

1. Virginia's paternal aunt, Caroline Emelia Stephen.
2. *Elizabeth and Essex*.
3. Pillars of the English society at Cassis.

A thousand thanks for the photographs [of Angelica]—which havent
yet come, but will I expect be perfect. O dear I wish you were here and I
could talk to you, instead of going to Armide[1] in the gallery—Nobody is
like you—I dry into middle aged desiccatry without you.

B

(you'll never understand that word)
The Singer has been garaged in Judd Street for 17/6, which includes cleaning
—But I don't know how much one will use it—We went to St Albans
last Sunday—and I think of going to Cambridge for the day and shall
sponge on Julian for lunch.

Berg

1894: TO VANESSA BELL   52 *Tavistock Sqre.* [*W.C.*1]
Saturday May 12th [1928]

Dearest,
    You will be sickening of the sight of the Wolves purple ink—I have
at last caught Mrs Goldsmith [Voigt] who says that two rooms will be
empty after Friday and you could send Angelica there at any time—She
has got a flat and could leave after the 18th I gather if you like—She seems
only anxious to fulfil your slightest wish. Would it be any use your com-
municating with Morgan [Forster] who is staying with [Charles] Mauron
at Mas Blanc Tarascon (but you will know the address) and comes back I
think at the end of May: He might be able to escort Angelica. It seems
absurd that you should have to make two journeys. Perhaps Angus has
written to you. He talked vaguely of a job at Newcastle—temporary—
Raymond has just sprung up to say that his time at Cassis was divine, in
spite of the weather: whereas Dolphin says that she dont mind how hard
it rains so long as Raymond aint there—such is the diversity of human
opinion in this world.
    The photographs [of Angelica for *Orlando*] are most lovely, and I
cannot thank you sufficiently for the pains you have been at, I think with
a little re-arrangement one or two might do: a trifle young, thats all, but
I'm showing them to Vita, who doesn't want to be accused of raping the
under age. My God—I shall rape Angelica one of these days: she is the
jasper of jocundity, of all your brood: a per se. Do you remember the
poem that comes from,[2] and how in the old days in the dawn of Bloomsbury,
Saxon used to say it?

1. The opera (1777) by Christoph Gluck.
2.   "London, thou art the Flower of cities all!
             Gemme of all joy, Jasper of jocunditie."
                    From *London*, by William Dunbar (1465?-1530?).

497

I've been in very odd society—partly owing to the Prize giving, which was of a horror indescribable; and after it, out crept from various corners old derelicts like Elizabeth Robins, and Beatrice Harraden, and a woman called Tupman.[1] E. Robins fascinated me by describing the extreme beauty combined with viciousness of mother. She looked like a saint and then said something so witty one was shocked—She combined complete sanctity with complete woman of the worldliness; and was extremely reserved. She used to come to Miss Robin's flat in Bayswater on hot summer evenings carrying jellies in pots—Then, in order to get her to write her memoirs, I had to go to tea yesterday with Lady Horner. That also was fascinating, though a little hard work—She is grown very old, but has all the airs of a great beauty, and got gossipey about Burne Jones, who was obviously her lover; but the Mackails wouldn't let it appear, and so though they read through 15 volumes of the most intimate letters, which I looked at, and saw "my darling" over and over again, this was completely ignored; and a respectable family man evolved, which, says Lady Horner, who should know, Burne Jones was not.[2] Most of her sons were killed in the war, and she is a little obliterated by sorrows, but has great charm, and would have wandered on for hours about the horrors of county family life in the 80ties, and how she was never allowed to move a pot, and every old rook or owl ever shot by a Horner had to be kept in one corner for ever, but unfortunately Cecily, a perfect dull glass-eyed beauty who married Lambton, Nelly Cecils brother, came in, hot from the races; and I fled. The whole house billows and undulates with Burne Jones'es—incredibly shiny and slick: but dull as a mosaic in a railway station waiting room—So I thought —All briars and flowing mantles—O and then I went to your show and spent an hour making some extremely interesting theories: which I will condense into one paean of admiration for your Three Women and Duncans Tree: (but why in God's name do they call it that?) I had forgotten the extreme brilliancy and flow and wit and ardour of these works—I am greatly tempted to write "Variations on a Picture by Vanessa Bell" for Desmonds paper—I should run the three women and the pot of flowers on a chair into one phantasmagoria. I think you are a most remarkable painter. But I maintain you are into the bargain, a satirist, a conveyer of impressions about human life: a short story writer of great wit and able to bring off a situation in a way that rouses my envy. I wonder if I could write the Three Women in prose. Would Roger let me have it here for a

1. Elizabeth Robins (d. 1952) was the American actress and novelist. Beatrice Harraden (1864-1936), a novelist and suffragette. Tupman unidentified.
2. Frances Horner (d. 1940), whose house at Mells, Somerset, was a centre of cultural society in the late Victorian and Edwardian periods. Her daughter Cicely married George Lambton, the son of the Earl of Durham. J. W. Mackail, the classical scholar and biographer, married the only daughter of the painter Edward Burne-Jones in 1888.

week or so? I think Lessore is very good: but I am tremendously impressed, most of all, by your and Duncans epic greatness and now I have made myself sufficiently ridiculous in the eyes of two cold blooded creatures who only draw me out to pour salt on my horns and see a little blob of foam (which causes intense pain to the snail) form on the tips:

Desmond told me that he had had two letters, by the same post, one from Bobo [Mayor] who is in Paris with Clive, saying that he is in roaring spirits; the other from Clive saying that his life is over, and he is tired of the sun. Don't you think it possible that Bobo is the Leicestershire lady— and the whole concoction is mere camouflage to salve his vanity? Anyhow, he will be back tomorrow, and I shall be I suppose, made to pay for my remarks one way or t'other.

We had a most curious evening last night with Lydia and Hugh Walpole. Lydia, Leonard says, has now been perfectly trained, and is invaluable. She does her trick; then goes under the table, and leaves before eleven— But Hugh stayed on till 12.30—pouring out his sorrows, which are that he can never sell less than 20,000 copies of his books, but nobody of any intelligence can bear them. It cuts him to the heart when his chauffeur praises them—He has 10 letters every day from enthusiastic Americans. But Bloomsbury sees that he is a fake, and he now sees it too. It all comes from being the son of a Bishop and so taught to tell lies from his infancy. He gave us a long analysis of his soul and his lies and his popularity which was very amusing—considering I'd only met him at the prize giving. But Lord! I must stop.

John Strachey has gone mad and been taken to an asylum. Adrian and Karin dashed their new car into a motor lorry and smashed it (but the driver was drunk): Alice says she will have the Law on them; and won't cash their cheque—thats all the Bloomsbury gossip at present: its bitter cold again. Roger seems to be staying on. Helens mother is ill—

Yr B

Berg

1895: To Vanessa Bell   *Monk's House, Rodmell*
[Sussex]

Saturday May 25th [1928]

Dearest,
   Business:
(1)   We have sold Hyde Park Gate for £4925—I hope you'll think this all right. Somebody of Halseys[1] has been after it for some weeks. They suddenly agreed to give this,—which we had beat them up to;

1. Of the family solicitors Halsey, Lightly and Hemsley, in which Jack Hills (who married Virginia's half-sister Stella) had been a partner.

and so we accepted. Leonard thinks we ought to get rather more from the money invested than from the rent; and we have no agents fees to pay, and shant pay Halsey for collecting either.

(2) I will put a notice of the La Bergère[1] in the Nation and bruit it abroad among the snobs; who think Cassis next to Bloomsbury—I dont see why Bunny or Colefax or Hope, or someone of that ilk shouldn't take it.

(3) I shall try to seduce Angelica.

(2B) but wouldn't it be a good thing to advertise it in a French paper?

I saw Angus for a moment. He seemed to feel that the highest and greenest of laurels had descended upon him;[2] and so it has—But how you can be so splendidly generous I cant conceive, to whom such company —not that he's not charming in every way—but such a damn flop, such an empty suit of clothes—I get the feeling I used to have with Adrian, of utter lackadaisicalness, which plunges me into the mirk of ten November fogs. Still, as I say, he has every virtue; and don't please leave this on the studio table—but I see I began this sentence "to whom such company" and so I must hastily finish it, would be somnolent in the extreme—What astonishing good hearts at core you and Duncan have! I was vastly amused by the Strachey panic; Carrington is said by Eddy to be perhaps the most tortuous, evil, and dishonest of all the people he knows—And I used to think her honest as a haystack!

We are in rather a turmoil about Rodmell. They've started a race course down at the Halt, which wouldn't so much matter; but now Alinson has bought our terrace, and threatens to build. This was done by some hanky panky with the agent behind our backs, and the owner, whose son was killed last year and has a very high opinion of us because we wrote him such a nice letter, is now much ashamed, and says he will talk Alinson out of it. But I doubt it. So Leonard is inclined to sell and go. But then I shall never see you again: What do you advise? I see from advertisements one can get the most ravishing old houses with gardens and orchards in Dorset, Suffolk or Norfolk for a mere song. Would you consider moving, for if so, I would willingly spend more time in the country, London being almost intolerable, what with Colefaxes, etc: and we might settle, of course not too near, in houses which would be our own for ever, and the apples of our eyes. They're selling all Cuckmere I see, and Laughton, so I cant help thinking Sussex is doomed. But give us your opinion.

I had a long rambling very indirect talk with Clive, who kept making allusions to my having told someone I saw too much of him, but wouldn't come to facts; and was rather apologetic; and also affectionate. But he

1. Vanessa's villa at Cassis.
2. Vanessa had asked Angus Davidson to come to Cassis and drive her car back to England.

says he cant help these outbursts, which date back to old horrors in the past; and as I am also scarred and riddled with complexes about you and him, and being derided and insulted and sacrificed and betrayed, I don't see how we can hope for a plain straightforward relationship. In fact, having kissed each other passionately, we met two days later and quarrelled—or rather he sneered and I became sarcastic—about my seeing Hugh Walpole. So it will go on till the daisies grow over us. But he told me he is much more settled and content; and talked of Mary as if she were under the earth for ever. I have had no dealings with her, nor shall, unless she makes the move.

I am feeling extremely barren and dry without you—Angelica will be a small shower of rain;[1] but not enough—What happens when you leave me too long is that I go gadding wherever I'm asked and finally end in a rage of misery against my kind—I saw nothing but celebrities last week; Rebecca West at Todds; Maurois and Arnold Bennett at Colefaxes, and had Rose Macaulay to dine alone. Rebecca was much the most interesting, though as hard as nails, very distrustful, and no beauty. She is a cross between a charwoman and a gipsy, but as tenacious as a terrier, with flashing eyes, very shabby, rather dirty nails, immense vitality, bad taste, suspicion of intellectuals, and great intelligence. She gave me the true history of Isadora Duncan's[2] life—(I sent you the life, by the way, which is rather valuable, as the libraries are banning it). Rebecca has knocked about with all the mongrels of Europe. She talks openly of her son [Anthony], who has got consumption: They say she is a hardened liar, but I rather liked her—The [Dorothy] Todd ménage is incredibly louche: Todd in sponge bag trousers; Garland[3] in pearls and silk; both rather raddled and on their beam ends. Maurois was disappointing, but then Sibyl makes everyone stony, and breaks up talk with a hammer—good, deserving, industrious, kindhearted woman as she is. Rose Macaulay was a great disappointment —Some houses have gone too far to be repaired—she is one. If we had rescued her before she was 30—but she is now 45—has lived with the riff raff of South Kensington culture for 15 years; become a successful lady novelist, and is rather jealous, spiteful, and uneasy about Bloomsbury; can talk of nothing but reviews, yet being the daughter of a Cambridge Don, knows she shouldn't; and has her tail between her legs. She made me determined not to allow Angelica, whatever happens, to become a novelist. All this fame that writers get is obviously the devil; I am not so nice as I was, but I am nicer than Rose Macaulay—also she is a spindle shanked withered virgin: I never felt anyone so utterly devoid of the sexual parts. Raymond

1. She was returning from Cassis with Angus Davidson several days before Vanessa.
2. The American dancer whose autobiography had just been published. She was killed in a car accident at Nice on 14 September 1927.
3. Madge Garland, previously the Fashion Editor of *Vogue*, later Lady Ashton.

gave one of his parties that night, and as Leonard was dining with Clive, I was alone with Rose; and as Raymond is really a male Colefax just out of the shell of course he insisted that Rose and I should come,—which flung me into a temper—Why do these young men all run to vulgarity, snobbery, shoddery, Toddery? However, Vita came in on her way to Raymonds, and I rubbed Rose off on her, and I saw them up Raymonds staircase, and heard him chopping the air like a woodpecker and ran off home. This was very brilliant on my part, as I picked out the soul of the party on a pin.

Leonard says you'll never get through this letter. He says I am to say he will do anything he can about 37,[1] but it is rather difficult, without seeing the letters. But send him any business you want done. James [Strachey] told me he has his house from the same people, and they never trouble him; yet he sublets every floor. Our Square gardener says the Bedford estate tries to tyrannise over everyone, even the old woman who sells papers; but if you stand up, they turn tail. Oh dear, how nice to see you again:

B.

Berg

1896: To Duncan Grant   [*Monk's House, Rodmell, Sussex*]

[27? May 1928]

Dearest Duncan,

Would you be an angel and buy me a small birthday present for Nessa? I enclose a cheque—(I am extremely rich—) as I dont think my taste is as good as yours and you might know some object—hat, bag, pot, anything—that she wants. I am rather distracted by the need of changing into respectability after missing Mr Snaiths[2] poetry to give tea to the editor of a paper which pays so well that I have to see him—Such is life. But all the more essential then is it that you and Nessa should come back and compose us into sanity.

Ott: by the way was enchanted by a letter you wrote her—"Dear, dear Duncan—one knows what it *costs* him to write—and he wrote me such a *charming kind, wonderful* letter . . ." She keeps it by her side, with a kind of chamber pot beneath. Teeth are drawn daily, but she seems in the best of spirits and reads nothing but Shakespeare. "Suddenly Margots head peers round the corner, with her lips like that (pointing to cherry on the walnut cake) and a hat like *that* (pointing to a walnut on the cake). *Money* is all she talks about—There is a certain *beauty* in illness—one is

1. See p. 494, note 1.
2. Stanley Snaith (b. 1903) published *A Flying Scroll* with the Hogarth Press in June 1928.

502

alone—one reads—one thinks—one sees only the people one likes seeing"
—Now its a very odd thing how spirited the old thing is, how beautiful,
with her jaw in a nosebag like an old horse, and yet so idiotic. One cant
stand very much of it.

You had better make Nessa get a present for herself—now I come to
think of it.

Ott. told me she knew for a fact, name and all, that Ethel [Sands] loved
a man; he loved Ethel; Nan came between. Ethels conscience pricked her.
I wouldn't have let it prick me! said Ottoline with a kind of neigh. Indeed,
I thought—talking of pricks—but one couldn't say that aloud to her.

I must give over, and work as I said.

A thousand loves. Angelica is adorable, very distinguished, debonaire,
aloof, intimate, erratic, passionate, reserved, lovely like her Aunt—(you
thought I was going to say father)

Duncan Grant

1897: To V. Sackville-West   *Monk's House [Rodmell,*
                                     Sussex]
Sunday [27 May 1928]
(the finest day of the year)

This is to say that we expect Harold to dine on Wednesday, 7.45:
and Vita to come in afterwards, and to bring the photographs of Orlando
in breeches. And are you making an appointment to be penetrated on
Friday?[1] And I'm alone Friday night.

I will briefly sketch 3 moods of horror: Raymond's lunch party—pretty
desperate; Sibyls tea party; then Rose to dinner—incredibly disillusioning
and terrifying—for I think I shall be like that and I thought her awful; so
cheap peevish and petty; and then you come in and say she's to go to
Raymonds: and I think what a damned snob Raymond is—how I detest
his hair and his clothes—so when you call in the morning I'm furious,
not with you, with Raymond: and so, when it comes to going to his party
I say I'm tired when I'm really furious—and these are my moods, only
very much more violent: and I cant bear seeing people any more; except
that I should like to see you—And its divine here, but the field is sold,
and we've seen the Byng Stampers[2] who are very contrite and the races
begin in the meadows tomorrow, and we go up by motor at dawn on
Tuesday, with the mist on the ground and you asleep.

                                                           V.

Berg

1. Virginia and Vita had their ears pierced on Monday, 4 June.
2. Mrs Byng Stamper and her sister Miss Caroline Byng Lucas, descendants of
   Admiral Byng. They had bought Allinson's farm at Rodmell in 1925.

52 *Tavistock Square* [*W.C.*1]

May 30th [1928]

Dearest Ottoline,

How difficult it is to write to you! I have thought about it ever so many times—that is I have thought of you and wanted to tell you how sorry I was about your illness and how fond of you. But its just these words one can't say. I think perhaps if one had never written a word one would then be able to say what one meant. I dread so getting tangled in a mass of words that when I want most to write, I dont. So you must write all my affection for me; and make it very strong and also the real odd, recurring discomfort it is to me to think of you in pain. How horrible it is that this should have happened to you. I have this silly romantic but impossible to avoid sense of your beauty; and then to combine this with the idea of you in pain—but you'll say I dont really know you. But enough, you must allow, to be very anxious if I could do anything for you, to do it. We brought some books, but Philip said you already had them.

I like Max [Beerbohm] in Desmonds new magazine [*Life and Letters*] —so neat and exact;—I ran into Desmond in Kingsway this evening, coming back from Leonards hairdresser. For here we are rather dusty and bedraggled in the midst of hairdressers, omnibuses and so on, after Whitsun at Rodmell, where I walked on the downs. Very foolishly we've come back to see people like Mr Leach and Miss McAfee[1]—Americans: I dont know them, but they will come here one hot afternoon and sit and sit and ask me who are the most promising young English writers—which I'm sure I dont know. I've been meeting them all—Rebecca West, Arnold Bennett, Rose Macaulay. Rebecca is the most interesting to me. I liked her vitality and inquisitiveness and hardness—or so I thought it, but we never got within 20 miles of each other, and I dont suppose we shall ever meet again. She spoke of you with great affection—in spite of her hardness.

This needs no answer of any sort. It is only the most stiff dry absurd inadequate way of sending my love to you, and do please get well soon and let me come and see you

Your
Virginia

Leonard wants me to send his love too.

Texas

---

1. Henry G. Leach, Editor of the *Forum*, and Helen McAfee, Managing Editor of the *Yale Review*.

1899: To V. Sackville-West   52 *Tavistock Square, W.C.*1

Friday [1 June 1928]

The low opinion I have of Sinclair Lewis's[1] books is confirmed. Your life is merely the Daily Mirror in action—I've seen that caravan a dozen times—and you might be dining here alone with me this minute.

Very well—I will be at the place at the time punctually on Monday. Will you dine here, and go out, or sit in, as you like afterwards—I being alone again? A chop will be ordered for you.

If Harold would dine on Wednesday next, probably he would meet Tom Eliot—if he would send me a word by you.

                                              Yr
                                              Virginia

Love to Dottie, whom I hope some day to see. Please find me a house, not in Cornwall; Wales, or the Hebrides. Eddy says he is sending me a book of his own poems.

Berg

1900: To Lady Ottoline Morrell
                                    52 *Tavistock Square, W.C.*1

[2? June 1928]

Dearest Ottoline

I never meant you to bother to answer—but it was delightful all the same, and a very great pleasure. Yes, there are masses of things I should like to talk about, if it didn't tire you. Might I come one afternoon—any except Monday or Saturday—next week? Tomorrow I'm afraid is hopeless.

Leonard, with his love again, says he always thought you would be "very brave"—so did everyone: because of course you are.

                                              Yr
                                              Virginia W.

Texas

1901: To Quentin Bell   52 *Tavistock Square, W.C.*1

Typewritten
Derby Day. June 5th 1928

Dearest Quentin,

It is all very well for you to tell me to write to you at Poste Restante

---

1. Sinclair Lewis and his bride Dorothy Thompson had arrived at Long Barn in a caravan and stayed from 30 May until 2 June.

"there", when you dont say where there is. You will be there for a week you say. Maybe Jericho or the South Seas for anything I know. I will try to get your address from Clive, if I see him; but he is as hard to be seen as a mackerel in the sea, with the goings and comings that are now the way in London in May. Everybody is running as hard as they can.

The Derby has just been won by a complete outsider. So I have lost half a crown. It is extremely hot and we are having strawberry ice for dinner. Charlie Sanger is dining with us and Hubert Henderson. There will be a great deal of political discussion, and I shall look out of the window and wish you were there to say something flippant, foolish, but a little interesting. Then I am going to have tea with Ottoline, half of whose jaw has been cut away; and this will be awful, for I dont know what to say; your mother would put the matter in a nutshell; but being a writer, so many words are possible that one is almost bound to say the wrong ones. Also she is incurably romantic. Do you remember crying at the sight of her at Wissett?[1]

But to return. You ask for news of old Bloomsbury. Very little of old B. is left. What with Roger away and Nessa and Duncan away, B. scarcely exists. I never go into Gordon Square, because I hate to see places when the people I visit there are away from them. Such is my immense sentimentality. Angelica came back last week, but she is very dignified and aloof, and has I think taken her lodging with Louie in Cadogan Mews until Nessa comes back. She seemed quite on her own and not to wish for anything. Secure in the possession of beauty that will be her tack through life.

I have finished my bad joke—that is the last book I have written in which you occur in the preface. It should be written again; but it wont be. Unless indeed when I am old I get like Mr [George] Moore and re-write everything. What reason is there to think that one knows better at seventy though? I think it is a proof of a weak imagination. The Press is very vigorous at the moment. Young Mr Kennedy is here and old Mother Cartwright, and middle aged Miss Belcher. I have been working so hard that I have seen none of them very often. I peep in on my way up to tea, and say something cheerful. The Old Umbrella [the Singer] is stabled round the corner. We went to Rodmell in her and go to the New Forest on Saturday. But a dreadful tragedy is about to happen. They are building over the field at Rodmell. I feel sure we shall have to go. And then what will happen? I shall never see you again. I shall never be able to make wrote [sic] words for our books. What is to be done? I am in despair, and the garden is at its most perfect too—the orchard shorn, flowers everywhere, the fruit all growing. Its that damnable man Allinson, who is the advertiser of The Times and has every vice a man can have. He builds to sell; and leaves his horrid mess wherever he goes. Even a dog knows better.

1. Ottoline had visited Vanessa and Duncan at Wissett Lodge, Suffolk, in August 1916.

I have just read the preceding page and doubt that I shall send it. The truth is I cannot write on a typewriter; I make enemies whenever I do; ladies are insulted; gentle men furious: old friendships are broke off. But then as you cant read my hand writing—one must risk it. Its very odd how it rigidifies the mind; as if ones hands were half numb. This is the reason why instead of being ablaze with brilliance, wit, profundity, news, of every kind, it is flat as a charwomans back. One cant correct, thats it. Also it pecks one along like a hen.

Julian says he is so hard at work no one must visit him even for a moment. He may well be expelled from Kings through sheer laziness. Meanwhile he has time to fire off a play or two. Its as clear as the sun that he will never hang a man or do anything useful. Nessa tries to make him into a barrister; I egg him on to waste his time in every way. Whats examinations, degrees, fellowships and the rest compared with a happy lazy life? He has written a very good review of a French history for the Nation. But I darent go to Cambridge to see.

Leonard is full of Chinese. They come and ask him perfectly idiotic questions like Shall I write a dissertation upon the Cooperative Movement for Pekin? However, the Americans are worse. Two are coming to see me this week. So ugly, so dusty, so dull, so long winded—I would pay you ten and six to do it for me. Or a machine. All they want to know is who in your opinion is the most promising young writer? Then they go and ask someone else.

[*in Virginia's handwriting:*]
    P.S.
    I forgot to post this and its now June 15th and I must send it to Munich.
    Nessa comes back tomorrow, so old B[loomsbury] will resume its outworn skin forlorn—and I will write and tell you about it. Julian's back, as spry as a race horse, and hopes he has passed but is doubtful.
    So write quick again and give your address. All news of Roger and Helen thankfully received.

Yrs
Virginia

Quentin Bell

1902: To Vanessa Bell   [52 *Tavistock Square, W.C.*1]

Thursday June 7th [1928]

Dearest
    Angelica is very well and happy. I've just been round and found her Louie and Grace eating strawberries for lunch. Angelica said I was to give you her love, and to say that she is happy and good and doesn't know if she

likes Cassis or London best. When she arrived she was at first very distant with me, and called Duncan Mr Grant: however she suddenly flung her arms round me at which I was much touched. Her manners are so scrupulously polite that I had great difficulty in discovering if she wanted to come to tea with me or not. At last, with many formalities it was arranged that she should spend the week end with Louie, and come to tea here tomorrow. I rather think she may run in to Sibyl Colefax, but no doubt her manners will triumph again—She is looking very well, and has some mysterious joke she wants to play on Grace, and also we are all to go and fetch Clinker in the car—but thats a secret of yours apparently.

I am supposing that you have reached Paris safely. Now you will have the Frys, and a myriad things to do; and my letters will I know be stuffed into an old bag with a hole in it and pulled out at lunch and read half aloud. but mostly skipped and probably lost. Life has been rather vocal: too many people, as usual, all in a bunch. Ottoline yesterday. She looks extremely well though swaddled in bandages; and seemed in great spirits, for one thing because so many ruined friendships have been now repaired in moments of emotion. Lawrence has made it up.[1] But his letters are wildly phallic and philosophical; and mad, and I dont see much point in renewing that. All germs are devils which attack us because we lower our selfishness, and women can only live in the imaginations of men, and Ottoline lived once in his, and so on—what dammed but conceited nonsense it all is; but it seems he is dying, and is I suppose a genius and so on. And Tom [Eliot] is in a great taking, with Vivien as mad as a hare, but not confined, and they give parties, where she suddenly accuses him of being in love with Ottoline (and me, but this Ott: threw in as a sop) and Tom drinks, and Vivien suddenly says when talk dies down "You're the bloodiest snob I ever knew"—so I have refused to dine there.

Clive is coming to tea today, but he is so much engaged that I've not seen much of him. They say he is much quieter and happier and scarcely talks of himself—Mary is never seen or heard of. Lord! how glad I shall be to stop writing and gossip instead—I dont think you can ever go away again. Angelica really prefers London: I think I shall die of another 4 months absence. Its not only your kindness I miss; its your discipline. I get more and more disillusioned and random; often say the wrong things and have let my hair grow and wear it in a kind of sponge bag—Quentin implores me to write to him; but sends no address; Julian says he has had no letters from you, me, or Clive (except 4 words) for weeks. He has written a play—but not a very good one. He says are we coming to see him?

When shall you be back? Is there any use in asking? I'm frightfully

---

1. Ottoline had been greatly distressed by D. H. Lawrence's unflattering portrait of her in *Women in Love* (1921), but he now wrote her a sympathetic letter about her illness and indirectly apologised.

envious of your antiquities, but had no time to buy anything in our dash, and have had out of pity for my friends to buy a sofa, very expensive, but soft instead. Charlie Sanger dined here last night, and Oliver brought his Inez,[1] at their own request, for it wouldn't have been mine, amiable as the woman is; but I couldnt get her name right and called her sometimes Ferguson—sometimes Strachey. I have quarrelled with many people because of my bad manners; calling them wrong names by mistake, so you must take me to your arms and cover me with kisses—

                                                                Yr B

Berg

1903: To Vanessa Bell   *Hewer's Orchard, Minstead,*
                                        Lyndhurst, Hants.
Sunday [10 June 1928]

     Yes, our garage will take your car—
     Angelica very well and almost as charming as ——[2] We have the same sense of reality
     Staying with Janet and Emphie [Case]—lids on all the po's—
     Most charming, refined sprightly; and very glad to see you—(I mean I shall be)—but the post goes

                                                                VW

Berg

1904: To Janet Case   52 *Tavistock Square, W.C.*1
Wednesday [13 June 1928]

My dear Janet,
     We came back safely in time for lunch, but to such a shower of horrors —I mean Americans and others—that I couldn't write; only envy you and Emphie the New Forest.
     Also how difficult to thank you sufficiently for all your goodness, kindness, hot bottles, cream, salmon, old furniture, clean linen, comfort, conversation—I could go on for ever. Leonard and I have been saying at intervals it was one of the few week ends we enjoyed; you and Emphie are some of the only people we envy etc etc. I think instead of garden notes, (which must in time exhaust even your garden) you should write notes on how to live, for the Manchester [Guardian].

1. Inez Ferguson had been an intimate friend of Oliver Strachey since 1919. In 1923 she married Frederick Jenkins, and in World War II became national organiser of the Women's Land Army.
2. Blank in original, meaning Virginia.

We called in at Winchester and saw Jane Austen's tomb.

Here is the letter to the woman I wont see.

Love and a thousand more thanks from Pinker, Leonard and Virginia

The rhododendrons are very lovely and the moss green and—oh but I mustn't begin over again.

Sussex

1905: To V. SACKVILLE-WEST   52 *T.[avistock] S.[quare, W.C.*1]

Sunday [17 June 1928]

Dearest Creature,

I forgot to say—or did I forget?—that we must have 2 copies, on glossy paper of the Lord Lascelles picture.[1] Could you order another to be done and sent me with all *possible haste* when you go to get it tomorrow?

Oh heavens what a bore Orlando is—worse in his death than in his life: I think: I'm so tired of him.

One tomorrow

V.W.

Berg

1906: To EDWARD SACKVILLE WEST

52 *Tavistock Sqre* [*W.C.*1]

Sunday June 24th [1928]

Dear Eddy

I am a disgraceful wretch never to have answered your letter—and it was one I enjoyed immensely, with its complete illumination of the Arnold-Forster household [at Zennor, Cornwall]. I dropped a cigarette into a flower bed once and it had the same effect as your breaking the child's chair.

I have been blind and deaf: nothing but proofs do I see; and the entire worthlessness of my own words. I have been correcting for 6 hours daily, and must now write my name 800 times over.[2]

Pen and ink and my own words disgust me.

London is dusty and dowdy and rowdy and drab. I daresay you are at Knole again, out of the winds and whirlpools which so incessantly and

1. A Tudor portrait at Knole of a woman who represented the Archduchess Harriet in *Orlando*.

2. For the limited edition of *Orlando*, published in New York by Crosby Gaige.

510

tiresomely blow and boil about me here. Endless people drop in for an hour's talk. All their colours are rubbed after my weeks in London; and I am critical and bored and irritable.

I see that your book [*Mandrake Over the Water-Carrier*] is out, and I hope you feel that it is a good—what is the word? I can't think—I mean a blow in the face: an effort; something struck off and done with. I hope to hear all about it when it has been read by your friends. This weekend I suppose they are all devouring it. And one day I shall read it too.

And now I must go and correct proofs again.

Why does one write these books after all? The drudgery, the misery, the grind, are forgotten everytime; and one launches another, and it seems sheer joy and buoyancy.

Yours Ever
Virginia

Berg

1907: To Helen McAfee   52 *Tavistock Square, W.C.*1

Typewritten
June 29th 1928

Dear Miss McAfee,

I have just seen Desmond MacCarthy and have been arranging with him for a short story and an article called Dr Burneys Evening party— partly true, partly fictitious. This would appear in the December number. I could if you liked send you this for your Christmas number.[1]

But I wonder if you would think me very grasping if I asked what fee the Yale Review is able to pay for stories and articles? I ask because I have now made an arrangement with Curtis Brown for articles in various American papers. As I don't write many, I want of course to place my work as profitably as I can—but I shall of course quite understand if the Yale Review is not able to offer more than the twenty pounds which I think it paid me before.

I hope you enjoyed your stay here. We so much enjoyed seeing you. And I am so sorry that the rush of engagements at this season made it impossible for us to see you again. I hope you may come over again when we are not quite so busy.

Yours sincerely
Virginia Woolf

Yale University

1. In fact, *Dr Burney's Evening Party* was first published in the *New York Herald Tribune* on 21 and 28 July 1929, and reprinted by Desmond MacCarthy in *Life and Letters* for September 1929.

1908: To Hugh Walpole   *Monks House, Rodmell,*
                                          Lewes [Sussex]
1st July 1928

My dear Hugh,

Yes, I've had your letter and it was a great pleasure to get it. Its so seldom one gets an unsolicited letter which needn't have been written and they're the only ones worth getting.

I'm sorry there are so many decayed ladies in the north,[1] but I admire your energy in opening bazaars for them—as I gather you do from my Morning Post. What a lot of speaking and writing you manage! (this is said admiringly, not critically)

I am as dry as a bone and as barren as a burnt moor (or whatever is the barrenest thing) having written 60,000 words in 5 months. This is my record as a writer—and I am rather alarmed by it. But its only a joke, and a bad one, I fear.

Now I'm trying to fan up some interest in other people's writings and have subscribed to the Times Book Club. But I've no time for reading—indeed, I must confess that I began to write to you 10 days ago, and was so often interrupted that the letter turned a pale yellow, and I was ashamed to go on with it.

We are now at Rodmell for the week end, and have only had one visitor; so I have read Percy Lubbock on Miss Cholmondeley[2] which seems to me the writing of a butler about his missus—a first rate butler of course. And I have a novel given me by Maurice Baring called Comfortless Love (I think)[3] Shall I enjoy that or hate it?

And early tomorrow back we go again to be interrupted endlessly. Authoresses who want me to re-write their novels, mad poets, old ladies from Sweden[4]—so we go on: but I hope you are more composed, and will finish your book and enjoy it tremendously. As nobody can possibly tell me whether one's writing is bad or good, the only certain value is one's own pleasure. I am sure of that.

I hope we shall see you again. Let us know when.

                                          Yours
                                          Virginia Woolf

I had no stamp at Rodmell so this is another day late.

Texas

1. Hugh Walpole's country-house was near Keswick in the Lake District.
2. *Mary Cholmondeley, A Sketch from Memory*, 1928. She was the novelist (1859-1925), whose most famous book was *Red Pottage*, 1899.
3. *Comfortless Memory* (1928).
4. The Woolfs had been visited by Leonard's cousin from Sweden, Charlotte Mannheimer.

1909: To Lady Colefax   52 *Tavistock Square, W.C.*1

Monday [July 1928?]

Dearest Sibyl,

Its angelic of you, but owing to the cursed habits of landowners, we've got to go down to Lewes on the 18th and bid for as much of the Downs as we can afford to save them from the citymen's bungalows, and shan't be back for dinner. And we shall be bankrupt. I envy you Tuscany.

V.

Michael Colefax

1910: To Donald Brace   52 *Tavistock Square, W.C.*1

16th July 1928

Dear Mr Brace,[1]

It is extremely kind of you to write to me so generously about Orlando. I am specially glad to have your good opinion, as the book was written very much as a joke, and I did not know how far it had succeeded. I hope for both our sakes that it will be a success; but I am always perfectly confident that you on your part do all that can be done to make it one.

With many thanks,

Yours sincerely
Virginia Woolf

Columbia

1. Harcourt, Brace published the American trade edition of *Orlando* on 18 October 1928.

Letters 1911-1925 (July–September 1928)

Virginia spent a happy summer at Rodmell, writing mainly criticism, much of it intended for The Common Reader: Second Series, *published in 1932, although she was still turning* The Waves *over in her mind. She walked almost daily on the Downs, or paddled down the Ouse in a rubber dinghy, and there were many visitors, including Morgan Forster, Eddy Sackville West, Desmond MacCarthy, Vita, and Leonard's mother. Even with this last, there was much talk about Radclyffe Hall's* The Well of Loneliness, *a Sapphist novel which Virginia did not admire, but she put her name to a petition to remove the ban on it, and offered to give evidence in its defence.*

1911: To V. Sackville-West   [*Monk's House, Rodmell, Sussex*]

Wednesday, July 25th [1928]

As a matter of fact, Sunday will suit us better than Monday—so come then—shall expect you to tea (or water).

Only I am sorry that you won't find your new bed here, or the new mat: your room is even more disintegrated than usual, and Nelly's away; so cooking is only ham and tongue, but there's the garden of course, all a blowing: and the orchard to sit in—which you haven't got—not with pears and apples everywhere: and you haven't got a large yellow tin bath on the lawn, or a view, or a loving heart—come to think of it. For Promiscuous you are, and thats all there is to be said of you. Look in the Index to Orlando —after Pippin and see what comes next—Promiscuity *passim*.

I am in soaring health and spirits after one day here and have sat looking at cows for 3 hours instead of chasing round London buying scraps of meat and coming home to find Clive, Miss Jenkins, Sibyl: etc. But Edith Sitwell is waving her hand—the loveliest in London—at me: says I'm the only person she wants to know. Now how do you read "know": it has 2 senses.

But all that is shut off for 2 months.

And now I'm going to saunter down to the river with Pinker and Leonard will throw a stick in: Look here; no wine has yet come, so if you want some bring some.

Berg

*Monk's House [Rodmell,
Sussex]*

[7? August 1928]
    This seems to be the only piece of notepaper left in this house. Very
angry and sorry that Eddy should see you—and not I.
    But will come for day any time before you go[1]—if you'd like it. Only
communicate your will. But I expect life is too horribly crowded. I think
theres a chance of a week in France.

                                                                    V.

And let me have your address so that I may write long impassioned letters:
because 11th Oct.[2] sees the end of our romance.

Berg

*Monk's House, Rodmell
[Sussex]*

Aug 12th 1928

My dear Saxon,
    I gather from your postcard that I am a source of disappointment to
you, but you would mitigate your severity if you knew how much I *hate*
and *detest* writing letters. Every year I write fewer, and every year I enjoy
reading them more—so that the magnanimous among my friends now write
to me without being answered—a hint: observe. I have left it so long that
I doubt now if you are in the arms of Kohlus, who has shrunk, poor woman,
since our day, or in the comparative chastity of Great James Street, and I
have forgotten your number, since Gerald Brenan has one too; and they
cant be the same.
    Rodmell village is in a state of eruption and affliction—Mrs Malthouse
was stung under her spectacles by a wasp and has died; Mrs Allinson has
been burnt on her yatcht [*sic*]; and Mrs Grigs has died of the gangrene in
the legs.
    Meanwhile Leonard and I have bought a field, including a view of
Asheham cement works. Over at Charleston they are busy bottling wine
and shutting the door in the face of Lord Gage on the grounds that they
won't have callers in the country, not even landlords. Julian [Bell] and Janie
Bussy have been over to luncheon, it being a very fine day but with the
wind in the West which is said to be a sign of rain. On Friday we are
going to Bodiam in a fleet of motor cars; and on Sunday it is Quentin's

1. Vita and Harold rented a villa at Potsdam for a month from 15 August.
2. The publication date of *Orlando*.

birthday and on Tuesday Leonard will drive me up to London, and I shall go to the London Library and ask for the Maxims and Characters of Fulke Greville—not *the* F.G. but his descendant who occurs in connection with Miss Burney's father's marriage and playing the harpsichord.[1] Nothing pleases me more than to ferret out perfectly useless enquiries into the lives of completely valueless people; I see it might well usurp all other affections and employments, and is anyhow a refuge for old age, because employed at the British Museum one will scarcely notice deafness, blindness, the spring, the nightingale, or other infirmities or changes of season. Eddy Sackville West has been staying here, and we got talking (a propos of Clive) of refuges in old age; veils and disguises: such is the origin of this thought.

I am reading six books at once, the only way of reading; since, as you will agree, one book is only a single unaccompanied note, and to get the full sound, one needs ten others at the same time. So I'm reading—but I've no room to go into that.

It is, so far, very fine and nice here, and we are making all sorts of ambitious schemes for terraces, gazebos, ponds, water lilies, fountains, carp, goldfish, statues of naked ladies, and figureheads of battleships reflected in shadowy lakes. This was how Sir Walter Scott came to a bad end—and no one reads the Waverley Novels now except

                                                      Virginia Woolf

Sussex

1914: To Pernel Strachey   *Monk's House, Rodmell,*
                                    Lewes [Sussex]
[mid-August 1928]

My dear Pernel,

It is disgraceful of me not to have answered—indeed I can think of no excuse, but natural depravity.

We shall like very much to stay with you on October 20th, but I am afraid it will have to be for the night only, and please make no preparations —no parties. I should like solitary gossip for hours. Leonard is going to a Cambridge meeting after dinner on Saturday, and I pray that you too will either go to Church or put your legs up on the sofa—anything rather than attend my paper,[2] which is already beginning to shadow even the downs with its dulness; and is only remarkable for being the last I shall ever read in this hemisphere or the next.

1. Greville appears in Virginia's *Dr Burney's Evening Party*, which was reprinted in *The Common Reader: Second Series* (1932).
2. On women and fiction. This paper read at Newnham College, together with one read at Girton on 26 October, was published in a revised form as *A Room of One's Own* (1929). Pernel Strachey was Principal of Newnham.

I saw Janie Bussy the other day among apple trees and sheep—what an odd setting for her—and she said you said Miss Jenkins[1] said my party was a ghastly affair and Clive was a Bloody Bounder. What language the young use to be sure—the blueeyes fairhaired young! I went to tea with her, and she gave me virgin cakes (white sugar I mean) and cream, and then she spits venom thus!

I daresay it was a bit thick. Can one by the way be a bit thick in a paper at Newnham? What do you allow? How can you undertake education at all? And what d'you mean by it? Answer please.

Yr
V.W.

1915: To Hugh Walpole   *Monks House, Rodmell*
                                          [Sussex]

Aug 20th [1928]

My dear Hugh,

You always say I needn't answer—and so I never do. Thats one, not at all the only, pleasure of getting a letter from you. Now, as I ought to be reading a vast pile of I'm afraid meritorious manuscripts, I make this an occasion to write.

Yes, we're very well; very wet, have been plunging through the water meadows looking for mushrooms. Leonard and I together found precisely 3: the man in the next field filled an entire bag. And I have a rubber boat that you blow up like an airball. I sit in this and paddle down the tide till 23 swans circle round me with wings out spread. You see, I'm boasting, by way of putting up a fight against your Cornish adventures.[2] Secretly, all the romance in my heart is stirred by Cornwall. People say it is spoilt. I still think to catch a mackerel in a Cornish bay the greatest excitement under the moon. And then you tantalise me with talk of some unhappy love affair. Why not send me full details—barring names? I cant see why people set such store by chastity. I'm not sure though that they do, any longer. My nephews were here yesterday, Vanessa's boys, and the things they say, and the lives they lead, while still remaining as innocent as new laid eggs, make me suspect that the figure of Chastity has somehow shifted since our day. And we've had Sibyl Colefax down here, and Vita;—not that I connect them, particularly, with Chastity. Sibyl rather moves my pity, mistakenly, no doubt. What a life—to be harrying plumbers and paper hangers in London for 10 per cent (cant make the proper sign)

1. See p. 495, note 3.
2. Walpole had a cottage at Polperro.

517

commission.[1] Oh to have a country cottage she sighed; which she could have, surely, if she dismissed her chauffeur and sold her Rolls Royce, but then of course thats precisely what she cant do.

I'm glad you are writing about Scott, if only to keep me in countenance, who have just bought the Waverley novels in 25 large volumes, and am thought a sentimental mug—or is it muff?—by my friends in consequence. They say its because he was read aloud by my father when we were children —not altogether, I think. Yes, I shall read your book[2]—only dont expect enlightened criticism from me. I am rather now in the state of the cows who are munching the grass off our field—sleepy, contented, not much aware of goodness or badness. But I shall read it. And must now, alas, begin turning over that awful pile which represents at least three hearts ambitions—and the hearts of clerks in Paisley dont attract me.

Yrs V.W.

Texas

1916: To Ethel Sands   *Monks House, Rodmell,*
                                        Lewes, Sussex

22 Aug 1928

Dearest Ethel,

You and Nan are much, much, much too good. What is more, your goodness seems inspired by some magical sympathy for my distresses. I had just been saying to Leonard that I must give up all hope of a desk, for I had asked a beautiful young man to design one for me, and he has disappeared for ever, God knows where, when your letter drops from the skies and the desk is actually there! It seems too good to be true. But I must, I implore, I command you to let me pay for it, out of the vast cheques which your compatriots send me. Indeed I wouldn't have asked you to look for one otherwise. So please, dearest Ethel and Nan, tell me what I owe you, and accept my eternal gratitude for what is far the hardest part of buying desks—finding a desk to buy. If you would send it to Newhaven I would meet the boat, unless its too big to get inside my Singer saloon. In that case, I would get the carrier. Only send me a line to say when and which and I pray it may come soon. What angels you are!

Here we are enjoying rain at the moment, after weeks and weeks of the loveliest weather—painters weather, so full of changes and lights. We buzz about the country in our cars, and abuse the Keynese's; Clive is autumnal this year, I'm afraid, and seems to have lost his Leicestershire lady; but I think its time, when ones hair is half off to give up these violences.

1. Sibyl Colefax founded an interior-decoration business, in which she was later joined by John Fowler.
2. Hugh Walpole published two books this year, *Wintersmoon* and *Anthony Trollope* (English Men of Letters Series).

And he is very nice with his boys with whom I flirt. So we go on discussing everything endlessly, as usual; and this week end there is a great party at the Keynes' which will be fed off two second hand grouse—the kind people don't want to stew—so Nessa says. Bobo Mayor is going to have a play acted by Lydia—Lydia is said to be childish, foolish, dull and boring, and Clive had to tell her so.

I now remember, in the midst of this gossip which I am ashamed to send to your much higher moral and mental atmosphere, that I have another request to make. Can you advise me where I could spend a perfect week in France at the end of September? Not too far; but somewhere half way down, warm, beautiful, with a good inn, lovely country, and perhaps a ruin or a church—I don't mind much. But I want a weeks perfect happiness, drinking, before settling in for the winter—and if Leonard won't come, which I see he won't, for his blessed dog is going to have puppies, I shall get Vita to come. And perhaps if it suited you we might look in on you for a night on our way back: and some gossiping.

Am I on good terms with Jacques Blanche? I feel somehow that I'm not.[1] By the way, your praises are sung by the Sitwells all over London.

Leonard has just come in and wishes me to send you both his love; we are taking Pinker for a little gentle exercise—she is what they call "heavy"—up to the post, so I must stop. A thousand thanks.

Yours Virginia

Wendy Baron

1917: To ETHEL SANDS   52 *Tavistock Square, W.C.*1

Aug 20th [1928]

Dearest Ethel,

Well well—there's no arguing with you and Miss Hudson. I submit—in fact I lie flat at your feet in homage for ever. Its possible I may retaliate by working you a plush tea cosy which you would have to use, or I should be hurt, but I'll try not to. What angels you are! What an excitement unpacking [the desk] will be—and then the joy of clearing up this awful mess—letters, cigarettes, reels of cotton, photographs of our late rector, old envelopes—all now scattered on top of me. Leonard says the way to send it is Mrs Woolf, Monks House, Rodmell, near Newhaven, to be called for at Newhaven. That saves the extra journey by train.

Many thanks for the suggestions. I will look at the map. Nessa thought Brantôme a perfect place—is it too far? I daresay. And Auxerre is a name of great romance.

1. Virginia had suggested to Blanche that he should write his recollections of England for the Hogarth Press, but she did not pursue the idea.

I can't write to you—thats one of the ill effects of giving presents—because every sentence bursts into thanks and praise, which is against the natural tendency of my temperament. Its as if you had to put a carnation in the middle of every picture. So I cant tell you about the party where Lydia cried—but must end—

A million thanks and love to Nan and Ethel.

Yr
V.W

Wendy Baron

1918: To V. Sackville-West   *Monks House, Rodmell*
                                     [Sussex]
30th Aug 1928

How do you live the life you do? Sixty people to dinner [in Berlin]. One for three days entirely dissipates my soul, and sends it floating, like duckweed, down a dirty river. I am very hot. I have been mowing the lawn. It looks now like a calm sea through which several large ships have passed leaving wakes behind them. Then I ate two plums which make my hands sticky. For many days I have been so disjected by society that writing has been only a dream—something another woman did once. What has caused this irruption I scarcely know—largely your friend Radclyffe Hall (she is now docked of her Miss owing to her proclivities) they banned her book;[1] and so Leonard and Morgan Forster began to get up a protest, and soon we were telephoning and interviewing and collecting signatures —not yours, for *your* proclivities are too well known. In the midst of this, Morgan goes to see Radclyffe in her tower in Kensington, with her love [Lady Troubridge]: and Radclyffe scolds him like a fishwife, and says that she wont have any letter written about her book unless it mentions the fact that it is a work of artistic merit—even genius. And no one has read her book; or can read it: and now we have to explain this to all the great signed names—Arnold Bennett and so on. So our ardour in the cause of freedom of speech gradually cools, and instead of offering to reprint the masterpiece, we are already beginning to wish it unwritten.

I am observing with interest the fluctuations of my own feelings about France. Leonard says he can't come. Like an angel he says but of course go with Vita. Then he somehow conveys without a word the fact of his intolerable loneliness without me—upon which I give it all up; and then suddenly think, what an unwholesome sentimental state this is! I will go. And then visualise myself saying goodbye to him and cant face it; and then visualise a rock in a valley with Vita in an Inn: and *must* go. So it goes on. Meanwhile Ethel Sands advises us to go to Auxerre, Vézelay, Autun, Semur,

---

1. Radclyffe Hall's *The Well of Loneliness* (1928), the famous novel about lesbianism.

Saulieu (Hotel de la Poste has wonderful food) and we are to stay at least two nights with her and Nan. I think I must manage to come. But it will be the greatest proof of devotion. And Leonard may make it impossible—Can you put up with these vacillations:? Anyhow I shall see you before anything need be done.

I am very happy and not very happy. Do you like these states of mind to take precedence of all else in letters? I am happy because it is the loveliest August; downs so brown and grey, and the meadows so—I forget what. On the other hand, I have to work all day—it seems—grinding out a few notes like those a blunt knife makes on a whetstone, at novels and novels. I read Proust, Henry James, Dostoevsky; my happiness is wedged like (but I am using too many metaphors) in between these granite blocks (and now that they are granite blocks I can compare my happiness to samphire, a small pink plant I picked as a child in Cornwall).

Why need you be so timid and pride-blown, both at once, over writing your novel? What does donkey West mean about her ambition and failure?[1] Why should you fail at this prosy art, when you can please Jack Squire with poetry? (Thats a nasty one) I am entirely of your opinion that Heaven has made us and not we ourselves. I accept no responsibility for anything I write or do. I like your fecundity. And; surely, for the last ten years almost, you have cut back and pruned and root dug—What is it one should do to fig trees?—with the result that you write sometimes too much like a racehorse who has been trained till his tail is like a mouses tail and his ribs are like a raised map of the Alps. Please write your novel, and then you will enter into the unreal world, where Virginia lives—and poor woman, can't now live anywhere else.

I've not seen Dottie: but then I said very incautiously that I would like to buy some bricks off her, and that one mustn't say to a woman with ten thousand a year. For then she sighs to herself "Virginia only thinks of my possessions" Is this true psychology? At any rate it is true that Pinker is breeding. She has at least six inside her, and the lice and a bad paw, all of which occupy our time incessantly. "Are you sure lice don't travel—is this a louse—what are nits—" such is our talk; and we had a play by Bobo Mayor; made poor Lydia who acted in such despair that instead of spending the week end with Lloyd-George, she spent it with the Spinaches [unidentified]. We didn't clap loud enough: but then we were sitting in the rain.

Yes, I think I must come to France, and I dont think Leonard will miss me one scrap.

Yr

Berg

1. Vita was thinking about her next novel, *The Edwardians* (1930), and wrote to Virginia, "I would rather fail gloriously than dingily succeed" (21 August 1928, *Berg*).

FAMILY TREE OF THE WOOLFS

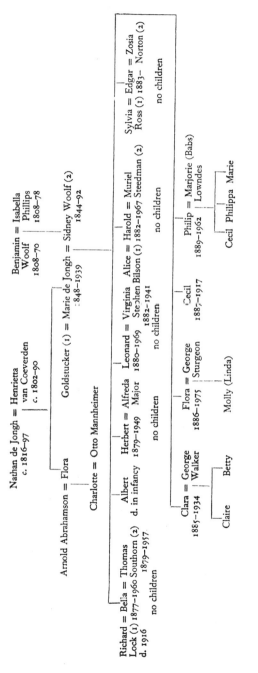

Sources: George A. Spater and Leonard Woolf's autobiographies

1919: To Vanessa Bell   [*Monk's House, Rodmell,*
                                          Sussex]
Typewritten
Sunday [2 September 1928]

Perhaps you would like some account of our conversation [with
Leonard's mother],[1] last night, which I will give you in a very hurried
way, as I am waiting to join my mother in law; but cannot write anything else.

First we discussed the enormous size of Julian.
"It is many years since I have seen your sister. I did not remember that
she was a very tall woman. Perhaps Mr Bell is very tall?" *V.* "No Mr Bell
is not very tall." "Then perhaps the men in your family are very tall?"
"Some of them are; but the women in my mothers family are not very
tall." *Mrs W.* You are very tall. *V.* I am not taller than my sister. *Mrs.
W.* It is many years since I have seen your sister. Is her little girl very tall?
V. No; she is very small. *Leonard.* I should say she is very big. *Mrs W.*
Sometimes children take after one parent; sometimes they take after another.
This is such pretty country. It has been a wonderful summer. I sit out on
my balcony all day long. At first they put me in a room without a balcony.
In fact it was not at all a nice room. It was over the kitchen. I heard the
servants going to bed at night. Then I heard them getting up in the morning.
So I went to the proprietor—but of course he is not the same man that
was there five years ago. He was a very nice man. Indeed Flora tells me
people came from all over the world to stay there on account of his cooking.
But he married a clever woman with a little money of her own. So they
bought a little place in Somerset. They keep chickens I believe. She was
the very woman to make a thing like that succeed. And what do you think
they gave for the house? I made enquiries because I sometimes feel so tired
of hotel life that I think I will buy a little house in the country of my own.
Then I could have my furniture from the warehouse. I have had my furniture
stored in a warehouse for fifteen years now. I have one lot stored at Paddington, and another at Staines. What do you think I spend every year on having
my furniture stored? *Leonard.* Fifty pounds. *V.* A hundred. *Mrs W.* No.
It comes to thirty two pounds every year. So I have now spent—how
much have I spent now Leonard, on having the furniture stored? *Leonard.*
Well over five hundred pounds. *Mrs W.* I daresay it is not worth more
than one hundred at most. It is what we bought when we first married.
We gave fifteen hundred pounds for that furniture. It was the very best
we could buy. We bought it at Gillows. We had a mahogany sideboard,
inlaid. We had a chandelier; but it was the trouble of my life, that chandelier,
for every part had to be unscrewed to clean it. *V.* But probably you could
get at least five hundred if you sold your furniture tomorrow. *Mrs W.* No

1. In the course of the conversation which follows, Leonard's mother mentions
    many of her relations. The family tree opposite provides a key to their identity.

523

Virginia, I should get nothing. And then I have sentiment. It was made by Gillows. It is not old furniture. It is very shabby too. My dear husband bought it when we first married. I should not like to part with it now. I have sentiment when perhaps it would be better not to have sentiment. . . . But I have also a complete set of the songs of Schubert. When I married my first husband we went for our marriage tour in Germany. My brother in law—that is my first husbands brother, no relation of Leonard of course, said he would give me what I liked to ask for my wedding present. So I said I would like the songs of Schubert. I used to sing in those days. But when one has a family, one soon gives it up; so I put the books away and then the other day Sylvia said to me how she would like to sing the songs of Schubert so I went to the warehouse and I had them taken out—and what do you think it cost me to have the furniture unstacked? *V.* Fifteen shillings. *Leonard.* One pound. *Mrs W.* No. it cost me six pounds—merely to have the furniture unstacked. So I said to the man, "But the things are not worth more than thirty five shillings." And he said "Madam it would be the same if they were worth five hundred pounds." (We played the gramophone) "What is that?" *Leonard.* Scheherazade. *Mrs W.* No. I have never heard of him. It is too sad. When one has had a lot of trouble in ones life one does not like sad music. Yes I have been very lucky in small things, Virginia, and very unlucky in big things. Did I tell you about my purse on the tram at Folkestone? No? I was staying with Charlotte. We make it a rule when we stay away together that one pays one day and the other the next day. So when we went on the tram I said it was my turn to pay and I took out my purse and I paid what ever the sum was—perhaps it was twopence perhaps more threepence—it does not matter. But now you know when one is staying in a hotel one does not know what to do —whether to leave ones money in ones room, or to take it with one. Well I had fourteen pounds in my purse; and I thought as I did not know the people at the hotel—they have changed since I was there last, which was twentyfive years ago—I would take my money with me. We went into a shop to have tea and behold! my purse was gone! Charlotte said I must have left it in the hotel. I said I knew I had it when I paid the tram. But I would not make a fuss, in order not to upset her. Still I thought how dreadful —it was fourteen pounds—a very large sum. But I said nothing so as not to upset Charlotte—she is always so kind—quiet, but very kind. So we had our tea, and I said nothing; but after tea we walked about; and then we went to get on a tram; and what do you think? It was the same tram we had come on. And we went on top. And we sat where we had sat. And Charlotte took her umbrella. And Charlotte poked under a piece of wood. And Charlotte said I think I feel something under this piece of wood. And it was the purse! Now what do you think of that? There was my fourteen pounds."

We played the gramophone for some time now; and suddenly in the middle of a song by Schubert, Mrs W. said Do you see that cat? It is a lovely black kitten with white paws in the fire. I do not know how it is, but I am always seeing faces. I see faces everywhere. *V.* That proves that you ought to write poetry. *Mrs W.* My dear Virginia, I could not dream of doing such a thing. If I were as clever as you are, I would love to write. I would love to write the beautiful things that have happened to me in my life; but not the sad ones; and I have had many sad ones. But one person has one gift; another another. And my gift has been [doing things domestically][1] bringing up my children. *V.* Well you have brought up eight. *Mrs W.* I have brought up ten [nine]. And they are all good men and women. They have all good characters. Len is a splendid man. He should have gone to the Bar. He has such a clear brain in so many directions. His father thought the world of Len. Have you read Radclyffe Hall's book? I have got it from Harrods. She was a friend of Bellas. They went to Mrs Coles school together and she used to come to our house sometimes—a regular society girl. Bella never liked her; but Bella did not dislike her. And now she has written this book. Of course I cannot say all that I would like to say if we were alone together. I may be foolish, but I cannot speak to you and Len as if Len were not there. But I would like very much to talk to you alone about it." (After some encouragement however she went on)—"It is a dreadful pity I think that such a book should have been published. I do not mean for the ordinary reasons. What I mean is there are many unmarried women living alone. And now it is very hard on them that such a book should have been written. That is what I think. And you may think me very foolish—I am seventy six—but until I read this book I did not know that such things went on at all. I do not think they do. I have never heard of such things. When I was at school there was nothing like that. I was at boarding school for two years and I never heard of such a thing. Once a girl was dispelled; but I never knew what she was dispelled for. It may have been for something unpleasant; but it may have been for nothing of the kind. And when I married my first husband—he was such a charming man, a Dutchman,—I assure you I knew no more about marriage than Flo's baby does. So it shows that we did not do such things at my boarding school. *Leonard.* We did at my boarding school. It was the most corrupt place I have ever been in. And you let me go there when I was twelve without knowing a thing. *Mrs W.* But I had given you good principles, Len. *Len.* You had given me no principles at all. *Mrs W.* Oh Len how can you say that, when you know what [a] splendid man your father was! And when your father died I said to myself that though I could not be to you what he was, I would do my utmost to bring you up good men and women; and sometimes, do you know Virginia, I would take a large basket of their socks to bed with me so that I might start mending them directly I woke

1. The bracketed phrase was crossed out by Virginia on the original.

in the morning. But I said that I did not mind any sacrifice to bring them up as their father would have wished. He was such a splendid man. But I think much of Miss Radclyffe Halls book is very beautiful. There is the old horse—that is wonderful—when she has to shoot the old horse after every vet. has been to see it; but it has grown to be so old they can do nothing. It is too old for them to do anything. And so she shoots the horse herself. That is beautiful. And William is a splendid character. He is the old groom. All that about the old horse and the old groom is very beautiful. But the rest of the book I did not care for. Still of course she is wonderfully clever; and I daresay there are not two people in the hotel at Bexhill who have ever heard of her. Of course when Mr Sturgeon bought his house at Bexhill it was not the same neighbourhood as it is now. His house was built by a Frenchwoman. In an old house like this you have so many cupboards. Do you use citronella oil for wasps stings? Some people dislike the smell. I hear there was a poor woman here who died of a wasp sting. And did I tell you the dreadful fright Babs had when the girl put the burning log back in the basket and the chair was burnt to ashes underneath the childrens nursery? And then you know they went to Somerset in the caravan: and the nurse—she came from Bexhill—Babs got her from a newspaper—she said it was the dream of her life to go in a caravan; and they were driving down I cant tell you exactly where, and Phil said—for they were all packed together in the caravan—Phil said, "I will move that box to make room for you;" and she said straight out "I will make room for you myself;" and she hailed a lorry which happened to be passing; and she jumped on to the lorry; and she was off. It was like a scene at the pictures, Phil said. And when she was gone Babs put her hand to her neck and you know that very pretty locket that her aunt gave her that she was so fond of? Well it was gone. And they cannot be sure the girl took it of course, but did you ever hear such a thing? She hailed the lorry and she was gone. So we will go to bed and I will lend you that book to read tonight if you like Virginia. For you are so clever. . . .

Berg

1920: To George Rylands   *Monk's House, Rodmell,*
                                           Lewes, Sussex

Sunday 2nd Sept [1928]

My dear Dadie,

  You said you might come to the Wolves in September. Could you manage the weekend of the 15th? I think I'm going away on the 22nd, so come before that.

  I suppose you are writing a novel and a poem and carrying on a vast complication of affairs.

I go on plodding with my poor nose to the grindstone. So please come and be charming to your poor drudge.

We have bought a field, and have all sorts of plans for planting and building.

Now I must go and entertain my mother in law.

Your aff
V.W.

George Rylands

1921: TO ETHEL SANDS   *Monks House, Rodmell,*
                                        Lewes [Sussex]
4th Sept 1928

Dearest Ethel and Nan

I was sitting in the garden this blazing hot day trying to read a manuscript when a battered old woman carrying a satchel of shiny books appeared, and asked me if I believed in God, because if I did I must buy her books, and if I did not, still more must I buy her books. So we began to argue about God and the soul, and she tried to convert me, and I tried to find out why she had left off being a governess and walked about converting people—in fact we were hard at it, and Leonard only throwing twigs at me from the cherry tree which he was scraping of ivy when in the very nick of time a man appeared with a case for Mrs Woolf from Newhaven. Out I ran; down Leonard came from his tree—the old woman with her books was swept aside, and I shall never know now anything more about her—for off we ran to the stable, Leonard with a big hammer, I with a small one, and began knocking and pulling and drawing out straw and paper and sometimes I cried out "I see it! I see it!" when an edge of the desk appeared, and at last there it was on the stable floor! But I must tell you it is not an ordinary desk, not such a desk as you might buy in London or Edinburgh or see in anybodies house when you go to lunch; this desk is a sympathetic one, full of character, trusty, discreet, very reserved: more like Nan than Ottoline; like Nan rather than Sibyl Colefax; not in the least like Philip Morrell; honourable and discreet, and if I may say so, not American (though there are some Americans—I love to be quite precise—there are two Americans I love; of the same sex too; I leave you to guess which) nor English even, but French at its heart, so that—I don't know where it came from, nor what its age is, but I think all the writers I most admire, and the people I like most—not the smart or the worldly, but the comfortable and those who enjoy eating and drinking—have sat under its shade (for it was a tree) or on its branches, if they were birds; in which case they were the birds I like, not starlings who are dirty, nor robins who are fierce, but nightingales, thrushes, wrens, and little owls. You see how it makes one enjoy the sound of ones own voice, which is the greatest pleasure in the world!

Years ago I wrote letters, when I was young and, though Clive won't have it, passionate, but for years now I have only written notes—"So sorry my dear Sibyl, but I cant come to tea"—but now I shall write letters, long long amorous letters. And it is also full of drawers, in which I shall hide the answers, the amorous answers; I have just counted them. There are 14 drawers. And I have twice shut the lid to look at it closed, and to admire the inlaid star. And what is so charming about it is that it does not force me to feel young, or to mind the hole in my stockings, as some desks would; and if it is trusty and discreet it is also distinguished and slightly scented and veined with romance, so that if it had eyes they would be red-brown like Ethel's, and it has something of her mothy ways, and her secret flights in her thick cape among the flowers in the garden. In short you see it combines the two women most aptly Nan and Ethel—Ethel and Nan, But you will be saying we regret the days when Virginia had only a deal table to write at, and so could never finish more than a single page. You will be wishing you had trod on your generosity as Nan treads on her slugs. If it is as fine on your side of the sea as on ours you will be wanting to stroll round the garden, or to feed the dog or to pour out the tea for M. Blanche and his nephew.[1] And still I go on writing, writing, for really it is so delightful to sit at your desk and think of you and write to you that I cant make up my mind to have done with it and say thank you and go in to dinner as I should. By the way, miraculously too, it fits my window to an inch; and it travelled unbroken. So thank you once more and finally, you'll be pleased to hear, thank you. V.

Wendy Baron

1922: To V. Sackville-West   *Monks House, Rodmell,*
                                     Sussex
Saturday, Sept 8th 1928

Concentrate your mind upon this, and give me your answer. Suppose we start (you and I and Potto) on Saturday 22nd. Sleep in Paris. Get to SAULIEU on Monday. Spend 2 nights, if we like more: go on to Auxerre, Semur, Vézelay; all within a stone's throw: and get back here on Sunday 30th. Would that suit you? Brantôme seems too far. Shall I take you a ticket to Saulieu? Do you want to go 2nd or 1st (I insist on 1st on the boat) If first is much more comfortable, first is advisable. Not otherwise; because first class travellers are always old fat testy and smell of eau de cologne, which makes me sick. As a guarantee of my good faith in coming, I went

1. George Nevil-Blanche, nephew, ward, and heir of Jacques-Emil Blanche.

to a travellers agency and found out about trains and they will get us tickets, if given notice—So, as I began by saying—and Lord knows I hate this business of being so precise—let me know. I confess I am in a state of violent excitement already. You see, dearest Creature, being now in the pink and prime of health, I could sit up all night: we might go to moonlight ruins, café's, dances, plays, junketings: converse for ever; sleep only while the moon covers herself for an instant with a thin veil; and by day traipse the vineyards. I am burnt chocolate brown. The sun blazes: but there—you are shuddering under quilts in a damned Teutonic fog [in Potsdam], and I'll say no more.

But I have a thousand things to say, and as usual am in a flying rush, Pinka having had four puppies yesterday so that I have to go and buy Lactol or something in Lewes. They are 2 male 2 female; and she is a model of all the maternal vices—absorbed, devoted, zealous, cowish, But I was going to say that I like your Tolstoy[1] very much. I think it is your best criticism, so far as I've seen. And as I always take credit for your good writing, I'm pleased with myself. I think you have got nearer the old Sphinx than any of the other anniversarists—who abound; but blither. The question you should have pushed home—had there been room—is precisely the one you raise, what made his realism which might have been photographic, not at all; but on the contrary, moving and exciting and all the rest of it. Some dodge there must have been; some very queer arrangement—I dont know what—of perspective. But I like you when you write such interesting things—and I have a great deal to say—if only the puppies could be fed without my going to Lewes—about your novel. I thought out, indeed, a long and it seemed then very profound essay upon writing novels, and how one can know if they are only foam and gush or not, on the downs the other evening: I cant remember it now. I believe that the main thing in beginning a novel is to feel, not that you can write it, but that it exists on the far side of a gulf, which words can't cross: that its to be pulled through only in a breathless anguish. Now when I sit down to an article, I have a net of words which will come down on the idea certainly in an hour or so. But a novel, as I say, to be good should seem, before one writes it, something unwriteable: but only visible; so that for nine months one lives in despair, and only when one has forgotten what one meant, does the book seem tolerable. I assure you, all my novels were first rate before they were written. If I felt I could write them easily (forgive the holes in this paper—it is torn from the handcuff book) then I should know they were plausible and ephemeral—as indeed Mr Swinnerton[2] says they are.

As for Radclyffe Hall, I agree: but what is one to do? She drew up a

1. *Tolstoy* (*Nation & Athenaeum*, 8 September 1928).
2. Frank Swinnerton, the novelist and critic, reviewed many of Virginia's novels, and found them beautiful but 'bloodless'.

letter of her own, protesting her innocence and decency, which she asked us to sign, and would have no other sent out. So nothing could be done, except indeed one rather comic little letter written by Morgan Forster, which he asked me to sign: and now it appears that I, the mouthpiece of Sapphism, write letters from the Reform Club![1] Nothing else can be done. Except that Desmond is writing an article—but, as Dottie says, whats the use of Desmond writing an article?

We saw Dottie yesterday, and she must sprinkle herself with some anti-aphrodisiac powder which gets into the male nostrils, for never have I seen Leonard in such a rage—yet she was much as usual to me: Nothing in particular, running about her [Penns-in-the] rocks. We drove home at 40 miles an hour—he was so furious with her vanity, conceit, egotism, vulgarity; ill breeding, violent temper. etc.

Now I must go.

But write please dearest; and encourage me to come with you; which is a venture; for suppose you're bored?

Yr

Berg

1923: To Miss Harper   52 *Tavistock Square, W.C.*1
                              [*Monk's House, Rodmell,*
                               Sussex]
Typewritten
14th Sept 1928

Dear Miss Harper,

Many thanks for sending me the translation of my story. Slaters Pins have no Points. I agree with you in thinking that "Les épingles de chez Slater n'ont pas de pointes" would be better than the title she has given it.[2] Still better would be "Les Epingles de Slater n'ont pas de pointes" but I do not know if the French of that is accurate.

The story otherwise reads well, but I have no copy of the original here (I am in the country) and so cannot check it. I agree that it is extremely difficult to give the feeling of modern English prose in French—indeed your plan of printing the original with the translation would certainly be the most satisfactory.

I think it would be best to say the "Serpentine" simply—unless that

1. A letter to the Editor, protesting against the banning of *The Well of Loneliness* and signed by E. M. Forster and Virginia, appeared in the *Nation* of 8 September.
2. *Les Epingles de chez Slater ne piquent pas* (*Echanges*, Paris, December 1929), translated by Georgette Camille.

would be too difficult for the French reader. It is not a river; it is more of the nature of a lake.

With many thanks

yours sincerely
Virginia Woolf

Texas

1924: To V. Sackville-West   52 *Tavistock Square, W.C.*1
                                  [*Monk's House, Rodmell,*
                                  Sussex]

Typewritten
Sunday [16 September 1928]

Dear Mrs N.

I have written for two first class tickets and cabin on boat for Monday Sept. 24th. Tickets to Saulieu via Paris. I am also writing to the Hotel recommended by Ethel at Saulieu to keep us two rooms for two nights.

Why dont you sleep here on Sunday night and leave your car in our stable? This would be much better, as if you dont, I may be unable to get off. As it is, what clothes do you expect me to take? None, I hope. [*in Virginia's handwriting to end:*] A fur coat? I cant come up on Tuesday I'm afraid—shall be up on Friday; but if there is anything to settle, I can telephone; only let me know when I could find you.

Isn't England nice compared with Germany? Look at my downs: even your weald.

Pinka and puppies very well. You could choose yours if you came here.

I am melancholy and excited in turn. You see, I would not have married Leonard had I not preferred living with him to saying good bye to him. But at the same time, the Roman ruins in Auxerre excite my interest. Also the stained glass.

(This is what I call my fun)
            and I'm very hurried going to a birthday
            party with Potto at Charleston and cursing
Desmond—Oh there's a lot to talk to you about: Orlando: Radclyffe Hall: etc.

I am getting a fish basket for Potto.

Shall you be bored with me?

As an experiment this journey interests me enormously.

Berg

1925: To Helen McAfee   52 *Tavistock Square, W.C.1*
                                         [*Monk's House, Rodmell,*
                                         Sussex]

Typewritten
23rd Sept. 1928

Dear Miss McAfee,

I should have written before but I have not been sure if I could get the article on Dr Burneys party ready for Oct. 1st as you suggest. I have been so busy that unfortunately I find that this is impossible. I should be able to let you have it early in November and go without seeing a proof if that suits you. I may, on getting to work, find it better to change the subject; but it would be an article of the same kind that I suggested to you. Unless I hear from you to the contrary, I will send you an article about the second week in November. It will appear here in December.

I am sorry to say that we have had to decide not to accept Mr Croly's invitation to America this time—my husbands engagements make it impossible. Otherwise we should have looked forward to seeing you.

                                         Yours very sincerely
                                         Virginia Woolf

Yale University

Letters 1926–1935 (end of September–early October 1928)

On 24 September Virginia went with Vita to Burgundy for a week's holiday. It was their only expedition abroad together, and the only occasion after her marriage when Virginia travelled alone with anyone except Leonard. Both were a little apprehensive before they started, and so was Leonard, but the holiday proved a great success. Vita's competence and fluent French shielded Virginia from the small difficulties of the journey, and they loved the country and little Burgundian towns, where Virginia, as usual on her travels, persuaded herself she wanted to settle for ever. Her only worry was the lack of letters from Leonard, to whom she wrote every day. Orlando, which was on the point of publication and of which Vita had not been allowed to read a single word, was scarcely mentioned between them. It was during this journey that Vita wrote to Harold Nicolson:

"Virginia is very sweet, and I feel extraordinarily protective towards her. The combination of that brilliant brain and fragile body is very lovable. She has a sweet and childlike nature, from which her intellect is completely separate. I have never known anyone who was so profoundly sensitive, and who makes less of a business of that sensitiveness."

1926: TO LEONARD WOOLF   Cafe Lutetia, [Rue de Sevres] Paris

9.30 Monday [24 September 1928]

Dearest,

Here we are taking a cup of coffee after dinner. A band is playing inside but alas I can only just hear it. We had a cold but calm voyage—except that the poor mots [marmots] sobbed for Dadyka the whole way and so did Mandrill. Lord, how I adore you, and how little you do![1] I believe you're glad to be quit of us! and to read all the evening without having beasts all over you.

I don't think a cabin is worth 37/-. It is very stuffy and smelly, and one is more comfortable in the smoking-room, certainly on a calm day when even the old women aren't sick. We dined fairly but cheaply at a modest restaurant, and then of course completely lost our way, and found

1. Vita's diary for 24 September 1928 reads: "She told me how she and Leonard had had a small and sudden row that morning about her going abroad with me" (*Berg*).

533

ourselves after walking for ½ an hour back in the Bd. Raspail. Vita's French is very competent, and having asked the way of a tobacconist, and appealing to a policeman, we are now within an arm's throw of the hotel. We are going back to bed at once, as we must get up at 6. I must say the first day has been completely ruined by parting with you. Vita is very kind and sympathetic and says she understands my affection.

Love to the Poos [Pinker's puppies]. I have bought a French novel[1] and this is the fly leaf.

The Dieppe boat gets to Newhaven at 4.30

V.

[*in Vita's handwriting:*]
Dear Leonard,

It is exactly ¼ to 10—and Virginia is now going to be made to go to bed.

V.

[*in Virginia's handwriting:*]
Vita says she is delighted to have Pinker and the Poos for as long as we like—

Sussex

1927: To Leonard Woolf   *Saulieu [France]*

Tuesday [25 September 1928]

Dearest Mongoose, darling Mongoose,

I am writing in a field overlooking Burgundy; 4.30: very hot and fine. It rained in Paris last night; but as usual completely cleared about 8 this morning. We got up at six and arrived at one, and then we had the vastest most delicious meal I have ever eaten. It is the usual small French inn, with farmers lunching; but as I say we began with paté of duck, went on to trout, gnocchi, stuffed chicken and spinach made with cream and then sour cream and a delicious cake and then pears ad lib; as the marmots say. Then it is the annual fair in Saulieu, and we walked about looking at roundabouts and paying twopence for a chance to win a live pigeon in a lottery. I am now getting melancholy for you, and thinking that perhaps the downs are more beautiful than Burgundy. What is odd is that there is no sign of vintage. We passed through vineyards this morning, and I saw some few black bunches hanging, but here there is nothing. It seems purely French, only two naval Englishmen at lunch, and some French motorists. Then—here it got so cold that we had to come back to the hotel. I am going to sit and read I think till dinner and then there are fireworks at the fair. You will be dining at Charleston, and I hope I may get some report of

1. *J'Adore*, by Jean Desbordes.

Lytton. I think we must come to France with the car, doing about 30 miles a day and seeing the small towns—it certainly has great advantages, not being in a hurry and walking about looking at the country.

Vita and I have not quarrelled, but then as we have been moving incessantly we have not had much chance. She has a permit from the Foreign office which got us through the customs unopened: otherwise, we have travelled fairly economically, though as she never asked the price of the rooms here, I daresay we shall be rooked. She says that Sydney Waterlow has been appointed to Abyssinia[1] (where Marjorie was once, I understand) and her mother has now taken to writing to anyone—her bookseller, or dressmaker, asking them to give her 'a tile for the roof of friendship' This is a method of asking for money for her new house and she has collected £400, but now decided not to build it, but to keep the money of course. I dont think I could stand more than a week away from you, as there are so many things to say to you, which I cant say to Vita—though she is most sympathetic and more intelligent than you think. At least we can discuss books for hours—perhaps I do most of the talking. Rather to my horror, Dotty is sending me here a new poem of hers to read, inspired by Rocks. On Vita's advice she is going to publish the Welsh Miner.[2]

Lord! I do hope you'll be careful motoring tonight!—and that you eat and sleep and dont give away all your affection to the poos. Poor Mandril does adore your every hair of your little body and hereby puts in a claim for an hour of antelope kissing the moment she gets back.

I forgot the timetable and my writing paper—nothing much else. This is a horrid, dull scrappy scratchy letter but all letters of real affection are dull. Do you think we are extremely intimate? I do; because, why should I, a born dandy as I am, write so carelessly—Have you done Dorothy Osborne?[3] Please write very long letters. You might send me a newspaper too.

Mandrill. DUSKY DARKY Marmot esquire.

Love to Nelly [Boxall].

Sussex

1928: TO LEONARD WOOLF

Hotel de la Poste, Saulieu
[France]

Wednesday [26 September 1928]

Dearest,

We have decided that we had better get back on Monday afternoon

1. Waterlow was British Minister in Addis Ababa, 1928-9.
2. Huw Menai, *The Passing of Guto and Other Poems*, published in March 1929 as No. 6 in the Hogarth Living Poets First Series, edited by Dorothy Wellesley.
3. Virginia reviewed Dorothy Osborne's *Letters* for the *New Republic*, New York, on 24 October 1928.

instead of Tuesday, as Vita finds that the boat train gets up too late on Tuesday for her broadcasting: The alternative is to come by the night boat, which arrives at 4 a.m. However this is too uncomfortable: also I want to see you: so we shall arrive on *Monday* and I could go up to London with you on *Tuesday* for the day—so please arrange this then I shouldn't have to think of you motoring alone. I hope you'll be glad to see me a day earlier. I am writing this to post it on our way out; but I'll write later—not that I daresay you read my letters; so long are they and so dull. But I have a lot to tell you about the circus last night.

Another fine day: a perfect night, and delicious food. I hope to get a letter tomorrow at Avallon.

Please settle to go up on *Tuesday* with me.

V.M.

We suggest dining with Ethel on Sunday night. Going straight through from Auxerre.

Sussex

1929: To Vanessa Bell   [*Saulieu, France*]

Postcard
[27 September 1928]

We are just leaving for Avallon, after eating the most perfect dinners and seeing a great circus with lions but no [grape] vines. We shall dine at Auppegard on Sunday, and hope to see you.

Berg

1930: To Leonard Woolf   *Avallon* [*France*]

Thursday [27 September 1928]

Dearest M,

I am sitting in an avenue after lunch while Vita tries to hire a motor to take us to Vézelay. I am rather melancholy because there is no letter from you, and Vita had two from Harold. But there is a post at 3, so we shall wait for that in hopes. We came from Saulieu this morning, and shall go straight on, so as to have two nights at Vézelay which looks more interesting, though Avallon is a very charming old place, and I am in the 7th Heaven (or would be if you had written) as I have bought a little dressing table for 650 f: how much is that, darling M? As you're not here to tell me, I am completely at sea; and Vita not much better. We have just had rather a terrific encounter with Valerie Taylor and Mr and Mrs John Balderston[1] who suddenly clapped me on the shoulder and of course I didnt recognise Valerie, and of course she had asked Vita to go abroad this very week with her and of course Vita hadn't written so there were endless explanations. They are motoring to the south, happily, in a Citroen which breaks down every 10 miles, so we shan't meet again I hope. But I rather think Mr Balderston is a playwright. Did I tell you I took the mots to a circus at Saulieu, where there was a gipsy girl on a ladder with a python bound about her head, and 8 lionesses and cubs in a green tent about as big as your greenhouse. The man was going to "dompt" them, with a stick—he was what he called a dompteur but I was too frightened to wait—also from the gimcrack arrangements I thought the whole boiling would be eating the marmots, so we withdrew. The fair was very very lovely—all lights and confetti and people firing guns at rabbits: if you hit one you had the choice of a bottle of wine or a live pigeon.

The Emperor's cook is, as far as being the Emperor's cook is concerned, rather a fraud—he was the scullion of the cook at the Kaiserhof: but the food was astonishing, only came again and again the same, as nobody except ourselves spends more than a night there. All the evening motors drove into the yard as we did, and they were off early. Here there is a sublime view; and tower, churches, old houses, palisseries and antiquaries *ad lib*, as the mots say, but if we dont motor, we shall catch the 3.30 to Vézelay Sermi [Sermizelles] something. God I shall be glad to see you again, am rather fidgeted not to have heard. You will meet me at Newhaven on *Monday* I hope. Then we'll have a day in London on Tuesday. My room last night was 40 fr. and lunch and dinner are about 30f. so you can calculate —which is more than I can do what I spend. So far we have not had to use any English notes.

It is a work of extreme difficulty, writing this letter, as it is rather hot, dusty, a little cloudy, and I have to hold the paper, which I have just bought with 4 envelopes on the edge of my knee. A fine mongrel dog is looking at me, yellow, with a short tail. The donkey population is large and in the highest degree monotonous. I think we are insufferably stupid not to have a house here. Probably we could get a perfect country house for about £20, and the country is superb—very large, rolling, wooded, watered, solitary; and then these delicious towns, with their shops and their restaurants. If I am left a widow I shall live here. But am I left a widow? That is what I ask. It is still only 2.15 so I cant go to the post, and Vita has disappeared—swallowed by Valerie I imagine.

Here is Vita and Valerie—Vita has hired a motor and we are going to drive straight to Vézelay—spend 2 nights there—one at Auxerre, then Dieppe Sunday night and Mongoose, Poos and Pinker on Monday thank

1. The American dramatist and chief correspondent in London of the *New York World*.

God tho' I admit I'm enjoying life, but not at all as much as with you, sweetest heart.

Yr Mandrill

Sussex

1931: To Leonard Woolf   *Avallon [France]*

Telegram
27 September 1928

No letters anxious wire Hotel de la Poste Vézelay

Sussex

1932: To Leonard Woolf   *Hotel de la Poste, Vézelay,*
                                     Yonne [France]

Friday 28th Sept [1928]

Dearest Mon,

I am afraid I must have seemed to you more than usually foolish to telegraph, but there were no letters at Avallon, and as we were coming here, without sleeping, I couldn't hear till Saturday at Auxerre. I wonder what happened? Vita heard from Harold, who wrote on Tuesday, by the first post; and we waited for the second and none came from you. I hope you didn't have to go into Lewes. But I admit I was ready to bother you any amount to be put out of my misery. Your answer came at 8.30 this morning. Mercifully it did, for its a pouring wet day: here we are cooped up in our bedrooms in a clean but primitive, cheap, but well cooking little inn, with Vézelay as black as London in November.

We had a lovely evening yesterday though, and saw the church—a magnificent great church, but too clean, on top of a steep hill, like an Italian hill, with the whole of France beneath, and even two or three little vineyards. Then in the night there was a violent thunder storm; we all crouched in our beds in fear;[1] and this morning the weather seems utterly destroyed. As we have no raincoats we daren't go out; nor should we see anything. So I am going to write to Tom [Eliot] and Saxon [Sydney-Turner] and to Florence Bishop,[2] and perhaps review Julian Hawthorne,[3] who turns out to be rather amusing in a dry way.

1. Vita's diary for 27 September records this event: "In the middle of the night I was woken up by a thunderstorm. Went along to V's room thinking she might be frightened. We talked about science and religion for an hour—and the ultimate principle—and then as the storm had gone over I left her to go to sleep again" (*Berg*).
2. See p. 495, note 2.
3. Review of *Shapes That Pass*, by Julian Hawthorne (*Nation & Athenaeum*, 17 November 1928).

I am extremely well, by the way: Vita is a perfect old hen, always running about with hot water bottles, and an amazingly competent traveller, as she talks apparently perfect French. I don't think we shall quarrel—indeed, I feel more established, now that we pay little attention to the others moods; not that she has many. The truth is she is an extremely nice, kind nature; but what I like, as a companion, is her memories of the past. She tells me stories of the departed world—Mrs Keppel,[1] King Edward, how she stayed with the Rothschilds at Chantilly and they ran over a big dog in a motor car and wouldn't stop because they were late for their polo. Then I tell her the life story of Saxon. Then I cross-examine her scientifically; and ask her what she thinks happens if a motor car in which one is travelling at 50 miles an hour is struck by lightning. She has been told that owing to its rubber tires it is a perfect non-conductor. Then we discuss her lectures on modern English poetry—which by the way, she is ready to let us have for a pamphlet if we like.[2] She thinks Lady Sackville may write me either a violent or a seducing letter about Orlando—may ask me to go and see her, and abuse Vita.

I wonder if Quentin finished the gramophone and what you think of it. I left my address here and may get your letter this evening, more likely tomorrow morning. Vézelay is 12 miles from Avallon, 8, I think from Sermizelles: and thus we are dependent upon motor buses which come twice a day for letters.

I wonder if Lytton was heckled [at Charleston]; whether you have "gathered" as you would say, being such a little prig—no daddies *not* a prig—we adore dadanko do-do—we want to talk with him; and kiss the poos. Have they really begun to play the violin, daddie? Are you fonder of them than of the marmoteski?—Now stop mots; go under the table. I cant hear myself speak for their chatter. How they sobbed when there was no letter from Dinkay at Avallon! Shall you be glad to see us all again? Remember I am coming by the *Monday* boat, not Tuesday: but if you have to go to London I suppose I could get a bus. Lord! how I adore you! and you only think of me as a bagfull of itching monkeys, and ship me to the Indies with indifference!

I think we shall have a very happy and exciting autumn, in spite of the complete failure of Orlando. It is clearing slightly—we may visit the museum.

Yrs Mandrill

D.D.

Sussex

1. Alice Keppel, the mother of Violet Trefusis, was for many years the mistress of King Edward VII.
2. Vita broadcast six talks on contemporary poetry for the B.B.C. between November 1928 and January 1929. The Hogarth Press did not publish them.

Friday [5 October 1928]

Dearest Ethel,

This is a belated attempt to thank you and Nan for being so kind and good to us and sending your car all that way and giving us such a delicious dinner.[1] I had been boasting to Vita of your house and of your food. Happily I had said not enough.

I came home to find an astonishing letter from Lady Sackville asking me to give her a small sum towards her new house. Have you also heard? Vita says she has already got £400 and doesn't mean to build one.

But perhaps this is a secret. Anyhow I hope you will soon come here and let us gossip over the gas fire.

Yours aff
V.W.

Wendy Baron

Sunday [7 October 1928]

Dearest Creature,

It was a very very nice letter you wrote by the light of the stars at midnight. Always write then, for your heart requires moonlight to deliquesce it. And mine is fried in gaslight, as it is only nine o'clock and I must go to bed at eleven. And so I shant say anything: not a word of the balm to my anguish—for I am always anguished—that you were to me. How I watched you! How I felt—now what was it like! Well, somewhere I have seen a little ball kept bubbling up and down on the spray of a fountain: the fountain is you; the ball me. It is a sensation I get only from you. It is physically stimulating, restful at the same time I feel suppled and anointed now—and then, here, in Tavistock Square, hour after hour passes, in rasping chatter. Oh I've seen so many people: talked so much, and woken up shot through the heart in the night by a sense of doom and frustration— I *must* see Clive, Mary, Dadie, Tom Eliot: cant escape: and why, and why?

But what I was about to say was, I have found my spectacles. Leonard says will you dose Pinka for worms. I cant decide what to say to your mother. Oh and if you're coming on Wednesday, let me know in good time.

I am horribly nervous about Thursday[2]—honestly I am—as Lydia

---

1. Virginia and Vita dined at Auppegard with Ethel Sands on 30 September, but spent the night in Dieppe. They returned home on 1 October.
2. The publication of *Orlando*.

would say. And why were you so bad in the summer and never told me?
Your father, I suppose, and that damned old witch [Lady Sackville]—

V.

Berg

1935: To Harold Nicolson   52 *Tavistock Sqre, W.C.*
7th Oct 1928

My dear Harold

I meant to write you a letter of thanks from Auxerre (Vita pronounces the X but you oughtn't to) then I didnt; and again at Rodmell; still I didnt; now at Tavistock I will—though Clive will be bursting in and as it is precisely a fortnight since we met we shall have the whole world to discuss.

But I was going to thank you for having married Vita; and so produced this charming and indeed inimitable mixture—But I wont describe her. I've written quite enough about her and got it all wrong too. (Yes—I'm very nervous about Thursday and Orlando—I'm sending you a copy; but be silent; I shant expect either thanks or praise).

Anyhow we had a perfect week, and I never laughed so much in my life, or talked so much. It went like a flash—Vita was an angel to me— looked out trains, paid tips, spoke perfect French, indulged me in every humour, was perpetually sweet tempered, endlessly entertaining, looked lovely; showed at every turn the most generous and magnanimous nature, even when there was only an old jug in the W.C. and she had lost her keys —in short, it was the greatest fun. Only I wish she were not so humble. It is perfect nonsense that she should think so lowly of her gifts and works. I cant persuade her that the nimbleness of Raymond, shall we say, the brilliance of Clive, and the incorrigible vanity of Virginia are all qualities we should be better without. I wish she would take up her poem again.[1] I wish that old she-devil (if you will excuse me for calling her so) would cease to poison the air of this sphere. and retire above or below, I dont mind which. I speak with some feeling, because I have just had a long letter from her—Lady Sackville I mean—somehow meretricious and unpleasant, though friendly on the surface, asking for a copy of Orlando and "a small cheque or postal order" for her house. What am I to do? If she hadn't written as she did to Vita, I would have stumped up £5 with pleasure: as it is, I feel hostile: I feel she is base and odious: I want to wring her neck.

I'm glad you are soon coming back. This is purely unselfish: I mean

1. See p. 297, note 3.

541

it is simply that I think Vita is not happy without you—She settles in at Long Barn, and has only Valerie [Taylor] who will talk about love incessantly, and Miss le Bosquet[1] who will probably soon mention the same subject. No answer of course needed to this—

Yr ever
Virginia

Berg

---

1. Audrey le Bosquet, Vita's secretary, who had just arrived, and remained with the Nicolsons for many years.

Letters 1936-1977 (early October–December 1928)

The day after Virginia and Vita returned from France, the Woolfs had gone to London until Christmas. On 11 October Orlando *was published. The majority of reviews were ecstatic, and the book sold better than any of Virginia's previous novels (over 6,000 by mid-December), but the opinion she awaited most anxiously was Vita's. She need not have worried. Vita was flattered, enchanted, and did not in the least mind the immediate public identification of herself with the hero-heroine. The success of* Orlando *made Virginia one of the best-known of contemporary writers, and she welcomed, to a point, the lionisation which followed, and the money which enabled her to add two rooms to Monk's House. In October she gave the two lectures at Cambridge which she published as* A Room of One's Own *in 1929, and finished in draft her long article* Phases of Fiction, *which she had laid aside to write* Orlando. *The other literary events of the autumn were the publication of Lytton Strachey's* Elizabeth and Essex, *which Virginia thought shoddy, and the continuing legal battle to save* The Well of Loneliness, *which ended in failure.*

1936: To Margaret Llewelyn Davies

52 *Tavistock Square*, W.C.1

Sunday Oct 7th [1928]

Dearest Margaret,

We are only just back and in a state of great chaos, so we shant attempt to come up this Sunday. But perhaps next week end—Saturday afternoon? —would that suit?

I agree it is shocking the length of time that passes—but I put it down to your habits, not mine. About the lecture on Tolstoi no NO NO Haven't I let myself in to go to Newnham and Girton [Cambridge] this month? And I am determined that these shall be my swan songs. I can't bear lecturing; it takes ages; and I do it vilely; and though I would do it for you, if for any human being—no, I can't. I can only advise Morgan Forster who lectures like an angel. Also, why do people want lectures? I wouldn't go, not if I were paid, to hear one.

Well, will you ring up sometime and settle a tea party. I've been in Burgundy to see the vintage, and never saw a vine; but I am convinced that we must all live in France.

543

Yes, Orlando is about to appear—but I dont believe in Margaret reading what I write. I'd much rather she didn't.

So goodbye till Saturday

Yrs V.W.

Could you lend me a copy of your Aunt's life,[1] for my lecture—we'll fetch it.

Sussex

1937: To Helen McAfee   52 *Tavistock Square, W.C.1*

Typewritten
7th Oct. 1928

Dear Miss McAfee,

I am so sorry you had the trouble of cabling. I am still more sorry to say that I dont see how I can possibly post the manuscript by October 25th. I have come back to find all sorts of things waiting to be done before I can start my Burney article. I think therefore I must hope that you will let me send it later and give up the idea of publishing it here in December. I will aim at sending it you early in December and if you will let me know when you will publish it, I will arrange about publication here. I am sorry to have been so changeable.

Yours very truly
Virginia Woolf

Yale University

1938: To V. Sackville-West   52 *Tavistock Square, W.C.1*

Friday [12 October 1928]

What an immense relief! I was half sick with fright till your telegram came.[2] It struck me suddenly with horror that you'd be hurt or angry, and I didn't dare open the post: Now let who will bark or bite; Angel that you are—But I'm rather rushed: and wont write, except this line. Sales much better. Enthusiasm in the Birmingham Post [Mail]. Knole is discovered. They hint at you.

1. Sarah Emily Davies (1830-1921), a pioneer campaigner for women's suffrage and education, and founder of Girton College.
2. Virginia sent Vita a copy of *Orlando* on publication day.

But look here—give me cold and considered criticism some time:[1]

We shall turn up about 11.30 or so—on Sunday—not lunch—in fact only 5 minutes, but you're coming on Tuesday

Berg

1939: To V. Sackville-West   52 *Tavistock Square, W.C.*1

Monday [15 October 1928]

Here is your mother [on *Orlando*]—milder than I expected.[2] But Heaven knows what she means.

I shan't answer. Perhaps you'd bring it back to add to my collection.

Might I beg some Saviour's flannel or rabbit ear—? only a few sprays, if you have any, and it aint too much bother.

Tomorrow then

V.

Berg

1940: To Helen McAfee   52 *Tavistock Square, W.C.*1

Typewritten
15th Oct. 1928

Dear Miss McAfee,

I am so sorry that you had again the trouble of cabling to me. I hope by this time you have had my letter. I am afraid that I cannot commit myself to write the article for any definite date. I have had to postpone it here too. I cannot at present get the time that I need for reading the books I want to read for it; nor do I feel sure when I shall be more at leisure.

Thus I fear I must leave it that I will let you know as soon as I can be certain. But I am extremely sorry that my half promise led you in any way to alter your plans. I am afraid that I must have been more optimistic than I had a right to be.

Believe me,

yours sincerely
Virginia Woolf

Yale University

1941: To Lady Ottoline Morrell
                    52 *Tavistock Square, W.C.*1

Oct 15 [1928]

Dearest Ottoline

Well but what is the criticism? It is all very well being heavenly, charit-

1. See Appendix for Vita's letter to Virginia.
2. But see Letter 1945.

545

able, and seductive, but I'm sure you have an asp up your sleeve which will take one bite—But when? My whole life is ravaged by having to go twice to Cambridge and speak. When that is over, next week, some time, then I hope for a cup of tea and a little poison.

However, I admit I was made very happy by your liking Orlando— At the same time, I'm reading Katherine Mansfields letters and feel desolated by them. What a waste!—and how wretched it is—her poverty, her illness —I didn't realise how gifted she was either. And now never to—but you will know all I mean. I never knew that she had been so intimate with you.

Are you better? Really better?

I have Philip's umbrella.

Many many thanks

Yr
Virginia

Texas

1942: TO VANESSA BELL   52 *Tavistock Square, W.C.*1

[16? October 1928]

Dearest Dolphin—blue nosed Dolphin—

it is entirely your fault, and Clives and Louies and Angelicas—They said you were coming Saturday last, Monday this, Tuesday today, and now you say Thursday.[1] So I thought I should miss you if I wrote or sent Orlando. But of course I pant for your opinion—the only one that has a grain of sense in it—you can't think what a fool's paradise I live in at the moment. But let us meet on Thursday in Gods name—here or at 37—I saw Angelica—She came to tea—cold almost gone—seemed in the highest spirits—fascinating—lovely—we had a most amusing tea—but she adores Leonard—This annoys me.

Lord! London is lovely; but the hubbub intolerable—Whatever you may say; I'm taking a site near Brantôme—cant endure even Sussex—We went to Rodmell for 2 hours—in come Hayward[2] and a prostitute—Now I'm off to Sibyl to meet Noel Coward, with whom I am slightly in love— Why?

But with you I am deeply passionately, unrequitedly in love—

B.

1. Vanessa was on her way back from a short stay at Cassis.
2. John Hayward, the critic and bibliographer, whom Virginia and Leonard had met in May 1925, when he was an undergraduate at King's, Cambridge.

and thank goodness your beauty is ruined, for my incestuous feeling may
then be cooled—yet it has survived a century of indifference.
I left a silk handkerchief given me by Nelly at the Londres [Hotel, Paris]
I suppose they haven't got it?

Berg

1943: To Hugh Walpole   52 *Tavistock Square, W.C.*1
21st Oct [1928]

My dear Hugh,
    I am ashamed—letters come from you that are charitable and charming
and full of things I like: and I swallowed them down—never say thank
you. But this may be a compliment—feeling sure that you wont take it
ill, for as it seems to me I have been perpetually doing necessary or dull
things, and could never find a moment to be merely loquacious.
    I am very glad that being in Orlando's preface did not annoy you. It
is very good indeed of you to be so generous about it. I am deep in your
debt, deeper and deeper.
    But what I am now writing to ask is, could you dine with us on Tuesday
6th Nov—7.45 without dressing, as before? This will have to go north
and then back to London, as I don't know your address. But I hope you
may manage it.
                                            Yours ever,
                                            Virginia Woolf
Texas

1944: To V. Sackville-West   [52 *Tavistock Square, W.C.*1]
Monday [22 October 1928]

    I'm so sorry old Squire annoyed you.[1] But I dont think he ought to.
And as for being angry with *him*—no, no, no. It was my fault largely—I
had a hit at him, which was silly.
    The sales are good—A very nice letter from Eddy.
                                            Yr
                                            V.

A thousand thanks for the rabbits ears. The only thing I should mind

1. In his review of *Orlando* (*Observer*, 21 October 1928), J. C. Squire called the
   book 'a pleasant trifle'.

547

about Squire is this—that it would make you or Harold[1] think less well of me or Orlando—But it wont, will it?

Arnold Bennett will be far worse than Squire—so be prepared.

P.M.

We've got to reprint—

Berg

1945: TO EDWARD SACKVILLE WEST

52 *Tavistock Sqre.* [*W.C.*1]

Oct. 22nd 1928

My dear Eddy,

I am immensely relieved that you like Orlando. I was rather worrying to think you probably wouldn't—and it is extremely nice of you to write. I think I agree about The Lighthouse—in fact I'm sure I do. It is for the moment the fashion to tell me Orlando is better. But The Lighthouse interested me more and troubled me more—and I enjoyed writing this more—and it rushed off like a rocket, which is not to say how brilliant it is, only how quick it went. Tell me, someday, with your wonted precision and destruction—qualities I so much value, (what I call your taking a line—) what offends you, and where I've bungled, and if its like Vita and if its like Knole etc. Oh yes, I'm overjoyed that you like it. A bitter letter from your Aunt at Brighton, has put a touch of quinine in my cup. She says its a *cruel* book;[2] but then I never sent her a cheque or postal order, as she asked, for her roof tree. I have been waiting for the American copies to come to send you what you so rightly demanded—a three guinea copy.

But they never came. At last, 4 weeks late, one miserable specimen, on pale green paper bound like a widows hymn book, has arrived. I dont

1. Harold's reaction, by telegram from Berlin on 13 October, was: "Orlando has filled me with amazed excitement. I feel deeply grateful to you Virginia for having written something so lovely and so strong." And in a letter to her of 15 October: "It really *is* Vita—her puzzled concentration, her absent-minded tenderness . . . She strides magnificent and clumsy through 350 years". (Both *Sussex.*)

2. Lady Sackville wrote: "You have written some beautiful phrases in Orlando, but probably you do not realise how *cruel* you have been. And the person who inspired the Book, has been crueller still." (14 October 1928, *Sussex.*) In her own copy of *Orlando* Lady Sackville pasted a photograph of Virginia and wrote alongside it: "The awful face of a mad woman whose successful mad desire is to separate people who care for each other. I loathe this woman for having changed my Vita and taken her away from me."

think you can wish for this; so I'll wait for the white paper ones, and send you what I trust may be less cadaverous. The Americans have surpassed themselves, in pretention, fuss, and incompetence.

This is only an Orlando letter. I wont embark on life and love, both of course teeming in Bloomsbury—Raymond silhouetted this evening in a white shirt doing his hair as I went by in the dark and the rain. And Clive fresh from Paris, and Duncan and Nessa back, and I lunching with Colefax to meet Noel Coward.

When shall I see another wad of diary? And did you enjoy the Tcheko-Slovakians? And are you writing? Of course you are, but what, and in what frame of mind? And reading? And thinking? What?

Any time you write, let it be a long letter full of a sort of tangle of everything, which I can browse upon, over my gas fire . . . making you up in Berlin—

Yr loving
Virginia

Berg

1946: To Julian Bell   52 *Tavistock Square* [*W.C.*1]
Typewritten
Thursday Oct 25th 1928

My dear Julian,
    I hope to turn up about five tomorrow, Friday, either with Vita, or without Vita—as she catches her train, or doesn't. And look forward to another tea.

    But now to the poems. I think the first nature poems still suffer to some extent from your old disease of crowded detail, so thick one cant see the whole.
            Of men and cities gathered in a war
is to me an agreeable change from
            And on black boughs in gold green foliage drops, etc
and the following lines. I think I see signs that you are changing your method, however, and I shall assume that you are now trying to con-glomerate words, like mosaic chips, together. Very well. But this method which is vivid and stark and has many advantages over fluent melody, asks extreme exactness, and more attention than you seem ready to give to sound. For example:
            Down winding narrow valleys seep unseen
            Trickles that slowly creep, to feed their depth
All those ees, seep, unseen, creep, feed, are ugly, I think, rather than descriptive. But I think that you carry out your idea very successfully sometimes. Still Life is one of the best and it is a very interesting attempt,

very pictorial, and I like the unpoeticallity (that is not the way to spell it) of the subject. I think that

Cool, heavy, porous, brown and white

is a very good line. It does what your very crowded, heaped, lines dont do. It is written at a little distance from the object. The variations on a Nursery Rhyme and an old Song are charming, but not very serious. The ones I like best and think most interesting are the Experiments in Association at the end. I like Ecbatana best. That seems to me to do its job very well— to transpose so that one gets the idea more vividly, more truly, than by actual transcription. Is that your idea? I think you might do more in that line with advantage. I like the odd combination of incongruous emotions, and the flickering angularity of it.

I am writing at a disadvantage with interruptions from Mrs Cartwright and Leonard. Clive's book [*Civilisation*] is coming out and doing very well.

I shall be seeing Desmond on Tusday, or Teusday, or Tuesday, and will ask him what in Gods name he is doing with your things. But he is worse than a sieve, a drain, a wastepaper basket, and amiable into the bargain, so that one gets nothing done, as with a crusty character. Nothing but smiles and promises.

If you want to make money to buy desks, I strongly advise you to write a political article and send it to Hubert Henderson at the Nation. I dont say he would take it straight off, but I think they are on the look out for some young politician, and might take an article now and then, which is much better paid than poetry. Also, I know your reviews were well thought of. Of course dont be too violent. Why not write something about politics at Cambridge? give an idea what the young are saying at the Union, or in private.

But we will talk of this tomorrow. Write more poems. I think they are very interesting.

Your affectionate and obedient

Virginia

[*in Virginia's handwriting:*]
This spelling is the spelling of a Portable Underwood not mine.

Quentin Bell

1947: To V. Sackville-West   52 *Tavistock Square, W.C.*1
Thursday [25 October 1928]

I think I must go by the 3 from Kings Cross, as I have promised to talk to Julian about his poetry—and you know what poets are—and this is the only train early enough.

But obviously its absurd for you to spoil Sibyls lunch party. She would foam with rage. So if I dont see you at Kings X at 3. I shall expect you to turn up at Kings: The porter will show you Julian's rooms. And Julian is agog to see you. Damn Sibyl and her lunch parties. Damn Girton and speeches.

Talking of idiotic reviews, your's in the Lit. Sup today was the limit[1]—some poor wretch who had mugged up a little history and wanted to show off.

Rebecca West has come out strong about Orlando.[2]

But we can talk about all this in the watches of the night at the Lion.

V.

Berg

1948: To Pernel Strachey   52 *Tavistock Sqre.* [*W.C.*1]

[25 October 1928]

My dear Pernel,

Julian said he would 'love' it if you asked him to tea—indeed it would be a kind act, and he is very talkative and merry.

A thousand thanks for our entertainment, and I now remember with pleasure (this is the outcome [?] of the disease I spoke of) the kind things Miss Strachey said of me—which I do little deserve.

Yrs aff

V.W.

You will I hope look in at Christmas.

And now you must pull yourself together, entertain the [Gilbert?] Murrays and bury Jane.[3]

Strachey Trust

1949: To Enid Bagnold   52 *Tavistock Square, W.C.*1

28 Oct 1928

Dear Lady Jones,

I came in from dining out the other night and found so cryptic a post-script from Claridges on my table with only an illegible initial to it abusing Jack Squire that I felt that the voice of God was speaking, and very likely

1. Vita's *Twelve Days: An Account of a Journey Across the Bakhtiari Mountains in South-west Persia* was published on this day by the Hogarth Press.
2. Her review was in the *New York Herald Tribune* of 21 October. She called it 'a poetic masterpiece of the first rank'.
3. Perhaps the memory of Jane Harrison, who had been a lecturer at Newnham.

551

Jack Squire was being roasted that instant. Next day your letter came, and I see with pleasure that it was Lady Jones and not God. Lady Jones writes, I think, better than the deity. I must say it was the most amusing and pleasing letter that I have yet had about Orlando, for, not only does it say what is to me very flattering, but says it so sharply and distinctly, and describes the situation at North End House so clearly and brilliantly that I cant help thinking how well *I* must write, if Lady Jones can like it. And I begin wanting to know about Mrs Elliot and who she was, and why she died in the bed at North End House; and whether the ghost of Burne Jones walks there:[1] in fact all sorts of questions rise in me.

But I won't ask them, for indeed I am as stupid as an owl, and only write to thank you very much for your letter. How very nice it was of you to write it, and I think to myself with wonder, could she really have liked Orlando as much as that? And the wind howls over the downs, and thin windows shake.

Yours,
Virginia Woolf

Enid Bagnold

1950: To Hugh Walpole   52 *Tavistock Square, W.C.*
Sunday [28 October 1928]

Dear Hugh,

A certain article on a Certain new book faces me.[2] Dare I add certain letters to your O-? Can I take to myself so much praise? I know I've no right to it, and yet I admit that I have wrapped myself round it, and refuse to be robbed of it. I wear it like an ermine fleece to protect me from the blast. But (except for Squire) they have been rather nice—the blast, I mean; only not so nice as you. How so rapid and various, and generally gifted and busy and successful a man can yet be so generous on such a large scale, I cant conceive. Seriously, I am more than grateful, and very proud into the bargain. Dont you, after all, share my passion for Waverley?— and lots of other things.

But I was writing about lunch on *Tuesday*—it is settled that it is Tuesday, I hear. I am trying to put someone off. If he is put off, as I hope to hear

1. North End House, Rottingdean, where Enid Bagnold lived, had belonged to Edward Burne-Jones. Mrs Elliott had owned Gothic House, next door to North End House, and Roderick Jones, Enid's husband, joined the two houses after Mrs Elliott's death.

2. In the *Morning Post* on 25 October, Hugh Walpole ecstatically reviewed *Orlando* under the title *On a Certain New Book*, without mentioning the name of the book or its author because he felt that posterity would not need to be reminded of either.

tomorrow, may I come, all the same, 1.30, Tuesday Oct 30th? I will let you know for certain. But tell me if you have changed your plans. Otherwise dont bother to write.

Again, please be thanked by yours ever

Virginia Woolf

Texas

1951: To Lady Cecil   52 *Tavistock Square, W.C.1*

Oct 28th [1928]

My dear Nelly,

It was very charming of you to write, and I assure you with my hand on my heart, if that is the correct position, that my motives in dragging you so impudently into my preface (Violet [Dickinson] says she doesn't like keeping such low company at all) were honourable affection, gratitude, esteem: Ought I to have asked your permission?

Why is Orlando difficult? It was a joke, I thought. Perhaps a bad one. I don't know. But I enjoyed writing it, and I should enjoy still more answering any questions about it, if put in person. I wont trust to the ink pot or the telephone. No, we must meet.

I had hoped somehow this summer that this would be accomplished. I still hope it, now that winter is here. Or shall I write a book about *you* next? What fun that would be! But writing about you won't do in place of seeing you. I am going to see your nephew next week, I think, Lord David. We shall talk about you. I shall tell him stories of the Grove End Road, and how you wore a particular white dress, and we used to sit in a window and there were branches across it, and you had a cat that ate the skin of turbot, and you were perfectly enchanting.

"But", he will say "she is still". Then he will tell me what you're like now. But just to anger him, I shall say that Nellie Cecil 20 years ago was better better far than any other Nelly. Think of us discussing you over my gas fire next Wednesday.

Ever affly
Virginia

And what have you been reading lately? And what is your opinion of ——— Everything in the whole world?

Hatfield

553

1952: To C. P. Sanger   52 *Tavistock Square, WC1*

[October 1928]

My dear Charlie,

It is very good of you to write—especially when I had taken such liberties with your venerated name (which I do seriously venerate).[1] Orlando was meant as a joke; and I daresay it gives a view of life which is not at all my own—if it gives a view of life at all. But I was having a holiday, and I am very glad that it amused you, when I am sure you are always seeing thousands of things which are not amusing. I feel somehow that I ought to apologise to people like yourself for scribbling these books. They sometimes seem to me to have no bearing upon anything that is really happening.

But I won't apologise any more; and hope some day we may see you. I'm so glad about Gavelkind.[2]

Yr affate
Virginia Woolf

Daphne Sanger

1953: To Dora Sanger   52 *Tavistock Square, W.C.1*

Tuesday [October 1928]

Dear Dora,

How nice of you to write—how delightful of you to like Orlando! I am so glad you do, because I remember you were made melancholy by the Lighthouse.

I hope Charlie didn't mind my using his name—it was a great support to me—and we were so sorry to be away when he came. I hope we may see you both soon.

Yours ever
Virginia Woolf

Daphne Sanger

1954: To Quentin Bell   52 *Tavistock Square, W.C.1*

Typewritten
1st Nov. 1928

My dear Quentin,

I quite agree that it is a dereliction on your part not to have written— Didnt I give you for nothing a nine shilling book [*Orlando*]? Not a word

1. In the Preface to *Orlando* Virginia wrote that she was "indebted to Mr C. P. Sanger, without whose knowledge of the law of real property this book could never have been written".
2. A law of inheritance, peculiar to Kent, which divided an intestate's property among all his sons. Virginia mentioned it in *Orlando*.

of thanks. Not a bark of criticism even. So this hidous [sic] typing of mine is an unsolicited act of purest mercy dropping from the azure on the coal black head etc of a nephew who don't deserve it. It is true you wrote a few lines once upon a time. If you could do without typing, many's the letter you'd get. But it means sitting high, on a chair, at a table, with cold hands, away from the fire. And then you'd never believe what a sterilising fracturing bone-cracking backaching effect on the style the typewriter has. No, for you dont know, being only a painter, what style is; what words are: nor mind more breaking the back of a sentence than snapping a flea.

I have been twice to Cambridge and given two lectures and seen Julian all in plus fours, brown, hairy, country-gentlemanly pouring out tea to his friends. He is a little shy, but very quick and hospitable. The grate is blocked with tin covers. He is however by no means as confident of immortality and happiness as we were at his age. The truth is there's no one to beat down in argument. They talk love where we talked God. I think our age though ossified was of the two the more sublime. But Julian has still many years before him. Only Cambridge will never be to him what it was, even to me. Oh the sound of Grace coming through Adrian's windows in Nevilles court [Trinity College] in the summer when we were young! But no more. You will laugh.

But what are you doing? I hear you are being attached to various studios. Yes. But life? How many old men, young girls, youths in blouses, have you seduced? What are you doing at this moment? Please be wildly indiscreet. And then I will be. At this moment our thoughts centre upon Sapphism—we have to uphold the morality of that Well of all that's stagnant and lukewarm and neither one thing or the other; The Well of Loneliness. I'm just off to a tea party to discuss our evidence.[1] Leonard and Nessa say I mustn't go into the box, because I should cast a shadow over Bloomsbury. Forgetting where I was I should speak the truth. All London, they say is agog with this. Most of our friends are trying to evade the witness box; for reasons you may guess. But they generally put it down to the weak heart of a father, or a cousin who is about to have twins.

Are you reading? No. Painting? Yes, all day. Roger is away, Clive gives parties at which each guest has a whole partridge, so that the waste of partridges legs is something heartbreaking. Legs upon legs are piled all around. Enough, they say, to keep the crossing sweepers of Bloomsbury in affluence till March. Now dearest Quentin write please, and I will answer by return. I have been madly busy; fingers worn to the bone. People to

1. The meeting was held in the studio of Clough Williams Ellis, the architect. Among those present were Virginia, Vita, Bernard Shaw and Rose Macaulay. Virginia was prepared to give evidence on behalf of the book, but on 9 November, the magistrate ruled that such evidence was inadmissable, and the novel was declared obscene on 16 November.

see every day. Americans, Germans. Never a moment worth throwing to a dog till now. But write me a long long loving letter.

Yrs
Virginia

Quentin Bell

1955: To Hugh Walpole   52 *Tavistock Sqre, W.C.*1

Sunday [4 November 1928]

My dear Hugh,

I didn't have a chance of putting your point to the [*Well of Loneliness*] meeting, which went on interminably and I had to leave in the middle. But what I am really writing to say, or to ask is, is there any chance of our having that book about the historical novel from you?[1] Can you possibly give us a date? Am I being too persistent? If so, say so. It is only that we very much want it.

Yours ever
Virginia Woolf

Texas

1956: To Lady Ottoline Morrell
52 *Tavistock Sqre* [*W.C.*1]

[early November 1928]

Dearest Ottoline

Would Thursday next about 5 suit you? If it does, dont bother to answer. Cambridge is over, but the Well of Loneliness is in full swing. I have to appear in favour of it, and have already wasted hours reading it and talking about it, but I hope to be free on Thursday. The dulness of the book is such that any indecency may lurk there—one simply can't keep one's eyes on the page—

Yr
V.

Texas

1957: To Julian Bell   52 *Tavistock Sqre.* [*W.C.*1]

[early November? 1928]

My dear Julian,

I saw Desmond yesterday who thinks very well of your poems and

---

1. In 1930 Walpole's *The Historical Novel* was announced as forthcoming in The Hogarth Lectures on Literature, but he never completed the book.

essay and hopes to do something with them (I dont know what this means). I think you had better write and ask him yourself.

Congratulations on your speech[1] and on being on the right side for once.

Yr Virginia

Quentin Bell

1958: To V. Sackville-West   [52 *Tavistock Square, W.C.*1]
Monday [12 November 1928]

Friday suits perfectly (only say what time—3.30 in studio, unless I hear to the contrary)

Providentially, I had just put off Sibyl.

Lord! What a curmudgeon you must think me!—you write as if you were a dog that had been hunting. But you're not a bad dog; you're a good dog; you needn't go under the table. How could you not be with Harold?

I shall be alone here, I think, on Thursday night, but I suppose you have to go back after seeing Harold off.[2]

I hope you get your rooms [in London]. I want to be given lobsters and crumpets there, as Clive used to give them, 20 years ago

V

in hurry, but lovesomely all the same.

Berg

1959: To Vanessa Bell   52 *Tavistock Square, W.C.*1
[15 November? 1928]

Dearest Dolphin;

Leonard and I were going to give you a moleskin coat for Christmas. But it seems silly to wait. So I'm sending you a small cheque, with the request that you will go *at once* and get it, and so save further colds. Stagg and Russells is the shop in Leicester Sqre—where I got mine, and it is the delight of my life.

So dearest Dolphin go at once.

B.

1. Perhaps at an Apostles meeting.
2. His father, Lord Carnock, had died on 5 November, and Harold returned to Berlin on the 15th.

[in Leonard's handwriting:]
Personally, if you do not carry out our wishes in this respect with your usual Stoicism, (I know you wont want to, but Stoics always do what they dont want to do, when it is their duty) I shall never speak to you again. So be a Stoic.

Leonard

[in Virginia's handwriting:]
We were so exhausted by George and Florence [Bishop] that we couldn't come in, but hope to see you soon and give full details.

Berg

1960: To Lady Ottoline Morrell

52 *Tavistock Square, W.C.*1

Friday [16 November 1928]

Dearest Ottoline

I can't come today, but could tomorrow, Saturday, about 5 if that suited you. I didn't come last week being in a rage with the world—Lady Cunard etc etc. and so shut myself up.

How do you manage not to hate everyone?

But I don't hate you—its this chatter chatter

Yr
Virginia

Texas

1961: To V. Sackville-West   [52 *Tavistock Square, W.C.*1]

Monday [19 November 1928]

Dearest,

Here's a letter from Eddy, and a draft of an answer to your Uncle.[1]

I should be greatly obliged if you would give me your opinion and any suggestions etc. I don't know if I ought to mention you, but I did think that you had thanked Lord Sackville—however, I ought to have done it—I'm very sorry: and yet, how could I have put him in the preface, or your father? Surely it wd. have been out of keeping

When shall I see you? Would you send the letters back.

V.

Berg

1. Edward Sackville West had complained that 'Mr S. W.' in *Orlando* might be mistaken for him; and his father, the new Lord Sackville, complained that the Knole pictures in the book had been used without his permission, although Vita had obtained it from her father before his death.

558

1962: To Edward Sackville West

52 *Tavistock Square, W.C.*1

21st Nov. [1928]

My dear Eddy,

All right. I have written a humble letter of apology to your father and sent him a copy of the Edition de luxe.

Mr S.W. was, (if anybody) Sydney Waterlow. How could it have been you?

Lord, Lord, why does one write books!

Yr
Virginia

Berg

1963: To V. Sackville-West   52 *T.[avistock] S.[quare, W.C.*1]

22nd Nov. [1928]

Would you, if its convenient, bring the puppy on Tuesday and then we might arrange to meet later—after your broadcasting. And, then all Wednesday I'm free—(for you: no one else, damn their souls) And (do you like sentences that begin with And?) we are going to have another biscuit tea party at Nessa's on Tuesday; so flee from Ethels which will be far too refined, and come to us. We had Hugh [Walpole] last Tuesday and he was much liked. That is the correct phrase for Hugh.

I've written Eddy one short sharp bark—what a housemaids mind he has, always thinking one 'means' him. And I've written a smooth silky letter to your Uncle. But I dont believe he minded—not if he's a man of sense, and not a niminy piminy housemaid. And tomorrow I have to go to Bow Street and stand surety for £40 for Jonathan Cape.[1] And then to Rodmell for Saturday night; back on Sunday. Youre *my* Towser, not Molly's [MacCarthy] Towser: Why go to tea with her?

Berg

1964: To Quentin Bell   52 *Tavistock Square, W.C.*1

22nd Nov 1928

My dear Quentin,

This is going to be written in such a hand that even you—even *you*—can read it. Because it is perishing cold and damp, and to sit at my typewriter is to become a polar bear rapidly drifting to destruction upon a block of ice. Even to please you I will not become a desolate she-bear.

1. The publisher of *The Well of Loneliness*.

I was much interested by your letter. I think we were arguing about sex. You have discovered you are sexless. Good God, how merciful! I am sure Bloomsbury is dull to extinction all because it will assume that life lives solely in those parts.

Up at Cambridge the young men all gossip, Julian says, and no one argues. No one tries to create or to destroy. We went up for Lydia's dance,[1] and the Keynes'es surpassed themselves in sharing one partridge among 70 guests—that is, they never paid Nessa and Duncan a penny; but it is all for the glory of art of course. Julian stands in the middle of the room like a church in the Strand. People pass under his arms.

I have been most frightfully busy doing silly things like writing to a gentleman in Peckham who wishes to know what authority I have for making dahlias flower in the reign of Charles the Second. And I have been to tea with 2 dozen, or perhaps even a gross of old ladies who want to know if my nephew Quentin is as clever as his Aunt. I raise my eyebrows. We will go and call on Ottoline together. She will pull your head down on her pillow. But as a relic—as something swept up on the beach after the defeat of the Spanish Armada she is admirable.

Nessa and I have been giving some little parties. We talk about life and eat biscuits till 2 A.M. Clive is very gloomy and thanks God for death. What is the use of life he says when one has a bald patch the size of a half crown on the top of ones' head? No virgin can love one again. Then we all look at Clives bald patch and he turns crusty and abuses us in French. But dont tell him; he would have out his rifle and murder me—all because of a virgin and bald patch on the top of his head.

Lytton's book is out tomorrow, and shops in the Strand are plastered with advertisements. I am not going to read it, because in that way I shall wear a glory round my head. There goes a woman what aint read Essex and Elizabeth the street urchins will say and the rumour will reverberate down Lambs Conduit Street.

I hear you are coming back to decorate Crichton Stuarts[2] rooms—Is that ail he expects you to do? Pardon me if I am too romantic. Come and see me—no, dont if you are in a hurry. We might see life together—that is go to the London Museum in a taxi: then have an ice at Gunters and so home to 37 to discuss life with dear old Roger, but he's away still.

Write an answer, and admit that my old crones hand—I am very old and talk in a husky whisper about my pains in my joints—is as clear as day.

Your loving
Aunt V.

Quentin Bell

1. Lydia Lopokova acted and danced in Rylands' production of Milton's *Comus*, for which Vanessa and Duncan had designed the scenery.
2. The report was inaccurate.

1965: To Daphne Sanger   52 *Tavistock Square, W.C.*1

Thursday [November? 1928]

Dear Daphne,

It was extremely nice of you to write. I am so glad you like Orlando
in spite of its being so untrue. However I agree with you that truth is not
very important in that particular book. I'm afraid I never thought about
going on a donkey to Broussa. By that time I was not bothering my head
at all to be accurate. Of course I am fond of the Country—don't you
remember how shocked I was by you and your father at Rodmell? But
it was very clever of you to see this in Orlando: I meant it to be there.

Thank you again for troubling to write.

Yours
Virginia Woolf

Daphne Sanger

1966: To V. Sackville-West   52 *T[avistock] S.[quare, W.C.*1]

Sunday [2 December 1928]

So you are just back [from Oxford] I suppose, it being after dinner,
and I had mine alone. What a good letter you wrote me! Do you know I
think about your writing with interest? All your feet seem to be coming
down on it now, not only the foreleg. Very few people interest me as
writers; but I think I shall read your next poem with care.

And I like the way you stand up resolute in the full flood of Tom's
[Eliot] and Reads:[1] a British Grenadier. I forget what I was going to say
now—something frightfully exciting, something that hit me between fore-
head and hair this afternoon: about Chaucer, it may have been. I am scraping
the slime off, the Cunards, the respectability of it all, reading Troilus, by
Chaucer. Thank God I still have the remnants of a mind to grate upon:
I've not read a thing, except as a bird flies through a bush, since Rodmell.
But I forget what I was going to say. I'm coming on Thursday, just as the
lamps are being lit in Sevenoaks, so that I can see you in the fishmongers
in a red jersey holding a paper bag, rather heavy and damp. Full of smelts.
And then we turn up the lights in your room, and I get into my chair and
you—ah well—too soon over, thats the worst of it. And I make it sooner
over by my terrific sense (aged 46—thats what it does) of the flight of time,
so that these moments are seen by me flying, flying; almost too distinct to
be bearable. I discovered that in Burgundy; and could not invent any way
of dimming my own eyes, which are, sometimes, too bright, aren't they?

1. Herbert Read (1893-1968), the poet and critic of literature and art. The Hogarth
   Press had published some of his early work. Vita was in despair about the
   distance which separated her own poetry from the moderns.

Couldn't we drop something into time to make it thick and dull? Lord—
but I must go round to Nessa instead of gossiping here: must brush my
hair; and Clive will say now Virginia tell us all the news. And the news
is we are coming to Berlin on the 15th January; but that I will talk about
on Thursday: but lets arrange it properly on Thursday: there must be one
perfectly empty compartment about Vita's poetry.

Coming down with all her feet at once—thats what I like in a writer.
Desmond shuffles, and I'm a jumper: never mind, I'll think it over and tell
you.

Lord! what a pleasure you are to me

Yr
Potto

Berg

1967: To Roger Fry   52 *Tavistock Square, W.C.*1
4th Dec [1928]

My dear Roger,

I have been going through the fog in a kind of ecstasy today—with a
luminous nose, perhaps—because of your letter [about *Orlando*]. Nothing
has given me so much pleasure, as, for reasons I will tell Helen one day
(when we're alone) I venerate and admire you to the point of worship:
Lord! you dont know what a lot I owe you!—About details you may be
wrong, but I agree entirely with what you say about the end. I got tired
and headachy and couldn't bring it off all in one fling, as I should have
done, and so had to write it over, and it got hard, where it should have
been all a rush and left in the air. But all the rest was great fun. I'm vaguely
in treaty with a French professor who wants to translate it, but Mauron
would be much better of course.[1]

But this is only a scrawl to thank you—not that I ever do thank you,
or express a thousandth part of the devotion I have for you—but that's
Helen's fault—devil take the woman!

Yours affly
Virginia

I had seen your pamphlet[2] and enjoyed your part—and entirely agree.

Sussex

1. Charles Mauron's French translation of *Orlando* was published in 1931.
2. Probably his introduction to R. R. Tatlock's *Port Sunlight Lady Lever Art
   Gallery: A Record of the Collection of English Painting from XVIIIth to XXth
   Century* (1928).

1968: To Edward Sackville West

52 *T.[avistock] S.[quare, W.C.*1]

9th Dec. 1928

My dear Eddy

What can I have said that makes you think I "wish to quarrel with you", and 'take things so seriously'? I can't conceive, though my habit of writing letters in a hurry is disastrous. I was afraid *you* were taking things seriously; but I hope, at any rate as far as your father is concerned, that you exaggerated—Anyhow here is his letter—perhaps merely polite, but I hope not, as I should be very sorry to annoy him—still more, you. If you had told me of Mr S.W. before, I would have altered it in the 2nd Edition; but it was too late. If there's another chance I will do it—so now I hope I have given no more signs of being annoyed or wishing to quarrel—but I'm terrified of letter writing: worse than writing books; all one's meanings get wrong; for which reason—and again I'm in a hurry—I'll end with the end of this page,

With love
Yr
Virginia

Berg

1969: To V. Sackville-West   [52 *Tavistock Square, W.C.*1]

Friday night [14 December 1928]

Dearest Creature,

I was very much upset to think you had been angry (as you said)) that I didn't go to the bloody womans trial[1]—(and yet I rather like you to be angry) Idiotically, I thought they would wire to you; and I rang up as early as I could this morning to ask you to lunch: and you'd gone—And then you were angry. And then I was wretched. And I waited all the afternoon for you. And I had lunch for you. And now you're off in the bitter black night with female unknown;[2] fresh, or stale and scented rather, from the arms, to put it euphemistically, of Mary—God! What a succession of flea bites and bug bites the life of a respectable hard working woman is!

And now Leonard has cut up rough about my having Elena[3] to tea on Tuesday if I lunch out and dine with people. So I won't ask Elena; and then again you'll be angry. But the truth is I've been rather headachy with rather a cold (both very mild) but, then, my life is all these easements

1. The appeal against the banning of *The Well of Loneliness* was heard on this day and disallowed.
2. Hilda Matheson, Talks Director of the B.B.C.
3. Elena Richmond, wife of Bruce Richmond, Editor of the *TLS*.

and dodges, not to my liking at all · but there—there—enough said on that point

The gist of the matter is that you'll turn up at 1.5 punctual on Tuesday and we'll lunch somewhere; and you shall take a carving knife to me if you like.

And we'll perhaps get to the bottom of this wretched affair—human friendship.

I rather wanted to see Elena too.

And I'll tell you about Max Beerbohm.[1]

Poor Potto—with a cold, crying, because Vita's angry.

V.

Berg

1970: To Angus Davidson   52 *Tavistock Square, W.C.*
Dec 22nd [1928]

My dear Angus,

A thousand thanks, though it is very wrong of you—for the honey, it lent a great lustre to our tea last night—I am, as they say, a very bear where honey is concerned.

We are sending you a small slice of Orlando,[2] which I always feel owed a great deal to you, and I hope it may come in handy for something or other.

There is poor old Cartwright toiling away (3.30 on Saturday) to find out how she can have spent 5/- more in coin and received 2/6 more in stamps (it may be the other way round) than she should. Nothing I can say is in the least help.

Well—our blessing for the new year, and may you soon be sitting in authority at the National Gallery.

Leonard sends his love.

Yrs
V.W.

Angus Davidson

1971: To Lytton Strachey   52 *T[avistock] Sqre [W.C.1]*
Xmas day [1928]

It was the greatest relief, getting your letter, dearest Lytton. I was so

1. Virginia had just met Max Beerbohm for the first time, dining with Ethel Sands. He had written to her in December 1927 to compliment her on *The Common Reader*, but complaining that her novels did not tell a story in the traditional manner.
2. A cheque for £10 or £20.

afraid I had said only commonplace things.[1] One can't say the things that matter—and it all seemed rather unreal.

She was very real to me,—oddly so, seeing how little I saw her; and I keep thinking of her. She used to descend upon me sometimes in Fitzroy Square and talk about you.

Love and blessings
Virginia

1972: To Lady Ottoline Morrell

52 T.[avistock] Sqre [W.C.1]

Boxing Day [26 December 1928]

Dearest Ottoline

What a wizard of an enchantress you are!—The difference between the two being that a wizard is wily and the other merely delightful—You cursed all present giving and then send me round the one thing I coveted (you had one on your table) so late at night that nothing could be done in retaliation. What an odd inspiration on your part! So much did I like your green smooth knife that I stopped in Oxford Street (buying a 3/6. present for Vivien Eliot) and looked if I could find one: naturally not. Heaven knows where you find things; even tinsel and silver braid are all dipped in fairy light.

But this shall always cut all my books.

And I cant think of anything to send you—and we go away tomorrow and shall be more or less away till the end of January: but then I shall come, I hope.

But do keep as happy as enchanting and lovely—

V.

1973: To Vanessa Bell

[Monk's House] Rodmell
[Sussex]

Thursday [27 December 1928]

Dearest Dolphin:

You are a bad beast—to hang my ears so magnificently Really they take my breath away and confer on me the lustre of a doomed Empress. I shall be shot and my body thrown into the Volga (river in Russia) if I wear them—A good riddance, you will say. But it was an astonishing

---

1. Virginia had written an obituary of Lytton's mother, Lady Strachey, who died on 15 December (*Nation & Athenaeum*, 22 December 1928).

inspiration, as I had only my red rings and specially coveted a pair of white ones. Being your choice, too, as Marny would say, makes them Quite Perfect—But if you shower ear rings, how will you educate Angelica? Bad wicked blue-nosed Dolphin—If you want to change your gloves and shoes by the way, Lafayette will do it.

I was enraptured by the account of Seend which is in its way masterly. The accounts in the dining room, the Keys—the lavatory: all my skill never produces that effect—We had a cloistered Christmas, in some ways: no posts; and the mercy of no proper keeping up; but we saw a good many odds and ends—Koteliansky, Roger, Gumbo, Gerald—Roger is the only civilised man I have ever met, and I continue to think him the plume in our cap; the vindication, asseveration—and all the rest of it—If Bloomsbury had produced only Roger, it would be on a par with Athens at its prime (little though this will convey to you) We dined with him, and came away—fed to the lips, but impressed almost to tears by his charm.

I gather that Pippa and Gumbo [Strachey sisters] don't hit it off. She said rather sourly that she didn't propose to live with Pippa. They will have about £200 each—but I daresay you've heard all this from Lytton.

We came here this evening and I am at present in the exalted state of the newly veiled nun. None of my friends and relations counts a straw. A large fire; books: peace; nobody to talk to—But [George] Kennedy arrives at 9.30 tomorrow, and stays the night, so there we shall be again tongue wagging. Still I am vastly excited about the building:[1] and will you have my chairs and things begun when I come back? I forward a letter from Dottie which I hope means that she has plunged.

I saw Ottoline and fell deeper and deeper into those sea green waters, till indeed the ancient carp, Philip to wit, turned up at Tavistock late at night with a jade paper knife, which I promptly broke.

B.

It strikes me with horror in the night that Angelica is the last child in the family. For Gods sake, consider how she can be stunted.

Berg

1974: To Hugh Walpole   *Monks House, Rodmell,*
                                          Lewes [Sussex]
29 Dec [1928]

My dear Hugh,
    Here we are rather chilly but on the whole happy and it becomes possible to write a letter. No sooner have I said this than Mrs Bartholomew

1. The Woolfs were planning an addition to Monk's House.

the village char appears and says the King refuses nourishment and Mrs Woolf has been mentioned on the wireless. Leonard has a bet about the King—£1 that he dies before Jan 1st[1]—so our excitement is great. Poor man—I cant help feeling that everyone wants him to die, merely to see black horses and plumes in Piccadilly. And in 10 minutes Mr Kennedy will be here, the gifted but almost inarticulate architect, to advise about adding a room to the cottage. This room will be called Orlando, and one window will be dedicated to St Hugh. It is financed by Orlando; and without St Hugh, should I have sold ten copies? But this reminds me of the—well I wont mention names since doubtless they are friends of yours: people of blameless character, good fathers, devoted husbands, who talk about royalties and sales; which in Bloomsbury, as you used to think, we dont. (This sentence is grossly ungrammatical, but the char is running in and out with blankets. She has been left £320 by an aunt; and has bought a set of false teeth and wireless: hence our news of the King. But she has broken into the current of my mind, and how to continue I know not—)

We shall go back next week, and then go on a family tour to Germany. Vita has promised to show us night life in Berlin; my sister and Duncan Grant have it on their conscience that German galleries should be visited. Leonard wants to hear every opera ever written. I shall go to a thing called the Planetarium (or some such name) where you see the stars as they are —so imagine us at our different occupations, meeting to drink at intervals, coffee, beer, all wrapped in rugs and bearskins for it is said you can't shock the Germans by uncouthness—and then we all come home again and start life afresh in February.

Shall you be in London? If so, come and dine.

(Here another interruption: old Moore [Almanac] has a picture of sentries at the palace and a deaths head in January.) Here's the architect too.

Yrs V.W.

Texas

1975: To Nan Hudson

Monk's House, Rodmell, Lewes [Sussex]

Saturday [29 December 1928]

My dear Nan,

Of course the choice of poems was deliberate,[2] and shows I think that in spite of your hedgehog character I have crept between the spines. Do you agree?

1. King George V had been desperately ill since 21 November. He was not expected to live, but he recovered and did not die until January 1936.
2. Virginia's Christmas present to Ethel and Nan.

567

How on earth you continue to send me the exact presents I want—gloves, from Ethel—a penwiper from you; and also to get them, the penwiper at least, embossed into the bargain—Heaven knows! It is a gift which goes with truffles, home craft, cookery, charm—all the inscrutable things which I associate with you.

Here we are in the depths of the country—heavenly after London: no telephone, nothing but a large fire and Pinker drowsing in an arm chair.

Your desk is the joy of my life. Will you give my love, thanks, blessing to Ethel, whose letter has just come, and hand on to her this cheque, which I was writing that second, and say that I shall be in Germany on the 18th but Francis Birrell thought they might lunch earlier—but it dont matter. And I hope to see you both before we go.

Yr
Virginia

Wendy Baron

1976: To V. Sackville-West   *Monk's House, Rodmell,*
Lewes [Sussex]
29th Dec. 1928

That wretched Potto is all slung with yellow beads.[1] He rolled himself round in them, and can't be dislodged—short of cutting off his front paws, which I know you wouldn't like. But may I say, once and for all, presents are not allowed: its written all over the cage. It spoils their tempers—They suffer for it in the long run—This once will be forgiven: but never never again—The night you were snared, that winter, at Long Barn [18 December 1925], you slipped out Lord Steyne's paper knife,[2] and I had then to make the terms plain: with this knife you will gash our hearts I said and the same applies to beads.

But I forget what I was about to say. We are sitting by the fire. Pinker snores like an old cook with a bad leg. Like a cook with white leg (wasn't that the joke at Gordon Square?) Leonard is furious, because a lamp I gave him to heat the motor wont screw up or down. He shakes it; he curses. Long long ago I should have thrown it to the ground. But the pertinacity of the Jewish race, to which we owe so much—Xtianity, among the rest (I had meant to write out a list, but Lord!—how ignorant I am) will not suffer him to give over; he is as a terrier worrying a very large rat which has him by the nose.

You never write to me, and your image has receded till it is like the thinnest shadow of the old moon: but just as Vita was about to vanish, a

1. Vita had given Virginia a string of amber beads as a Christmas present.
2. Vita always supposed that the character of Lord Steyne in Thackeray's *Vanity Fair* was based on her ancestor, the Duke of Dorset.

thin silver edge appeared, and you now hang like a sickle over my life again: thats why I am writing to you, hurry scurry, for Nelly'll be in with our gammon and eggs in a minute, instead of reading M: Maurois for an article, which, Mrs Nick, will be printed in England France and America, simultaneously—Why do I boast? Nothing impresses you. The truth is I boast because I'm modest. The sales of Orlando went very nicely till the end. Now they'll stop. Did you like my champagne party?[1] I was so proud of it. But I thought it made my dear Dadie red-nosed coarse and quarrelsome: Vita sails over champagne like a racing cutter: all sails, all flags, all bowing and curtseying. But then Vita has the blood of the Sackvilles in her, which is made of—which reminds me: Eddy. *His* blood is not his strong point. It's his damned aristocratic thin-blooded, bubbly prickly weakly temper that annoys one; so would you hand on to him, tactfully, (for I cant be bothered to write another letter and be snubbed for it) that we can't meet [Kurt] Wagenseil? Charming, virtuous, accomplished as Wagenseil is, it is to avoid Wagenseil that we come to Berlin—Yes Vita: we come to Berlin. It is still true; that moon increases. (Honestly, if I look out of the window, I see a moon among the apple trees: and there is an owl on my two big trees. God! We had the architect yesterday and the builder and I spent two hours in the attics, and we're planning rooms for me, rooms for Leonard; and a cabinet de toilette for Vita. The luxury etc. combined with the refinement etc. of Long Barn.) How are you? By the way (but this'll need a new sheet, and theyre double bed sheets, there, fit for Long Barn on a summer's night a June night with Ethel Smyths nightingales[2] whistling in the syringas by the swimming pool) by the way, Julian, my nephew, came out with a great burst of enthusiasm for The Land the other night. He said its frightfully good, he thinks; one of the best modern poems; the sort of poetry he likes; so solid; and she knows it all; and she has a sense of words; and she's honest; and thank God she doesn't imitate Tom Eliot; and I think her a real poet; one of the few now writing; and don't let her write like Tom Eliot; let her write like The Land again—all of which was so genuine and fervent I blushed and said well why don't you write and tell her? and he blushed and said he couldnt write to Vita (he calls you Vita very naturally, which rather pleases me)

Nelly is stumbling with the eggs in the kitchen, so I will hastily say that I have finished Troilus and Cressida (by Chaucer) and see now that long poems are the only things I want to read—Next Spenser; then Daniel; then Drayton, and so on, down one long long road after another, to

1. A party given by Virginia and Vanessa on 18 December, the night before Vita left for Berlin.
2. Virginia had seen Ethel Smyth, the composer, at a concert in 1919, but they did not become friends until 1930. Vita knew her well, and in June 1927 took her to Long Barn to hear the nightingales.

Cowper, whom I suspect of hidden divinities unnumbered, to Crabbe; and then?—Well Vita, you must be ready to lead me by the hand into daylight. It is perfectly true that I cannot read War and Peace now with any gusto or enchantment; yet 20 years ago, lying in bed one summer, I was enthralled and floated through week after week; and have lived in the recollection and called Tolstoi the greatest of novelists ever since. Not a patch on Chaucer! So what's to be done? What? What?

Virginia

P.S.

It is now Wednesday the 3rd of January 1929: and I find this rather incoherent letter still lying about: Shall I send it? Tolstoi has risen again.

Vita's moon is full. But its true that the image of ones loves forever changes: and gradually (you know how I like noticing physical symptoms) from being a sight, becomes a sense—a heaviness betwixt the 3rd and 4th rib; a physical oppression: These are the signs writers should watch for. Love is so physical; and so's reading—the exercise of the wits.

I do hope the spleens and the chills have left you. Both are—I was going to say prevalent here; but no: I am light headed at the moment; why, heaven knows. I have been walking alone down a valley to Rat Farm, if that means anything to you: and the quiet and the cold and the loveliness—one hare, the weald washed away to vapour—the downs blue green; the stacks, like cakes cut in half—I say all this so excited me; and my own life suddenly became so impressive to me, not as usual shooting meteor like through the sky, but solitary and still that, as I say—well how is the sentence to end?: figure to yourself that sentence, like the shooting star, extinct in an abyss, a dome, of blue; the colour of night: which, if dearest Vita you can follow, is now my condition: as I sit waiting for dinner, over the logs.

[Audrey] Le Boski writes to say how much she misses you. And then you pretend the woman is all typewriter within! all wires and ribbon, for writing your business letters on. No—Next month she will be flinging herself on your hearthrug. A tap at the window. Bosqi will be there—you see it all, dont you? And then a hurried removal.

I have not the face to write another double bedded sheet.

Do you really love me? Much? passionately not reasonably?

We go back tomorrow.

V.

Berg

1977: To V. Sackville-West   *Monk's House, Rodmell*
                                      [Sussex]
31st Dec. [1928]

Please be an angel and let me have one line on receipt of this to say how you are. I've just got your letter, sent on, and feel rather bothered as you say casually you've had a sort of influenza—You know how one worries about people abroad. So do, dearest, let me know any fact—ridiculous as it may seem to you; and if you are perfectly recovered. Gastric influenza was it? I've just seen someone afflicted thus: but hope you are not the same:

I wrote a long long letter two nights ago, and then found I had no address; but I will send it; It is rather dismal here—the weather. Snow and rain and cold, and we crouch over the single fire, and read and read. Lord I wish I were less fond of you! I hate being anxious: I hate being away. And why were you so splenetic? Haint you got Harold? So what do Potto and Virginia matter?

We go back to Tavistock on Thursday so write there. A long, long letter please. I hope you valued my self restraint in sitting still and not seeing you out of the door the other night.

The beads: yes; I like the beads: But no no—I wont be given things. In the very long letter I wrote all this is explained.

This is a very short letter; asking only for an answer, to say how you are.

If I dont hear, I shant sleep; then I shall get a headache; then I shant be able to come to Berlin:

So you see Love, love: and its the last day of the year by the way.

P

Berg

Appendix

FROM VANESSA BELL TO VIRGINIA WOOLF
On first reading "To the Lighthouse"

May 11 [1927]   *Villa Corsica [Cassis,*
                                        France]

My Billy,

So I am forgiven—what a relief: Even your stony and reasonable heart would be touched I think if you knew how anxiously I looked for a letter. But I was going to write to you even if you didnt forgive me, asking for a snub though it would be. All my pride was humbled and I was eating dust at your feet in any case and all owing to The Lighthouse.

I dont flatter myself that my literary opinion is really of any interest to you and it would be difficult or impossible to give it to you in a nutshell. In fact I think I am more incapable than anyone else in the world of making an aesthetic judgment on it—only I know that I have somewhere a feeling about it as a work of art which will perhaps gradually take shape and which must be enormously strong to make any impression on me at all beside the other feelings which you roused in me—I suppose I'm the only person in the world who can have these feelings, at any rate to such an extent— so though probably they dont matter to you at all you may be interested to know how much you did make me feel. Besides I daresay they do show something about aesthetic merits in your curious art of writing. Anyhow it seemed to me that in the first part of the book you have given a portrait of mother which is more like her to me than anything I could ever have conceived of as possible. It is almost painful to have her so raised from the dead. You have made one feel the extraordinary beauty of her character, which must be the most difficult thing in the world to do. It was like meeting her again with oneself grown up and on equal terms and it seems to me the most astonishing feat of creation to have been able to see her in such a way. You have given father too I think as clearly but perhaps, I may be wrong, that isn't quite so difficult. There is more to catch hold of. Still it seems to me to be the only thing about him which ever gave a true idea. So you see as far as portrait painting goes you seem to me to be a supreme artist and it is so shattering to find oneself face to face with those two again that I can hardly consider anything else. In fact for the last two days I have hardly been able to attend to daily life. Duncan and I have talked about them, as each had a copy, whenever we could get alone together, Roger too furious at being out of it for us to be able to do so when he was there. I

572

dont think it is only that I knew them though that makes me feel all this, for Duncan who didn't know them says too that for the first time he understands mother. So your vision of her stands as a whole by itself and not only as reminding one of facts.

But I am very bad at describing my feelings—I daresay you'll understand.

Then of course there is the relationship between the two, which perhaps is more your subject—but it is so mixed with the other that one can't feel only one alone. But that too is complete and seemed to me to be understood and imagined as a whole.

I agree with Leonard, I think it is your best work—you see I can't quite avoid an opinion. I know that in spite of all my personal interest I shouldn't have been moved as I was if it hadn't moved me impersonally too, only at the moment I dont feel capable of much analysis. I am excited and thrilled and taken into another world as one only is by a great work of art, only now also it has this curious other interest which I can't help feeling too.

I daresay you'll think all I've said nonsense. You can put it down to the imbecile ravings of a painter on paper. By the way surely Lily Briscoe must have been rather a good painter—before her time perhaps, but with great gifts really? No, we didn't laugh at the bits about painting—though I'm a little doubtful about covering paints with damp cloths, but it *might* be done. But how do you make Boeuf en Daube? Does it have to be eaten on the moment after cooking 3 days?

[The remainder of the letter deals with other matters]

Your VB

Berg

FROM V. SACKVILLE-WEST TO VIRGINIA WOOLF
On first reading "Orlando"

Oct. 11th 1928

Long Barn, Weald,
Sevenoaks [Kent]

My darling,

I am in no fit state to write to you—and as for cold and considered opinions, (as you said on the telephone) such things do not exist in such a connection. At least, not yet. Perhaps they will come later. For the moment, I can't say anything except that I am completely dazzled, bewitched, enchanted, under a spell. It seems to me the loveliest, wisest, *richest* book that I have ever read,—excelling even your own Lighthouse. Virginia, I really don't know what to say,—am I right? am I wrong? am I prejudiced? am in my senses or not? It seems to me that you have really shut up that "hard and rare thing" in a book; that you have a complete vision; and yet when you came down to the sober labour of working it out, have never lost sight of it nor faltered in the execution. Ideas come to me so fast that they trip over each other and I lose them before I can put salt on their tails; There is so much I want to say, yet I can only go back to my first cry that I am bewitched. You will get letters, very reasoned and illuminating, from many people; I cannot write you that sort of letter now, I can only tell you that I am really shaken, which may seem to you useless and silly, but which is really a greater tribute than pages of calm appreciation,—and then after all it does touch me so personally, and I don't know what to say about that either, only that I feel like one of those wax figures in a shop window, on which you have hung a robe stitched with jewels. It is like being alone in a dark room with a treasure chest full of rubies and nuggets and brocades. Darling, I don't know and scarcely even like to write it, so overwhelmed am I, how you could have hung so splendid a garment on so poor a peg. Really this isn't false humility; *really* it isn't. I can't write about that part of it, though, much less ever tell you verbally.

By now you must be thinking me too confused and illiterate for anything, so I'll just slip in that the book (in texture) seems to me to have in it all the best of Sir Thomas Browne and Swift,—the richness of the one, and the directness of the other.

There are a dozen details I should like to go into,—Queen Elizabeth's visit, Greene's visit, phrases scattered about, (particularly one on p. 160 beginning "High battlements of thought, etc" which is just what you did for *me*), Johnson on the blind, and so on and so on,—but it is too late today; I have been reading steadily all day, and it is now 5 o'clock, and I must catch the post, but I will try and write more sensibly tomorrow. It is your fault, for having moved me so and dazzled me completely, so that all my faculties have dropped from me and left me stark.

One awful thought struck me this morning: you didn't, did you, think for a second that it was out of indifference I didn't come to London yesterday? You *couldn't* have thought that? I had got it so firmly fixed in my head that Oct. 11th was the day I was to have it, that I was resigned (after all these months) to wait till then. But when I saw it in its lovely binding, with my initials, the idea rushed into my head and utterly appalled me. But on second thoughts I reflected that you could not possibly so have misunderstood.

Yes, I *will* write again tomorrow, in a calmer frame of mind I hope—now I am really writing against time—and, as I tell you, shaken quite out of my wits.

Also, you have invented a new form of Narcissism,—I confess,—I am in love with Orlando—this is a complication I had not foreseen.

Virginia, my dearest, I can only thank you for pouring out such riches.

V.

You made me cry with your passages about Knole, you wretch.

Berg

Index

time, 75; 'sepulchral voice', 94; publishes V.'s *Mr Bennett*, 106, 109-110; on V.'s fiction, 107*n*; Essays on Dryden, 107, 128; row with Murry, 108; at Garsington, 116*n*; *The Sacred Wood*, 129; remains at bank, 169; wants a cottage, 170, 173; *New Criterion*, 203-4; *Waste Land* reprinted by Faber & Gwyer, 204*n*; behaves like 'infuriated hen', 209; publishes V.'s *On Being Ill*, 220; abused by Murry, 238; visits Monk's House, 298; death of his wife's father, 367; *Fragments of an Agon*, 413; becomes Anglo-Catholic, 448; V. talks to about God, 455, 457-8; Vivien talks oddly, 508; *mentioned*, xviii, 37, 71, 80, 103, 156, 226, 310, 380, 505, 569

Letters to: Nos. *1397, 1466, 1468, 1470, 1472, 1495, 1577, 1597, 1802*

Eliot, Vivien (first Mrs T. S. Eliot), 12, 26, 38, 48, 52, 63, 110*n*, 170, 204, 508, 565

Elizabeth and Essex (Strachey), 242, 454, 496, 560

Elton, Charles, 443*n*

Elwes, Miss, 84

Endfield, D. E., 418, 489

Etang, Chevalier Antoine de l', 280*n*, 472

Eton College, Windsor, 273

Fairbanks, Douglas, 250

Farrell, Charles, 286

Fass, Marjorie, 81

Femina Vie Heureuse Prize, 337*n*; V. wins for *Lighthouse*, 338, 446, 479, 489; 'dog-show prize', 491; prize presented, 491-2, 495, 498

Ferguson, Inez, 509

Ferrier, Susan, 192*n*

Fielding, Henry, 153

Fisher, H. A. L., 9*n*, 146, 217, 375

Fisher, Aunt Mary, 146, 205, 318

Flecker, James Elroy, 4*n*

Fontcreuse, Cassis, 473

Forster, E. M. (Morgan): in Cambridge, 39; will not write for *Nation*, 43; lectures on India, 53; *A Passage to India*, 115; alone understands V.'s fiction, 189; stays with Hardy, 238; 'limp and damp', 266; V.'s article on, 321, 343, 384; time-table, 332; on

friendship, 352; at Rodmell, 420; corresponds with V. on *Aspects of the Novel*, 437, 438-9; likes Julian Bell, 439; at Cassis, 497; *The Well of Loneliness* case, 520, 530; a good lecturer, 543; *mentioned*, 185, 475

Letters to: Nos. *1832, 1835*

Forum, The, 193, 217, 397*n*

France: V. loves, 23, 25; V. in Paris, 29-31; at Cassis, 175-7, 477-83; in Normandy, 404-7; with Vita in Burgundy, 533-41; V. wishes to live there, 537

French language: V.'s ignorance of, 23, 29, 30; 'pining to speak', 134; taking lessons, 138; example of V.'s writing in French, 216; talks French to L., 304; V. envies, 417; more lessons, 438*n*, 467, 469, 472, 475

French literature: Benjamin Constant, 10; Rimbaud, 29; Proust, 39, 166; Giraudoux, 130; Valéry, 137, 145; Madame de Sévigné, 192; de Stael, 233; Gide, 309

Freshfield, Mrs Douglas (Augusta), 6

Freshwater (V.'s play), 61, 67, 72-3, 75

Freud, Sigmund: Hogarth Press publish works of, 119, 133; V. on, 134-5

Fry, Margery, 386, 419

Fry, Pamela, *see* Diamand, Pamela

Fry, Roger: invitation from Brenan to Spain, 28-9; one-man show, 29; ill in Nancy, 38; V. on his painting, 40; in Spain with VB., 42*n*, 50, 56; unjealous, 51; loves VB., 67; *A Sampler of Castile*, 68-9; 'gets richer and suppler', 80; *Duncan Grant*, 87, 133; tragedy of Josette Coatmellec, 110*n*; in France, 122; *The Artist and Psycho-Analysis*, 132-3; 'not a born painter', 150; on Raverat's painting, 154; at Karin Stephen's party, 168; growing surly, 187-8; on *Mrs Dalloway*, 189; at Pontigny conference, 208; translates Ronsard on train, 209, 212; does not need company, 209; accident to, 216; at Charleston, 225; at Sargent show, 229; in General Strike, 260; V. on his painting again, 271; *Transformations*, 317; with Sibyl Colefax, 331; 'improved vastly', 340; Helen Anrep, 341, 452, 454, 456; lectures, 354;

young Oxford admires, 372, 386; admires *Lighthouse*, 385-6; V. intends memoir about, 386; takes up meteorology, 419; lectures again, 453; does V.'s portrait, 457; lionized in London, 467; at Cassis with V. and VB., 480; giving up painting?, 496; on *Orlando*, 562; V.'s devotion to, 562; 'only civilised man', 566; *mentioned*, xviii, 2, 6, 25, 26, 252, 258, 475, 493 Letters to: Nos. *1380, 1390, 1420, 1488, 1498, 1583, 1764, 1967*

Furse, Charles, 256
Furse, Katherine, 489
Furst, Herbert, 34

Gage, 6th Viscount, 407, 476, 515
Gaige, Crosby, 308, 510n. Letter to: No. *1695*
Galsworthy, John, 25n
Garland, Madge (Lady Ashton), 463, 501
Garnett, David ('Bunny'): son born, 6n; *Lady into Fox*, 27n, 54; awarded Hawthornden Prize, 55; bookshop, 73, 122n, 327n; *A Man in the Zoo*, 74n; V. praises, 99-100; V. dispraises, 120; runs Square Club, 153; Colefax orders books by, 179; V. on *The Sailor's Return*, 212-13; *Go she Must!*, 332, 335
Letters to: Nos. *1377, 1408, 1427, 1459, 1523, 1634*
Garsington (Ottoline Morrell): V.'s visits to, 45, 50, 116, 278
Garvin, J. L., 260
Gates, Barrington, 298
Gathorne-Hardy, Robert, 185
Generalife (Granada), 26
General Strike (1926), 259-62
Genoux, Louise, 344, 352
George V, King, 567
Georgian Poetry, 1n
Germans and Germany, 364, 460, 567
Gide, André, 309
Gilchrist, Mrs, 265
Giraudoux, Jean, 130n
Gissing, George, 30-1
Glasgow, Ellen, 409
Goddard, Mrs, 443
Godrevy Lighthouse (St Ives), 310
Goldenveizer, A. B., 18n
Goldsmith, Margaret (Voigt), 473n, 485, 487-8, 494, 497

Goldstucker (Mrs Woolf's first husband), 525
Goodman, Victor, 269
Gosse, Edmund, 15, 234, 242, 254, 260, 344, 356, 372, 412
Gottschalk, Laura, *see* Riding, Laura
Gould, Gerald, 251
Granada, Spain, 25-7
Grant, Major Bartle, 84, 99, 103
Grant, Mrs Bartle, 77, 99, 329, 467. Letter to: No. *1458*
Grant, Duncan: stays in Monk's House, 27, 33; in Spain with VB. and Fry, 42n, 56; successful exhibition, 51; reads *Freshwater*, 72, 75; character in 1923, 77; book by Fry about, 87, 133; decorates Tavistock Square, 88, 95, 97; his father dies, 99; his sympathy, 102; Charleston character, 103; transvestite ballet, 120; 'Dunciad', 152; accepts society patronage, 158; 'august and austere', 187; 'humming with happiness', 209; 'creamy grace', 216; pleasure in life, 237; 'living with' VB., 241; exhibits, 265, 270; decorates Hutchinson house, 266; talkative in youth, 270; V. on his painting, 271, 274; suspected typhoid at Cassis, 317-18; recovers, 329; 'great genius', 350; painting at Cassis, 358; 'marmoreally chaste', 363; V. invents his talk with VB. about *Lighthouse*, 375-6; exhibits, 377; 'androgynous', 381; on *Lighthouse*, 383; 'painters highminded', 400; first occupies Cassis villa, 452; V.'s new character for, 478; life at Cassis, 480; does V. really know him?, 486; if V. had married him, 490; another exhibition, 498-9; *mentioned*, 13, 18n, 34, 236, 254, 573
Letters to: Nos. *1758, 1896*
Graves, Robert, 36, 226
Greece, 310, 326, 339
Greek Literature, 80, 186, 191, 364
Gregory, J. D., 460n
Greville, Fulke, 516
Greville, Ursula, 343
Grigg, Maurice and Elsie, 312
Grizzle (dog), 119, 167, 226, 245-6, 249, 253, 264, 294
Grosvenor, Mrs Norman, 39
Grubb, G. H., 313-14. Letter to: No. *1702*

585

Squire, J. C. ('Jack'), 19n, 41, 260, 297, 394, 547, 552
Stagg, Mrs, 411
Stawell, Melian, 143
Stein, Gertrude, 87, 198, 209, 268, 269-70
Stephen, Adrian: mental state, 43; *Freshwater*, 72, 75; in Gordon Square, 84n; temporary estrangement from Karin, 92-3; at Monk's House, 134, 137; separated from Karin, 144; reunited, 265, 377; work as psychoanalyst, 381; lackadaisical, 500; as former undergraduate, 555
Stephen, Anne, 134
Stephen, Caroline Emelia, 63n, 101-2, 496
Stephen, Dorothea, 324
Stephen, Sir Herbert, 318, 324
Stephen, Julia (V.'s mother): see *Lighthouse, To the* for Mrs Ramsay; V.'s memory of, 383; VB.'s memory, 572
Stephen, Karin (Mrs Adrian Stephen): on Adrian's mental state, 43; in Gordon Square, 84n; estrangement from Adrian, 92-3; in Italy, 105; character, 137, 156; separated from Adrian, 144; reunited, 265; gives party with V., 156, 160, 164-5, 168; operation for deafness, 216; her sterling qualities, 377; to live in America?, 496
Stephen, Katharine: death and funeral of, 121n, 122, 124, 126, 182
Stephen, Sir Leslie (V.'s father): Hardy on, 37, 283; mountaineering, 126; walks with V., 247; Mr Ramsay in *Lighthouse*, 374, 379, 572
Stephen, Thoby (V.'s brother), 152, 180, 259
Stephens, James, 469
Sterne, Laurence, 308
Stevenson, R. L., 201, 211
Stillman, Lisa, 380
Stokes, Adrian, 365
Stoop, Bertha and Frank, 467
Stopes, Marie, 6
Strachey, Alix, 76, 77, 363, 377
Strachey, James, 77, 119n, 265, 502
Strachey, Lady, 565
Strachey, Lytton: V. asks to contribute to *Nation*, 14; visits Brenan in Spain, 23; 'poor article', 36; gets RSL medal, 43; Carrington and Partridge, 51, 65; imitated by H. Nicolson, 62; buys

Ham Spray, 77, 105; *Books and Characters*, 94-5; satirised by Wyndham Lewis, 108; moves to Ham Spray, 122; relations with Carrington and Partridge, 129-30; V. sends bill to, 141; love for Philip Ritchie, 160, 335; at Karin's party, 164, 168; loves Angus Davidson, 182; on *Mrs Dalloway*, 189; on *Common Reader*, 206; V.'s relations with, 213; praises V.'s *On Being Ill*, 236; V. lunches with, 242; at Charleston, 294; conversation, 330; Roger Senhouse, 335, 343, 351; his homosexuality, 342; on Clive, 383; desperate about Senhouse, 384, 448, 451; his influence, 418-19; *Portraits in Miniature*, 454; *Elizabeth and Essex*, 242, 454, 496, 560; his mother dies, 565; *mentioned*, xviii, 18n, 21, 40, 332, 496, 539
Letters to: Nos. *1360, 1424, 1454, 1465, 1509, 1530, 1580, 1615, 1733, 1807, 1971*
Strachey, Marjorie ('Gumbo'): at Bloomsbury party, 6; gossip about, 103; character, 144, 468; at Charleston, 186, 277; *The Counterfeit*, 381, 386; upset, 489, 566
Strachey, Oliver, 300, 315, 317, 448, 509
Strachey, Pernel: Principal of Newnham College, 61, 126; V.'s view of, 62, 126, 470; *A Room of One's Own*, 516-517
Letters to: Nos. *1415-16, 1492, 1869, 1914, 1948*
Strachey, Philippa ('Pippa'), 103, 144, 470, 566. Letter to: No. *1841*
Strachey, Rachel ('Ray'), 380
Strachey, Ralph, 381n
Strachey, Richard, 350
Strep, Mrs, 39
Studland, Dorset, 70, 76
Sturgeon, George and Flora (Woolf), 67, 523, 526
Summer Fields, Oxford (school), 346
Swanwick, Helena, 464
Swinnerton, Frank, 529n
Sydney-Turner, Saxon: to opera with V., 39; in Spain with Fry, 50-1, 52; rents Hogarth House from Woolfs, 82, 90, 93, 122; 'diplomatic, fastidious', 122; ancestor's memoirs, 186, 286;

holiday with Vita in France, 520-1, 533n; his mother's chatter, 523-6; pertinacity, 568
Letters to: Nos. *1382, 1648, 1926-8, 1930-2*
Woolf, Marie (L.'s mother), 197, 523-6
Woolf, Philip and 'Babs', 248, 273, 526
Woolf, Sylvia, 524
Woolf, Virginia
Life (main events only; summary of this period, xvi)
1923: writing *Mrs Dalloway*, 1; organises T. S. Eliot fund 7-8*ff*; has flu, 5-6, 8, 10, 12; Katherine Mansfield's death, 5, 8, 9, 17-18; Twelfth Night party, 6; tries to obtain Lit. Editorship for Eliot, 11-12*ff*; visit to Gerald Brenan in Spain, 23-29; in Paris, 30-2; progress with *Mrs Dalloway* and *Common Reader*, 32, 36; visits Garsington, 44-5, 50; Cooperative Guild, 53-4; sets type for *The Waste Land*, 56; decision to leave Hogarth House, 61; visits Lytton Strachey, 65; writes *Freshwater*, 67, 72-3, 75; stays in Dorset with Keynes etc, 70, 76
1924: move from Hogarth House to Tavistock Square, 82, 94-6; meets Vita again, 85-6; *Mr Bennett and Mrs Brown*, 99, 106, 108; lectures at Cambridge, 108-9, 114-15; first visit to Knole and Long Barn, 118; Bloomsbury party, 120; 'rather famous', 130; opinion of Vita's *Seducers*, 131; 'almost done' *Mrs Dalloway*, 133; finishes it, 147; Christmas at Monk's House, 149, 151
1925: sends Raverat *Mrs Dalloway* proofs, 154, 163; gets flu, 157, 161; misses Karin's party, 164-5, 168; Raverat's death, 171-2; holiday at Cassis, 175-7; to Cambridge, 181-182; *Common Reader* published, 182; *Mrs Dalloway* published, 183; writing stories, 185, 187; begins *To the Lighthouse*, 189; taken ill at Charleston, 197-8; planning four more books, 202; lectures on reading, 211, 236-7; ill again in London, 221; beginning

of love-affair with Vita, 223-4; Christmas at Charleston, 225
1926: flu again, 227; German measles, 228; Vita leaves for Persia, 231; V. misses her dreadfully, 231, 237, 241; writing *Lighthouse* fast, 232, 235; holiday in Oxfordshire, 243; holiday in Dorset, 252; General Strike, 259-62; Vita returns, 264; on VB.'s painting, 270-1, 274-5; headaches, 272; Vita to Rodmell, 275; visits Robert Bridges, 278; writes about Julia Cameron, 278, 280; visits Hardy, 281; to Long Barn, 281-2; summer at Monk's House, 284; on Vita's *Passenger to Teheran*, 290-1; depressed, 294; 'finished' *Lighthouse*, 296; retyping, 299; to Long Barn again, 300-301; again, 305-6; Christmas in Cornwall, 308-12; invited to U.S.A., 311, 313
1927: second visit to Knole, 307n; Harold 'not jealous', 316; Vita goes to Persia again, 319; weekend with Webbs, 319-20; involved in end of Bell-Hutchinson affair, 319-20, 322-4, 327-8; misses Vita, 325, 332, 352; *Phases of Fiction*, 325; helps raise fund for MacCarthy, 327-8, 330; typical day, 330; hair shingled, 334; *Lighthouse* proofs, 332; more journalism, 344; idea for *Jessamy Brides*, 344; 'a precipice marked V.', 352; journey to France and Italy, 358-368; *Lighthouse* published, 372n; idea for *The Waves* (The Moths), 372; lectures at Oxford, 374-5; at eclipse in Yorkshire, 377, 382; illness, 387; to Long Barn, 394, 397-8; 'come then' telegram to Vita, 391-2; buys car, 397; broadcasts, 397n, 403; driving-lessons, 400-1; stays with Ethel Sands in Normandy, 404-7; loved by Philip Morrell, 404, 408, 441; journalism for America, 416; Laughton Place, 420; starts *Orlando*, 427, 428-9; visits Knole again, 434n; comforts Vita about Mary Campbell, 435
1928: Resumes *Orlando*, 449; misses VB. (in Cassis), 452; headaches,